MILESTONE DOCUMENTS OF WORLD RELIGIONS

Exploring Traditions of Faith
Through Primary Sources

MILESTONE DOCUMENTS OF WORLD RELIGIONS

Exploring Traditions of Faith
Through Primary Sources

Volume 1
2404 BCE – 200 CE

David M. Fahey, Editor in Chief

Schlager Group
Dallas, Texas

Milestone Documents of World Religions
Copyright © 2011 by Schlager Group Inc.

Schlager Group Inc.
2501 Oak Lawn Avenue, Suite 440
Dallas, Tex. 75219
USA

You can find Schlager Group on the World Wide Web at
http://www.schlagergroup.com
Text and cover design by Patricia Moritz

Printed in the United States of America

10 9 8 7 6 5 4 3 2 1

ISBN: 978-0-9797758-8-8

This book is printed on acid-free paper.

CONTENTS

VOLUME 1: 2404 BCE–200 CE

Volume 2: 240–1570

Editorial and Production Staff

Copy Editors, Fact Checkers, Proofreaders

Larry Baker, Barbara Bigelow, John Fitzpatrick, Gretchen
Gordon, Carol Holmes, Jennifer Holmes, Michael Allen
Holmes, Michael J. O'Neal, Karen Schader

Indexer

Michael J. O'Neal

Imaging and Design

Patricia Moritz

Schlager Group Editorial Staff

R. Lynn Naughton, Benjamin Painter

Project Manager

Marcia Merryman-Means

Publisher

Neil Schlager

CONTRIBUTORS

Christopher Abram
University College London, U.K.

Mary A. Afolabi
Independent Scholar, Kaduna, Nigeria

Chandra Alexandre
Institute of Transpersonal Psychology

Shatha Almutawa
University of Chicago

Claudia Arno
University of Michigan

Jakub Basista
Jagiellonian University, Kraków, Poland

Marc A. Beherec
University of California, San Diego

Michael W. Blastic
Washington Theological Union

Jeremy Bonner
Independent Scholar, Pittsburgh, Pennsylvania

Samuel Brenner
University of Michigan

Prudence F. Bruns
Independent Scholar, Seagrove Beach, Florida

Kristina Buhrman
University of Southern California

William Burns
George Washington University

Nawaraj Chaulagain
Harvard University

Tobias Churton
University of Exeter, U.K.

Cynthia Col
Independent Scholar, Boston, Massachusetts

Brian Collins
University of Chicago

Adam W. Darlage
Oakton Community College

Tim J. Davis
Columbus State and Otterbein University

Susan de Gaia
Independent Scholar, Los Angeles, California

Jason H. Driver
Crestview High School, Florida

Caroline Fraser
Independent Journalist, Santa Fe, New Mexico

Alexandria Frisch
New York University

Christopher Garbowski
Maria Curie-Sklodowska University, Lublin, Poland

Robert Gnuse
Loyola University, New Orleans

Lyn Green
Society for the Study of Egyptian Antiquities, Montréal, Canada

Aaron J. Gulyas
Mott Community College

Melissa Harrington
Independent Scholar, Cumbria, U.K.

Dale A. Hueber
East Bay High School, Gibsonton, Florida

Hillary Kaell
Harvard University

Dana Evan Kaplan
Temple B'nai Israel, Albany, Georgia

Joseph Abraham Levi
George Washington University

Richard Lines
Swedenborg Society, London, U.K.

Kirk R. MacGregor
Quincy University

Tereasa Maillie
University of Alberta, Canada

Eric L. May
Independent Scholar, Chicago, Illinois

Amy K. Milligan
Pennsylvania State University

Jeffrey L. Morrow
Seton Hall University

Salvador Jimenez Murguia
Miyazaki International College, Japan

Aisha Y. Musa
Florida International University

Michael J. O'Neal
Independent Scholar, Moscow, Idaho

David Ownby
Université de Montréal

Lisa J. M. Poirier
Miami University, Ohio

Janine Larmon Peterson
Marist College

Timothy Pettipiece
University of Ottawa, Canada

Rupa Pillai
University of Oregon

Andrew Polk
Florida State University

Raymond A. Powell
LCC International University, Klaipeda, Lithuania

Luca Prono
Independent Scholar, Bologna, Italy

C. D. Rodkey
Lebanon Valley College

Michael D. Royster
Prairie View A&M University

Steven Schroeder
University of Chicago

Allison Sellers
University of Central Florida

LaChelle E. M. Schilling
Claremont Graduate University

James Mark Shields
Bucknell University

Bradley A. Skeen
Independent Scholar, St. Louis, Missouri

Carl B. Smith II
Cedarville University

Tamara Shircliff Spike
North Georgia College & State University

Steven Stannish
State University of New York, Potsdam

Lieve M. Teugels
Radboud University, Nijmegen, Netherlands

Stephen E. Thompson
Independent Scholar, Coral Springs, Florida

Joel E. Tishken
Washington State University

Lisa Tran
California State University, Fullerton

David Treviño
Independent Scholar, Boca Raton, Florida

Andrew J. Waskey
Dalton State College

Cy Ashley Webb
Stanford University

Jonathan M. Wooding
University of Wales, Trinity Saint David, Lampeter

Agnes Veto
Vassar College

Andrei G. Zavaliy
American University of Kuwait, Safat (Kuwait City)

Dong Zhao
Beijing Foreign Studies University, China

ACKNOWLEDGMENTS

♦ **Cover Image Credits**

Indra, king of the gods (gouache on paper), Indian School, (18th century) / Bibliotheque Nationale, Paris, France / Archives Charmet / The Bridgeman Art Library International. **Tlaloc** (stone), Toltec / Museo Nacional de Antropologia, Mexico City, Mexico / Photo: Michel Zabe / AZA INAH / The Bridgeman Art Library International. **Papyrus 1531, Sayings of Jesus**, from the Gospel of Thomas (ink on papyrus), Egyptian School, (3rd Century AD) / British Library, London, UK / The Bridgeman Art Library International. **Page from the *Mishneh Torah***, c.1351 (vellum) / National Library, Jerusalem, Israel / Giraudon / The Bridgeman Art Library International. **Shakyamuni Buddha**, Ming Dynasty, Xuande Period (1426-65) (gilt bronze), Chinese School, (15th century) / Museum of Fine Arts, Boston, Massachusetts, USA / Gift of Miss Lucy T. Aldrich / The Bridgeman Art Library International. **Kufic calligraphy from a Koran manuscript** (parchment), Islamic School, (9th century) / Private Collection / The Bridgeman Art Library International

♦ **Text Credits**

Schlager Group also gratefully acknowledges the permission granted to reproduce the copyrighted textual material in this book. Every effort has been made to trace copyright holders and to obtain their permission for the use of copyrighted material. The publisher apologizes for any errors or omissions in the list below and would be grateful if notified of any corrections that should be incorporated in future reprints or editions of this set. In addition, an updated version of this list of acknowledgments can be found on our website: http://www.schlagergroup.com/.

Ba'al Shem Tov: "The Holy Epistle": From *Founder of Hasidism: A Quest for the Historical Ba'al Shem Tov*, by Moshe Rosman. Copyright (c) 1996 University of California Press. Reprinted courtesy of the publisher.

Egyptian Book of the Dead: From *Ancient Egyptian Literature: A Book of Readings*, by Miriam Lichtheim. Copyright (c) 1976 University of California Press. Reprinted courtesy of the publisher.

Francis of Assisi: "Canticle of the Creatures": From *Francis of Assisi: Early Documents*, Vol I: *The Saint*, edited by Regis Armstrong. Copyright (c) 2000 New City Press. Reprinted courtesy of the publisher.

"Great Hymn to the Aten": From *Texts from the Amarna Period in Egypt*, by William J. Murnane. Copyright (c) 1995 Society of Biblical Literature. Reprinted courtesy of the publisher.

Han Feizi: From *Sources of Chinese Tradition*, Volume 1, 2nd edition, edited by Wm. Theodore de Bary and Irene Bloom. Copyright (c) 1999 Columbia University Press. Reprinted with permission of the publisher.

Humanist Manifesto: Reprinted courtesy of the American Humanist Association.

"Instructions of Ptahhotep": From *Ancient Egyptian Literature: A Book of Readings*, by Miriam Lichtheim. Copyright (c) 1975 University of California Press. Reprinted courtesy of the publisher.

Mani: Evangelion: From *New Light on Manichaeism*, by Jason David BeDuhn. Copyright (c) 2009 Koninklijke BRILL NV. Reprinted courtesy of the publisher.

Meher Baba: *Discourses*: From *Discourses* by Meher Baba, 7th edition, 1987. Copyright (c) 1987 Avatar Meher Baba Perpetual Public Charitable Trust. Reprinted courtesy of the Trust.

Orphic Tablets and Hymns: From *Ancilla to the Pre-Socratic Philosophers*, by Kathleen Freeman. Blackwell Publishers, 1948. Used by permission of John Wiley & Sons.

Popol Vuh: Reprinted with the permission of Simon & Schuster, Inc., from *Popol Vuh* by Dennis Tedlock. Copyright (c) 1985, 1996 Dennis Tedlock. All Rights Reserved.

Pseudo-Sibylline Oracles: From *The Old Testament Pseudepigrapha*, Vol. 1: *Apocalyptic Literature and Testaments*, edited by James H. Charlesworth. Copyright (c) 1983 Yale University Press. Reprinted courtesy of the publisher.

Pyramid Texts: From *The Ancient Egyptian Pyramid Texts*. Copyright (c) 2005 Society of Biblical Literature.

Rig Veda: From *The Rig Veda: An Anthology of One Hundred and Eight Hymns*, selected, translated and annotated by Wendy Doniger O'Flaherty (London: Penguin Classics, 1981). Copyright (c) Wendy Doniger O'Flaherty, 1981. Reprinted by permission of Penguin Books Ltd.

Shulchan Arukh: Reprinted courtesy of Torah.org and Project Genesis.

Snorra Edda: From *Snorri Sturluson, Edda*. Translated and edited by Anthony Faulkes. London: Everyman. J.M. Dent, Orion Publishing Group. Copyright (c) 1995.

Tirumular: "Atbudha Dance": From *Tirumular*, Tamil text with English translation by Dr. B. Natarajan. Sri Ramakrishna Math, Chennai, 1991.

Overview

Milestone Documents of World Religions represents a unique and innovative approach to history reference. Combining full-text primary sources with in-depth expert analysis, the ninety-four entries in the set cover the world's religions from the third millennium BCE to the twenty-first century and include documents that range from hymns and praise poems to sacred scriptures, from religious laws and commentaries to essays and manifestos.

Organization

The set is organized chronologically in three volumes:

- Volume 1: 2404 BCE–200 CE
- Volume 2: 240–1570
- Volume 3: 1604–2002

Within each volume, entries likewise are arranged chronologically by year.

Entry Format

Each entry in *Milestone Documents of World Religions* follows the same structure using the same standardized headings. The entries are divided into two main sections: analysis and document text. Following is the full list of entry headings:

- **Overview** gives a brief summary of the primary source document and its importance in history.

- **Context** places the document in its historical framework.

- **Time Line** chronicles key events surrounding the writing of the document.

- **About the Author** presents a brief biographical profile of the person or persons who wrote the document.

- **Explanation and Analysis of the Document** consists of a detailed examination of the document text, generally in section-by-section or paragraph-by-paragraph format.

- **Audience** discusses the intended audience of the document's author.

- **Impact** examines the historical influence of the document.

- **Questions for Further Study** proposes study questions for students.

- **Essential Quotes** offers a selection of key quotes from the document and, in some cases, about the document.

- **Further Reading** lists articles, books, and Web sites for further research.

- **Document Text** gives the actual text of the primary document.

- **Glossary** defines important, difficult, or unusual terms in the document text.

Each entry features the byline of the scholar who wrote the analysis. Readers should note that for most entries, key portions of the Document Text have been excerpted for analysis. In a few cases, the entry includes the full text of the primary source document.

Features

In addition to the text of the ninety-four entries, the set includes nearly two hundred photographs and illustrations. The front matter of Volume 1 comprises an "Introduction" to the set, written by Editor in Chief David M. Fahey; a list of "Contributors"; "Editorial and Production Staff"; and "Acknowledgments." At the end of Volume 3, readers will find an "Index of Documents by Religious Tradition" and a cumulative "Subject Index."

Questions

We welcome questions and comments about the set. Readers may address all such comments to the following address:

The Editor
Milestone Documents of World Religions
Schlager Group Inc.
2501 Oak Lawn Avenue, Suite 440
Dallas, Texas 75219
USA

Religions offer to their adherents an explanation of the world around them and enrich their lives, giving them meaning. Throughout history, religions have been important in secular as well as spiritual life. In fact, outside modern Judeo-Christian societies religion has been part of a seamless web of everyday life as opposed to something entirely separate. In many cultures the idea of a nonreligious sphere exists blurrily if at all, although certain persons, places, and times might be regarded as especially holy.

For thousands of years in every culture, religions have provided themes for the arts and literature and defined for society what is proper behavior. Religions were intertwined with the legitimacy of government and law, with family relationships, with popular and high culture, even with what one could eat and drink. Religions devised rituals to worship the divine and, when they became complex institutions, also created a clergy and constructed sacred buildings. In ancient times nearly all people believed in many gods, often identified with nature. In contrast, the Abrahamic religions (Judaism and later Christianity and then Islam) were monotheistic.

Defining what constitutes a religion is difficult. Ordinarily we identify religion with the worship of God (or of gods). A few religions, from ancient Daoism to modern Unitarian Universalism, attract both people who worship and people who do not, because they are either atheists (who say that there is no God) or agnostics (who say that nobody can know for certain). Theravada Buddhism, the oldest form of that religious tradition, lacks a belief in a personal god or a creator god.

Before the nineteenth century, nearly every human being identified with one religion or another. Since then irreligion has become increasingly common among educated elites in secularized industrialized countries. This has been particularly true in Europe. In addition to this general rise of skepticism in the West, new political philosophies sometimes embraced atheism (Communism) or at least were compatible with it (ideologies ranging from Socialism to Nazism). As a result, many educated people in Europe began to assume that religion had retreated to the private sphere, had become unimportant, and in fact was dying out. It was thought that the entire world would follow the European model. The Iranian revolution of 1979 showed how wrong this idea was. Iran became an Islamic republic, with Shia Muslim religious leaders overseeing state policies.

In retrospect, many other examples of the power of religion in the public sphere can be found both before and after the Ayatollah Khomeini ousted Mohammad Reza Pahlavi, the shah of Iran. Mohandas Gandhi put a religious face on the nationalist cause in British-ruled India, perhaps

an overly Hindu face for most Muslims. The partition of the Indian Subcontinent in 1947 that created a Muslim state of Pakistan and a predominantly Hindu state of India demonstrates the political importance of religion in the aftermath of World War II, as did the creation of the Jewish State of Israel in 1948.

In modern times religion plays many roles. Often it is associated with bloodshed: between Catholics and Protestants in Northern Ireland, between Muslims and Christians in Nigeria, between Sunni and Shia Muslims in Iraq, and between Muslims and Catholics in the Philippines. Sikh bodyguards assassinated an Indian prime minister who was a Hindu. Al Qaeda justified its acts of terrorism with an appeal to Islam. Sometimes religion provides a rallying place for resistance to an unpopular government or its policies. This is the case for the African American civil rights movement in the southern American states; for Poland, where the Roman Catholic Church supported the resistance to a Communist dictatorship; and for Myanmar (also known as Burma), where Buddhist monks sometimes led nonviolent protests against the military junta. Liberation theology inspired Catholic priests in Latin America to criticize injustice. Religious conflict often is cultural and social, as exemplified by the tensions between Muslims and the non-Muslim majority in some Western European countries. A vague sense of a Christian or Judeo-Christian culture underlies anti-Muslim fears in France and elsewhere in Europe, although fewer and fewer Europeans are believing or practicing Christians or Jews.

After the collapse of the Soviet Union and the rise of the international Communist movement, religion seemed to be (together with ethnic nationalism) the most important ideology wielding the power to motivate people to sacrifice. Probably most Europeans and many Americans think of Islam when they talk about the deep influence of religion on society today. Such an emphasis overlooks the shift of Christianity from a less-religious Europe to Africa, Latin America, and parts of East Asia. Christianity is now increasingly a third world religion, as is demonstrated by splits in the Anglican (Episcopal) Church that prompted conservative white American parishes to put themselves under the jurisdiction of like-minded black East African bishops.

Intellectuals read the newspapers. The large role of religions in contemporary political and social conflicts has persuaded historians, sociologists, and others that religion matters. As a result, religious history and the sociology of religion are growing fields within these scholarly disciplines. Journalists, too, are fascinated with the so-called religious right in the United States and, above all, with Islam everywhere. Scholarly and journalistic reports about contemporary religion abound. For instance, newspapers tell us that in the English-speaking world, ordinary people often shift from one religion to another, including to New Age religions that combine Christianity with Eastern religions such as Buddhism. Wicca and other neopagan religions often emphasize a goddess figure or the divine feminine. Pentecostalism and charismatic Christian sects flourish, including denominations that promise prosperity to their followers, particularly in Africa.

The large role of religion in the public sphere today is important. Its importance has legitimized its study. Not even nonbelievers regard religion as irrelevant. Unfortunately, the new interest in religion suffers from a weakness. It is present-minded and offers only a superficial examination of the doctrines that are the basis for any religion. It is time to look at the doctrinal foundations of contemporary and past religions, to go beyond the headlines to examine and analyze doctrinal texts.

Our set, *Milestone Documents of World Religions*, pays special attention to today's five major religious traditions (Buddhism, Christianity, Hinduism, Islam, and Judaism) without neglecting other living religions with many adherents (for example, the Sikhs) or only a few (for instance, Baha'i). The set also offers a generous sampling of the many historic religions that have come and gone, such as ancient Mediterranean and pre-Columbian traditions.

Religions have endless variants. They have changed over time. They have adapted to new cultural environments when they expanded geographically. Buddhism was transformed when it entered China, where ancestor worship was universal, and then again when it entered Tibet, where it met and mingled with the Tibetan Bon religion. Missionary expansion results in syncretism, borrowing from other religions and adjusting to them. Although it has many sects with their own doctrines, Buddhism is divided basically between the Theravada and the Mahayana schools. Even terminology is fraught with controversy. Many Theravada Buddhists, for instance, resent the name Mahayana (meaning "Great Vehicle") because it implicitly relegates other Buddhists to a lesser status.

Similar complexities in creed and makeup affect the other major religious traditions. Christianity includes Roman Catholics, Protestants, and Eastern Orthodox adherents. Nearly thirty years ago a leading scholar counted more than twenty thousand Christian denominations, nearly all of them Protestant. Probably there are more sects now. For Hinduism, diversity is even more extreme. Is it a single religion or a family of related religions, worshipping different gods? Although some Hindus see one creator god behind a pantheon of deities, Hinduism certainly is not monotheistic in the way that the Abrahamic

religions are. We can count Mahayana Buddhism as polytheistic too. Islam is divided between the Sunni and the Shia, with numerous subgroups. Who is a Muslim? Most Islamic people reject as heretical a few sects claiming to be Muslim. Judaism includes the Reformed, Conservative, and Orthodox, with many further variations and subgroups. It would take a reference work larger than ours to do justice to the diversity in any one of these religious traditions, but to the extent that it is practical our set attempts to suggest the variety within major religions and how new generations have reinterpreted them.

The documents that follow remain important in the spiritual lives of millions of people. Our perspective is that of the scholarly observer, essentially that of a historian, but *Milestone Documents of World Religions* treats all religions respectfully. Some documents declare doctrinal principles directly. In other instances the documents offer a narrative or story, rather than explicitly imparting doctrines. In still other cases, the documents are aphorisms or parables or hymns of praise. The line between what we might strictly consider a religion and other belief systems is difficult to draw, so our set includes such documents as a Chinese Legalist text, an African praise poem, an essay on atheism, and works concerned with witchcraft and magic.

It is unlikely that anybody will read *Milestone Documents of World Religions* from cover to cover. Instead, one may choose to read documents from a single religious tradition or from a particular time period or region of the world. Most readers will simply browse. Within the set, any educated reader will be attracted to many documents, both familiar and unfamiliar. Each entry follows the same format, designed to facilitate an understanding of what will be new material for many readers. All the entries follow a set format, outlined here with pertinent examples.

Overview. The Overview encapsulates basic information about the document. Who wrote it, when and why was it written, and how is important? For the Qur'an, the Overview tells how Muhammad received this scripture as a revelation from the angel Gabriel and places it in the context of related foundational Muslim writings: the Hadith, which interprets the Qur'an; Sharia law, which applies its teachings; and the Sita, or traditions about the life of the Prophet. For the Westminster Confession, the Overview explains that in 1646, during the English Civil War, Parliament asked a group of English and Scottish ministers to prepare creedal statement to reform the Church of England on Calvinist lines. The thirty-three chapters of the resulting work were meant to cover all the major issues of Christian theology as they existed in the mid-seventeenth century.

Context. The Context grounds the document in its place and time, explaining the historical circumstances surrounding its creation. The Popol Vuh is an example of a document with a long and complex history. The original manuscript—if one ever existed—is lost to us. The story survived from ancient times in artifacts from the Mayan culture and in oral tradition until the 1550s, when it was recorded as epic poetry by the Mayan group known as the Quiché, to preserve its creation story. It then survived the Spanish conquest of what is now Guatemala (during which many manuscripts were destroyed). In the early 1700s a Dominican priest copied this rare document and translated it into Spanish. *The Life of St. Teresa of Jesus* is the spiritual autobiography of the Carmelite nun and mystic Teresa of Ávila. Written during the sixteenth-century transformation and revival of Catholicism that paralleled the Protestant Reformation and did battle with it, the document serves a double purpose. It records the spiritual journey of Teresa but also grounds us in the reasoning behind her efforts to reform the Carmelite Order—efforts that showed the way to a more disciplined and effective Catholic Church.

Time Line. Sometimes *Milestone Documents of World Religions* can provide only approximate dates for the history surrounding a document—which might include such wide-ranging information as political events, biographical details, and publication information. The Egyptian Book of the Dead is a collection of magical spells meant to help deceased persons proceed to the afterlife and later return when they desired to visit the world of the living. This time line begins a thousand years before the Book of the Dead, with a reference to the analogous Pyramid Texts and Coffin Texts. The texts known as the Book of the Dead appear in about 1600–1425 BCE, reappear in about 664–525 BCE, and finally disappear when Christianity replaced the traditional Egyptian religion in the early years of the Common Era. The time line ends in 1867, when the first English translation was published. A very different kind of time line, with precise years, is possible for Francis of Assisi, author of the "Canticle of the Creatures." It begins with his birth in 1182 and ends with his canonization in 1228, only two years after his death.

About the Author. This section looks at the historical person, group, or culture that created the document or, when the author is unknown, investigates the origin of the document. For instance, the life of John Bunyan (1628–1688) is known: his religious conversion, his work as a minister who preached outside the state church, his frequent imprisonments, and the eventual publication of *Pilgrim's Progress*. The Canons and Decrees of the Council of Trent, on the other hand, was the work of a large group of Roman Catholic clergy, working over the course of twenty years. While historians know the participants of the council at various stages

of its work, with their particular backgrounds and theological beliefs, the final document was presented by the Catholic Church as an entity. Many documents have no identifiable author. The Heart Sutra, one of the scriptures of Mahayana Buddhism, is the subject of debate as to its authorship. Mahayana Buddhists regard the Buddha as its author, but other Buddhists believe it to have been the work of poets.

Explanation and Analysis of the Document. The Explanation and Analysis is the lengthiest and meatiest section of each entry and its most important part. The extracts are chosen to highlight the essential aspects of a particular spiritual path. For example, *Milestone Documents of World Religions* excerpts just three of the 138 "revelations," or sections, from the Doctrine and Covenants of the Church of Jesus Christ of Latter-day Saints, looking deeply into their content. The sections reprinted here speak to the church's organization and two of the more controversial aspects of their early doctrine and practice: plural marriage (polygamy) and the baptism of the dead by proxy. The Explanation and Analysis relates the latter practice to the Mormon belief that those who are dead still have an opportunity to hear and believe in the Gospel of Jesus Christ. Moreover, since Mormons believe that family members are intimately connected, even after death, baptism is done on behalf of the entire group—which is the basis for the enormous collection of genealogical records created by the Church of Latter Day Saints.

Essential Quotes. The Essential Quotes single out the pithiest statements of a document. The massive work of Moses Maimonides, the *Mishneh Torah*, which explains the Jewish oral law, for example, has this to say: "Every Israelite has a duty to study whether he is poor or rich, whether healthy or suffering, whether young or very old and in failing strength, even if he is poor and supported by charity or begs from door to door. Even if he is a married man with a wife and children, it is a duty to set aside time to study, day and night, as the verse says: 'Thou shalt meditate therin day and night'." A signature document of the founder of Hasidism, Ba'al Shem Tov, "The Holy Epistle" reports: "I asked the Messiah, 'When will the master come?' And he answered me, 'Once your Torah will have spread throughout the world'." The quotes can admonish, instruct, and predict, but they can also instill fear, as does the *Malleus maleficarum* (popularly known as "The Hammer of Witches"): "Here it should be noted that since the Devil's intent and appetite are greater in tempting the good than the evil . . . he makes greater efforts to lead astray all the holiest virgins and girls."

Questions for Further Study. Readers are advised look at these questions before reading the document itself, to penetrate its significance. The questions take up issues of content and language, style and substance—and how one reflects the other: "The Dao De Jing relies heavily on metaphors. Select one such metaphor and be prepared to explain its significance in the text." A favorite Daoist metaphor is water. ("Best to be like water, which benefits the ten thousand things and does not contend.") The questions also ask the reader to make comparisons through the ages and across religious paths and intellectual traditions, as in *Summa theologiae*, written by the medieval theologian and philosopher Thomas Aquinas. The questions there include these: "Over the centuries, numerous cultures throughout the world have produced at least one major work that outlines a theology and a philosophy that influenced people well into the future. Select a milestone work from another culture—the Analects of Confucius, for example, or the Baghavad Gita—and, in comparing it with the *Summa theologiae*, explain why each work had such an impact on the culture that produced it."

Audience. The audience for religious texts can range widely and include the gods themselves, priests and others engaged in performing sacred rites, a faith's adherents, or even society's political groups and governmental bodies. Mani's Evangelium (or "Living Gospel") is an early quasi-Christian text that is fundamental for understanding Manichaeanism, a religion that once had adherents in the Mediterranean lands, the Middle East, Central Asia, and China. (The great Christian thinker Augustine had been a Manichaean for nine years before he converted.) One of Mani's other books was directed at the Persian court, but the Evangelium was written for the Manichaean community only. The Book of the Cave of Treasures, a Christian document composed under the threat of persecution within the hostile Persian Empire and meant to present a unified narrative of Christian history, was directed at all the Syriac-speaking peoples of Mesopotamia. Martin Luther's provocative *Ninety-five Theses* was directed at the academic and ecclesiastical community in the small university town of Wittenberg, but its message of reform soon spread and sparked the Protestant Reformation throughout Europe. For some documents we can only surmise the intended audience.

Impact. How much did these documents matter at the time they were written? Whom did they affect and how? Does their influence reach us today? Those answers may come easily for a text such as Exodus or Revelation or even the Qur'an, but they become more elusive for documents like the Orphic Tablets and Hymns and Enuma Elish. The ancient philosophy of Epicureanism is represented by *On the Nature of Things*, a work of the Roman thinker Lucretius. Lucretius addressed his book to Gaius Memmius, a Roman aristocrat who is thought to have been his patron. Its impact at the time, if any, is unknown. But after the fifteenth century, the work's influence on the literary world was consider-

able, extending from the poets John Milton to Alfred Lord Tennyson and Walt Whitman. Lucretius's ideas were also felt in scientific and philosophical circles, among those, like Jean-Baptiste Lamarck, Charles Darwin, and Pierre Teilhard de Chardin, engaged in evolutionary studies.

Further Reading. A section offering suggested further readings appears at the end of each entry. This listing is particularly helpful for less-familiar documents such as the Jain Sutras, representing a minority Indian religious tradition that emphasizes asceticism and nonviolence, and the Sufi mystical text *Meccan Illuminations*.

Document. What matters most is the original document itself. Our excerpts range widely and broadly. They are as brief as the 250-word Emerald Tablet, a summary statement of alchemical principles, or a much more substantial portion of a set of documents, such as the twentieth-century declarations, constitutions, and decrees promulgated by the Second Vatican Council. The reproduced texts might derive from fragments of ancient tablets, such as the ancient Babylonian *Hymn of the Righteous Sufferer*, or they might be collections such as the medieval Japanese myths of the *Nihongi* or Francis Barrett's compilation of many occult works in *The Magus*.

Glossary. For the most part, the original document is followed by a glossary explaining terms or identifying persons and places found in the document text. The glossaries are essential aids to the understanding of most, if not all, of the texts, which include many terms specific to a time or a place or a culture.

A reference work that strives to cover the world's religions will necessarily fall short. No such set can be exhaustive. We have aimed instead to be inclusive and representative, covering all regions of the world, balancing documents from Western and Eastern paths and ancient and modern streams, and showcasing the obscure as well as the more well known. We were challenged in certain arenas. The historical record is silent, for example, in the area of preliterate societies, whose religious views may only be deduced from artifacts and the descriptions and interpretations of those who came later. Then, too, there are the stumbling blocks that arise in the present day, among them the difficulty of locating authentic versions of ancient texts and the scholars to write about them and acquiring permission to reprint copyrighted items. Featuring entries on ninety-four documents, with scholarly analysis provided by specialists, *Milestones Documents of World Religions* is a rich introduction to an enormous topic. No comparable work exists.

David M. Fahey
Professor Emeritus of History
Miami University

MILESTONE DOCUMENTS OF WORLD RELIGIONS

Exploring Traditions of Faith
Through Primary Sources

Hieroglyphs of the earliest Pyramid Texts on the wall and roof of the tomb of Unas
(Roof and wall of the tomb chamber of the Pyramid of Unas, Old Kingdom [painted stone], Egyptian 5th Dynasty [c.2494-2345 BC] / Saqqara, Memphis, Egypt / The Bridgeman Art Library International)

Pyramid Texts

"Let there be none of you who will turn his back to Atum as he saves . . . this his work from all the gods and from all the dead."

Overview

The Pyramid Texts are the oldest religious texts preserved from ancient Egypt, dating to between 2404 and 2193 BCE. They are called the Pyramid Texts because they were carved on the walls of the subterranean chambers and corridors of the pyramids of ten kings and queens of Old Kingdom Egypt (ca. 2687–2191 BCE), beginning with Unas, the last king of the Fifth Dynasty. These pyramids are located at Saqqara, which served as the cemetery for Memphis, the capital of Egypt during the Old Kingdom. The texts were mostly written in vertical columns of hieroglyphs and have been divided into sections called *spells* by scholars. Each section begins with the hieroglyphs for *djed medu*, or "words to be spoken," and ends with the hieroglyph for the word meaning "chapter." The number of spells varied from pyramid to pyramid, with the pyramid of Unas containing 227, while the pyramid of Pepi II Neferkare contained over 600. There was considerable repetition of spells among the pyramids, and the total number of individual spells is now thought to be around 750. The location of the spells within each pyramid is significant and helps to determine the order in which the spells should be read. The purpose of these texts was to permit the deceased king (or queen) to make a successful transition to the next life and to continue to enjoy a royal existence there.

Following the end of the Old Kingdom, the Pyramid Texts began to be inscribed on tombs, sarcophagi, coffins, papyri, and other funerary monuments of nonroyal Egyptians, and this practice continued up until the end of pharaonic civilization. As a result, the Pyramid Texts can boast of an almost-continuous period of use of over two thousand years. The French Egyptologist Gaston Maspero discovered the Pyramid Texts in 1880, beginning with the pyramid of Pepi I, and since that time they have been a subject of constant study and publication by scholars. Through these efforts Egyptologists have been able to gain insight into the earliest beliefs and rituals of the ancient Egyptians.

Context

The Old Kingdom is a term applied to the Third through Sixth Dynasties (sometimes extended to the Eighth), the first lengthy period of centralized government in ancient Egypt. The first king of the Third Dynasty (ca. 2687–2649 BCE), Djoser, and his counselor and architect, Imhotep, are famous for having constructed the first monumental building out of stone, the step pyramid complex at Saqqara. There, Imhotep transformed the existing large rectangular structure of brick and rubble—today called a mastaba—which was built over the underground burial chambers of the kings of the First and Second Dynasties, into a step pyramid, so called because it consisted of what appears to be six mastabas of descending size stacked one on top of the other. The step pyramid covered the underground burial chambers of the king, which would have contained the king's tomb as well as the grave goods he expected to need in the afterlife. It has been theorized that the steps of the pyramid would have served as a means for the deceased king's spirit to ascend to the sky, as Egyptians then believed that the afterlife of the king involved his ascending to become one of the group of northern stars that never disappear from the night sky (the circumpolar "Imperishable Stars"). The use of the step pyramid in royal burials continued throughout the Third Dynasty.

The Fourth Dynasty (ca. 2649–2513 BCE) was a time of religious change in ancient Egypt. Beginning with this dynasty, there is evidence of increasing emphasis on the worship of the sun, deified as Re, and the sun begins to play a larger role in the nature of the king's afterlife. This is seen most dramatically in the shift from the use of step pyramids to the use of true pyramids—that is, with flat surfaces—as first built for King Snefru, of the Fourth Dynasty. This dynasty was the great age of pyramid building, and the most recognizable monuments from ancient Egypt, the pyramids of Kings Khufu, Khafre, and Menkure, as well as the Great Sphinx of Khafre, all located at Giza, belong to this period. The pyramid itself was a solar symbol. One hypothesis for the conceptual origin of the pyramid is that if one looks to the sky on a mostly cloudy day, one can observe sunbeams descending as if forming the sides of a pyramid. One of the terms used by the Egyptians to refer to a pyra-

CA. 2687 –2668 BCE	■ Djoser, the first king of the Third Dynasty, the first dynasty of the Old Kingdom, reigns. He and his architect, Imhotep, build the step pyramid complex at Saqqara, the world's first monumental architecture built of stone.
CA. 2649 –2609 BCE	■ Snefru, the first king of the Fourth Dynasty, reigns. Snefru replaces the use of the step pyramid with a true pyramid in his funerary monuments.
CA. 2609 –2584 BCE	■ Khufu, of the Fourth Dynasty, reigns, building the Great Pyramid at Giza.
CA. 2513 –2374 BCE	■ During the Fifth Dynasty, the sun (Re) comes to play a larger role in beliefs regarding the king's afterlife. Kings of this dynasty adopt names indicating that they see themselves as the son of Re and build special monuments called sun temples.
CA. 2404 –2374 BCE	■ Unas, the last king of the Fifth Dynasty and the first king to inscribe Pyramid Texts on the walls of the underground chambers of his pyramid, reigns.
CA. 2109 –2107 BCE	■ Ibi, a king of the Eighth Dynasty, reigns. Ibi is the last Old Kingdom king to have Pyramid Texts inscribed within his pyramid.
CA. 1991 –1786 BCE	■ During the Twelfth Dynasty, numerous officials use Pyramid Texts in their tombs or on their coffins.
CA. 755 –525 BCE	■ During the Twenty-fifth and Twenty-sixth Dynasties, rulers of Egypt make use of the Pyramid Texts to associate themselves with the great kings of Egypt's distant past.
1880 CE	■ The French Egyptologist Gaston Maspero opens the pyramid of Pepi I and discovers texts carved on the walls of the burial chambers, now known as Pyramid Texts.

mid was *akhet*, or "horizon," the place from which the sun, and therefore also the dead king's spirit, ascended into the sky. The relationship between the Egyptian king and the sun was emphasized even further during the Fifth Dynasty (ca. 2513–2374 BCE), when the kings adopted the use of a title that explicitly referred to the king as the "son of Re," a practice that continued throughout the rest of pharaonic history. In addition to building pyramid complexes for their burials, the kings of the Fifth Dynasty also built special temples, called sun temples, which served to further join the deceased king with the sun in the afterlife.

Beginning with Unas, the last king of the Fifth Dynasty, and continuing into the Eighth Dynasty (ca. 2190–2165), the kings introduced the practice of inscribing hieroglyphic texts within the underground chambers of their pyramids at Saqqara. Although the Pyramid Texts did not appear as such until the Fifth Dynasty, there are indications that some of the texts are older. According to the modern Egyptologist James Allen, the grammar of the texts reflects a stage of the Egyptian language that ended about fifty years prior to the appearance of the texts in the pyramid of Unas. Some of the texts may be even older, as they refer to burial practices in use during the First and Second Dynasties, when the kings were buried in graves beneath mud-brick mastabas. Newer spells that appear for the first time in the Sixth Dynasty (ca. 2374–2191) pyramids reflect features of the contemporary language, indicating the composite nature of this collection of texts.

The Pyramid Texts can be divided into two types: mortuary liturgies and mortuary literature. Mortuary liturgies are short texts that were recited as part of the funerary rituals that accompanied the burial of the king. These texts address the king in the second person ("you are"/"you will") and were recited by a priest who played the role of the dead king's son. The spells of this group belong to three main rituals: the offering and insignia ritual, the resurrection ritual, and the morning ritual. The offering and insignia ritual combined what were originally two separate rituals and entailed the presentation of a large meal and items of royal dress and regalia (for example, scepters, staffs, bows and arrows, crowns) to a statue of the deceased king. The resurrection ritual was performed in order to release the dead king's spirit from its body and allow him to journey daily with the gods. The morning ritual was based on the daily morning routine of the king during life—the king would awake, cleanse himself, dress, and eat breakfast; items involved in these activities would be presented to a statue of the dead king. By recording the texts of these rituals on the walls of the king's pyramid, it was as if their performance at the king's burial had been frozen in time, and the king would continue to benefit from the performance of these rituals throughout eternity.

Spells belonging to the genre of mortuary literature had a different purpose: to equip the deceased with the ability to magically overcome any obstacles that might confront him as he continued to exist after death. These were composed in the first person ("I") and were addressed to the gods by the spirit of the deceased king. Over time, the first-person pronouns were replaced by the name of

Step pyramid of Djoser

(The Step Pyramid of King Djoser, c.2630-2611 BC [photo], Egyptian 3rd Dynasty [2700-2620 BC] / Saqqara, Egypt / The Bridgeman Art Library International)

the king in whose pyramid the text occurred. These spells could provide the deceased with protection from such harmful agents as snakes and worms (which could harm the king's body or the contents of his tomb), serve to protect the pyramid itself, or allow the deceased's spirit to leave the tomb safely each morning and spend the day in the company of the gods.

The Egyptian view of the afterlife involved the concept of travel by the deceased's spirit. The path of the deceased was symbolically represented by the structure of the underground chambers of the pyramid, on whose walls the Pyramid Texts were carved. The burial chamber represented the *duat*, the underworld, the place where both the body of Osiris, god of the underworld, and the dead king lay. West of the burial chamber and connected to it by a passageway was the antechamber, representing the *akhet*, the horizon, from which the sun god Re and the deceased were reborn each day and in which the deceased made the transition into an *akh*, a glorified or effective spirit. The *akh* was the aspect of an individual that received a glorified or

exalted status after death, provided the proper rituals were performed. A sharp turn to the north in the antechamber brought one to a long corridor broken up by a vestibule and ascending corridor. This was the pathway that the *akh* would take as it ascended into the sky each day.

The spells of the offering and insignia ritual always appear on the north wall of the burial chamber of a pyramid, and the spells of the resurrection ritual always appear on the south wall. The location of the morning ritual varied, and its spells could be found on the east wall of the burial chamber or antechamber. Most of the texts in the burial chamber are intended to release the spirit from its body so that it can begin its journey toward rebirth at dawn. Many of the texts found in the antechamber belonged to the category "mortuary literature" and were meant to be used by the dead king's spirit while making the transition into an *akh*. The spells found within the corridor, vestibule, and ascending corridor are similar to those in the antechamber, being mostly concerned with allowing the spirit to cross the *akhet* and ascend into the sky to be with Re and the other gods.

About the Author

There is nothing known regarding the authors of the Pyramid Texts, as the ancient Egyptians did not credit any individual with composing any of the spells. Given the composite nature of the texts and the considerable span of time over which they were composed, one must imagine many authors rather than a single author. Certain characteristics of the texts indicate that they would have circulated orally before being written down. Those spells belonging to the category of mortuary liturgy were intended primarily for recitation, and inscribing them within the pyramids was a means used to make a permanent record of their performance. A building called the "House of Life" was attached to many temples, and in this building priests would study, compose, and copy the texts used in rituals. Scholars have deduced from the types of errors that occurred in the carving of the Pyramid Texts on the walls of the chambers that these texts were taken from papyrus copies, and it is possible that these copies were made and stored in a House of Life. So even though the Pyramid Texts had their origin as oral texts recited in rituals, at some point they were written down, copied, and recopied by priests laboring at such an institution.

Explanation and Analysis of the Document

Though the Pyramid Texts were discovered in 1880, the first English translation, by S. A. B. Mercer, did not appear until 1952. Alexandre Piankoff published the hieroglyphic texts and a translation into English from the pyramid of Unas in 1968, and in 1969 R. O. Faulkner published a translation into English of all the available Pyramid Texts. In 2005, James Allen published what is considered the most useful and up-to-date translation of the Pyramid Texts, treating each pyramid as a separate document, and his years of careful study have yielded numerous insights, drawn on extensively here. The bracketed wording represents gaps in the hieroglyphic text that the translator has filled with wording from parallels at other pyramids. The parenthetical wording has no equivalent in the underlying Egyptian text but was added to give the sense in English.

♦ Invoking Osiris

The first excerpt from the Pyramid Texts is commonly known as spell 477, here entitled "Invoking Osiris." This translation is based on the texts appearing in the pyramid of Pepi I, where this spell is seen on the west wall of the antechamber, among other spells to allow the deceased to enter the *akhet* (horizon). This spell belongs to the genre of mortuary literature, serving to introduce the deceased king Pepi I to Osiris. In order to do so, the text makes allusions to events from the myth of Osiris and Seth. Myths are often stories that describe the activities of gods or superhuman beings; in many instances, they explain why the world is the way it is and why people behave in certain ways. In Egyptian mortuary liturgies and literature, the deceased Egyptian—whether an Old Kingdom king or a New Kingdom

official buried with a copy of the Book of the Dead—played a role in mythical events, and, as a result, certain benefits or privileges accrued to the individual. The authors of these texts did not consider it necessary to describe these myths in detail but merely made allusions to the various events that made up a particular myth. Full narrative myths are rare in ancient Egypt, not appearing until the New Kingdom. By piecing together the mythical allusions made in the funerary literature of the Old and Middle Kingdoms, scholars have been able to assemble coherent accounts of many ancient Egyptian myths. A full understanding of spell 477 requires familiarity with the story of Osiris and Seth, one of the great myths from ancient Egypt.

Osiris and Seth were brothers, sons of the god Geb and the goddess Nut. Osiris was said to have inherited the rule of the Two Lands (that is, Upper and Lower Egypt) from his father, Geb. Seth then killed Osiris, although exactly how he did this is rarely mentioned in Egyptian texts. But Osiris's wife, Isis, and her sister Nephthys managed to restore the deceased Osiris's sexual potency long enough to allow Isis to conceive a son, Horus. Seth was tried for his crime before a court made up of the major gods of Egypt, presided over by Atum, while Geb served as Osiris's advocate. The tribunal decided in favor of Osiris, who was awarded kingship of the underworld and the dead who inhabit it, and the kingship of Egypt was taken from Seth and conferred on Horus.

As the present spell opens, all creation is in an uproar because Osiris has been murdered by Seth (who "threw Osiris to the Earth"). Horus and Thoth, the god of wisdom and writing, are said to raise Osiris up and make him stand up before the "Dual Ennead," a term referring to the gods of both Upper Egypt (the southerly Nile Valley) and Lower Egypt (the northerly Nile Delta). The tribunal takes place in the "Official's Enclosure in Heliopolis," which refers to the sanctuary of the sun temple at Heliopolis. Paragraph 2 reports remarks made by Seth to this tribunal, and each comment of Seth's becomes an explanation for an epithet applied to Osiris. Seth's claim that Osiris has been attacking him leads to Osiris's epithet "earth-attacker." Seth's accusation that Osiris has been kicking (*sah*) him is given as the reason for associating the constellation called *sah* by the Egyptians—now known as Orion—with Osiris. The Egyptians did not believe that similarities in sound between words were coincidental, but rather revealed essential information about the relationship between entities.

In paragraph 4, the verdict of the tribunal is given; Osiris is awarded the kingship of the underworld. The "Marsh of Reeds" was a region of the night sky south of the ecliptic, the path traveled by the sun through the sky in the course of the year, which the Egyptians thought of as a canal of water bisecting the sky. The Horus Mounds and Seth Mounds were located at the edge of the sky and were inhabited by the gods and *akh*s.

Paragraph 5 represents a transition in the text, demonstrating how this recounting of myth will serve to benefit the dead king, Pepi. Thoth is said to be armed with a knife and will "remove the heads" and "cut out

"Recitation. The sky has become disheveled, the earth has trembled. Horus has come, Thoth has appeared, that they might raise Osiris from off his side and make him stand up in the Dual Ennead. Remember, Seth, and put in your heart this speech that Geb has said, this curse that the gods have made against you in the Official's Enclosure in Heliopolis, because you threw Osiris to the earth."

"So says Horus, your son to whom you gave birth. He will not put this Pepi at the head of the dead, but will put him among the gods who have become divine. Their water is the water of this Pepi, their bread is the bread of this Pepi, their cleansing is this Pepi's cleansing. What Horus has done for Osiris, [he will do for this Pepi] likewise."

"Atum Beetle! You became high, as the hill; you rose as the benben in the Benben Enclosure in Heliopolis. You sneezed Shu and spat Tefnut. You put your arms around them as ka-arms so that your ka might be in them. Atum, put your arms around Pepi Neferkare as ka-arms, so that the ka of Pepi Neferkare might be in it, firm for the course of eternity."

"Ho, Big Ennead in Heliopolis—Atum, Shu, Tefnut, Geb, Nut, Osiris, Isis, Seth, and Nephthys, Atum's children! His heart was stretched for (you), his children, in your identity of the Nine Bows. Let there be none of you who will turn his back to Atum as he saves this Pepi Neferkare, as he saves this pyramid of Pepi Neferkare, as he saves this his work from all the gods and from all the dead."

"Pepi Neferkare is Geb, the persuasive mouth, the god's elite one, whom Atum put at the fore of the Ennead, he with whose speech the gods are content. All the gods shall be content with everything this Pepi Neferkare says, through which it will be good for him for the course of eternity, for Atum has said about Pepi Neferkare; 'See our most persuasive mouth calling us! Let us go and be gathered to him.'"

the hearts" of any who would prevent Pepi from joining Osiris. In the following paragraphs, Pepi claims that he will perform certain services for Osiris—wipe his face, clothe him, amputate a limb from Osiris's opponent—tasks that he is qualified to accomplish through having

undergone the proper rituals ("having become clean") in the necropolis (cemetery) of Heliopolis, called Djedit. In the final paragraph, Horus declares that, as a result, Pepi will be counted not among the dead but among the dead who have become gods after death. The Egyptian term *netjer*, often translated as "god," had a far wider frame of reference than the English *god*. *Netjer* could refer to the Egyptian king, certain living animals, and dead people or animals; here it refers to the glorified dead. Because of his status, Pepi will enjoy the same nourishment and purification—water, bread, cleansing—that these gods receive throughout eternity.

♦ **Spells for the Protection of the Pyramid**

There are three spells contained within this excerpt from the Pyramid Texts: numbers 600, 601, and 599. Each new spell begins with the word "recitation," from the Egyptian *djed medu*, "words to be spoken." These spells are translated from the versions found in the pyramid of Pepi II, Pepi Neferkare, where they are located on the east wall and gable of the burial chamber. The purpose of the pyramid and its attendant structures was to provide for the burial and cult (daily rituals) of the dead king. It was necessary for this cult to continue if the king was to enjoy a pleasant afterlife, and the spells in this selection were intended to protect the pyramid from harm. These spells belong to the category of mortuary literature, but the original first-person pronouns have been replaced by the name of the deceased king, Pepi Neferkare.

The first spell in this group contains a recounting of one of the Egyptian stories of creation. The ancient Egyptians had several creation accounts, each one attributing the creation of the universe to a different god or group of gods. Scholars usually refer to these accounts by referencing the city important to the major god in the account. For example, the Memphite cosmogony attributes creation to the god Ptah, of Memphis. The creation account described here is called the Heliopolitan cosmogony, because the main creator god is the sun god Atum, associated with Heliopolis, near modern-day Cairo.

In the Heliopolitan account, before creation the universe existed as an infinite, dark, watery expanse called Nun. Within this vast ocean a god, Atum, created himself. The name *Atum* means both "complete, finished" and "the undifferentiated one." Here he is called "Atum Beetle." The beetle (scarab), particularly the dung beetle, called by the Egyptians *khepri*, was an aspect of the sun and represented the rising morning sun. The association with the dung beetle came from this insect's habit of rolling a ball of dung across the desert floor, an image that was transformed into the god Khepri pushing the sun across the sky. Once Atum came into existence within Nun, he needed a place to stand. For this, again, the Egyptians drew on an image observed in the natural world. Each year the Nile River overflowed its banks and flooded the valley; as the floodwaters began to recede, the highest points of ground would emerge from the floodwaters first. The first dry ground to emerge from Nun was called the *benben*, the "primeval mound," thought to have been located at Heliopolis. The reason this myth is recounted in a spell to protect the pyramid is that the pyramid was thought to be an architectural representation of the *benben*; its pyramid-shaped capstone was called the *benbenet*.

As related in spell 600, once the sun god Atum Beetle emerges from Nun—essentially the first sunrise—and stands on the primeval hill, he begins the work of creation by sneezing out the god Shu and spitting out the goddess Tefnut. The names of the gods and their method of creation represent wordplay. Shu, whose name means "void" or "emptiness" and who represented the atmosphere, was created by sneezing. Tefnut was created by spitting, and while the meaning of *Tefnut* is uncertain, one tradition associates her with moisture. Atum is said to put his arms around his children as *ka*-arms (the hieroglyph of two extended arms had the phonetic value *ka*) and, by doing so, places his *ka* in them. The *ka* was one of the components that made up an individual and represented the life force, the difference between a living and a dead body. It was thought of as a double of the living person, coming into existence when the body came into being. It was transmitted from parent to child, and it represented the aspect of the deceased that was able to make use of food and drink offerings that were presented. Here Atum is portrayed as passing on his "life force" to his children Shu and Tefnut. Atum is then said to do the same for the deceased Pepi Neferkare, and by putting his arms around the deceased king and his pyramid, he grants them protection for eternity.

The fourth paragraph mentions the Big Ennead of Heliopolis. An *ennead* is literally a group of nine gods. Atum, Shu, and Tefnut are the first three. Geb (male) and Nut (female) were the children of Shu and Tefnut, with Geb representing dry land and Nut the sky. Originally Geb and Nut were locked in an embrace, and Geb impregnated Nut. A significant act of creation takes place when Shu (the atmosphere) steps in and separates Geb and Nut, essentially creating a space in which life can take place, a bubble within the vast watery expanse of Nun. This act is frequently depicted in Egyptian religious iconography as Shu standing on a prone Geb while lifting the arching body of a woman spangled with stars high overhead. Nut then gives birth to two pairs of gods and goddesses, Osiris and Isis and Seth and Nephthys, whose mythical origins are relevant to spell 477. Atum's children are referred to as the Nine Bows, a term the Egyptians used to refer to all the lands outside of Egypt—essentially the whole world as was known to them at the time. The members of the Big Ennead, also called the Heliopolitan Ennead, thus include Atum, Shu, Tefnut, Geb, Nut, Osiris, Isis, Seth, and Nephthys.

Paragraph 5 equates Pepi Neferkare with Osiris and commands Horus to look after him and his pyramid. Paragraph 6 features two instances of wordplay, as the Egyptian terms for "put," "ferry," and "guide" are related to the names of the two enclosures, *dedja* and *demaa*, but there is nothing more known about these two structures. In the last paragraph is an allusion to the myth of Osiris, in which Horus defends his father in the tribunal and wins for Osiris the kingship of the beatified dead (here called the gods). Again, wordplay is involved, between the words for "elevated" and "reeds" and for "brighten" and "White Palaces."

The next spell, 601 (again beginning with "Recitation"), is a series of injunctions to the members of the Big

Ennead to protect the pyramid of the king and make his name endure throughout eternity. Each deity is associated with a particular location, some identifiable with geographic locations in Egypt and others not. In paragraph 7 of this spell, Osiris is referred to as "Foremost of the Westerners." For the Egyptians, the West was the direction of the dead; it was the direction in which the sun set each night. As a result, most cemeteries were located on the west of the Nile, and the dead could be referred to as "Westerners." In paragraph 11, the god "Eyes Forward" was a form of the falcon-headed god Horus from the city of Letopolis (modern-day Ausim) in northern Egypt. Wadjet (paragraph 12) is a goddess thought of as a rearing cobra and, as part of his headdress, also thought to protect the king. Her cult center was also in northern Egypt, at Buto (present-dayTell el-Fara'in).

The last spell, 599, begins by equating the deceased Pepi Neferkare with Geb, called "the persuasive mouth" because of his role as advocate for Osiris in the tribunal of the gods. As a result, Pepi is also endowed with the power to persuade the gods to protect him and his pyramid throughout eternity. In the second paragraph of this spell, the king and Geb promise the gods food offerings in return for their protection of the pyramid of Pepi. The final paragraph continues this theme. The gods are promised food, drink, clothing, ointment (used as a deodorant), and even the rulership of the gods, at the head of the Dual Ennead, in return for protecting Pepi's pyramid. The verb phrase "will be ba" is understood to mean "will become impressive," yet another characteristic the gods are promised.

Audience

The Pyramid Texts can be divided into two types of text, mortuary liturgies and mortuary literature. The mortuary liturgies were the scripts of rituals recited on behalf of the dead king and so were addressed to him. Mortuary literature was addressed to the gods by the deceased king. While there is evidence that the offering ritual of the Pyramid Texts would have been recited for nonroyal individuals during the Old Kingdom, there is no evidence that these texts would have been read and studied by the living for their own benefit. It is apparent, however, that later scribes had access to papyrus copies of the texts carved in several Old Kingdom pyramids. Beginning in the First Intermediate Period (ca. 2165–2061 BCE) and continuing to the end of pharaonic Egyptian history, private individuals made use of Pyramid Texts in their burials, and, at times, details of the texts allow modern scholars to identify the Old Kingdom pyramid serving as the source of a particular Pyramid Text.

Impact

The Pyramid Texts were intended for use by royalty. With the collapse of the Old Kingdom, the afterlife previously available only to kings and queens gradually became available to all Egyptians with the means to prepare a proper burial for themselves. As a result, Pyramid Texts were used by nonroyal Egyptians during the Middle Kingdom in their coffins or on their tomb walls. Portions of the Pyramid

Questions for Further Study

1. Read this entry in conjunction with the Egyptian Book of the Dead. Taken together, what do the two documents tell you about Egyptian conceptions of death and the afterlife? How did the Pyramid Texts contribute to the evolution of the later Book of the Dead?

2. The sun played a significant role in the religious worldviews of many ancient cultures. How is the Egyptian view of the sun similar to, or different from, that of Amaterasu, as described in the entry on the Yengishiki?

3. Most religious cultures have some conception of an "underworld," a place distinct from "heaven." Compare the Egyptian underworld, ruled over by Osiris, with other conceptions of the underworld in Greek, Roman, Christian, and other religious cultures. How do these conceptions of an underworld reflect religious anxieties?

4. Why were most Egyptian cemeteries located on the west bank of the Nile River, as opposed to the east bank? How did this practice reflect something about Egyptian religious belief?

5. Compare the account of the creation of the world with creation accounts in other religious traditions, including Christianity (Genesis) and Jewish mysticism (Sefer Yetzirah). Do you see any similarities in these creation accounts? How do they fundamentally differ? Explain.

Texts were used by later scribes when they created new funerary compositions such as the Coffin Texts and the Book of the Dead. Later dynasties—the Twenty-fifth and Twenty-sixth—returned to the use of Pyramid Texts in their tombs as a conscious attempt to emulate the great rulers of the Old Kingdom.

In modern times, the Pyramid Texts have not had the same impact on the popular imagination as has the Book of the Dead, and they remain largely unknown to any but students of ancient Mediterranean religions. This is possibly due to the fact that there are literally hundreds of papyrus copies of the Book of the Dead scattered in museums throughout the world, where they can be viewed by the visiting public, while the Pyramid Texts have been available only in specialized publications not easily accessible to the general public prior to the growth of the Internet. Because of the practice of illustrating the Book of the Dead, many of these papyri are veritable works of art. Nevertheless, the Pyramid Texts, as the earliest religious texts from ancient Egypt, have been of the utmost importance in reconstructing Egypt's foundational religious beliefs and practices. The practice of burying the dead with texts to ease their transition to the afterlife began with the Pyramid Texts, and this practice ultimately led to the creation of the Coffin Texts and Book of the Dead, which are both likewise important sources of knowledge of ancient Egyptian religion.

Further Reading

■ Books

Allen, James P., trans. *The Ancient Egyptian Pyramid Texts*, ed. Peter Der Manuelian. Atlanta: Society of Biblical Literature, 2005.

Assmann, Jan. *The Mind of Egypt History and Meaning in the Time of the Pharaohs*, trans. Andrew Jenkins. New York: Metropolitan Books, 2002.

Assmann, Jan. *Death and Salvation in Ancient Egypt*, trans. David Lorton. Ithaca, N.Y.: Cornell University Press, 2005.

Bleiberg, Edward, ed. *Arts and Humanities through the Eras*. Vol. 3: *Ancient Egypt, 2675–332 B.C.E.* New York: Thomson/Gale, 2005. Faulkner, R. O., trans. *The Ancient Egyptian Pyramid Texts*. Oxford, U.K.: Oxford University Press, 1969.

Hornung, Erik. *The Ancient Egyptian Books of the Afterlife*, trans. David Lorton. Ithaca, N.Y.: Cornell University Press, 1999.

Lesko, Leonard. "Ancient Egyptian Cosmogonies and Cosmology." In *Religion in Ancient Egypt: Gods, Myths, and Personal Practice*, ed. Byron E. Shafer. Ithaca, N.Y.: Cornell University Press, 1991.

Pinch, Geraldine. *Egyptian Myth: A Very Short Introduction*. Oxford, U.K.: Oxford University Press, 2004.

—Stephen E. Thompson

PYRAMID TEXTS

Invoking Osiris

Recitation. The sky has become disheveled, the earth has trembled. Horus has come, Thoth has appeared, that they might raise Osiris from off his side and make him stand up in the Dual Ennead.

Remember, Seth, and put in your heart this speech that Geb has said, this curse that the gods have made against you in the Official's Enclosure in Heliopolis, because you threw Osiris to the earth, when you said, Seth: "It was not against him that I did this," so that you might take control thereby when your control was taken away for Horus; when you said, Seth: "In fact, he has been attacking [me]," and his identity of earth-attacker came into being; when you said, Seth: "In fact, he has been kicking me," and his identity of Orion came into being, wide of foot, spread of stride, and foremost of the Nile-Valley land.

Raise yourself, Osiris, for Seth has raised himself, having heard the curse of the gods, who spoke on behalf of the god's father. (Give) your arm to Isis, Osiris, and your hand to Nephthys, and you will go between them.

You have been given the sky, you have been given the earth, the Marsh of Reeds, the Horus Mounds and the Seth Mounds; you have been given the towns and the countryside has been joined together for you—by Atum. Geb is the one who argued for it.

Thoth's blade has been sharpened, and the knife that removes heads and cuts out hearts has been honed, and [it] will remove the heads and cut out the hearts of those who will cross this Pepi when he goes to you, Osiris, and of those who will bar this Pepi when he goes to you, Osiris.

This Pepi has come to you, lord of the sky. This Pepi has come to you, Osiris. This Pepi will wipe your face and clothe you with a god's clothing, having become clean for you in Djedit, Sothis, your daughter whom you have desired, [who makes] your [fresh vegetables in] her identity of the year, is the one who led this Pepi when this Pepi came to you.

[This Pepi] has come [to you, lord of the sky]. This Pepi [has come] to you, [Osiris], This Pepi [will wipe] your face and this Pepi will clothe you with a god's clothing, for this Pepi has become clean for you in Iadi. He will annihilate a limb from your opponent: when he butchers it for Osiris, he will put him at the fore of the butchers.

This Pepi has come to you, lord of the sky. This Pepi has come to you, Osiris. This Pepi will wipe your face and this Pepi will clothe you with a god's clothing. This Pepi will do for you that which [Geb] has commanded [he do for you: this Pepi will establish your arm upon life, this Pepi will lift your arm with authority].

This Pepi has come to you, lord of the sky. Pepi has come to you, Osiris. This Pepi will wipe your face and this Pepi will clothe you with a god's clothing, for this Pepi is clean for you.

So says Horus, your son to whom you gave birth. He will not put this Pepi at the head of the dead, but will put him among the gods who have become divine. Their water is the water of this Pepi, their bread is the bread of this Pepi, their cleansing is this Pepi's cleansing. What Horus has done for Osiris, [he will do for this Pepi] likewise.

Spells for Protection of the Pyramid

Recitation. Atum Beetle! You became high, as the hill; you rose as the *benben* in the *Benben* Enclosure in Heliopolis. You sneezed Shu and spat Tefnut. You put your arms around them as *ka*-arms so that your *ka* might be in them.

Atum, put your arms around Pepi Neferkare as *ka*-arms, so that the *ka* of Pepi Neferkare might be in it, firm for the course of eternity.

Ho, Atum! May you extend protection over this Pepi Neferkare, over this his pyramid and this work of Pepi Neferkare, and prevent anything bad from happening to it for the course of eternity, like you extended protection over Shu and Tefnut.

Ho, Big Ennead in Heliopolis—Atum, Shu, Tefnut, Geb, Nut, Osiris, Isis, Seth, and Nephthys, Atum's children! His heart was stretched for (you), his children, in your identity of the Nine Bows. Let there be none of you who will turn his back to Atum as he saves this Pepi Neferkare, as he saves this pyramid of Pepi Neferkare, as he saves this his work from all the gods and from all the dead, as he prevents anything bad from happening to it for the course of eternity.

Ho, Horus! This Pepi Neferkare is Osiris, this pyramid of Pepi Neferkare and this his work are Osiris.

Betake yourself to him and don't be far from him in his identity of the pyramid.

(Osiris), you have become very black in your identity of the Great Black One's Enclosure. Thoth has put the gods under you, ferried in the *dedja*-enclosure and guided in the *demaa*-enclosure.

Horus, here is your father Osiris, in his identity of the Sovereign's Enclosure.

(Osiris), Horus has given you the gods: he has elevated them to you as reeds so that they may brighten your face in the White Palaces.

Recitation. O, Big Ennead in Heliopolis! You will make Pepi Neferkare be firm as you make this pyramid of Pepi Neferkare and this his work be firm for the course of eternity as the name of Atum, foremost of the Big Ennead, is firm.

As the name of Shu, lord of Upper Menset in Heliopolis, is firm, Pepi Neferkare shall be firm, and this his pyramid and this his work shall be firm likewise, for the course of eternity.

As the name of Tefnut, lady of Lower Menset in Heliopolis, remains, the name of this Pepi Neferkare shall remain, and this pyramid shall remain likewise, for the course of eternity.

As the name of Geb at the earths *ba* is firm, the name of Pepi Neferkare shall be firm, and this pyramid of Pepi Neferkare shall be firm and this his work shall be firm likewise, for the course of eternity.

As the name of Nut is firm in the Enclosure of Shenit in Heliopolis the name of this Pepi Neferkare shall be firm, and this his pyramid shall be firm and this his work shall be firm likewise, for the course, of eternity.

As the name of Osiris is firm in Great Land, the name of this Pepi Neferkare shall be firm, and this pyramid of Pepi Neferkare shall be firm and this his work shall be firm likewise, for the course of eternity.

As the name of Osiris as Foremost of Westerners is firm, the name of this Pepi Neferkare shall be firm, and this pyramid of Pepi Neferkare shall be firm and this his work shall be firm likewise, for the course of eternity.

As the name of Seth is firm in Ombos, the name of this Pepi Neferkare shall be firm, and this pyramid of Pepi Neferkare shall be firm and this his work shall be firm likewise, for the course of eternity.

As the name of Horus of Seal-ring is firm, the name of this Pepi Neferkare shall be firm, and this pyramid of Pepi Neferkare shall be firm and this his work shall be firm likewise, for the course of eternity.

As the name of the Sun is firm at the Akhet, the name of this Pepi Neferkare shall be firm, and this pyramid of Pepi Neferkare shall be firm and this his work shall be firm likewise, for the course of eternity.

As the name of Eyes-Forward remains at Akhmim, the name of this Pepi Neferkare shall be firm, and this

Akhet	horizon
Atum	the sun god Atum, associated with Heliopolis, near modern-day Cairo
benben	the primeval mound where the gods could first stand
Djedit	the cemetery of Heliopolis, near modern-day Cairo
Dual Ennead	a term referring to a group of gods of both Upper Egypt (the southerly Nile Valley) and Lower Egypt (the northerly Nile Delta)
Eyes Forward	a form of the falcon-headed god Horus from the city of Letopolis (modern-day Ausim) in northern Egypt
Geb and Nut	the children of Shu and Tefnut, with Geb representing dry land and Nut the sky
Horus	the son of Osiris and Isis; according to myth, Osiris was murdered by his brother Seth, his body dismembered, and the pieces scattered throughout Egypt. Isis collected the pieces of her dead husband and with the help of the god Thoth reassembled and revivified Osiris; she then conceived a son, Horus, with him.
Horus Mounds and Seth Mounds	places at the edge of the sky inhabited by the gods

his pyramid shall be firm and this work of Pepi Neferkare shall be firm likewise, for the course of eternity.

As the name of Wadjet is firm in Dep, the name of this Pepi Neferkare shall be firm, and this pyramid of Pepi Neferkare shall be firm and this [his] work shall be firm likewise, for the course of eternity.

Recitation. Pepi Neferkare is Geb, the persuasive mouth, the god's elite one, whom Atum put at the fore of the Ennead, he with whose speech the gods are content. All the gods shall be content with everything this Pepi Neferkare says, through which it will be good for him for the course of eternity, for Atum has said about Pepi Neferkare; "See our most persuasive mouth calling us! Let us go and be gathered to him."

Ho, all you gods! Come, combine; come, gather, like when you combined and gathered for Atum in Heliopolis. He is calling you to come and do everything good for Pepi Neferkare for the course of eternity. A king-given offering, a Geb-given offering,

of these select-cuts of meat, and an invocation offering of bread, beer, and fowl for all the gods who will make everything good happen for Pepi Neferkare, who will make this pyramid of Pepi Neferkare be firm, who will make this work of Pepi Neferkare be firm, like the state in which he loves to be for the course of eternity.

All the gods who will make this pyramid and this work of Pepi Neferkare be good and firm—they are the ones who will be sharp; they are the ones who will be esteemed; they are the ones who will be *ba*; they are the ones who will have control; they are the ones to whom will be given a king-given offering of bread, beer, cattle, fowl, clothing, and ointment; they are the ones who will receive their gods' offerings; they are the ones for whom will be selected their select cuts of beef and fowl; they are the ones for whom will be made their feasts; they are the ones who will acquire the crown amongst the Dual Ennead.

Glossary

ka	life force
Marsh of Reeds	a region of the night sky south of the ecliptic, the path traveled by the sun through the sky in the course of the year
Nine Bows	a term the Egyptians used to refer to all the lands outside Egypt—essentially the whole world
Nun	the infinite, dark, watery expanse that existed before creation
Official's Enclosure in Heliopolis	the sanctuary of the sun temple at Heliopolis.
Osiris	god of the underworld
Seth	the brother of Osiris
Shu	the atmosphere, or void and emptiness, sneezed out by Atum as an act of creation
Wadjet	a goddess thought of as a rearing cobra and, as part of his headdress, also thought to protect the king
will be *ba*	will become impressive

Tomb relief of Osiris

(Relief depicting Osiris, from the Tomb of Horemheb, New Kingdom [painted limestone], Egyptian 18th Dynasty [c.1567-1320 BC] / Valley of the Kings, Thebes, Egypt / Photo © BEBA/AISA / The Bridgeman Art Library International)

"It is the god who gives advancement, / He who uses elbows is not helped."

Overview

The document known today as the "Instructions of Ptahhotep" is one of the oldest wisdom texts surviving from ancient Egypt, perhaps composed sometime around 2200 BCE during the Old Kingdom period. It consists of a prologue, a series of thirty-seven maxims, and an epilogue. It is written in verse, in one of the older forms of the ancient Egyptian language. Although an author and a time period are mentioned in the document, many modern scholars doubt that it was composed when, and by whom, the text claims it was written. Based on the number of ancient copies that survive, it was copied and studied for at least a thousand years. It provides important insight into the development of ethics and morality in the Egypt of the pharaohs.

Context

The "Instructions of Ptahhotep" belongs to a category of ancient Egyptian literature that is known today as "wisdom literature" or "didactic literature." Modern scholars who refer to this genre as "didactic literature" do so because the texts were used in the training of young scribes or young officials. Didactic literature offers advice for living a good and moral life; such texts are not necessarily intended as meditations on larger philosophical or religious themes. In the ancient Egyptian language the name for this genre of literature was *sebayt*, which means "teachings" or "instructions." The "Instructions of Ptahhotep" is also known today as the "Maxims of Good Discourse," a phrase that appears in the document itself. However, all such names are modern additions, since the ancient Egyptians rarely recorded titles for their compositions.

The "Instructions of Ptahhotep" is a document about which many things remain mysterious. For example, according to the opening lines of the text, the document was composed during the reign of the Egyptian king Isesi (also known as Djedkare Isesi, who ruled ca. 2414 BCE–ca. 2375 BCE) or shortly thereafter. This would date the document to about 2400 BCE. However, the form of the ancient Egyptian language used in the piece suggests a date about two hundred years later. (The difference in the language might be compared roughly to the difference between the English of the twentieth century and that of the King James version of the Bible.) The earliest surviving copy of the "Instructions" comes from the ancient Egyptian Middle Kingdom, dating to about 1900 BCE. This version, which is one of the texts on the Prisse Papyrus, is today kept in the Bibliothèque Nationale in Paris. It is considered to be the most complete and correct version.

The date of the composition of this document is an important factor in any consideration of its importance to the history of pharaonic Egyptian thought, for two reasons. First, if the document was, in fact, created in the Middle Kingdom (ca. 2040–1785 BCE), then it is obviously not an important and influential *precursor* of the *sebayt* of later periods. Rather, it would represent one of many similar texts, sharing many of their themes and points of view. Moreover, if the "Instructions of Ptahhotep" was not actually written during the Old Kingdom (ca. 2650–2135 BCE), there is much less evidence that the genre of Egyptian wisdom literature originated in the mid-third millennium BCE.

Second, the two periods of Egyptian history in which it might have been composed are very different. If "Instructions of Ptahhotep" dates to the Fifth Dynasty (ca. 2494 BCE–ca. 2345 BCE), it was composed at a period of great political stability, during which the kings had access to the vast resources necessary to build awe-inspiring monuments such as the pyramids of Giza. Although different lines of pharaohs came and went, Egypt seemingly never experienced the dissolution of central power or any serious challenge to the godlike status of its rulers during this period. It was also a time during which worship of the sun god was supreme, and the vision of the Egyptian afterlife familiar to us today was in its formative stages.

In the Middle Kingdom, by contrast, the Egyptians had memory of a period of breakdown of central government, famine, and civil war that continued to haunt them. The aftermath of this period, known to modern scholars as the First Intermediate Period, inspired some works of pessimistic and almost apocalyptic literature. Although those compositions were the product of a reunited and stable Egypt, they show the lasting influence of the period of chaos. The

CA. 2414 BCE −2375 BCE	■ Djedkare Isesi reigns as pharoah, during the Fifth Dynasty of the Egyptian Old Kindgom.
CA. 2400 BCE	■ Ptahhotep is vizier under King Isesi.
CA. 2375 BCE	■ Ptahhotep's grandson, also named Ptahhotep, is vizier under King Unas.
CA. 2200 BCE	■ Some scholars believe that "Instructions of Ptahhotep" was composed at this time.
CA. 1900 BCE	■ The Prisse Papyrus, containing the oldest extant copy of the "Instructions," dates from this time.

sebayt that we know were composed in the Middle Kingdom are occasionally attributed to kings, and they sometimes reflect suspicion and lack of trust. Even some of the fiction of the period, such as the famous story of Sinuhe, deals with themes of betrayal, exile, loneliness, and loss.

Although the worship of the sun remained important during the Middle Kingdom, new deities rose to prominence and the capital of the country was relocated farther south. In addition, the concept of the afterlife was articulated more clearly. It could even be said that Egyptian ideas about access to the afterlife became more egalitarian. In the Old Kingdom, the vast majority of texts concerning the soul and the afterlife come from royal monuments. Although the wealthy had beautifully decorated tombs, which they obviously expected would lead them into the next world, there are few religious or mythological references in them. In the Middle Kingdom, by contrast, guidebooks to the afterlife were painted on the inside of coffins, making the magic necessary to ensure a safe eternity accessible even to non-royal individuals.

The "Instructions of Ptahhotep" makes fairly frequent references to a divine being, or beings. Unfortunately, they are never specifically named except for Osiris, ruler of the afterlife and the god of death and rebirth. It would be useful to scholars who wish to date the composition if even one other god's name had been mentioned. Osiris was so popular at all stages of Egyptian history that the appearance of his name in a text is not helpful in dating it.

Some scholars who believe that the text was written in the Old Kingdom focus on the clear representation of hier-

archy and the importance of maintaining the cosmic order. Egyptologists who believe that the work was written five hundred years later point to what they describe as elements of a more egalitarian and open spirit. For proof, they refer to the statements in the "Instructions" regarding wisdom and justice as qualities that are universal and not the preserve of the educated and wealthy.

If the "Instructions of Ptahhotep" was written around 1800 BCE, the motive of the ancient author for ascribing the "Instructions" to the Old Kingdom would have been to give the instructions the added authority of having originated in a golden age. Making the instructions of Ptahhotep come from such a perfect era might have implied that following these maxims would lead Egypt back to that ideal.

About the Author

The opening lines of "Instructions of Ptahhotep" assert that the author is the "Mayor of the city," Ptahhotep, under the reign of King Isesi. A few lines later, more titles and honorifics are given, some of them quite lofty: "Prince, Count, God's Father, God's Beloved, Eldest Son of the King, [of] his body." Although some of the titles, such as "Eldest Son of the King," should perhaps not be taken at face value, they place Ptahhotep very close to the royal family.

Ptahhotep was a fairly common name in the Old Kingdom, particularly in the royal court at the capital city of Memphis. Ptah, god of craftsmen and a creator god, was the patron of the city of Memphis. Several tombs belonging to men called Ptahhotep are known today in the cemeteries of Saqqara and Giza near Memphis, and some of those date to approximately the right period corresponding with the text. One French Egyptologist has claimed that the tomb of the mayor and vizier Ptahhotep who is named in the "Instructions" may be found at Saqqara. The time period is the right one, and the tomb owner's list of titles is very similar to that mentioned in the "Instructions." However, some Egyptologists believe that the man who actually wrote the "Instructions" was the grandson of the vizier of Isesi, a man who had the same name and was also a vizier. This theory maintains that the younger Ptahhotep wrote the "Instructions" under the name of his grandfather.

Explanation and Analysis of the Document

The "Instructions of Ptahhotep" follows a pattern familiar from other ancient Egyptian instructions, and the themes are also those repeated over and over in many other Egyptian wisdom texts. These themes include the importance of demonstrating respect and maintaining the etiquette of the social hierarchy; the importance of the qualities of moderation, thoughtfulness, judiciousness, honesty, respectfulness, and modesty; the contrast between the ideal man, who manifests these qualities, and his opposite; and the way in which these qualities will be rewarded. The main difference between the "Instructions of Ptahhotep" and

Tombs at Saqqara, dating to Egypt's golden age
(AP/Wide World Photos)

other wisdom and didactic texts is that Ptahhotep's teachings seem to be far less specifically focused toward becoming a high court official.

The similar themes found in many wisdom texts should make it easy to interpret the meaning of the "Instructions of Ptahhotep." However, many lines have proved difficult to translate or to interpret once translated. Several sentences in which meaning is clear might be followed by a phrase or sentence that is difficult to understand. This may be because of the use of ancient idioms in the text, or sometimes it is because the form of the language is not quite like that of the classic Old Kingdom or the Middle Kingdom either. Despite the best efforts of many Egyptologists, using the many copies and editions of Ptahhotep's maxims that are available, some parts of the text remain puzzling.

♦ Prologue

The opening lines of the document briefly identify the author and then proceed directly into a poignant lament of the infirmities and indignities of old age. Although the author's dwelling on his age and infirmity might seem merely a bit of autobiography, it likely served another purpose. The ancient Egyptians had great respect for tradition and age, both in people and in things. Ptahhotep's age would have reinforced his authority.

The next dozen or so lines set the scene and give a context for the composition of the "Instructions." Ptahhotep wishes to appoint a successor, or "staff of old age," so that he may pass on his wisdom and save the people of Egypt from strife. The king responds by ordering Ptahhotep to instruct his son in the "sayings of the past" so that he may become a model for the children of the other officials.

♦ The Maxims: "The Formulations of Good Discourse"

The opening section of the maxims reintroduces the author at slightly greater length, providing him with an impressive set of titles, and says that these "formulations of excellent discourse" will be addressed to the son of Ptahhotep. The text then proceeds directly to a series of instructions (maxims).

Maxim 1: The first maxim deals with the importance of modesty in assessing one's abilities and counsels the reader to listen to the ignorant and the wise, noting that "good speech" may be found among kitchen maids. The "greenstone" to which good speech is compared is malachite. Malachite is a dark-green copper mineral that was mined in Sinai and imported into Egypt from the most ancient times. It was used occasionally in jewelry but also ground to a fine powder to make eye paint and, later, pigment for statues. It is here apparently referenced only for its value

"Consult the ignorant and the wise."

"Do not scheme against people, / God punishes accordingly."

"If you plow and there's growth in the field, / And god lets it prosper in your hand, / Do not boast at your neighbors' side."

"Follow your heart as long as you live."

"It is the god who gives advancement, / He who uses elbows is not helped."

"A short moment is like a dream, / then death comes for having known them."

"Kindness is a man's memorial."

and universal usefulness. Some modern scholars believe that this comparison reflects a classless viewpoint, reiterating the king's statement at the end of the prologue: "No one is born wise."

Maxim 2: The next stanzas counsel self-control and silence, particularly in dispute with a superior. It is the first of a series of maxims that address how the ideal man conducts himself in dealing with different classes of people. Throughout these maxims, the contrast is between the silent, self-controlled man and the "hot" man.

Maxim 3: The author then assures his audience that the same qualities that served in good stead with those more powerful will win out in disputes with one's equals. It also introduces the idea that a good name is something of preeminent importance. The idea of maintaining a good name was so important to the ancient Egyptians that its loss could lead to suicidal depression: In a Middle Kingdom composition that is sometimes called "The Man Who Was Tired of Life," the protagonist describes how the loss of his good name is so destructive that he cannot imagine living with the shame.

Maxim 4: When it comes to disputation with a poor man, however, the reader is especially advised to stand back from aggressive argument. The fourth maxim stigmatizes "he who injures a poor man." This section of the "Instructions" establishes the importance of controlling both one's speech and one's temper, themes that will recur throughout the text, along with the duty of those with power to mix justice with fairness and compassion.

Maxim 5: The fifth maxim introduces the concept that the powerful have a special duty to behave blamelessly in the maintenance of *maat*. *Maat*, an Egyptian concept translated variously as "truth," "cosmic order," or "justice," seems in this document to be closest in meaning to the latter. This maxim is one of the few that makes reference to reward or punishment in the afterlife, by mentioning Osiris, god of the dead, and it also refers directly to the guiding principle of morality in ancient Egyptian life: "justice," or *maat*.

Maxim 6: This teaching states that schemes and cleverness cannot prevail over divine will and that a person's success is dependent upon this. The maxim is the first one to refer to punishment by "god," a deity that is unnamed.

Maxim 7: Maxim 7 offers instructions in both table manners and the inevitability of social order and hierarchy. It also offers a glimpse of the ancient Egyptian view of human psychology when it says, "The nobleman . . . behaves as his *ka* commands him." *Ka* is one of the terms used by the ancient Egyptians to describe the component parts of a human being: physical, mental, emotional, and spiritual. Although *ka* is often translated as "soul," some Egyptologists prefer to describe it as a man or woman's personality or individuality. Scholars also increasingly refer to *ka* as the life force inherent in all human beings. The use of the term *god* (*ntr*) in this maxim refers to the fact that these rules of etiquette are more or less divinely ordained, as is the hierarchy they reinforce.

Maxim 8: This saying counsels against misrepresentation and slander, saying "the *ka* abhors it." As noted, there can be many interpretations of what the term *ka* meant to the ancient Egyptians. Whichever interpretation is chosen, it is certain that slander was regarded as a heinous crime.

Maxim 9: The ninth instruction advises against boasting about the fertility of one's land and thus raising the jealousy or anger of neighbors. In a parallel idea, the reader is advised not to flaunt one's personal fertility in front of those less fortunate in their families. This maxim has been interpreted in various ways. The fact that it refers to crops has sometimes been taken as proof that the "Instructions" were intended to be read to a wide audience. The first and second halves of the maxim can be read as shifting in topic from farming to family. However, it is also possible that the reference to fertile fields actually refers to the readers' own fertility in producing a family. For comparison, maxim 21 refers to a woman as a "fertile field" for her husband or lord. The reference to "praying" here just connotes asking the gods for a "follower" or successor; the gods determine the fertility of both fields and human beings.

Maxim 10: The tenth maxim is puzzling if taken at face value, because it seems to indicate a possible future in which the son of a vizier might end up as a poor man. Some Egyptologists have argued that the wording of the text indicates that it is addressing a wider audience than merely the high-status sons of officials. The mention of "god" here is another reference to the fact that an unnamed god or gods have determined this person's character.

Maxim 11: Unlike the other teachings, which advise against putting oneself first, this maxim urges the audience to pursue happiness and advises against becoming preoccupied with work. In ancient Egyptian thought, the heart is the seat of both intellect and emotion: In this maxim about the value of following the heart, it is clear that trusting emotion is what is meant.

Maxim 12: This teaching takes up the theme of the tenth maxim and develops the idea of how a good son should be treated: with love for good behavior and punishment for disobedience. It also reintroduces the theme that the gods in some sense determine the fate and character of mortals.

Maxim 13: This is another instruction on the importance of keeping to one's place in the hierarchy, even in such behavior as standing and sitting at the right times. An antechamber, as used here, is an outer chamber or waiting room in a palace or administrative building.

Maxim 14: Maxim 14 deals both with the qualities that make a man trusted and a leader and those that lead him to be despised: A trusted man does not think only of the needs of his belly (that is, his body) but also pays attention to the needs of other people.

Maxim 15: This maxim advises that a person should not falter in making a report or giving advice in the council of a supervisor.

Maxim 16: This teaching states that a leader should do outstanding things and remember "the day that comes after." This is another, indirect, reference to the importance of reputation.

Maxim 17: This maxim continues the advice on how to be a good leader. The reader is counseled to listen carefully and in silence to petitions and pleas, advising that even if the request cannot be granted, the petitioner will feel better for having his case heard. This maxim, like the one dealing with greed, shows considerable understanding of psychology.

Maxim 18: Maxim 18 is a warning against taking up with women of another household. It warns that death and failure are the rewards for trifling with these women, and it contains several almost untranslatable lines, including the one rendered here as "Poor advice is 'shoot the opponent.'"

Maxim 19: The fourteen lines that make up this teaching warn of the danger of greed, which is described as "a grievous sickness without cure."

Maxim 20: Maxim 20 repeats the warning of maxim 19 and especially mentions the dangers of greed towards one's relatives. It also repeats the theme that the moderate person is more deserving: "The mild has greater claim than the harsh."

Maxim 21: This maxim, which instructs a man in how to deal with his wife, is one of the most famous in all of Egyptian literature. This is largely because so little direct information describing the attitude of the ancient Egyptians toward women has survived. A man is enjoined to love his wife, clothe her, feed her, and "gladden her heart" because she is a "fertile field for her lord." It also warns a man against contending with his wife in court or allowing her to gain power.

Maxim 22: The next verses urge the reader to support his friends. It begins a theme that is picked up again in Maxim 35.

Maxim 23: This maxim is almost identical in sense to the eighth maxim and deals with the evil of slander. As with maxim 3, the importance of keeping a good reputation is stressed.

Maxim 24: In this instruction a "man of worth" is once again defined as one who is silent. This section has attracted the attention of scholars studying the history of rhetoric, because it states that "speaking is harder than all other work," thus indicating the importance of knowledgeable and accomplished speech in ancient Egyptian society.

Maxim 25: The twenty-fifth maxim nicely sums up how to be a great man in ancient Egypt: Be knowledgeable, gentle of speech, modest, not too commanding, and self-controlled. Although elsewhere the reader is counseled to be silent, this instruction warns, "Don't be mute, lest you be chided." This is not contradictory, as it is part of a theme developed in the next few lines. One should neither fret all day nor be too happy so that nothing gets done.

Maxim 26: This maxim and the next one deal with the ways in which a wise man should deal with his superior. In the first of these instructions, the reader is advised not to oppose those more powerful than he.

Maxim 27: Maxim 27 urges the student to become the teacher to the great, advising them on the best way to act to impress their own superiors. (Presumably this refers to the king and higher officials.) As a result, the text says, "as the favourite's belly is filled, so your back will be clothed." Because this particular instruction is equally, if not more, applicable to those lower down the social pyramid than the son of a vizier, some scholars view this as one of the maxims offering proof that the "Instructions" were intended for a wide audience.

Maxim 28: This instruction is specifically intended for one who is acting as a magistrate, and it urges the audience to avoid favoritism. A portion of one of the verses contains an unknown phrase, but it seems to be an expression for remaining impartial.

Maxim 29: Despite the urging to impartiality in maxim 28, the instruction of maxim 29 seems to advise that a judge or magistrate be forgiving of a man who has been otherwise upright and has not tried to argue his way out of punishment for a misdeed.

Maxim 30: This teaching warns against trusting in wealth, because wealth comes as a gift of the god. The theme that reward (in the form of wealth) and punishment are divinely given is continued from maxims 5 and 12. The punishment that awaits wrongdoers is never specified, unless it is to be understood that they will never prosper.

Maxim 31: Maxim 31 returns to the theme of deference to a superior as the gateway to success. The references here to "bending the back" and "baring the arm" refer to a position of respect or respectful greeting sometimes shown in Egyptian art. Inferiors greet someone greater than themselves by leaning forward with arms outstretched at knee level. This same posture of respect is mentioned in maxim 2.

Maxim 32: The next stanzas have not been included here, but later versions of the "Instructions" seem to indicate that they referred to a specific form of sexual misconduct.

Maxim 33: At the outset, maxim 33 contains advice on how to make and keep friends. It may be paired with maxims 22 and 35, which also deal with friendship.

Maxim 34: This maxim instructs the reader to be generous because "kindness is a man's memorial." It reiterates that the Egyptian ideal is someone clement and charitable.

Maxim 35: This instruction returns to the theme of knowing one's friends. It compares them in value to a well-watered field. The use of this term could be compared to the expression "to cultivate a friendship." This is no doubt a reflection of the importance of agricultural fertility to survival in ancient Egyptian society.

Maxim 36: This maxim counsels the reader not to stint on punishment but to punish only if a crime has been committed. This reiterates the advice of maxims 28 and 29.

Maxim 37: This last maxim offers marital advice about what to do if one's wife is a *shepnet,* a word whose meaning is uncertain but that may suggest a frivolous or flirtatious woman. (This meaning may be guessed from the description in the next line: "who is joyful and known by her town.") It recommends that a wise man should not be put off by such a woman but that rather he should "let her eat" and enjoy her company instead.

♦ Epilogue

The epilogue opens with the assurance that those who follow the maxims will prosper. There is special emphasis on the importance of learning good speech and of being mindful of history. As in the maxims, the onus is on a leader to learn wisdom. These stanzas mention that the *ba,* or soul of a person, should be fed "with what endures." In other words, the personality of an individual should be shaped by things that are permanent in their value.

The epilogue then proceeds to describe and define at length the qualities of the "good son," who is described as "a son who hears"; that is to say, a good son listens and takes note of what he is taught, and he follows the precepts he has learned from his father. The text describes such a son as "a follower of Horus," in a reference to the son of Osiris, who was viewed by the Egyptians as epitomizing the ideal son. The epilogue reiterates at great length and repetitiously that the premier qualities of such a son are his attention and obedience, his self-control, and his judicious and wise speech.

Audience

Like all wisdom texts, the primary audience for the "Instructions of Ptahhotep" would have been the very small literate proportion of Egyptian society. This group was overwhelmingly male and very largely destined for careers in public life. However, compared to other ancient Egyptian didactic wisdom texts, Ptahhotep's instructions are not always addressed specifically to this group. Many of the maxims are applicable to the conditions of life in general and would be of value to a much wider audience: Copies of this text were found in an artists' community, for instance, indicating clearly that even though the maxims ostensibly were written for the sons of viziers, their wisdom was considered to be of value to the children of ordinary people.

Impact

Whatever their actual date of composition, the "Instructions of Ptahhotep" were undoubtedly among the most influential documents written in ancient Egypt, evidenced by the fact that numerous partial copies of the text exist. Some are written on papyrus—obviously the work of qualified scribes and intended as good copies—but others are written on plaster-covered boards or even on scraps of pottery. The latter are excerpts from the longer document and were probably the work of students.

Another proof of the ancient impact of the "Instructions of Ptahhotep" is that at least two editions exist. Papyrus versions of the text in the British Museum contain some quite significant differences, in the form of additional lines, from the version that is translated here. Finally, some of the excerpts and school-text copies of the maxims that survive were written about two thousand years after the original document would have been composed. The latest versions are excerpts found on sherds of pottery at Deir el-Medina, the village that housed the artists who worked on the royal tombs, which was occupied from about 1500 BCE until about 1100 BCE. Quotations or references to specific maxims are also found in writings from the eighth century BCE during the time of the Kushite kings of Egypt.

The impact of the "Instructions of Ptahhotep" on modern scholarship is also considerable. The document itself has greatly contributed to our knowledge of the evolution of ancient Egyptian philosophy and ethics. There are, however, other wisdom texts that have much the same content. Part of what has made "Instructions of Ptahhotep" so important to modern scholars are the small red dots that appear in the margins. These have been identified as verse points, markings used to indicate the end of sections of poetry. Analysis of these points in the "Instructions" shows that the verses were arranged in pairs. These pairs of verses may also be found in some other examples of ancient Egyptian wisdom literature. This is an important clue to the nature of Egyptian wisdom and teaching literature because composing instructions in song or poetry is often used as an aid to memorization. If these maxims were passed on by memorization, then not everyone who learned them needed to be literate. This supports modern theories that hold that the "Instructions of Ptahhotep" was intended for a wide audience.

Further Reading

■ Books

Foster, John L. "Wisdom Texts." In *The Oxford Encyclopedia of Ancient Egypt*, ed. Donald B. Redford. Vol. 3. New York: Oxford University Press, 2001.

Lichtheim, Miriam. *Ancient Egyptian Literature.* Vol. 1. Berkeley: University of California Press, 2006.

Parkinson, R. B. *Voices from Ancient Egypt: An Anthology of Middle Kingdom Writings.* London: British Museum Press, 1991.

Raver, Wendy. "Instruction of Ptahhotep." In *The Oxford Encyclopedia of Ancient Egypt*, ed. Donald B. Redford. Vol. 3. New York: Oxford University Press, 2001.

Simpson, William Kelly, ed. *The Literature of Ancient Egypt: An Anthology of Stories, Instructions, Stelae, Autobiographies, and Poetry.* 3rd ed. New Haven, Conn.: Yale University Press, 2003.

■ Journals

Hutto, David. "Ancient Egyptian Rhetoric in the Old and Middle Kingdoms." *Rhetorica* 20, no. 3 (Summer 2002): 213–233.

—L. Green

Questions for Further Study

1. As an example of "wisdom literature," how does this document compare with other, similar wisdom texts, such as *Han Feizi*, the Dao De Jing, or the gZi-brjid? What similar—and differing—wisdom do the documents present?

2. The "Instructions of Ptahhotep" was written some four thousand years ago. What difference does it make whether the text can be dated accurately? Put differently, what difference do a few hundred years make for a document that is four millennia old?

3. How applicable do you think the "Instructions of Ptahhotep" are today? Do you think that contemporary people could profit from any of the maxims? If so, what does this tell you about the common humanity of people in the twenty-first century CE and the twenty-third century BCE?

4. Why should modern readers care about ancient Egyptian texts, including not only "Instructions of Ptahhotep" but also such documents as the Egyptian Book of the Dead, the Pyramid Texts, and "Great Hymn to the Aten"?

"INSTRUCTIONS OF PTAHHOTEP"

Instruction of the Mayor of the city, the Vizier Ptahhotep, under the Majesty of King Isesi, who lives for all eternity. The mayor of the city, the vizier Ptahhotep, said:

O king, my lord!
Age is here, old age arrived,
Feebleness came, weakness grows,
"Childlike" one sleeps all day.
Eyes are dim, ears deaf,
Strength is waning through weariness,
The mouth, silenced, speaks not,
The heart, void, recalls not the past,
The bones ache throughout.
Good has become evil, all taste is gone,
What age does to people is evil in everything.
The nose, clogged, breathes not,
"Painful" are standing and sitting.

May this servant be ordered to make a staff of old age,
So as to tell him the words of those who heard,
The ways of the ancestors,
Who have listened to the gods.
May such be done for you,
So that strife may be banned from the people,
And the Two Shores may serve you!
Said the majesty of this god:
Instruct him then in the sayings of the past,
May he become a model for the children of the great,
May obedience enter him,
And the devotion of him who speaks to him,
No one is born wise.

Beginning of the formulations of excellent discourse spoken by the Prince, Count, God's Father, God's beloved, Eldest Son of the King, of his body, Mayor of the city and Vizier, Ptahhotep, in instructing the ignorant in knowledge and in the standard of excellent discourse, as profit for him who will hear, as woe to him who would neglect them. He spoke to his son:

1. Don't be proud of your knowledge,
Consult the ignorant and the wise;
The limits of art are not reached,
No artist's skills are perfect;

Good speech is more hidden than greenstone,
Yet may be found among maids at the grindstones.

2. If you meet a disputant in action,
A powerful man, superior to you,
Fold your arms, bend your back,
To flout him will not make him agree with you.
Make little of the evil speech
By not opposing him while he's in action;
He will be called an ignoramus,
Your self-control will match his pile (of words).

3. If you meet a disputant in action
Who is your equal, on your level,
You will make your worth exceed his by silence,
While he is speaking evilly,
There will be much talk by the hearers,
Your name will be good in the mind of the magistrates.

4. If you meet a disputant in action,
A poor man, not your equal,
Do not attack him because he is weak,
Let him alone, he will confute himself,
Do not answer him to relieve your heart,
Do not vent yourself against your opponent,
Wretched is he who injures a poor man,
One will wish to do what you desire,
You will beat him through the magistrates' reproof.

5. If you are a man who leads,
Who controls the affairs of the many,
Seek out every beneficent deed,
That your conduct may be blameless.
Great is justice, lasting in effect,
Unchallenged since the time of Osiris,
One punishes the transgressor of laws,
Though the greedy overlooks this;
Baseness may seize riches.
Yet crime never lands its wares;
In the end it is justice that lasts,
Man says: "It is my father's ground,"

6. Do not scheme against people,
God punishes accordingly:
If a man says: "I shall live by it,"
He will lack bread for his mouth.

If a man says; "I shall be rich,"
He will have to say: "My cleverness has snared me."
If he says: "I will snare for myself,"
He will be unable to say: "I snared for my profit."
If a man says: "I will rob someone,"
He will end being given to a stranger.
People's schemes do not prevail,
God's command is what prevails;
Live then in the midst of peace,
What they give comes by itself.

7.   If you are one among guests
At the table of one greater than you,
Take what he gives as it is set before you;
Look at what is before you,
Don't shoot many glances at him,
Molesting him offends the *ka*.
Don't speak to him until he summons,
One does not know what may displease;
Speak when he has addressed you,
Then your words will please the heart.
The nobleman, when he is behind food,
Behaves as his *ka* commands him;
He will give to him whom he favors,
It is the custom when night has come.
It is the *ka* that makes his hands reach out,
The great man gives to the chosen man;
Thus eating is under the counsel of god,
A fool is who complains of it.

8.   If you are a man of trust,
Sent by one great man to another,
Adhere to the nature of him who sent you,
Give his message as he said it.
Guard against reviling speech,
Which embroils one great with another;
Keep to the truth, don't exceed it,
But an outburst should not be repeated.
Do not malign anyone,
Great or small, the ka abhors it.

9.   If you plow and there's growth in the field,
And god lets it prosper in your hand,
Do not boast at your neighbors' side,
One has great respect for the silent man;
Man of character is man of wealth.
If he robs he is like a crocodile in court.
Don't impose on one who is childless,
Neither decry nor boast of it;
There is many a father who has grief,
And a mother of children less content than another;
It is the lonely whom god fosters,

While the family man prays for a follower.

10. If you are poor, serve a man of worth,
That all your conduct may be well with the god.
Do not recall if he once was poor,
Don't be arrogant toward him
For knowing his former state;
Respect him for what has accrued to him,
For wealth does not come by itself.
It is their law for him whom they love,
His gain, he gathered it himself;
It is the god who makes him worthy
And protects him while he sleeps.

11. Follow your heart as long as you live,
Do no more than is required,
Do not shorten the time of "follow-the-heart,"
Trimming its moment offends the *ka*.
Don't waste time on daily cares
Beyond providing for your household;
When wealth has come, follow your heart,
Wealth does no good if one is glum!

12. If you are a man of worth
And produce a son by the grace of god,
If he is straight, takes after you,
Takes good care of your possessions,
Do for him all that is good,
He is your son, your *ka* begot him,
Don't withdraw your heart from him.
But an offspring can make trouble:
If he strays, neglects your counsel,
Disobeys all that is said,
His mouth spouting evil speech,
Punish him for all his talk!
They hate him who crosses you,
His guilt was fated in the womb;
He whom they guide can not go wrong,
Whom they make boatless can not cross.

13. If you are in the antechamber,
Stand and sit as fits your rank,
Which was assigned you the first day.
Do not trespass—you will be turned back,
Keen is the face to him who enters announced,
Spacious the seat of him who has been called.
The antechamber has a rule,
All behavior is by measure;
It is the god who gives advancement,
He who uses elbows is not helped.

14. If you are among the people,

Gain supporters through being trusted;
The trusted man who does not vent his belly's speech,
He will himself become a leader.
A man of means—what is he like?
Your name is good, you are not maligned,
Your body is sleek, your face benign,
One praises you without your knowing.
He whose heart obeys his belly
Puts contempt of himself in place of love,
His heart is bald, his body unanointed;
The great-hearted is god-given,
He who obeys his belly belongs to the enemy.

15. Report your commission without faltering,
Give your advice in your master's council.
If he is fluent in his speech,
It will not be hard for the envoy to report,
Nor will he be answered, "Who is he to know it?"
As to the master, his affairs will fail
If he plans to punish him for it,
He should be silent upon (hearing): "I have told."

16. If you are a man who leads,
Whose authority reaches wide,
You should do outstanding things,
Remember the day that comes after.
No strife will occur in the midst of honors,
But where the crocodile enters hatred arises.

17. If you are a man who leads,
Listen calmly to the speech of one who pleads;
Don't stop him from purging his body
Of that which he planned to tell.
A man in distress wants to pour out his heart
More than that his case be won.
About him who stops a plea
One says: "Why does he reject it?"
Not all one pleads for can be granted,
But a good hearing soothes the heart.

18. If you want friendship to endure
In the house you enter
As master, brother, or friend,
In whatever place you enter,
Beware of approaching the women!
Unhappy is the place where it is done,
Unwelcome is he who intrudes on them.
A thousand men arc turned away from their good:
A short moment like a dream,
Then death comes for having known them.
Poor advice is "shoot the opponent,"
When one goes to do it the heart rejects it.

He who fails through lust of them,
No affair of his can prosper.

19. If you want a perfect conduct,
To be free from every evil,
Guard against the vice of greed:
A grievous sickness without cure,
There is no treatment for it.
It embroils fathers, mothers,
And the brothers of the mother,
It parts wife from husband;
It is a compound of all evils,
A bundle of all hateful things.
That man endures whose rule is rightness,
Who walks a straight line;
He will make a wilt by it,
The greedy has no tomb.

20. Do not be greedy in the division,
Do not covet more than your share;
Do not be greedy toward your kin,
The mild has a greater claim than the harsh.
Poor is he who shuns his kin,
He is deprived of "interchange."
Even a little of what is craved,
Turns a quarreler into an amiable man.

21. When you prosper and found your house,
And love your wife with ardor,
Fill her belly, clothe her back,
Ointment soothes her body.
Gladden her heart as long as you live,
She is a fertile field for her lord.
Do not contend with her in court,
Keep her from power, restrain her—
Her eye is her storm when she gazes—
Thus will you make her stay in your house.

22. Sustain your friends with what you have,
You have it by the grace of god;
Of him who fails to sustain his friends
One says, "a selfish *ka*."
One plans the morrow but knows not what will be,
The (right) *ka* is the *ka* by which one is sustained.
If praiseworthy deeds are done,
Friends will say, "welcome!"
One does not bring supplies to town,
One brings friends when there is need.

23. Do not repeat calumny,
Nor should you listen to it,
It is the spouting of the hot-bellied,

Report a thing observed, not heard,
If it is negligible, don't say anything,
He who is before you recognizes worth.
"If a seizure is ordered and carried out,
Hatred will arise against him who seizes;
Calumny is like a dream against which one covers
   the face.

24. If you are a man of worth
Who sits in his master's council,
Concentrate on excellence,
Your silence is better than chatter.
Speak when you know you have a solution,
It is, the skilled who should speak in council;
Speaking is harder than all other work,
He who understands it makes it serve.

25. If you are mighty, gain respect through knowledge
And through gentleness of speech.
Don't command except as is fitting,
He who provokes gets into trouble.
Don't be haughty, lest you be humbled,
Don't be mute, lest you be chided.
When you answer one who is fuming,
Avert your face, control yourself.
The flame of the hot-heart sweeps across,
He who steps gently, his path is paved.
He who frets all day has no happy moment.
He who's gay all day can't keep house.

26. Don't oppose a great man's action,
Don't vex the heart of one who is burdened;
If he gets angry at him who foils him,
The *ka* will part from him who loves him.
Yet he is the provider along with the god,
What he wishes should be done for him.
When he turns his face back to you after raging,
There will be peace from his *ka*;
As ill will comes from opposition,
So goodwill increases love.

27. Teach the great what is useful to him,
Be his aid before the people;
If you let his knowledge impress his lord,
Your sustenance will come from his *ka*.
As the favorite's belly is filled,
So your back will be clothed by it,
And his help will be there to sustain you.
For your superior whom you love
And who lives by it,
He in turn will give you good support.
Thus will love of you endure

In the belly of those who love you,
He is a *ka* who loves to listen.

28. If you are a magistrate of standing,
Commissioned to satisfy the many,
Hew a straight line.
When you speak don't lean to one side,
Beware lest one complain:
"Judges, he distorts the matter!"
And your deed turns into a judgment (of you).

29. If you are angered by a misdeed,
Lean toward a man on account of his rightness;
Pass it over, don't recall it,
Since he was silent to you the first day.

30. If you are great after having been humble,
Have gained wealth after having been poor
In the past, in a town which you know,
Knowing your former condition,
Do not put trust in your wealth,
Which came to you as gift of god;
So that you will not fall behind one like you,
To whom the same has happened.

31. Bend your back to your superior,
Your overseer from the palace;
Then your house will endure in its wealth,
Your rewards in their right place.
Wretched is he who opposes a superior,
One lives as long as he is mild,
Baring the arm does not hurt it.
Do not plunder a neighbor's house,
Do not steal the goods of one near you,
Lest he denounce you are before you are heard.
A quarreler is a mindless person,
If he is known as an aggressor
The hostile man will have trouble in the neighborhood.

32. *This maxim is an injunction against illicit sexual intercourse. It is very obscure and has been
   omitted here.*

33. If you probe the character of a friend,
Don't inquire, but approach him,
Deal with him alone,
So as not to suffer from his manner.
Dispute with him after a time,
Test his heart in conversation;
If what he has seen escapes him,
If he does a thing that annoys you,
Be yet friendly with him, don't attack;

Be restrained, don't! let fly,
Don't answer with hostility.
Neither part from him nor attack him;
His time does not fail to come,
One does not escape what is fated.

34. Be generous as long as you live,
What leaves the storehouse does not return;
It is the food to be shared which is coveted,
One whose belly is empty is an accuser;
One deprived becomes an opponent,
Don't have him for a neighbor.
Kindness is a man's memorial
For the years after the function.

35. Know your helpers, then you prosper,
Don't be mean toward your friends,
They are one's watered field,
And greater then one's riches,
For what belongs to one belongs to another.
The character of a son-of-man is profit to him;
Good nature is a memorial,

36. Punish firmly, chastise soundly,
Then repression of crime becomes an example;
Punishment except for crime
Turns the complainer into an enemy.

37. If you take to wife a *spnt*
Who is joyful and known by her town,
If she is fickle and likes the moment,
Do not reject her, let her eat,
The joyful brings happiness.

Epilogue

If you listen to my sayings,
All your affairs will go forward;
In their truth resides their value,
Their memory goes on in the speech of men,
Because of the worth of their precepts;
If every word is carried on,
They will not perish in this land.
If advice is given for the good,
The great will speak accordingly;
It is teaching a man to speak to posterity,
He who hears it becomes a master-hearer;
It is good to speak to posterity,
It will listen to it,

If a good example is set by him who leads,
He will be beneficent for ever,

His wisdom being for all time.
The wise feeds his *ba* with what endures,
So that it is happy with him on earth.
The wise is known by his wisdom,
The great by his good actions;
His heart matches his tongue,
His lips are straight when he speaks;
He has eyes that see,
His ears are made to hear what will profit his son.
Acting with truth he is free of falsehood.

Useful is hearing to a son who hears;
If hearing enters the hearer,
The hearer becomes a listener,
Hearing well is speaking well.
Useful is hearing to one who hears.
Hearing is better than all else,
It creates good will.
How good for a son to grasp his father's words,
He will reach old age through them.

He who hears is beloved of god,
He whom god hates does not hear.
The heart makes of its owner a hearer or non-hearer,
Man's heart is his life-prosperity-health!
The hearer is one who hears what is said,
He who loves to hear is one who does what is said.
How good for a son to listen to his father,
How happy is he to whom it is said:
"The son, he pleases as a master of hearing."
The hearer of whom this is said,
He is well-endowed
And honored by his father;
His remembrance is in the mouth of the living,
Those on earth and those who will be.

If a man's son accepts his father's words,
No plan of his will go wrong.
Teach your son to be a hearer,
One who will be valued by the nobles;
One who guides his speech by what he was told,
One regarded as a hearer.
This son excels, his deeds stand out,
While failure follows him who hears not.
The wise wakes early to his lasting gain,
While the fool is hard pressed.

The fool who does not hear,
He can do nothing at all;
He sees knowledge in ignorance,
Usefulness in harmfulness.
He does all that one detests

And is blamed for it each day;
He lives on that by which one dies,
His food is distortion of speech.
His sort is known to the officials,
Who say: "A living death each day."
One passes over his doings,
Because of his many daily troubles.

A son who hears is a follower of Horus,
It goes well with him when he has heard.
When he is old, has reached veneration,
He will speak likewise to his children,
Renewing the teaching of his father.
Every man teaches as he acts,
He will speak to the children,
So that they will speak to their children:
Set an example, don't give offense,
If justice stands firm your children will live.

As to the first who gets into trouble,
When they see (it) people will say:
"That is just like him."
And will say to what they hear:
"That's just like him too."

To see everyone is to satisfy the many,
Riches are useless without them.
Don't take a word and then bring it back,
Don't put one thing in place of another.
Beware of loosening the cords in you,
Lest a wise man say:
"Listen, if you want to endure in the mouth of the hearers,
Speak after you have mastered the craft!"
If you speak to good purpose,
All your affairs will be in place.

Conceal your heart, control your mouth,
Then you will be known among the officials;
Be quite exact before your lord,
Act so that one will say to him: "He's the son of that one."
And those who hear it will say:
"Blessed is he to whom he was born!"
Be deliberate when you speak,
So as to say things that count;
Then the officials who listen will say:
"How good is what comes from his mouth!"
Act so that your lord will say of you:
"How good is he whom his father taught;
When he came forth from his body,
He told him all that was in (his) mind,
And he does even more than he was told."

Lo, the good son, the gift of god,
Exceeds what is told him by his lord,
He will do right when his heart is straight.
As you succeed me, sound in your body,
The king content with all that was done,
May you obtain (many) years of life!
Not small is what I did on earth,
I had one hundred and ten years of life
As gift of the king,
Honors exceeding those of the ancestors,
By doing justice for the king,
Until the state of veneration!
Colophon: It is done from its beginning to its end as
    it was found in writing.

Glossary

Colophon	a publisher's emblem or inscription at the end of a manuscript
greenstone	malachite, a dark-green copper mineral
Horus	the son of Osiris, an ideal son
ka	"soul," personality or individuality, or the life force inherent in all human beings
King Isesi	the Egyptian king also known as Djedkare Isesi, who ruled from about 2414 BCE to about 2375 BCE
Osiris	the Egyptian god of the afterlife, the underworld, and the dead
spnt	shepnet, possibly a frivolous or flirtatious woman
Two Shores	probably a reference to the east and west banks of the Nile River
Vizier	a high official in ancient Egypt

Two images of the god Hapy, depicting the symbolic unity of Upper and Lower Egypt

(Relief depicting symbolic union of Upper and Lower Egypt, from the base of a colossal statue of Ramesses II, New Kingdom [stone], Egyptian 19th
Dynasty [c.1297-1185 BC] / Abu Simbel, Egypt / Photo © AISA / The Bridgeman Art Library International)

"HYMN TO THE NILE"

"Hail to you, Hapy, / Sprung from earth, / Come to nourish Egypt!"

Overview

The "Hymn to the Nile" is an ancient Egyptian composition also known as the "Hymn to the Inundation" or the "Hymn to Hapy," dating to the early twentieth century BCE and attributed to a scribe called Khety. Consisting of about two hundred of lines of verse written in short columns, it is an unusual sort of hymn in that it was not part of any known temple ritual. Hapy, god of the Nile River and its flood, had no temple and perhaps no priests or temple ritual particular to his worship. Nonetheless, he was a very popular and extremely important god. This hymn was likewise very popular, and many ancient copies exist. It was no doubt sung or recited at festivals in honor of the god and the Nile's life-giving inundation.

Context

It is almost impossible to read a modern book on Egypt without coming across the quotation "Egypt is the gift of the Nile." This famous saying originated with the ancient Greek travel writer and historian Herodotus in about 455 BCE. His famous quote was as true three millennia earlier, at the dawn of Egyptian civilization, as it was in his time. In the thirty-fifth century BCE, the Nile was the heart of Egypt, and its yearly floods spread fertilized new soil through the fields much in the same way that blood circulates life-giving oxygen and nutrients through the body. This fertile new soil washed down from the mountains in the highlands of East Africa, far beyond any lands familiar to the ancient Egyptians. The mystery of the Nile's sources sparked the imaginations of the Egyptians, and they sought to explain where the river came from. However, they seem to have been content to seek the source of the river within their own borders, or close to them, and to explain its origins through myth.

The Nile was not only the heart of Egypt but its highway as well. South of the Nile Delta, the river is closely bounded on either side by cliffs and desert, which do not make for easy travel. In the delta itself, the months-long rise and fall of the floodwaters over the surrounding dry land discour-

aged the building of bridges. The river, on the other hand, facilitated the movement of people and goods, whether from one riverbank to the other or from the cataracts of Egypt's southernmost border to the shore of the Mediterranean Sea. In fact, the Nile made it relatively easy to move multiton blocks of stone from one part of the country to another. The toil and sweat needed to move massive pieces of granite or limestone across dry land would have stood in stark contrast to the ease with which they could be moved down the country by water, with the river itself helping in the task by bearing part of the burden. At such times, the river would surely have been perceived as a friendly and powerful entity. Without the Nile, there would have been no pyramids in the north and no monumental temples in the south, and the Egyptians were well aware of this fact.

The Nile defined Egypt in almost every way. It split the country in half, into the east and west banks, and also provided other clear geographical distinctions: the flat, wide delta versus the narrow river valley bounded by cliffs and the sere red-brown desert versus the lush black soil left by the flood's retreat. In most of the Nile Valley, this layer of fertile soil was heaviest along the riverbanks, soon meeting the harsh and rocky soil of the desert. Only in the delta did the fertile soil encompass the whole landscape. The Egyptians acknowledged these contrasts by referring to their country as the "Two Lands," which could allude to any one of these pairs: east and west, upriver and downriver, valley and delta, or desert and fertile land. Each ecosystem had its own distinct characteristics, its flora and fauna and even its own gods. The Nile was the one geographical feature common to all of Egypt.

Even the turning of the year and the passage of time were delimited for the ancient Egyptians by the Nile's changes. Many cultures have timed their new year to an astronomical event such as a solstice or equinox. For example, New Year's Day in modern Western culture happens close to the winter solstice, or shortest day of the year. However, in the Middle Ages, the New Year was celebrated around the time of the spring equinox, when day and night are of equal length. By contrast, the ancient Egyptians began their new year with the rising of the Nile, in mid-July. The seasons as well were defined by the Nile and its floods. Akhet, the first season, was that of the inundation, lasting for four months from

Time Line

CA. 2150 BCE	The Egyptian Old Kingdom ends.
CA. 2150 −2100 BCE	■ The beginning of the First Intermediate Period is a time of chaos and breakdown of central government.
CA. 2100 −2040 BCE	■ Through the end of the First Intermediate Period, order is gradually restored; several kings called Khety rule Egypt.
CA. 2040 BCE	■ The Middle Kingdom begins, to last until 1650 BCE.
CA. 1990 −1950 BCE	■ During the early Twelfth Dynasty, the "Hymn to the Nile" is possibly composed by an unknown author, perhaps named Khety.
CA. 1550 BCE	■ The New Kingdom begins, to last until 1080 BCE.
CA. 1500 −1350 BCE	■ During the Eighteenth Dynasty, academic copies of the "Hymn to the Nile" are made.
CA. 1200 −1100 BCE	■ Through the Nineteenth and Twentieth Dynasties, also known as the Ramesside Period, copies and extracts of the "Hymn to the Nile" are made on scraps of pottery by beginner scribes in the artisan village of Deir el-Medina.
CA. 460 −454 BCE	■ Herodotus comes to Egypt, to call Egypt "the gift of the Nile."

July onward. During this season, no agricultural work could be done, and so the pharaohs conscripted labor for work on monuments. The second season, Peret, which came after the flood's retreat and ended around March, was given a name that means "Going Out" and was devoted to planting and growing crops. The last season, called Shemu, which means "Heat" or "Drought," saw the harvest of grain and other important crops and was a time when the Nile water level began to sink.

Although they may not have depended upon astronomy to determine the year's end and beginning, the fact that their calendar followed the Nile's flooding did not mean that the ancient Egyptians paid no attention to the skies. Each year in midsummer the Egyptians eagerly scanned the heavens, watching for the heliacal rising—or the first rising just before sunrise after a period of invisibility—of the star Sirius, which they called Sepdet. They knew that around the time when this star rose into the sky in conjunction with the sun, the waters of the Nile would begin to rise in volume. This tied the Nile's flooding cycle, which might otherwise have been seen as strictly terrestrial, with events in the heavens.

The importance of the flooding and its regular, cyclical nature contributed to the ancient Egyptians' basic ideas about the proper nature of the universe. The cosmos was seen as unchanging and yet moving through a series of predestined stages. The last of these stages did not mean an end or even a settling into a static and eternal state. It was quite the opposite, in fact: The final act of one cycle was always the prelude to the opening stage of a new cycle.

The Nile, however, was not always predictable and could be a fickle friend. If it failed to rise or did not flood sufficiently, famine and disease were the inevitable outcome. If, on the other hand, it produced an overabundance of floodwaters, the result was destruction of property and the drowning of animals. The ideal inundation was neither too high nor too low, neither too late nor too early. The delicate balance between disaster and prosperity inherent in each year's flooding may have helped shape the Egyptian belief in the necessity of equilibrium in the universe. With respect to the outcome of a human being's life, the Egyptians applied the same idea of balance. Wisdom texts such as the "Instructions of Ptahhotep" speak of the necessity of moderation and fairness.

The Nile, and especially the Nile in flood, was personified as a god called Hapy. He was often depicted as a man with pendulous breasts and a large, drooping stomach and was shown wearing a false beard and a crown in the form of a marsh plant on his head. He was often represented with blue or green skin, which might even have rippled or zigzag lines to represent the current of the river. There is a certain amount of controversy about Hapy: Some Egyptologists claim that he embodies only the inundation and that the Nile itself has no name nor any deity representing it. Still others claim that he is not a god at all but a personification of the fertility of the earth.

Hapy had no regular temple and therefore no liturgy or priests. In this hymn, it is also mentioned that he had no shrines. Nonetheless, several sites in Egypt claimed to be special to Hapy because those very sites were the places where the Nile sprang from the earth. Different groups of priests at Egypt's southern borders tried to claim the source of the Nile for their temple, in order to tie the importance of the river to pharaonic society. One such group was at Elephantine (near modern-day Aswan), in southernmost Egypt. Another was at a site close to ancient Memphis and near present-day Cairo, in the north. The priests in this area claimed that there was a "second Nile" for the delta area of Egypt, which had its sources there. Also indicating the importance of Hapy and the inundation were the religious festivals held in their honor. Despite his having no temples or specialized priests, celebrations honoring

Nilometer at the mortuary temple of Ramses III
(Nilometer, from the Mortuary Temple of Ramesses III [c.1184-1153 BC] New Kingdom [photo], Egyptian 20th Dynasty [1200-1085 BC] / Medinet Habu,
Thebes, Egypt / Giraudon / The Bridgeman Art Library International)

Hapy were huge events. Ancient records confirm that over a thousand goats were sacrificed at one festival alone.

In the absence of shrines or temples, one sort of site must have been particularly associated with the Nile god: the Nilometer. The term *Nilometer* is used to describe several different kinds of ancient structures used to measure the rise of the Nile River during flood time. The simplest sort of Nilometer was a vertical column in the river with measurement markings on its side. Some Nilometers consisted of a flight of stairs leading down to the water, with measurement markings engraved into the walls of the stairway. Another type of Nilometer was a well that would fill with water as the flood rose. The rise of the Nile was measured in cubits (each approximately 21 inches in length) and palms, which were sections of cubits.

Numerous Nilometers were built in ancient Egypt. One of the best known and undoubtedly most important was the Nilometer at Elephantine Island, one of the sites where the Nile was claimed to spring forth from the underworld. This was also the home territory of the ram-headed god Khnum, who was said to create living beings and their souls on his potter's wheel. In the Eleventh Dynasty, not long before the period in which the "Hymn to the Nile" is said to have been composed, a sanctuary was built on Elephantine Island especially to celebrate the start of the inundation.

The Egyptians of the Middle Kingdom, when the "Hymn to the Nile" was written, still had vivid collective memories of the breakdown of order that followed the end of the Old Kingdom, around 2150 BCE. Many of the ideas expressed in the sections of the hymn mentioning the results of an insufficient inundation, such as the abandonment of friends and family and the lack of food and clothing, are reflected in the texts written about the time of chaos that lasted from approximately 2150 to 2050 BCE. Archaeological and paleogeological research

"Hail to you, Hapy, / Sprung from earth, / Come to nourish Egypt!"

"Who floods the fields that Re has made, / To nourish all who thirst; / Lets drink the waterless desert, / His dew descending from the sky."

"If he is heavy, the people dwindle, / A year's food supply is lost."

"No one beats his hand with gold, / No man can get drunk on silver, / One can not eat lapis lazuli, / Barley is foremost and strong!"

have confirmed that low inundations were a contributing factor in the end of the age of the Great Pyramids.

About the Author

As there are many versions of this important text, it is difficult to identify an author. The ancient Egyptian scribes of the Ramesside Period of the New Kingdom (ca. 1200–1100 BCE) declared that the "Hymn to the Nile" was the work of a great scribe of the Middle Kingdom. This author was supposedly a man called Khety who lived in the early Twelfth Dynasty of ancient Egypt, around 1990–1950 BCE. Virtually nothing is known about this ancient author, except that a variety of instructional texts are also attributed to him. Some of the kings of Egypt around 2100–2050 BCE were called Khety, and the name was very popular in the early Middle Kingdom.

Explanation and Analysis of the Document

The "Hymn to the Nile" was an important document, not only for its religious content but also because it was used in the education of scribes, alongside the wisdom texts and satirical commentaries on nonscribal professions. At least thirty copies of the text or extracts from the text have survived, all dating from the New Kingdom (ca. 1550–1080 BCE); most are incomplete. Unfortunately, many are corrupted by errors and omissions, and various texts can be seen as significantly different from one another. The abundance of mistakes and alternate lines has been explained as a result of scribes-in-training either writing the text from memory or taking dictation from an instructor. The translation used here has been compiled from a number of different versions.

Although no copy of the "Hymn to the Nile" has yet been found that can be dated to before the Eighteenth Dynasty (ca. 1550–1300 BCE), the form of the language used is that of a much older period. The "Hymn to the Nile" is written in Middle Egyptian, a form of ancient Egyptian that was the spoken language of around 1990–1600 BCE. Later Egyptians of the pharaonic period regarded Middle Egyptian as the classical form of the language, and people continued to learn it and even to attempt to write in it until the first centuries of the Common Era, over two thousand years later. (A comparison in the modern world might be the way that Latin has been taught in schools for over a thousand years since the end of the Roman Empire.)

While numerous ancient copies of the "Hymn to the Nile" have survived, only one divides the text into sections. The scribe who made a partial copy of the hymn on Papyrus Chester Beatty V (named after the wealthy collector who donated it to the British Museum in London) divided the document into stanzas of about ten to a dozen lines. Each line consists of a complete sentence or a clause from a longer sentence. In other versions, however, the meaning of the verses dictates that they be grouped into stanzas varying from eight to eighteen lines.

♦ **Stanza 1**

Unlike most of the other lines of the text, the first line is not part of a clause or sentence; it merely reads, "Adoration of Hapy." It is unusual for the ancient name of a text to be preserved. As mentioned, this hymn is known today by several different names, including "Hymn to Hapy." This opening phrase is probably closest to the way the ancient Egyptians might have referred to the composition.

Most of the first stanza enumerates the qualities and domains of Hapy. His many gifts to the world are listed, such as nourishing those who thirst, fertilizing the fields, and causing the crops to grow. He is considered responsible even for dew and rain. Egypt sees rain very rarely, and in the ancient language there was no name for it. In the famous "Great Hymn to the Aten" of the pharaoh Akhenaten, rain is referred to as the "inundation in heaven." That image is very similar to the one conjured here by the mention of Hapy's "dew descending from the sky." The "Great Hymn to the Aten" was composed around 1360 BCE, at a time when numerous copies of the "Hymn to the Nile" were being made, and the Nile hymn might possibly have influenced the Aten hymn.

In the opening lines of this hymn, the author notes that Hapy is "sprung from earth." Ancient Egyptian images of the origins of the Nile seem to show an underground source, with drawings or carvings depicting a kneeling god over an underground pool from which the water flows. Several cities claimed to be the place where this happened. However, the hymn itself says here and in the fourth stanza that the Nile god is "of secret ways," stressing the mystery of the river's origins.

The first stanza makes reference to several other gods. Re is the sun god and leader of the Egyptian pantheon. Over the course of pharaonic history the Egyptians would write down several competing creation stories, including some in which Atum, a god often identified with Re, is described as the Creator. In that version of creation, nine primordial deities are brought into being by the first one. This hymn makes reference to Re as creator, saying that he made the fields that Hapy waters with his flood. In a later stanza, the Nine Gods are mentioned.

Geb is the god of the Earth and is one of the primordial deities created in the aforementioned creation story. Along with his wife, the sky goddess Nut; Shu, god of air; and Tefnut, goddess of moisture, he represents the elements of the universe. It is from these four that other gods will be born. Since the Nile both springs from and flows over Geb, the relationship between him and Hapy must be close. Accordingly, he is described here as a "friend" of the Earth God (and the ancient Egyptian word translated here as "friend" can also mean "beloved").

Nepri is the divine personification of grain or the grain harvest. He, like Hapy as the Nile flood, had a cyclical existence. He was born with the sowing and sprouting of crops, died with their harvest, and was reborn when the grain seed was sown again. His life cycle was an interesting parallel and complement to Hapy's, since his regeneration came immediately after the retreat of the floodwaters, while the end of his life cycle preceded the Nile flood. Over time, as the myth of Osiris—who died and yet was reborn—became more dominant, it came to be equated symbolically with the growth cycle of the crops. Once this happened, Nepri lost his individual identity and became merely an aspect of Osiris. If this text was, in fact, written later than the Middle Kingdom, as some scholars have suggested, "Nepri" here is just another name for Osiris.

The ensuing line mentions Ptah, god of craftsmen and lord of Memphis, the ancient capital of Egypt. Ptah also has his own version of a myth that names him creator of the universe. Here, however, he is the patron deity of arts and crafts.

♦ Stanza 2

This section of the hymn describes three different types, or "modes," of Nile flooding. First, there is the low Nile, in which the river flows sluggishly. When this happens, insufficient fertile soil is deposited, and poor crops will result. In time, the soil dries out and blows away—hence the phrase "noses clog" in the first line of the stanza. Low Niles affected the whole country and not just the immediate valley. Failure of the flood would cause the oasis at el-Faiyûm, in Upper Egypt, to shrink in size, and the important surrounding agricultural area would also fail in productivity. Famine was the inevitable result. The second mode of flooding was also disastrous. When the Nile floodwaters were too high, irrigation infrastructure, dikes, and even buildings could be destroyed. Sometimes, when the flood reached too far beyond the banks of the river, whole villages could be washed away.

The third type of Nile flood was the perfect inundation. It is said in the hymn that the life-creating god Khnum has "fashioned" Hapy when this occurs. (The implication might be that when the flood is too low or too high, Khnum has not been involved, but this is not specifically stated.) Khnum's main cult center was in Elephantine at the southernmost tip of Egypt. This is the first place in the country where the rise of the Nile in flood would have been noticed.

♦ Stanza 3

These lines return to the theme of praising Hapy and enumerating his blessings upon the earth and its inhabitants. Even the other divine beings benefit from Hapy's actions, as the fertility left by his floods "gives sacrifice for every god." This stanza also speaks of Hapy as "dwelling in the netherworld." The ancient Egyptians conceived of the cosmos as being surrounded by the waters of chaos, or Nun. Creation happened when a hump of dry land emerged from these waters—a clear parallel to the inundation's subsiding to leave behind fertile land ready for life to spring forth. Nun existed before the origins of the universe and continued to exist even after the Creator-God brought order to chaos. The implication here and in the following verses is that the Nile or its floodwaters or both originate in this outer area of the universe. The Nile flood is also imbued with the symbolism of rebirth, in that it re-creates the moment of the birth of the orderly cosmos every year.

♦ Stanza 4

In the verses of this stanza, the themes of the power and secret origins of Hapy are reiterated. These are contrasted with the statements that Hapy has no temples or regular worship. The expressions "no portions" and "no service of his choice" refer to the fact that other deities would receive daily offerings of food and drink. The stanza then draws another contrasting picture: that of Hapy being received like a pharaoh. (The Egyptian words translated as "king" actually mean "one who rules Upper Egypt [the South] and Lower Egypt [the North].")

♦ **Stanza 5**

While continuing to praise Hapy, these verses make reference to a number of different deities. Neith was a delta-based goddess, one of the oldest in Egyptian religion. However, she was also connected with Esna, a city in the south of Egypt. This city was closely associated with fish, specifically the Nile perch, and in later Egyptian history it is clear that these fish were considered sacred at Esna. The association of this city with fish recalls Hapy's title of "Lord of the Fishes." Although Neith was connected both with war and with weaving, the goddess was also sometimes shown nursing baby crocodiles; this may be because in some myths she seems to personify primordial waters of creation.

Sobek (spelled "Sobk" in the document) is a crocodile deity whose cult center was later in the Faiyûm area. Like a number of other gods, he is credited with being a creator god; in one story he comes out of the primeval waters to create the world. If Neith is regarded as a personification of these waters, this explains how Sobek is seen as her son. On a more practical level, crocodiles were dangerous animals, and ancient Egyptians who traveled on the Nile would have hoped that a god like Sobek, who was both human and crocodile, might protect them.

The "Nine Gods," or "Ennead," is a name for the main Egyptian pantheon. The gods of the Ennead included Geb, Nut, Shu, Tefnut, Osiris, Isis (the sister-wife of Osiris, who raised him from the dead), Set (the brother and murderer of Osiris—just as Osiris came to symbolize the fertile land, Set represented the natural forces of the desert), Nephthys (sister of Osiris, who aided Isis in her quest to restore her husband's body), and the original deity, Atum. Interestingly, Hapy himself is never included in any ancient grouping of important Egyptian gods. Only a few of the Nine Gods are mentioned by name in this hymn, but all ancient Egyptians would have known who they were.

♦ **Stanza 6**

In this stanza, certain ideas are repeated from elsewhere in the hymn, such as that Hapy comes from darkness and is essential to life. Plants and animals alike are dependent upon the Nile. The rest of the stanza rather interestingly deals first with clothing and makeup and later with books. Ptah is mentioned once more, along with Hedj-hotep, the deity in charge of weaving and cloth making, who is described in some modern books as male, in some as female. Hedj-hotep is said to "serve" Hapy because the latter is the one who makes the flax fields fertile. Since linen, which is made from flax, was the main material for making clothing for the living and wrappings for the dead, the failure of this crop would have been disastrous. (Cotton was not grown in pharaonic Egypt, silk was unknown until Roman times, and wool was rarely used.) Unguents, or ointments, made from oils and animal fats scented with flower extracts, were also necessary in the intensely arid climate of ancient Egypt. The making of these perfumes links Hapy with Ptah, god of crafts. The papyrus plants that grew along the banks of the Nile were also

necessary to pharaonic civilization. They were the source of the materials from which books were made, and Hapy is thus linked also with knowledge and wisdom.

♦ **Stanza 7**

In this stanza, the words "if he is heavy" return to the theme of the low Nile, or insufficient flood, painting a picture of a sluggishly moving creature. Famine, death, and civil unrest ("everyone is seen with weapons") are the results of a low Nile. The ancient Egyptians would have offered their prayers to Hapy to bring necessary protection from both natural disaster and political chaos.

♦ **Stanza 8**

In this stanza, the verses elaborate on the theme of the importance of the freshwater of the Nile. This is contrasted with the saltwater of the sea, which cannot help humans grow grain, and the desert, which does not attract birds to drink—and thus to be caught and eaten. There are many ancient scenes of the Egyptians hunting birds, with the great majority set in marshes.

♦ **Stanza 9**

This stanza and also the eleventh stanza describe the celebrations made in honor of the arrival of the inundation. Music by harpists and singing by choirs of youths are important parts of the celebration mentioned here. Another much shorter hymn to the Nile written in Greek at least two thousand years later mentions similar celebration, particularly the procession of singing children. It seems very likely that the traditions, if not the actual original "Hymn to the Nile" itself, were passed on almost unchanged for millennia.

♦ **Stanza 10**

In these lines, the spontaneous and natural festivities of people enjoying a perfect inundation are set out, as they enjoy the bounty brought by the Nile. It is worth noting that food is not the only thing they "feast" upon: These verses describe flowers and herbs being taken up for their aromatic pleasure, a counterpoint to the dust-clogged noses that result from a low Nile.

♦ **Stanza 11**

In the hymn's eleventh stanza the different types of sacrifices made to the Nile are listed. These are of interest because they include not only animals that might live close to the Nile, such as oxen or fowl, but desert animals as well. These lines thus continue the theme of Hapy as ruler of the "Two Lands" in all their permutations.

♦ **Stanza 12**

The last verses of the hymn return to the motif of Hapy "mighty . . . in his cavern" and mention that his name is "unknown to those below"—that is, that he has a different name in the underworld. This exalts Hapy's position among the gods by equating him with the great deities whose real names must be kept secret, such as Re. The last few lines are clearly meant to be sung or chanted and bring the hymn to a vigorous end, while also serving as a kind of appeal to the god, reminding him of the joy he brings.

Audience

Although a few scholars have suggested that the "Hymn to the Nile" was never meant to be performed in a ritual, most would agree that it was intended to be sung at the festivals of the god. Since festivals were attended by all classes of pharaonic society, much of the audience for its performance would not have been literate and would not have had access to the written text. However, the existence of practice versions written by scribes-in-training implies that learning the hymn was considered essential knowledge for the educated for hundreds of years beyond its composition.

Impact

The impact of the "Hymn to the Nile" may be judged not only by the sheer number of copies that exist, and the long time span over which they were written, but also by the purpose for which many were made. The hymn was an essential school text, probably learned by heart and written out from memory by thousands of aspiring scribes from the early second millennium BCE until a thousand years later. It may be that copies continued to be made or the hymn recited from memory for another thousand years after that. A short hymn to the Nile written in Greek in about the fourth century CE shows some slight influence from this classic version, including mention of some of the same festival celebrations. The "Hymn to the Nile" thus served for thousands of years as the anthem for the single most important event of the pharaonic Egyptian calendar year. It was sung, or heard, by many millions of ancient Egyptians during that time. Without doubt, no matter what the date of its composition or the identity of its author, this work was among the most influential in ancient Egyptian religion.

Further Reading

■ Books

Assmann, Jan. *The Search for God in Ancient Egypt*, trans. David Lorton. Ithaca, N.Y.: Cornell University Press, 2001.

Baines, John. *Fecundity Figures: Egyptian Personification and the Iconology of a Genre*. Chicago: Bolchazy-Carducci, 1985.

Questions for Further Study

1. In what ways did the Nile River define ancient Egypt? Can you think of a more modern instance in which a geographical feature—a river, a mountain, a desert, a lake—"defines" the local community or nation?

2. Given the importance of the Nile to the ancient Egyptians, why do you think no temple was built to the Nile River god, Hapy; no priests were devoted to his worship; and, as the entry states, "Hapy himself is never included in any ancient grouping of important Egyptian gods"?

3. Floods and the movement of waters played an important role in many early civilizations. How does this document, as well as the story of Noah's flood in Genesis and the Book of Enoch and the flood account in the *Epic of Gilgamesh*, reflect the importance of flooding and attach theological significance to it?

4. The entry states that the ancient Egyptians "seem to have been content to seek the source of the [Nile] river within their own borders, or close to them, and to explain its origins through myth." Why do you suppose this was the case? Given the importance of the Nile, why was a party of explorers not dispatched to follow the river southward to its source, just to find out?

5. The ancient Egyptians worshipped the goddess Hathor, the mother-goddess of the world. She was also known by the name *Mehturt*, meaning "great flood," a reference to the Milky Way, which the Egyptians saw as a waterway on which the gods could travel. Hathor was believed to be responsible for the yearly flooding of the Nile. She was associated with motherhood, for the breaking of the amniotic sac as a signal that a woman is about to give birth was thought of as analogous to the flooding of the Nile, with the "birth" of the crops that would grow after it receded. Explain how and why this type of mythology would evolve in a place like ancient Egypt.

Foster, John L., ed. and trans. *Ancient Egyptian Literature: An Anthology*. Austin: University of Texas Press, 2001.

Hart, George. *The Routledge Dictionary of Egyptian Gods and Goddesses*. London: Routledge, 2005.

Lichtheim, Miriam. *Ancient Egyptian Literature: A Book of Readings*. Vol. 1: *The Old and Middle Kingdoms*. 2nd ed. Berkeley: University of California Press, 2006.

Pinch, Geraldine. *Egyptian Mythology: A Guide to the Gods, Goddesses, and Traditions of Ancient Egypt*. Oxford, U.K.: Oxford University Press, 2004.

Wilkinson, Richard. *The Complete Gods and Goddesses of Ancient Egypt*. London: Thames & Hudson, 2003.

■ **Journals**

Forbes, D. "The Egyptian Pantheon, Third of a Series: Hapi, Essence of the Nile." *KMT: A Modern Journal of Ancient Egypt* 10, no. 3 (Fall 1999): 52–55.

■ **Web Sites**

Hassan, Fekri A. "A River Runs through Egypt: Nile Floods and Civilization." Geotimes Web site.
   http://www.geotimes.org/apr05/feature_NileFloods.html

"The Hymn to the Nile Flood." University College London "Digital Egypt for Universities" Web site.
   http://www.digitalegypt.ucl.ac.uk/literature/floodindex.html

—Lyn Green

"HYMN TO THE NILE"

Adoration of Hapy:
Hail to you, Hapy,
Sprung from earth,
Come to nourish Egypt!
Of secret ways
A darkness by day,
To whom his followers sing!
Who floods the fields that Re has made,
To nourish all who thirst;
Lets drink the waterless desert,
His dew descending from the sky.
Friend of Geb, lord of Nepri,
Promoter of the arts of Ptah.
Lord of the fishes,
He makes fowl stream south,
No bird falling down from heat.
Maker of barley, creator of emmer,
He lets the temples celebrate.

When he is sluggish noses clog,
Everyone is poor;
As the sacred loaves are pared,
A million perish among men.
When he plunders, the whole land rages,
Great and small roar;
People change according to his coming,
When Khnum has fashioned him.
When he floods, earth rejoices,
Every belly jubilates,
Every jawbone takes on laughter,
Every tooth is bared.

Food provider, bounty maker,
Who creates all that is good!
Lord of awe, sweetly fragrant,
Gracious when he comes.
Who makes herbage for the herds,
Gives sacrifice for every god.
Dwelling in the netherworld,
He controls both sky and earth.
Conqueror of the Two Lands,
He fills the stores,
Makes bulge the barns,
Gives bounty to the poor.

Grower of all delightful trees—

He has no revenue;
Barges exist by his might
He is not hewn in stone.
Mountains cleave by his surge—
One sees no workmen, no leader;
He carries off in secrecy.
No one knows the place he's in,
His cavern is not found in books.
He has no shrines, no portions,
No service of his choice;
But youths, his children, hail him,
One greets him like a king.
Lawful, timely, he comes forth,
Filling Egypt, South and North;
As one drinks, all eyes are on him,
Who makes his bounty overflow.

He who grieved goes out in joy,
Every heart rejoices;
Sobk, Neith's child, bares his teeth, The Nine Gods exult.
As he spouts, makes drink the fields,
Everyone grows vigorous.
Rich because another toils,
One has no quarrel with him;
Maker of food he's not defied,
One sets no limits for him.

Light-maker who comes from dark,
Fattener of herds,
Might that fashions all,
None can live without him.
People are clothed with the flax of his fields,
For he made Hedj-hotep serve him;
He made anointing with his unguents,
For he is the like of Ptah.
All kinds of crafts exist through him,
All books of godly words,
His produce from the sedges.

Entering the cavern,
Coming out above,
He wants his coming secret.
If he is heavy, the people dwindle,
A year's food supply is lost.
The rich man looks concerned,
Everyone is seen with weapons,

Milestone Documents

Friend does not attend to friend.
Cloth is wanting for one's clothes,
Noble children lack their finery;
There's no eye-paint to be had,
No one is anointed.

This truth is fixed in people's hearts:
Want is followed by deceit.
He who consorts with the sea,
Does not harvest grain.
Though one praises all the gods,
Birds will not come down to deserts.
No one beats his hand with gold,
No man can get drunk on silver,
One can not eat lapis lazuli,
Barley is foremost and strong!

Songs to the harp are made for you,
One sings to you with clapping hands;
The youths, your children hail you,
Crowds adorn themselves for you,
Who comes with riches, decks the land,
Makes flourish every body;
Sustains the pregnant woman's heart,
And loves a multitude of herds.

When he rises at the residence,
Men feast on the meadows' gifts,
Decked with lotus for the nose,
And all the things that sprout from earth.
Children's hands are filled with herbs,
They forget to eat.
Good things are strewn about the houses,
The whole land leaps for joy.

When you overflow, O Hapy, Sacrifice is made for you;
Oxen are slaughtered for you,
A great oblation is made to you.
Fowl is fattened for you,
Desert game snared for you,
As one repays your bounty.
One offers to all the gods
Of that which Hapy has provided,
Choice incense, oxen, goats,
And birds in holocaust.

Mighty is Hapy in his cavern,
His name unknown to those below,
For the gods do not reveal it.
You people who extol the gods, Respect the awe his
    son has made,

Glossary

emmer	a type of wheat
Geb	the god of the earth
Hapy	the god of the Nile River
Hedj-hotep	the deity in charge of weaving and cloth making
Khnum	the life-creating god
lapis lazuli	a blue semiprecious stone
Neith	a goddess based in the delta area of the Nile and possibly associated with the primordial waters of creation
Nepri	the divine personification of grain or the grain harvest
Nine Gods	the main Egyptian pantheon: Geb, Nut, Shu, Tefnut, Osiris, Isis, Set, Nephthys, and Atum
Ptah	the god of craftsmen
Re	the sun god and chief god of the Egyptian pantheon
Sobk	a crocodile deity and a creator god
Two Lands	the two portions of Egypt, east and west, divided by the Nile River

The All-Lord who sustains the shores!
Oh joy when you come!
Oh joy when you come, O Hapy,
Oh joy when you come!
You who feed men and herds
With your meadow gifts!
Oh joy when you come!
Oh joy when you come, O Hapy,
Oh joy when you come!

Dragon, symbol of the god Marduk

(Dragon, symbol of the god Marduk, Late Assyrian Period, c.800-600 BC [bronze], / Louvre, Paris, France / The Bridgeman Art Library International)

"Those endowed with life, who walk upright, / Teeming mankind as many they be, give praise to Marduk!"

Overview

The *Hymn of the Righteous Sufferer* is an ancient work from Mesopotamia. As with most ancient works, little is known about its specific origins. We do not know who wrote it or when it was written. In fact, we do not even have the entire text. Some scholars place it in the second millennium BCE, but others place it in the middle of the first millennium BCE. At best, we can place it in about 1770–600 BCE. These gaps in our knowledge notwithstanding, this text must have been very popular, because fragments of it have been found in both Assur, in what is now Iraq, and Sultantepe, in what is now the Urfa (or Sanhurfa) province of Turkey.

The *Hymn of the Righteous Sufferer* was written to celebrate the god Marduk, who was the primary Babylonian deity. Marduk held a central position in this polytheistic culture because he ruled over all other gods and is credited with creating humans. Although the Sumerians recognized Marduk as a lesser god, his popularity grew throughout the latter half of the second millennium until he became the patron god of Babylon. For this reason, sometimes the text is referred to as the *Hymn to Marduk*. Scholars refer to it as the *Ludlul bel Nemeqi*, after the initial words in the first line.

The most complete version of this poem was found in 1952 by the archaeologist Seton Lloyd at a site called Sultantepe. The treasure trove of six hundred unbaked tablets found by Lloyd included a nearly complete first tablet of the *Hymn of the Righteous Sufferer*, containing previously unknown text, as well a second tablet that confirmed material already known from other sources. (Legible unbaked tablets are exceedingly rare, as they tend to crumble upon exposure to the air.) Although the beginning and end of the first tablet are missing, the great bulk of the text is well preserved, as is the text of the second tablet. The third tablet is less intact, as large portions are obscured. Two fragments from Assur and a third found in Sultantepe make up what we know of the fourth tablet. These pieces make sense in terms of content, but their order and placement remain unclear. This text is important because it is a classic Babylonian tale describing the relationship between humans and the gods.

Context

The second millennium in Mesopotamia was a profoundly militaristic period that saw the decline of Sumer and the rise and fall of Babylon. The first laws were codified under Hammurabi, and the first great stories, such as Atrahasis (also known as the Mesopotamian Flood Story) were committed to writing. This period also saw the rise of the Assyrians, a Semitic group whose control of the area began with Sargon of Akkad in 2371 BCE and eventually included the creation of the first empire that the West had ever seen. It was during this time that the *Hymn of the Righteous Sufferer* was written.

Clues to the context of *Hymn of the Righteous Sufferer* can be gleaned by looking to the locations where it was found and the language in which it was written. The technique used was cuneiform, which involves the impression of wedge shapes into clay; many different dialects and languages have been written in cuneiform, providing clues to dates. The first tablets featuring the hymn were found in Assur, capital of the Assyrian Empire, where King Ashurbanipal maintained a great library. Other tablets were found later in Sultantepe, the site of an Assyrian city that was located at the western reaches of the empire in Asia Minor in the seventh and eighth centuries BCE. Archaeologists also found a cache of tablets in what is believed to have been a priestly family house. Priests, being literate, were often the keepers of literary works, as were astronomers and healers. The culture was polytheistic, so maintaining tablets that elevated Babylonian deities such as Marduk was not inconsistent with their beliefs. Moreover, the Assyrians often found it politically expedient to recognize the local gods of areas they conquered. Other tablets in the priestly cache include medical texts and fragments of astronomy texts as well as an abundance of wisdom literature of the type that was common throughout Egypt and the Middle East. This wisdom literature includes religious texts, literary poems, prayers, incantations, and rituals. The inclusion of medical and astronomy works reflects the priest's dual role as healer and astronomer. Not surprisingly, the dates associated with these tablets end sharply with the fall of the nearby city of Haran to the Babylonians in approximately 608 BCE as the Assyrian Empire crumbled.

CA. 2334 −2279 BCE	■ King Sargon of Akkad unites all of Mesopotamia under a single ruler—conquering Sumer, Syria, and Elam.
CA. 1900 −1700 BCE	■ Assyrians create a web of trading posts throughout the Middle East.
CA. 1792 −1750 BCE	■ With his capital in Babylon, Hammurabi rules a large kingdom and compiles his code of law.
1285 BCE	■ The Assyrian king Adadnirari I starts a series of conquests that give rise to the Assyrian Empire.
CA. 685 −627 BCE	■ Ashurbanipal, the last great king of the Assyrian Empire, reigns.
610 BCE	■ The Assyrian outpost Haran (near Sultantepe) falls to the Babylonians as the Assyrian Empire crumbles.
1952 CE	■ The archaeologist Seton Lloyd finds the most complete version of this poem in Sultantepe.

The *Hymn of the Righteous Sufferer* was written in Akkadian, a language that had largely replaced Sumerian by approximately 2000 BCE. The use of Akkadian flourished with several variants until approximately 1000 BCE, when Aramaic began to dominate. Clay tablets continued to be written in Akkadian, but new writings on papyrus and leather were inscribed in Aramaic.

About the Author

Although the author of this poem is otherwise unknown, the text itself provides many clues if one assumes that the author and the narrator are the same person. In fact, the author identifies himself in line 44 of the third tablet as Shubshi-meshre-Sakkan, while more substantive information about Shubshi-meshre-Sakkan can be found in the first and second tablets. Looking to lines 78–79 of the first tablet, the narrator speaks of his former self as "so grand" with a "vast family." This sense of having been a person of authority is echoed in lines 29 through 32 of the second tablet, where he refers to instructing his people on his land to respect the gods and the king. Shubshi-meshre-Sakkan

may have been a governor, an important functionary, or a feudal lord of some sort who supported the king. He appears to have been wealthy, learned, and secure in his position in his family and with his immediate ruler. While it is conceivable that Shubshi-meshre-Sakkan was a fictional creation, it is reasonable to speculate that he represented the author. Ultimately, the truth is unknown.

Explanation and Analysis of the Document

The *Hymn of the Righteous Sufferer* recounts the story of the suffering of Shubshi-meshre-Sakkan and his eventual rescue by Marduk. The reader sees Shubshi-meshre-Sakkan become progressively isolated, outcast, and ill. The first tablet begins with a paean to Marduk. The arc of the plot begins when Shubshi-meshre-Sakkan is abandoned by the gods, his family, and his colleagues. He becomes terminally ill and in a delirious state begins to dream of his recovery. Ultimately, Marduk rescues him and restores his health and social position.

With ancient texts, the use of many tablets for large documents is done intentionally with regard to logical breaks in the subject matter. Thus, the first tablet can be thought of as the first chapter or first canto, and readers can expect a shift in the subject as the story advances from one tablet to the next. Given the condition of many ancient tablets, gaps in the text are inevitable. As such, translators follow certain conventions when translating a text with gaps or illegible passages. If a word or two is missing, the translator indicates the gap with an ellipsis. If a larger section is missing, the translator indicates the gap with brackets, often including information such as the number of lines that are unclear. Parenthetical or bracketed question marks indicate places where the translator has provided suggested words to restore the text.

◆ Tablet I

The first tablet can be divided into two sections. The first section (lines 1–36) is an objective discourse on the personality and powers of Marduk. The second, subjective section (lines 37–120) speaks directly of the narrator's experiences.

The initial lines set the tone and literary style of the entire work. It is obvious at the outset that this is a sophisticated poem. Many Akkadian cuneiform tablets have a limited vocabulary and a paucity of descriptive imagery; perhaps such tablets were used as mere guidelines to be fleshed out by skilled narrators rather than as literary works in themselves. Here, however, the range of vocabulary is wider than most religious texts. Moreover, the *Hymn of the Righteous Sufferer* shows substantial foreshadowing between the tablets as well as the use of opposing contrasts between various attributes.

The use of contrasting extremes in the opening quatrain is obvious at first glance. In line 2, Marduk is described as both "furious" and "calming." In lines 7 and 8, we see him in his fury and in his mercy. In lines 9 and 10, we learn that he is so heavy-handed that "the skies cannot sustain the weight of his hand," but he also has "a gentle palm." These contrasting pairs often refer to the weather and light. Just as daylight and mild weather are routinely associated with positive attributes, evening and storms are associated with negative ones.

These sudden shifts from night to day and from furious to calming moods parallel sudden shifts in mood that recur throughout the rest of the poem. The transitions are important because they are used only to describe Marduk. They are not found in other parts of the poem pertaining to the narrator or his situation. Only Marduk has the power to embody two completely opposite attributes.

Marduk's powers and attributes are described in surprisingly physical terms. He has a "gentle palm" and "quickly feels pain like a mother in labor." He has the power to heal as "his bandages are soothing, they heal the doomed." By establishing Marduk's powers as a divine healer, the narrator foreshadows his own physical suffering and delivery by Marduk that will be fully described in the second and third tablets.

This paean to Marduk establishes him as a wise and merciful god whose wrath is to be feared because he has the power of life and death. This is consistent with the view of him set forth in the Babylonian creation story, the Enuma Elish, in which Marduk is a fearsome warrior god who creates man while simultaneously destroying his enemy. However, the Marduk described in the Enuma Elish seems adolescent and two-dimensional compared with the Marduk portrayed in this work. Here Marduk is invested with great mystery, which is emphasized by the repeated phrases in lines 28–32 to the effect that no other god can understand him.

The objective portion of the hymn comes to an abrupt conclusion at line 37. Up to this point the author has pointedly left himself out of the text and dwelt instead on Marduk's attributes. Now the focus suddenly shifts as the narrator tells how Marduk has inexplicably become angry with him. This change in circumstances leaves no aspect of the narrator's life unaltered. Psychologically, he is thrown into a world that makes no sense to him, leaving him with a sense of existential trauma. The very tools that the narrator uses to make the world comprehensible have stopped working. This sense of loss is not merely psychological and spiritual. Having lost his "protecting spirit," the narrator also loses his vigor and manly appearance. Beset by "terrifying signs," he wanders the streets by day like a lost soul and by night is terrorized by dreams.

The suffering narrator moves through a world that has become polarized against him. Not only is the "king, incarnation of the gods," enraged with him, but he has become the focus of public animosity. A group of courtiers plot against him and launch schemes to strip him of his position and his house. Taken together, this group assumes a supernatural power "equal to demons."

The focus of the first tablet changes once more at line 70. While maintaining the subjectivity established in line 37, the narrator shifts from describing how the authorities have maligned him to the effect that this treatment

Stone slab depicting King Ashurbanipal
(Stone slab depicting King Ashurbanipal I [668-626 BC] [stone], Assyrian, [7th century BC] / Magdalen College, Oxford, UK / The Bridgeman Art Library International)

has on him. The physicality hinted at in the early lines of the poem recurs in a more developed form as the narrator describes his reduced circumstances by referring to his mouth, lips, heart, breast, and arms in lines 70–76. References to the physical expression of his reduced status recur later in this first tablet, particularly with regard to his face. The narrator's eyes cannot see because he is constantly crying. His eyelids smart through the tears. His face has become jaundiced by terror and pain. His mouth and lips are no longer functional, as his speech becomes gibberish when he tries to talk.

The narrator's position in his family and community changes. He becomes a loner, since his family, friends, comrades, colleagues, and slaves are united in their open animosity to him. A social pariah, he has no champions; "death came early" to anyone who tried to help him. Stripped of his social position, he says that his opponents "appointed an outsider to my prerogatives." The final insult—the ravaging of his farm and means of subsistence—appears close to the end of the tablet. Striking at the heart and source of Mesopotamian life, his opponents destroy his irrigation system.

The first tablet comes to an abrupt end with an unconvincing expression of hope in the future. The reference to the moon in line 120 most likely has astrological significance. This conclusion notwithstanding, the narrator's hope in a better future remains unpersuasive.

"I will praise the lord of Wisdom, solicitous god, / Furious in the night, calming in the daylight; / Marduk! Lord of wisdom, solicitous god, / Furious in the night, calming in the daylight."

"What seems good to one's self could be an offence to a god, / What in one's own heart seems abominable, could be good to one's god / Who could learn the reasoning of the gods in heaven?"

"An evil vapor has blown against me from the ends of the earth."

"Those endowed with life, who walk upright, / Teeming mankind as many they be, give praise to Marduk!"

◆ **Tablet II**

Tablet II takes a different approach to Shubshi-meshre-Sakkan's suffering. Whereas the first tablet spoke to his suffering at the hands of others, the second opens with lines that suggest supernatural agencies may be at work. This change is particularly fascinating because it sheds light upon Mesopotamian religious practices and spiritual beliefs and reveals how intertwined they are with physical health.

Medicine has a long history in the Middle East. Six hundred and sixty tablets from Ashurbanipal's library in Nineveh describe the treatment of disease and preparation of different drugs. According to these works, individual gods and lesser deities control particular parts of the body, which explains why Shubshi-meshre-Sakkan obsessively lists individual body parts in lines 52–105. Two different types of medical practitioner—the *ashipu* and the *asu*—are well known in the literature. Whereas the *asu* deals with mechanics of bandages and herbs, the *ashipu* is more like a spiritual healer who diagnoses disease and tries to determine if it is the result of some sin on the part of the invalid. The practitioners that Shubshi-meshre-Sakkan refers to in lines 6 through 9 seem to be some variety of *ashipu*. He catalogs their inadequacies, saying that none of them relieved his situation.

This shifts to a long passage in which Shubshi-meshre-Sakkan likens his suffering to those who neglected appropriate religious practices. Once again, the comparison sheds light on the customary rites and practices. We learn that prostration and prayer were common, as were obser-

vances of holy days, offerings of flour to the gods, along with oaths. Prayers and praises for the king were routine.

Shubshi-meshre-Sakkan argues that his present straits are undeserved because he did all these things and went to lengths to encourage others to do the same. Frustrated, he complains, saying that his fate is identical to that of people who failed to make the proper observances. He ponders the inexplicability of his fate, saying he can make no sense of the gods' reasoning.

An extended head-to-toe description of his debilitated physical condition begins at line 52. The narrator claims that supernatural agencies such as a "malignant specter," a "relentless ghost," and a "she-demon" are responsible for his condition. Shubshi-meshre-Sakkan describes his condition in the conventional Babylonian manner, starting with his head ("they struck my head, they closed around my pate"), and working his way down to the afflictions in his chest, bowels, and limbs. The graphic description of that narrator's physical state leaves no doubt that he is very close to death, as he describes himself as completely incapable of response. His eyes cannot see, his ears cannot hear, and a bolt bars his lips. Paralyzed, his "feet forgot how to move." The physical portrait he paints is that of a dying man.

The second tablet ends with a curious reversal of the light-and-dark imagery mentioned earlier. In line 117, the narrator tells us, "when my ill-wisher heard, his face lit up." This continues in line 118: "When the tidings reached her, my ill-wisher, her mood became radiant." Here the pattern established earlier in which positive events were associated with light has become as topsy-turvy as the behavior of the gods.

♦ **Tablet III**

The critical turning point of the drama is found in the third tablet. At first, the narrator speaks of his cosmic oppressor but fails to give him a name. Shubshi-meshre-Sakkan is being coy with his reader in not naming the one whom he blames for his trials. However, despite his invocation of various demons, goddesses, and lesser deities, it is clear whom he is referring to because the phrase "heavy was his hand" (line 1) echoes the earlier language about Marduk's "heavy palm" in the first tablet. However, by refraining here from directly blaming Marduk for his condition, the narrator can later praise him for his recovery.

Beginning with line 9, the narrator recounts three dreams. It is not clear whether these are ordinary dreams, vision states, or merely sick delirium. However, each episode is marked by the visitation of a supernatural character. In the first dream, the visitor is "A remarkable young man of extraordinary physique. / Magnificent in body, clothed in new garments." The second visitor is an exorcist of some sort, and the third is a beautiful young woman.

Each of these three characters works a form of magic upon Shubshi-meshre-Sakkan. The tablets are so crum-bling that it is impossible to tell exactly what the first messenger does, although it appears that he may be a forerunner sent to announce the impending arrival of the other two. The second figure is clearly a healer in the tradition of the *ashipu* mentioned earlier. It is he who pronounces "the resuscitating incantation" (line 28). The narrator builds the suspense slowly and carefully; it is not until the third dream that an exorcist, specifically sent by Marduk, works the final healing cure. If Shubshi-meshre-Sakkan is reluctant to blame Marduk for his trials, he is quick to credit him with his release. While the exact content of lines 54–61 has been obscured, it is obvious that "the feelings of merciful Marduk were appeased" and the situation is reversed.

In a second portion of the third tablet, the sufferer is released from the physical and spiritual woes that tormented him. The "evil vapor," "malignant specter," "relentless ghost," and "she-demon" that had beset him are overthrown and "dissipated like smoke filling the sky." Just as the narrator's physical woes were cataloged from the head down, his relief begins at his eyes and ears and moves down to his gullet until his abilities to breathe, speak, hear, and see are completely restored.

♦ **Tablet IV**

All that is known of Tablet IV are various separate fragments from which it is not possible to divine the plotline.

Questions for Further Study

1. "Marduk" is also the name of a black metal rock band formed in Sweden in 1990. Many of the band's lyrics feature Satanist and anti-Christian motifs as well as historical themes having to do with war, Nazism, and the like. The band is named specifically after the Babylonian god Marduk. "Sarpanitum," the name of Marduk's consort, is also the name of a contemporary black metal band. Why do you think these bands took these names? What connection, if any, might their type of music have with the Babylonian god?

2. Imagine that you are an archaeologist and you have set as your goal determining more precisely when *Hymn of the Righteous Sufferer* was composed. How would you set about this task? What types of evidence would you look for? Where would you look for this evidence?

3. *Hymn of the Righteous Sufferer* invites comparison with the *Epic of Gilgamesh,* which came from the same region of the world during very roughly the same time period. What do the two documents, taken together, tell you about the worldview of the people living at this time and in this place, particularly with regard to the role of suffering in human life?

4. In what ways, if any, is Marduk as depicted in *Hymn of the Righteous Sufferer* similar to the conception of God in the biblical book of Genesis?

5. Compare this entry with that on Cleanthes' "Hymn to Zeus," which also discourses on the powers and attributes of a major god. How do the conceptions of Marduk and Zeus differ? Are there any similarities? What do these differences and similarities tell you about ancient polytheistic religions and the cultures that produced them?

Fragments A, B, and C are entirely different pieces. As of 2010, scholars remained unclear as to which portions belong on the obverse or reverse (front or back, respectively) of the tablet or where they fit together. It has even been speculated that there may be more than four tablets. Taken together, these fragments seem to document the narrator's grateful recognition of Marduk as his savior. It was Marduk "who put a muzzle on the mouth of the lion that was devouring me." The reader learns more about Babylonian religious practices, such as the various ritual offerings of oil, butterfat, and grain that are made in Marduk's honor.

Audience

Unlike the Enuma Elish creation epic, there are no contemporaneous references to this poem, so we simply do not know the intended audience. Since several copies exist, we can speculate that it was a classic tale widely known from Nineveh to Sultantepe. Today, the hymn is studied by scholars specializing in Akkadian studies, religion, ancient history, and many other disciplines.

Impact

Since there are no contemporaneous references, it is unclear what impact, if any, the *Hymn of the Righteous Sufferer* may have had during its time. When it was first translated in the 1950s, some scholars struggled to make connections with the biblical book of Job, thinking that the Babylonian sufferer may have been the model for Job. Indeed, the "righteous sufferer" is commonly referred to as the "Babylonian Job" because both suffered the loss of social position and health, only to have them restored by their respective gods. Similar efforts were also made to historically connect the Mesopotamian creation story known as the Enuma Elish and the Mesopotamian flood story Atrahasis with events occurring in the Old Testament. This approach has fallen out of favor. Modern scholars are unlikely to use such ancient documents to bolster fundamentalist Judeo-Christian history; instead of using one story to support any one particular belief, they evaluate the stories comparatively, tracing story lines and patterns and determining how they relate to each other. People study these stories today to learn about Mesopotamian beliefs and practices and how they fit into the rich cultural world of the Middle East. By studying the specific language usage, one learns about the transmission of stories throughout the Neo-Assryian Empire. As new scholarship evolves, more will be learned about how this story, and others like it, were used in their own time; in particular with respect to the *Hymn of the Righteous Sufferer*, historians hope that new scholarship will shed more light on the configuration of the fourth tablet.

Further Reading

■ Books

Dalley, Stephanie, et al. *The Legacy of Mesopotamia*. New York: Oxford University Press, 1998.

Lambert, W. G. *Babylonian Wisdom Literature*. Winona Lake, Ind.: Eisenbrauns, 1996.

■ Journals

Lambert, W. G., and O. R Gurney. "The Poem of the Righteous Sufferer." *Anatolian Studies* 4 (1954): 65–99.

Moran, William L. "Notes on the Hymn to Marduk in *Ludlul Bel Nemeqi*." *Journal of the American Oriental Society* 103, no. 1 (January–March 1983): 255–260.

■ Web Sites

"Ancient Mesopotamia: This History, Our History." Oriental Institute of the University of Chicago Web site.
  http://mesopotamia.lib.uchicago.edu/

BetBasoo, Peter. "Brief History of Assyrians." Assyrian International News Agency Web site.
  http://www.aina.org/aol/peter/brief.htm

—Cy Ashley Webb

HYMN OF THE RIGHTEOUS SUFFERER

Tablet I

1. I will praise the lord of Wisdom, solicitous god,
2. Furious in the night, calming in the daylight;
3. Marduk! lord of wisdom, solicitous god,
4. Furious in the night, calming in the daylight;
5. Whose anger engulfs like a tempest,
6. Whose breeze is sweet as the breath of morn
7. In his fury not to be withstood, his rage the deluge,
8. Merciful in his feelings, his emotions relenting.
9. The skies cannot sustain the weight of his hand,
10. His gentle palm rescues the moribund.
11. Marduk! The skies cannot sustain the weight of his hand,
12. His gentle palm rescues the moribund.
13. When he is angry, graves are dug,
14. His mercy raised the fallen from disaster.
15. When he glowers, protective spirits take flight,
16. He has regard for and turns to the one whose god has forsaken him.
17. Harsh is his punishments, he . . . in battles (?)
18. When moved to mercy, he quickly feels pain like a mother in labor.
19. He is bull-headed in love of mercy
20. Like a cow with a calf, he keeps turning around watchfully.
21. His scourge is barbed and punctures the body,
22. His bandages are soothing, they heal the doomed.
23. He speaks and makes one incur many sins,
24. On the day of his justice sin and guilt are dispelled.
25. He is the one who makes shivering and trembling,
26. Through his sacral spell chills and shivering are relieved.
27. Who raises the flood of Adad, the blow of Erra,
28. Who reconciles the wrathful god and goddess
29. The Lord divines the gods' inmost thoughts
30. But no god understand his behavior,
31. Marduk divines the gods' inmost thoughts
32. But no god understands his behavior!
33. As heavy his hand, so compassionate his heart
34. As brutal his weapons, so life-sustaining his feelings,
35. Without his consent, who could cure his blow?
36. Against his will, who could sin and escape?
37. I will proclaim his anger, which runs deep, like a fish,
38. He punished me abruptly, then granted life
39. I will teach the people, I will instruct the land to fear
40. To be mindful of him is propitious for . . .
41. After the Lord changed day into night
42. And the warrior Marduk became furious with me,
43. My own god threw me over and disappeared,
44. My goddess broke rank and vanished
45. He cut off the benevolent angel who walked beside me
46. My protecting spirit was frightened off, to seek out someone else
47. My vigor was taken away, my manly appearance became gloomy,
48. My dignity flew off, my cover leaped away.
49. Terrifying signs beset me
50. I was forced out of my house, I wandered outside,
51. My omens were confused, they were abnormal every day,
52. The prognostication of diviner and dream interpreter could not explain what I was undergoing.
53. What was said in the street portended ill for me,
54. When I lay down at nights, my dream was terrifying
55. The king, incarnation of the gods, sun of his people
56. His heart was enraged with me and appeasing him was impossible
57. Courtiers were plotting hostile against me,
58. They gathered themselves to instigate base deeds:
59. Says the first "I will make him end his life"
60. Says the second "I ousted him from his command"
61. So likewise the third "I will get my hands on his post!"
62. "I will force his house!" vows the fourth
63. As the fifth pants to speak
64. Sixth and seventh follow in his train! (literally in his protective spirit)
65. The clique of seven have massed their forces,
66. Merciless as fiends, equal to demons.
67. So one is their body, united in purpose,
68. Their hearts fulminate against me, ablaze like fire.
69. Slander and lies they try to lend credence against me
70. My mouth once proud was muzzled like a . . .
71. My lips, which used to discourse, became those of a dead man.
72. My resounding call struck dumb,

73. My proud head bent earthward,
74. My stout heart turned feeble for terror,
75. My broad breast brushed aside by a novice,
76. My far-reaching arms pinned down by flimsy matting,
77. I, who walked proudly, learned slinking,
78. I, so grand, became servile,
79. To my vast family, I became a loner,
80. As I went through the streets, ears were pricked up at me,
81. I would enter the palace, eyes would squint at me,
82. My city was glowering at me like an enemy,
83. Belligerent and hostile would seem my land!
84. My brother became my foe,
85. My friend became a malignant demon,
86. My comrade would denounce me savagely,
87. My colleague was constantly keeping the taint to his weapons,
88. My best friend would pinch off my life.
89. My slave cursed me openly in the assembly of gentlefolk
90. My slave girl defamed me before the rabble.
91. An acquaintance would see me and make himself scarce,
92. My family disowned me,
93. A pit awaited anyone speaking well of me,
94. While he who was uttering defamation of me forged ahead.
95. One who relayed base things about me had a god for his help
96. For the one who said "What a pity about him!" death came early,
97. The one of no help, his life became charmed,
98. I had no one to go at my side, nor saw I a champion.
99. They parceled my possessions among the riffraff,
100. The sources of my watercourses they blocked with muck,
101. They chased the harvest song from my fields,
102. They left my community deathly still, like that of a ravaged foe.
103. They let another assume my duties,
104. They appointed an outsider to my prerogatives.
105. By day sighing, by night lamentation,
106. Monthly, trepidation, despair the year,
107. I moaned like a dove all my days,
108. I let out groans as my song,
109. My eyes are forced to look through constant crying,
110. My eyelids are smarting through of tears.
111. My face is darkened from the apprehensions of my heart,
112. Terror and pain have jaundiced my face.

113. The . . . of my heart is quaking in ceaseless apprehension.
114. . . . like a burning fire,
115. Like the bursting of a flame falsehood beset me,
116. . . . lamentation, my imploring!
117. The speech of lips was senseless, like a moron´s,
118. When I tried to talk, my conversation was gibberish.
119. I watch, that in daylight good will come upon me!
120. The moon will change, the sun will shine!

Tablet II

1. One whole year to the next! The normal time passed.
2. As I turned around, it was more and more terrible,
3. My ill luck was on the increase, I could find no good fortune.
4. I called to my god, he did not show his face,
5. I prayed to my goddess, she did not raise her head.
6. The diviner with his inspection did not get the bottom of it,
7. Nor did the dream interpreter with his incense clear up my case
8. I beseeched a dream spirit, but it did not enlighten me,
9. The exorcist with his ritual did not appease divine wrath.
10. What bizarre actions everywhere!
11. I looked behind: persecution, harassment!
12. Like one who had not made libations to his god,
13. Nor invoked his goddess with a food offering,
14. Who was not wont to prostrate, nor seen to bow down,
15. From whose mouth supplication and prayer were wanting,
16. Who skipped holy days, despised festivals,
17. Who was neglectful, omitted the gods´ rites,
18. Who had not taught his people reverence and worship,
19. Who did not invoke his god, but ate his food offering,
20. Who snubbed his goddess, brought her no flour offering,
21. Like one possessed, who forgot his lord,
22. Who casually swore a solemn oath by his god; I indeed seemed such a one!
23. I, for my part, was mindful of supplication and prayer,
24. Prayer to me was the natural recourse, sacrifice my rule.
25. The day for reverencing the gods was a source of satisfaction to me,

26. The goddess's procession day was my profit and return.
27. Praying for the king, that was my joy,
28. His sennet was as if for my own good omen.
29. I instructed my land to observe the god's rites,
30. The goddess's name did I drill my people to esteem
31. I made my praises of the king like a god's,
32. And taught the populace reverence for the palace.
33. I wish I knew that these things were pleasing to a god!
34. What seems good to one's self could be an offence to a god,
35. What in one's own heart seems abominable, could be good to one's god!
36. Who could learn the reasoning of the gods in heaven?
37. Who could grasp the intentions of the gods of the depths?
38. Where might human beings have learned the ways of a god?
39. He who lived by his brawn died in confinement.
40. Suddenly one is downcast, in a trice full of cheer,
41. One moment he sings in exaltation,
42. In a trice he groans like a professional mourner.
43. People's motivations change in a twinkling!
44. Starving, they become like corpses,
45. Full, they would rival their gods.
46. In good times, they speak of scaling heaven,
47. When it goes badly, they complain of going down to hell.
48. I have pondered these things; I have made no sense of them.
49. But as for me, in despair a whirlwind is driving me!
50. Debilitating disease is let loose upon me.
51. An evil vapor has blown against me from the ends of the earth,
52. Head pain has surged upon me from the breast of hell,
53. A malignant specter has come forth from its hidden depth,
54. A relentless ghost came out of its dwelling place.
55. A she-demon came down from the mountain,
56. Ague set forth with the flood and sea,
57. Debility broke through the ground with the plants.
58. They assembled their host, together they came upon me:
59. They struck my head, they closed around my pate,
60. My features were gloomy, my eyes ran a flood,
61. They wrenched my muscles, made my neck limp,
62. They thwacked my chest, pounded my breast,
63. They affected my flesh, threw me into convulsion,
64. They kindled a fire in my epigastrium,

65. They churned up my bowels, they twisted my entrails
66. Coughing and hacking infected my lungs,
67. They infected my limbs, made my flesh pasty,
68. My lofty stature they toppled like a wall,
69. My robust figure they flattened like a bulrush,
70. I was dropped like a dried fig, I was tossed on my face.
71. A demon has clothed himself in my body for a garment,
72. Drowsiness smothers me like a net,
73. My eyes stare, they cannot see,
74. My ears prick up, they cannot hear.
75. Numbness has spread over my whole body,
76. Paralysis has fallen upon my flesh.
77. Stiffness has seized my arms,
78. Debility has fallen upon my loins,
79. My feet forgot how to move.
80. A stroke has overcome me, I choke like one fallen
81. Signs of death have shrouded my face!
82. If someone thinks of me, I can't respond to the enquirer,
83. "Alas" they weep, I have lost consciousness,
84. A snare is laid on my mouth,
85. And a bolt bars my lips,
86. My way in is barred, my point of slaking blocked,
87. My hunger is chronic, my gullet constricted.
88. If it be of grain, I choke it down like stinkweed,
89. Beer, the sustenance of mankind, is sickening to me.
90. Indeed, the malady drags on!
91. For lack of food my features are unrecognizable,
92. My flesh is waste, my blood has run dry,
93. My bones are loose, covered only with skin,
94. My tissues are inflamed, afflicted with gangrene.
95. I took to bed, confined, going out was exhaustion,
96. My house turned into my prison.
97. My flesh was a shackle, my arms being useless,
98. My person was a fetter, my feet having given way.
99. My afflictions were grievous, the blow was severe!
100. A scourge full of barbs thrashed me,
101. A crop lacerated me, cruel with thorns,
102. All day long tormentor would torment me,
103. Nor a night would he let me breathe freely a moment
104. From writhing, my joints were separated,
105. My limbs were splayed and thrust apart.
106. I spent the night in my dung like an ox,
107. I wallowed in my excrement like a sheep.
108. The exorcist recoiled from my symptoms,
109. While my omens have perplexed the diviner.

110. The exorcist did not clarify the nature of my complaint,
111. While the diviner put no time limit on my illness.
112. No god came to the rescue, nor lent me a hand,
113. No goddess took pity on me, nor went at my side.
114. My grave was open, my funerary gods ready,
115. Before I had died, lamentation for me was done.
116. All my country said, "How wretched he was!"
117. When my ill-wisher heard, his face lit up,
118. When the tidings reached her, my ill-wisher, her mood became radiant,
119. The day grew dim for my whole family
120. For those who knew me, their sun grew dark.

Tablet III

1. Heavy was his hand upon me, I could not hear it!
2. Dread of him was oppressive, it . . . me.
3. His fierce punishment . . . the deluge,
4. His stride was . . . , it . . .
5. Harsh, severe illness does not . . . my person,
6. I lost sight of alertness, . . . make my mind stray,
7. I groan day and night alike,
8. Dreaming and waking I am equally wretched.
9. A remarkable young man of extraordinary physique,
10. Magnificent in body, clothed in new garments,
11. Because I was only half awake, his features lacked form.
12. He was clad in splendor, robed in dread—
13. He came in upon me, he stood over me,
14. When I saw him my flesh grew numb.
15. [ ] "The Lady has sent me,
16. "[ ]."
17. [ ] I tried to tell my people
18. "[ ] sent [ ] for me."
19. They were silent and did not speak,
20. They heard me in silence and did not answer.
21. A second time I saw a dream
22. In the dream I saw at night
23. A remarkable purifier [ ]
24. Holding in his hand a tamarisk rod of purification.
25. "Laluralimma, resident of Nippur,
26. Has sent me to cleanse you."
27. He was carrying water, he poured it over me,
28. He pronounced the resuscitating incantation, he massaged my body.
29. A third time I saw a dream,
30. In my dream I saw at night:
31. A remarkable young woman in shining countenance,
32. Clothed like a person, being like a god,
33. A queen among peoples [ ]

34. She entered upon me and sat down. . . .
35. She ordered my deliverance [ ]
36. "Fear not," She said, " I will . . . ,
37. "Whatever one sees of a dream. . . ."
38. She ordered my deliverance, "Most wretched indeed is he,
39. "Whoever he might be, . . . the one who saw the vision at night"
40. In the dream was Ur-Nintinugga, a Babylonian. . . .
41. A bearded young man wearing a tiara,
42. He was an exorcist, carrying a tablet,
43. "Marduk has sent me!
44. "To Shubshi-meshre-Sakkan [the sufferer] I have brought swathe,
45. "From his pure hands I have brought a swathe."
46. He has entrusted me into the hands of my ministrant.
47. In waking hours he sent a message,
48. He revealed his favorable sign to my people.
49. I was awake in my sickness, a healing serpent slithered by
50. My illness was quickly over, my fetters were broken
51. After my lord´s heart had quieted,
52. And the feelings of merciful Marduk were appeased,
53. And he had accepted my prayers,
54. His sweet relenting. . . .
55. He ordered my deliverance: "He is greatly tried"
56. . . . to extol . . .
57. . . . to worship and . . .
58. . . . my guilt . . .
59. . . . my iniquity . . .
60. . . . my transgression . . .
61. He made the wind bear away my offenses

(The exact placement of the following lines is unknown.)

1. He applied to me his spell which binds debilitating disease
2. He drove back the evil vapor to the ends of the earth,
3. He bore off the head pain to the breast of hell,
4. He sent down the malignant specter to its hidden depth,
5. The relentless ghost he returned to its dwelling
6. He overthrew the she-demon, sending her off to a mountain,
7. He replaced the ague in flood and sea.
8. He eradicated debility like a plant,
9. Uneasy sleep, excessive drowsiness,
10. He dissipated like smoke filling the sky.
11. The turning towards people with "Woe!" and "Alas!" he drove away like a cloud, earth. . . .

12. The tenacious disease in the head, which was heavy as a millstone,

13. He raised like dew of night, he removed it from me.

14. My beclouded eyes, which were wrapped in the shroud of death,

15. He drove the cloud a thousand leagues away, he brightened my vision.

16. My ears, which were stopped and clogged like a deaf man's,

17. He removed their blockage, he opened my hearing.

18. My nose, whose breathing was choked by symptoms of fever,

19. He soothed its affliction so I could breathe freely.

20. My babbling lips, which had taken on a hard crust,

21. He wiped away their distress and undid their deformation.

22. My mouth, which was muffled, so that proper speech was difficult,

23. He scoured like copper and removed its filth.

24. My teeth, which were clenched and locked together firmly,

25. He opened their fastening, freed the jaws.

26. My tongue, which was tied and could not converse,

27. He wiped off its coating and its speech became fluent.

28. My windpipe, which was tight and choking, as though on a gobbet,

29. He made well and let it sing its songs like a flute.

30. My gullet, which was swollen so it could not take food,

31. Its swelling went down and he opened its blockage

32. My . . . which . . .

33. . . . above . . .

34. . . . which was darkened like

(Three damaged lines, then gap.)

Tablet IV

♦ **(Fragment A)**

1. The Lord . . . me

2. The Lord took hold of me,

3. The Lord set me on my feet,

4. The Lord revived me,

5. He rescued me from the pit

6. He summoned me from destruction

7. . . . he pulled me from the river of death,

8. . . . he took my hand.

9. He who smote me,

10. Marduk, he restored me!

11. It was Marduk who made him drop his weapon.

12. He . . . the attack of my foe,

13. It was Marduk who . . .

(Two fragmentary lines, then gap. Insert here, perhaps, two lines known only from an ancient commentary.)

At the place of the river ordeal, where people's fates are decided, I was struck on the forehead, my slave marks removed.

♦ **(Fragment B)**

1. [ ] which in my prayers. . . .

2. With prostration and supplication [ ] to Esagila [ ]

3. I who went down to the grave have returned to the Gate of Sunrise

4. In the Gate of Prosperity prosperity was given me

5. In the Gateway of the Guardian Spirit, a guardian spirit drew nigh to me,

1. In the Gate of Well-being I beheld well-being

2. In the Gate of Life I was granted life

3. In the Gate of Sunrise I was reckoned among the living

4. In the Gate of Splendid Wonderment my signs were plain to see.

5. In the Gate of Release from Guilt, I was released from my bond.

6. In the Gate of Petition my mouth made inquiry.

7. In the Gate of Release from Sighing my sighs were released.

8. In the Gate of Pure Water, I was sprinkled with purifying water.

9. In the Gate of Conciliation, I appeared with Marduk,

10. In the Gate of Joy I kissed the foot of Sarpanitum,

6. I was assiduous in supplication and prayer before them,

7. I placed fragrant incense before them,

8. An offering, a gift, sundry donations I presented,

9. Many fatted oxen I slaughtered, butchered many. . . .

10. Honey-sweet beer and pure wine I repeatedly libated,

11. The protecting genius, the guardian spirit, divine attendants of the fabric of Esagila,

12. I made their feelings glow with libation,

13. I made them exultant with lavish meals.

14. To the threshold, the bolt socket, the bolt, the doors

15. I offered oil, butterfat, and choicest grain,

16. [ ] the rites of the temple

(large gap)

Insert here four lines quoted in an ancient commentary.

1. I proceeded along Kunush-kadru Street in a state of redemption,
2. He who has done wrong by Esagila, let him learn from me.
3. It was Marduk who put a muzzle on the mouth of the lion that was devouring me.
4. Marduk took away the sling of my pursuer and deflected the slingstone.

♦ **(Fragment C)**
1. [ ] golden grain
2. He anointed himself with sweet cedar perfume upon him,
3. A feast for the Babylonians. . . .
4. His tomb he had made was set up for a feast!
5. The Babylonians saw how Marduk can restore to life,
6. And all mouths proclaimed his greatness,
7. "Who would have said he would see his sun?
8. "Who would have imagined that we would pass through his street?

9. "Who but Marduk revived him as he was dying?
10. "Besides Sarpanitum, which goddess bestowed his breath of life?
11. "Marduk can restore to life from the grave,
12. "Sarpanitum knows how to rescue from annihilation,
13. "Wherever earth is founded, heavens are stretched wide,
14. "Wherever sun shines, fire ablazes,
15. "Wherever water runs, wind blows,
16. "Those whose bits of clay Aruru pinched off to from them,
17. "Those endowed with life, who walk upright,
18. "Teeming mankind as many they be, give praise to Marduk!
19. "[. . .] those who can speak
20. "[. . .] may he rule all the peoples
21. "[. . .] shepherd of all habitations
22. "[. . .] floods from the deep.
23. "[. . .] the gods [ ]
24. "[. . .] the extent of heaven and netherworld
25. "[. . .]
26. "[. . .] was getting darker and darker for him."

Glossary

Adad	a storm god
Aruru	the mother goddess of creation
epigastrium	the upper-central region of the abdomen
Erra	a god of pestilence, plague, and mayhem
Esagila	an ancient Babylonian temple dedicated to Marduk
gobbet	a chunk of meat
Laluralimma	possibly a Sumerian king
Nippur	an ancient Mesopotamian city in modern-day Iraq
Sarpanitum	a mother goddess and Marduk's consort
sennet	a signal call on a trumpet
Shubshi-meshre-Sakkan	the name of the hymn's narrator
swathe	an enveloping bandage or cloth covering
tamarisk	a type of shrub or small tree
Ur-Nintinugga	the name of a young man

Brahma holds a page of the Vedas.

(Brahma, attended by a devotee, holds a page of the Vedas [paint on paper], Indian School / India Office Library, London / Ann & Bury Peerless Picture Library / The Bridgeman Art Library International)

RIG VEDA

"His mouth became the Brahmin; his arms were made into the Warrior, his thighs the People, and from his feet the Servants were born."

Overview

The earliest stratum of Indian literature, called the Vedas, consists of four books: the Rig Veda, the Yajur Veda, the Sama Veda, and the Atharva Veda. Of these, the Rig Veda is the oldest and longest. As the word *rig* means "verse" and the word *veda* means "knowledge," the Rig Veda, composed in poetic verse, is considered the source of all sacred knowledge.

Consisting of 1,028 metrical hymns, the Rig Veda was composed in roughly two stages. Books 2–9, the core of the text, were composed between 1700 and 1500 BCE, while books 1 and 10 were composed around 1200 BCE. The hymns of the Rig Veda cover a wide range of topics. Some of them praise the virtues of the Vedic gods, the most important of which were Indra, king of the gods; Mitra-Varuna, the pair of gods who enforced oaths and maintained cosmic order; and Agni, the deified sacrificial fire and the priest of the gods. Other hymns contain instructions on how to perform the rituals that were at the center of the Vedic religion, while still others are magic spells, accounts of the creation of the universe, or paeans to worldly things like gambling.

Beginning around 800 BCE, Brahmin priests began to supplement the Rig Veda and the other Vedas with commentarial texts called Brahmanas that explain the meanings of the rituals and elaborate on the rules for performing them. The Brahmanas later gave way to mystical and speculative philosophical texts called the Upanishads. Taken together, the four Vedas, the Brahmanas, and the Upanishads make up the class of texts called *shruti*, or "heard." Unlike *smriti*, or "remembered" texts (the class including all other Indian scripture), *shruti* were considered infallible, eternal, and revealed to men rather than composed by them.

Around 500 BCE new religious movements like Buddhism and Jainism challenged the authority of the Vedas and the Brahmin priests who had exclusive access to them. The influence of Buddhism combined with the growing popularity of religious practice centered on devotion and sectarianism caused the traditions associated with the Rig Veda to go into decline. Classical Hinduism maintained the authority of the Vedas, but their actual content became less important than other texts like the Mahabharata and the Ramayana, the two great Sanskrit epics. Sectarian gods like Vishnu and Shiva (who were only minor players in the Rig Veda) supplanted Indra and Agni, and the expensive and elaborate Vedic sacrifices ceased to be performed. In the present day, small groups of Brahmins continue to memorize the Rig Veda and perform the household rites, and although it is rarely read, the Rig Veda functions as a symbol of modern Hinduism's continuity with a religion practiced more than three thousand years ago.

Context

Linguistic evidence suggests that the earliest books of the Rig Veda were composed around 1700 BCE, when the Aryans, as the people who composed the Vedas called themselves, were in the part of India now known as the Punjab, in the north. Books 1 and 10 were composed when the Aryans had moved farther east, around 1200 BCE, and were making the transition from a pastoral to an agricultural lifestyle, though they still had deep connections with cattle and horses, which figure predominantly in the hymns.

The Rig Veda is generally unconcerned with what happens after death, as the rituals it contains are used to gain wealth and power on earth. Vegetarianism had not yet become a part of Indian religion, and the rituals described in the Rig Veda call for the sacrifice of animals. The most elaborate was the horse sacrifice, used to sanctify a king's dominion.

The world of the early Rig Veda predated the great empires of India. Instead of kings, loosely federated clans or tribes held political power. But by the time the first and tenth books were written, the Aryans had become more settled, and their chiefs began to resemble kings. The later portions of the Rig Veda describe a hierarchical class system with Brahmin priests on top, followed by kings and warriors, then merchants and craftsmen, and finally slaves. The top two classes were in a relationship that was both mutually antagonistic and mutually beneficial. Kings needed Brahmins to perform the rituals that legitimized their power in the eyes of the people, while Brahmins needed kings to protect them and support them financially. But the struggle between spiritual authority and worldly power often put kings and Brahmins at odds with each other.

CA. 2000 −1500 BCE	■ India's first great agricultural civilizations in the Indus Valley decline as tribes of pastoral nomads calling themselves "Aryans" begin to migrate into the subcontinent from Central Asia.
CA. 1700 −1500 BCE	■ Vedic sages compose books 2–9 of the Rig Veda in Vedic Sanskrit.
CA. 1200 BCE	■ Books 1 and 10 of the Rig Veda are composed.
CA. 1200 −900 BCE	■ The Yajur, Sama, and Atharva Vedas are composed.
CA. 800 −600 BCE	■ The Brahmanas, commentaries on the Vedas, are composed.
CA. 600 −400 BCE	■ The Aranyakas and Upanishads, mystical Vedic commentaries, are composed.
CA. 500 BCE	■ The grammarian Panini codifies classical Sanskrit, which supplants Vedic Sanskrit; meanwhile, ascetic reform movements, especially Jainism and Buddhism, reject the centrality of the Vedic sacrifice and the authority of the Vedas.
CA. 300 BCE −300 CE	■ The Mahabharata epic is composed.
CA. 200 −100 BCE	■ Brahmin priests compose the Dharma Sutras, codifying the absolute authority of the Vedas.
CA. 200 BCE −200 CE	■ The Ramayana epic is composed.
CA. 200 −1800 CE	■ Brahmin clans continue to transmit Vedic knowledge orally, while mainstream Hinduism develops along sectarian lines.

The language of the Rig Veda is closely related to Greek, Latin, Lithuanian, Hittite, English, and the other ancient and modern languages that make up the Indo-European family. The text's mythology, in turn, bears a close resemblance to myths of the ancient Greek, Roman, and Norse civilizations. For example, Indra, who is both the thunderbolt-wielding storm deity and the king of the gods, is a Vedic counterpart to the Greek Zeus, the Roman Jupiter, and the Norse Thor. Thus, there are elements in the Rig Veda that reflect a culture borrowed from and shared by peoples living thousands of miles apart.

About the Author

The seers or *rishis* that composed the Rig Veda were grouped into different priestly lineages. They were responsible for composing new hymns to commemorate special occasions, like a tribal chief's successful cattle raid, as well as transmitting and preserving their clan's lore and sacred knowledge. Different parts of the Veda were ascribed to different priestly clans, but eventually they were all compiled to create the Rig Vedic canon.

There are two kinds of Vedic rites: the domestic, which were small and performed privately in one's own household, and the solemn, which were performed publicly and sometimes took days or weeks to complete. One of the most sacred rituals was the pressing of the *soma* plant to make a ceremonial drink. The *rishis* often composed their hymns after they had imbibed the drink. *Soma* is mentioned many times in the Rig Veda and is described as a plant whose stalks are pressed to make a sacred drink that is offered to the gods as part of the solemn sacrificial rites. This *soma* is the favorite beverage of Indra, king of the gods, but Soma is also mentioned as a god himself. The identity of the *soma* plant has been lost, but most scholars think it was related either to the psychedelic psilocybin mushroom, which causes the user to hallucinate, or to the plant ephedra, which acts as a stimulant. Either way, the *soma* drink caused the *rishis* to enter an ecstatic state in which to compose their hymns.

By the time they invested the Vedas with absolute authority, the Brahmin priests of the Vedic religion began to hold that the hymns were not "composed" at all but instead "seen" by the divinely inspired *rishis*. The Brahmins considered the Vedas beyond human authorship, and they also taught that they were not even written by the gods but were instead eternal and unchanging revelation.

Explanation and Analysis of the Document

The following selections from the Rig Veda represent the variety of subjects addressed by the text. "The Killing of Vritra" relates one of the most well known of Indra's heroic feats, utilizing the widespread Indo-European motif of the dragon slayer. "The Three Strides of Vishnu" is the first story of a minor Vedic god who will later become an important sectarian deity. "The Sacrifice of the Horse" describes

***Indra being annointed with* soma**

(Indra, king of the gods, being anointed with *soma* [gouache on paper], Indian School, [18th century] / Bibliotheque Nationale, Paris, France / Archives Charmet / The Bridgeman Art Library International)

one of the most elaborate of the solemn Vedic rituals. "The Riddle of Sacrifice" is another sacrificial hymn, but one filled with obscure passages that prefigure the philosophical discourse of the Upanishads. "The Demons in Hell," is a magic spell or charm used to ward off evil. "The Hymn of the Cosmic Man" is a creation myth, describing the birth of the universe from the sacrifice of a primordial giant.

♦ The Killing of Vritra

"The Killing of Vritra" tells the story of one of Indra's most famous heroic deeds. Like his Greek counterpart Zeus, Indra is not only the king of the gods but also the god of the storm. This hymn can be read as a description of a warrior slaying a monster with his spear or as a mythic account of the lightning that seems to pierce the thunderclouds and release the rain.

The first verse offers a synopsis of the myth: "He killed the dragon and pierced an opening for the waters; he split open the bellies of mountains." The second verse expands on this story, explaining that the dragon was in the mountains and that Indra did the deed with his thunderbolt weapon, forged by Tvastr, the blacksmith of the gods. It also describes the waters set loose when Indra struck Vritra, waters the dragon had apparently been holding back, possibly a metaphor for a rainstorm.

By using the epithet "Indra the Generous," verse 3 links the divine king Indra with mortal kings on earth, who are always expected to be generous (especially to Brahmins). It also tells us that he is a drinker of the sacrificial beverage *soma* and is intoxicated with *soma* when he kills Vritra.

Verse 4 relates that Indra is able to fight with magic as well as his thunderbolt weapon and that Vritra is the ancestor of all dragons and presumably the greatest of them. This verse also casts the myth as a creation story. The next verse describes Vritra as "like the trunk of a tree." Indra, according to verse 6, experiences the intoxicating effect of the *soma* to the point that he is "muddled by drunkenness like one who is no soldier" before, in the ensuing verses, he kills Vritra's mother and releases the waters held back by the dragon. Verse 11 explains that Vritra was holding back the waters and makes reference to another famous Indra story, his cattle raid against the Panis. The line about Indra turning into the hair of a horse's tail in verse 12 is obscure.

In the closing verses, after describing his heroism, the hymn unexpectedly shows Indra as a coward, fleeing from some unknown avenger after slaying Vritra. The later tradition explains the line by adding that Indra's killing of Vritra was an evil act because the two had previously made a treaty in which Indra would rule heaven and Vritra would rule

"Let me now sing the heroic deeds of Indra, the first that the thunderbolt-wielder performed. He killed the dragon and pierced an opening for the waters; he split open the bellies of mountains."

"Would that I might reach his dear place of refuge, where men who love the gods rejoice. For there one draws close to the wide-striding Vishnu; there, in his highest footstep, is the fountain of honey."

"Let this racehorse bring us good cattle and good horses, male children and all-nourishing wealth. Let Aditi make us free from sin. Let the horse with our offerings achieve sovereign power for us."

"This altar is the farthest end of the earth; this sacrifice is the navel of the universe. This Soma is the semen of the stallion bursting with seed; this Brahmin priest is the final abode of Speech."

"Whoever has spoken against me with false words when I was acting with a pure heart, O Indra let him become nothing even as he talks about nothing, like water grasped in one's fist."

"His mouth became the Brahmin; his arms were made into the Warrior, his thighs the People, and from his feet the Servants were born."

the earth. The line about flying like an eagle is a reference to another story in which Indra took the form of an eagle to steal the *soma* plant.

♦ The Three Strides of Vishnu

This hymn is one of only five (or possibly six) hymns addressed to Vishnu in the Rig Veda. Vishnu is definitely a minor deity in the Rig Veda—in comparison, Indra alone has 250 hymns—but by 300 CE, he was worshipped across southern Asia, while Indra and Agni were barely remembered. The story of Vishnu's three strides later formed the basis of the myth of his incarnation as Vamana the dwarf: When a demon conquers the whole world, the gods send Vishnu to get it back. Vishnu takes the form of a dwarf and approaches the demon during a sacrifice, when he is obligated to grant requests from his guests. The dwarf asks for only as much land as he can cover in three strides and since the dwarf is so small, the demon readily agrees. But then Vishnu assumes his giant cosmic form and covers the earth, the sky, and the heaven of the gods in three enormous strides.

The first verse of the hymn mentions the three strides of Vishnu as one of his heroic deeds, but not as performed to win back the universe for the gods. Instead, he seems to be portrayed as separating the universe into an upper half (for the gods) and a lower half (for men) and standing between them to keep them apart.

Verses 2 and 3 describe Vishnu as being like a wild animal and living in the mountains, which is more typically a way of describing Shiva, the other great post-Vedic god who appears briefly in the Rig Veda. But the last three verses all praise Vishnu's benevolence toward humankind as he props up the sky and measures out the earth, and he is included as a recipient of sacrificial offerings. The mention of his "highest footstep" in verse 5 is a reference to heaven, which is described as a place of refuge full of cows and honey to which the poets aspire to go, emphasizing the benevolent nature of Vishnu.

♦ The Sacrifice of the Horse

"The Sacrifice of the Horse" gives a detailed description of one of the most elaborate Vedic rites. The ritual lasted one year, during which the sacrificial horse was allowed to roam free, probably followed by soldiers from the king's army, to prevent anyone from capturing or stopping the horse. When it returned, all the land that the horse had crossed belonged to the king.

The first verse of the hymn calls together the gods to partake in the sacrifice. Aryaman is probably another name for Agni, the Rbhus are the divine craftsmen, and the Maruts are a band of demigods that make up Indra's army. Verses 2–4 describe the first sacrificial offering, a dappled goat covered with expensive cloth and other ornaments (which may have been taken as gifts by the officiating priests after the ritual). Two more gods are also named: Pushan, the shepherd god to whom the goat is offered, and Tvastr, the blacksmith and craftsman of the gods.

Verse 5 lists the types of priests needed to perform the sacrifice, each specializing in a different branch of the Veda. The next verse lists still more sacrificial technicians that must be employed, giving an idea of the money and resources needed to perform a horse sacrifice. The priests send the horse into the realm of the gods in verse 7, and verses 8–11 and verses 13, 14, and 16 describe everything that will accompany the sacrificed horse into heaven. Verse 12 refers to the priests, who apparently eat some of the horse's flesh as a sacrificial meal.

In verse 15, the priests pray that nothing will go wrong in the cooking of the horse to make it unacceptable to the gods. And in verse 17, the priest makes right all the harms that may have been done to the horse, to make it a more worthy offering. Verses 18 and 19 describe the killing of the horse, and after that the priests dismember it, dedicating each part of the carcass to a different deity. The balls offered into the fire were probably rice balls, still used today as an offering to the spirits of one's departed ancestors.

The priests appease the horse in verses 20 and 21, explaining that it is being sent to live with the gods. In Vedic thought, the sacred fire is the intermediary between humans and gods, and the smoke that rises upward from it is the path that leads from earth to heaven. This idea is also expressed in hymn 10.16, "The Funeral Fire." The last verse describes the worldly benefits the sacrificer expects to get from the ritual.

♦ The Riddle of Sacrifice

"The Riddle of Sacrifice" illustrates the ways in which the *rishis* who composed the hymns of the Rig Veda demonstrated their knowledge of the mystical meaning of the sacrifice and challenged rival *rishis* to solve their complex riddles at the same time. This kind of composition, in which words are used to mean many things at once, served to hide esoteric teachings too dangerous for the uninitiated to learn and became part of the philosophical tradition of the Upanishads.

In the first verse, the three brothers each represent one of the sacred fires used in a sacrifice. The "beloved grey priest" refers to the fire that receives the sacrificial offering, the "middle brother who is hungry" is the southern fire where nothing is offered, and the "brother with butter on his back" is the fire into which the priest pours an offering of clarified butter. The "Lord of All Tribes with his seven sons" refers to the fire god Agni and the seven priests who perform the ritual.

Verses 2 and 3 make use of Vedic numerology, while verses 4–8 pose a series of riddles, concluding with one that may be a description of the sunrise, in which the mother (dawn) embraces the father (the sky) and is pierced so that she spills out the embryo (the sun). The last line, "The reverent came to praise," may refer to the rituals that Brahmin priests performed at dawn to greet the sun. Verse 9 continues the solar mythology, with the sun as a "many-coloured cow" and the "three stages of the journey" being the three eight-hour periods of the day—morning, evening, and night.

Verses 10–18 continue with a long series of riddles that can refer to the sacrificial ritual, to the path of a man's soul after death, to the cycle of the sun, or to all three at once. Verse 19 introduces the idea of cyclical time, which is less concerned with reincarnation than the regular repetition of sacrifices to keep the universe in order. With each performance, the world is born anew.

The two birds in verses 20–22 may refer to the sacrificial fires, and the phrase "the wise one, entered me, the fool," seems to describe a mystical experience or revelation at the sacrificial altar. Verses 23–25 identify the three main poetic meters in the Rig Veda and describe their roles in the composition of Vedic poetry.

The motif of sun as cow is reintroduced in verses 26–29, while verses 30–33 connect the sun's cyclical rising, setting, and rising again with the birth, death, and rebirth of a mortal man. Another riddle about the sacrifice is asked and answered in verses 34 and 35; verse 36 may refer either to a Vedic creation myth or the path of the sun. The cyclical nature of life and death is likened to the sun cycle again in verses 37–39, and the cow reappears in verses 40–42, but this time it represents the sacred speech of the priests. The dappled bull in verse 43 refers to the *soma* plant, while the "three long-haired ones" in verse 44 may be the three forms of Agni: fire (which "shaves" the earth), sun (which is visible), and wind (which is invisible).

Verse 45 emphasizes the sacred and powerful nature of the great domain of speech, of which even the wise know only a quarter. The riddles posed in verses 46–48 probably all refer to the sun. Sarasvati, in verse 49, is a sacred river and a goddess of speech. Verse 50 reiterates the last line from the "Purusha Sukta," emphasizing the importance of sacrifice for the maintenance of cosmic order. The final two verses are a prayer to the sun for rain.

♦ The Demons in Hell

Unlike the other hymns in this selection, "The Demons in Hell" has little to do with the performance of sacrifice or the heroic deeds of the Vedic gods. Instead, it is a magic spell of the kind usually found in the Atharva Veda. The background seems to be that one Brahmin priest has accused another of black magic, so the accused priest is (ironically) cursing him for making false accusations.

The first six verses call on the powerful Vedic deities Indra and Soma to banish the demons to hell. These demons are probably not the Asuras, the Vedic anti-gods, but *rakshasas*, earthly demons that might be considered goblins or ogres. In verse 7, the priest singing this hymn continues to curse the demons but also curses his own rival in the last line. Verse 8 specifically refers to the human target of the spell, someone who has made false accusations against the priest.

The next four verses call upon the gods to punish all evildoers and those who would disrupt the sacrifice. Then, in verses 13–15, the priest asks Soma to witness his own innocence of the accusations against him and to deprive the one who made them of ten generations of sons. In verse 16 he calls upon Indra to kill his accuser, whom he then accuses of being a black magician himself.

Verse 17 describes a type of witch who takes the shape of an owl, a bird of bad omen in India. Verse 18 calls upon the Maruts, the demigods of Indra's army, to destroy the witch and all other shape-shifting magicians, and the next verse asks Indra to use a mountain as a giant discus weapon. Verses 20–22 list all of the types of shape-shifters and ask Indra to destroy them again, as he has done in the past. The hymn suggests in verses 23 and 24 that these demons are vulnerable to the daylight and that they fly through the air, and it ends with a final prayer for Indra and Soma to be vigilant against the forces of the demons.

♦ **The Hymn of the Cosmic Man**

Probably the most famous hymn of the Rig Veda, "The Hymn of the Cosmic Man," is in book 10 and is generally considered to be one of the latest passages in the text. It has parallels in many other Indo-European myths, including the dismemberment of the giant Ymir in Norse mythology.

The hymn begins with a description of Purusha. The word *purusha* generally means "person," but here it refers to the primordial figure who is the subject of this story, so it is translated with the proper noun "Man." Verses 1 and 2 describe him as a giant who fills the entire universe and who is sustained through "food," which probably refers to sacrificial offerings. When the hymn states in verses 3 and 4 that only one-quarter of the Man covers the earth while the rest is in the heavens, it illustrates the vastness of the universe well beyond what can be known on earth, a prevalent concept in Indian thought.

It is not clear at the beginning of the hymn whether or not the Man is in an already-manifested universe or whether he is in a void, as with the God of the Hebrew Bible in the first Creation account of Genesis. Verse 5 introduces another paradox regarding the Man when it states that "from him Viraj was born, and from Viraj came the Man." One interpretation is that the Man represents matter, while

Viraj represents the energy or force that shapes and animates matter, later called *prakriti*. Later Indian philosophy divides the world into *prakriti* ("spirit") and *purusha* ("person" or "matter"), while some schools of Yoga see *purusha* and *prakriti* as complementary male and female energies like the yin and yang of Chinese thought.

Verses 6 and 7 tell that the Man is a sacrificial victim, apparently a willing one, and verses 8–10 describe how the gods took the Man's body apart and used it to create the world, beginning with the sacred chants and meters found in the Rig Veda, whose recitation is vital in keeping the universe in order. All the animals listed in verse 10 are also connected to ritual, since they are all animals that were sacrificed.

Verse 11 asks a question that is answered in the next verse. This question-and-answer structure appears throughout the Rig Veda and may reflect the verbal contests that the Vedic *rishis* held among themselves. Verse 12 is one of the most famous lines of the Rig Veda, laying out the four-tier hierarchy of Indian society. This division of the Man's body into groups of people defines the four classes in two ways. First, it identifies each class with a particular function. The Brahmins come from the mouth because they are responsible for speech, specifically the sacred chants of the Vedas. The warriors come from the arms, indicating that their chief virtue should be strength, while the people come from the thighs (probably a euphemistic reference to the genitals), as their job is to produce and grow. The servants come from the feet because they hold up everyone else with their labor. In a second sense, this division of the Man's body ranks the classes according to ancient Indian ideas about purity and pollution. The head is the highest part of the body and also the most pure, while the feet are the lowest and the least pure. In India today it is still common to show respect for someone by touching their feet and then your own head, as if to say, "The most pure part of me is equal to the most pure part of you." These standards of purity and pollution were used to govern the relationships between castes. Soon after the Vedic people entered India, in the early second millennium BCE, they encountered groups of outsiders that they tried to incorporate into their *varna* system, representing the beginning of the modern caste system.

Verses 13 and 14 describe the creation of the gods and the universe from the other parts of the Man. Verse 15 brings back the sacrificial motif, giving a picture of a physical altar surrounded by green sticks to keep the fire from spreading.

The final verse establishes the sacrifice of the Man as the paradigm for all future sacrifices—the sacrifice offered to itself. It is also tells us that the sacrifice of the Man is the source of the ritual laws that govern how the sacrifices are performed. Whenever the Brahmins carried out a sacrifice, they were repeating the original act of creation and thus restoring order to the universe, so that the sun and moon would continue to rise and set, the rains would come, and the social hierarchy would be maintained.

The audience of the Rig Veda was limited almost exclusively to kings and especially Brahmins; they are the people who are primarily represented in the text. Indeed, the Rig Veda can give only an incomplete picture of the ancient Indian society that produced it because it was composed by and for an elite class of men, leaving out the voices of women and people outside the Aryan class system. But since the Aryans were nomadic and built temporary dwellings out of wood, they left behind no archaeological evidence revealing anything about the society that produced the Rig Veda beyond Brahmins and kings.

The Vedas were too sacred to write down, so the Brahmins invented ingenious mnemonic devices that allowed them to transmit the texts orally for millennia with great accuracy. The archaic language of the Vedas, while closely related to classical Sanskrit, was generally only known to the Brahmin lineages who transmitted them orally and who maintained exclusive control over the Vedas and the Vedic rites. These rites were expensive and required rich patrons, usually tribal chiefs or, later, kings, to sponsor the sacrifices and pay the Brahmins who presided over them. Up to the present day, small groups of Brahmins have continued to memorize the Rig Veda and perform the household rites, and the Rig Veda functions as a symbol of Hinduism's roots in traditions that existed three thousand years ago.

The Rig Veda and the sacrificial rituals it prescribed were the foundation of the Vedic religion that preceded it and had a profound influence on the Hindu tradition that followed. By the time of the Mahabharata, between 300 BCE and 300 CE, a wide array of clans, guilds, and tribes were being absorbed into the Vedic class system, resulting in a complex hierarchy of hereditary social groups that formed the basis of the modern caste system. The ideology of "The Hymn of the Cosmic Man" was part of a system of Brahmin rules of purity and pollution that governed divisions of labor, marriage, and who could eat with whom. The Rig Veda was also the source of many later intellectual developments. Determining the exact specifications and proper times for performing the Vedic rituals demanded the rigorous application of geometry and astronomy, giving birth to the sciences in ancient India. And as they speculated on the meaning of the sacrifice in more and more esoteric ways, the Brahmins began to develop schools of philosophy, including Yoga and the mystical traditions of the Upanishads.

Questions for Further Study

1. Outline the distinctions between the three major sacred texts of Hinduism: the Vedas, the Upanishads, and the Puranas.

2. Compare "The Demons in Hell," a magic spell or charm used to ward off evil, with "The Ritual for Evil Spirits," one of the rituals contained in the Yengishiki. How are the two rituals similar and how do they differ? What do the differences tell you about the differences between early Hindu society and Japanese Shinto society?

3. The god Indra can be thought of as a parallel to the Greek god Zeus. Compare Indra as portrayed in "The Killing of Vritra" with Zeus as portrayed in Cleanthes' "Hymn to Zeus." Again, what do the differences in the texts tell you about the differences between the early Hindu culture and Greek religious beliefs?

4. Compare "The Three Strides of Vishnu" with the Vishnu Purana. How did the conception of Vishnu change in the intervening millennium? Why do you think this change took place?

5. The Rig Veda documents the emergence and development of the Indian caste system. Why do you think issues of social class, occupation, and the like became bound up with religious beliefs during this period?

Further Reading

■ Books

Elizarenkova, Tatyana J. *Language and Style of the Vedic Rishis*. Albany: State University of New York Press, 1995.

Griswold, H. D. *The Religion of the Rig Veda*. Delhi: Motilal Banarsidass, 1999.

Heesterman, J. C. *The Broken World of Sacrifice: An Essay in Ancient Indian Ritual*. Chicago: University of Chicago Press, 1993.

Mahony, William K. *The Artful Universe: An Introduction to the Vedic Religious Imagination*. Albany: State University of New York Press, 1998.

O'Flaherty, Wendy Doniger. *The Rig Veda: An Anthology*. New York: Penguin Books, 1981.

Smith, Brian K. *Reflections on Resemblance, Ritual, and Religion*. New York: Oxford University Press, 1989.

—Brian Collins

RIG VEDA

1.32 The Killing of Vritra

1 Let me now sing the heroic deeds of Indra, the first that the thunderbolt-wielder performed. He killed the dragon and pierced an opening for the waters; he split open the bellies of mountains.

2 He killed the dragon who lay upon the mountain; Tvastr fashioned the roaring thunderbolt for him. Like lowing cows, the flowing waters rushed straight down to the sea.

3 Wildly excited like a bull, he took the Soma for himself and drank the extract from the three bowls in the three-day Soma ceremony. Indra the Generous seized his thunderbolt to hurl it as a weapon; he killed the firstborn of dragons.

4 Indra, when you killed the first-born of dragons and overcame by your own magic the magic of the magicians, at that very moment you brought forth the sun, the sky, and dawn. Since then you have found no enemy to conquer you.

5 With his great weapon, the thunderbolt, Indra killed the shoulderless Vritra, his greatest enemy. Like the trunk of a tree whose branches have been lopped off by an axe, the dragon lies flat upon the ground.

6 For, muddled by drunkenness like one who is no soldier, Vritra challenged the great hero who had overcome the mighty and who drank Soma to the dregs. Unable to withstand the onslaught of his weapons, he found Indra an enemy to conquer him and was shattered, his nose crushed.

7 Without feet or hands he fought against Indra, who struck him on the nape of the neck with his thunderbolt. The steer who wished to become the equal of the bull bursting with seed, Vritra lay broken in many places.

8 Over him as he lay there like a broken reed the swelling waters flowed for man. Those waters that Vritra had enclosed with his power—the dragon now lay at their feet.

9 The vital energy of Vritra's mother ebbed away, for Indra had hurled his deadly weapon at her. Above was the mother, below was the son; Danu lay down like a cow with her calf.

10 In the midst of the channels of the waters which never stood still or rested, the body was hidden. The waters now over Vritra's secret place; he who found Indra an enemy to conquer him sank into long darkness.

11 The waters who had the Dasa for their husband, the dragon for their protector, were imprisoned like the cows imprisoned by the Panis. When he killed Vritra he split open the outlet of the waters that had been closed.

12 Indra, you became a hair of a horse's tail when Vritra struck you on the corner of the mouth. You, the one god, the brave one, you won the cows; you won the Soma; you released the seven streams so that they could flow.

13 No use was the lightning and thunder, fog and hail that he had scattered about, when the dragon and Indra fought. Indra the Generous remained victorious for all time to come.

14 What avenger of the dragon did you see, Indra, that fear entered your heart when you had killed him? Then you crossed the ninety-nine streams like the frightened eagle crossing the realms of earth and air.

15 Indra, who wields the thunderbolt in his hand, is the king of that which moves and that which rests, of the tame and of the horned. He rules the people as their king, encircling all this as a rim encircles spokes.

1.154 The Three Strides of Vishnu

1 Let me now sing the heroic deeds of Vishnu, who has measured apart the realms of earth, who propped upthe upper dwelling-place, striding far as he stepped forth three times.

2 They praise for his heroic deeds Vishnu who lurks in the mountains, wandering like a ferocious wild beast, in whose three wide strides all creatures dwell.

3 Let this song of inspiration go forth to Vishnu, the wide-striding bull who lives in the mountains, who alone with but three steps measured apart this long, far-reaching dwelling-place.

4 His three footprints, inexhaustibly full of honey, rejoice in the sacrificial drink. Alone, he supports threefold the earth and the sky—all creatures.

5 Would that I might reach his dear place of refuge, where men who love the gods rejoice. For there one draws close to the wide-striding Vishnu; there, in his highest footstep, is the fountain of honey.

6 We wish to go to your dwelling-places, where there are untiring, many-horned cattle. There the highest footstep of the wide-stepping bull shines brightly down.

1.162 The Sacrifice of the Horse

1 Mitra, Varuna, Aryaman the Active, Indra the ruler of the Rbhus, and the Maruts—let them not fail to heed us when we proclaim in the assembly the heroic deeds of the racehorse who was born of the gods.

2 When they lead the firmly grasped offering in front of the horse that is covered with cloths and heirlooms, the dappled goat goes bleating straight to the dear dwelling of Indra and Pushan.

3 This goat for all the gods is led forward with the race-horse as the share for Pushan. When they lead forth the welcome offering with the charger, Tvastr urges him on to great fame.

4 When, as the ritual law ordains, the men circle three times, leading the horse that is to be the oblation on the path to the gods, the goat who is the share for Pushan goes first, announcing the sacrifice to the gods.

5 The Invoker, the officiating priest, the atoner, the fire-kindler, the holder of the pressing-stones, the reciter, the priest who prays—fill your bellies with this well-prepared, well-sacrificed sacrifice.

6 The hewers of the sacrificial stake and those who carry it, and those who carve the knob for the horse's sacrificial stake, and those who gather together the things to cook the charger—let their approval encourage us.

7 The horse with his smooth back went forth into the fields of the gods, just when I made my prayer. The inspired sages exult in him. We have made him a welcome companion at the banquet of the gods.

8 The charger's rope and halter, the reins and bridle on his head, and even the grass that has been brought up to his mouth—let all of that stay with you even among the gods.

9 Whatever of the horse's flesh the fly has eaten, or whatever stays stuck to the stake or the axe, or to the hands or nails of the slaughterer—let all of that stay with you even among the gods.

10 Whatever food remains in his stomach, sending forth gas, or whatever smell there is from his raw flesh let the slaughterers make that well done; let them cook the sacrificial animal until he is perfectly cooked.

11 Whatever runs off your body when it has been placed on the spit and roasted by the fire, let it not lie there in the earth or on the grass, but let it be given to the gods who long for it.

12 Those who see that the racehorse is cooked, who say, "It smells good! Take it away!," and who wait for the doling out of the flesh of the charger—let their approval encourage us.

13 The testing fork for the cauldron that cooks the flesh, the pots for pouring the broth, the cover of the bowls to keep it warm, the hooks, the dishes—all these attend the horse.

14 The place where he walks, where he rests, where he rolls, and the fetters on the horse's feet, and what he has drunk and the fodder he has eaten—let all of that stay with you even among the gods.

15 Let not the fire that reeks of smoke darken you, nor the red-hot cauldron split into pieces. The

gods receive the horse who has been sacrificed, worshipped, consecrated, and sanctified with the cry of "Vasatl."

16 The cloth that they spread beneath the horse, the upper covering, the golden trappings on him, the halter and the fetters on his feet—let these things that are his own bind the horse among the gods.

17 If someone riding you has struck you too hard with heel or whip when you shied, I make all these things well again for you with prayer, as they do with the oblation's ladle in sacrifices.

18 The axe cuts through the thirty-four ribs of the racehorse who is the companion of the gods. Keep the limbs undamaged and place them in the proper pattern. Cut them apart, calling out piece by piece.

19 One is the slaughterer of the horse of Tvastr; two restrain him. This is the rule. As many of your limbs as I set out, according to the rules, so many balls I offer into the fire.

20 Let not your dear soul burn you as you go away. Let not the axe do lasting harm to your body. Let no greedy, clumsy slaughterer hack in the wrong place and damage your limbs with his knife.

21 You do not really die through this, nor are you harmed. You go to the gods on paths pleasant to go on. The two bay stallions, the two roan mares are now your chariot mates. The racehorse has been set in the donkey's yoke.

22 Let this racehorse bring us good cattle and good horses, male children and all-nourishing wealth. Let Aditi make us free from sin. Let the horse with our offerings achieve sovereign power for us.

1.164 The Riddle of Sacrifice

1 This beloved grey priest has a middle brother who is hungry and a third brother with butter on his back. In him I saw the Lord of All Tribes with his seven sons.

2 Seven yoke the one-wheeled chariot drawn by one horse with seven names. All these creatures rest on the age-less and unstoppable wheel with three naves.

3 Seven horses draw the seven who ride on this seven-wheeled chariot. Seven sisters call out to the place where the seven names of the cows are hidden.

4 Who saw the newborn one, the one with bones who was brought forth by the boneless one? Where was the breath and blood and soul of the earth? Who can go to ask this from someone who knows ?

5 An ignorant fool, I ask in my mind about the hidden footprints of the gods. Over the young calf the poets stretched out seven threads to weave.

6 Unknowing, ignorant, I ask for knowledge about it from the poets who know: What is the One who in the form of the unborn propped apart these six realms of space?

7 Let him who really knows proclaim here the hidden place of that beloved bird. The cows give milk from his head; wearing a cloak, they drank water with their feet.

8 The mother gave the father a share in accordance with the Order, for at the beginning she embraced him with mind and heart. Recoiling, she was pierced and flowed with the seed of the embryo. The reverent came to praise.

9 The mother was harnessed to the chariot pole of the priest's cow; the embryo remained within the cowpens. The calf lowed and looked for the many-coloured cow on the three stages of the journey.

10 The One has risen up, holding up three mothers and three fathers, who never wear him down. On the back of the distant sky they speak of Speech, who knows all but does not move all.

11 The twelve-spoked wheel of Order rolls around and around the sky and never ages. Seven hundred and twenty sons in pairs rest on it, O Agni.

12 Some say that the father with his five feet and twelve shapes dwells in his fullness in the farther half of the sky. But others here say that the far-seeing one in the seven-wheeled, six-spoked chariot moves in the near half.

13 All the worlds rest on this five-spoked wheel that rolls around and around. Though heavy-laden,

its axle does not get hot, nor has it ever broken in its naves.

14 The unageing wheel rolls out on its rim; the ten yoked horses draw it up the outstretched path. All the worlds are kept in motion on the eye of the sun, that moves on though shrouded in dark space.

15 They say that besides those born in pairs there is a seventh born alone, while the six sets of twins are the sages born from the gods. The sacrifices for them are firmly set, but they change their forms and waver as he stands firm.

16 They are female, but people tell me they are male. He who has eyes sees this, but the blind one does not understand. The poet who is his son has understood this well; the one who knows it would be his father's father.

17 Beneath what is above, and above what is beneath, the cow went upward, holding her calf by the foot. In what direction and to what half of the sky has she gone away? Where did she give birth? Not within the herd.

18 Whoever here knows his father beneath what is above and above what is beneath—who with such mystical insight can here proclaim the source from which the mind of god was born?

19 Those that are in the future they say are in the past; those that are in the past they say are in the future. The things that you and Indra did, Soma, still pull the axle pole of space as though yoked to it.

20 Two birds, friends joined together, clutch the same tree. One of them eats the sweet fruit; the other looks on without eating.

21 Where the birds sing unblinkingly about their share of immortality among the wise, there the mighty herdsman of the whole world, the wise one, entered me, the fool.

22 The birds that eat honey nest and brood on that tree on whose tip, they say, is the sweet fruit. No one who does not know the father eats that.

23 Only those gain immortality who know that the Gayatri foot is based on the Gayatri hymn, or that

the Tristubh foot is made from the Tristubh hymn, or that the Jagat foot is based on the Jagat hymn.

24 With the Gayatri foot they fashion a hymn; with the hymn, a chant; with the Tristubh foot a strophe; with the strophe of two feet or four feet they fashion a speech. With the syllable they fashion the seven tones.

25 With the Jagat he fixed the stream in the sky. In the Rathantara chant he discovered the sun. They say the Gayatri has three kindling-sticks, and so its power and magnificence excels.

26 I call to the cow who is easy to milk, so that the milker with clever hands may milk her. Let Savitr inspire us with the finest vigour. The pot of milk is set on the fire—this is what I would happily proclaim.

27 The mistress of riches has come, snuffling and longing in her heart for her calf. Let this cow give milk for the Asvins and grow greater for good fortune.

28 The cow has lowed at her blinking calf, snuffling at his head to make him low. Longing for his warm mouth, she lows and swells with milk.

29 The one that encloses the cow hums; she that is set over the spluttering flame lows. With her hissing she has put down the mortal; becoming lightning, she has thrown off the cloak.

30 Life that breathes now lies still and yet moves fast, rushing but firmly fixed in the midst of the resting places. The life of the dead one wanders as his nature wills. The immortal comes from the same womb as the mortal.

31 I have seen the cowherd who never tires, moving to and fro along the paths. Clothing himself in those that move toward the same centre but spread apart, he rolls on and on inside the worlds.

32 He who made him knows nothing of him. He who saw him—he vanishes from him. Enclosed within the mother's womb, yet full of progeny, he entered Destruction.

33 The sky is my father; here is the navel that gave me birth. This great earth is my mother, my close kin. The womb for me was between the two bowls

stretched apart; here the father placed the embryo in the daughter.

34 I ask you about the farthest end of the earth; I ask you about the navel of the universe. I ask you about the semen of the stallion bursting with seed; I ask you about the final abode of Speech.

35 This altar is the farthest end of the earth; this sacrifice is the navel of the universe. This Soma is the semen of the stallion bursting with seed; this Brahmin priest is the final abode of Speech.

36 The seven half-embryos portion out the semen of the world at Vishnu's command. Wise in their thoughts and their heart, themselves surrounded, they surround it on all sides.

37 I do not know just what it is that I am like. I wander about concealed and wrapped in thought. When the first born of Order came to me, I won a share of this Speech.

38 The one who is compelled as his own nature wills goes away and comes back; the immortal came from the same womb as the mortal. The two constantly move in opposite directions; when people perceive the one, they do not perceive the other.

39 The undying syllable of the song is the final abode where all the gods have taken their seat. What can one who does not know this do with the song ? Only those who know it sit together here.

40 Be happy eating good fodder, and then we will be happy too. O inviolable cow, eat grass and drink pure water as you graze for ever.

41 The buffalo-cow lowed as she fashioned the flowing waters; she who has a thousand syllables in the final abode became one-footed, two-footed, eight-footed, nine-footed.

42 The quarters of the sky live on the oceans that flow out of her in all directions. The whole universe exists through the undying syllable that flows from her.

43 In the distance I saw the cowdung smoke midway between what is above and what is below. The heroes roasted the dappled bull. These were the first ritual laws.

44 The three long-haired ones reveal themselves at the right moment. During the year, one of them shaves; one looks upon everything with his powers; of one the onrush is visible, but the form is not.

45 Speech was divided into four parts that the inspired priests know. Three parts, hidden in deep secret, humans do not stir into action; the fourth part of Speech is what men speak.

46 They call it Indra, Mitra, Varuna, Agni, and it is the heavenly bird that flies. The wise speak of what is One in many ways; they call it Agni, Yama, Matarisvan.

47 The yellow birds clothed in waters fly up to the sky on the dark path. They have now returned from the home of Order, and at once the earth was drenched with butter.

48 Twelve fellies, one wheel, three naves—who has understood this? Three hundred and sixty are set on it like poles that do not loosen.

49 Your inexhaustible breast, Sarasvati, that flows with the food of life, that you use to nourish all that one could wish for, freely giving treasure and wealth and beautiful gifts—bring that here for us to suck.

50 The gods sacrificed to the sacrifice with the sacrifice. These became the first ritual laws. These great powers went to the dome of heaven where dwell the Sadhyas, the ancient gods.

51 The same water travels up and down day after day. While the rain-clouds enliven the earth, the flames enliven the sky.

52 The great heavenly bird with wonderful wings, the beautiful embryo of the waters and the plants, that delights us with rains overflowing—I call to him for help.

7.104 The Demons in Hell

1 Indra and Soma, burn the demon and crush him; bulls, hurl down those who thrive on darkness. Shatter those who lack good thoughts; scorch them, kill, drive out, cut down the devourers.

2 Indra and Soma, let evil heat boil up around him who plots evil, like a pot set on a fire. Set unrelenting hatred against the fiend, the flesh-eating Brahmin-hater with the evil eye.

3 Indra and Soma, pierce the evil-doers and hurl them into the pit, the bottomless darkness, so that not a single one will come up from there again. Let this furious rage of yours overpower them.

4 Indra and Soma, together roll the shattering weapon from the sky, from the earth, upon the one who plots evil. Carve out of the mountains the hissing thing with which you burn down the demon who thrives.

5 Indra and Soma, roll it from the sky. With unageing weapons of heat that burn like fire and strike like stone pierce the devourers and hurl them into the abyss. Let them go into silence.

6 Indra and Soma, let this prayer embrace you all around like the girth around two prize-winning horses. Like a pair of princes, urge on these prayers, this invocation that I send to you by meditation.

7 Plot against them. Swooping down swiftly, kill the demons who hate us and would break us to bits. Indra and Soma, let nothing good happen to the evil-doer who has ever tried to injure me with his hatred.

8 Whoever has spoken against me with false words when I was acting with a pure heart, O Indra let him become nothing even as he talks about nothing, like water grasped in one's fist.

9 Those who casually seduce the man of pure heart or wilfully make the good man bad, let Soma deliver them over to the serpent, or let him set them in the lap of Destruction.

10 Agni, whoever wants to injure the sap of our drink, of our horses, of our cows, of our own bodies, he is our enemy, a thief and a robber; let him fall upon hard times; let him perish with his own body and his offspring.

11 Let him with his own body and his offspring be beyond, let him be below all three earths. Gods, dry up the glory of the one who wants to injure us by day or by night.

12 For the clever man it is easy to distinguish: true and false words fight against one another. Soma favours the one of them that is true, that is straight; he kills the false.

13 Surely Soma does not push forward the one who is dishonest, nor the ruler who holds power falsely. He kills the demon, he kills the one who speaks lies. Both of these lie in Indra's snare.

14 As if I worshipped false gods, or considered the gods useless—why, Agni knower of creatures, why are you angry with us? Gather into your destruction those who speak hateful words.

15 Let me die at once if I am a sorcerer, or if I have burnt up a man's span of life. Let the one who falsely calls me a sorcerer be cut off from ten heroes.

Glossary

Aditi	a mother principle identified with mystic speech
Agni	the deified sacrificial fire and the priest of the gods
Aryaman	probably another name for Agni
Asvins	divine twin horsemen and chariot warriors
beloved grey priest	the fire that receives a sacrificial offering in "The Riddle of Sacrifice"
Danu	Vrita's mother
Dasa	another name for Vritra
fellies	the rims or sections of the rim of a wheel supported by spokes
Gayatri foot	a mantra
Indra	the king of the gods and the god of the storm
Jagat foot	a metrical unit

16 The one who calls me a sorcerer, though I am not a sorcerer, or the one who says he is pure, though he is demonic—let Indra strike him with his great weapon. Let him fall to the lowest depths under all creation.

17 She who ranges about at night like an owl, hiding her body in a hateful disguise, let her fall into the endless pits. Let the pressing-stones slay the demons with their rumblings.

18 Maruts, scatter yourselves among all the peoples. Seek out, grab, and crush the demons who become birds and fly about at night, the ones who have injured the sacrifice of the gods.

19 Roll the stone from the sky, generous Indra. Sharpen it completely when Soma has sharpened it. From in front, from behind, from below, from above, strike the demons with the mountain.

20 There they go! The dog-sorcerers are flying away. Viciously they wish to harm Indra, who cannot be harmed. Indra sharpens his weapon against the slanderers. Now let him loose his bolt at the sorcerers.

21 Indra shattered the sorcerers who snatched away the oblation and waylaid him. Indra splits them as an axe splits a tree, bursting apart the demons as if they were clay pots.

22 Kill the owl-sorcerer, the owlet-sorcerer, the dog-sorcerer, the cuckoo-sorcerer, the eagle-sorcerer, the vulture-sorcerer. Indra, crush the demon to powder as if with a millstone.

23 Do not let the demon of the sorcerers get close to us. Let the light blot out the fiends who work in couples. Let the earth protect us from earthly anguish, and the middle realm of space protect us from the anguish of the sky.

24 Indra, kill the male sorcerer and the female who deceives by her power of illusion. Let the idol-worshippers sink down with broken necks; let them never see the rising sun.

25 Look here, look there, Indra and Soma; stay awake! Hurl the weapon at the demons; hurl the thunderbolt at the sorcerers!

10.90 The Hymn of the Cosmic Man

1 The Man has a thousand heads, a thousand eyes, a thousand feet. He pervaded the earth on all sides and extended beyond it as far as ten fingers.

2 It is the Man who is all this, whatever has been and whatever is to be. He is the ruler of immortality, when he grows beyond everything through food.

Glossary

Lord of All Tribes with his seven sons	Agni and the seven priests who perform the sacrificial ritual
Maruts	a band of demigods that make up Indra's army
Matarisvan	a name for Agni or a divine being closely associated with her
middle brother who is hungry	the southern fire where nothing is offered in "The Riddle of Sacrifice"
Mitra	one of the gods who, with Varuna, enforces oaths and maintains cosmic order
Panis	enemies of Indra
Pushan	the shepherd god to whom a goat is offered in "The Sacrifice of the Horse"
Rbhus	divine craftsmen
Sadhyas	the ancient gods
Sarasvati	a sacred river and a goddess of speech
Savitr	a beneficent god who acts as protector of all beings

3 Such is his greatness, and the Man is yet more than this. All creatures are a quarter of him; three quarters are what is immortal in heaven.

4 With three quarters the Man rose upwards, and one quarter of him still remains here. From this he spread out in all directions, into that which eats and that which does not eat.

5 From him Viraj was born, and from Viraj came the Man. When he was born, he ranged beyond the earth behind and before.

6 When the gods spread the sacrifice with the Man as the offering, spring was the clarified butter, summer the fuel, autumn the oblation.

7 They anointed the Man, the sacrifice born at the beginning, upon the sacred grass. With him the gods, Sadhyas, and sages sacrificed.

8 From that sacrifice in which everything was offered, the melted fat was collected, and he made it into those beasts who live in the air, in the forest, and in villages.

9 From that sacrifice in which everything was offered, the verses and chants were born, the metres were born from it, and from it the formulas were born.

10 Horses were born from it, and those other animals that have two rows of teeth; cows were born from it, and from it goats and sheep were born.

11 When they divided the Man, into how many parts did they apportion him? What do they call his mouth, his two arms and thighs and feet?

12 His mouth became the Brahmin; his arms were made into the Warrior, his thighs the People, and from his feet the Servants were born.

13 The moon was born from his mind; from his eye the sun was born. Indra and Agni came from his mouth, and from his vital breath the Wind was born.

14 From his navel the middle realm of space arose; from his head the sky evolved. From his two feet came the earth, and the quarters of the sky from his ear. Thus they set the worlds in order.

15 There were seven enclosing-sticks for him, and thrice seven fuel-sticks, when the gods, spreading the sacrifice, bound the Man as the sacrificial beast.

16 With the sacrifice the gods sacrificed to the sacrifice. These were the first ritual laws. These very powers reached the dome of the sky where dwell the Sadhyas, the ancient gods.

Glossary

soma	an unidentified plant that produced a drink that may have had hallucinogenic properties
Tristubh foot	a metrical unit, the most common in the Rig Veda
Tvastr	the blacksmith of the gods
twelve-spoked wheel of Order	the celestial wheel, signifying the months and analogous to the zodiac
Varuna	one of the gods who, with Mitra, enforces oaths and maintains cosmic order
Vasatl	literally, "abode," "house"
Viraj	possibly a representation of the energy or force that shapes and animates matter
Vishnu	a minor god in the Rig Veda, conceived as a figure who uses trickery to recover the world from a demon
Vritra	a monster or dragon
Yama	the demigod of death

Stele of Unas

(Stele of Unas [c.2375-2345 BC] Old Kingdom [stone], Egyptian 5th Dynasty [c.2494-2345 BC] / Saqqara, Egypt / Giraudon / The Bridgeman Art Library International)

EGYPTIAN BOOK OF THE DEAD

"He for whom this scroll is recited will prosper, and his children will prosper."

Overview

The compilation of texts and figures that the world knows as the Book of the Dead was known to the ancient Egyptians as the "Spells for Going Forth by Day." The original title is descriptive of its purpose. The texts and images constituting the Book of the Dead were intended to enable the deceased Egyptian to make a successful transition to the next life at death and to return to the world of the living—"go forth by day"—when he so desired. By being buried with a copy of the Book of the Dead, the deceased was assured of having the knowledge needed to successfully overcome the dangers encountered in the afterlife. The Book of the Dead first appeared during the Eighteenth Dynasty (ca. 1569–1315 BCE) of the New Kingdom and remained in almost continuous use for the next seventeen hundred years.

Context

Spells belonging to the collection known as the Book of the Dead are first attested in the early New Kingdom in Egypt. The tradition of burying the deceased with texts began with Unas, the last king of the Fifth Dynasty (ca. 2404–2374 BCE). These earliest religious texts, which scholars call the Pyramid Texts because they were inscribed on the walls of the pyramids of the kings (and some queens) of the late Old Kingdom (ca. 2404–2206 BCE), were copies of the texts that had been recited during the rituals accompanying the death and burial of the king. With the collapse of the central government at the end of the Old Kingdom, we find some of these texts, which were previously used only by royalty, inscribed on the coffins of nonroyal noblemen. This is one indication of the process known as the "democratization of the afterlife," during which the type of afterlife previously available only to royalty became available to nonroyal Egyptians. In addition to the Pyramid Texts is the appearance of a new type of texts, called by scholars Coffin Texts, inscribed on the coffins of noblemen during the First Intermediate Period (ca. 2190–2061 BCE) and the Middle Kingdom (ca. 2061–1650 BCE). These texts were

also intended to assist the deceased in his transition to and existence in the afterlife. One innovation found in the Coffin Texts is the occasional use of illustrations to accompany some of the spells.

At the end of the Seventeenth Dynasty (ca. 1600–1569 BCE), many of the spells that made up the Coffin Texts underwent subtle changes and began to be copied on the sides of coffins and on papyri buried with the dead. In addition to those spells carried over from the Coffin Texts, new compositions were added to this corpus of texts, reflecting changes in Egyptian religion. One new development was the wider use of illustrations, called vignettes, to accompany the texts written on papyri. It is this collection of texts and images that is now known as the Book of the Dead. Calling this collection of spells a book is somewhat of a misnomer. There was originally no set collection of texts, or order of spells, that made up a Book of the Dead. Approximately 190 spells make up the corpus of the Book of the Dead, but no single papyrus copy contains them all. During the Twenty-sixth Dynasty (664–525 BCE) the spells of the Book of the Dead achieved a canonical order including 165 spells, but even after this time not all examples of the Book of the Dead contained all 165 spells, nor were the spells used always found in the canonical order.

The opportunity to be buried with a copy of the Book of the Dead was limited only by one's ability to afford an inscribed papyrus. Middle- and upper-class Egyptians would have purchased a copy of the book as preparation for their burial, and it is possible that a husband and wife may have shared a single copy of the book, since frequently both members of a couple are depicted in the scenes contained within copies of the Book of the Dead. A copy of the book would be purchased ready-made from a workshop, and the length of a papyrus and the spells it contained would be limited by the amount a person could afford. Only the wealthiest could commission a custom-made Book of the Dead. The cost of a copy of the Book of the Dead (of unknown dimensions) was given as 1 deben (91 grams) of silver, equivalent to the cost of two cows or about 7.5 acres of land. Copies of the book were created in advance, with blank spaces left for the name of the eventual owner. From the number of blank spaces left in copies of the book found in burials, it is apparent that the scribes were not conscien-

Time Line	
2375– 2345 BCE	■ King Unas, last king of the Fifth Dynasty in the Egyptian Old Kingdom and the first king to have Pyramid Texts inscribed in his pyramid, reigns.
2160– 2055 BCE	■ Pyramid Texts, and new compositions called Coffin Texts, begin to appear on the coffins and in the tombs of upper-class Egyptians.
CA. 1600 BCE	■ The earliest spells of the Book of the Dead appear on the coffin of King Mentuhotep.
1479– 1425 BCE	■ Beginning in the reign of King Thutmose III (1504–1450 BCE) of the Eighteenth Dynasty of the New Kingdom, papyrus copies of the Book of the Dead come into common use by officials.
945– 715 BCE	■ During the Twenty-second Dynasty, the Book of the Dead falls into disuse.
664– 525 BCE	■ Use of the Book of the Dead resumes, and it assumes the "canonical order" of spells 1–165, called by modern scholars the "Saite Recension" of the Book of the Dead.
30 BCE –395 CE	■ Toward the end of this period— the period of Roman rule in Egypt—the Book of the Dead falls out of use as a result of the replacement of the ancient Egyptian religion by Christianity.
1798	■ Napoléon invades Egypt, and European scholars accompanying him first become aware of the existence of the Book of the Dead papyri.
1805	■ The French scholar J. Marc Cadet first publishes a copy of the Book of the Dead.
1822	■ The French Egyptologist Jean-François Champollion deciphers the hieroglyphic writing system.

tious about filling in the name of the beneficiary in every place it should have occurred. It is assumed that a client would be shown several different patterns of the Book of the Dead from which to choose.

An important aspect of the Book of the Dead was the illustrations, or vignettes, which accompanied most of the spells. Vignettes could be simple monochrome stick figures or elaborately colored works of art, depending on how much one was willing to spend on a copy of the book. The excerpt featured here, spell 125, was typically accompanied by an elaborate vignette that illustrated the context in which the declarations of innocence were made. This scene showed many minor variations, but certain elements were common to these variations. The deceased Egyptian was usually shown being led by the hand to a large two-pan scale by the jackal-headed god of embalming, Anubis. Anubis also served to ensure that the scale was reading accurately, by checking the plum bob indicating the scale was level. In one pan of the scale we find a hieroglyph representing the heart of the deceased. The Egyptians viewed the heart rather than the brain as the seat of intellect and emotions. Great care was taken during embalming to remove the heart, wrap it carefully, and then reinsert it into the chest cavity of the corpse. At times, a beetle-shaped amulet called a scarab was inscribed on its base with spell 30 from the Book of the Dead. This amulet was intended to protect the heart of the deceased and replace it in the event the original organ was destroyed. The spell on the amulet, addressed to the heart of the deceased, conveys what the Egyptian feared might happen: "Do not stand as a witness against me; do not oppose me in the court; do not incline (the scale) against me before the keeper of the balance."

The other pan of the scale was occupied by a feather representing the Egyptian word *maat*, frequently translated as "truth" or "justice." The feather thus represented the true order of the universe, the way things ought to be, and the way a person ought to behave. (These concepts were personified in the goddess Maat.) Proper order was established by the gods at the time of creation, and it was the human being's duty to maintain this order. The gods required the king to rule in accordance with *maat*; otherwise calamities would befall Egypt. Similarly, a person had to live a life in accordance with *maat* if he or she wanted to have success in this life and a pleasant existence in the next.

Crouching near the scale was a hybrid monster called Ammit, "the swallower of the dead." This creature, possessing the head of a crocodile, a lion's mane and forequarters, and the hindquarters of a hippopotamus, was thought to gobble up any heart that failed to balance against *maat*. When this happened, the deceased suffered what the Egyptians termed "the second death" and ceased to exist. The ibis-headed god of wisdom and writing, Thoth, was shown observing the weighing of the heart and recording the results of the test. Once past this ordeal, the successful deceased is shown being introduced by the falcon-headed god Horus to Osiris, seated on a throne within an elaborate booth, flanked by his sister-wives Isis and Nephthys. In some vignettes a number of seated gods are shown as witnesses to the entire process. Other scenes show forty-two seated gods before whom the deceased Egyptian made protestations of innocence.

About the Author

As with many texts from ancient Egypt, the authors of the spells of the Book of the Dead are unknown. Authors must be thought of in the plural, because it is probable that many individuals played a role in the composition and compilation of the numerous spells that could appear in a copy of the Book of the Dead. The individual spells did not derive their authority from an author but rather from the fact that they had been proved effective (although how this was known is never made clear) "a million times," according to the last line of the text. The authority of a spell could be enhanced by an account of its discovery by a famous figure from Egypt's distant past. Even in these instances, the spell was not written by but found by such an individual. The identity of the individuals who actually composed these texts was of no interest to the ancient Egyptians.

Explanation and Analysis of the Document

Book of the Dead spell 125 is one of the most important texts from the collection. This text and its accompanying scene give the most complete expression of the Egyptian belief in a postmortem judgment of the dead. Egyptians believed that they could be subject to litigation after death, just as they were during life. Egyptians would write letters to their dead relatives asking them to take action in the court of the afterlife against other deceased individuals whom they felt were harming them on earth. Another example of a divine tribunal is found in the myth of Osiris. After he is murdered by his brother Seth, Osiris successfully pursues a claim against Seth in the divine court; as a result, Osiris becomes the ruler of the underworld, and his son Horus inherits the throne of Egypt. Osiris established the pattern that each Egyptian wanted to follow after death: vindication in the tribunal of the afterlife leading to eternal life in the world to come. By the time of the New Kingdom, this view of the court of the afterlife had changed somewhat. Now each Egyptian expected to appear before the tribunal of Osiris to be judged for his behavior during life and, through a combination of proper behavior and adequate preparation, receive the designation of "justified" (in Egyptian, "true of voice"), which entitled the deceased to a beatific afterlife.

◆ The Declaration of Innocence

The titles included in this excerpt do not appear in the original Egyptian text but were added by the translator. The opening lines of the text indicate that what follows is to be recited by the deceased when he reaches the "Hall of the Two Truths" in order to purify himself of any sins he may have committed during his lifetime. The Hall of the Two

Time Line

1842
- The German scholar Carl R. Lepsius publishes the first major study of the Book of the Dead, publishing a copy from the Ptolemaic (Greek) Period in Egypt and introducing the system of numbering spells still in use today. He coined the name *Totenbuch*, in English translated as "Book of the Dead," for this collection of texts.

1867
- Samuel Birch publishes the first English translation of the Book of the Dead, based on the papyrus published by Lepsius.

Truths was where Osiris presided over his court of assessors. The declarations of innocence to follow, also called the negative confession, resemble oaths that priests had to take when being accepted into the priesthood of a temple. In both instances, the purpose of the declarations was the same, to purify the speaker and prepare him to behold the gods.

The deceased addresses Osiris, whom he refers to as "great God," "Lord of the Two Truths," "He-of-Two-Daughters," and "He-of-Maat's-Two-Eyes." He claims to know the names of the forty-two gods who will serve as his assessors. For the Egyptians, names were thought to refer to the essence of a person or deity, and manipulation of an entity's name was thought to grant control over that entity. Knowing the true name of a god granted one power over that god. The names of gods were the building blocks for expanding knowledge of the deities, and the more names a god had the more aspects to his being he possessed. The deceased's knowledge of the names of the forty-two gods grants him power over them, and given their function—that of warding off, and drinking the blood of, those unworthy to enter Osiris's presence—such power would be useful to the deceased. The deceased brings *maat* to Osiris. *Maat* represented the archetypal offering to the gods; the gods were said to live on *maat*, and *maat* was described as the "food of the gods."

The first list of sins that the deceased denies having committed constitute what is known as list A in the declarations of innocence, or the negative confession. List A, consisting of nearly forty sins, is recited by the deceased before Osiris. List B is found in the section labled "The Declaration to the Forty-two Gods." An attempt to bring some order to both lists has been made by the Egyptologist Jan Assmann, who suggested that the forbidden acts found in the two lists fall into three categories: very general rules, such as "I have not killed"; more specific taboos, such as "I have not dammed a flowing stream"; and rules of correct professional behavior, especially in connection with weights and measures. He also suggests that the two lists are related, in that a theme specified in one list by several sins will be mentioned

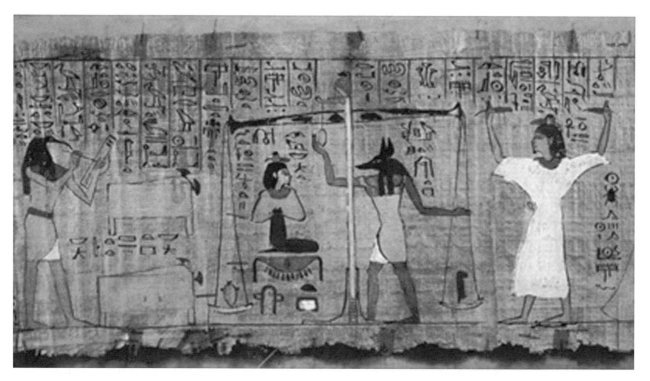

A scene from the Book of the Dead, showing the weighing of the heart

(The Weighing of the Heart against Maat's Feather of Truth, from the Book of the Dead of Heruben / Egyptian National Museum, Cairo, Egypt / Photo © AISA / The Bridgeman Art Library International)

in only a summary fashion in the other list and vice versa. List B places emphasis on traditional and general rules that affect social solidarity and communication, while list A focuses more on sins against the gods. One should think of the two lists as being recited by the deceased Egyptian while standing in front of the scale of justice, with his heart in one pan and the feather of *maat* in the other. At any point in his recitation, if his heart sank because of a lie, it would have been swallowed up by Ammit, and he would have suffered annihilation.

The confession that reads "I have not known what should not be known" is better translated as "I do not know the nonexistent." For the ancient Egyptians, creation emerged from the nonexistent. Before creation, everything was a limitless, watery, dark expanse. Within this dark, watery abyss a god—frequently, but not only, the sun god—came into being by himself and then began the process of differentiation that led to creation. Chaos, however, did not cease to exist, but rather it continued to exist at the boundary of the created world, and it constantly posed a threat to creation. One symbol of this threat was the snake god Apophis, who threatened to bring the voyage of the sun god to a halt every day and thereby bring an end to creation. The Egyptologist Erik Hornung has interpreted this line to mean that the deceased has lived his life within the boundaries of order and has not overstepped the limits laid down by the gods at creation.

"Meat offerings" refers to offerings made to the gods. Every day in temples throughout Egypt, the gods were presented with three meals a day. The main meal of the day,

and the most elaborate ritual, was the morning ritual at which the god was presented his breakfast. An enormous meal was prepared for the gods worshipped in each temple, consisting of meat, bread, cakes, beer, milk, honey, vegetables, and fruit. Only a small part of this feast was actually placed before the god. An offering formula was recited by the priest, listing the various items of the feast, while incense was burned and libations made to purify and sanctify the offerings. Since the god did not actually consume the meal, it could be shared with the other deities worshipped in the temple, until ultimately it was consumed by the priests who served in the temple, their share being determined by their rank in the priestly hierarchy. Temples owned land, herds, and flocks from which the contents of these meals derived. It is this divine property that is referred to in references to cattle, birds, and fish later in the declarations.

The dead as well as the gods received daily offerings of food and drink, and an Egyptian with the means would leave behind an endowment of land from which his daily offerings would derive, it was hoped, perpetually. As in the temples, this food would have been consumed by the priests who performed the daily offering ritual on behalf of the deceased. "Cakes of the dead" means the food offered to the dead at their tombs.

The Egyptians viewed sexual activity as potentially defiling, and therefore abstinence from sex was a precondition for purity. For instance, priests and priestesses were required to abstain when serving in the temple. In list A of the delarations, therefore, the deceased proclaims that he

"To be said on reaching the Hall of Two Truths so as to purge [the deceased] of any sins committed and to see the face of every god: / Hail to you great God, Lord of the Two Truths! / . . . Lo, I come before you, / Bringing Maat to you, / Having repelled evil for you. / I have not done crimes against people, /. . . I have not done any harm. / . . . I have not blasphemed a god, / I have not robbed the poor."

"Behold me, I have come to you, / Without sin, without guilt, without evil, /. . . I have done what people speak of, / What the gods are pleased with, / . . . I have given bread to the hungry, / Water to the thirsty, / Clothes to the naked, / A ferryboat to the boatless. / I have given divine offerings to the gods, / Invocation-offerings to the dead. / Rescue me, protect me, / Do not accuse me before the great god!"

"'Come,' says Thoth, / 'Why have you come?' / 'I have come here to report.' / 'What is your condition?' / 'I am free of all wrongdoing, / I avoided the strife of those in their day, / I am not one of them.' / 'To whom shall I announce you?' / 'To him whose roof is of fire. . . .' 'Who is he?' / 'He is Osiris.' / 'Proceed, you are announced. / . . .' So says he to me."

"He for whom this scroll is recited will prosper, and his children will prosper. He will be the friend of the king and his courtiers. He will receive bread, beer, and a big chunk of meat from the altar of the great god. He will not be held back at any gate of the west. He will be ushered in with the kings of Upper and Lower Egypt. He will be a follower of Osiris."

has not copulated, presumably on those occasions when such activity was prohibited because of the need for purity.

The phrase translated as "defiled myself" would be more accurately rendered as "I did not have penetrative sex with a man on whom a sexual act is performed." This line, along with the declaration in list B, "I have not copulated with a boy," introduces us to Egyptian notions regarding homosexuality. The Egyptians did not view an individual as either homosexual or heterosexual, but rather they focused on the type of sexual act involved. For a man to be the passive participant in a sexual act with another man was considered a sign of weakness and was associated with the place of an enemy. Apparently no stigma was attached to the act of penetration, but what may be referred to here is that the deceased denies having exerted authority or control over another male or a boy through a sexual act.

A major method of travel in ancient Egypt was by boat. Accordingly, the sun god was understood to sail through the sky by day and through the underworld by night. The kings of the Old Kingdom were buried with full-sized boats for their use in the afterlife. Egyptian gods always traveled by boat; in reality, their statues were carried either in boats over water or in bark shrines over land on the shoulders of priests. During festivals, gods could leave their temples in their bark shrines to visit other gods in their temples. People would line the processional routes to get a glimpse of the god in his bark shrine. On these occasions the average person would have had his closest encounter with a god, since only the priests were allowed into the inner rooms of an Egyptian temple. When the deceased proclaims that he has never "stopped a god in his procession," he is referring to a procession on one of these festival occasions.

After having declared himself innocent of the sins in list A, the deceased now declares himself pure. This passage makes two references to the completion of the Eye in On (the Egyptian name for the city of Heliopolis). The eye is the *udjat* (sound) eye. Originally this eye was thought of as the eye of the sky god, Horus (who originally was distinct from Horus, the son of Osiris and Isis), which was wounded in his battle with the god Seth but was restored to wholeness by Thoth, the god of writing and wisdom. The eye could be associated with both the sun and moon, and the reference to the completing of the eye is a reference to the full moon. The deceased claims that because of his state of purity, his experience of witnessing the restoration of the wounded eye of Horus in Heliopolis, and his knowledge of the names of the gods in the Hall of the Two Truths, nothing harmful will happen to him in the afterlife ("this land").

♦ The Declaration to the Forty-two Gods

These declarations (list B) are addressed to the forty-two assessor gods of the Hall of the Two Truths. Each declaration is directed to a particular deity addressed by name. Many scholars believe that the number forty-two derives from the fact that at times ancient Egypt was divided into forty-two administrative districts called nomes. Jan Assmann has argued that by announcing his innocence to the forty-two gods of the Hall of the Two Truths, the deceased is symbolically announcing his innocence to all of Egypt. These deities possessed names such as "Blood-eater," "Entrail-eater," "Fiend who comes from slaughterhouse," and "Accuser" and could pose a threat to the deceased if he were not able to address them by name and deny committing the acts that they found offensive.

The ancient Egyptians viewed adultery somewhat differently than it is viewed in modern America. Adultery was not necessarily a punishable offense, and an affair between a married man and a single woman caused little notice. Adultery was viewed as a crime against property (the wife) committed by one man against another (her husband). A married woman guilty of adultery would forfeit the one-third share of the marital property she would normally be entitled to should the couple divorce.

♦ The Address to the Gods

In the text of the spell discussed so far, the deceased has proclaimed his innocence and declared that he has not done certain deeds, and therefore he maintains that he should be judged worthy of entering the afterlife. As a result of his declarations of innocence, the deceased proclaims himself to be "without sin, without guilt, without evil." The deceased then declares those deeds that he *has* done that make him worthy of protection from the dangers of the afterlife. The deceased proclaims that he has lived a life in accordance with *maat* (he lives on *maat*, and he feeds on *maat*), has cared for the poor (given bread to the hungry, water to the thirsty, clothing to the naked), and has made offerings to the gods and the dead. These lines derive from what scholars call the "reflective autobiography" of an Egyptian, and they were inscribed on the walls of tombs during the Old Kingdom to convince those who visited that the deceased had lived a meritorious life and was worthy of receiving offerings.

There is an obscure allusion in this section to a conversation held between a donkey and a cat. The cat frequently represented the sun god in Egyptian iconography, but the role of the donkey is unclear. The donkey perhaps represents the enemy of the sun god, but it may also represent the god Seth, who played a role in protecting the sun god as he sailed through the sky in his solar boat.

♦ The First Interrogation

The gods of the Hall of the Two Truths interrogate the deceased concerning his identity and his knowledge of certain cultic activities. Many of the questions and answers refer to events that took place during the Mysteries of Osiris. In the myth of Osiris, Osiris had been murdered by his brother Seth, his body dismembered, and the pieces scattered throughout Egypt. Osiris's sister and wife, Isis, collected the pieces of her dead husband and with the help of the god Thoth reassembled and revivified Osiris; she then conceived a son, Horus, with him. The Mysteries of Osiris was a ritual reenactment of the reassembling and revivifying of Osiris. Various parts of Osiris were thought to be buried throughout Egypt. The leg and the thigh mentioned are those of Osiris. The other actions mentioned in these lines are references to activities that took place during the performance of the mysteries.

♦ The Second Interrogation

Here the deceased demonstrates his knowledge of the Hall of the Two Truths by showing that he knows the names of the gate of the hall and its parts, the keeper of the gate, the floor of the hall, and the guardians of the hall. As noted, for the Egyptians names were not random collections of letters and sounds, but revealed something about the essence of the entity named. By knowing the names of the parts of the Hall of the Two Truths and its guardians, the deceased demonstrates that he deserves safe passage through the hall to the god enthroned therein, Osiris. After having passed the ordeal of the weighing of the heart, having declared his innocence of numerous sins and transgressions, having announced the good deeds he had done while alive, and finally having demonstrated his knowledge of the Mysteries of Osiris and the Hall of the Two Truths, the deceased is ushered into the presence of Osiris as one "true of voice" and worthy of becoming a "follower of Osiris"—that is, of entering the afterlife.

♦ Instructions for Use

The final paragraph of the text contains ritual instructions for its use. Before reciting the text, the deceased should be prepared with a ritual cleansing and dressed in the proper attire. The text is said to have been successful "a million times" for those who have used it properly.

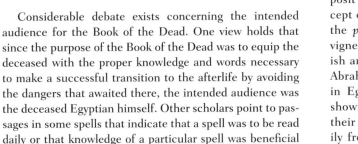

Audience

Considerable debate exists concerning the intended audience for the Book of the Dead. One view holds that since the purpose of the Book of the Dead was to equip the deceased with the proper knowledge and words necessary to make a successful transition to the afterlife by avoiding the dangers that awaited there, the intended audience was the deceased Egyptian himself. Other scholars point to passages in some spells that indicate that a spell was to be read daily or that knowledge of a particular spell was beneficial to one who knew it "on earth," as an indication that the living would have had reason to study some spells during their lifetimes. We know that at least one Egyptian claimed to have taken the contents of spell 125 as a guide for living his life, because he tells us in a stele that his plan for gaining entrance into the realm of the dead was to fulfill the laws of the Hall of the Two Truths while he was alive.

Impact

When considering the impact of the text known in modern times as the Egyptian Book of the Dead, one has to keep in mind that there was actually no such thing as a canonical Book of the Dead in the time of the pharaohs. Many spells made up the collection from which the contents of any particular copy of the Book of the Dead could be drawn, and so the impact of the Book of the Dead has to be considered spell by spell. Based on the currently available documentation, it appears that the Egyptians were the first culture in the world to posit a judgment of the individual after death. The concept of the weighing of the souls of the deceased (called the *psychostasia*) that is so graphically depicted in the vignette accompanying spell 125 influenced early Jewish and Christian texts and images. In the Testament of Abraham, an apocryphal Jewish work written in Greek in Egypt in the early second century CE, Abraham is shown a vision of the judgment of the dead by weighing their souls, and the description of the scene draws heavily from the imagery of the vignette of spell 125. Early Christian writers such as Saint Augustine and Saint John Chrysostom used this image in their descriptions of the final judgment, and the weighing of souls is also depicted in medieval Christian art, with the archangel Michael playing the role of Anubis as the tender of the scale.

When Napoléon invaded Egypt in 1798, European scholars accompanying him first became aware of the existence of the Book of the Dead papyri. The French scholar J. Marc Cadet published the first copy of a Book of the Dead in 1805. After Jean-François Champollion deciphered the hieroglyphic writing system in 1822, it became possible to translate the text of the book, and in 1842 the German scholar Carl R. Lepsius produced the first major study of the Book of the Dead, publishing a copy from the Ptolemaic (Greek) period in Egypt (323–30 BCE) and introducing the system of numbering spells still in use today. He coined the term *Totenbuch*, in English "Book of the Dead," for this collection of texts. The first English translation of the Book of the Dead, based on the papyrus published by Lepsius, appeared in 1867.

Questions for Further Study

1. What analogues for the Book of the Dead, if any, do you think are used by modern religions? Give examples from your experience.

2. Why were the ancient Egyptians so concerned with the afterlife? How did the Book of the Dead reflect the particular concerns that ancient Egyptians had about life after death?

3. Why do you think the Book of the Dead eventually fell into disuse? What historical circumstances might have contributed to this decline?

4. The Book of the Dead is part of many funerary rites and objects that are associated with the ancient Egyptians. For example, excavations of tombs, particularly (but not exclusively) of those of royalty, have revealed many beautiful and costly objects, and the process of mummification is widely known. What do these burial practices tell us about the ancient Egyptians and their beliefs?

5. What impact, if any, did ancient Egyptian religious beliefs, as reflected in burial practices, have on the development of Judaism and Christianity? Explain.

Early translations of the Book of the Dead served as inspiration for a growing body of esoteric literature beginning in the late nineteenth century. Helena Blavatsky, the founder of the modern theosophical movement, viewed the Book of the Dead as an initiatory text in her book *Isis Unveiled: A Master Key to the Mysteries of Ancient and Modern Science and Theology* (1877). E. A. Wallis Budge's translation, *The Book of the Dead: The Papyrus of Ani,* which appeared in 1895, inspired such modern poets as Ezra Pound and James Joyce. Most scholars today would view the Book of the Dead as a key source of knowledge regarding ancient Egyptian religion but not as a source of esoteric knowledge.

Further Reading

■ Books

Allen, Thomas George, trans. *The Book of the Dead; or, Going Forth by Day.* Chicago: Oriental Institute of the University of Chicago, 1974.

Assmann, Jan. *The Mind of Egypt: History and Meaning in the Time of the Pharaohs,* trans. Andrew Jenkins. New York: Metropolitan Books, 2002.

Assmann, Jan. *Death and Salvation in Ancient Egypt,* trans. David Lorton. Ithaca, N.Y.: Cornell University Press, 2005.

Bleiberg, Edward, ed. *Arts and Humanities through the Eras: Ancient Egypt 2675–332 BCE.* Detroit: Thomson Gale, 2005.

Brandon, S. F. G. *The Judgment of the Dead: The Idea of Life after Death in the Major Religions.* New York: Charles Scribner's Sons, 1967.

Faulkner, R. O., trans. *The Egyptian Book of the Dead: The Book of Going Forth by Day.* San Francisco: Chronicle Books, 1998.

Hornung, Erik. *The Ancient Egyptian Books of the Afterlife,* trans. David Lorton. Ithaca, N.Y.: Cornell University Press, 1999.

Kemp, Barry. *How to Read the Egyptian Book of the Dead.* New York: W. W. Norton, 2008.

—Stephen E. Thompson

EGYPTIAN BOOK OF THE DEAD

♦ The Declaration of Innocence

To be said on reaching the Hall of the Two Truths so
　as to purge N of any sins committed and to see the
　face of every god:
Hail to you, great God, Lord of the Two Truths!
I have come to you, my Lord,
I was brought to see your beauty.
I know you, I know the names of the forty-two gods,
Who are with you in the Hall of the Two Truths,
Who live by warding off evildoers,
Who drink of their blood,
On that day of judging characters before Wennofer.
Lo, your name is "He-of-Two-Daughters,"
(And) "He-of-Maat's-Two-Eyes."
Lo, I come before you,
Bringing Maat to you,
Having repelled evil for you.
I have not done crimes against people,
I have not mistreated cattle,
I have not sinned in the Place of Truth.
I have not known what should not be known,
I have not done any harm.
I did not begin a day by exacting more than my due,
My name did not reach the bark of the mighty ruler.
I have not blasphemed a god,
I have not robbed the poor.
I have not done what the god abhors,
I have not maligned a servant to his master.
I have not caused pain,
I have not caused tears.
I have not killed,
I have not ordered to kill,
I have not made anyone suffer.
I have not damaged the offerings in the temples,
I have not depleted the loaves of the gods,
I have not stolen the cakes of the dead.
I have not copulated nor defiled myself.
I have not increased nor reduced the measure,
I have not diminished the arura,
I have not cheated in the fields.
I have not added to the weight of the balance,
I have not falsified the plummet of the scales.
I have not taken milk from the mouth of children,
I have not deprived cattle of their pasture.
I have not snared birds in the reeds of the gods,
I have not caught fish in their ponds.

I have not held back water in its season,
I have not dammed a flowing stream,
I have not quenched a needed fire.
I have not neglected the days of meat offerings,
I have not detained cattle belonging to the god,
I have not stopped a god in his procession.
I am pure, I am pure, I am pure, I am pure!
I am pure as is pure that great heron in Hues.
I am truly the nose of the Lord of Breath,
Who sustains all the people,
On the day of completing the Eye in On,
In the second month of winter, last day,
In the presence of the lord of this land.
I have seen the completion of the Eye in On!
No evil shall befall me in this land,
In this Hall of the Two Truths;
For I know the names of the gods in it,
The followers of the great God!

♦ The Declaration to the Forty-two Gods

O Wide-of-stride who comes from On: I have not
　done evil.
O Flame-grasper who comes from Kheraha: I have
　not robbed.
O Long-nosed who comes from Khmun: I have not
　coveted.
O Shadow-eater who comes from the cave: I have
　not stolen.
O Savage-faced who comes from Rostau: I have not
　killed people.
O Lion-Twins who come from heaven: I have not
　trimmed the measure.
O Flint-eyed who comes from Khem: I have not
　cheated.
O Fiery-one who comes backward: I have not stolen
　a god's property.
O Bone-smasher who comes from Hnes: I have not
　told lies.
O Flame-thrower who comes from Memphis: I have
　not seized food.
O Cave-dweller who comes from the west: I have
　not sulked.
O White-toothed who comes from Lakeland: I have
　not trespassed.
O Blood-eater who comes from slaughterplace: I
　have not slain sacred cattle.

O Entrail-eater who comes from the tribunal: I have not extorted.

O Lord of Maat who comes from Maaty: I have not stolen bread rations.

O Wanderer who comes from Bubastis: I have not spied.

O Pale-one who comes from On: I have not prattled.

O Villain who comes from Anjdty: I have contended only for my goods.

O Fiend who comes from slaughterhouse: I have not committed adultery.

O Examiner who comes from Min's temple: I have not defiled myself.

O Chief of the nobles who comes from Imu: I have not caused fear.

O Wrecker who comes from Huy: I have not trespassed.

O Disturber who comes from the sanctuary: I have not been violent.

O Child who comes from the nome of On: I have not been deaf to Maat.

O Foreteller who comes from Wensi: I have not quarreled.

O Bastet who comes from the shrine: I have not winked.

O Backward-faced who comes from the pit: I have not copulated with a boy.

O Flame-footed who comes from the dusk: I have not been false.

O Dark-one who comes from darkness: I have not reviled.

O Peace-bringer who comes from Sais: I have not been aggressive.

O Many-faced who comes from Djefet: I have not had a hasty heart.

O Accuser who comes from Utjen: I have not attacked and reviled a god.

O Horned-one who comes from Siut: I have not made many words.

O Nefertem who comes from Memphis: I have not sinned, I have not done wrong.

O Timeless-one who comes from Djedu: I have not made trouble.

O Willful-one who comes from Tjebu: I have not [waded] in water.

O Flowing-one who comes from Nun: I have not raised my voice.

O Commander of people who comes from his shrine: I have not cursed a god.

O Benefactor who comes from Huy: I have not been boastful.

O Nehebkau who comes from the city: I have not been haughty.

O High-of-head who comes from the cave: I have not wanted more than I had.

O Captor who comes from the graveyard: I have not cursed god in my town.

◆ The Address to the Gods

Hail to you, gods!
I know you, I know your names,
I shall not fall in fear of you,
You shall not acccuse me of crime to this god whom you follow!
No misfortune shall befall me on your account!
You shall speak rightly about me before the All-Lord,
For I have acted rightly in Egypt.
I have not cursed a god,
I have not been faulted,
Hail to you, gods in the Hall of the Two Truths,
Who have no lies in their bodies,
Who live on maat in On,
Who feed on their Tightness before Horus in his disk.
Rescue me from Babi, who feeds on the entrails of nobles,
On that day of the great reckoning.
Behold me, I have come to you,
Without sin, without guilt, without evil,
Without a witness against me,
Without one whom I have wronged.
I live on maat, I feed on maat,
I have done what people speak of,
What the gods are pleased with,
I have contented a god with what he wishes.
I have given bread to the hungry,
Water to the thirsty,
Clothes to the naked,
A ferryboat to the boatless.
I have given divine offerings to the gods,
Invocation-offerings to the dead.
Rescue me, protect me,
Do not accuse me before the great god!

I am one pure of mouth, pure of hands,
One to whom "welcome" is said by those who see him;
For I have heard the words spoken by the Donkey and the Cat,
In the house of the Open-mouthed;
I was a witness before him when he cried out,
I saw the splitting of the ished-tree in Rostau.
I am one who is acquainted with the gods,
One who knows what concerns them,
I have come here to bear witness to maat,
To set the balance in right position among the dead,

O you who are high upon your standard,
Lord of the atef-crown,
Who is given the name "Lord of Breath"
Rescue me from your messengers,
Who inflict wounds,
Who mete out punishment,
Who have no compassion,
For I have done maat for the Lord of maat!
I am pure,
My front is pure,
My rear is pure,
My middle has been in the well of maat,
No limb of mine is unclean.
I have washed in the well of the South,
I have halted at the town of the North,
In the meadow of the grasshoppers,
Where the crew of Re bathes by day and by night,
Where the gods enjoy passing by day and by
    night.

◆ The First Interrogation

"Let him come," they say to me,
"Who are you?" they say to me,
"What is your name?" they say to me.
"I am the stalk of the papyrus,
He-who-is-in-the-moringa is my name."
"Where have you passed by?" they say to me,
"I have passed by the town north of the moringa."
"What have you seen there?"
"The Leg and the Thigh."
"What did you say to them?"
"I have witnessed the acclaim in the land of the
    Fenkhu."
"What did they give you?"
"A firebrand and a faience column."
"What did you do with them?"
"I buried them on the shore of the pool Maaty,
At the time of the evening meal."
"What did you find there on the shore of the pool
    Maaty?"
"A scepter of flint whose name is 'Breath-giver'."
"What did you do to the firebrand and the faience
    column,
When you had buried them?"
"I lamented over them,
I took them up,
I extinguished the fire,
I broke the column,
Threw it in the pool."
"Come then, enter the gate of this Hall of the Two
    Truths,
For you know us."

◆ The Second Interrogation

"I shall not let you enter through me,"
Says the beam of this gate,
"Unless you tell my name."
"'Plummet-of-the-Place-of-Truth' is your name."
"I shall not let you enter through me,"
Says the right leaf of this gate,
"Unless you tell my name."
"'Scale-pan-that-carries-maat' is your name."
"I shall not let you enter through me,"
Says the left leaf of this gate,
"Unless you tell my name."
"'Scale-pan-of-wine' is your name."
"I shall not let you pass over me,"
Says the threshold of this gate,
"Unless you tell my name."
"'Ox-of-Geb' is your name."
"I shall not open for you,"
Says the bolt of this gate,
"Unless you tell my name."
"'Toe-of-his-mother' is your name."
"I shall not open for you,"
Says the bolt-clasp of this gate,
"Unless you tell my name."
"'Eye-of-Sobk-Lord-of-Bakhu' is your name."
"I shall not open for you,
I shall not let you enter by me,"
Says the keeper of this gate,
"Unless you tell my name."
"'Breast-of-Shu-given-him-to-guard-Osiris' is your
    name."
"We shall not let you pass over us,"
Say the cross-timbers,
"Unless you tell our name."
"'Offspring-of-Renenutet' is your name."
"You know us, pass over us,"

"You shall not tread upon me,"
Says the floor of this hall.
"Why not, since I am pure?"
"Because we do not know your feet,
With which you tread on us;
Tell them to me,"
"'Who-enters-before-Min' is the name of my right foot,
'Wnpt-of-Nephthys' is the name of my left foot."
"Tread upon us, since you know us."
"I shall not announce you,"
Says the guard of the Hall,
"Unless you tell my name."
"'Knower-of-hearts Examiner-of-bellies' is your name."
"To which god present shall I announce you?"
"Tell it to the Interpreter of the Two Lands."

"Who is the Interpreter of the Two Lands?"
"It is Thoth."

"Come," says Thoth,
"Why have you come?"
"I have come here to report."
"What is your condition?"
"I am free of all wrongdoing,
I avoided the strife of those in their day,
I am not one of them."
"To whom shall I announce you?"
"To him whose roof is of fire,
Whose walls are living cobras,
The floor of whose house is in the flood."
"Who is he?"
"He is Osiris."

"Proceed, you are announced,
The Eye is your bread,
The Eye is your beer,
The Eye is your offering on earth,"
So says he to me.

♦ **Instructions for Use**

This is the way to act toward the Hall of the Two Truths. A man says this speech when he is pure, clean, dressed in fresh clothes, shod in white sandals, painted with eye-paint, anointed with the finest oil of myrrh. One shall offer to him beef, fowl, incense, bread, beer, and herbs. And you make this image in drawing on a clean surface in red paint mixed with soil on which pigs and goats have not trodden.

Glossary

atef	feathered white crown of Osiris
Babi	a baboon god in Egyptian mythology
cakes of the dead	food offered to the dead at their tombs
Eye in On	the Egyptian name for the city of Heliopolis
faience	a type of pottery
Fenkhu	a Syrian tribe
great God, Lord of the Two Truths, He-of-Two-Daughters, He-of-Maat's-Two-Eyes	all variant names for Osiris
Hall of the Two Truths	the place where Osiris presided over his court of assessors
Horus	the son of Osiris and Isis; according to myth, Osiris was murdered by his brother Seth, his body dismembered, and the pieces scattered throughout Egypt. Isis collected the pieces of her dead husband and with the help of the god Thoth reassembled and revivified Osiris; she then conceived a son, Horus, with him.
maat	food of the gods
Maaty	the gate keeper of the royal treasury during the reign of King Nebhepetre Montuhotep II
moringa	a flowering plant
Osiris	the ruler of the underworld
Re	the Egyptian sun god
Rostau	the underground tunnels of the pyramids
Thoth	one of the two main deities of ancient Egypt
Wennofer	a high priest of Amun during the reigns of Tutankhamen and Horemheb

He for whom this scroll is recited will prosper, and his children will prosper. He will be the friend of the king and his courtiers. He will receive bread, beer, and a big chunk of meat from the altar of the great god. He will not be held back at any gate of the west. He will be ushered in with the kings of Upper and Lower Egypt. He will be a follower of Osiris.

Effective a million times.

Marduk sets out to attack Tiamat

(Merodach sets forth to attack Tiamat, illustration from 'Myths of Babylonia and Assyria' by Donald A. Makenzie, 1915 / The Stapleton Collection / The Bridgeman Art Library International)

ENUMA ELISH

"O Marduk, thou art our avenger! / We give thee sovereignty over the whole world."

Overview

The civilization of ancient Mesopotamia that emerged around six thousand years ago is the earliest ancestor of Western culture, and its religion is the precursor of all later Western religion. Perhaps the single most important religious text of Mesopotamian culture is the Babylonian hymn that tells of Marduk, the chief god of Babylon, creating the universe. Like many ancient books, it has no title in the modern sense, but it is known by three different names: It is called Enuma Elish, its first two words (meaning "When in the height"); the Epic of Creation, after its subject matter; and the Seven Tablets of Creation, after its length. Its main themes are the emergence of order from chaos and the imposition of civilization on a hostile and destructive world—themes that relate to the precarious security of Mesopotamia in its natural and political environment.

Enuma Elish was a hymn sung on New Year's Day (which fell toward the middle of April on the Babylonian calendar) each year for nearly two thousand years. About 1750 BCE, the Babylonian king Hammurabi unified the earlier independent Mesopotamian city-states. Thereafter, Babylon was culturally dominant and vied for political supremacy for the next thousand years with Assyria, a kingdom to the northwest of Mesopotamia, until the outside power of Persia conquered the entire region in the mid-sixth century BCE. Enuma Elish was composed after Babylon's rise in order to elevate Marduk to the status of a national, even a universal, god. It may have been composed during the reign of the Babylonian king Agum-Kakrime (ca. 1500 BCE), who secured the return of the cult statue of Marduk, which had been lost earlier during a period of war. The poem was also adopted outside Babylon, notably by the Assyrians, who simply replaced Marduk with their national god, Assur. Enuma Elish had a wide influence on other cultures down to Roman times; the Neoplatonist philosopher Damascius commented on it as late as the sixth century CE.

Context

Unlike many modern religions, including Zoroastrianism, Buddhism, Christianity, and Islam, the Mesopotamian religion was not the creation of a single virtuoso at a specific moment in time. Rather, it was a traditional part of the culture of its peoples going back to prehistory. It was not a creed of belief; it was simply part of the description of the world, inextricably bound up with the people's understanding of history, science, government, and every other part of life. As a hymn in a traditional religion, Enuma Elish is not a fixed source of religious orthodoxy but an evolving expression of belief. In Babylon, the hymn was sung to Marduk; later, it was sung in Assyria to Assur. As the Assyrians and Babylonians vied for what seemed to them dominance of the world empire, their national gods assumed a central role as the head of the pantheon. The gods were imagined as human beings who were larger than life. The ideal image of the Mesopotamian family was a large landowner as a patriarch, with a wife, concubines, children, and a larger number of dependents and slaves. Many households together, in turn, gave rise to the king, who ruled all of the families in the state.

The king, for all his earthly power, was only the chief slave of the gods. The purpose of the universe was to guarantee a blessed existence to the gods by providing them with all the physical goods they could want (in the form of sacrifices) without any labor or worry on their part. In order to fulfill this purpose, individuals were allotted their own places within the universe, their destinies. Before any other consideration, each person in Mesopotamian society first had obligations to the gods, who needed to be praised and sacrificed to just as the king had to be praised and paid taxes. Enuma Elish is about human and national identity as much as the origin of the world itself. The poem also demonstrates a traditional view of nature, whose various parts are alive and conceived of as anthropomorphic, having a nearly human god in charge of it: An for the sky, Enlil for the atmosphere, Ea for the earth, and Marduk for sovereignty among many others.

Mesopotamia was certainly not immune to influence from outside. While it was the geopolitical center of the Near East (as India and China were too far distant to be of direct concern), Mesopotamia did not enjoy an overwhelming military superiority against its less civilized (that is, nonurban) neighbors. Mesopotamian civilization could thus be secure only if it also dominated the surrounding

CA. 6000 BCE	■ Mesopotamian culture and religion emerges.
CA. 1750 BCE	■ Babylon rises to a preeminent position in Mesopotamia.
CA. 1500 BCE	■ Enuma Elish is thought to have been composed.
627 BCE	■ A copy of Enuma Elish exists in the library of the Assyrian king Ashurbanipal.
CA. 275 BCE	■ Berossus, explaining Babylonian religion to the Greek world, summarizes and quotes from Enuma Elish.
CA. 100–300 CE	■ Enuma Elish ceases to be performed in public in Babylon.
CA. 500	■ Damascius is the last classical author to cite Enuma Elish.
1849	■ The archaeologist Austen Layard discovers fragments of Enuma Elish while excavating the palace of Ashurbanipal in Nineveh.
1876	■ George Smith publishes the first modern translation of Enuma Elish.

mountainous regions to the east, north, and west and the deserts to the south. This happened only twice, very late in the history of the region, under the Persian Empire in the sixth century BCE and the Arab Empire in the seventh century CE, when forces from the periphery came to dominate the entire region. Consequently, Mesopotamia was as often conquered by people from surrounding regions as it was able to control them. (While Egypt was a serious potential rival, Mesopotamia usually had the upper hand and eventually conquered Egypt.) For instance, between about 2000 and 1600 BCE, Mesopotamia was conquered and ruled by Amorites, a Northwest Semitic people from Syria with a culture similar to the Canaanites (in modern-day Lebanon and Israel-Palestine). The chief myth of the Northwest Semitic region was the battle of the thunder god with the sea, owing to the violent thunderstorms that sweep in from the Mediterranean, whereas the sea and storms played very little role in traditional Mesopotamian geography or culture. It is likely, therefore, that the battle between Marduk

and Tiamat—one of the main themes in Enuma Elish—was based on this foreign combat myth, however thoroughly it was integrated into Mesopotamian belief. One hypothesis for the composition of the text has the older myth of the gods' battle with the monstrous Anzu bird being combined with the Northwest Semitic combat myth.

About the Author

The author of Enuma Elish is unknown but was undoubtedly male and a priest of Marduk in Babylon. Mesopotamian texts were inscribed on clay tablets. Although new fragments of Enuma Elish have been found frequently by archaeologists over the past 150 years, the chief witness to the text is a single group of tablets originally found in Babylon in 1849. These tablets are signed by the scribe who wrote them, Nabubalatsuiqbi, son of Naidmarduk. His name indicates that he was from a family of priests of Marduk. The colophon, or signature, also indicates that the text was checked for error by a supervisor, so the text was produced in a well-organized professional scriptorium.

When the Assyrian king Sennacherib (704–681 BCE) refurbished the Babylonian temple of the New Year's Festival, he decorated the doors with detailed illustrations of the story of Enuma Elish, including scenes and details not present in the written text of the poem. This suggests that the story might also have existed in an oral tradition. In that case, it would seem that bards, or professional reciters, would have had the poem in their repertoire and were capable of elaborating and transforming it as they chose. If Enuma Elish arose in such a practice of oral performance over many generations, it would not be correct to speak of a single author of the poem. Rather, it would imply a tradition of poets who learned and could recite the poem in different variants. One version of it was eventually set down in writing, as was the case with the *Iliad* and the *Odyssey* of Homer or *Beowulf*—becoming the document that survives. Nevertheless, the carefully protected text of the New Year's Festival became a canonized version, and all surviving manuscripts of the poem show remarkably little variation.

Explanation and Analysis of the Document

Enuma Elish tells one continuous story, beginning with the world coming into being, continuing through conflict between the generations of the gods, and culminating in Marduk's being enthroned as the champion and ruler of the gods and his creation of human beings. The seventh and last tablet of Enuma Elish (which is not treated here directly) gives a list of Marduk's cultic names and epithets. Note that the text is highly repetitious compared with most modern writing (perhaps owing to the conditions of performance of the original work). This often takes the form of one character's giving a speech in which he quotes what was said by another, and then a third character finds occasion later to repeat the whole verbatim. The reader must be careful not to become lost in the many levels of quotation. Note, too, that ellipses in the text indicate gaps due to damage of the original manuscripts.

Impression of a cylinder seal with a prayer to Marduk

(Impression of a cylinder seal with a prayer to Marduk, 14th-12th century BC [plaster], Mesopotamian / Ancient Art and Architecture Collection Ltd. / The Bridgeman Art Library International)

◆ The First Tablet

The first tablet begins before the existence of the world order as it was envisioned by ancient Mesopotamians. That order starts to emerge slowly in the first lines of the poem and is complete by its end. The basis of creation is Tiamat, the salt ocean. In the middle of this ocean floats Apsu, the freshwater of springs and rivers. The earth floats atop that—a flat disk with Babylon in the center. Heaven is a dome of solid material above it, while the underworld is another dome below it. This is also the worldview of the Hebrew Bible and of earliest Greek literature. However, in the beginning of Enuma Elish, only Tiamat and Apsu already exist. They slowly resolve from being chaotic cosmic forces to becoming anthropomorphic gods, that is, they take on a form with many recognizable human characteristics. Note that the hymn indicates that heaven and earth do not yet exist by saying they are not yet named. In the magical thought that dominates the text's worldview, things and their names are identical. To control a thing's name is to control the thing. This mythological cosmography lies as much behind the first lines of Enuma Elish as it does the book of Genesis, which describes the fundamental constituents of the world in the same order (first the sky, then the earth, then the chaotic waters).

Tiamat and Apsu swiftly breed a new generation of gods by a process analogous to biological procreation: "Their waters were mingled together." The beginning of creation as the imposition of order on a watery chaos is also a feature of the creation myth in Genesis (1:1–2), an account that proves to have many similarities to Enuma Elish. These new gods, in turn, have offspring, including Anu (the sky) and his son Ea. As the first king of the gods, Apsu soon takes one of his descendants, Mummu, as his prime minister. Already, the divine world is becoming established as a greater type of the royal courts of Mesopotamia.

The genealogy of the divine family presented in Enuma Elish is taken up in the Greek world by Hesiod's *Theogony*, a poem composed in the first millennium BCE that introduced many Near Eastern theological ideas into Greek thought. In Hesiod, too, the world begins in a primordial chaos from which gods emerge and proceed through many generations and assassinate and fight with each other. Tiamat and Apsu may be compared directly to Tethys and Oceanus in Homer and more generally to Gaia and Uranus in Hesiod as the first divine pair. Similarly, the preexisting "deep" in Genesis (1:2) is in Hebrew *tehom,* which is cognate with Tiamat.

The conflict in Enuma Elish begins when Tiamat complains of being constantly disturbed by the noise and turbulence created by the younger gods, and Apsu (her husband) and his minister Mummu go to consult with her about what is to be done. This introduces what will seem a paradox to the modern reader. On the one hand, the text leads us to imagine something like a royal throne room with anthropomorphic gods meeting in council. On the other hand, the young gods

"When in the height heaven was not named, / And the earth beneath did not yet bear a name, / And the primeval Apsu, who begat them, / And chaos, Tiamat, the mother of them both / Their waters were mingled together, / And no field was formed, no marsh was to be seen."

"Ummu-Hubur [Tiamat], who formed all things, / Hath made in addition weapons invincible; she hath spawned monster-serpents, / Sharp of tooth, and merciless of fang. / With poison, instead of blood, she hath filled their bodies. / Fierce monster-vipers she hath clothed with terror, / With splendor she hath decked them; she hath made them of lofty stature. / Whoever beholdeth them is overcome by terror, / Their bodies rear up and none can withstand their attack."

"'I have uttered thy spell, in the assembly of the gods I have raised thee to power. / The dominion over all the gods have I entrusted unto him. / Be thou exalted, thou my chosen spouse, / May they magnify thy name over all of them the Anunnaki.' / She gave him the Tablets of Destiny, on his breast she laid them, saying: / 'Thy command shall not be without avail, and the word of thy mouth shall be established.'"

"O Marduk, thou art our avenger! / We give thee sovereignty over the whole world. / Sit thou down in might; be exalted in thy command. / Thy weapon shall never lose its power; it shall crush thy foe. / O Lord, spare the life of him that putteth his trust in thee, / But as for the god who began the rebellion, pour out his life."

"My blood will I take and bone will I fashion / I will make man, that man may / I will create man who shall inhabit the earth, / That the service of the gods may be established, and that their shrines may be built."

are disturbing Tiamat because they are inside her. She is the ocean, and so far no other place than the ocean exists, so indeed where else could they be? But this kind of cognitive dissonance did not disturb the Babylonian audience. In any case, though Tiamat herself wishes to treat her offspring with more patience, Apsu and Mummu conspire to bring Tiamat peace by killing the troublesome young gods.

Naturally, the Anunnaki (the gods loyal to Anu) immediately perceive this threat, and Ea, the most cunning of

them, tries to forestall it by poisoning Apsu (as becomes clearer in fragments of the text found since the first effort at translation). This may be compared to Kronos's castrating of Uranus in Hesiod. Note also that Ea is the son of the sky (Anu) and the father of the storm god Marduk, just as the Greek Kronos is the son of the sky (Uranus) and the father of Zeus. The murder of her consort infuriates Tiamat, who now decides to make war on Anu, Ea, and the other gods, using as an army another race of gods that are loyal to her. She makes Kingu commander over these gods and over a new race of monsters that she brings forth. These creatures are the literary ancestors of the monsters that populated the Judeo-Christian apocalyptic texts like the book of Revelation. The remains of Apsu became Ea's heavenly palace; Apsu was also the name applied to his temples on earth.

♦ The Second Tablet

Ea reports on what has occurred to Ansar (whose name refers to the celestial North Pole), who is Anu's father and ultimately the leader of the gods opposed to Tiamat. Ea confesses that he was unable to withstand the terrifying display of Tiamat's army. Ansar is also overcome. He calls on some god to step forward and offer to fight against and overcome Tiamat on behalf of the other gods. Ea's son Marduk answers this call. Many of the gods refashioned into a single family in Enuma Elish were originally the chief gods of individual cities (for example, Ea in Eridu and Anu in Uruk). One purpose of Enuma Elish was to define a relationship between these various deities. Marduk was the particular god of Babylon, and his elevation in the poem reflects the Babylonian conquest of the other Mesopotamian cities.

♦ The Third and Fourth Tablets

Amid much negotiation among the gods about what is to be done to fight Tiamat, Marduk calls for a council of all the gods to come together so that he may address them. For the first time, the Igigi are mentioned, a group of lesser gods who have the task of serving the Anunnaki to make their lives entirely blessed.

The gods build a temple for Marduk and come together in it to confer absolute sovereignty on him in return for his protecting them from Tiamat. This models the kinds of negotiation for power between king, aristocrats, and urban populations that often went on in Mesopotamian cities in times of crisis. Marduk's power is described in relation to language, similar to the claim of kings to have their will obeyed absolutely. Marduk's word has the same determinative power over not mere law but, indeed, reality: "To destroy and to create; speak thou [Marduk] the word, and thy command shall be fulfilled. / Command now and let the garment vanish; / And speak the word again and let the garment reappear!"

Marduk's word is absolutely creative or destructive. What he says becomes reality. And this power operates on a cosmic scale: The garment spoken of is one of the constellations of the night sky. This kind of magical authority is echoed very strongly in Genesis, where the god also creates merely by speaking: "And God said, Let there be light: and there was light" (Genesis 1:3).

Marduk sets off to go to battle with Tiamat. This part of the poem is most likely drawn from the Northwest Semitic combat myth. In that story, which is common to the peoples living on the Syrian coast of the Mediterranean, the thunder god establishes his rule by defeating a monster symbolic of the sea. The tale survives in very ancient form in the religious texts of the Canaanite city of Ugarit (ca. 1200 BCE)

and in the Bronze Age Hurrian myth of Kumarbi. There are reflexes also in Hesiod, but these are closer to the Hurrian version than to Enuma Elish. The combat myth is of central importance in the Hebrew bible (which itself is a Northwest Semitic document) and occurs in many different forms (for example, Psalms 104, 124; Habbakuk 3). Marduk overcomes Tiamat's general Kingu merely by the power of his glance and then destroys Tiamat herself with his storm winds. The rest of her army is captured in his net like so many fish.

After the battle is over, Marduk dissects Tiamat's body and employs it to complete the creation of the universe. He uses the upper half of her body to create the dome of the sky and the lower half to create the earth. In particular, he regulates the discharge of water from heaven in his capacity as the storm god. It was generally believed in antiquity that there was a supply of water in heaven that the gods could allow to pass through to become rain (nothing was known about the hydrological cycle). Compare the similar action taken by the creator god in Genesis: "And God made the firmament, and divided the waters which were under the firmament from the waters which were above the firmament: and it was so" (Genesis 1:7–8).

Of more fundamental importance, the universe of Enuma Elish is made from an anthropomorphic body split in two, with half used for heaven and the other half for earth. This is a very elegant explanation of how the universe operates in the Mesopotamian worldview. An action taken of earth (such as a prayer or ritual) can have a direct effect on heaven, because the two are part of the same system and there is a real physical connection between them. Tiamat has been killed, but, because she is a god, she is also in some sense immortal (like Apsu), and her body is still a single interconnected living being. Because of this essentially living unity of the whole world, an action on earth affects a corresponding part of heaven, to which it is connected by virtue of the original divine union of the different parts.

♦ The Fifth Tablet

Marduk goes on with creation, making the heavenly bodies (stars, luminaries, and planets) and time, which they govern. The creator in Genesis carries out the same operation (1:14–19). Thus the pattern of creation in Enuma Elish and Genesis are parallel: chaos, the separation of the waters by the firmament, the earth and its contents and the sky, and finally the heavenly bodies and time. Hesiod's *Theogony* also begins with chaos, but rather than dealing thereafter with physical creation, it concentrates on the generation of the gods, echoing Enuma Elish in great detail.

♦ The Sixth Tablet

Only a very small and damaged copy of the sixth tablet was available in the first find of the text made by archaeologists in the nineteenth century. But, according to more recently discovered intact copies, the sixth tablet does describe Marduk's overseeing of the creation of humanity. Ea, acting on Marduk's orders, makes the first man, using not Marduk's blood but that of the captured god Kingu. After Kingu is slaughtered, his blood is poured out on the ground like that of an animal sacrificed in the ritual cult of Mesopotamian religion. This blood is mixed with bones and flesh to create humanity, beings that are partly physical and partly divine (albeit incorporating the corrupt and hostile divinity of Kingu, the enemy of the other gods). As in the account in Genesis 1, humanity is the last thing created. The purpose of people in the order of the world described in Enuma Elish is to serve as the gods' slaves, supplying them with everything the divinities need to enjoy life through offerings made in the sacrificial cult. They take over the original role of the Igigi, who are now freed to become blessed gods alongside the Anunnaki. This story has points of contact with both the stories of the creation of human beings in Genesis (1:27; 2:7), but there is no clear parallel in the *Theogony*. However, the creation myth does have echoes in the Greek world. While Hesiod represents the ordinary religion that was generally accepted by Greek society, other teachings were attributed to the poet Orpheus that were secret and considered subversive by the centers of Greek culture, although that did not keep them from being accepted by many Greeks. Orphic tradition taught that humanity was in need of salvation because it was made with blood and ashes left over after Zeus used the thunderbolt to destroy the Titans, an older generation of gods opposed to his rule. If this teaching is indeed based on Enuma Elish, then this work is the basis of many later esoteric ideas about the condition of humanity, including the Christian idea of the fallen nature of humankind, and Platonic and Gnostic ideas about the possibility of redemption of a secretly divine part of human nature.

Audience

Enuma Elish has had an ever-changing audience throughout its history. The poem was originally composed for performance during the New Year's Festival in the city of Babylon in celebration of the city's patron god, Marduk, sometime in the second half of the second millennium BCE. Not much is known about its performance, but it was unlikely to have been a simple reading. At a minimum, it would have been sung by a musician accompanying himself on a lyre, but it is also conceivable that it received a much fuller performance, perhaps with an orchestra and a group of singers, though any specific reconstruction must remain speculative. The high degree of repetition should also be considered in this light, compared to the choruses of modern songs. In any case, its primary audience would have been the people of Babylon, who likely heard it each year in something like the manner modern Americans listen to Handel's *Messiah* every Christmas. The audience would seem to have been extended early in the first millennium BCE, when Enuma Elish was adopted for performance during the New Year's Festival in other cities, notably at Nineveh, the capital of the Assyrian Empire. Copies of the text have been found in official libraries throughout Mesopotamia, so its performance may have been widespread. It may also have been performed by bards apart from the New Year's Festival and in other Near Eastern cities, gaining an even wider audience. In Babylon, at least, the performance of the poem probably went on down into the first centuries CE.

Questions for Further Study

1. Enuma Elish emerged during the same era and in the same region of the world as the tales that would make up the *Epic of Gilgamesh.* What similarities and differences do you see between the two works, particularly in the role of a king and in the conception of the gods?

2. What importance did warfare and conquest have for the outlook expressed in Enuma Elish?

3. Notice that in the nineteenth century, Enuma Elish and the *Epic of Gilgamesh* were both discovered by the same archaeologist and rendered into English by the same translator. These were major finds, both made at roughly the same time. How do you think the two documents revolutionized knowledge of and thinking about Mesopotamian civilization among historians and archeologists in the nineteenth century?

4. Why was Enuma Elish read during the New Year's Day Festival? Why do you think the people regarded it as important at that time of year?

5. Compare the creation account of Enuma Elish with that contained in the Old Testament book of Genesis. How are the accounts similar? How do they differ? What do the two accounts, taken together, tell you about conceptions of creation in antiquity?

In the midfirst millennium BCE, Enuma Elish received a second kind of audience as religious authors outside Mesopotamia became aware of it and incorporated its teachings into their own religious documents. This is reflected in the hymn's influence on the biblical book of Genesis and on Hesiod's *Theogony*. After Alexander the Great conquered the Near East, the Babylonian priest Berossus wrote a history of his country in Greek, the *Bablyoniaca*, which contained a summary of and quotations from Enuma Elish. In this form, the poem continued to be studied by scholars in the Hellenistic and Roman eras down to the sixth century CE. Since the recovery of original manuscripts of Enuma Elish in the nineteenth century, the hymn again became the subject of scholarly investigation and has become part of the canon of world literature.

Impact

Enuma Elish today seems obscure. It is written in the dead language of Akkadian. It is not part of any extant religious tradition and can be found only through rather out-of-the-way studies. Enuma Elish was lost for most of two millennia, its existence barely suspected except for a few recondite clues, until its discovery by archaeologists a century and a half ago. Its text has been built up over that time only by further archaeological discoveries and is still not completely known. For all its apparent unfamiliarity, few works have had so profound an impact on Western civilization. At one time it was fashionable to describe Western culture as oscillating between two poles: Athens and Jerusalem, or classical culture and Judeo-Christian religion. Both of those cultural currents were profoundly influenced by Enuma Elish. Greece underwent a renaissance in the first half of the first millennium BCE, going from an illiterate culture of isolated farming villages to the greatest cosmopolitan culture in the world. During this rise, it was profoundly influenced by the cultures of the Near East, to the extent that the seventh century in Greece is often called the Orientalizing Revolution; art, literature, religion, philosophy, and every other part of Greek life was profoundly changed by the contacts Greeks made in the older, dominating cultures of the East as merchants and mercenaries. In that era, the poet Hesiod composed his *Theogony* (genealogy of the gods) in which he explains how gods worshipped throughout Greece—such as Zeus, Apollo, and Athena—came into existence and, indeed, how the world came to be. To do so, he largely abandoned whatever he knew of Greek tradition on these points and adopted myths from western Asia—both Northwest Semitic material, such as the combat myth and a good deal of material from Enuma Elish, especially in the structure and general history of his cosmogony. The *Theogony* became one of the most important books on religious subjects in Greece and an authority for all later Greeks. The ideas in the *Theogony* quickly became defining of Greek thought, and any knowledge that its myths were originally foreign were soon forgotten. At the same time, a new religious phenomenon developed in Greece that is given the name Orphism. Orphic priests gave initiations to their followers, promising them secret knowledge, healing, and salvation. Much of their lore was simply telling mysteriously in Greece what was openly known in Babylon, namely, ideas about the nature of humanity and other topics sung about in Enuma Elish.

The final form of the biblical book of Genesis was probably not edited until the Babylonian Captivity (traditionally 587–538 BCE), when members of the elite class of the kingdom of Judah were forcibly deported to Babylon, or after the return, when the Persian king Cyrus conquered Mesopotamia and allowed the self-identified Jewish exile community to settle in Jerusalem. At this time (if not earlier), the prestige of Babylonian civilization caused its myths to find their way into the text of Genesis, for instance, in the famous story of a worldwide flood in chapter 6, or the divine confusion of languages in chapter 11. Enuma Elish, in particular, is reflected in the first creation story in Genesis 1 in its basic idea of a single divine creator working on preexistent matter and in many details of his creation. The rejection of other elements of Enuma Elish, especially its polytheism, is just as important a reaction to the work and a formative influence on the Jewish tradition. Genesis, especially its first chapter, is perhaps the most widely known text in the world today. Through this mediator, as well as the *Theogony* of Hesiod and the arts of Orpheus, Enuma Elish became a foundational text of Western civilization.

Further Reading

■ Books

Bottéro, Jean. *Mesopotamia: Writing, Reasoning, and the Gods*, trans. Zainab Bahrani and Marc van de Mieroop. Chicago, Ill.: University of Chicago Press, 1992.

Burkert, Walter. *The Orientalizing Revolution*, trans. Margaret E. Pinder and Walter Burkert. Cambridge, Mass.: Harvard University Press, 1992.

Burkert, Walter. *Babylon, Memphis, Persepolis: Eastern Contexts of Greek Culture*. Cambridge, Mass.: Harvard University Press, 2004.

Clifford, R. J. *Creation Accounts in the Ancient Near East and in the Bible*. Washington, D.C.: Catholic Biblical Association, 1994.

Dalley, Stephanie. *Myths from Mesopotamia: Creation, the Flood, Gilgamesh, and Others*. Oxford, U.K.: Oxford University Press, 1989.

Dalley, Stephanie, ed. *The Legacy of Mesopotamia*. Oxford, U.K.: Oxford University Press, 1998.

Day, John. *God's Conflict with the Dragon and the Sea: Echoes of a Canaanite Myth in the Old Testament*. Cambridge, U.K.: Cambridge University Press, 1985.

Fowden, Garth. *Empire to Commonwealth*. Princeton, N.J.: Princeton University Press, 1993.

Horowitz, Wayne. *Mesopotamian Cosmic Geography*. Winona Lake, Ind.: Eisenbrauns, 1998.

Jacobsen, Thorkild. *The Treasures of Darkness: A History of Mesopotamian Religion*. New Haven, Conn.: Yale University Press, 1976.

King, L. W., trans. *The Seven Tablets of Creation; or, The Babylonian Legends concerning the Creation of the World and of Mankind*. 2 vols. London: Luzac, 1902.

Speiser, E. A. *Genesis: Anchor Bible*. Garden City, N.Y.: Doubleday, 1964.

Verbrugghe, Gerald P., and John M. Wickersham. *Berossos and Manetho, Introduced and Translated: Native Traditions in Ancient Mesopotamia and Egypt*. Ann Arbor: University of Michigan Press, 1996.

West, Martin L. *The East Face of Helicon: West Asiatic Elements in Greek Poetry and Myth*. Oxford, U.K.: Clarendon, 1997.

■ **Journals**

Kapelrud, Arvid S. "The Mythological Features in Genesis Chapter I and the Author's Intentions." *Vetus Testamentum* 24, no. 2 (1974): 178–186.

■ **Web Sites**

Etana: Electronic Tools and Ancient Near Eastern Archives Web site.
    http://www.etana.org/

Hesiod, *Theogony*, trans. H. G. Evelyn-White. Perseus Digital Library Web site.
    http://www.perseus.tufts.edu/hopper/

—Bradley A. Skeen

ENUMA ELISH

♦ **The First Tablet**

When in the height heaven was not named,
And the earth beneath did not yet bear a name,
And the primeval Apsu, who begat them,
And chaos, Tiamat, the mother of them both
Their waters were mingled together,
And no field was formed, no marsh was to be seen;
When of the gods none had been called into being,
And none bore a name, and no destinies were ordained;
Then were created the gods in the midst of heaven,
Lahmu and Lahamu were called into being [. . .]
Ages increased, [. . .]
Then Ansar and Kisar were created, and over them [. . .]
Long were the days, then there came forth [. . .]

Anu, their son, [. . .]
Ansar and Anu [. . .]
And the god Anu [. . .]
Nudimmud, whom his fathers, his begetters [. . .]
Abounding in all wisdom, [. . .]
He was exceeding strong [. . .]
He had no rival—
Thus were established and were [. . .] the great gods.
But Tiamat and Apsu were still in confusion [. . .]
They were troubled and [. . .]
In disorder [. . .]
Apsu was not diminished in might [. . .]
And Tiamat roared [. . .]
She smote, and their deeds [. . .]
Their way was evil [. . .]
Then Apsu, the begetter of the great gods,
Cried unto Mummu, his minister, and said unto him:
"O Mummu, thou minister that rejoicest my spirit,
Come, unto Tiamat let us go!"
So they went and before Tiamat they lay down,
They consulted on a plan with regard to the gods,
    their sons.
Apsu opened his mouth and spake,
And unto Tiamat, the glistening one, he addressed the
    word:

"[. . .] their way [. . .]
By day I can not rest, by night I can not lie down in
    peace.
But I will destroy their way, I will [. . .]

Let there be lamentation, and let us lie down again
    in peace."
When Tiamat heard these words,
She raged and cried aloud [. . .]
She [. . .] grievously [. . .],
She uttered a curse, and unto Apsu she spake:
"What then shall we do?
Let their way be made difficult, and let us lie down
    again in peace."
Mummu answered, and gave counsel unto Apsu,
[. . .] and hostile to the gods was the counsel Mum-
mu gave:
"Come, their way is strong, but thou shalt destroy it;
Then by day shalt thou have rest, by night shalt thou
lie down in peace."
Apsu harkened unto him and his countenance grew
bright,
Since he (Mummu) planned evil against the gods his
sons.
[. . .] he was afraid [. . .],
His knees became weak; they gave way beneath him,
Because of the evil which their first-born had
planned.
[. . .] their [. . .] they altered.
[. . .] they [. . .],
Lamentation they sat in sorrow
[. . .]
Then Ea, who knoweth all that is, went up and he
beheld their muttering.

[about 30 illegible lines]

[. . .] he spake:
[. . .] thy... he hath conquered and
[. . .] he weepeth and sitteth in tribulation.
[. . .] of fear,
[. . .] we shall not lie down in peace.
[. . .] Apsu is laid waste,
[. . .]and Mummu, who were taken captive, in [. . .]
[. . .] thou didst [. . .]
[. . .] let us lie down in peace.
[. . .] they will smite [. . .]
[. . .] let us lie down in peace.
[. . .] thou shalt take vengeance for them,
[. . .] unto the tempest shalt thou [. . .]!"

And Tiamat harkened unto the word of the bright god, and said:

[. . .] shalt thou entrust! let us wage war!"

[. . .] the gods in the midst of [. . .]

[. . .] for the gods did she create.

They banded themselves together and at the side of Tiamat they advanced;

They were furious; they devised mischief without resting night and day.

They prepared for battle, fuming and raging;

They joined their forces and made war,

Ummu-Hubur [Tiamat] who formed all things,

Made in addition weapons invincible; she spawned monster-serpents,

Sharp of tooth, and merciless of fang;

With poison, instead of blood, she filled their bodies.

Fierce monster-vipers she clothed with terror,

With splendor she decked them, she made them of lofty stature.

Whoever beheld them, terror overcame him,

Their bodies reared up and none could withstand their attack.

She set up vipers and dragons, and the monster Lahamu,

And hurricanes, and raging hounds, and scorpion-men,

And mighty tempests, and fish-men, and rams;

They bore cruel weapons, without fear of the fight.

Her commands were mighty, none could resist them;

After this fashion, huge of stature, she made eleven [kinds of] monsters.

Among the gods who were her sons, inasmuch as he had given her support,

She exalted Kingu; in their midst she raised him to power.

To march before the forces, to lead the host,

To give the battle-signal, to advance to the attack,

To direct the battle, to control the fight,

Unto him she entrusted; in costly raiment she made him sit, saying:

"I have uttered thy spell, in the assembly of the gods

I have raised thee to power.

The dominion over all the gods have I entrusted unto him.

Be thou exalted, thou my chosen spouse,

May they magnify thy name over all of them the Anunnaki."

She gave him the Tablets of Destiny, on his breast she laid them, saying:

"Thy command shall not be without avail, and the word of thy mouth shall be established."

Now Kingu, thus exalted, having received the power of Anu,

Decreed the fate among the gods his sons, saying:

"Let the opening of your mouth quench the Fire-god;

Whoso is exalted in the battle, let him display his might!"

♦ **The Second Tablet**

Tiamat made weighty her handiwork,

Evil she wrought against the gods her children.

To avenge Apsu, Tiamat planned evil,

But how she had collected her forces, the god unto Ea divulged.

Ea harkened to this thing, and

He was grievously afflicted and he sat in sorrow.

The days went by, and his anger was appeased,

And to the place of Ansar his father he took his way.

He went and, standing before Ansar, the father who begat him,

All that Tiamat had plotted he repeated unto him,

Saying, "Tiamat our mother hath conceived a hatred for us,

With all her force she rageth, full of wrath.

All the gods have turned to her,

With those, whom ye created, they go at her side.

They are banded together and at the side of Tiamat they advance;

They are furious, they devise mischief without resting night and day.

They prepare for battle, fuming and raging;

They have joined their forces and are making war.

Ummu-Hubur, who formed all things,

Hath made in addition weapons invincible; she hath spawned monster-serpents,

Sharp of tooth, and merciless of fang.

With poison, instead of blood, she hath filled their bodies.

Fierce monster-vipers she hath clothed with terror,

With splendor she hath decked them; she hath made them of lofty stature.

Whoever beholdeth them is overcome by terror,

Their bodies rear up and none can withstand their attack.

She hath set up vipers, and dragons, and the monster Lahamu,

And hurricanes and raging hounds, and scorpion-men,

And mighty tempests, and fish-men and rams;

They bear cruel weapons, without fear of the fight.

Her commands are mighty; none can resist them;

After this fashion, huge of stature, hath she made eleven monsters.

Among the gods who are her sons, inasmuch as he hath given her support,

She hath exalted Kingu; in their midst she hath raised him to power.

To march before the forces, to lead the host,

To give the battle-signal, to advance to the attack.

To direct the battle, to control the fight,

Unto him hath she entrusted; in costly raiment she hath made him sit, saying:

"I have uttered thy spell; in the assembly of the gods I have raised thee to power,

The dominion over all the gods have I entrusted unto thee.

Be thou exalted, thou my chosen spouse,

May they magnify thy name over all of them

She hath given him the Tablets of Destiny, on his breast she laid them, saying:

'Thy command shall not be without avail, and the word of thy mouth shall be established.'

Now Kingu, thus exalted, having received the power of Anu,

Decreed the fate for the gods, her sons, saying:

'Let the opening of your mouth quench the Fire-god;

Whoso is exalted in the battle, let him display his might!'"

When Ansar heard how Tiamat was mightily in revolt,

he bit his lips, his mind was not at peace,

[. . .], he made a bitter lamentation:

[. . .] battle,

[. . .] thou [. . .]

Mummu and Apsu thou hast smitten

But Tiamat hath exalted Kingu, and where is one who can oppose her?

[. . .] deliberation

[. . .] the [. . .] of the gods,—Nudimmud.

[A gap of about a dozen lines occurs here.]

Ansar unto his son addressed the word:

"[. . .] my mighty hero,

Whose strength is great and whose onslaught can not be withstood,

Go and stand before Tiamat,

That her spirit may be appeased, that her heart may be merciful.

But if she will not harken unto thy word,

Our word shalt thou speak unto her, that she may be pacified."

He heard the word of his father Ansar

And he directed his path to her, toward her he took the way.

Anu drew nigh, he beheld the muttering of Tiamat,

But he could not withstand her, and he turned back.

[. . .] Ansar

[. . .] he spake unto him:

[A gap of over twenty lines occurs here.]

an avenger [. . .]

[. . .] valiant

[. . .] in the place of his decision

[. . .] he spake unto him:

[. . .] thy father

"Thou art my son, who maketh merciful his heart.

[. . .] to the battle shalt thou draw nigh,

he that shall behold thee shall have peace."

And the lord rejoiced at the word of his father,

And he drew nigh and stood before Ansar.

Ansar beheld him and his heart was filled with joy,

He kissed him on the lips and his fear departed from him.

"O my father, let not the word of thy lips be overcome,

Let me go, that I may accomplish all that is in thy heart.

O Ansar, let not the word of thy lips be overcome,

Let me go, that I may accomplish all that is in thy heart."

[Marduk answered:] "What man is it, who hath brought thee forth to battle?

[. . .] Tiamat, who is a woman, is armed and attacketh thee.

[. . .] rejoice and be glad;

The neck of Tiamat shalt thou swiftly trample under foot.

[. . .] rejoice and be glad;

The neck of Tiamat shalt thou swiftly trample under foot.

O my son, who knoweth all wisdom,

Pacify Tiamat with thy pure incantation.

Speedily set out upon thy way,

For thy blood shall not be poured out; thou shalt return again."

The lord rejoiced at the word of his father,

His heart exulted, and unto his father he spake:

"O Lord of the gods, Destiny of the great gods,

If I, your avenger,

Conquer Tiamat and give you life,

Appoint an assembly, make my fate preeminent and proclaim it.

In Upsukkinaku seat yourself joyfully together,

With my word in place of you will I decree fate.

May whatsoever I do remain unaltered,

May the word of my lips never be chanced nor made of no avail."

♦ The Third Tablet

Ansar opened his mouth, and
Unto Gaga, his minister, spake the word.
"O Gaga, thou minister that rejoicest my spirit,
Unto Lahmu and Lahamu will I send thee.
[. . .] thou canst attain,
[. . .] thou shalt cause to be brought before thee.
[. . .] let the gods, all of them,
Make ready for a feast, at a banquet let them sit,
Let them eat bread, let them mix wine,
That for Marduk, their avenger they may decree
    the fate.
Go, Gaga, stand before them,
And all that I tell thee, repeat unto them, and say:
Ansar, your son, hath sent me,
The purpose of his heart he hath made known unto me.
He saith that Tiamat our mother hath conceived a
    hatred for us,
With all her force she rageth, full of wrath.
All the gods have turned to her,
With those, whom ye created, they go at her side.
They are banded together, and at the side of Tiamat
    they advance;
They are furious, they devise mischief without rest-
    ing night and day.
They prepare for battle, fuming and raging;
They have joined their forces and are making war.
Ummu-Hubur, who formed all things,
Hath made in addition weapons invincible; she hath
    spawned monster-serpents,
Sharp of tooth and merciless of fang.
With poison, instead of blood, she hath filled
    their bodies.
Fierce monster-vipers she hath clothed with terror,
With splendor she hath decked them; she hath made
    them of lofty stature.
Whoever beholdeth them, terror overcometh him,
Their bodies rear up and none can withstand their
    attack.
She hath set up vipers, and dragons, and the monster
    Lahamu,
And hurricanes, and raging hounds, and scorpion-men,
And mighty tempests, and fish-men, and rams;
They bear merciless weapons, without fear of the fight.
Her commands are mighty; none can resist them;
After this fashion, huge of stature, hath she made
    eleven monsters.
Among the gods who are her sons, inasmuch as he
    hath given her support,
She hath exalted Kingu; in their midst she hath
    raised him to power.
To march before the forces, to lead the host,

To give the battle-signal, to advance to the attack,
To direct the battle, to control the fight,
Unto him hath she entrusted; in costly raiment she
    hath made him sit, saying:
"I have uttered thy spell; in the assembly of the gods
I have raised thee to power,
The dominion over all the gods have I entrusted
    unto thee.
Be thou exalted, thou my chosen spouse,
May they magnify thy name over all of them [. . .] the
    Anunnaki."
She hath given him the Tablets of Destiny, on his
    breast she laid them, saying:
"Thy command shall not be without avail, and the
    word of thy mouth shall be established."
Now Kingu, thus exalted, having received the power
    of Anu,
Decreed the fate for the gods, her sons, saying:
"Let the opening of your mouth quench the Fire-god;
Whoso is exalted in the battle, let him display his
    might!"
I sent Anu, but he could not withstand her;
Nudimmud was afraid and turned back.
But Marduk hath set out, the director of the gods,
    your son;
To set out against Tiamat his heart hath prompted him.
He opened his mouth and spake unto me, saying: "If
    I, your avenger,
Conquer Tiamat and give you life,
Appoint an assembly, make my fate preeminent and
    proclaim it.
In Upsukkinaku seat yourself joyfully together;
With my word in place of you will I decree fate.
May whatsoever I do remain unaltered,
May the word of my lips never be changed nor made
    of no avail."
Hasten, therefore, and swiftly decree for him the fate
    which you bestow,
That he may go and fight your strong enemy.
Gaga went, he took his way and
Humbly before Lahmu and Lahamu, the gods, his
    fathers,
He made obeisance, and he kissed the ground at
    their feet.
He humbled himself; then he stood up and spake
    unto them saying:
"Ansar, your son, hath sent me,
The purpose of his heart he hath made known unto me.
He saith that Tiamat our mother hath conceived a
    hatred for us,
With all her force she rageth, full of wrath.
All the gods have turned to her,

With those, whom ye created, they go at her side.

They are banded together and at the side of Tiamat they advance;

They are furious, they devise mischief without resting night and day.

They prepare for battle, fuming and raging;

They have joined their forces and are making war.

Ummu-Hubur, who formed all things,

Hath made in addition weapons invincible; she hath spawned monster-serpents,

Sharp of tooth and merciless of fang.

With poison, instead of blood, she hath filled their bodies.

Fierce monster-vipers she hath clothed with terror,

With splendor she hath decked them, she hath made them of lofty stature.

Whoever beholdeth them, terror overcometh him,

Their bodies rear up and none can withstand their attack.

She hath set up vipers, and dragons, and the monster Lahamu,

And hurricanes, and raging hounds, and scorpion-men,

And mighty tempests, and fish-men, and rams;

They bear merciless weapons, without fear of the fight.

Her commands are mighty; none can resist them;

After this fashion, huge of stature, hath she made eleven monsters.

Among the gods who are her sons, inasmuch as he hath given her support,

She hath exalted Kingu; in their midst she hath raised him to power.

To march before the forces, to lead the host,

To give the battle-signal, to advance to the attack, To direct the battle, to control the fight,

Unto him hath she entrusted; in costly raiment she hath made him sit, saying:

"I have uttered thy spell; in the assembly of the gods I have raised thee to power,

The dominion over all the gods have I entrusted unto thee.

Be thou exalted, thou my chosen spouse,

May they magnify thy name over all of them [. . .] the Anunnaki.

She hath given him the Tablets of Destiny on his breast she laid them, saying:

Thy command shall not be without avail, and the word of thy mouth shall be established."

Now Kingu, thus exalted, having received the power of Anu,

Decreed the fate for the gods, her sons, saying:

"Let the opening of your mouth quench the Fire-god;

Whoso is exalted in the battle, let him display his might!"

I sent Anu, but he could not withstand her;

Nudimmud was afraid and turned back.

But Marduk hath set out, the director of the gods, your son;

To set out against Tiamat his heart hath prompted him.

He opened his mouth and spake unto me, saying:

"If I, your avenger,

Conquer Tiamat and give you life,

Appoint an assembly, make my fate preeminent and proclaim it.

In Upsukkinaku seat yourselves joyfully together;

With my word in place of you will I decree fate.

May, whatsoever I do remain unaltered,

May the word of my lips never be changed nor made of no avail."

Hasten, therefore, and swiftly decree for him the fate which you bestow,

That he may go and fight your strong enemy!"

Lahmu and Lahamu heard and cried aloud

All of the Igigi [the elder gods] wailed bitterly, saying:

"What has been altered so that they should

We do not understand the deed of Tiamat!"

Then did they collect and go,

The great gods, all of them, who decree fate.

They entered in before Ansar, they filled [. . .]

They kissed one another, in the assembly [. . .];

They made ready for the feast, at the banquet they sat;

They ate bread, they mixed sesame-wine.

The sweet drink, the mead, confused their [. . .]

They were drunk with drinking, their bodies were filled.

They were wholly at ease, their spirit was exalted;

Then for Marduk, their avenger, did they decree the fate.

♦ **The Fourth Tablet**

They prepared for him a lordly chamber,

Before his fathers as prince he took his place.

"Thou art chiefest among the great gods,

Thy fate is unequaled, thy word is Anu!

O Marduk, thou art chiefest among the great gods,

Thy fate is unequaled, thy word is Anu!

Henceforth not without avail shall be thy command,

In thy power shall it be to exalt and to abase.

Established shall be the word of thy mouth, irresistible shall be thy command,

None among the gods shall transgress thy boundary.

Abundance, the desire of the shrines of the gods,

Shall be established in thy sanctuary, even though they lack offerings.

O Marduk, thou art our avenger!

We give thee sovereignty over the whole world.

Sit thou down in might; be exalted in thy command.

Thy weapon shall never lose its power; it shall crush thy foe.

O Lord, spare the life of him that putteth his trust in thee,

But as for the god who began the rebellion, pour out his life."

Then set they in their midst a garment,

And unto Marduk,—their first-born they spake:

"May thy fate, O lord, be supreme among the gods,

To destroy and to create; speak thou the word, and thy command shall be fulfilled.

Command now and let the garment vanish;

And speak the word again and let the garment reappear!

Then he spake with his mouth, and the garment vanished;

Again he commanded it, and. the garment reappeared.

When the gods, his fathers, beheld the fulfillment of his word,

They rejoiced, and they did homage unto him, saying, "Marduk is king!"

They bestowed upon him the scepter, and the throne, and the ring,

They give him an invincible weaponry which overwhelmeth the foe.

Go, and cut off the life of Tiamat,

And let the wind carry her blood into secret places."

After the gods his fathers had decreed for the lord his fate,

They caused him to set out on a path of prosperity and success.

He made ready the bow, he chose his weapon,

He slung a spear upon him and fastened it [. . .]

He raised the club, in his right hand he grasped it,

The bow and the quiver he hung at his side.

He set the lightning in front of him,

With burning flame he filled his body.

He made a net to enclose the inward parts of Tiamat,

The four winds he stationed so that nothing of her might escape;

The South wind and the North wind and the East wind and the West wind

He brought near to the net, the gift of his father Anu.

He created the evil wind, and the tempest, and the hurricane,

And the fourfold wind, and the sevenfold wind, and the whirlwind, and the wind which had no equal;

He sent forth the winds which he had created, the seven of them;

To disturb the inward parts of Tiamat, they followed after him.

Then the lord raised the thunderbolt, his mighty weapon,

He mounted the chariot, the storm unequaled for terror,

He harnessed and yoked unto it four horses,

Destructive, ferocious, overwhelming, and swift of pace;

[. . .] were their teeth, they were flecked with foam;

They were skilled in [. . .], they had been trained to trample underfoot.

[. . .] mighty in battle,

Left and right [. . .]

His garment was... , he was clothed with terror,

With overpowering brightness his head was crowned.

Then he set out, he took his way,

And toward the raging Tiamat he set his face.

On his lips he held [. . .],

[. . .] he grasped in his hand.

Then they beheld him, the gods beheld him,

The gods his fathers beheld him, the gods beheld him.

And the lord drew nigh, he gazed upon the inward parts of Tiamat,

He perceived the muttering of Kingu, her spouse.

As Marduk gazed, Kingu was troubled in his gait,

His will was destroyed and his motions ceased.

And the gods, his helpers, who marched by his side,

Beheld their leader's [. . .], and their sight was troubled.

But Tiamat [. . .], she turned not her neck,

With lips that failed not she uttered rebellious words:

"[. . .] thy coming as lord of the gods,

From their places have they gathered, in thy place are they!"

Then the lord raised the thunderbolt, his mighty weapon,

And against Tiamat, who was raging, thus he sent the word:

Thou art become great, thou hast exalted thyself on high,

And thy heart hath prompted thee to call to battle.

[. . .] their fathers [. . .]

[. . .] their... thou hatest [. . .]

Thou hast exalted Kingu to be thy spouse,

Thou hast [. . .] him, that, even as Anu, he should issue decrees.

Thou hast followed after evil,

And against the gods my fathers thou hast contrived thy wicked plan.

Let then thy host be equipped, let thy weapons be girded on!

Stand! I and thou, let us join battle!

When Tiamat heard these words,

She was like one possessed; she lost her reason.
Tiamat uttered wild, piercing cries,
She trembled and shook to her very foundations.
She recited an incantation, she pronounced her spell,
And the gods of the battle cried out for their weapons.
Then advanced Tiamat and Marduk, the counselor of the gods;
To the fight they came on, to the battle they drew nigh.
The lord spread out his net and caught her,
And the evil wind that was behind him he let loose in her face.
As Tiamat opened her mouth to its full extent,
He drove in the evil wind, while as yet she had not shut her lips.
The terrible winds filled her belly,
And her courage was taken from her, and her mouth she opened wide.
He seized the spear and burst her belly,
He severed her inward parts, he pierced her heart.
He overcame her and cut off her life;
He cast down her body and stood upon it.
When he had slain Tiamat, the leader,
Her might was broken, her host was scattered.
And the gods her helpers, who marched by her side,
Trembled, and were afraid, and turned back.
They took to flight to save their lives;
But they were surrounded, so that they could not escape.
He took them captive, he broke their weapons;
In the net they were caught and in the snare they sat down.
The [. . .] of the world they filled with cries of grief.
They received punishment from him, they were held in bondage.
And on the eleven creatures which she had filled with the power of striking terror,
Upon the troop of devils, who marched at her [. . .],
He brought affliction, their strength he [. . .];
Them and their opposition he trampled under his feet.
Moreover, Kingu, who had been exalted over them,
He conquered, and with the god Dug-ga he counted him.
He took from him the Tablets of Destiny that were not rightly his,
He sealed them with a seal and in his own breast he laid them.
Now after the hero Marduk had conquered and cast down his enemies,
And had made the arrogant foe even like
And had fully established Ansar's triumph over the enemy
And had attained the purpose of Nudimmud,
Over the captive gods he strengthened his durance,

And unto Tiamat, whom he had conquered, he returned.
And the lord stood upon Tiamat's hinder parts,
And with his merciless club he smashed her skull.
He cut through the channels of her blood,
And he made the North wind bear it away into secret places.
His fathers beheld, and they rejoiced and were glad;
Presents and gifts they brought unto him.
Then the lord rested, gazing upon her dead body,
While he divided the flesh of the [. . .], and devised a cunning plan.
He split her up like a flat fish into two halves;
One half of her he stablished as a covering for heaven.
He fixed a bolt, he stationed a watchman,
And bade them not to let her waters come forth.
He passed through the heavens, he surveyed the regions thereof,
And over against the Deep he set the dwelling of Nudimmud.
And the lord measured the structure of the Deep,
And he founded E-sara, a mansion like unto it.
The mansion E-sara which he created as heaven,
He caused Anu, Bel, and Ea in their districts to inhabit.

♦ The Fifth Tablet

He [Marduk] made the stations for the great gods;
The stars, their images, as the stars of the Zodiac, he fixed.
He ordained the year and into sections he divided it;
For the twelve months he fixed three stars.
After he had [. . .] the days of the year [. . .] images,
He founded the station of Nibir [the planet Jupiter] to determine their bounds;
That none might err or go astray,
He set the station of Bel and Ea along with him.
He opened great gates on both sides,
He made strong the bolt on the left and on the right.
In the midst thereof he fixed the zenith;
The Moon-god he caused to shine forth, the night he entrusted to him.
He appointed him, a being of the night, to determine the days;
Every month without ceasing with the crown he covered him, saying:
"At the beginning of the month, when thou shinest upon the land,
Thou commandest the horns to determine six days,
And on the seventh day to divide the crown.
On the fourteenth day thou shalt stand opposite, the half [. . .]

When the Sun-god on the foundation of heaven [. . .] thee,

The [. . .] thou shalt cause to [. . .], and thou shalt make his...

[. . .] unto the path of the Sun-god shalt thou cause to draw nigh,

And on the [. . .] day thou shalt stand opposite, and the Sun-god shall [. . .]

[. . .] to traverse her way.

[. . .] thou shalt cause to draw nigh, and thou shalt judge the right.

[. . .] to destroy [. . .]"

[Nearly fifty lines are here lost.]

The gods, his fathers, beheld the net which he had made,

They beheld the bow and how its work was accomplished.

They praised the work which he had done [. . .]

Then Anu raised the [. . .] in the assembly of the gods. He kissed the bow, saying, "It is [. . .]!"

And thus he named the names of the bow, saying,

"'Long-wood' shall be one name, and the second name shall be [. . .],

And its third name shall be the Bow-star, in heaven shall it...!"

Then he fixed a station for it [. . .]

Now after the fate of [. . .]

He set a throne [. . .]

[. . .]in heaven [. . .]

[The remainder of this tablet is missing.]

♦ The Sixth Tablet

When Marduk heard the word of the gods,

His heart prompted him and he devised a cunning plan.

He opened his mouth and unto Ea he spake

That which he had conceived in his heart he imparted unto him:

"My blood will I take and bone will I fashion

I will make man, that man may

I will create man who shall inhabit the earth,

That the service of the gods may be established, and that their shrines may be built.

But I will alter the ways of the gods, and I will change their paths;

Together shall they be oppressed and unto evil shall they [. . .]

And Ea answered him and spake the word:

"[. . .] the [. . .] of the gods I have changed

[. . .] and one...

[. . .] shall be destroyed and men will I [. . .]

[. . .] and the gods .

[. . .] and they [. . .]"

[The rest of the text is wanting with the exception of the last few lines of the tablet, which read as follows.]

They rejoiced [. . .]

In Upsukkinnaku they set their dwelling.

Of the heroic son, their avenger, they cried:

"We, whom he succored [. . .]!"

They seated themselves and in the assembly they named him [. . .],

They all cried aloud, they exalted him [. . .]

Glossary

Ansar	Anu's father and the leader of the gods opposed to Tiamat
Anu	the sky god
Anunnaki	the gods who are loyal to Anu
Apsu	the first king of the gods and the god of the freshwater of springs and rivers
Ea	the son of Anu and the father of Marduk, the storm god
Kingu	a captured god whose blood Ea uses to make the first human
Marduk	the storm god and the chief god of the Babylonians
Mummu	a descendant of Apsu and Apsu's prime minister
Tiamat	the salt ocean

Moses, holding the tablet with the Ten Commandments

(Library of Congress)

"I am come down to deliver them out of the hand of the Egyptians, and to bring them up out of that land unto a . . . land flowing with milk and honey."

Overview

The book of Exodus, conjectured by religious scholars to have been written by Moses in the fifteenth century BCE, is the second book of what is commonly called the Old Testament, although among Jews the Old Testament is called the Tanakh. The first five books of the Tanakh—Genesis, Exodus, Leviticus, Numbers, and Deuteronomy—are referred to collectively in Judaism as the Torah ("law"). While Genesis focuses on the creation of the world and the events that followed (such as Noah's Flood), Exodus serves two primary purposes. It tells the story of the Israelites' deliverance from slavery and their flight from Egypt under the leadership of Moses. At the same time, it documents the formation of the Jewish nation—the Israelites—and the covenant between God and the Israelites—that is, God's agreement to treat the Israelites as his chosen people in exchange for certain behaviors such as those enumerated in the Ten Commandments; this covenant is often referred to as the Mosaic Covenant to distinguish it from other covenants arrived at under other biblical figures such as Abraham and David.

The events of Exodus cover a time period of about 145 years, and the book of Exodus falls into three major parts. The first fifteen chapters outline Egypt's treatment of the Israelites, which was often cruel and harsh. It then chronicles the life and career of Moses from his birth through his exile in Midian. It highlights Moses's final victorious contest with the Egyptian pharaoh, during which Moses becomes God's spokesman and leads the Israelites out of Egyptian captivity. The Egyptians give chase but are destroyed as they try to cross the Reed (Red) Sea. Chapters 16–40 tell of the march of the Israelites through the wilderness and then to Mount Sinai, where God gives Moses his law in the form of the commandments.

Some scholars believe that Exodus is the most important book in the Bible because of the seminal events it records and because of its ongoing legacy to religion and history. Another book in the Torah, Deuteronomy, states that the exodus and the revelation of the laws and covenant at Mount Sinai demonstrate that there is no other God but the one of the Hebrews. Thus, it could be argued that Exodus forms the foundation of the world's first great monotheistic religion.

Context

The name Exodus, emphasizing the Israelites' flight out of Egypt, is the Greek name for the book; it translates roughly as "going out." In Hebrew, the name of the book is taken from its first two words, which in English mean "here are the names," and thus the book of Exodus is often also known as the "Book of Names." In Exodus, God takes different names as he interacts with the Hebrew people, and the book also lists the many names of the tribes of Israel and other figures in Old Testament history. In the Exodus story, God shows himself in various ways to the Israelites: there are pillars of clouds and fire, the thunder at Mount Sinai, the daily supply of manna (the miraculous food that God gave to the Israelites during their flight), and God's instructions to Moses to build the Ark of the Covenant (that is, the vessel that would contain the stone tablets on which the Ten Commandments were inscribed).

The Jewish Torah narrates the history of the Jews from Creation through the death of Moses. Exodus, the second book of the Torah, begins where Genesis left off, as the descendants of Joseph moved to Egypt to escape famine and hardship. The Israelites actually thrived for a time under the rule of the Egyptian pharaoh, but when a new pharaoh ascended the throne, the Israelites were enslaved and forced to work on the pharaoh's building projects. The "exodus" of the book is the Israelites' flight from Egyptian servitude.

In Exodus, the Israelites in Egypt have greatly increased in number, and the new Egyptian leadership feels threatened by them. Accordingly, the Egyptians issue a decree that all Hebrew boys must be killed at birth, by being drowned in the Nile River. One Hebrew woman refuses to do this and sets her newborn son afloat on the river in a basket. The pharaoh's daughter discovers the baby, and although she recognizes him as Hebrew she raises him as her own, naming him Moses. Over the years, Moses becomes aware of his Hebrew roots and grows troubled by the subjugation of the Jewish people and concerned about their welfare. Then God appears to Moses in the form of a burning

CA. 1526 BCE	■ Some scholars argue for this early date for the birth of Moses; others contend he lived in the thirteenth and early part of the twelfth century BCE.
1491 BCE	■ The plagues of Egypt described in Exodus may have occurred in this year; other theories contend that the plagues occurred in 1450 BCE, when the Egyptians may have been subjected to a locust plague.
CA. 1453 BCE	■ Amenhotep II, whose reign would end around 1419 BCE, is born; he may have been the pharaoh at the time of Exodus (as based on the chronology given in the Bible in 1 Kings 6:1).
1446 BCE	■ As believed by some scholars, Moses writes the book of Exodus.
CA. 1304 BCE	■ Rameses II, who would die in 1237 BCE, is born; Rameses II may have been the pharaoh at the time of Exodus (as based on conclusions by Egyptologists counter to 1 Kings 6:1).
1828	■ A papyrus is found near the pyramids of Memphis, Egypt, that appears to give a detailed description, from the Egyptian point of view, of the plagues described by Moses in the Old Testament book of Exodus.
1848	■ **January 6** Some scholars conclude that the north end of the Red Sea was much farther north in biblical times than it is today, supporting the view that the Israelites might have crossed it by following the itinerary given in Exodus.

bush and informs him that the Israelites need to return to Canaan, the ancient name for the region of modern-day Israel and surrounding lands. At first, Moses is hesitant about helping the Israelites accomplish this aim, but God gives him a staff he can use to perform miracles and encourages him to take his brother Aaron, whose breastplate contains twelve stones representing the Twelve Tribes of Israel.

The Egyptians refuse to let the Israelites leave. In response, God sends ten plagues on Egypt to demonstrate his wrath and power. (Among the most persuasive theories, dates of either 1491 or 1450 BCE are given by Bible historians for these events.) After Moses and the Israelites take flight, the pharaoh and his army give chase. A key event in this narrative is the parting of the Red Sea. As the Israelites seem trapped by the sea, Moses miraculously parts it, and the people pass through. When the Egyptians follow, Moses closes the waters, drowning the Egyptians.

Several months after their departure from Egypt, the Israelites arrive at Mount Sinai, where God gives Moses the Ten Commandments and establishes his covenant with the Jews: If the Israelites obey the commandments, God promises to help them win the land of Canaan. When Moses returns from the mountain after forty days and forty nights, he discovers that the Israelites have begun worshipping a golden calf made by Aaron in his absence. God is displeased, and Moses orders the Israelites to build a tabernacle to God. This tabernacle would house the Ark of the Covenant.

All dates connected with Exodus and the Israelites' flight from Egypt are conjectural and thus often inconsistent. Scholars have offered various theories about the date of Moses's birth, the date of the flight, the dates of the plagues that occurred in Egypt, who was the pharaoh at the time of Egyptian slavery, and when the book of Exodus was written. Since no pharaoh is identified in the book, conclusions about who was pharaoh differ depending on whether a particular historian accepts an earlier or a later date for the events of Exodus. The Bible, at 1 Kings 6:1, indicates that the date when Solomon built his Temple to God, in the fourth year of his reign—identified as 966 BCE—was 480 years after the Exodus. This situates the Exodus around 1446 BCE, perhaps during Amenhotep II's reign. Some Egyptologists consider the 480-year span of 1 Kings 6:1 to have been only 284 years. They then date the Exodus to around 1250 BCE, the middle of Rameses II's reign.

About the Author

Moses, sometimes called Moshe, is traditionally viewed as the author of the book of Exodus, although it is possible that Moses appropriated parts of already existing written documents or that Exodus was written by another author altogether. Some scholars argue that Exodus was written many years after the events outlined in the book and after the time of Moses, pointing to the fact that the book was written in a relatively late form of the Hebrew language, a form that Moses would not have used. Yet another argument suggests that inconsistencies in the book are evidence that Exodus was written by different authors using different sources.

Various dates are given for Moses's life; some scholars contend that he was born in about 1526 BCE, while others claim that he lived in the thirteenth and early part of the twelfth century BCE. Moses is considered a major prophet and lawgiver not only by Judaism and Christianity but also by Islam, Rastafari, Baha'i, and numerous

auff dy erde. Vnd do pharaon sah das der regen hett auffgehört vnd der hagel vñ dy thunner er meret dye sunde. vnnd seyn hertz war Be‖

got sendet die hewschrecken vber alles egipten land. vnd wie vinster das ward. das nymant de andern gesehen kund.

[Illuminated initial U] ND der herr sprach zu moyses. Gee ein zu pharaō. Wann ich haß erherttet seyn hertz vnnd seyner knecht. das ich thun dyse meyne zeychen in im

im. Bis wie lanng erleyden wir dyse schande. Laß die leut das sy opffern irē herren got. Sihstu den nicht das egipt verdirbet. Vnd sy rüfften wider dem moyses vnnd aaron zu pharaon

The plague of locusts, from the Nuremburg Bible

(Exodus: The plague of locusts, from the 'Nuremberg Bible [Biblia Sacra Germanaica]' [coloured woodcut], German School, [15th century] / Private Collection / The Stapleton Collection / The Bridgeman Art Library International)

other faiths. He was born during a period when the Israelites were growing in number; worried that the Israelites might lend aid to Egypt's enemies, the pharaoh had ordered that all Hebrew male babies be drowned in the Nile River. According to legend, Moses's Hebrew mother, Jochebed, saved her baby by hiding him in a basket and setting it afloat on the Nile. The child was discovered and raised as a member of the royal family. As an adult, he killed a slave master and fled to Midian, a region on the eastern shore of the Gulf of Aqaba and the northern Red Sea in Arabia. There he tended the flocks of the priest Jethro on Mount Horeb, but after the Egyptian plagues he led the Israelites out of bondage across the Red Sea to Mount Sinai, where he received the Ten Commandments. According to the Old Testament, he lived to the age of 120, but his biggest disappointment in life was that he died before reaching Israel.

Explanation and Analysis of the Document

The reproduced excerpt consists of chapters 1–6 of Exodus. These chapters are extremely important to both Jews and Christians, for they document a central belief in Judaism: God's covenant with the Jews.

♦ Chapter 1

Verses 1–10: The first five verses name and enumerate the Jewish people who came into Egypt. These verses also provide a link with the closing scenes of the previous book of the Bible, Genesis, in which Joseph and other descendants of the patriarch Jacob are established in Egypt. The passage mentions that the Jewish people multiplied in Egypt and soon became a cause of concern for the new pharaoh, who said that the Israelites were "more and mightier than we." This section lays the groundwork for the rift that was

"And the children of Israel were fruitful, and increased abundantly, and multiplied, and waxed exceeding mighty; and the land was filled with them. Now there arose up a new king over Egypt, which knew not Joseph. And he said unto his people, Behold, the people of the children of Israel are more and mightier than we."

"And the daughter of Pharaoh came down to wash herself at the river; and her maidens walked along by the river's side; and when she saw the ark among the flags, she sent her maid to fetch it. And when she had opened it, she saw the child: and, behold, the babe wept. And she had compassion on him, and said, 'This is one of the Hebrews' children.'"

"And it came to pass in those days, when Moses was grown, that he went out unto his brethren, and looked on their burdens: and he spied an Egyptian smiting a Hebrew, one of his brethren. And he looked this way and that way, and when he saw that there was no man, he slew the Egyptian, and hid him in the sand."

"And it came to pass in process of time, that the king of Egypt died: and the children of Israel sighed by reason of the bondage, and they cried, and their cry came up unto God by reason of the bondage. And God heard their groaning, and God remembered his covenant with Abraham, with Isaac, and with Jacob. And God looked upon the children of Israel, and God had respect unto them."

"And the LORD said, I have surely seen the affliction of my people which are in Egypt, and have heard their cry by reason of their taskmasters; for I know their sorrows; And I am come down to deliver them out of the hand of the Egyptians, and to bring them up out of that land unto a good land and a large, unto a land flowing with milk and honey."

"And Moses and Aaron went and gathered together all the elders of the children of Israel: And Aaron spake all the words which the LORD had spoken unto Moses, and did the signs in the sight of the people. And the people believed: and when they heard that the LORD had visited the children of Israel, and that he had looked upon their affliction, then they bowed their heads and worshipped."

about to occur between the Egyptians, led by the pharaoh, and the Israelites, led by Moses.

Verses 11–22: These verses explain the rigorous life the Israelites led in Egypt as slaves, building cities and statues for the pharaoh. The pharaoh, however, is still concerned about the growing number of Jews, so he issues a decree that every newborn Jewish boy be put to death. The Hebrew midwives and the mothers do not want to comply, for in addition to the personal grief such murders would cause, killing the future generation of Israelites would go against everything they believed in as a religious community and they feared the wrath of God. This chapter begins to highlight the Jewish connection with God and the Egyptians' lack of connection with him. In much the same way as any epic does, Exodus narrates a conflict between good and evil—in this case, between God's chosen people and the polytheistic Egyptians, who do not recognize the one God of the Israelites.

♦ **Chapter 2**

Verses 1–10: The opening verses of chapter 2 narrate the birth of Moses, whose mother tries to evade the decree of the pharaoh and save her son's life by hiding him in an "ark of bulrushes" (similar to a wicker basket). She then places the ark on the bank of the Nile River and lets it float away. The pharaoh's daughter and her maidens discover the basket and bring in a Hebrew nurse to take care of the infant. The daughter names the boy Moses, a name that means "drawn from the waters."

Verses 11–25: By this point in Exodus, Moses has grown to adulthood. The pharaoh hears word that Moses has slain an Egyptian and buried him in the sand. In fear for his life, Moses leaves Egypt and flees to Midian, where he meets a priest named Reuel who, with his daughters, tends a flock of sheep. Reuel gives one of his seven daughters, Zipporah, to Moses as a bride. She and Moses produce a son name Gershom. The pharaoh dies, and the chapter ends with God acknowledging the hardship of the Jewish people, underlining the special relationship God has with "the children of Israel." God remembers his special bond with previous Jewish patriarchs such as Abraham, Isaac, and Jacob. It is now time for Moses to take over the role of Jewish patriarch.

♦ **Chapter 3**

Verses 1–10: God appears to Moses in the form of a bush that burns without ever being consumed by the flames. God reminds a fearful Moses of his relationship with Abraham, Isaac, and Jacob; the bond between God and the Israelites is hundreds of years old. God then tells Moses of his plans to free the Israelites from the bondage of Egypt and bring them to Canaan, the land of "milk and honey." God promised the land of Canaan to Abraham, and he is now ready to fulfill that promise, having chosen Moses to be the one who will deliver the Israelites out of slavery. God shows love and compassion for the Hebrew people in these verses, as though he regards their suffering in Egypt as a form of preparation for the departure to the Promised Land.

Verses 11–22: God, called Yahweh in Genesis, tells Moses another of his many names by saying "I am that I am," a name that suggests that God simply is and that there was never a time when he did not exist and nor will there be a time when he ceases to exist. The name "I Am" conveys that God is completely independent and relies on nothing for life or existence. With the name "I Am," God is "the becoming one"—that is, he becomes whatever he needs to become or wishes to become. Moses seems hesitant to fulfill his role as savior of the Jewish people, but God has a plan laid out for him. Some scholars argue that the many Israelites had no desire to go to the Promised Land but rather wanted a better life in Egypt. God tells Moses that he will strike Egypt with whatever "wonders" are needed to help the Israelites flee the land. These miraculous "wonders" are the plagues and calamities that afflicted Egypt.

♦ **Chapter 4**

Verses 1–10: God performs a miracle by turning Moses's rod into a snake and then back into a rod again. These supernatural signs confirm that Moses was sent by God and that harm will be done to the Egyptians if they resist the departure of the Israelites. The rod, or staff, will also help Moses perform miracles, and God will speak and act through Moses. Thus begins the legation of Moses, as he becomes God's diplomat on earth with a mission to deliver God's people to the Promised Land. The miracles that God performs enable Moses to gain confidence in his mission and work.

Verses 11–20: God states that he will teach Moses what to say to the pharaoh and to the Israelites. Once the miracles are performed and God proclaims the staff powerful and ready to perform miracles, Moses prepares to depart from Midian and head to Egypt to lead the Israelites. A key moral element in these verses is that those who decline the call of God may forfeit the blessing they desire. Moses is apprehensive at first to go speak to the pharaoh, so God loses his patience and says he will have Aaron (Moses's brother) serve as Moses's spokesman.

Verses 21–31: Moses does not yet know what type of miracles he is going to perform. He does know that he will have to go to the pharaoh and perform wonders before him. God talks about the final stage of the confrontation Moses will have with the pharaoh. The overall message in these verses is that God has become aware of Israel's plight. The chapter concludes with the submission of the Israelites to God's commands: "And the people believed: and when they heard that the LORD had visited the children of Israel, and that he had looked upon their affliction, then they bowed their heads and worshipped."

♦ **Chapter 5**

Verses 1–14: Controversy arises between God and the pharaoh, who is portrayed as an arrogant heathen who dares to go against the wishes of God, the creator of the universe. The pharaoh dismisses Moses's intentions, believing that Moses is in exile in a foreign land and therefore is insignificant. By refusing to let the Israelites go, the pharaoh seals his destruction. This is the first time the phrases

"God of Israel" or the "God of the Hebrews" is used in the scriptures. This is significant because God is not afraid to be called the God of the suppressed and enslaved. The pharaoh treats Moses and the Jewish elders not as statesmen but as intruders and disturbers of the peace. The pharaoh sees the Jews as lazy troublemakers, and he puts out the order that they be treated more harshly and be made to work even more unremittingly.

Verses 15–23: Moses and Aaron see that their efforts to persuade the pharoah have failed. There are new persecutions against the Jews, and their hardships increase. Moses rightfully feels that no steps have been taken to deliver the Jews from their present state and is surprised that their burdens have multiplied. In a prefiguration of Christ's words on the Cross in the New Testament, Moses asks, "Lord, wherefore hast thou *so* evil entreated this people? why *is* it *that* thou hast sent me?" Moses, the lawgiver and patriarch, acts in a very human fashion by questioning God and wondering why he has been burdened with the task of carrying out God's will.

♦ **Chapter 6**

Verses 1–10: God tells Moses that one of his names is "Jehovah." Some scholars argue that the name Jehovah (or Yahweh) was not known to the older Jewish patriarchs and that the name was first revealed to Moses at the site of the burning bush. These scholars propose that when God says "I am that I am," he uses a phrase that is of the same origin as "Jehovah." Others maintain that the name Jehovah was known to the Jewish patriarchs before Moses but that God's omnipotence and omnipresence were not, because God had not fulfilled his promise to them. Still, it is probable that the name was not new to Moses or to the Israelites. God begins to make good on his promise by stating that the Israelites will be brought out "from under the burdens of the Egyptians." God assures them that he will be their God and bring them to the lands promised to Abraham, Isaac, and Jacob. His covenant with the Jews is reaffirmed and reestablished.

Verses 11–20: God again gives Moses a charge in this passage: "Go in, speak unto Pharaoh king of Egypt, that he let the children of Israel go out of his land." This section also

Questions for Further Study

1. On what basis could it be said that Exodus is the most important book in the Hebrew Bible? In what ways did the book lay the foundations for the Judeo-Christian tradition in the West?

2. In what ways might the Israelites' flight from Egypt have parallels centuries later when Muhammad and his Islamic followers fled the city of Mecca for Medina? (For reference, see the discussions surrounding *The Meccan Illuminations* and Sahih al-Bukhari.) How do the events, studied side by side, illustrate the theme of a chosen people setting itself apart?

3. The book of Exodus is scriptural, but it is also historical. How accurate as a historical narrative do you think Exodus is? How important is it to determine the historical accuracy of a narrative such as that contained in Exodus? Would its underlying truth be called into question if it could be proved that the book contains historical inaccuracies?

4. Many of the miracles recounted in Exodus, such as the parting of the Red Sea, are at least vaguely familiar to people who grew up in countries with a Judeo-Christian tradition. Some scholars have attempted to demonstrate a scientific basis for these miracles—for example, that Moses's parting of the Red Sea was really a natural event that took place in a marshy area that was intermittently dried out, then covered with water. What is your response to this type of effort on the part of scientists and others? Do miracles really occur? Why would the ancient Israelites have interpreted such an event as a miracle from God?

5. What is your position on the concept of separation of church and state, given that the Old Testament in general and the book of Exodus in particular have provided numerous symbols, concepts, and names that seem woven into American thought? In some municipalities, for example, the Ten Commandments are displayed; a famous hospital in New York City is called Mount Sinai, as are towns in at least five states; place names throughout the United States have Old Testament origins (Noah, the name of a town in four states; Moses, the name of a town in two states; Mount Zion, the name of a town in some twenty-one states); and so on. Do you think these biblical connections create an impermissible connection between church and state?

lists the names of purported chiefs of the families Moses brought out of Egypt. Moses speaks to God like someone who is timid and discouraged and lacks the confidence needed to carry out his task. Moses is frustrated by the Israelites and, more than likely, the pharaoh. In these verses, the descendants of Jacob's three sons are listed, particularly those of Levi, Jacob's third son; Jacob was the grandson of the patriarch Abraham, and the stories of Jacob are told in Genesis.

Verses 21–30: More names of Israelite families are listed within this passage of Exodus, adding to the foundation for this book's alternate title, the Book of Names. The Israelite tribes are numerous at this point in history and can be said to constitute their own armies; God commands that the exodus of the Hebrew people be organized along these tribal lines: "Bring out the children of Israel from the land of Egypt according to their armies." Some scholars suggest that Moses could have never carried out the task of leading these tribes (armies) out of Egypt without divine guidance.

Audience

The primary audience for the book of Exodus was the Israelites. As part of the first five books of the Old Testament, the book is a record of the history of the Israelites, their flight from servitude, and their special relationship with God. In subsequent years, Exodus, as part of the Torah, established the foundations of Judaism—its customs and traditions, its laws, its conception of God and the nature of God, and the relationship between God and the Jewish people. After the advent of Christianity, Exodus, along with the other canonical books of the Old Testament, became firmly embedded in the Judeo-Christian tradition. Many of the incidents recorded in the Old Testament, including Exodus, were seen to prefigure the coming of Jesus Christ as the Messiah. God's law, particularly as expressed in the Ten Commandments, continues to play an important role in the Judeo-Christian tradition. Additionally, those who read the Bible as a work of literature, irrespective of any personal religious beliefs, regard the story of Moses and the Israelites as an important example of the type of heroic literature produced by early civilizations. In this respect, they read Exodus alongside such works as the *Epic of Gilgamesh* and the works of Homer to gain insight into the minds of people who lived in this part of the world in past millennia. The book provides one piece of the historical, geographical, and archeological record of the ancient world.

Impact

The Book of Exodus holds significant spiritual value, for it delves into complex problems of religion and society, par-

ticularly the relationship between God and a community of people—in this case, the Israelites. It could be argued that without the book of Exodus there would be no Jewish people and no Judaism.

Judaism was the world's first great monotheistic religion, and the book of Exodus establishes the concept of a single God. The God of the Old Testament is male, and he acts on his own. He does not have to consult with, or quarrel with, other gods. He is omniscient, all-powerful, and the creator of the universe. Evil, or calamities in the natural world, are not the result of petty quarrels among multiple gods. The one God is the source of all that happens in the world. Further, God is not always rational, and he acts in mysterious ways. He feels no need to explain his purposes to humans. If there is a grand plan in the world, God is under no obligation to share that plan. Accordingly, any attempt by humans to explain God, reason with him, or question his purposes is futile. God is above all human standards.

In the modern world, people who belong to a monotheistic religion such as Christianity, Judaism, or Islam would find this conception of God to be a matter of course. It takes considerable imagination to cast one's mind back to a time three thousand or more years ago when people explained natural phenomena—illness, death, earthquakes, storms, crop failures—as a product of the activities of multiple gods—gods who in many ways were like humans, subject to jealousy, vindictiveness, desire, anger, pettiness, and other human failings. For the books of the Old Testament, including Exodus, to expound on the nature of a single, all-powerful God would have been perhaps shocking, or at least perplexing, for the concept of monotheism would have been foreign to every culture in that region of the world.

Also of significance in the Judeo-Christian tradition is one key difference between Exodus and such works as the *Epic of Gilgamesh* and Homer's *Iliad* and *Odyssey*. The latter works are essentially about returning home. Gilgamesh, for example, returns to his home, the city of Uruk, a better king for the experiences he has had. In Exodus, though, there is no return home. The people of Israel have to find a new home for themselves, and this notion of a Promised Land somewhere over the horizon is one that has played an important role in Western thought. The New World, for example, was viewed by Europeans of the early modern period as a new Eden, where people could find a Promised Land of "milk and honey" and live out their lives under the strictures of their covenant with God—and escape the cruelty of their masters in the Old World. Among the Jewish people, the search for a home continued long after the book of Exodus was written, and that search to find and preserve a home remains crucial to Jewish identity in the twenty-first century.

Further Reading

■ Books

Berlin, Adele, and Marc Zui Brettler, eds. *The Jewish Study Bible: Featuring the Jewish Publication Society Tanakh Translation.*Oxford, U.K.: Oxford University Press, 2004.

Childs, Brevard S. *The Book of Exodus: A Critical, Theological Commentary*. Louisville, Ky.: Westminster Press, 1974.

Dozeman, Thomas B., ed. *Methods for Exodus*. Cambridge, U.K.: Cambridge University Press, 2010.

Propp, William H. C. *Exodus 1–18*. New Haven, Conn.: Yale University Press, 1999.

Telushkin, Joseph. *Jewish Literacy*. New York: William Morrow, 1991.

■ Journals

Eberstadt, Fernanda. "The Uses of Exodus." *Commentary* 83, no. 6 (June 1987): 25.

■ Web Sites

Malick, David. "An Introduction to the Book of Exodus." Bible. org Web site.
   http://bible.org/article/introduction-book-exodus

Roberts, J. J. M. "Book of Exodus." BELIEVE Religious Information Source Web site.
   http://mb-soft.com/believe/txs/exodus.htm

—David Treviño

BIBLE: EXODUS

Chapter 1

1 Now these *are* the names of the children of Israel, which came into Egypt; every man and his household came with Jacob. 2 Reuben, Simeon, Levi, and Judah, 3 Issachar, Zebulun, and Benjamin, 4 Dan, and Naphtali, Gad, and Asher. 5 And all the souls that came out of the loins of Jacob were seventy souls: for Joseph was in Egypt *already.* 6 And Joseph died, and all his brethren, and all that generation.

7 And the children of Israel were fruitful, and increased abundantly, and multiplied, and waxed exceeding mighty; and the land was filled with them. 8 Now there arose up a new king over Egypt, which knew not Joseph. 9 And he said unto his people, Behold, the people of the children of Israel *are* more and mightier than we: 10 Come on, let us deal wisely with them; lest they multiply, and it come to pass, that, when there falleth out any war, they join also unto our enemies, and fight against us, and *so* get them up out of the land. 11 Therefore they did set over them taskmasters to afflict them with their burdens. And they built for Pharaoh treasure cities, Pithom and Raamses. 12 But the more they afflicted them, the more they multiplied and grew. And they were grieved because of the children of Israel. 13 And the Egyptians made the children of Israel to serve with rigour: 14 And they made their lives bitter with hard bondage, in morter, and in brick, and in all manner of service in the field: all their service, wherein they made them serve, *was* with rigour.

15 And the king of Egypt spake to the Hebrew midwives, of which the name of the one *was* Shiphrah, and the name of the other Puah: 16 And he said, When ye do the office of a midwife to the Hebrew women, and see *them* upon the stools; if it *be* a son, then ye shall kill him: but if it *be* a daughter, then she shall live. 17 But the midwives feared God, and did not as the king of Egypt commanded them, but saved the men children alive. 18 And the king of Egypt called for the midwives, and said unto them, Why have ye done this thing, and have saved the men children alive? 19 And the midwives said unto Pharaoh, Because the Hebrew women *are* not as the Egyptian women; for they *are* lively, and are delivered ere the midwives come in unto them. 20 Therefore God dealt well with the midwives: and the people multiplied, and waxed very mighty. 21 And it came to pass, because the midwives feared God, that he made them houses. 22 And Pharaoh charged all his people, saying, Every son that is born ye shall cast into the river, and every daughter ye shall save alive.

Chapter 2

1 And there went a man of the house of Levi, and took *to wife* a daughter of Levi. 2 And the woman conceived, and bare a son: and when she saw him that he *was a* goodly *child*, she hid him three months. 3 And when she could not longer hide him, she took for him an ark of bulrushes, and daubed it with slime and with pitch, and put the child therein; and she laid *it* in the flags by the river's brink. 4 And his sister stood afar off, to wit what would be done to him.

5 And the daughter of Pharaoh came down to wash *herself* at the river; and her maidens walked along by the river's side; and when she saw the ark among the flags, she sent her maid to fetch it. 6 And when she had opened *it,* she saw the child: and, behold, the babe wept. And she had compassion on him, and said, This *is one* of the Hebrews' children. 7 Then said his sister to Pharaoh's daughter, Shall I go and call to thee a nurse of the Hebrew women, that she may nurse the child for thee? 8 And Pharaoh's daughter said to her, Go. And the maid went and called the child's mother. 9 And Pharaoh's daughter said unto her, Take this child away, and nurse it for me, and I will give *thee* thy wages. And the woman took the child, and nursed it. 10 And the child grew, and she brought him unto Pharaoh's daughter, and he became her son. And she called his name Moses: and she said, Because I drew him out of the water.

11 And it came to pass in those days, when Moses was grown, that he went out unto his brethren, and looked on their burdens: and he spied an Egyptian smiting an Hebrew, one of his brethren. 12 And he looked this way and that way, and when

he saw that *there was* no man, he slew the Egyptian, and hid him in the sand. 13 And when he went out the second day, behold, two men of the Hebrews strove together: and he said to him that did the wrong, Wherefore smitest thou thy fellow? 14 And he said, Who made thee a prince and a judge over us? intendest thou to kill me, as thou killedst the Egyptian? And Moses feared, and said, Surely this thing is known. 15 Now when Pharaoh heard this thing, he sought to slay Moses. But Moses fled from the face of Pharaoh, and dwelt in the land of Midian: and he sat down by a well. 16 Now the priest of Midian had seven daughters: and they came and drew *water,* and filled the troughs to water their father's flock. 17 And the shepherds came and drove them away: but Moses stood up and helped them, and watered their flock. 18 And when they came to Reuel their father, he said, How *is it that* ye are come so soon to day? 19 And they said, An Egyptian delivered us out of the hand of the shepherds, and also drew *water* enough for us, and watered the flock. 20 And he said unto his daughters, And where *is* he? why *is* it *that* ye have left the man? call him, that he may eat bread. 21 And Moses was content to dwell with the man: and he gave Moses Zipporah his daughter. 22 And she bare *him* a son, and he called his name Gershom: for he said, I have been a stranger in a strange land.

23 And it came to pass in process of time, that the king of Egypt died: and the children of Israel sighed by reason of the bondage, and they cried, and their cry came up unto God by reason of the bondage. 24 And God heard their groaning, and God remembered his covenant with Abraham, with Isaac, and with Jacob. 25 And God looked upon the children of Israel, and God had respect unto *them.*

Chapter 3

1 Now Moses kept the flock of Jethro his father in law, the priest of Midian: and he led the flock to the backside of the desert, and came to the mountain of God, *even* to Horeb. 2 And the angel of the LORD appeared unto him in a flame of fire out of the midst of a bush: and he looked, and, behold, the bush burned with fire, and the bush *was* not consumed. 3 And Moses said, I will now turn aside, and see this great sight, why the bush is not burnt. 4 And when the LORD saw that he

turned aside to see, God called unto him out of the midst of the bush, and said, Moses, Moses. And he said, Here *am* I. 5 And he said, Draw not nigh hither: put off thy shoes from off thy feet, for the place whereon thou standest is holy ground. 6 Moreover he said, I *am* the God of thy father, the God of Abraham, the God of Isaac, and the God of Jacob. And Moses hid his face; for he was afraid to look upon God.

7 And the LORD said, I have surely seen the affliction of my people which *are* in Egypt, and have heard their cry by reason of their taskmasters; for I know their sorrows; 8 And I am come down to deliver them out of the hand of the Egyptians, and to bring them up out of that land unto a good land and a large, unto a land flowing with milk and honey; unto the place of the Canaanites, and the Hittites, and the Amorites, and the Perizzites, and the Hivites, and the Jebusites. 9 Now therefore, behold, the cry of the children of Israel is come unto me: and I have also seen the oppression wherewith the Egyptians oppress them. 10 Come now therefore, and I will send thee unto Pharaoh, that thou mayest bring forth my people the children of Israel out of Egypt.

11 And Moses said unto God, Who *am* I, that I should go unto Pharaoh, and that I should bring forth the children of Israel out of Egypt? 12 And he said, Certainly I will be with thee; and this *shall be* a token unto thee, that I have sent thee: When thou hast brought forth the people out of Egypt, ye shall serve God upon this mountain. 13 And Moses said unto God, Behold, *when* I come unto the children of Israel, and shall say unto them, The God of your fathers hath sent me unto you; and they shall say to me, What is his name? what shall I say unto them? 14 And God said unto Moses, I AM THAT I AM: and he said, Thus shalt thou say unto the children of Israel, I AM hath sent me unto you. 15 And God said moreover unto Moses, Thus shalt thou say unto the children of Israel, The LORD God of your fathers, the God of Abraham, the God of Isaac, and the God of Jacob, hath sent me unto you: this *is* my name for ever, and this *is* my memorial unto all generations. 16 Go, and gather the elders of Israel together, and say unto them, The LORD God of your fathers, the God of Abraham, of Isaac, and of Jacob, appeared unto me, saying, I have surely visited you, and *seen* that which is done to you in Egypt: 17 And I have said, I will bring you up out of the affliction of Egypt unto the land of the Canaanites, and the

Hittites, and the Amorites, and the Perizzites, and the Hivites, and the Jebusites, unto a land flowing with milk and honey. 18 And they shall hearken to thy voice: and thou shalt come, thou and the elders of Israel, unto the king of Egypt, and ye shall say unto him, The LORD God of the Hebrews hath met with us: and now let us go, we beseech thee, three days' journey into the wilderness, that we may sacrifice to the LORD our God.

19 And I am sure that the king of Egypt will not let you go, no, not by a mighty hand. 20 And I will stretch out my hand, and smite Egypt with all my wonders which I will do in the midst thereof: and after that he will let you go. 21 And I will give this people favour in the sight of the Egyptians: and it shall come to pass, that, when ye go, ye shall not go empty: 22 But every woman shall borrow of her neighbour, and of her that sojourneth in her house, jewels of silver, and jewels of gold, and raiment: and ye shall put *them* upon your sons, and upon your daughters; and ye shall spoil the Egyptians.

Chapter 4

1 And Moses answered and said, But, behold, they will not believe me, nor hearken unto my voice: for they will say, The LORD hath not appeared unto thee. 2 And the LORD said unto him, What *is* that in thine hand? And he said, A rod. 3 And he said, Cast it on the ground. And he cast it on the ground, and it became a serpent; and Moses fled from before it. 4 And the LORD said unto Moses, Put forth thine hand, and take it by the tail. And he put forth his hand, and caught it, and it became a rod in his hand: 5 That they may believe that the LORD God of their fathers, the God of Abraham, the God of Isaac, and the God of Jacob, hath appeared unto thee.

6 And the LORD said furthermore unto him, Put now thine hand into thy bosom. And he put his hand into his bosom: and when he took it out, behold, his hand *was* leprous as snow. 7 And he said, Put thine hand into thy bosom again. And he put his hand into his bosom again; and plucked it out of his bosom, and, behold, it was turned again as his *other* flesh. 8 And it shall come to pass, if they will not believe thee, neither hearken to the voice of the first sign, that they will believe the voice of the latter sign. 9 And it shall come to pass, if they will not believe also these two signs, neither hearken unto thy voice, that thou shalt take of the water of the river, and pour *it* upon the dry *land:* and the water which thou takest out of the river shall become blood upon the dry *land.*

10 And Moses said unto the LORD, O my Lord, I *am* not eloquent, neither heretofore, nor since thou hast spoken unto thy servant: but I *am* slow of speech, and of a slow tongue. 11 And the LORD said unto him, Who hath made man's mouth? or who maketh the dumb, or deaf, or the seeing, or the blind? have not I the LORD? 12 Now therefore go, and I will be with thy mouth, and teach thee what thou shalt say. 13 And he said, O my Lord, send, I pray thee, by the hand *of him whom* thou wilt send. 14 And the anger of the LORD was kindled against Moses, and he said, *Is* not Aaron the Levite thy brother? I know that he can speak well. And also, behold, he cometh forth to meet thee: and when he seeth thee, he will be glad in his heart. 15 And thou shalt speak unto him, and put words in his mouth: and I will be with thy mouth, and with his mouth, and will teach you what ye shall do. 16 And he shall be thy spokesman unto the people: and he shall be, *even* he shall be to thee instead of a mouth, and thou shalt be to him instead of God. 17 And thou shalt take this rod in thine hand, wherewith thou shalt do signs.

18 And Moses went and returned to Jethro his father in law, and said unto him, Let me go, I pray thee, and return unto my brethren which *are* in Egypt, and see whether they be yet alive. And Jethro said to Moses, Go in peace. 19 And the LORD said unto Moses in Midian, Go, return into Egypt: for all the men are dead which sought thy life. 20 And Moses took his wife and his sons, and set them upon an ass, and he returned to the land of Egypt: and Moses took the rod of God in his hand. 21 And the LORD said unto Moses, When thou goest to return into Egypt, see that thou do all those wonders before Pharaoh, which I have put in thine hand: but I will harden his heart, that he shall not let the people go. 22 And thou shalt say unto Pharaoh, Thus saith the LORD, Israel *is* my son, *even* my firstborn: 23 And I say unto thee, Let my son go, that he may serve me: and if thou refuse to let him go, behold, I will slay thy son, *even* thy firstborn.

24 And it came to pass by the way in the inn, that the LORD met him, and sought to kill him. 25 Then Zipporah took a sharp stone, and cut off the foreskin of her son, and cast *it* at his feet, and said, Surely a bloody husband *art* thou to me. 26 So he let him go: then she said, A bloody husband *thou art,* because of the circumcision.

27 And the LORD said to Aaron, Go into the wilderness to meet Moses. And he went, and met him in the mount of God, and kissed him. 28 And Moses told Aaron all the words of the LORD who had sent him, and all the signs which he had commanded him.

29 And Moses and Aaron went and gathered together all the elders of the children of Israel: 30 And Aaron spake all the words which the LORD had spoken unto Moses, and did the signs in the sight of the people. 31 And the people believed: and when they heard that the LORD had visited the children of Israel, and that he had looked upon their affliction, then they bowed their heads and worshipped.

Chapter 5

1 And afterward Moses and Aaron went in, and told Pharaoh, Thus saith the LORD God of Israel, Let my people go, that they may hold a feast unto me in the wilderness. 2 And Pharaoh said, Who *is* the LORD, that I should obey his voice to let Israel go? I know not the LORD, neither will I let Israel go. 3 And they said, The God of the Hebrews hath met with us: let us go, we pray thee, three days' journey into the desert, and sacrifice unto the LORD our God; lest he fall upon us with pestilence, or with the sword. 4 And the king of Egypt said unto them, Wherefore do ye, Moses and Aaron, let the people from their works? get you unto your burdens. 5 And Pharaoh said, Behold, the people of the land now *are* many, and ye make them rest from their burdens. 6 And Pha-

raoh commanded the same day the taskmasters of the people, and their officers, saying, 7 Ye shall no more give the people straw to make brick, as heretofore: let them go and gather straw for themselves. 8 And the tale of the bricks, which they did make heretofore, ye shall lay upon them; ye shall not diminish *ought* thereof: for they *be* idle; therefore they cry, saying, Let us go *and* sacrifice to our God. 9 Let there more work be laid upon the men, that they may labour therein; and let them not regard vain words.

10 And the taskmasters of the people went out, and their officers, and they spake to the people, saying, Thus saith Pharaoh, I will not give you straw. 11 Go ye, get you straw where ye can find it: yet not ought of your work shall be diminished. 12 So the people were scattered abroad throughout all the land of Egypt to gather stubble instead of straw. 13 And the taskmasters hasted *them,* saying, Fulfil your works, *your* daily tasks, as when there was straw. 14 And the officers of the children of Israel, which Pharaoh's taskmasters had set over them, were beaten, *and* demanded, Wherefore have ye not fulfilled your task in making brick both yesterday and to day, as heretofore?

15 Then the officers of the children of Israel came and cried unto Pharaoh, saying, Wherefore dealest thou thus with thy servants? 16 There is no straw given unto thy servants, and they say to us, Make brick: and, behold, thy servants *are* beaten; but the fault *is* in thine own people. 17 But he said, Ye *are* idle, *ye are* idle: therefore ye say, Let us go *and* do sacrifice to the LORD. 18 Go therefore now, *and* work; for there shall no straw be given you, yet shall ye deliver the tale of bricks. 19 And

Abraham . . . Isaac . . . Jacob	the Old Testament patriarchs who preceded Moses
Canaan	a region roughly encompassing modern-day Israel and surrounding territories
Canaanites, Hittites, Amorites, Perizzites, Hivites, Jebusites	a listing of various pre-Israelite peoples
Midian	a place possibly in northwestern Arabia on the east shore of the Gulf of Aqaba and the northern Red Sea
priest of Midian	Jethro, Moses's father-in-law
Reuben, Simeon, Levi . . .	the Hebrew people who came into Egypt

the officers of the children of Israel did see *that* they *were* in evil *case*, after it was said, Ye shall not minish *ought* from your bricks of your daily task.

20 And they met Moses and Aaron, who stood in the way, as they came forth from Pharaoh: 21 And they said unto them, The LORD look upon you, and judge; because ye have made our savour to be abhorred in the eyes of Pharaoh, and in the eyes of his servants, to put a sword in their hand to slay us. 22 And Moses returned unto the LORD, and said, Lord, wherefore hast thou *so* evil entreated this people? why *is* it *that* thou hast sent me? 23 For since I came to Pharaoh to speak in thy name, he hath done evil to this people; neither hast thou delivered thy people at all.

Chapter 6

1 Then the LORD said unto Moses, Now shalt thou see what I will do to Pharaoh: for with a strong hand shall he let them go, and with a strong hand shall he drive them out of his land. 2 And God spake unto Moses, and said unto him, I *am* the LORD: 3 And I appeared unto Abraham, unto Isaac, and unto Jacob, by *the name of* God Almighty, but by my name JEHOVAH was I not known to them. 4 And I have also established my covenant with them, to give them the land of Canaan, the land of their pilgrimage, wherein they were strangers. 5 And I have also heard the groaning of the children of Israel, whom the Egyptians keep in bondage; and I have remembered my covenant. 6 Wherefore say unto the children of Israel, I *am* the LORD, and I will bring you out from under the burdens of the Egyptians, and I will rid you out of their bondage, and I will redeem you with a stretched out arm, and with great judgments: 7 And I will take you to me for a people, and I will be to you a God: and ye shall know that I *am* the LORD your God, which bringeth you out from under the burdens of the Egyptians. 8 And I will bring you in unto the land, concerning the which I did swear to give it to Abraham, to Isaac, and to Jacob; and I will give it you for an heritage: I *am* the LORD.

9 And Moses spake so unto the children of Israel: but they hearkened not unto Moses for anguish of spirit, and for cruel bondage. 10 And the LORD spake unto Moses, saying, 11 Go in, speak unto Pharaoh king of Egypt, that he let the children of Israel go out of his land. 12 And Moses spake be-

fore the LORD, saying, Behold, the children of Israel have not hearkened unto me; how then shall Pharaoh hear me, who *am* of uncircumcised lips? 13 And the LORD spake unto Moses and unto Aaron, and gave them a charge unto the children of Israel, and unto Pharaoh king of Egypt, to bring the children of Israel out of the land of Egypt.

14 These *be* the heads of their fathers' houses: The sons of Reuben the firstborn of Israel; Hanoch, and Pallu, Hezron, and Carmi: these *be* the families of Reuben. 15 And the sons of Simeon; Jemuel, and Jamin, and Ohad, and Jachin, and Zohar, and Shaul the son of a Canaanitish woman: these *are* the families of Simeon.

16 And these *are* the names of the sons of Levi according to their generations; Gershon, and Kohath, and Merari: and the years of the life of Levi *were* an hundred thirty and seven years. 17 The sons of Gershon; Libni, and Shimi, according to their families. 18 And the sons of Kohath; Amram, and Izhar, and Hebron, and Uzziel: and the years of the life of Kohath *were* an hundred thirty and three years. 19 And the sons of Merari; Mahali and Mushi: these *are* the families of Levi according to their generations. 20 And Amram took him Jochebed his father's sister to wife; and she bare him Aaron and Moses: and the years of the life of Amram *were* an hundred and thirty and seven years.

21 And the sons of Izhar; Korah, and Nepheg, and Zichri. 22 And the sons of Uzziel; Mishael, and Elzaphan, and Zithri. 23 And Aaron took him Elisheba, daughter of Amminadab, sister of Naashon, to wife; and she bare him Nadab, and Abihu, Eleazar, and Ithamar. 24 And the sons of Korah; Assir, and Elkanah, and Abiasaph: these *are* the families of the Korhites. 25 And Eleazar Aaron's son took him *one* of the daughters of Putiel to wife; and she bare him Phinehas: these *are* the heads of the fathers of the Levites according to their families. 26 These *are* that Aaron and Moses, to whom the LORD said, Bring out the children of Israel from the land of Egypt according to their armies. 27 These *are* they which spake to Pharaoh king of Egypt, to bring out the children of Israel from Egypt: these *are* that Moses and Aaron.

28 And it came to pass on the day *when* the LORD spake unto Moses in the land of Egypt, 29 That the LORD spake unto Moses, saying, I *am* the LORD: speak thou unto Pharaoh king of Egypt all that I say unto thee. 30 And Moses said before the LORD, Behold, I *am* of uncircumcised lips, and how shall Pharaoh hearken unto me?

View of the caves at Khirbat Qumran

(View of the Qumran Caves, where the Dead Sea Scrolls were discovered in 1947 [photo], / Qumran, Israel / Ancient Art and Architecture Collection Ltd. / The Bridgeman Art Library International)

"So God created man in his own image, in the image of God he created him; male and female he created them."

Overview

The book of Genesis is one of the most significant books in the Bible and is considered sacred scripture for Jews, Samaritans, and Christians. It is the first book of the Bible and begins the section often called the Pentateuch, from the Greek for *Five Books*: Genesis, Exodus, Leviticus, Numbers, and Deuteronomy. Traditionally, Jews and Christians have held that Moses was the primary author responsible for compiling and composing Genesis as well as the rest of the Pentateuch, although some medieval Jewish scholars favored the scribe Ezra. The Samaritans, descendants of the northern tribes of Israel whose central sanctuary is on Mount Gerizim and not in Jerusalem, use their own version of the Pentateuch as sacred scripture. Contemporary scholars remain divided over the identity of the author, or authors, of Genesis.

Genesis is a complex document that embraces many diverse literary genres. Portions of it, like Genesis 1, are highly stylized and include poetic elements like repetition and parallelism. Genesis also features historical narratives that involve characters and a plot, with protagonists and antagonists. In addition, Genesis contains elaborate and complex genealogies. Although Muslims do not view Genesis as sacred, many of the characters that appear in Genesis also appear in the Qur'an and are viewed as prophets in Islam, and some of the stories found in Genesis, with variations, are also found in the Qur'an. Some of the most famous passages in the Bible are found in Genesis: the Creation of the world; the Fall of Adam and Eve; Cain's murder of his brother Abel; Noah's ark and the Flood; and the life stories of Abraham, Isaac, and Jacob, as well as the lengthy Joseph narratives that set the stage for the Jews' sojourn in the land of Egypt and the later departure depicted in the very next biblical book, Exodus.

Context

The book of Genesis shares genres and themes with other literature of the end of the third millennium and the second millennium BCE. The account in Genesis 1–2 unfolds with a brief outline of Creation (1:1–2:3), followed by a more detailed description of the creation of humanity and the introduction of plant and animal life into the Garden of Eden (2:4–25). This follows a basic pattern discernible in other ancient Near Eastern creation accounts, such as the Akkadian Atrahasis Epic (ca. 1750 BCE) and the Sumerian Epic of Enki and Ninmah (from the early second millennium BCE). The link between creation and flood material is also paralleled in other ancient Near Eastern texts. Moreover, there are several parallels between the Creation account and the accounts later in the Old Testament of the construction of the Tabernacle and Temple, accounts that in turn share much in common with other ancient Near Eastern descriptions of temple-building linked to creation, such as the Sumerian Gudea cylinders (ca. 2100 BCE). More recently, scholars have begun to point out previously unrecognized parallels with the creation accounts in Egyptian texts. Although these texts are polytheistic, Egyptian creation accounts, like the account in Genesis, depict one creator God. It is only in Egyptian creation accounts and in Genesis that one hears about the creation of "heaven and earth." In both Egyptian creation accounts and in Genesis, the divine creator is depicted as a skilled worker crafting creation as one would construct a temple.

In the material concerning Abraham, there are numerous parallels in the ancient Near East to the types of covenants found in Genesis. In many instances, the types of personal and place names encountered in these narratives fit the types of personal and place names from the ancient Near East in the early second millennium BCE (roughly 2000–1700 BCE) when the events purport to take place. Moreover, the description of the battle of the five armies in Genesis 14 fits the geopolitical context of that time. Earlier than this time period, the rule of the Sumerian Empire would have made such a battle impossible; later, the Babylonian and Assyrian empires would have likewise rendered this description untenable.

No one knows for certain how the text of Genesis was promulgated. Those scholars who argue that the text is the work of primarily one author tend to link it either with Moses or with Ezra. For those who link it with Moses, they see Moses' promulgation of it, along with the rest of the Pen-

Time Line	
CA. 2000 –1900 BCE	■ This is believed to be the approximate time period for Abraham and the beginning of the patriarchal narratives in Genesis.
CA. 1446 –1406 BCE	■ According to one traditional Jewish and Christian view, this is when the Exodus and subsequent Israelite wandering in the wilderness took place, and thus when Moses may have compiled or composed Genesis.
CA. 1250 –1210 BCE	■ This is the most widely accepted proposal for when the Exodus took place.
CA. 950 BCE	■ This is a commonly accepted date for the Yahwist (J) source of Genesis.
CA. 850 BCE	■ This is a commonly accepted date for the Elohist (E) source.
CA. 586 BCE	■ The Temple in Jerusalem, along with the city, is destroyed by the armies of King Nebuchadnezzar of Babylon. The Jews are taken into captivity in Babylon.
CA. 400s BCE	■ Ezra the scribe, who many scholars in the medieval, Renaissance, and early-modern period thought was responsible for the final form of Genesis, lived during this time. This is also the time from which the Priestly source (P) dates.

tateuch, as an explanation of the history of God's relationship with the world and the people of Israel's relationship with neighboring peoples, as well as of the history of how the people of Israel entered Egypt in the first place prior to the Exodus initiated by Moses. For those scholars who link it with Ezra, they see Ezra's composition of Genesis or redaction of it from various earlier texts after the Babylonian exile as explaining Israel's prehistory. The Babylonian exile, or captivity, occurred when the Babylonians invaded Jerusalem in the early part of the sixth century BCE, destroyed the Temple in Jerusalem, and took the majority of the inhabitants—mainly from the southern Israelite tribes of Judah, Benjamin, and Levi—into captivity in Babylon (modern-day Iraq). Roughly seventy years later, after the Persian king Cyrus the Great defeated the Babylonians, the Persians brought many of the Israelites back from exile to Jerusalem to begin rebuilding the city and eventually to begin rebuilding the Temple.

Many scholars, possibly most, hold to a much more complicated history of promulgation for Genesis, involving many (at least three) fragmented texts or groups of texts with diverse origins, which came together in a unified whole only sometime after the Babylonian exile. The earliest manuscript of Genesis, which comes from the Dead Sea Scrolls of Khirbat Qumran (on the West Bank), is written in Hebrew and dates to perhaps as early as 200 BCE, although no scholar argues for such a late date for the composition of Genesis. The text is fragmentary, consisting of only about ten chapters of Genesis, all from the patriarchal narratives, and also including the beginning of the book of Exodus. There are several other Genesis texts, which are again fragmentary, offering only later portions of the patriarchal narratives, and also written in Hebrew and from Khirbat Qumran, probably from the first half of the first century BCE.

Most scholars maintain that Genesis, like the majority of the rest of the Old Testament, was originally written in Hebrew. Some maintain that the script used was the paleo-Hebrew script, whereas others maintain that it was Hebrew in the more recent Aramaic script, which the manuscript tradition has preserved. A few scholars argue that the book of Genesis was written very early, and thus in a proto-Hebrew Semitic language related to Canaanite and possibly in a cuneiform script. This latter view is extremely rare and there is no hard evidence for such a hypothesis.

Overall, then, scholars know nothing with any certainty about the creation, promulgation, publication, or distribution of Genesis. There is no external evidence for any of the scholarly views concerning these matters until the much later fragmentary copies from Khirbat Qumran, and even then the debate rages. There is no direct evidence outside of the Bible that Moses ever existed and little outside of the Bible to suggest that Ezra ever existed. Various scholars debate the probability of these figures and their roles based on other indirect corroborating evidence. In turn, no external evidence exists to support any of the proposed theories of documentary composition, since the only extant copies of Genesis are found in their final form (even if fragmented). Thus, the portions of the patriarchal narratives from the first two centuries BCE cannot be divided into component texts but rather represent the final form of those chapters. Moreover, these early manuscripts support different textual traditions. The oldest complete text of the book of Genesis comes from the fourth-century CE Greek Septuagint translations.

About the Author

Since the 1600s, the authorship of Genesis has been one of the most controversial questions in biblical scholarship. Early and medieval Jewish and Christian traditions commonly assumed that Moses was the primary author of Genesis, compiling or composing it at some point after the Exodus, when Moses received the Law from God at Mount Sinai. However, a number of Muslim scholars in the medi-

Fifteenth-century colored woodcut of Noah's ark

(Genesis 6:11-24 Noah's Ark, from the Nuremberg Bible [coloured woodcut], German School [15th century] [after] / Private Collection / The Stapleton Collection / The Bridgeman Art Library International)

eval period attributed Genesis to the later (ca. 400s BCE) Israelite scribe Ezra, a returnee to Jerusalem from the Babylonian exile. This view of Ezra as author was expressed by several individuals in the Latin Christian west as well and became very popular among scholars like Thomas Hobbes and Baruch Spinoza in the early-modern period.

In 1711 Henning Bernhard Witter maintained that the book of Genesis was the work of more than a single author, and in 1753 Jean Astruc argued that he was able to detect several sources underlying the text of Genesis. Astruc adhered to the traditional idea of Mosaic authorship but was convinced that Moses had compiled Genesis from several prior sources. Other scholars in the early nineteenth century, such as Johann Gottfried Eichhorn, Alexander Geddes, and Johann Vater, suggested that the Pentateuch was a piecing together of numerous disparate fragments from various unknown authors. In 1805 Wilhelm Martin Leberecht de Wette claimed that the book of Deuteronomy was the result of its own separate source (D), and his dating of Deuteronomy to the later part of the seventh century BCE became an important landmark study.

In the 1830s scholars like Georg Heinrich August Ewald were dissatisfied with this explanation of authorship, which was becoming known as the Fragmentary Hypothesis. Ewald and others constructed the Supplementary Hypoth-

esis, which viewed the bulk of the Pentateuch, including Genesis, as the result of one primary source, supplemented by various smaller, less significant sources. In 1853 Hermann Hupfeld began to revive an approach called the Documentary Hypothesis, which envisioned discrete documents lying behind the text of the Pentateuch.

Near the end of the nineteenth century the Documentary Hypothesis reached its classical expression. The most famous proponent of this is also the figure responsible for the standard textbook formulation, Julius Wellhausen, a former student of Ewald's. His Documentary Hypothesis is often known as the JEDP Hypothesis, with each letter representing one source: Yawhist, Elohist, Deuteronomist, and Priestly (with the letter *J* used in accord with the German spelling of "Yahweh"). Few scholars follow Wellhausen exactly, but variations on this hypothesis remain prevalent today.

One of the most important critics of the classic Documentary Hypothesis was the Jewish scholar Yehezkel Kaufmann. Kaufmann was particularly critical of the elaborate editorial schemes posited by scholars and also of the late dating of material pertaining to ritual, liturgical, and sacrificial regulation. He attributed these in part to anti-Jewish philosophical influences as opposed to disinterested scholarship; that is, he believed that such scholars were intentionally minimizing aspects of the Bible that were important historically to

"In the beginning God created the heavens and the earth."

"Then God said, 'Let us make man in our image, after our likeness. . . .' So God created man in his own image, in the image of God he created him; male and female he created them. And God blessed them, and God said to them, 'Be fruitful and multiply, and fill the earth and subdue it.'"

"And on the seventh day God finished his work which he had done, and he rested on the seventh day from all his work which he had done. So God blessed the seventh day and hallowed it, because on it God rested from all his work which he had done in creation."

"Then the LORD said to Noah, 'Go into the ark, you and all your household, for I have seen that you are righteous before me in this generation.'"

"After these things the word of the LORD came to Abram in a vision, 'Fear not, Abram, I am your shield; your reward shall be very great.'"

"By myself I have sworn . . . because you have done this, and have not withheld your son, your only son, I will indeed bless you, and I will multiply your descendants as the stars of heaven and as the sand which is on the seashore. And your descendants shall possess the gate of their enemies, and by your descendants shall all the nations of the earth bless themselves, because you have obeyed my voice."

Jews and to Judaism. A number of twentieth-century scholars have also departed from views of multiple authorship, arguing for a core unity for the bulk of the entire Pentateuch, including Genesis. These scholars maintain that the Pentateuch is the work primarily of a single author who was a skilled literary artist, using repetition and parallelism as did other authors in the ancient Near East. Variation in names and vocabulary, such scholars claim, is better accounted for by their parallels in other ancient literature and on stylistic grounds. Many scholars have argued for a primary unity in the Pentateuch, including the Jewish scholar Cyrus Gordon, the Catholic scholar Augustin Bea, and the Protestant scholar Roger Norman Whybray. In many instances, as with Gordon, these scholars do not believe that the Pentateuch goes back to Moses, but they do think that it is primarily the work of a single author.

Explanation and Analysis of the Document

The excerpts included here from the Revised Standard Version of Genesis represent various passages from roughly the first half of the book. They include important passages discussing the Creation of the world and of humanity, the Fall of Adam and Eve, and Noah and the Flood, as well as key events in the life of Abraham.

♦ Chapters 1–2:3

At the opening of Genesis, Creation unfolds in a very orderly fashion, using similar phrases and themes that link this text to the later creation of the Tabernacle and Temple. The text flows to the seventh day, which becomes known in later biblical passages as the Sabbath, the day of rest set aside for worship. Key phrases recur in the accounts of the construction of the Tabernacle in Exodus 39–40. Like the Creation, the Tabernacle was consecrated over seven days. The focus on the number 7 is important, because, in the Hebrew tradition reflected in the Old Testament, the number 7 is closely related to the swearing of oaths, the forging of covenants, and thus the extending of family relationships. The emphasis on the number 7 and on the theme of rest recurs with the construction of the Temple in 1 Kings 6 and 8, Psalm 132, and 1 Chronicles 22, where the Temple takes seven years to complete, it is dedicated during the seven-day feast of Tabernacles, and King Solomon's prayer of dedication is seven petitions long. When placed in the ancient Near Eastern and Egyptian context, where temple construction is often linked with creation, Genesis becomes one of several texts depicting God as the master builder constructing the temple of creation. The six days of Creation in Genesis solve the problem for God the builder announced in the second verse: The world was formless and void. In the first three days God creates the form, and in the last three days God fills the void. On the first day, God creates light and darkness. On the fourth day God fills the light and the darkness with the sun, moon, and stars. On the second day God separates the sky from the water. On the fifth day God creates animals to populate the sky and the water. On the third day God creates the land and vegetation. On the sixth day God creates animals and humanity to populate the land and vegetation.

♦ Chapters 2:4–3:24

In the second chapter the creation of humanity is the focus, and Adam is depicted as a royal priest. His royalty is emphasized in the dominion he is given over all of creation, and his priestly role is indicated by the dual command to keep and till the land. The verb *to keep* is also translated as "guard" or "watch," and the verb *to till* is also translated as "work" or "serve." Those two verbs occur together again in the Pentateuch only with the dual command given to the priestly Levites who are to guard and serve in the Tabernacle (Numbers 3, 8, and 18). Moreover, the connections between the Garden of Eden and the Holy of Holies, the inner sanctuary in the Temple in Jerusalem, suggest that Eden is to be viewed as the Holy of Holies, just as the Temple was viewed as a new creation and the inner sanctum as a garden in later Jewish interpretations. Eden, the Tabernacle, and the Temple were all entered from the East. The description of God walking through the Garden of Eden in Genesis 3 uses the same verb that is used to describe God's presence in the Tabernacle. Finally, cherubim angels, who guard the Tree of Life in Genesis 3, are found again carved on the entrance to the inner sanctum of the Temple, on the inner walls of the Temple, and on the Ark of the Covenant, which was in both the tabernacle and the Temple.

At its core, Genesis 2 sets the stage for Genesis 3. In Genesis 2 we are introduced to the Tree of Life as well as the Tree of the Knowledge of Good and Evil. We are also introduced to the idea that Adam is meant to keep, watch, and guard the garden, implying the possibility of threat from an intruder. In Genesis 3 we find the intruder is a serpent,

which ancient Jewish and Christian traditions sometimes depicted as a fierce dragon or biting serpent. Apparently, Adam is silent but present when the intruder enters. Adam's presence might be implied in the fact that the serpent speaks using the Hebrew dual form, which implies that he is speaking to two individuals; only the woman responds. Both man and woman eat the forbidden fruit of the Tree of the Knowledge and thus experience some form of spiritual death, which in western Christian traditions since the time of Saint Augustine (354–430 CE) has been understood as original sin. God enters into dialogue with Adam and Eve. God asks them questions, not in order to find out information so much as to help them recognize what they did. Later biblical texts and Jewish and Christian traditions indicate that perhaps God questions them in order to provide an opportunity for them to repent. If God were being depicted as gathering information, one might expect that God would ask the serpent questions, but instead God simply curses the serpent (and only the serpent). Man and woman are told of various repercussions, indicating that their sin changed their relationships with each other and with the world around them. Later Jewish and Christian interpreters understood these repercussions or punishments as penitential and redemptive.

The full capitalization of the word "LORD" is found beginning in Genesis 2. The normal Hebrew word for Lord is "Adonai" (and sometimes Ba'al), so when the name Adonai appears, it is translated into English as "Lord." However, when religious Jews read "Yahweh," the Hebrew word for God's name, they do not pronounce it. They usually instead say "Adonai," or very Orthodox Jews will sometimes instead say "HaShem" (the Name). Most English translations, Christian or otherwise, follow a similar scheme and translate Yahweh as "LORD," in all-capital letters, while translating Adonai and also Ba'al, when referring to the God of Israel, as "Lord."

♦ Chapter 4

Next we are introduced to Cain and his brother, Abel. Cain is the firstborn son, which is the privileged family status throughout the Pentateuch, but as so often happens in Genesis, the firstborn son is found lacking the necessary qualities of family heir. In this case, Cain's sacrifice is displeasing to God. According to traditional Jewish and Christian interpreters, this is because, unlike Abel, Cain does not offer his best in sacrifice to God. In envy, Cain murders Abel. As in Genesis 3, God again enters into dialogue with the perpetrator. Unlike Adam and Eve, however, who answer God's questions, Cain does not give any answer, he simply shirks responsibility, never admitting that he murdered his brother. God's response makes it clear that God knows what happened to Abel even though Cain never explains it. The rest of chapter 4 traces the family of Cain, the focal point being the seventh generation from Adam through Cain, namely, Lamech, who exceeds Cain in wickedness by committing two murders. The chapter ends with Adam and Eve's righteous son Seth. The remaining chapters until the time of Noah follow the two families, the children of Cain and the children of Seth.

Chapters 6–8

Chapter 6 sets up the stories concerning Noah and the Flood by emphasizing human wickedness. Although many commentators understand the phrase "sons of God" to refer to angelic beings, the more proximate reference would be to the children from Seth's line. Adam is described as being created in the image and likeness of God (1:26) and that phraseology of being in the "image and likeness" of one's father occurs again in Genesis with reference to Seth being in Adam's own "likeness" and "image" (5:3). The "daughters of men" on this reading would be descendants of Cain. Thus we see here the mixing of Seth's righteous line with Cain's unrighteous line, producing the "men of renown," literally in Hebrew the "men of the name," which could be a reference for notorious individuals who made a bad name for themselves. This would account for the context of and transition to the story about Noah, where the Flood comes in response to human wickedness. Noah is depicted as a righteous man who obeys God, and God saves Noah and his family from the flood's destruction. Noah obeys God's command and builds the ark that becomes the instrument of their salvation. Parallels with the Creation account abound, with the land emerging from the waters and the command to be fruitful and multiply. In response to Noah's fidelity, God makes a covenant with him, renewing the covenant with the creation implied in God's Sabbath rest at Creation in 2:2–3.

Chapters 12, 14–17, and 22

These chapters form the essential core of the Abrahamic stories. In chapter 12, God calls Abram to move from Ur (in modern-day Iraq) to Canaan (in present-day Israel). (Only after Genesis 17, when God reemphasizes that he will make Abram's name great, does his name change for the remainder of the narratives to Abraham.) God makes three basic promises to Abram: great nation; great name; and a blessing to all nations, that is, all the families of the world. The remainder of chapter 12 finds Abram taking his family, his entire tribe, to Canaan, foreshadowing the history of Israel in telling how Abram goes down into Egypt and then comes out of Egypt back into the Promised Land. In chapter 14 we encounter the battle of the five armies, over which Abram stands victorious. At the end of this passage the mysterious figure of Melchizedek appears, whose name is actually a descriptive title that means "righteous king." In the Bible, the figure of Melchizedek occurs again only in Psalm 110 and in the New Testament book of the Letter to the Hebrews. Like Adam, Melchizedek is depicted as a royal priest. He is royal in that he is explicitly identified as a king of the city of Salem, which elsewhere in the Old Testament becomes identified with the city of Zion (Jerusalem). He is priestly in that he blesses Abram, blessing being a priestly action; Abram pays him a tithe, which is what Israelites were commanded to pay priests in the Pentateuch. Melchizedek also presents an offering of bread and wine, which was interpreted by the early rabbinic traditions of Judaism as foreshadowing the nonbloody sacrifices of the bread of the presence in the Tabernacle and Temple, which was consumed by the priests on the Sabbath along with wine.

Chapter 15 depicts the first covenant God makes with Abram, where God elevates the first promise from chapter 12—the promise of a great nation—to the status of a covenant, wherein two parties enter into a family relationship. In the ancient Near East covenants were made through oath-swearing rituals, and they were the means of extending family relationships. In this initial covenant, Abram's oath of fidelity is implied in his splitting of the animal carcasses in two—the action communicated something like, "May I be split in half like these animals if I do not remain faithful to the covenant"—whereas God's part in the oath is implied in passing through the split animals like fire. In chapter 16 Abram has intercourse with his wife's Egyptian maidservant Hagar. Ishmael is the son of that union, but God intends to fulfill his promises to Abram through his wife Sar'ai. In chapter 17 God elevates the first two promises made in chapter 12 into a covenant with Abram, whose name is changed to Abraham (17:5). In both chapters 15 and 17 nationhood is implied in the promise of land and descendants, and in chapter 17 the great name is highlighted by the royal dynasty implied in the promise as well as by the change in name to Abraham. Abram means something like "exalted father," whereas Abraham means something more like "father of a great multitude." The name change thus emphasizes that Abraham will be the father of many nations through dynastic succession.

Finally, chapter 22 describes the binding of Isaac, known in Jewish tradition as the Akedah. This passage was understood in Jewish and Christian traditions as pointing forward to the hope of a future resurrection. Abraham is told to offer his son Isaac as a sacrifice on Moriah, but Isaac's life is given back when, through angelic mediation, God stops Abraham from killing Isaac. When Isaac asks his father where the animal for sacrifice is to be found, Abraham responds that God will provide the lamb. In Jewish traditions this passage is interpreted in light of the Passover event, where God saved Israelite firstborn sons from the plague visited on the Egyptians through the Israelites' sacrificial offering of lambs (Exodus 11:4–12:30). In Christian interpretive traditions, the binding of Isaac points forward to Jesus's death and Resurrection, where, like Isaac, Jesus bore the wood to the place of sacrifice and Jesus' life, too, was given back; unlike Isaac, however, he had to complete the sacrifice.

Audience

Because we do not know when Genesis was written or when it received its final form, we cannot know for certain who was its original audience. If Moses was the figure primarily responsible for Genesis, then the audience would have been the early Israelites after their Exodus from slavery in Egypt before they entered Canaan, the Promised Land. If Ezra was the author, then the audience would have been primarily the southern Israelite tribes of Judah, Benjamin, and Levi, who had returned from captivity in Babylon. In either case, the stories about Creation and the Fall, Noah and the Flood, and the patriarchal ancestors would be depicting in story form many of the laws God gave the Israelites after the Exodus. The Genesis narratives would chronicle the history of God's dealings with the ancestors of the Israelites. If Genesis is the result of the compilation of multiple sources, the audience for this final form was initially believing Jews or Israelites, including Samaritans, and later Christians who accepted Genesis as a divinely inspired book. For all these audiences, the book functioned primarily in communal liturgical worship. In modern times, passages from Genesis are read regularly in Jewish, Catholic, Orthodox Christian, Anglican, Lutheran, Methodist, Presbyterian, and many other Christian traditions.

Impact

Scholars are uncertain what impact Genesis had in its own time. Portions of the text may have influenced early Jewish liturgical celebrations, and many scholars have argued that such liturgical services helped shape the final form of the text. The Genesis stories exerted a tremendous influence on later biblical texts in both the Old and New Testaments. Themes within the initial chapters of Genesis, particularly concerning Adam in Genesis 2–3, provide the backdrop to Ezekiel's description of the Prince of Tyre (Ezekiel 28:1–19). The description of wisdom in chapter 24 of the book of Sirach (part of the Deuterocanon, or "second canon," in Catholic and Orthodox Christian Bibles) appears to be an elaborate theological meditation inspired in part by the Genesis account of Creation. And the Psalms also reflect elements and themes from these initial chapters of Genesis. In the New Testament, numerous passages include reflections and arguments based upon these opening chapters. The prologue to the Gospel of John is a rereading of Genesis 1 characterizing Jesus as the Word of God through which all things were created (John 1:1–3). The apostle Paul constructs elaborate theological arguments based upon the Fall account in Genesis 3 (Romans 5 and 1 Corinthians 15). Later Jewish and Christian interpreters spent a great deal of time reflecting on the Genesis Creation and Fall accounts. The rabbinic commentary *Genesis Rabbah* (ca. 300–600) as well as the later varied textual versions of the *Life of Adam and Eve* (ca. 200–700) represent two significant examples of Jewish and Christian reflection on Genesis 1–3.

Other than a very few references and allusions, the stories concerning Noah do not appear to have had much impact on other Old Testament texts. Reference to Noah and the Flood, however, is made in a few significant New Testament passages. Jesus makes reference to Noah and the Flood in his comments about his future coming (Matthew 24:37–39 and Luke 17:26–27). Moreover, the New Testament makes a comparison between baptism and how Noah and his family were saved through the Flood (1 Peter 3:19–21).

By far, the patriarchal narratives concerning Abraham receive the most attention in both the Old and New Testaments. In the books of Exodus, Leviticus, Numbers, and Deuteronomy, God's covenant with Abraham is mentioned frequently. In some instances, God reminds the Israelites of the covenant he made with Abraham, and at other times Moses asks God to remember his fidelity to the Israelites based on the covenant oath he swore to Abraham. Throughout the historical books, wisdom literature, and prophets' writings of the Old Testament, the Israelites are known as the descendants of Abraham. In the New Testament, the Gospels depict Jesus as a descendant of Abraham. Throughout the books of Romans, Galatians, and James, Abraham and the stories concerning Abraham (mainly Genesis 15–22) are employed in theological discussions concerning the doctrine of justification, the Christian doctrine regarding how one becomes a child of God (such as through baptism).

Throughout the centuries, the stories in Genesis have played a significant part in the debate between various religious communities and within western society more broadly speaking. With the advent of Islam in the medieval period, the religious traditions that traced themselves back to Abraham expanded. At the center of Muslim and Jewish interpretative debates lies the differing traditions concerning which of Abraham's sons became the son of the blessing. For Jewish and Christian traditions, following the book of Genesis, Isaac was the son of the promise. In Muslim traditions, however, Ishmael is viewed as the son of the promise. In the Reformation period, the question of Abraham's justification became a major theological concern between Catholic and Protestant traditions. In the modern period, and especially since the nineteenth century, debates about how to interpret Genesis 1–3 and questions about the relationship between science and religion, especially regarding theories of evolution, have come to the fore. All these issues relate in some way to Genesis and its reception, and all these debates continue in the present.

Further Reading

■ Books

Anderson, Gary A. *The Genesis of Perfection: Adam and Eve in Jewish and Christian Imagination*. Louisville, Ky.: Westminster John Knox Press, 2001.

Arnold, Bill T. *Genesis*. Cambridge, U.K.: Cambridge University Press, 2009.

Averbeck, Richard E. "Factors in Reading the Patriarchal Narratives: Literary, Historical, and Theological Dimensions." In *Giving the Sense: Understanding and Using Old Testament Historical Texts*, eds. David M. Howard, Jr., and Michael A. Grisanti. Grand Rapids, Mich.: Kregel, 2003.

Cassuto, Umberto. *The Documentary Hypothesis: And the Composition of the Pentateuch*. Jerusalem: Shalem Press, 2006.

Hahn, Scott W. *Kinship by Covenant: A Canonical Approach to the Fulfillment of God's Saving Promises*. New Haven, Conn.: Yale University Press, 2009.

Hamilton, Victor P. *The Book of Genesis: Chapters 1–17*. Grand Rapids, Mich.: Eerdmans, 1990.

Hamilton, Victor P. *The Book of Genesis: Chapters 18–50*. Grand Rapids, Mich.: Eerdmans, 1995.

Kitchen, Kenneth A. "Genesis 12–50 in the Near Eastern World." In *He Swore an Oath: Biblical Themes from Genesis 12–50*, ed. Richard S. Hess, et al. Grand Rapids, Mich.: Baker Book House, 1994.

Kugel, James L. *How to Read the Bible: A Guide to Scripture, Then and Now*. New York: Free Press, 2007.

Rendsburg, Gary A. *Redaction of Genesis*. Winona Lake, Ind.: Eisenbrauns, 1986.

Ska, Jean-Louis. *Introduction to Reading the Pentateuch*. Winona Lake, Ind.: Eisenbrauns, 2006.

Tsumura, David Toshio. "Genesis and Ancient Near Eastern Stories of Creation and Flood: An Introduction." In *"I Studied Inscriptions from before the Flood": Ancient Near Eastern, Literary, and Linguistic Approaches to Genesis 1–11*, ed. Richard S. Hess and David Toshio Tsumura. Winona Lake, Ind.: Eisenbrauns, 1994.

Wiseman, D. J., and A. R. Millard, eds. *Essays on the Patriarchal Narratives*. Eugene, Ore.: Wipf and Stock, 2007.

Yamauchi, Edwin. "The Current Status of Old Testament Historiography." In *Faith, Tradition, and History: Old Testament Historiography in Its Near Eastern Context*, eds. A. R. Millard, James K. Hoffmeier, and David W. Baker. Winona Lake, Ind.: Eisenbrauns, 1994.

Yamauchi, Edwin M. "Abraham and Archaeology: Anachronisms or Adaptations?" In *Perspectives on Our Father Abraham: Essays in Honor of Marvin R. Wilson*, ed. Steven A. Hunt. Grand Rapids, Mich.: Eerdmans, 2010.

■ **Journals**

Levenson, Jon D. "The Temple and the World." *Journal of Religion* 64, no. 3 (1984): 275–298.

Morrow, Jeff. "Creation as Temple-Building and Work as Liturgy in Genesis 1-3." *Journal of the Orthodox Center for the Advancement of Biblical Studies* 2, no. 1 (2009): 1–13.

Wenham, Gordon J. "Sanctuary Symbolism in the Garden of Eden Story." *Proceedings of the Ninth World Congress of Jewish Studies, Division A: The Period of the Bible* (1986): 19–25.

—Jeffrey L. Morrow

Questions for Further Study

1. In contemporary life, conflict exists between those who believe literally in the Creation account of Genesis and those who believe that the universe and life on earth evolved over immense periods of time. What is your position on this issue? Do you think that the views of the "creationists" and those of the "evolutionists" are necessarily at odds? Explain how they might be reconciled.

2. Why do you think that flood stories played such a prominent part in the mythology of this region of the world thousands of years ago? Compare this account, for example, with the entry on the *Epic of Gilgamesh*.

3. Many of the most widely known "Bible stories" in the Judeo-Christian tradition come from the book of Genesis; in contrast, much of the rest of the Old Testament is perhaps somewhat less familiar among laypeople. Why do you think this is so? What is the fundamental appeal of Genesis to many people, even those who might not practice a traditional religion or any religion at all? Why are the Bible stories from Genesis so compelling?

4. In what respect can Genesis be regarded as a foundational document for Western civilization? Consider such issues as monotheism, law, tradition, the origin of evil, and the role of God in human affairs.

5. Compare the account of Creation in Genesis with that discussed in the entry on the Yengishiki. How do the accounts differ? Are there any similarities? What differences in historical events, geography, and other factors might have accounted for the different creation accounts?

BIBLE: GENESIS

Chapter 1

[1] In the beginning God created the heavens and the earth.

[2] The earth was without form and void, and darkness was upon the face of the deep; and the Spirit of God was moving over the face of the waters.

[3] And God said, "Let there be light"; and there was light.

[4] And God saw that the light was good; and God separated the light from the darkness.

[5] God called the light Day, and the darkness he called Night. And there was evening and there was morning, one day.

[6] And God said, "Let there be a firmament in the midst of the waters, and let it separate the waters from the waters."

[7] And God made the firmament and separated the waters which were under the firmament from the waters which were above the firmament. And it was so.

[8] And God called the firmament Heaven. And there was evening and there was morning, a second day.

[9] And God said, "Let the waters under the heavens be gathered together into one place, and let the dry land appear." And it was so.

[10] God called the dry land Earth, and the waters that were gathered together he called Seas. And God saw that it was good.

[11] And God said, "Let the earth put forth vegetation, plants yielding seed, and fruit trees bearing fruit in which is their seed, each according to its kind, upon the earth." And it was so.

[12] The earth brought forth vegetation, plants yielding seed according to their own kinds, and trees bearing fruit in which is their seed, each according to its kind. And God saw that it was good.

[13] And there was evening and there was morning, a third day.

[14] And God said, "Let there be lights in the firmament of the heavens to separate the day from the night; and let them be for signs and for seasons and for days and years,

[15] and let them be lights in the firmament of the heavens to give light upon the earth." And it was so.

[16] And God made the two great lights, the greater light to rule the day, and the lesser light to rule the night; he made the stars also.

[17] And God set them in the firmament of the heavens to give light upon the earth,

[18] to rule over the day and over the night, and to separate the light from the darkness. And God saw that it was good.

[19] And there was evening and there was morning, a fourth day.

[20] And God said, "Let the waters bring forth swarms of living creatures, and let birds fly above the earth across the firmament of the heavens."

[21] So God created the great sea monsters and every living creature that moves, with which the waters swarm, according to their kinds, and every winged bird according to its kind. And God saw that it was good.

[22] And God blessed them, saying, "Be fruitful and multiply and fill the waters in the seas, and let birds multiply on the earth."

[23] And there was evening and there was morning, a fifth day.

[24] And God said, "Let the earth bring forth living creatures according to their kinds: cattle and creeping things and beasts of the earth according to their kinds." And it was so.

[25] And God made the beasts of the earth according to their kinds and the cattle according to their kinds, and everything that creeps upon the ground according to its kind. And God saw that it was good.

[26] Then God said, "Let us make man in our image, after our likeness; and let them have dominion over the fish of the sea, and over the birds of the air, and over the cattle, and over all the earth, and over every creeping thing that creeps upon the earth."

[27] So God created man in his own image, in the image of God he created him; male and female he created them.

[28] And God blessed them, and God said to them, "Be fruitful and multiply, and fill the earth and subdue it; and have dominion over the fish of the sea and over the birds of the air and over every living thing that moves upon the earth."

[29] And God said, "Behold, I have given you every plant yielding seed which is upon the face of all the earth, and every tree with seed in its fruit; you shall have them for food.

[30] And to every beast of the earth, and to every bird of the air, and to everything that creeps on the earth, everything that has the breath of life, I have given every green plant for food." And it was so.

[31] And God saw everything that he had made, and behold, it was very good. And there was evening and there was morning, a sixth day.

Chapter 2

[1] Thus the heavens and the earth were finished, and all the host of them.

[2] And on the seventh day God finished his work which he had done, and he rested on the seventh day from all his work which he had done.

[3] So God blessed the seventh day and hallowed it, because on it God rested from all his work which he had done in creation.

[4] These are the generations of the heavens and the earth when they were created. In the day that the LORD God made the earth and the heavens,

[5] when no plant of the field was yet in the earth and no herb of the field had yet sprung up—for the LORD God had not caused it to rain upon the earth, and there was no man to till the ground;

[6] but a mist went up from the earth and watered the whole face of the ground—

[7] then the LORD God formed man of dust from the ground, and breathed into his nostrils the breath of life; and man became a living being.

[8] And the LORD God planted a garden in Eden, in the east; and there he put the man whom he had formed.

[9] And out of the ground the LORD God made to grow every tree that is pleasant to the sight and good for food, the tree of life also in the midst of the garden, and the tree of the knowledge of good and evil.

[10] A river flowed out of Eden to water the garden, and there it divided and became four rivers.

[11] The name of the first is Pishon; it is the one which flows around the whole land of Havilah, where there is gold;

[12] and the gold of that land is good; bdellium and onyx stone are there.

[13] The name of the second river is Gihon; it is the one which flows around the whole land of Cush.

[14] And the name of the third river is Tigris, which flows east of Assyria. And the fourth river is the Euphrates.

[15] The LORD God took the man and put him in the garden of Eden to till it and keep it.

[16] And the LORD God commanded the man, saying, "You may freely eat of every tree of the garden;

[17] but of the tree of the knowledge of good and evil you shall not eat, for in the day that you eat of it you shall die."

[18] Then the LORD God said, "It is not good that the man should be alone; I will make him a helper fit for him."

[19] So out of the ground the LORD God formed every beast of the field and every bird of the air, and brought them to the man to see what he would call them; and whatever the man called every living creature, that was its name.

[20] The man gave names to all cattle, and to the birds of the air, and to every beast of the field; but for the man there was not found a helper fit for him.

[21] So the LORD God caused a deep sleep to fall upon the man, and while he slept took one of his ribs and closed up its place with flesh;

[22] and the rib which the LORD God had taken from the man he made into a woman and brought her to the man.

[23] Then the man said, "This at last is bone of my bones and flesh of my flesh; she shall be called Woman, because she was taken out of Man."

[24] Therefore a man leaves his father and his mother and cleaves to his wife, and they become one flesh.

[25] And the man and his wife were both naked, and were not ashamed.

Chapter 3

[1] Now the serpent was more subtle than any other wild creature that the LORD God had made. He said to the woman, "Did God say, 'You shall not eat of any tree of the garden'?"

[2] And the woman said to the serpent, "We may eat of the fruit of the trees of the garden;

[3] but God said, 'You shall not eat of the fruit of the tree which is in the midst of the garden, neither shall you touch it, lest you die.'"

[4] But the serpent said to the woman, "You will not die.

[5] For God knows that when you eat of it your eyes will be opened, and you will be like God, knowing good and evil."

[6] So when the woman saw that the tree was good for food, and that it was a delight to the eyes, and

that the tree was to be desired to make one wise, she took of its fruit and ate; and she also gave some to her husband, and he ate.

[7] Then the eyes of both were opened, and they knew that they were naked; and they sewed fig leaves together and made themselves aprons.

[8] And they heard the sound of the LORD God walking in the garden in the cool of the day, and the man and his wife hid themselves from the presence of the LORD God among the trees of the garden.

[9] But the LORD God called to the man, and said to him, "Where are you?"

[10] And he said, "I heard the sound of thee in the garden, and I was afraid, because I was naked; and I hid myself."

[11] He said, "Who told you that you were naked? Have you eaten of the tree of which I commanded you not to eat?"

[12] The man said, "The woman whom thou gavest to be with me, she gave me fruit of the tree, and I ate."

[13] Then the LORD God said to the woman, "What is this that you have done?" The woman said, "The serpent beguiled me, and I ate."

[14] The LORD God said to the serpent, "Because you have done this, cursed are you above all cattle, and above all wild animals; upon your belly you shall go, and dust you shall eat all the days of your life.

[15] I will put enmity between you and the woman, and between your seed and her seed; he shall bruise your head, and you shall bruise his heel."

[16] To the woman he said, "I will greatly multiply your pain in childbearing; in pain you shall bring forth children, yet your desire shall be for your husband, and he shall rule over you."

[17] And to Adam he said, "Because you have listened to the voice of your wife, and have eaten of the tree of which I commanded you, 'You shall not eat of it,' cursed is the ground because of you; in toil you shall eat of it all the days of your life;

[18] thorns and thistles it shall bring forth to you; and you shall eat the plants of the field.

[19] In the sweat of your face you shall eat bread till you return to the ground, for out of it you were taken; you are dust, and to dust you shall return."

[20] The man called his wife's name Eve, because she was the mother of all living.

[21] And the LORD God made for Adam and for his wife garments of skins, and clothed them.

[22] Then the LORD God said, "Behold, the man has become like one of us, knowing good and evil; and now, lest he put forth his hand and take also of the tree of life, and eat, and live for ever"—

[23] therefore the LORD God sent him forth from the garden of Eden, to till the ground from which he was taken.

[24] He drove out the man; and at the east of the garden of Eden he placed the cherubim, and a flaming sword which turned every way, to guard the way to the tree of life.

Chapter 4

[1] Now Adam knew Eve his wife, and she conceived and bore Cain, saying, "I have gotten a man with the help of the LORD."

[2] And again, she bore his brother Abel. Now Abel was a keeper of sheep, and Cain a tiller of the ground.

[3] In the course of time Cain brought to the LORD an offering of the fruit of the ground,

[4] and Abel brought of the firstlings of his flock and of their fat portions. And the LORD had regard for Abel and his offering,

[5] but for Cain and his offering he had no regard. So Cain was very angry, and his countenance fell.

[6] The LORD said to Cain, "Why are you angry, and why has your countenance fallen?

[7] If you do well, will you not be accepted? And if you do not do well, sin is couching at the door; its desire is for you, but you must master it."

[8] Cain said to Abel his brother, "Let us go out to the field." And when they were in the field, Cain rose up against his brother Abel, and killed him.

[9] Then the LORD said to Cain, "Where is Abel your brother?" He said, "I do not know; am I my brother's keeper?"

[10] And the LORD said, "What have you done? The voice of your brother's blood is crying to me from the ground.

[11] And now you are cursed from the ground, which has opened its mouth to receive your brother's blood from your hand.

[12] When you till the ground, it shall no longer yield to you its strength; you shall be a fugitive and a wanderer on the earth."

[13] Cain said to the LORD, "My punishment is greater than I can bear.

[14] Behold, thou hast driven me this day away from the ground; and from thy face I shall be hidden;

and I shall be a fugitive and a wanderer on the earth, and whoever finds me will slay me."

[15] Then the LORD said to him, "Not so! If any one slays Cain, vengeance shall be taken on him sevenfold." And the LORD put a mark on Cain, lest any who came upon him should kill him.

[16] Then Cain went away from the presence of the LORD, and dwelt in the land of Nod, east of Eden.

[17] Cain knew his wife, and she conceived and bore Enoch; and he built a city, and called the name of the city after the name of his son, Enoch.

[18] To Enoch was born Irad; and Irad was the father of Me-hu'ja-el, and Me-hu'ja-el the father of Me-thu'sha-el, and Me-thu'sha-el the father of Lamech.

[19] And Lamech took two wives; the name of the one was Adah, and the name of the other Zillah.

[20] Adah bore Jabal; he was the father of those who dwell in tents and have cattle.

[21] His brother's name was Jubal; he was the father of all those who play the lyre and pipe.

[22] Zillah bore Tubal-cain; he was the forger of all instruments of bronze and iron. The sister of Tubal-cain was Na'amah.

[23] Lamech said to his wives: "Adah and Zillah, hear my voice; you wives of Lamech, hearken to what I say: I have slain a man for wounding me, a young man for striking me.

[24] If Cain is avenged sevenfold, truly Lamech seventy-sevenfold."

[25] And Adam knew his wife again, and she bore a son and called his name Seth, for she said, "God has appointed for me another child instead of Abel, for Cain slew him."

[26] To Seth also a son was born, and he called his name Enosh. At that time men began to call upon the name of the LORD.

…

Chapter 6

[1] When men began to multiply on the face of the ground, and daughters were born to them,

[2] the sons of God saw that the daughters of men were fair; and they took to wife such of them as they chose.

[3] Then the LORD said, "My spirit shall not abide in man for ever, for he is flesh, but his days shall be a hundred and twenty years."

[4] The Nephilim were on the earth in those days, and also afterward, when the sons of God came in to the daughters of men, and they bore children to them. These were the mighty men that were of old, the men of renown.

[5] The LORD saw that the wickedness of man was great in the earth, and that every imagination of the thoughts of his heart was only evil continually.

[6] And the LORD was sorry that he had made man on the earth, and it grieved him to his heart.

[7] So the LORD said, "I will blot out man whom I have created from the face of the ground, man and beast and creeping things and birds of the air, for I am sorry that I have made them."

[8] But Noah found favor in the eyes of the LORD.

[9] These are the generations of Noah. Noah was a righteous man, blameless in his generation; Noah walked with God.

[10] And Noah had three sons, Shem, Ham, and Japheth.

[11] Now the earth was corrupt in God's sight, and the earth was filled with violence.

[12] And God saw the earth, and behold, it was corrupt; for all flesh had corrupted their way upon the earth.

[13] And God said to Noah, "I have determined to make an end of all flesh; for the earth is filled with violence through them; behold, I will destroy them with the earth.

[14] Make yourself an ark of gopher wood; make rooms in the ark, and cover it inside and out with pitch.

[15] This is how you are to make it: the length of the ark three hundred cubits, its breadth fifty cubits, and its height thirty cubits.

[16] Make a roof for the ark, and finish it to a cubit above; and set the door of the ark in its side; make it with lower, second, and third decks.

[17] For behold, I will bring a flood of waters upon the earth, to destroy all flesh in which is the breath of life from under heaven; everything that is on the earth shall die.

[18] But I will establish my covenant with you; and you shall come into the ark, you, your sons, your wife, and your sons' wives with you.

[19] And of every living thing of all flesh, you shall bring two of every sort into the ark, to keep them alive with you; they shall be male and female.

[20] Of the birds according to their kinds, and of the animals according to their kinds, of every creeping thing of the ground according to its kind, two of every sort shall come in to you, to keep them alive.

[21] Also take with you every sort of food that is eaten, and store it up; and it shall serve as food for you and for them."

[22] Noah did this; he did all that God commanded him.

Chapter 7

[1] Then the LORD said to Noah, "Go into the ark, you and all your household, for I have seen that you are righteous before me in this generation.

[2] Take with you seven pairs of all clean animals, the male and his mate; and a pair of the animals that are not clean, the male and his mate;

[3] and seven pairs of the birds of the air also, male and female, to keep their kind alive upon the face of all the earth.

[4] For in seven days I will send rain upon the earth forty days and forty nights; and every living thing that I have made I will blot out from the face of the ground."

[5] And Noah did all that the LORD had commanded him.

[6] Noah was six hundred years old when the flood of waters came upon the earth.

[7] And Noah and his sons and his wife and his sons' wives with him went into the ark, to escape the waters of the flood.

[8] Of clean animals, and of animals that are not clean, and of birds, and of everything that creeps on the ground,

[9] two and two, male and female, went into the ark with Noah, as God had commanded Noah.

[10] And after seven days the waters of the flood came upon the earth.

[11] In the six hundredth year of Noah's life, in the second month, on the seventeenth day of the month, on that day all the fountains of the great deep burst forth, and the windows of the heavens were opened.

[12] And rain fell upon the earth forty days and forty nights.

[13] On the very same day Noah and his sons, Shem and Ham and Japheth, and Noah's wife and the three wives of his sons with them entered the ark,

[14] they and every beast according to its kind, and all the cattle according to their kinds, and every creeping thing that creeps on the earth according to its kind, and every bird according to its kind, every bird of every sort.

[15] They went into the ark with Noah, two and two of all flesh in which there was the breath of life.

[16] And they that entered, male and female of all flesh, went in as God had commanded him; and the LORD shut him in.

[17] The flood continued forty days upon the earth; and the waters increased, and bore up the ark, and it rose high above the earth.

[18] The waters prevailed and increased greatly upon the earth; and the ark floated on the face of the waters.

[19] And the waters prevailed so mightily upon the earth that all the high mountains under the whole heaven were covered;

[20] the waters prevailed above the mountains, covering them fifteen cubits deep.

[21] And all flesh died that moved upon the earth, birds, cattle, beasts, all swarming creatures that swarm upon the earth, and every man;

[22] everything on the dry land in whose nostrils was the breath of life died.

[23] He blotted out every living thing that was upon the face of the ground, man and animals and creeping things and birds of the air; they were blotted out from the earth. Only Noah was left, and those that were with him in the ark.

[24] And the waters prevailed upon the earth a hundred and fifty days.

Chapter 8

[1] But God remembered Noah and all the beasts and all the cattle that were with him in the ark. And God made a wind blow over the earth, and the waters subsided;

[2] the fountains of the deep and the windows of the heavens were closed, the rain from the heavens was restrained,

[3] and the waters receded from the earth continually. At the end of a hundred and fifty days the waters had abated;

[4] and in the seventh month, on the seventeenth day of the month, the ark came to rest upon the mountains of Ar'arat.

[5] And the waters continued to abate until the tenth month; in the tenth month, on the first day of the month, the tops of the mountains were seen.

[6] At the end of forty days Noah opened the window of the ark which he had made,

[7] and sent forth a raven; and it went to and fro until the waters were dried up from the earth.

[8] Then he sent forth a dove from him, to see if the waters had subsided from the face of the ground;

[9] but the dove found no place to set her foot, and she returned to him to the ark, for the waters were still on the face of the whole earth. So he put forth

his hand and took her and brought her into the ark with him.

[10] He waited another seven days, and again he sent forth the dove out of the ark;

[11] and the dove came back to him in the evening, and lo, in her mouth a freshly plucked olive leaf; so Noah knew that the waters had subsided from the earth.

[12] Then he waited another seven days, and sent forth the dove; and she did not return to him any more.

[13] In the six hundred and first year, in the first month, the first day of the month, the waters were dried from off the earth; and Noah removed the covering of the ark, and looked, and behold, the face of the ground was dry.

[14] In the second month, on the twenty-seventh day of the month, the earth was dry.

[15] Then God said to Noah,

[16] "Go forth from the ark, you and your wife, and your sons and your sons' wives with you.

[17] Bring forth with you every living thing that is with you of all flesh—birds and animals and every creeping thing that creeps on the earth—that they may breed abundantly on the earth, and be fruitful and multiply upon the earth."

[18] So Noah went forth, and his sons and his wife and his sons' wives with him.

[19] And every beast, every creeping thing, and every bird, everything that moves upon the earth, went forth by families out of the ark.

[20] Then Noah built an altar to the LORD, and took of every clean animal and of every clean bird, and offered burnt offerings on the altar.

[21] And when the LORD smelled the pleasing odor, the LORD said in his heart, "I will never again curse the ground because of man, for the imagination of man's heart is evil from his youth; neither will I ever again destroy every living creature as I have done.

[22] While the earth remains, seedtime and harvest, cold and heat, summer and winter, day and night, shall not cease."

. . .

Chapter 12

[1] Now the LORD said to Abram, "Go from your country and your kindred and your father's house to the land that I will show you.

[2] And I will make of you a great nation, and I will bless you, and make your name great, so that you will be a blessing.

[3] I will bless those who bless you, and him who curses you I will curse; and by you all the families of the earth shall bless themselves."

[4] So Abram went, as the LORD had told him; and Lot went with him. Abram was seventy-five years old when he departed from Haran.

[5] And Abram took Sar'ai his wife, and Lot his brother's son, and all their possessions which they had gathered, and the persons that they had gotten in Haran; and they set forth to go to the land of Canaan. When they had come to the land of Canaan,

[6] Abram passed through the land to the place at Shechem, to the oak of Moreh. At that time the Canaanites were in the land.

[7] Then the LORD appeared to Abram, and said, "To your descendants I will give this land." So he built there an altar to the LORD, who had appeared to him.

[8] Thence he removed to the mountain on the east of Bethel, and pitched his tent, with Bethel on the west and Ai on the east; and there he built an altar to the LORD and called on the name of the LORD.

[9] And Abram journeyed on, still going toward the Negeb.

[10] Now there was a famine in the land. So Abram went down to Egypt to sojourn there, for the famine was severe in the land.

[11] When he was about to enter Egypt, he said to Sar'ai his wife, "I know that you are a woman beautiful to behold;

[12] and when the Egyptians see you, they will say, 'This is his wife'; then they will kill me, but they will let you live.

[13] Say you are my sister, that it may go well with me because of you, and that my life may be spared on your account."

[14] When Abram entered Egypt the Egyptians saw that the woman was very beautiful.

[15] And when the princes of Pharaoh saw her, they praised her to Pharaoh. And the woman was taken into Pharaoh's house.

[16] And for her sake he dealt well with Abram; and he had sheep, oxen, he-asses, menservants, maidservants, she-asses, and camels.

[17] But the LORD afflicted Pharaoh and his house with great plagues because of Sar'ai, Abram's wife.

[18] So Pharaoh called Abram, and said, "What is this you have done to me? Why did you not tell me that she was your wife?

[19] Why did you say, 'She is my sister,' so that I took her for my wife? Now then, here is your wife, take her, and be gone."

[20] And Pharaoh gave men orders concerning him; and they set him on the way, with his wife and all that he had.

. . .

Chapter 14

[1] In the days of Am'raphel king of Shinar, Ar'ioch king of Ella'sar, Ched-or-lao'mer king of Elam, and Tidal king of Goi'im,

[2] these kings made war with Bera king of Sodom, Birsha king of Gomor'rah, Shinab king of Admah, Sheme'ber king of Zeboi'im, and the king of Bela (that is, Zo'ar).

[3] And all these joined forces in the Valley of Siddim (that is, the Salt Sea).

[4] Twelve years they had served Ched-or-lao'mer, but in the thirteenth year they rebelled.

[5] In the fourteenth year Ched-or-lao'mer and the kings who were with him came and subdued the Reph'aim in Ash'teroth-karna'im, the Zuzim in Ham, the Emim in Sha'veh-kiriatha'im,

[6] and the Horites in their Mount Se'ir as far as El-paran on the border of the wilderness;

[7] then they turned back and came to Enmish'pat (that is, Kadesh), and subdued all the country of the Amal'ekites, and also the Amorites who dwelt in Haz'azon-ta'mar.

[8] Then the king of Sodom, the king of Gomor'rah, the king of Admah, the king of Zeboi'im, and the king of Bela (that is, Zo'ar) went out, and they joined battle in the Valley of Siddim

[9] with Ched-or-lao'mer king of Elam, Tidal king of Goi'im, Am'raphel king of Shinar, and Ar'ioch king of Ella'sar, four kings against five.

[10] Now the Valley of Siddim was full of bitumen pits; and as the kings of Sodom and Gomor'rah fled, some fell into them, and the rest fled to the mountain.

[11] So the enemy took all the goods of Sodom and Gomor'rah, and all their provisions, and went their way;

[12] they also took Lot, the son of Abram's brother, who dwelt in Sodom, and his goods, and departed.

[13] Then one who had escaped came, and told Abram the Hebrew, who was living by the oaks of Mamre the Amorite, brother of Eshcol and of Aner; these were allies of Abram.

[14] When Abram heard that his kinsman had been taken captive, he led forth his trained men, born in his house, three hundred and eighteen of them, and went in pursuit as far as Dan.

[15] And he divided his forces against them by night, he and his servants, and routed them and pursued them to Hobah, north of Damascus.

[16] Then he brought back all the goods, and also brought back his kinsman Lot with his goods, and the women and the people.

[17] After his return from the defeat of Ched-or-lao'mer and the kings who were with him, the king of Sodom went out to meet him at the Valley of Shaveh (that is, the King's Valley).

[18] And Mel-chiz'edek king of Salem brought out bread and wine; he was priest of God Most High.

[19] And he blessed him and said, "Blessed be Abram by God Most High, maker of heaven and earth;

[20] and blessed be God Most High, who has delivered your enemies into your hand!"

[21] And the king of Sodom said to Abram, "Give me the persons, but take the goods for yourself."

[22] But Abram said to the king of Sodom, "I have sworn to the LORD God Most High, maker of heaven and earth,

[23] that I would not take a thread or a sandal-thong or anything that is yours, lest you should say, 'I have made Abram rich.'

[24] I will take nothing but what the young men have eaten, and the share of the men who went with me; let Aner, Eshcol, and Mamre take their share."

Chapter 15

[1] After these things the word of the LORD came to Abram in a vision, "Fear not, Abram, I am your shield; your reward shall be very great."

[2] But Abram said, "O Lord GOD, what wilt thou give me, for I continue childless, and the heir of my house is Elie'zer of Damascus?"

[3] And Abram said, "Behold, thou hast given me no offspring; and a slave born in my house will be my heir."

[4] And behold, the word of the LORD came to him, "This man shall not be your heir; your own son shall be your heir."

[5] And he brought him outside and said, "Look toward heaven, and number the stars, if you are able to number them." Then he said to him, "So shall your descendants be."

[6] And he believed the LORD; and he reckoned it to him as righteousness.

[7] And he said to him, "I am the LORD who brought you from Ur of the Chalde'ans, to give you this land to possess."

[8] But he said, "O Lord GOD, how am I to know that I shall possess it?"

[9] He said to him, "Bring me a heifer three years old, a she-goat three years old, a ram three years old, a turtledove, and a young pigeon."

[10] And he brought him all these, cut them in two, and laid each half over against the other; but he did not cut the birds in two.

[11] And when birds of prey came down upon the carcasses, Abram drove them away.

[12] As the sun was going down, a deep sleep fell on Abram; and lo, a dread and great darkness fell upon him.

[13] Then the LORD said to Abram, "Know of a surety that your descendants will be sojourners in a land that is not theirs, and will be slaves there, and they will be oppressed for four hundred years;

[14] but I will bring judgment on the nation which they serve, and afterward they shall come out with great possessions.

[15] As for yourself, you shall go to your fathers in peace; you shall be buried in a good old age.

[16] And they shall come back here in the fourth generation; for the iniquity of the Amorites is not yet complete."

[17] When the sun had gone down and it was dark, behold, a smoking fire pot and a flaming torch passed between these pieces.

[18] On that day the LORD made a covenant with Abram, saying, "To your descendants I give this land, from the river of Egypt to the great river, the river Euphra'tes,

[19] the land of the Ken'ites, the Ken'izzites, the Kad'monites,

[20] the Hittites, the Per'izzites, the Reph'aim,

[21] the Amorites, the Canaanites, the Gir'gashites and the Jeb'usites."

Chapter 16

[1] Now Sar'ai, Abram's wife, bore him no children. She had an Egyptian maid whose name was Hagar;

[2] and Sar'ai said to Abram, "Behold now, the LORD has prevented me from bearing children; go in to my maid; it may be that I shall obtain children by her." And Abram hearkened to the voice of Sar'ai.

[3] So, after Abram had dwelt ten years in the land of Canaan, Sar'ai, Abram's wife, took Hagar the Egyptian, her maid, and gave her to Abram her husband as a wife.

[4] And he went in to Hagar, and she conceived; and when she saw that she had conceived, she looked with contempt on her mistress.

[5] And Sar'ai said to Abram, "May the wrong done to me be on you! I gave my maid to your embrace, and when she saw that she had conceived, she looked on me with contempt. May the LORD judge between you and me!"

[6] But Abram said to Sar'ai, "Behold, your maid is in your power; do to her as you please." Then Sar'ai dealt harshly with her, and she fled from her.

[7] The angel of the LORD found her by a spring of water in the wilderness, the spring on the way to Shur.

[8] And he said, "Hagar, maid of Sar'ai, where have you come from and where are you going?" She said, "I am fleeing from my mistress Sar'ai."

[9] The angel of the LORD said to her, "Return to your mistress, and submit to her."

[10] The angel of the LORD also said to her, "I will so greatly multiply your descendants that they cannot be numbered for multitude."

[11] And the angel of the LORD said to her, "Behold, you are with child, and shall bear a son; you shall call his name Ish'mael; because the LORD has given heed to your affliction.

[12] He shall be a wild ass of a man, his hand against every man and every man's hand against him; and he shall dwell over against all his kinsmen."

[13] So she called the name of the LORD who spoke to her, "Thou art a God of seeing"; for she said, "Have I really seen God and remained alive after seeing him?"

[14] Therefore the well was called Beer-la'hai-roi; it lies between Kadesh and Bered.

[15] And Hagar bore Abram a son; and Abram called the name of his son, whom Hagar bore, Ish'mael.

[16] Abram was eighty-six years old when Hagar bore Ish'mael to Abram.

Chapter 17

[1] When Abram was ninety-nine years old the LORD appeared to Abram, and said to him, "I am God Almighty; walk before me, and be blameless.

[2] And I will make my covenant between me and you, and will multiply you exceedingly."

[3] Then Abram fell on his face; and God said to him,

[4] "Behold, my covenant is with you, and you shall be the father of a multitude of nations.

[5] No longer shall your name be Abram, but your name shall be Abraham; for I have made you the father of a multitude of nations.

[6] I will make you exceedingly fruitful; and I will make nations of you, and kings shall come forth from you.

[7] And I will establish my covenant between me and you and your descendants after you throughout their generations for an everlasting covenant, to be God to you and to your descendants after you.

[8] And I will give to you, and to your descendants after you, the land of your sojournings, all the land of Canaan, for an everlasting possession; and I will be their God."

[9] And God said to Abraham, "As for you, you shall keep my covenant, you and your descendants after you throughout their generations.

[10] This is my covenant, which you shall keep, between me and you and your descendants after you: Every male among you shall be circumcised.

[11] You shall be circumcised in the flesh of your foreskins, and it shall be a sign of the covenant between me and you.

[12] He that is eight days old among you shall be circumcised; every male throughout your generations, whether born in your house, or bought with your money from any foreigner who is not of your offspring,

[13] both he that is born in your house and he that is bought with your money, shall be circumcised. So shall my covenant be in your flesh an everlasting covenant.

[14] Any uncircumcised male who is not circumcised in the flesh of his foreskin shall be cut off from his people; he has broken my covenant."

[15] And God said to Abraham, "As for Sar'ai your wife, you shall not call her name Sar'ai, but Sarah shall be her name.

[16] I will bless her, and moreover I will give you a son by her; I will bless her, and she shall be a mother of nations; kings of peoples shall come from her."

[17] Then Abraham fell on his face and laughed, and said to himself, "Shall a child be born to a man who is a hundred years old? Shall Sarah, who is ninety years old, bear a child?"

[18] And Abraham said to God, "O that Ish'mael might live in thy sight!"

[19] God said, "No, but Sarah your wife shall bear you a son, and you shall call his name Isaac. I will establish my covenant with him as an everlasting covenant for his descendants after him.

[20] As for Ish'mael, I have heard you; behold, I will bless him and make him fruitful and multiply him exceedingly; he shall be the father of twelve princes, and I will make him a great nation.

[21] But I will establish my covenant with Isaac, whom Sarah shall bear to you at this season next year."

[22] When he had finished talking with him, God went up from Abraham.

[23] Then Abraham took Ish'mael his son and all the slaves born in his house or bought with his money, every male among the men of Abraham's house, and he circumcised the flesh of their foreskins that very day, as God had said to him.

[24] Abraham was ninety-nine years old when he was circumcised in the flesh of his foreskin.

[25] And Ish'mael his son was thirteen years old when he was circumcised in the flesh of his foreskin.

[26] That very day Abraham and his son Ish'mael were circumcised;

[27] and all the men of his house, those born in the house and those bought with money from a foreigner, were circumcised with him.

. . .

Chapter 22

[1] After these things God tested Abraham, and said to him, "Abraham!" And he said, "Here am I."

[2] He said, "Take your son, your only son Isaac, whom you love, and go to the land of Mori'ah, and offer him there as a burnt offering upon one of the mountains of which I shall tell you."

[3] So Abraham rose early in the morning, saddled his ass, and took two of his young men with him, and his son Isaac; and he cut the wood for the burnt offering, and arose and went to the place of which God had told him.

[4] On the third day Abraham lifted up his eyes and saw the place afar off.

[5] Then Abraham said to his young men, "Stay here with the ass; I and the lad will go yonder and worship, and come again to you."

[6] And Abraham took the wood of the burnt offering, and laid it on Isaac his son; and he took in his hand the fire and the knife. So they went both of them together.

[7] And Isaac said to his father Abraham, "My father!" And he said, "Here am I, my son." He said, "Behold, the fire and the wood; but where is the lamb for a burnt offering?"

[8] Abraham said, "God will provide himself the lamb for a burnt offering, my son." So they went both of them together.

[9] When they came to the place of which God had told him, Abraham built an altar there, and laid the wood in order, and bound Isaac his son, and laid him on the altar, upon the wood.

[10] Then Abraham put forth his hand, and took the knife to slay his son.

[11] But the angel of the LORD called to him from heaven, and said, "Abraham, Abraham!" And he said, "Here am I."

[12] He said, "Do not lay your hand on the lad or do anything to him; for now I know that you fear God, seeing you have not withheld your son, your only son, from me."

[13] And Abraham lifted up his eyes and looked, and behold, behind him was a ram, caught in a thicket by his horns; and Abraham went and took the ram, and offered it up as a burnt offering instead of his son.

[14] So Abraham called the name of that place The LORD will provide; as it is said to this day, "On the mount of the LORD it shall be provided."

[15] And the angel of the LORD called to Abraham a second time from heaven,

[16] and said, "By myself I have sworn, says the LORD, because you have done this, and have not withheld your son, your only son,

[17] I will indeed bless you, and I will multiply your descendants as the stars of heaven and as the sand which is on the seashore. And your descendants shall possess the gate of their enemies,

[18] and by your descendants shall all the nations of the earth bless themselves, because you have obeyed my voice."

[19] So Abraham returned to his young men, and they arose and went together to Beer-sheba; and Abraham dwelt at Beer-sheba.

[20] Now after these things it was told Abraham, "Behold, Milcah also has borne children to your brother Nahor:

[21] Uz the first-born, Buz his brother, Kemu'el the father of Aram,

[22] Chesed, Hazo, Pildash, Jidlaph, and Bethu'el."

[23] Bethu'el became the father of Rebekah. These eight Milcah bore to Nahor, Abraham's brother.

[24] Moreover, his concubine, whose name was Reumah, bore Tebah, Gaham, Tahash, and Ma'acah.

Glossary

Cush	possibly Ethiopia
Gihon	literally, "bursting forth, gushing"
Havilah	literally, "stretch of sand," used in the Old Testament to refer to various lands
land of Canaan	a region roughly commensurate with modern-day Israel and surrounding territories
Moreh	variously identified as a tree, a grove, or a plain
mountains of Ar'arat	mountains located in modern-day Turkey
Pishon	a river variously identified as the Nile, the Indus, the Ganges, and other rivers
Sar'ai	generally spelled "Sarah"
Shechem	the first capital of the Kingdom of Israel
Ur	a city in ancient Sumer

Scene of Akhenaten worshipping Aten

(Scene of Akhenaten worshipping the Aten [painted limestone], Egyptian 18th Dynasty [c.1567-1320 BC] / Egyptian National Museum, Cairo, Egypt / Ancient Art and Architecture Collection Ltd. / The Bridgeman Art Library International)

"GREAT HYMN TO THE ATEN"

ca. 1348 BCE

"Beautifully you appear from the horizon of heaven,

O living Aten who initiates life."

Overview

The "Great Hymn to the Aten" is one of the most important texts from the Egyptian Eighteenth Dynasty (ca. 1550–1295 BCE). It offers insight into the revolution of the "heretic pharaoh" Akhenaten (ca. 1352–1336 BCE). Based in part on the "Great Hymn," many scholars have argued that the king's faith was a form of monotheism, or belief in only one god. Although this characterization may be too simplistic, the text does focus on a single deity, the Aten or "Solar Orb." The "Great Hymn" consists of thirteen columns of damaged hieroglyphic text in the entrance of the tomb of Ay (the penultimate pharaoh of the Eighteenth Dynasty) at Amarna, in middle Upper Egypt. The document certainly predates Akhenaten's tumultuous ninth regnal year, when he orchestrated large-scale revisions to remove written references to certain gods, for it uses the early didactic form of the Aten's name.

Context

Located in northeastern Africa and bordering the Mediterranean Sea, Egypt is the site of one of the ancient world's earliest civilizations. The Nile, the longest river in the world, runs northward through Egypt and into the Mediterranean Sea. Because of the northerly flow of the river, the Nile Delta region—located in the northern part of Egypt—is known as Lower Egypt; the valley region in the south is known as Upper Egypt.

Egypt's Eighteenth Dynasty emerged from the strife that erupted at the end of the Second Intermediate Period (ca. 1650–1550 BCE). Semitic immigrants called the Hyksos—a name derived from the Egyptian expression *heqau khasut*, meaning "rulers of foreign lands"—gained control of the Nile Delta and projected their influence up the river valley. Theban princes of the Seventeenth Dynasty (ca. 1580–1550 BCE) rose to challenge them from Upper Egypt, and a series of fierce battles ensued. Under Ahmose (ca. 1550–1525 BCE), a scion of the Seventeenth Dynasty and the founder of the Eighteenth Dynasty, the Thebans sacked

the Hyksos stronghold of Avaris, in the delta region near the Mediterranean coast. The Thebans pursued the Hyksos refugees eastward toward Canaan (roughly modern-day Palestine), massacring them at Sharuhen, in southern Canaan.

The victorious Eighteenth Dynasty viewed the Hyksos ascendancy as a period of foreign oppression and sought to improve national security by "extending the boundaries of Egypt," which effectively became a motto. Especially noteworthy in this respect is Thutmose III (ca. 1479–1425 BCE), who campaigned seventeen times in the Near East. As a result of such adventures, later pharaohs ruled an empire that included Egypt, Nubia, and vassal territories in Canaan and Syria. They also inherited diplomatic ties with other great powers, including Mitanni, Babylon, and the Hittites.

Egyptian empire-building led to a new cosmopolitan spirit. Simply put, kings were now too involved in the wider world to pursue a traditional policy of isolationism. They still may have viewed outsiders with contempt and apprehension, but they had to receive foreign envoys at their palaces and take foreign princesses into their harems. With these political obligations went economic and cultural exchange, such that exotic merchandise and strange customs—including the worship of foreign gods like Baal and Astarte and foreign artistic motifs like the running spiral—flowed into the Nile Valley as never before. The Thebans had, in effect, butchered the Hyksos at Sharuhen, only to cohabit, barter, and worship with their confederates.

Cosmopolitanism in turn sparked reflections on the nature of the divine. Without renouncing their old polytheism (belief in many gods), the Egyptians began thinking about a more universal type of supernatural being. Moreover, they evolved a new conception of the solar creator, Re, as a deity who acts alone, rather than in concert with others. Finally, the Egyptians started to focus on the sun god's visible journey across the sky and his generation of life and time. The German Egyptologist Jan Assmann has labeled the latter two trends "the New Solar Theology."

The hymn of the brothers Suti and Hor illustrates these new ideas. Dating to the first half of the fourteenth century BCE, it glorifies Amen, the creator god of Thebes, as he appears in various solar guises. (The Egyptians were not at all averse to combining divinities in this way.) The hymn triumphantly proclaims that Amen, as the Aten—both deity and

CA. 1650 BCE	■ The Hyksos ascendancy begins in the Nile Delta.
CA. 1560 BCE	■ Strife erupts between the Hyksos and Theban princes.
CA. 1530 BCE	■ Ahmose, the founder of the Eighteenth Dynasty, sacks the Hyksos capital at Avaris and pursues the Hyksos into Canaan; Egyptian imperialism begins.
CA. 1458 BCE	■ Thutmose III fights the first of his seventeen campaigns in the Near East.
CA. 1400 BCE	■ Thutmose IV restores the Great Sphinx at Giza.
CA. 1390 BCE	■ Amenhotep III assumes the throne.
CA. 1360 BCE	■ Amenhotep III celebrates the first of his three Sed Festivals.
CA. 1352 BCE	■ Amenhotep IV assumes the throne. (The following dates are especially provisional, given the possibility of a coregency with Amenhotep III.)
CA. 1349 BCE	■ Amenhotep IV changes his name to Akhenaten, meaning "Effective for the Solar Orb," and starts building a new residence at Amarna; there, he worships the Aten, sponsors a naturalistic style of art, and vernacularizes official writing.
CA. 1348 BCE	■ The "Great Hymn" is composed, most likely by Akhenaten or Ay.
CA. 1344 BCE	■ Akhenaten launches a persecution of traditional gods, most notably Amen.
CA. 1341 BCE	■ Akhenaten celebrates a durbar at Amarna, attended by diplomats from the Near East and Africa.
CA. 1336 BCE	■ Akhenaten dies.

orb—captures and encompasses foreign lands. It does not refer to any nonsolar deities except one, the sky goddess Nut. In addition, it emphasizes the sun's rays and their life-giving energy, declaring that the god's unseen aspects—his self-creation and his character—are mysterious and unknown.

Before turning to the reign of Akhenaten, two other developments are worth mentioning. The Eighteenth Dynasty's military campaigns resulted in plunder, a good deal of which went directly to Amen's cult. By the fourteenth century BCE, Amen's priests may have acquired so much power that they became a threat to royal authority. Also significant is the Eighteenth Dynasty's antiquarian focus—its effort to revitalize the culture of the distant past. Thutmose IV (ca. 1400–1390 BCE), for example, restored the Great Sphinx at Giza in Lower Egypt, while Akhenaten's father, Amenhotep III (ca. 1390–1352 BCE), researched the Sed Festival, an ancient rite of rejuvenation intended for a king's thirtieth regnal year. (Contrary to custom, however, Amenhotep III celebrated a total of three Sed Festivals.)

There were thus several intriguing developments, but no major crises, when Amenhotep IV assumed the throne around 1352 BCE. (Egyptologists are divided over whether Amenhotep III was still alive at this point and participating in a coregency.) In his fourth regnal year, however, the new pharaoh, together with his wife, Queen Nefertiti, began a revolution. Changing his name to Akhenaten, which means "Effective for the Solar Orb," he built a new residence at the barren site of Amarna, about two hundred miles north of Thebes on the eastern bank of the Nile River. There, in open-roofed temples, he mixed contemporary theology with titles and symbols from the old sun cult of Heliopolis and worshiped the Aten. He also patronized a flowing, naturalistic style of art and allowed vernacular words into official documents, initiating the literary transition from Middle to Late Egyptian. (Middle Egyptian did not employ definite articles like *pa*, for example, and scribes tended to regard their use as inelegant, but Late Egyptian did include them.)

Akhenaten took another major step during his ninth regnal year, ordering the names of traditional gods, most notably Amen, hacked out of inscriptions. Some deities, like Ptah and Osiris, were spared the chisel and simply ignored. This persecution doubtless angered conservative elements in Egyptian society, but it does not seem to have affected popular religion.

In his twelfth regnal year, Akhenaten held a durbar, or reception, at Amarna. Envoys from throughout the Near East and Africa attended the event, but what they celebrated is today uncertain. The British Egyptologist Cyril Aldred believed that Akhenaten's durbar marked the beginning of his sole rule, following the death of his father, Amenhotep III.

Unfortunately, modern scholars have little information about the end of Akhenaten's reign. The defeat of Egypt's closest ally, the Kingdom of Mitanni (in modern-day Syria), by the Hittites of central Anatolia (present-day Turkey), together with the squabbling of vassal princes in Canaan and Syria, may have exacerbated domestic tensions caused by the persecution of Amen and other traditional gods. Recent scholarship suggests that Nefertiti became Akhenaten's coregent before his death in his seventeenth regnal year.

Amarna, on the bank of the Nile (Bank of the Nile [photo], / Tell el-Amarna, Egypt / The Bridgeman Art Library International)

Almost nothing is known about the successor Smenkhkare (ca. 1338–1336 BCE), except for the fact that he married the eldest of the king's six daughters, Meritaten.

About the Author

The "Great Hymn" does not have a byline or an inscriber's mark, so we cannot be sure about its authorship. Nonetheless, a reasonable theory is that Akhenaten himself composed it. Akhenaten was the son of King Amenhotep III and Queen Tiyi. He had an older brother, Thutmose V, and only became crown prince after this sibling died. Scholars have speculated that Akhenaten was introduced to sun worship by his maternal uncle, Anen, who served as a priest at Heliopolis, the "City of the Sun," in Lower Egypt. Based on the king's curious, elongated portraits, some scholars have also argued that he suffered from a disease that affected his growth, such as Fröhlich's syndrome or Marfan's syndrome. Neither hypothesis has been proved, however, and the latter seems exceedingly hypothetical given the absence of Akhenaten's mummy from the archaeological record. It is important to remember that Egyptian art was never intended to look "realistic" and therefore should not be used as a basis for medical diagnoses.

One thing that can be said with confidence is that Akhenaten disliked traditional religion from the outset of his reign. He gives the reason in an early speech that is partly preserved on two *talatat*. (*Talatat* are Akhenaten's distinctive 27-by-27-by-54-centimeter stone blocks, which are relatively small and easy to handle.) The king states that he has studied sacred writings and has learned that cult statues—the "bodies" of the gods—fall to ruin, no matter what costly materials go into their construction. He declares that the single exception to this rule is the heavenly vessel of the mysterious solar creator.

Akhenaten's speech is significant because it contains the germ of his later thought. The king's temples at Amarna did not have roofs or cult statues, for he believed that the one true divine body was the sun itself. Indeed, in relief carving and hieroglyphic writing, Akhenaten eventually discarded all of the old images of the gods, depicting only the Solar Orb, with its rays ending in hands holding the symbols for life (*ankhs,* or looped crosses) and dominion (*waset* scepters). As far as the authorship of the "Great Hymn" is concerned, another possibility is that the tomb owner, Ay, wrote it. A likeness of Ay, who himself became a pharaoh, was found near the text of the "Great Hymn."

Explanation and Analysis of the Document

The "Great Hymn" is accompanied by the kneeling figures of Ay and his wife, Tiyi (not to be confused with Akhenaten's mother), as well as a list of their titles. Among other duties, Ay served as cavalry commander and "God's

"Beautifully you appear from the horizon of heaven, O living Aten who initiates life."

"For you are risen from the eastern horizon and have filled every land with your beauty; / For you are fair, great, dazzling and high over every land, / And your rays enclose the lands to the limit of all you have made; / For you are Re, having reached their limit and subdued them your beloved son."

"How manifold it is, what you have made, although mysterious in the face (of humanity), / O sole god, without another beside him!"

"You make millions of developments from yourself, (you who are) a oneness: cities, towns, fields, the path of the river."

"You are in my heart, and there is none who knows you except your son, NEFERKHEPRURE-WAENRE, / For you make him aware of your plans and your strength. / The land develops through your action, just as you made them (= people): / When you have risen they live, (but) when you set they die. You are lifetime in your (very) limbs, and one lives by means of you."

Father"—that is, the tutor of princes. Bracketed wording in the document text denotes restored text, while parentheses contain explanatory material.

♦ Introduction and Stanzas 1 and 2

The introduction and first two stanzas of the "Great Hymn" hail the Aten and the royal couple and summarize the god's role in maintaining the cosmos. Names originally in cartouches (oval rings that denote sovereignty) are rendered here in capital letters.

HOR-ATEN is an abbreviation of the Aten's early didactic name, "The Living One, Sun (Re), Horus of the Horizon (Harakhty) who Becomes Excited in the Horizon, in His Name which is Light (Shu) that is in the Solar Orb." Note that the god's cartouches and titles identify him as the ruler of the world as well as the Lord of Akhet-Aten, the "Horizon of the Solar Orb" (Amarna). Also note that his early didactic name alludes to three other deities—Re, Harakhty, and Shu—and that it specifies *light* as the proper object of veneration. As such, the usual state-

ment that Akhenaten exclusively worshiped the Aten is not quite correct.

NEFERKHEPRURE-WAENRE, "Perfect are the Forms of the Sun (Re)—The Only One of the Sun (Re)," is Akhenaten's throne name. Among the king's epithets, "(he) who lives on Maat" is the most obscure. *Maat* means at once "truth," "justice," and "order." (Before the persecution, it was embodied in a goddess wearing an ostrich feather in her hair.) The title thus implies that Akhenaten offers his followers a uniquely valid religious system. The "Two Lands" are Upper and Lower Egypt. NEFERNEFRUATEN-NEFERTITI, "Perfect is the Beauty of the Solar Orb—The Beautiful One is Come," is Nefertiti's full name.

Stanzas 1 and 2 reveal that the Aten is primarily a life god. When he rises, the world lives; when he sets, darkness, danger, and death prevail. Significantly, stanza 1 echoes the imperialism and universalism of the hymn of Suti and Hor, declaring that the Aten envelops and subdues all lands. It also mentions the god's far-near paradox. He is distant, but his rays are on earth.

♦ **Stanzas 3 and 4**

This section of the "Great Hymn" describes a typical day in the Aten's cosmos. The god's rising signals a festival of light. Humanity goes to work, flocks set off to pasture, grasses sway in the breeze, birds soar from their nests, and fish leap about in the Nile. The Aten's rays even penetrate the depths of the "Great Green" (the Mediterranean and Red seas). Every morning thus sees a dance of gratitude, the wings of birds adoring the divine *ka*, or "essence."

The Aten does not merely invigorate the world, however; he also creates it. The god forms fetuses in women, causes blood to flow, and provides the breath of life. (The expression "descends from the womb" refers to the Egyptian custom of giving birth while squatting or seated on a stool.) Acting as a time god, the Aten fixes the very day on which the chick emerges from the egg.

♦ **Stanzas 5 and 6**

Next, the "Great Hymn" celebrates the diversity of the Aten's creation. Alone, the mysterious god separates Egypt from Kharu (Syria) and Kush (Upper Nubia) and distinguishes every human from his fellow. He sets life spans and differentiates nations. While the Aten provides Egypt with a river that springs from the underworld, he gives foreign lands "an inundation in heaven"—rainfall.

The preceding reference to the underworld betrays Akhenaten's contempt for traditional funerary religion. Where others imagined the abode of Osiris, the god of the underworld, and of the blessed dead, the king saw only the source of the Nile. Such naturalistic thinking probably influenced Akhenaten's decision to cut tombs in the eastern cliffs and bluffs at Amarna, over which the sun rises, rather than in the west, the old gateway to the Osiran realm.

Stanza 6 describes the Aten's plans as effective and calls him the "lord of continuity (*heh*)." The word *heh* denotes an endless cycle of events, so the mention of recurring natural phenomena—floods, sunrises, and seasons—is logical.

♦ **Stanza 7**

Stanza 7 is arguably the most important part of the "Great Hymn." After reiterating the Aten's far-near paradox, it proclaims, "You make millions of developments (*kheperu*) from yourself, (you who are) a oneness: cities, towns, fields, the path of the river." Interestingly, the word *kheperu*, here written with the upright mummy sign, also designates cult statues. The verse's implication seems to be that the Aten fashions the world from himself and that his creatures replace the traditional images in temples. The "Great Hymn" thus diverges from the typically monotheistic idea—present in Judaism, Christianity, and Islam—that God created the world out of nothing, and stood apart from it. Indeed, the text seems more representative of pantheism (literally, "all-god-ism"), the belief that a divine principle—in this case, sunlight—permeates nature.

♦ **Stanza 8**

The "Great Hymn" concludes with a declaration that the Aten abides in the hymnist's heart and that his only son and prophet is Akhenaten. Until this point, the god has seemed impersonal and mute, but now he explicitly consoles the believer and communicates with an earthly representative. Finally, the "Great Hymn" reemphasizes the Aten's role as a life and time god, and says that he acts for the sake of the king and queen.

Audience

It is difficult to determine the audience of the "Great Hymn," the present version of which comes from a burial site. The extant text was obviously intended for the deceased Ay and Tiyi, for when they went forth to bask in the Aten's radiance at dawn. This assumption seems logical in light of Akhenaten's conception of the afterlife, which was austere in that he removed the elaborate Osiran elements. There is, however, no reason that the "Great Hymn" could not have been disseminated—wholly or in part—throughout Egypt, as Aten temples were also found in other cities, such as Memphis, in Lower Egypt.

Impact

Akhenaten's revolution was the pivotal event in the period of the Egyptian New Kingdom (ca. 1550–1069 BCE), yet its influence was largely negative. During the reigns of Tutankhamen (ca. 1336–1327 BCE) and Ay (ca. 1327–1323 BCE), the Egyptians restored traditional religion and returned to conventional art. The reversal continued under Horemheb (ca. 1323–1295 BCE), who started dismantling Akhenaten's buildings and using the *talatat* as building blocks for new projects. The fact that the king's own kin (Tutankhamen) and courtiers (Ay and probably Horemheb) oversaw this about-face attests to the bitterness that his ideas engendered.

Long-term, Akhenaten's fate was even more dismal. No later than the time of Ramesses II (ca. 1279–1213 BCE)—and perhaps as early as that of Horemheb—the king and his immediate heirs were struck from official records. When scribes needed to refer to Akhenaten, they did so in a roundabout, pejorative way, calling him "the rebel" or "the enemy of Amarna" rather than by his name.

Although Akhenaten's revolution failed, traces of it did survive. After the king's death, the vernacularization of official writing proceeded apace. Moreover, funerary religion began to stress the sun's passage through the underworld at night. Members of the Anglo-Dutch archaeological mission at Saqqara, the necropolis of Memphis, discovered a beautiful representation of this solarized afterlife in the tomb of Maya and Meryt, dating to the later fourteenth century BCE.

On the reactionary level, Akhenaten's heresy contributed to the rise of personal piety, the individual aspect of religion, and a shift away from serving the pharaoh. Recall that stanza 8 of the "Great Hymn" describes the king as the sole intermediary between the Aten and humanity. Such a claim was unprecedented, even in the autocratic history of the Nile Valley, and it provoked a severe response. Out of either disgust or guilt, the Egyptians shifted control over the individual's destiny from the king to the gods—especially to the resurgent Amen. As a result, everyone from the lowest washerwoman to the pharaoh himself was obliged to bow in contrite prayer before a volatile and omnipotent divine will.

More complex is the possible relationship between Akhenaten's ideas and "Ba Theology." The word ba, written with the human-headed bird hieroglyph, denotes the ability to travel between this world and the next. By extension, it also designates a god's power to reside in kheperu—idols, animals, and so forth—as well as the kheperu themselves. After Akhenaten's reign, the Egyptians began to equate ba with Amen, calling him the "one god who makes himself into millions" and speaking of four elements—water, earth, air, and light—that emanate from him. One text says that Amen "hides himself in the Solar Orb," while another stresses his seclusion, remoteness, and inscrutability.

Akhenaten's religion and Ba Theology do have striking similarities. Both the Aten and Amen were unique, distant, and mysterious deities. Some papyrus manuscripts even characterize Amen as the "ba of gods and human beings," expressing a measure of pantheism. Of course, the two movements have differences too. The "Great Hymn" never uses the word ba to characterize the Aten's light, while Ba Theology does not object to cult images.

Nonetheless, if Akhenaten's heresy and Ba Theology are linked, it is significant that the latter flourished for over a millennium. Indeed, by the Roman era (30 BCE–395 CE), Ba Theology fed into the conceptions of Isis and Bes Pantheos. Egyptians referred to Isis as "the One," the queen of matter and fate. The Greek polymath Plutarch reports that she "is called by many names, since … she turns herself into this thing or that and is receptive to all manner of shapes and forms." Likewise, the North African writer Apuleius calls her the "mother of the universe" and the "mistress of the elements." As for Bes Pantheos, a document from the Saite

Period (ca. 664–525 BCE) portrays him as the embodiment of Amen's ba elements.

In the end, Ba Theology—and hence, Akhenaten's religion—may have influenced the late antique notion of a high god who fills the world from within. Writings in the Corpus Hermeticum, part of the Hermetica—the body of philosophical and mystical works attributed to the mythical divine sage Hermes Trismegistus—say that this deity is "the One and the All," that he is hidden yet manifest, and that he creates life alone. Several passages associate the high god with the sun, and one even describes him as "the incorporeal light." The most intriguing part of the Corpus Hermeticum, however, is an exchange between Hermes and his son Tat on the subject of "everlasting bodies":

> Tat. What then can we call real, father?—Hermes. The Sun alone; because the Sun, unlike all other things, does not suffer change, but continues to be as he is. Wherefore the Sun alone has been entrusted with the task of making all things in the universe; he rules over all things, and makes all things. Him do I worship, and I adore his reality, acknowledging him, next after the one supreme God, as the Maker.

This excerpt clearly echoes Akhenaten's thinking. Like Tat, the king sought the real and the lasting. He learned that cult statues decay and perish, while the Aten endures. He thus worshiped that body which held the light-energy that sustains all living things.

A last way in which Akhenaten may have shaped the future is through Psalm 104 of the Hebrew Bible. The American Egyptologist James Henry Breasted noticed a number of parallels between this text and the "Great Hymn." Psalm 104 associates God with the sun, imbues him with a universal quality, gives him power over life and time, and celebrates the multiplicity of his creation. Breasted maintained that the biblical song was, in fact, derived from the Egyptian one. Others have gone even further, arguing that Akhenaten was

Questions for Further Study

1. How did historical events surrounding the Eighteenth Dynasty in Egypt contribute to the emergence of the "Great Hymn to the Aten"?

2. In what sense could it be said that the "Great Hymn to the Aten" represents a first step away from polytheism toward later monotheism? What influence might the hymn and the reign of Akhenaten have had on Jewish conceptions of God?

3. Why do you think that the sun or a sun god was often a central figure in early polytheistic religions?

4. In what sense was Akhenaten a religious rebel in ancient Egypt? Why do you think his successors tried to undo Akhenaten's religious innovations?

the tutor of Moses and the father of Judaism. Today, however, most scholars eschew such theories as flights of fancy.

Further Reading

■ Books

Aldred, Cyril. *Akhenaten, King of Egypt.* New York: Thames and Hudson, 1988.

Assmann, Jan. *The Search for God in Ancient Egypt*, trans. David Lorton. Ithaca, N.Y.: Cornell University Press, 2001.

Breasted, James Henry. *The Dawn of Conscience.* New York: Charles Scribner's Sons, 1933.

Davies, Norman de Garis. *The Rock Tombs of El Amarna.* Part VI: *Tombs of Parennefer, Tutu and Aÿ.* London: Egypt Exploration Fund, 1908.

Hornung, Erik. *Akhenaten and the Religion of Light*, trans. David Lorton. Ithaca, N.Y.: Cornell University Press, 1999.

Martin, Geoffrey Thorndike. *The Hidden Tombs of Memphis: New Discoveries from the Time of Tutankhamun and Ramesses the Great.* London: Thames and Hudson, 1991.

Murnane, William J., and Edmund S. Meltzer. *Texts from the Amarna Period in Egypt.* Atlanta: Scholars Press, 1995.

Plutarch. *Isis and Osiris.* In *Plutarch's Moralia.* Vol. 5: *351C–438E*, trans. Frank Cole Babbitt. Cambridge, Mass.: Harvard University Press, 1936.

Redford, Donald B. *Akhenaten: The Heretic King.* Princeton, N.J.: Princeton University Press, 1984.

Scott, Walter. *Hermetica: The Ancient Greek and Latin Writings Which Contain Religious or Philosophic Teachings Ascribed to Hermes Trismegistus.* 4 vols. Boston: Shambhala, 1985.

Witt, R. E. *Isis in the Graeco-Roman World.* Ithaca, N.Y.: Cornell University Press, 1971.

■ Journals

Dodson, Aidan. "Were Nefertiti & Tutankhaten Coregents?" *KMT* 20, no. 3 (Fall 2009): 41–49.

—Steven M. Stannish

"Great Hymn to the Aten"

The fanbearer at the right hand of the king, the commander of all the horse of his Person, the confidant throughout the entire land, the favorite of the Good God, the God's Father Ay, and his wife, The favorite of the Good God, the great nurse of the King's Chief Wife NEFERNEFRUATEN-NEFERTITI—may she live forever continually—the king's ornament, Tiyi.

Adoration of HOR-ATEN, [living] forever [continually—Great living Aten] who is in jubilee, Lord of all that Aten encircles, Lord of Heaven, Lord of Earth, Lord of the House of Aten in Akhet-Aten; and the King of Upper and Lower Egypt, who lives on Maat, the Lord of the Two Lands, NEFERKHEP-RURE-WAENRE, the Son of Re who lives on Maat, Lord of Crowns, AKHENAT-EN, long [in his lifetime]; and the King's Chief Wife, his beloved, the Lady of the Two Lands, NEFERNEFRU-ATEN-NEFERTITI, may she live, be healthy and youthful everlastingly forever. He says:

"Beautifully you appear from the horizon of heaven, O living Aten who initiates life—
For you are risen from the eastern horizon and have filled every land with your beauty;
For you are fair, great, dazzling and high over every land,
And your rays enclose the lands to the limit of all you have made;
For you are Re, having reached their limit and subdued them your beloved son;
For although you are far away, your rays are upon the earth and you are perceived."

"When your movements vanish and you set in the western horizon,
The land is in darkness, in the manner of death.
(People), they lie in bedchambers, heads covered up, and one eye does not see its fellow.
All their property might be robbed, although it is under their heads, and they do not realize it.
Every lion is out of its den, all creeping things bite.
Darkness gathers, the land is silent.
The one who made them is set in his horizon."

"(But) the land grows bright when you are risen from the horizon,
Shining in the orb (= Aten) in the daytime, you push back the darkness and give forth your rays.

The Two Lands are in a festival of light—
Awake and standing on legs, for you have lifted them up:
Their limbs are cleansed and wearing clothes,
Their arms are in adoration at your appearing.
The whole land, they do their work:
All flocks are content with their pasturage,
Trees and grasses flourish.
Birds are flown from their nests, their wings adoring your Ka;
All small cattle prance upon their legs.
All that fly up and alight, they live when you rise for them.
Ships go downstream, and upstream as well, every road being open at your appearance.
Fish upon the river leap up in front of you, and your rays are (even) inside the Great Green (sea)."

"(O you) who brings into being foetuses in women,
Who makes fluid in people,
Who gives life to the son in his mother's womb, and calms him by stopping his tears;
Nurse in the womb, who gives breath to animate all he makes
When it descends from the womb to breathe on the day it is born—
You open his mouth completely and make what he needs.
When the chick is in the egg, speaking in the shell,
You give him breath within it to cause him to live;
And when you have made his appointed time for him, so that he may break himself out of the egg,
He comes out of the egg to speak at his appointed time and goes on his two legs when he comes out of it."

"How manifold it is, what you have made, although mysterious in the face (of humanity),
O sole god, without another beside him!
You create the earth according to your wish, being alone—
People, all large and small animals,
All things which are on earth, which go on legs, which rise up and fly by means of their wings,
The foreign countries of Kharu and Kush, (and) the land of Egypt.
You set every man in his place, you make their requirements, each one having his food and the

reckoning of his lifetime. Their tongues differ in speech, their natures likewise. Their skins are distinct, for you have made foreigners to be distinct.

You make the inundation from the underworld,

And you bring it to (the place) you wish in order to cause the subjects to live,

Inasmuch as you made them for yourself, their lord entirely, who is wearied with them,

the lord of every land, who rises for them,

The orb (= Aten) of the daytime, whose awesomeness is great!

(As for) all distant countries, you make their life:

You have granted an inundation in heaven, that it might come down for them

And make torrents upon the mountains, like the Great Green, to soak their fields with what suits them."

"How functional are your plans, O lord of continuity!

An inundation in heaven, which is for the foreigners (and) for all foreign flocks which go on legs;

(And) an inundation when it comes from the underworld for the Tilled Land (= Egypt),

While your rays nurse every field:

When you rise, they live and flourish for you.

You make the seasons in order to develop all you make:

The Growing season to cool them, and heat so that they might feel you."

"You made heaven far away just to rise in it, to see all you make,

Being unique and risen in your aspects of being as 'living Aten'—manifest, shining, far (yet) near.

You make millions of developments from yourself, (you who are) a oneness: cities, towns, fields, the path of the river.

Every eye observes you in relation to them, for you are Aten of the daytime above the earth (?).

When you have gone, nobody can exist.

You create their faces so that you might not see [your] self [as] the only (thing) which you made."

"You are in my heart, and there is none who knows you except your son, NEFERKHEPRURE-WAENRE,

For you make him aware of your plans and your strength.

The land develops through your action, just as you made them (= people):

When you have risen they live, (but) when you set they die. You are lifetime in your (very) limbs, and one lives by means of you.

Until you set, (all) eyes are upon your beauty (but) all work is put aside when you set on the western side.

(You) who rise and make [all creation] grow for the king, (as for) everyone who hurries about on foot since you founded the land,

You raise them up for your son, who issued from your limbs, the King of Upper and Lower Egypt, who lives on Maat,

The Lord of the Two Lands, NEFERKHEPRURE-[WAENRE],

Son of Re, who lives on Maat, Lord of Crowns, AKHENATEN, long in his lifetime;

(And) the King's Chief Wife, his beloved, the Lady of the Two Lands,

NEFERNEFRUATEN-NEFERTITI."

Glossary

Maat	the personification of the fundamental order of the universe, encompassing truth, morality, balance, order, law, and the like
Re	the Egyptian sun god
Two Lands	Upper and Lower Egypt

Stone relief of Gilgamesh from the Palace of Sargon II at Khorsabad (Iraq)

(The hero Gilgamesh holding a lion that he has captured, stone relief from the Palace of Sargon II at Khorsabad [Iraq], c.725 BC [gypsum], Assyrian School / Louvre, Paris, France / Giraudon / The Bridgeman Art Library International)

EPIC OF GILGAMESH

"Supreme over other kings, lordly in appearance. . . .

He walks out in front, the leader."

Overview

The *Epic of Gilgamesh* is one of the world's earliest surviving written texts, and its author, Sinleqeunnini, is the earliest author of a surviving text whose name is known—although he was less a writer and more a compiler and adapter of stories that already existed. These stories were written, or passed along orally, in Sumerian probably beginning sometime around 2000 BCE. At about the turn of the thirteenth century BCE—though scholars differ about the date—Sinleqeunnini (also written Sin-leqe-unini) recorded the version that survives in Akkadian, a Semitic language related to Hebrew, the language of the Jewish people. It is his version that is regarded as the "standard" version of the epic. The story was lost for more than two millennia until it was rediscovered near modern-day Mosul, a city in Iraq on the eastern bank of the Tigris River. In ancient times, this was the site of the city of Nineveh. The first of the tablets upon which the epic was inscribed was found in about 1853 during an expedition led by Sir Austen Henry Layard of the British Museum.

The *Epic of Gilgamesh* is the world's first-known epic poem, that is, a long narrative poem chronicling the adventurous deeds of heroic, and often partly divine, individuals. These deeds were of significance to the culture that produced the epic—in this case, ancient Mesopotamia—for they had legendary, religious, and historical importance. The story of Gilgamesh, who is not a fictional character but an actual king who ruled the city of Uruk (or Erech) in Babylonia sometime around 2750 BCE, continues to be read in large part because it is gripping, an adventure yarn that celebrates the bonds between men and that raises questions about the price people pay to become civilized, about the role of a king, and about the value of fame on earth. Primarily, the *Epic of Gilgamesh* chronicles the struggles of a man who must discover meaning in life while accepting the inevitability of his own mortality. For this reason, it had profound religious significance in Mesopotamia, for it offered both an object lesson about rulers who fail their people and a view of eternal life not in heaven but through accomplishments on earth.

Context

Ancient Mesopotamia was situated within the Fertile Crescent, a hook of agriculturally productive land on the northern part of the Arabian Peninsula that extended northward from the city of Jericho (just east of Jerusalem) and then curved around the peninsula to the southeast to Sumer, near the northwest coast of the Persian Gulf. Mesopotamia was not a country, as the word is understood today, but rather a large region that comprised a number of areas dominated by different civilizations that rose and fell over the centuries. One of the most prominent was Sumer, located at the southern end of the alluvial plain between the Tigris and Euphrates rivers. (Rivers flood an alluvial plain during the rainy season, leaving behind fertile silt in which crops can be easily grown.)

Much of the history of the Sumerians was dictated by this geography. Because the land was fertile, the Sumerians were able to grow ample food crops. At the same time, that fertility was the result of rivers that frequently overran their banks and caused widespread destruction. Furthermore, the region, because it was flat, was susceptible to invasion. Because of these difficulties, a strain of pessimism and gloom runs through Sumerian thought, a gloom that is reflected in Gilgamesh's quest for some kind of immortality in the face of the arbitrariness of the gods. The Sumerians were polytheistic, believing in a number of gods who created the world and the standards by which people were to live. In addition to the sky god Anu, they recognized the storm god Enlil, a normally benevolent god who gave Sumerians the plow and made the land fertile. Enlil, however, could be terrifying, forced to carry out the wishes of other gods when they were displeased with humans. It is Enlil who inflicts the Flood that dominates Tablet XI of the *Epic of Gilgamesh*. Meanwhile, the goddess Ishtar represented a creative, feminine principle, one that would play a key role in Gilgamesh's epic quest.

For the ancient Sumerians, fate totally depended on the will of the gods. In their worldview, life was a cycle in which the gods granted and then withdrew their favor—a view that was likely a reflection of the natural cycle of flooding and then growth: When the floods came, the Sumerians believed they had angered the gods, who flooded

Time Line	
CA. 3000 BCE	■ In southern Mesopotamia, the Sumerian kingdom emerges out of political rivalries.
CA. 2750 BCE	■ Gilgamesh is the ruler of Uruk (or Erech), in Babylonia.
CA. 2000 BCE	■ Tales of Gilgamesh begin to circulate, both orally and in writing.
CA. 1760 BCE	■ King Hammurabi of Babylon gains control of Sumer.
CA. 1720 BCE	■ The Euphrates River shifts, and Sumerian cities such as Nippur collapse.
CA. 1595 BCE	■ Sumer collapses with the invasion of the Hittites.
CA. 1300 BCE	■ Sinleqeunnini records the *Epic of Gilgamesh*.
CA. 612 BCE	■ The library of Ashurbanipal, king of Assyria from 669 to 633 BCE, at Nineveh is destroyed by Persian invaders, and the tablets recording the *Epic of Gilgamesh* are damaged.
CA. 1853 CE	■ The first tablets of the *Epic of Gilgamesh* are discovered at the library of Ashurbanipal by Austen Henry Layard and Hormuzd Rassam.
CA. 1873 CE	■ George Smith of the British Museum publishes the first translation of the *Epic of Gilgamesh*.

primarily to obtain lumber and stone in exchange for foodstuffs. To make the record keeping needed for trade easier, the Sumerians also developed a system of mathematical notation based on the number 60, which is easily divisible by many other numbers: 2, 3, 4, 5, 6, 10, 12, 15, 20, and 30. Sumerian mathematics is reflected in many aspects of modern systems of measurements. Still today, the hour consists of sixty minutes and the minute of sixty seconds; the day consists of two twelve-hour periods; a foot has twelve inches; and a circle consists of 360 (6 × 60) degrees. All of these seemingly peculiar units of measurement are lasting legacies of the ancient Sumerians.

The chief contribution of the Sumerians to civilization was the development of writing. The earliest Sumerians used pictographs, or symbols that were essentially pictures of the things represented. Later, Sumerian writing developed into a form based on ideographs, which are more symbolic or abstract representations than pictographs. Still later, the Sumerians developed writing based partially on an alphabet. The *Epic of Gilgamesh* is a good example of this kind of writing. The epic was recorded on twelve stone tablets, the most common Sumerian means of preserving written texts. They used a stylus—a pen-shaped instrument—made of reed or bone and impressed the written characters into wet clay, which then dried into stone. The form the writing took was cuneiform—from the Latin *cuneus*, designating the marks as "wedge-shaped." Cuneiform writing was also used by other civilizations in that part of the world.

Sometime during the twenty-first century BCE, the Sumerian city of Ur was ruled by Shulgi, who was a patron of the arts and encouraged the preservation of older literature. He also established academies both at Ur and at the city of Nippur. What is noteworthy about Shulgi is that he claimed Gilgamesh as his brother (despite the obvious discrepancy in eras). In the centuries that followed, much of the literature that Shulgi assembled disappeared, and Sumerian no longer was a spoken language. However, Sumerian literature continued to be studied in Babylonian academies, and at least five stories about Gilgamesh were copied at these academies. It is also known that the stories were sung at the royal court at the city of Ur. At the same time, scholars transcribed oral stories about Gilgamesh. But by the end of the eighteenth century BCE the Euphrates River had shifted, and many areas of Mesopotamia, including Nippur, were abandoned and the academies closed. New Babylonian dynasties arose, with their own academies and scribes. Although Babylonian literature dominated, some scholars resurrected the old tales, including the story of Gilgamesh. Numerous translations and adaptations were made—including that of Sinleqeunnini. The stone tablets on which the *Epic of Gilgamesh* were written were stored at the library of Ashurbanipal, the king of Assyria from 669 to 633 BCE. The library was destroyed by Persian invaders in 612 BCE, and all of the tablets were damaged. They remained lost until archaeologists discovered them in the nineteenth century. In 1873 George Smith of the British Museum published the first translation of the *Epic of Gilgamesh*.

the land to show their displeasure. On the other hand, when the crops grew, Sumerians believed they had won back the gods' favor. In this kind of geographical setting, it is not surprising that the flood would be a major manifestation of the state of mind of the gods.

The Sumerians developed one of the world's earliest civilizations. By about 3000 BCE the region had some twelve independent cities, each ruled by its own king. The Sumerians developed a law code, had a fixed social structure, and carried on trade with other parts of the known world,

About the Author

Little is known about the author of the *Epic of Gilgamesh*. What is known is that around the beginning of the thirteenth century BCE, a Babylonian scholar and scribe named Sinleqeunnini assembled a number of oral and written versions of the tales about Gilgamesh that had been in circulation for centuries and thus recorded what would become the classic version of the epic. Sinleqeunnini did not simply write down older versions of the story but rather updated it to reflect the literary trends of the day. One of the earlier versions of the tale was titled "Surpassing All Other Kings"; Sinleqeunnini's version was titled "He Who Saw the Deep." A major change he made was to make Enkidu Gilgamesh's companion instead of just a wild man who functions in opposition to Gilgamesh. Further, Sinleqeunnini gave greater emphasis to such issues as morality, the nature of wisdom, heroism, the responsibilities of a king, and the purpose of life. His new version of the epic depicts Gilgamesh as an impulsive, arrogant, and sometimes irresponsible king who makes a futile attempt to find eternal life and emerges from his quest with the realization that achievements, not immortality, serve as a person's legacy. As for Sinleqeunnini, his legacy consists entirely of his version of the Gilgamesh epic, as nothing else is known about any other works of his or the remainder of his life.

Explanation and Analysis of the Document

The stone tablets that contain the *Epic of Gilgamesh* were discovered in about 1853, by Austen Henry Layard of the British Museum and the Assyrian Hormuzd Rassam at the site of the ancient city of Nineveh (in modern-day Iraq) in the ruins of the library of the Assyrian king Ashurbanipal. Persian invaders destroyed the library in 612 BCE, damaging all of the tablets, some more than others, such that no complete text of the epic remains. Where gaps exist in the text, scholars have suggested missing words and phrases, so different editions of the work are likely to vary in relatively minor matters of phrasing. Reproduced here are Tablets I and XI. The former introduces Gilgamesh and his relationship with Enkidu; the latter is an account of the flood that almost destroyed humanity. Scholars have had to restore the complete text of *Gilgamesh*. In the excerpts, words in square brackets are added words or translated words that are obscure but about which the translator can be fairly certain. The question mark, on the other hand, indicates additions that are more conjectural. Text in parentheses indicates wording that the translator has added for sense.

♦ Tablet I

A prelude introduces the hero. The reader learns that Gilgamesh's mother was a minor goddess, Rimat-Ninsun; her husband was Lugalbanda, but it is not entirely clear whether Lugalbanda is Gilgamesh's actual father. Lugalbanda was a historical figure, an earlier Sumerian king, and records suggest that he may have been the grandfather of

Hormuzd Rassam

(Portrait of Hormuzd Rassam, 1869 [oil on canvas], Hunt, Arthur Ackland [fl.1863-1913] / Private Collection / The Bridgeman Art Library International)

Gilgamesh. In any event, Gilgamesh is presented as part human and part divine. He ordered the building of the city of Uruk (Erech), which was surrounded by magnificent walls. He also built temples for Anu, the god of the heavens, and for Anu's daughter Ishtar, the goddess of war and love. Uruk had orchards, ponds, and irrigated fields. As an explorer, Gilgamesh found mountain passes, sunk wells, and traveled widely. During his travels he met Utanapishtim, the lone survivor of the enormous flood that almost destroyed the world. He returned from his travels and then wrote everything down on a tablet of lapis lazuli, which he locked in a copper chest. Thus, the story takes place in the past and purports to be in Gilgamesh's own written words.

As the story proper begins, Gilgamesh is presented as all-powerful, even terrifying. When he wants to fight, he sacrifices warriors. He forces himself upon the wives of his nobles and takes whatever he wants. The people of Uruk, especially the city's elders, complain; they believe that the proper role of a king is to be a shepherd and guard over his subjects, not exploit them. They appeal to Aruru, the "Great Goddess" of creation, to make someone who would be an equal match for Gilgamesh. Accordingly, Aruru fashions Enkidu out of clay moistened with her saliva. Enkidu is depicted as a shaggy, hairy wild man who lives in the wilderness with the animals and grazes with them; like Gilgamesh, he is a powerful force of nature. Ninurta, who gave him his strength, was the god of war and also of wells; Ashnan was the goddess of grain; and Sumukan was the god of wild animals.

"Supreme over other kings, lordly in appearance, / he is the hero, born of Uruk, the goring wild bull. / He walks out in front, the leader, / and walks at the rear, trusted by his companions. / Mighty net, protector of his people, / raging flood-wave who destroys even walls of stone! / Offspring of Lugalbanda, Gilgamesh is strong to perfection."

"Then he, Enkidu, offspring of the mountains, / who eats grasses with the gazelles, / came to drink at the watering hole with the animals, / with the wild beasts he slaked his thirst with water."

"All day long the South Wind blew . . . , / blowing fast, submerging the mountain in water, / overwhelming the people like an attack. / No one could see his fellow, / they could not recognize each other in the torrent. / The gods were frightened by the Flood, / and retreated, ascending to the heaven of Anu."

"Urshanabi, this plant is a plant against decay(!) by which a man can attain his survival(!). / I will bring it to Uruk-Haven, / and have an old man eat the plant to test it. / The plant's name is 'The Old Man Becomes a Young Man.' / Then I will eat it and return to the condition of my youth."

One day a trapper encounters Enkidu at a watering hole. He returns to his home, where he informs his father that he has seen a powerful giant who has dismantled his trapping devices and filled in his pit traps. The father instructs his son to go to Uruk and petition Gilgamesh, who will lend him a harlot, or prostitute, from the temple of Ishtar, who will be able to subdue Enkidu. The young trapper agrees, and soon he returns to the forest with Shamhat, a temple harlot. He and Shamhat wait for three days by the watering hole. Enkidu appears, and over the next six days and seven nights, Enkidu satisfies his lust with her. He turns back to the forest, but the animals no longer see him as one of their own and flee from him. Shamhat, as a representative of a sophisticated city culture, in effect tames Enkidu, and it is through her sexuality that Enkidu passes from a savage existence to one that is more self-aware and civilized.

Enkidu tries to follow the animals, but he has become weak and is unsuccessful, so he returns to the watering hole. Shamhat is still there, and she urges him to go to the city of Uruk, where he will see many wonders, such as festivals, food, music, and Gilgamesh himself.

Enkidu is intrigued by Gilgamesh and wants not only to meet him but also to engage in a contest of strength with him. Shamhat is skeptical that Enkidu would be able to prevail in such a contest, but she tells Enkidu that Gilgamesh is lonely and would like a friend. She then recounts how Gilgamesh told his mother, Rimat-Ninsun, about two dreams he has had about Enkidu. In the first, a meteorite strikes the ground in a field outside Uruk. Gilgamesh finds the rock and with great effort lifts it and carries it to his mother, who made it compete with him. His mother interprets this dream as meaning that "there will come to you a mighty man, a comrade who saves his friend." The mighty man is Enkidu, who has the strength of the meteorite. In the second dream, Gilgamesh finds an ax in the city, which he likewise carries to his mother, who likewise makes it compete with him. As before, Gilgamesh's mother sees the ax as prefiguring the arrival of a trustworthy companion—Enkidu.

In the portions of the epic that follow, the sexual relationship between Enkidu and Shamhat is replaced by the love that Gilgamesh and Enkidu have for each other, love that is based on comradeship and equality. During their adventures, Gilgamesh must find a balance between his earthly and divine traits, just as Enkidu finds a balance between his animal nature and his human nature. As Enkidu becomes more civilized, Gilgamesh undergoes a moral education. The two travel northward, to an area probably located in modern-day Iran, perhaps Syria. Their purpose is to bring back precious cedarwood from the Cedar Forest, but to do so they will have to overcome the guardian of the Cedar Forest, Humbaba the Terrible. During the journey, Enkidu is killed by the storm-god Enlil. Gilgamesh, mourning the loss of his companion, is haunted by the possibility of his own death, so he travels throughout the world in search of eternal life.

♦ Tablet XI

After searching at great length for him, Gilgamesh encounters Utanapishtim and puts to him the fundamental questions he wants answered: How did Utanapishtim, a mortal, become a god? How had he escaped death? How can Gilgamesh, too, escape death? In response, Utanapishtim, who survived the flood that almost destroyed humankind, narrates his story. He explains to Gilgamesh that he had been the king of Shuruppak, which had been a thriving city on the banks of the Euphrates River. But the gods met secretly and ordered the massive flood to wipe out humankind, though no reason is ever given for their doing so. The gods included Anu, the god of the firmament; Enlil, the god of earth, wind, and air; Ninurta, the god of war and of wells; Ennugi, the god of irrigation; and Ea, the cleverest god and the god of wisdom. The council was sworn to secrecy, but Ea revealed the gods' plan to Utanapishtim by speaking to the walls of Utanapishtim's house, instructing him to build a boat. Apsu is known to have been the goddess of freshwater, but the meaning of the phrasing "Roof it over like the Apsu" is obscure.

Utanapishtim is concerned about what he is going to tell the people of the city, who will necessarily be involved in the construction of the boat. Ea suggests a clever lie: Utanapishtim is to tell them that he is leaving because Enlil is angry with him and that after he leaves the gods will bless the people of the city with good fortune. During the construction of the boat, Utanapishtim gives the workers food and drink in a festival-like atmosphere. The boat has a length and width of ten dozen cubits (a cubit being an ancient unit of measurement about the length of one's forearm) and thus about an acre of floor space, and Utanapishtim loads the boat with his family, living things, and all his possessions. Seven days later, the boat is ready and Utanapishtim and his family are sealed inside.

The flood comes, and even the gods are frightened by its destructive force. Ishtar weeps as she watches the destruction of her children. After the storm and flooding end a week later, the boat runs aground on the peak of Mount Nimush, and after another week Utanapishtim releases a dove, which returns when it cannot find dry ground on which to land. Later he releases a swallow, then a raven. Finally, Utanapishtim offers a sacrifice

to the gods and burns incense for them, and they convene over the "sweet savor." When Enlil sees the boat and Utanapishtim, he grows angry, for his intention was for there to be no survivors. Ninurta reveals the role Ea played in Utanapishtim's survival, and in response to Enlil's anger, Ea explains that in his view, the flood was disproportionate to the crimes of humanity. Enlil is swayed by Ea's words and turns Utanapishtim and his family into gods, with eternal life.

Utanapishtim finishes his story, then asks Gilgamesh what reason the gods should have for convening and deciding to grant him immortality. Utanapishtim proposes a sort of test: Can Gilgamesh go seven days without sleeping? Gilgamesh then sits but promptly falls asleep—a clear indication of his humanity. Utanapishtim and his wife discuss the matter; Utanapishtim believes that if he wakes Gilgamesh, the king will just deny that he has slept. He thus instructs his wife to bake bread and leave a loaf by Gilgamesh's side each day; the bread will be proof that Gilgamesh has slept. After seven days, Utanapishtim awakens Gilgamesh and proves to the king that he has slept by noting the condition of the loaves of bread, which have progressively grown more stale. Gilgamesh despairs because he has not found the secret to eternal life.

Gilgamesh is taken away by Utanapishtim's boatman, Urshanabi, to cleanse himself, a purifying ritual resembling that of baptism. Urshanabi's instructions are to have Gilgamesh bind up his hair, dispose of the animal skin he wears, and don a royal robe so that he can reenter Uruk. But first, at the urging of his wife, Utanapishtim reveals to Gilgamesh one of the secrets of the gods. He tells Gilgamesh of a thorny sea plant that will give him back his youth. Gilgamesh dives into the sea; retrieves the plant, which he names "'The Old Man Becomes a Young Man"; and tells the boatman that he will give the plant to an elder in Uruk to test it, after which he, too, will eat it and become young again. But after he and the boatman stop to camp, Gilgamesh goes swimming; in his absence, a snake comes and steals the plant, a prefigurement of the biblical tale of Adam and Eve and the serpent in the Garden of Eden. Gilgamesh is heartbroken. However, the snake's theft of the plant is to be seen as a good thing, for it frees Gilgamesh from his obsessions and gets him to think about his mortal responsibilities.

Tablet XI ends as Gilgamesh and the boatman arrive at Uruk and Gilgamesh shows the boatman the city and the temple of Ishtar. As Tablet XII reveals, Gilgamesh has found an answer to the question of immortality: he has learned that he cannot elude death. He begins to think more like a king, focusing on his responsibilities to his people, and is less concerned about his own mortality, which is unavoidable. His place is in the city, and he will gain a kind of immortality if he rules the city well and frees his people to pursue beauty and prosperity. In the Judeo-Christian tradition, the ending of the story might be considered pessimistic, since there is no heaven and no promise of eternal life with God. In the context of the times, though, the ending was optimistic, for Gilgamesh has been reformed and his city is seen as a place of beauty, industry, and prosperity.

Audience

Epic tales of Gilgamesh's life first began circulating around the twenty-first century BCE during the Sumerian rule of Shulgi, who claimed Gilgamesh as a relation. In the centuries that followed, the epic was studied at academies devoted to the preservation of older literature, even after Sumerian was no longer a spoken language. The stories on which the epic was founded were sung at the royal court at Ur, and scholars transcribed these stories. Although in later years Babylonian literature was predominant, scholars and scribes continued to preserve the stories and issue translations of them.

It is impossible to state with any certainty who comprised the specific audience for Sinleqeunnini's *Epic of Gilgamesh*. It is highly likely that the epic, or portions of it, were read aloud, perhaps by priests, for the benefit of their followers. Thus, the place the *Epic of Gilgamesh* occupied in Mesopotamian culture was little different from the place occupied by other ancient epics in their cultures.

Impact

Modern scholars can infer that readers and hearers of the *Epic of Gilgamesh* at the time of its production, over three thousand years ago, were inspired by the story of their ancient king and moved to ponder the philosophical and proto-religious issues it raises—just as modern readers can still be moved by the heroism, adventure, and literary depth of the tale. Further, the *Epic of Gilgamesh* was in effect a historical document, for it recorded the exploits of a former ruler and the history of the community. It is likely that such writers as Homer knew of the epic tales of Gilgamesh and were at least partly influenced by them.

The *Epic of Gilgamesh*, specifically Tablet XI and the story of the flood, has raised one major question: Was the epic the source, or perhaps one of the sources, for the story of the Great Flood survived by Noah in Chapters 6 through 9 of the biblical book of Genesis? Scholars continue to debate the question, offering three possibilities: that the *Epic of Gilgamesh* inspired the writer of Genesis, that the writer of Genesis inspired the *Epic of Gilgamesh,* or that both relied on another common source. Whichever possibility is the truth, it is clear that the flood accounts in the two texts bear many similarities: The flood was divinely planned; it was revealed to the hero; the hero was divinely instructed to build a boat; the hero and his family were spared; and birds were sent out to measure the lowering of the floodwaters, among numerous other parallels. At the same time, there are noteworthy differences between the two accounts; in particular, Genesis is written in the context of a monotheistic conception of God, while the *Epic of Gilgamesh* reflects the polytheistic culture from which it emerged. Further, in Genesis, Noah is saved because he alone is righteous among humans; in the *Epic of Gilgamesh*, no particular reason is given for Utanapishtim's survival, which is the result of a combination of Ea's betrayal of his fellow gods and Utanapishtim's shrewd devotion to heeding Ea's advice.

Interestingly, flood stories can be found the world over. Even the Pawnee of Nebraska have a flood account in their mythology, as do, for example, the Miao of southwestern China; scholars have identified at least two hundred such accounts throughout the world. A large proportion of these accounts share similar characteristics: the notion of a favored family that was forewarned, sin and corruption as motivation for the flood, the notion that the flood was global, and many others. Thus, while it is difficult to ascertain the specific impact of the *Epic of Gilgamesh* on later

---

Questions for Further Study

1. What role did geography play in the lives of the ancient Sumerians? What influence did geography have on the *Epic of Gilgamesh?*

2. In many ways, Gilgamesh is not a very appealing king, unlike, perhaps, the heroes of other epics. How does Gilgamesh change? Why does he change?

3. The *Epic of Gilgamesh* is frequently studied as a work of literature, similar to the epics of Homer or the epics associated with King Arthur and the Knights of the Round Table. In what sense, though, is *Gilgamesh* a religious document? What does it tell us about the religious beliefs of the ancient Sumerians?

4. What vision of immortality does *Gilgamesh* present? How does that vision differ from the vision of immortality in such religions as Christianity, Judaism, or Islam?

5. What role does Enkidu play in the *Epic of Gilgamesh?* Why is he an important character?

---

epics and later scriptural and mythological narratives, it is safe to say that it became part of a literary and philosophical tradition that the human community has shared for millennia. Further, the discovery of the *Epic of Gilgamesh* in the nineteenth century gave students of history, archaeology, and religion a first glimpse into an ancient world that they had previously known only through the Bible. In large measure, then, the *Epic of Gilgamesh* helped to redefine biblical history and historians' understanding of the culture and civilization of ancient Mesopotamia.

After the first publication of *Gilgamesh* in English in 1873, scholars and writers began to recognize that a masterpiece had been discovered. One of the principal figures who brought the work to the attention of others was the Austrian art critic and poet Rainer Maria Rilke, who in 1916 read the epic for the first time and enthusiastically recommended it to others. In the decades that followed, *Gilgamesh* became standard reading for those interested in ancient epics.

Further Reading

■ Books

Black, Jeremy, and Anthony Green. *Gods, Demons and Symbols of Ancient Mesopotamia: An Illustrated Dictionary*. Austin: University of Texas Press, 1992.

Dalley, Stephanie, ed. and trans. *Myths from Mesopotamia: Creation, the Flood, Gilgamesh, and Others*. New York: Oxford University Press, 1989.

Damrosch, David. *The Buried Book: The Loss and Rediscovery of the Great Epic of Gilgamesh*. New York: Henry Holt, 2007.

Foster, Benjamin R., ed. and trans. *The Epic of Gilgamesh: A New Translation, Analogues, Criticism*. New York: W. W. Norton, 2001.

Heidel, Alexander. *Gilgamesh Epic and Old Testament Parallels*. Chicago: University of Chicago Press, 1963.

Kluger, Rivkah Schärf. *The Archetypal Significance of Gilgamesh: A Modern Ancient Hero*. Einsiedeln, Switzerland: Daimon Verlag, 2004.

Maier, John, ed. *Gilgamesh: A Reader*. Wauconda, Ill.: Bolchazy-Carducci, 2001.

Tigay, Jeffrey H. *The Evolution of the Gilgamesh Epic*. Wauconda, Ill.: Bolchazy-Carducci, 2002.

■ Web Sites

Brown, Arthur A. "Storytelling, the Meaning of Life, and the *Epic of Gilgamesh*." Exploring Ancient World Cultures Web site. http://eawc.evansville.edu/essays/brown.htm

—Michael J. O'Neal

EPIC OF GILGAMESH

Tablet I

He who has seen everything, *I will make known* (?)
to the lands.
I will teach (?) about him who experienced all things
. . . alike,
Anu granted him the totality of knowledge of *all*.
He saw the Secret, discovered the Hidden,
he brought information of (the time) before the Flood.
He went on a distant journey, pushing himself to
exhaustion,
but then was brought to peace.
He carved on a stone stela all of his toils,
and built the wall of Uruk-Haven,
the wall of the sacred Eanna Temple, the holy sanctuary.
Look at its wall which gleams like *copper* (?),
inspect its inner wall, the likes of which no one can
equal!
Take hold of the threshold stone—it dates from
ancient times!
Go close to the Eanna Temple, the residence of Ishtar,
such as no later king or man ever equaled!
Go up on the wall of Uruk and walk around,
examine its foundation, inspect its brickwork
thoroughly.
Is not (even the core of) the brick structure made of
kiln-fired brick,
and did not the Seven Sages themselves lay out its plans?
One league city, one league palm gardens, one league
lowlands, the open area (?) of the Ishtar Temple,
three leagues and the open area (?) of Uruk it (the
wall) encloses.
Find the copper tablet box,
open the . . . of its lock of bronze,
undo the fastening of its secret opening.
Take and read out from the lapis lazuli tablet
how Gilgamesh went through every hardship.

Supreme over other kings, lordly in appearance,
he is the hero, born of Uruk, the goring wild bull.
He walks out in front, the leader,
and walks at the rear, trusted by his companions.
Mighty net, protector of his people,
raging flood-wave who destroys even walls of stone!
Offspring of Lugalbanda, Gilgamesh is strong to
perfection,

son of the august cow, Rimat-Ninsun; . . . Gilgamesh
is awesome to perfection.
It was he who opened the mountain passes,
who dug wells on the flank of the mountain.
It was he who crossed the ocean, the vast seas, to the
rising sun,
who explored the world regions, seeking life.
It was he who reached by his own sheer strength
Utanapishtim, the Faraway,
who restored the sanctuaries (or: cities) that the
Flood had destroyed!
. . . for teeming mankind.
Who can compare with him in kingliness?
Who can say like Gilgamesh: "I am King!"?
Whose name, from the day of his birth, was called
"Gilgamesh"?
Two-thirds of him is god, one-third of him is human.
The Great Goddess [Aruru] designed (?) the model
for his body,
she prepared his form . . .
. . . beautiful, handsomest of men,
. . . perfect
. . .
He walks around in the enclosure of Uruk,
Like a wild bull he makes himself mighty, head raised
(over others).
There is no rival who can raise his weapon against
him.
His fellows stand (at the alert), attentive to his (orders ?),
and the men of Uruk become anxious in . . .
Gilgamesh does not leave a son to his father,
day and night he arrogantl[y(?)] . . .

[The following lines are interpreted as rhetorical, perhaps spoken by the oppressed citizens of Uruk.]

Is Gilgamesh the shepherd of Uruk-Haven,
is he the shepherd . . .
bold, eminent, knowing, and wise!
Gilgamesh does not leave a girl to her mother (?)
The daughter of the warrior, the bride of the young man,
the gods kept hearing their complaints, so
the gods of the heavens implored the Lord of Uruk [Anu]

"You have indeed brought into being a mighty wild
bull, head raised!

There is no rival who can raise a weapon against him.
His fellows stand (at the alert), attentive to his (orders),
Gilgamesh does not leave a son to his father,
day and night he arrogantly . . .
Is he the shepherd of Uruk-Haven,
is he their shepherd. . .
bold, eminent, knowing, and wise,
Gilgamesh does not leave a girl to her mother (?)!"

The daughter of the warrior, the bride of the young man,
Anu listened to their complaints,
and (the gods) called out to Aruru:
"it was you, Aruru, who created mankind (?),
now create a *zikru* to it/him.
Let him be equal to his (Gilgamesh's) stormy heart,
let them be a match for each other so that Uruk may
     find peace!"
When Aruru heard this she created within herself the
     zikrtt of Anu.
Aruru washed her hands, she pinched off some clay,
     and threw it into the wilderness.
In the wildness (?) she created valiant Enkidu,
born of Silence, endowed with strength by Ninurta.
His whole body was shaggy with hair,
he had a full head of hair like a woman,
his locks billowed in profusion like Ashnan.
He knew neither people nor settled living,
but wore a garment like Sumukan.
He ate grasses with the gazelles,
and jostled at the watering hole with the animals;
as with animals, his thirst was slaked with (mere)
     water.

A notorious trapper came face-to-face with him op-
     posite the watering hole.
A first, a second, and a third day
he came face-to-face with him opposite the watering
     hole.
On seeing him the trapper's face went stark with fear,
and he (Enkidu?) and his animals drew back home.
He was rigid with fear; though stock-still
his heart pounded and his face drained of color.
He was miserable to the core,
and his face looked like one who had made a long
     journey.
The trapper addressed his father saying:

"Father, a certain fellow has come from the mountains.
He is the mightiest in the land,

his strength is as mighty as the meteorite (?) of Anu!
He continually goes over the mountains,

he continually jostles at the watering place with the
     animals,
he continually plants his feet opposite the watering
     place.
I was afraid, so I did not go up to him.
He filled in the pits that I had dug,
wrenched out my traps that I had spread,
released from my grasp the wild animals.
He does not let me make my rounds in the wilderness!"

The trapper's father spoke to him saying:
"My son, there lives in Uruk a certain Gilgamesh.
There is no one stronger than he,
he is as strong as the meteorite (?) of Anu.
Go, set off to Uruk,
tell Gilgamesh of this Man of Might.
He will give you the harlot Shamhat, take her with you.
The woman will overcome the fellow (?) as if she
     were strong.
When the animals are drinking at the watering place
have her take off her robe and expose her sex.
When he sees her he will draw near to her,
and his animals, who grew up in his wilderness, will
     be alien to him."

He heeded his father's advice.
The trapper went off to Uruk,
he made the journey, stood inside of Uruk,
and declared to . . . Gilgamesh:
"There is a certain fellow who has come from the
     mountains—
he is the mightiest in the land,
his strength is as mighty as the meteorite (?) of Anu!
He continually goes over the mountains,
he continually jostles at the watering place with the
     animals,
he continually plants his feet opposite the watering
     place.
I was afraid, so I did not go up to him.
He filled in the pits that I had dug,
wrenched out my traps that I had spread,
released from my grasp the wild animals.
He does not let me make my rounds in the wilderness!"
Gilgamesh said to the trapper:
"Go, trapper, bring the harlot, Shamhat, with you.
When the animals are drinking at the watering place
have her take off her robe and expose her sex.
When he sees her he will draw near to her,
and his animals, who grew up in his wilderness, will
     be alien to him."

The trapper went, bringing the harlot, Shamhat, with him.

They set off on the journey, making direct way.
On the third day they arrived at the appointed place,
and the trapper and the harlot sat down at their posts (?).
A first day and a second they sat opposite the watering
hole.
The animals arrived and drank at the watering hole,
the wild beasts arrived and slaked their thirst with
water.
Then he, Enkidu, offspring of the mountains,
who eats grasses with the gazelles,
came to drink at the watering hole with the animals,
with the wild beasts he slaked his thirst with water.
Then Shamhat saw him—a primitive,
a savage fellow from the depths of the wilderness!
"That is he, Shamhat! Release your clenched arms,
expose your sex so he can take in your voluptuousness.
Do not be restrained—take his energy!
When he sees you he will draw near to you.
Spread out your robe so he can lie upon you,
and perform for this primitive the task of womankind!
His animals, who grew up in his wilderness, will become alien to him,
and his lust will groan over you."
Shamhat unclutched her bosom, exposed her sex,
and he took in her voluptuousness.
She was not restrained, but took his energy.
She spread out her robe and he lay upon her,
she performed for the primitive the task of womankind.
His lust groaned over her;
for six days and seven nights Enkidu stayed aroused,
and had intercourse with the harlot
until he was sated with her charms.
But when he turned his attention to his animals,
the gazelles saw Enkidu and darted off,
the wild animals distanced themselves from his body.
Enkidu . . . his utterly depleted (?) body,
his knees that wanted to go off with his animals
went rigid;
Enkidu was diminished, his running was not as before.
But then he drew himself up, for his understanding
had broadened.
Turning around, he sat down at the harlot's feet,
gazing into her face, his ears attentive as the harlot spoke.
The harlot said to Enkidu:
"You are beautiful, Enkidu, you are become like a god.
Why do you gallop around the wilderness with the
wild beasts?
Come, let me bring you into Uruk-Haven,
to the Holy Temple, the residence of Anu and Ishtar,
the place of Gilgamesh, who is wise to perfection,
but who struts his power over the people like a wild bull."

What she kept saying found favor with him.
Becoming aware of himself, he sought a friend.
Enkidu spoke to the harlot:
"Come, Shamhat, take me away with you
to the sacred Holy Temple, the residence of Anu and
Ishtar,
the place of Gilgamesh, who is wise to perfection,
but who struts his power over the people like a
wild bull.
I will challenge him . . .
Let me shout out in Uruk: 'I am the mighty one!'
Lead me in and I will change the order of things;
he whose strength is mightiest is the one born in the
wilderness!"
[Shamhat to Enkidu:]
"Come, let us go, so he may see your face.
I will lead you to Gilgamesh—I know where he will be.
Look about, Enkidu, inside Uruk-Haven,
where the people show off in skirted finery,
where every day is a day for some festival,
where the lyre (?) and drum play continually,
where harlots stand about prettily,
exuding voluptuousness, full of laughter
and on the couch of night the sheets are spread."
Enkidu, you who do not know, how to live,
I will show you Gilgamesh, a man of extreme feelings.
Look at him, gaze at his face—
he is a handsome youth, with freshness,
his entire body exudes voluptuousness
He has mightier strength than you,
without sleeping day or night!
Enkidu, it is your wrong thoughts you must change!
It is Gilgamesh whom Shamhat loves,
and Anu, Enlil, and La have enlarged his mind.
Even before you came from the mountain
Gilgamesh in Uruk had dreams about you."

Gilgamesh got up and revealed the dream, saying to
his mother:
"Mother, I had a dream last night.
Stars of the sky appeared,
and some kind of meteorite (?) of Anu fell next to me.
I tried to lift it but it was too mighty for me,
I tried to turn it over but I could not budge it.
The Land of Uruk was standing around it,
the whole land had assembled about it,
the populace was thronging around it,
the Men clustered about it,
and kissed its feet as if it were a little baby.
I loved it and embraced it as a wife.
I laid it down at your feet,
and you made it compete with me."

The mother of Gilgamesh, the wise, all-knowing, said
    to her Lord;
Rimat-Ninsun, the wise, all-knowing, said to Gilgamesh:
"As for the stars of the sky that appeared
and the meteorite (?) of Anu which fell next to you,
you tried to lift but it was too mighty for you,
you tried to turn it over but were unable to budge it,
you laid it down at my feet,
and I made it compete with you,
and you loved and embraced it as a wife."
"There will come to you a mighty man, a comrade
    who saves his friend—
he is the mightiest in the land, he is strongest,
his strength is mighty as the meteorite of Anu!
You loved him and embraced him as a wife;
and it is he who will repeatedly save you.
Your dream is good and propitious!"
A second time Gilgamesh said to his mother: "Moth-
    er, I have had another dream:
At the gate of my marital chamber there lay an axe,
and people had collected about it.
The Land of Uruk was standing around it,
the whole land had assembled about it,
the populace was thronging around it.
I laid it down at your feet,
I loved it and embraced it as a wife,
and you made it compete with me."
The mother of Gilgamesh, the wise, all-knowing, said
    to her son;
Rimat-Ninsun, the wise, all-knowing, said to Gilgamesh:
"The axe that you saw (is) a man.
. . . (that) you love him and embrace as a wife,
but (that) I have compete with you."
"There will come to you a mighty man,
"a comrade who saves his friend—
"he is the mightiest in the land, he is strongest,
"he is as mighty as the meteorite of Anu!"
Gilgamesh spoke to his mother saying:
"By the command of Enlil, the Great Counselor, so
    may it to pass!
"May I have a friend and adviser, a friend and adviser
    may I have!
"You have interpreted for me the dreams about him!"
After the harlot recounted the dreams of Gilgamesh
    to Enkidu
the two of them made love. . . .

Tablet XI

♦ The Story of the Flood
Gilgamesh spoke to Utanapishtim, the Faraway:

"I have been looking at you,
but your appearance is not strange—you are like me!
You yourself are not different—you are like me!
My mind was resolved to fight with you,
(but instead?) my arm lies useless over you.
Tell me, how is it that you stand in the Assembly of
    the Gods, and have found life!"
Utanapishtim spoke to Gilgamesh, saying:
"I will reveal to you, Gilgamesh, a thing that is hidden,
a secret of the gods I will tell you!
Shuruppak, a city that you surely know,
situated on the banks of the Euphrates,
that city was very old, and there were gods inside it.
The hearts of the Great Gods moved them to inflict
    the Flood.
Their Father Anu uttered the oath (of secrecy),
Valiant Enlil was their Adviser,
Ninurta was their Chamberlain,
Ennugi was their Minister of Canals.
Ea, the Clever Prince (?), was under oath with them
so he repeated their talk to the reed house:
'Reed house, reed house! Wall, wall!
O man of Shuruppak, son of Ubartutu:
Tear down the house and build a boat!
Abandon wealth and seek living beings!
Spurn possessions and keep alive living beings!
Make all living beings go up into the boat.
The boat which you are to build,
its dimensions must measure equal to each other:
its length must correspond to its width.
Roof it over like the Apsu.'
I understood and spoke to my lord, Ea:
'My lord, thus is the command which you have uttered
I will heed and will do it.
But what shall I answer the city, the populace, and
    the Elders!'
Ea spoke, commanding me, his servant:
'You, well then, this is what you must say to them:
"It appears that Enlil is rejecting me
so I cannot reside in your city (?),
nor set foot on Enlil's earth.
I will go down to the Apsu to live with my lord, Ea,
and upon you he will rain down abundance,
a profusion of fowl, myriad fishes.
He will bring to you a harvest of wealth,
in the morning he will let loaves of bread shower down,
and in the evening a rain of wheat!'"
Just as dawn began to glow
the land assembled around me—
the carpenter carried his hatchet,
the reed worker carried his (flattening) stone,
. . . the men . . .

The child carried the pitch,
the weak brought whatever else was needed.
On the fifth day I laid out her exterior.
It was a field in area,
its walls were each 10 times 12 cubits in height,
the sides of its top were of equal length, 10 times 12
    cubits each.
I laid out its (interior) structure and drew a picture
    of it (?).
I provided it with six decks,
thus dividing it into seven (levels).
The inside of it I divided into nine (compartments).
I drove plugs (to keep out) water in its middle part.
I saw to the punting poles and laid in what was nec-
    essary.
Three times 3,600 (units) of raw bitumen I poured
    into the
bitumen kiln,
three times 3,600 (units of) pitch . . . into it,
there were three times 3,600 porters of casks who
    carried (vegetable) oil,
apart from the 3,600 (units of) oil which they consumed
and two times 3,600 (units of) oil which the boatman
    stored away.
I butchered oxen for the meat,
and day upon day I slaughtered sheep.
I gave the workmen (?) ale, beer, oil, and wine, as if
    it were river water,
so they could make a party like the New Year's Festival.
. . . and I set my hand to the oiling.
The boat was finished by sunset.
The launching was very difficult.
They had to keep carrying a runway of poles front
    to back,
until two-thirds of it had gone into the water (?).
Whatever I had I loaded on it:
whatever silver I had I loaded on it,
whatever gold I had I loaded on it.
All the living beings that I had I loaded on it,
I had all my kith and kin go up into the boat,
all the beasts and animals of the field and the crafts-
    men I had go up.
Shamash had set a stated time:
'In the morning I will let loaves of bread shower down,
and in the evening a rain of wheat!
Go inside the boat, seal the entry!'
That stated time had arrived.
In the morning he let loaves of bread shower down,
and in the evening a rain of wheat.
I watched the appearance of the weather—
the weather was frightful to behold!
I went into the boat and sealed the entry.

For the caulking of the boat, to Puzuramurri, the
    boatman,
I gave the palace together with its contents.
Just as dawn began to glow
there arose from the horizon a black cloud.
Adad rumbled inside of it,
before him went Shullat and Hanish,
heralds going over mountain and land.
Erragal pulled out the mooring poles,
forth went Ninurta and made the dikes overflow.
The Anunnaki lifted up the torches,
setting the land ablaze with their flare.
Stunned shock over Adad's deeds overtook the heavens,
and turned to blackness all that had been light.
The . . . land shattered like a . . . pot.
All day long the South Wind blew . . . ,
blowing fast, submerging the mountain in water,
overwhelming the people like an attack.
No one could see his fellow,
they could not recognize each other in the torrent.
The gods were frightened by the Flood,
and retreated, ascending to the heaven of Anu.
The gods were cowering like dogs, crouching by the
    outer wall.
Ishtar shrieked like a woman in childbirth,
the sweet-voiced Mistress of the Gods wailed:
'The olden days have alas turned to clay,
because I said evil things in the Assembly of the Gods!
How could I say evil things in the Assembly of the Gods,
ordering a catastrophe to destroy my people!!
No sooner have I given birth to my dear people
than they fill the sea like so many fish!'
The gods—those of the Anunnaki—were weeping
    with her,
the gods humbly sat weeping, sobbing with grief (?),
their lips burning, parched with thirst.
Six days and seven nights
came the wind and flood, the storm flattening the land.
When the seventh day arrived, the storm was pounding,
the flood was a war—struggling with itself like a
    woman writhing (in labor).
The sea calmed, fell still, the whirlwind (and) flood
    stopped up.
I looked around all day long—quiet had set in
and all the human beings had turned to clay!
The terrain was as flat as a roof.
I opened a vent and fresh air (daylight) fell upon the
    side of my nose.
I fell to my knees and sat weeping,
tears streaming down the side of my nose.
I looked around for coastlines in the expanse of the sea,
and at twelve leagues there emerged a region (of land).

On Mt. Nimush the boat lodged firm,

Mt. Nimush held the boat, allowing no sway.

One day and a second Mt. Nimush held the boat, allowing no sway.

A third day, a fourth, Mt. Nimush held the boat, allowing no sway.

A fifth day, a sixth, Mt. Nimush held the boat, allowing no sway.

When a seventh day arrived

I sent forth a dove and released it.

The dove went off, but came back to me;

no perch was visible so it circled back to me.

I sent forth a swallow and released it.

The swallow went off, but came back to me;

no perch was visible so it circled back to me.

I sent forth a raven and released it.

The raven went off, and saw the waters slither back.

It eats, it scratches, it bobs, but does not circle back to me.

Then I sent out everything in all directions and sacrificed (a sheep).

I offered incense in front of the mountain-ziggurat.

Seven and seven cult vessels I put in place,

and (into the fire) underneath (or: into their bowls) I poured reeds, cedar, and myrtle.

The gods smelled the savor,

the gods smelled the sweet savor,

and collected like flies over a (sheep) sacrifice.

Just then Beletili arrived.

She lifted up the large flies (beads) which Anu had made for his enjoyment:

'You gods, as surely as I shall not forget this lapis lazuli around my neck,

may I be mindful of these days, and never forget them!

The gods may come to the incense offering,

but Enlil may not come to the incense offering,

because without considering he brought about the Flood

and consigned my people to annihilation.'

Just then Enlil arrived.

He saw the boat and became furious,

he was filled with rage at the Igigi gods:

'Where did a living being escape?

No man was to survive the annihilation!'

Ninurta spoke to Valiant Enlil, saying:

'Who else but Ea could devise such a thing?

It is Ea who knows every machination!'

Ea spoke to Valiant Enlil, saying:

'It is yours, O Valiant One, who is the Sage of the Gods.

How, how could you bring about a Flood without consideration

Charge the violation to the violator,

charge the offense to the offender,

but be compassionate lest (mankind) be cut off,

be patient lest they be killed.

Instead of your bringing on the Flood,

would that a lion had appeared to diminish the people!

Instead of your bringing on the Flood,

would that a wolf had appeared to diminish the people!

Instead of your bringing on the Flood,

would that famine had occurred to slay the land!

Instead of your bringing on the Flood,

would that (Pestilent) Erra had appeared to ravage the land!

It was not I who revealed the secret of the Great Gods,

I (only) made a dream appear to Atrahasis, and (thus) he heard the secret of the gods.

Now then! The deliberation should be about him!'

Enlil went up inside the boat

and, grasping my hand, made me go up.

He had my wife go up and kneel by my side.

He touched our forehead and, standing between us, he blessed us:

'Previously Utanapishtim was a human being.

But now let Utanapishtim and his wife become like us, the gods!

Let Utanapishtim reside far away, at the Mouth of the Rivers.'

They took us far away and settled us at the Mouth of the Rivers."

"Now then, who will convene the gods on your behalf, that you may find the life that you are seeking!

Wait! You must not lie down for six days and seven nights."

soon as he sat down (with his head) between his legs

sleep, like a fog, blew upon him.

Utanapishtim said to his wife:

"Look there! The man, the youth who wanted (eternal) life!

Sleep, like a fog, blew over him."

his wife said to Utanapishtim the Faraway:

"Touch him, let the man awaken.

Let him return safely by the way he came.

Let him return to his land by the gate through which he left."

Utanapishtim said to his wife:

"Mankind is deceptive, and will deceive you.

Come, bake loaves for him and keep setting them by his head

and draw on the wall each day that he lay down."

She baked his loaves and placed them by his head

and marked on the wall the day that he lay down.

The first loaf was dessicated,

the second stale, the third moist (?), the fourth turned white, its . . . ,

the fifth sprouted gray (mold), the sixth is still fresh.
The seventh—suddenly he touched him and the man awoke.
Gilgamesh said to Utanapishtim:
"The very moment sleep was pouring over me
you touched me and alerted me!"
Utanapishtim spoke to Gilgamesh, saying:
"Look over here, Gilgamesh, count your loaves!
You should be aware of what is marked on the wall!
Your first loaf is dessicated,
the second stale, the third moist, your fourth turned white, its . . .
the fifth sprouted gray (mold), the sixth is still fresh.
The seventh—at that instant you awoke!"
Gilgamesh said to Utanapishtim the Faraway:
"O woe! What shall I do, Utanapishtim, where shall I go!
The Snatcher has taken hold of my flesh,
in my bedroom Death dwells,
and wherever I set foot there too is Death!"
Home Empty-Handed
Utanapishtim said to Urshanabi, the ferryman:
"May the harbor reject you, may the ferry landing reject you!
May you who used to walk its shores be denied its shores!
The man in front of whom you walk, matted hair chains his body,
animal skins have ruined his beautiful skin.
Take him away, Urshanabi, bring him to the washing place.
Let him wash his matted hair in water like ellu.
Let him cast away his animal skin and have the sea carry it off,
let his body be moistened with fine oil,
let the wrap around his head be made new,
let him wear royal robes worthy of him!
Until he goes off to his city,
until he sets off on his way,
let his royal robe not become spotted, let it be perfectly new!"
Urshanabi took him away and brought him to the washing place.
He washed his matted hair with water like ellu.
He cast off his animal skin and the sea carried it oh.
He moistened his body with fine oil,
and made a new wrap for his head.
He put on a royal robe worthy of him.
Until he went away to his city,
until he set off on his way,
his royal robe remained unspotted, it was perfectly clean.
Gilgamesh and Urshanabi bearded the boat,

they cast off the magillu-boat, and sailed away.
The wife of Utanapishtim the Faraway said to him:
"Gilgamesh came here exhausted and worn out.
What can you give him so that he can return to his land (with honor)!"
Then Gilgamesh raised a punting pole
and drew the boat to shore.
Utanapishtim spoke to Gilgamesh, saying:
"Gilgamesh, you came here exhausted and worn out.
What can I give you so you can return to your land?
I will disclose to you a thing that is hidden, Gilgamesh,
a . . . I will tell you.
There is a plant . . . like a boxthorn,
whose thorns will prick your hand like a rose.
If your hands reach that plant you will become a young man again."
Hearing this, Gilgamesh opened a conduit (to the Apsu)
and attached heavy stones to his feet.
They dragged him down, to the Apsu they pulled him.
He took the plant, though it pricked his hand,
and cut the heavy stones from his feet,
letting the waves (?) throw him onto its shores.
Gilgamesh spoke to Urshanabi, the ferryman, saying:
"Urshanabi, this plant is a plant against decay by which a man can attain his survival.
I will bring it to Uruk-Haven,
and have an old man eat the plant to test it.
The plant's name is 'The Old Man Becomes a Young Man.'
Then I will eat it and return to the condition of my youth."
At twenty leagues they broke for some food,
at thirty leagues they stopped for the night.
Seeing a spring and how cool its waters were,
Gilgamesh went down and was bathing in the water.
A snake smelled the fragrance of the plant,
silently came up and carried off the plant.
While going back it sloughed off its casing.'
At that point Gilgamesh sat down, weeping,
his tears streaming over the side of his nose.
"Counsel me, O ferryman Urshanabi!
For whom have my arms labored, Urshanabi!
For whom has my heart's blood roiled!
I have not secured any good deed for myself,
but done a good deed for the 'lion of the ground'!
Now the high waters are coursing twenty leagues distant,
as I was opening the conduit (?) I turned my equipment over into it.
What can I find (to serve) as a marker (?) for me!
I will turn back (from the journey by sea) and leave the boat by the shore!"
At twenty leagues they broke for some food,

at thirty leagues they stopped for the night.

They arrived in Uruk-Haven.

Gilgamesh said to Urshanabi, the ferryman:

"Go up, Urshanabi, onto the wall of Uruk and walk around.

Examine its foundation, inspect its brickwork thoroughly—

is not (even the core of) the brick structure of kiln-fired brick,

and did not the Seven Sages themselves lay out its plan!

One league city, one league palm gardens, one league lowlands, the open area (?) of the Ishtar Temple,

three leagues and the open area (?) of Uruk it encloses."

Glossary

Anu	the god of the firmament, the heavens
Anunnaki	the great gods
Aruru	the great goddess of creation
Ashnan	the grain goddess
Atrahasis	king of the Sumerian city Shuruppak in the years before the flood
Beletili	a mother goddess
bitumen	a viscous tarlike substance
cubit	an ancient unit of length based on the length of the forearm
Ea	the cleverest god and the god of wisdom
ellu	possibly a reference to the brightness and shininess of copper and bronze
Enlil	the god of earth, wind, and air
Ennugi	the god of irrigation
Erra	god of mayhem and pestilence
Hanish	a mountain herald
Igigi gods	great gods of the younger generation, headed by Enlil
Ishtar	Anu's daughter, the goddess of war and love
lapis lazuli	an azure blue semiprecious stone
league	a unit of length, roughly one and a half miles
magillu-boat	a type of oceangoing boat typically used to travel long distances
Ninurta	the god of war and of wells
Shullat	a mountain herald
Sumukan	the anointed priest of the gods
ziggurat	a tiered or terraced temple
zikru	word, speech

Buddha seated on a lotus throne and surrounded by scenes from his life

(Buddha seated upon a lotus throne, 12th/13th century (red-stained steatite), Burmese School / British Library, London, UK / © British Library Board.

All Rights Reserved / The Bridgeman Art Library International)

Noble Eightfold Path

"This is the Middle Path which the Perfect One has found out, which makes one both to see and to know, which leads . . . to Nirvana."

Overview

The Noble Eightfold Path, one of the principal teachings of the Buddha (Siddhartha Gautama), is a chief text in the canonical scriptures of Theravada Buddhism. Its primary purposes were to help followers end suffering and achieve enlightenment and self-awakening. The discourse on the Noble Eightfold Path is part of the Pali canon, the standard collection of scriptures in Theravada Buddhism; it is called "Pali" because it was preserved in the Pali language, a largely literary language of India that no one actually spoke. The Pali canon remains the only early Buddhist canon that survives in its entirety and was the first Buddhist canon to be written down (by the Fourth Buddhist Council, held in Sri Lanka in 29 BCE, some four and a half centuries after the death of the Buddha). Until then it was preserved in oral tradition.

Description of the Pali canon necessarily involves a considerable amount of nomenclature and classification. First, the canon comprises three general categories. Each of these is called a *pitaka,* a Pali word that means "basket." This word is the root of the term *Tipitaka,* which means "three baskets" or "threefold basket," so the canon is often referred to as the Tipitaka or the Pali Tipitaka (often rendered *Tripitika*). The three baskets are the Vinaya Pitaka, or "Discipline Basket," which contains rules for nuns and monks; the Sutta Pitaka, or "Sayings Basket" (literally, the "basket of threads"), which contains discourses primarily of the Buddha but those of some of his disciples as well; and the Abhidhamma Pitaka, or "beyond the dhamma," which contains seven books of philosophy covering such topics as the nature of mind, time, and matter.

The second of the three baskets, the Sutta Pitaka, consists of five *nikayas,* or collections. The third of these is the Samyutta Nikaya, which means "connected discourses" or "kindred sayings." This *nikaya,* in turn, is divided into sections called *vaggas.* The fifth *vagga,* called Maha-vagga, is the largest of the *vaggas* in the Sutta Pitaka; the word *maha* means "great" in Pali. Finally, one arrives at the Noble Eightfold Path, which (in most editions) is chapter 45 of the Samyutta Nikaya.

It is impossible to attach a precise date to the Noble Eightfold Path—and even its authorship is to some extent unclear. The documents in the Pali canon were passed down orally. While they largely represent the teachings of the Buddha, it is unclear to what extent later disciples may have modified them. Some scholars, as well as Buddhist tradition, argue for an early date for the canon and specifically the Sutta Pitaka, fixing its origin during the Buddha's lifetime. They maintain that the Sutta Pitaka is a record of the Buddha's own words, or possibly those of a follower, and note that the Buddha first expounded the Noble Eightfold Path in his "first discourse" delivered to a small group of followers in July 528 BCE. Other scholars would date the text to a later period, perhaps around 250 BCE, arguing that the entire Pali canon evolved over a lengthy period after the Buddha's death. Still others give a later date, arguing that the text continued to take shape up to the Sri Lankan council held in 29 BCE. It is quite possible that there are elements of truth to each of these dates. The text, passed down orally, undoubtedly reflects the teachings of the Buddha but was likely augmented by the Buddha's followers after his death until it was preserved in written form at the Fourth Buddhist Council.

Context

At the time of Gautama's birth in northern India in 563 BCE, the region was in a state of turmoil. During the second millennium BCE, this region had been invaded by Indo-Aryan groups from the west. These peoples spoke a variety of Indo-European languages derived from a common tongue on the Eurasian landmass. The invaders had brought with them their own religious beliefs and customs. Prominent ong these practices was adherence to ritual sacrifice and to a priestly cult that evolved into orthodox Hinduism. They claimed religious superiority over the indigenous Indian tribes, and conflicts between these tribes and the invaders occasioned violence and political instability.

In response to the death and destruction around them, many people embarked on a quest for religious truth. They sought the meaning of life and religious institutions that would guide them through troubled times. The young Gau-

Time Line

563 BCE	■ **April 8** (by tradition)—Siddhartha Gautama is born in Lumbini in Nepal, though he spends most of his early life in nearby Kapilavastu.
533 BCE	■ Gautama begins to live as a wandering student, philosopher, and teacher.
528 BCE	■ **April** Gautama has a mystical revelation and becomes the Buddha; he preaches his first sermon. ■ **July** The Buddha delivers his "first discourse," in which he propounds the Noble Eightfold Path.
483 BCE	■ The Buddha dies near Kushinagar, India; during the year following his death, the First Buddhist Council is held in Rajgir, India, to preserve the words of the Buddha.
CA. 383 BCE	■ The Second Buddhist Council is convened at the Indian city of Vaishali.
250 BCE	■ The Third Buddhist Council is convened at Patiliputta (or Pataliputra) in north-central India, possibly under the patronage of Emperor Ashoka, to rid Buddhism of corruption and heresy; meanwhile (as believed by some scholars), the Samyutta Nikaya, of which the Noble Eightfold Path is a part, takes its final shape at roughly this time as part of Buddhist oral tradition.
29 BCE	■ The Fourth Buddhist Council in Sri Lanka initiates the recording of the Pali canon over a three-year period.

fold Path. At first, his followers were few. In time, however, he began attracting hundreds of followers, then thousands.

Because Buddhism is a religion whose roots extend back more than two millennia, it is nearly impossible to trace with any accuracy its history and development through a universally accepted body of texts. While Judaism and Christianity, for example, are based on the Bible, and the Qur'an is the foundation of Islam, Buddhism has produced an overwhelming number of texts, many of them having scriptural authority. Many of these texts are lost, many survive only in translation, and many have become the core scriptures of various and numerous sects of Buddhism.

Within the complex set of Buddhist beliefs, one traditional form of Buddhism is referred to as Theravada, a term that means "doctrine of the elders" or "ancient wisdom." The only early Buddhist scriptural canon that exists today in its entirety is that of the Theravada Buddhists. According to Buddhist tradition, a council of Buddhist elders met shortly after the death of the Buddha in about 483 BCE. The goal of the council was to remember the truths that the Buddha preached and to implant these truths in the minds of his followers. Lacking any written texts, the elders formalized the Buddha's pronouncements as verses for oral recitation. This meeting is now referred to as the First Buddhist Council.

About a century later, the Second Buddhist Council was convened to affirm the purity of Buddhist doctrine. During this council, however, a major split emerged between two broad schools of Buddhist thought. The Northern School was referred to by the term *Mahayana* (literally "Great Vehicle" or "Great Ox-Cart"). This school was progressive; the goal of its proponents was bodhisattva ("enlightened existence"), the process of becoming a compassionate, heroic person dedicated to saving all beings. The Mahayanas referred to the other school of thought, the Southern School, by the disparaging term *Hinayana* ("Deficient/ Abandoned/ Defective Vehicle"). Its followers practiced a traditional form of Buddhism that they believed to have descended from the teachings of the Buddha himself. Its goal was arhat, or the process of becoming saintlike and achieving through enlightenment a form of salvation called nirvana. The Theravadins are a branch of the Southern School. The practitioners of Theravada believe that their form of Buddhism is more closely descended from the teachings of the Buddha himself and is based on his actual words. The Theravadins, or course, do not use the pejorative term *Hinayana*, which was created by the Mahayanas, because it suggests that their version of Buddhism is somehow inferior.

Very early Theravadin discourses were not written down for a variety of reasons. One practical reason was the lack of workable writing materials. But deeper causes explain the emphasis on oral transmission. Early Buddhist sages believed that the path to enlightenment and contact with a divine reality was best achieved through intuition and self-deprivation; this is why the Buddha lived the life of a wandering mendicant. They believed that the contemplation of wisdom heard rather than read provided a purer path to enlightenment and that writing actually debased the wisdom of the words. Further, while historical events

tama was such a person, and according to Buddhist tradition and belief, in 528 BCE he had a mystical experience that revealed to him a form of religious truth. He proclaimed himself the Buddha, a name that means "awakened one" or "enlightened one." In the years that followed, he traveled about preaching his message, including the Noble Eight-

were typically recorded in writing, the belief at the time was that philosophical and spiritual truths were best grasped through oral poetry, which was more easily remembered. Accordingly, the Theravadin texts in Pali were passed down through an oral tradition, making it nearly impossible for modern scholars to state with any certainty whether the words of the documents, including Noble Eightfold Path, are actually those of the Buddha.

The texts were eventually written down because a number of calamities, notably poor harvests, resulted in the death of a large number of the monks charged with remembering the canon. Fear grew that the oral tradition would be lost, especially because the number of texts was increasing. Accordingly, the texts were recorded at the Fourth Buddhist Council of 29 BCE, held in Sri Lanka under the patronage of King Vattagamani. Working in a cave near the modern-day mountain town of Matale, five hundred monks recited the texts so that they could be written down on palm leaves. Palm-leaf copies of the canon were then circulated in such places as Laos, Cambodia, Thailand, and Burma. (Another "Fourth" Buddhist Council took place in Kashmir, India, around 100 CE but Theravadins do not regard it as authoritative.)

About the Author

The Buddha was born Siddhartha Gautama on April 8, 563 BCE (according to tradition), near the town of Lumbini in Nepal. His father, Suddhodana, was the king of a local tribe called the Shakyas, so one of the Buddha's traditional names is Shakyamuni, meaning "sage (or wise man) of the Shakyas." His mother was Queen Mayadevi (sometimes given as Maya Devi). From 563 to 547 Prince Gautama grew up in his father's palace, where he was raised primarily by an aunt, learned and practiced the skills of warfare, and was expected to follow in his father's footsteps and ascend to the throne as king. In 547, at the age of sixteen, Gautama married his cousin, Princess Yasodhara, and the two had a son. After thirteen years of a life of luxury—his father had built three palaces for him—he announced on his twenty-ninth birthday that he was abandoning his worldly ties, leaving home, and launching a quest for spiritual truth. He said that what sparked this decision was an outing he had taken one day when he saw a diseased person, a corpse being cremated, a decrepit old man, and a holy man—the so-called Four Sights in Buddhist tradition. At this point, he said, he came to fully understand the pain, suffering, and death of the world.

From 533 to 528, Gautama lived the life of a wandering student, philosopher, and teacher. During these years he practiced various forms of Yoga, but he was not certain that any of them were providing him with enlightenment. Tradition holds that one night in April 528, in Bodh Gaya, a city in the state of Bihar, India, he engaged in intensive meditation and achieved a breakthrough, a mystical experience that gave him the answers he sought. At this point he became the Buddha, a name that means "the enlightened one." He remained in the city, meditating under a bodhi tree for seven weeks.

Buddhist stupa that was the site of Buddha's first sermon
(Buddhist stupa [photo], / Sarnath, Uttar Pradesh, India / Dinodia / The Bridgeman Art Library International)

The Buddha preached his first sermon in 528, and in the years that followed his revelation, he and his small community of followers preached their message to anyone who would listen. The community gained converts and created monastic centers. The Buddha resisted any kind of hierarchy because he wanted to ensure that every monk could pursue his own path to enlightenment, and every monk had an equal vote on matters affecting the community. He ignored caste, social class, background, race, and gender. His first woman convert, the aunt who had raised him, joined his followers when he returned to the royal palace after the death of his father in 523.

From the time of his enlightenment until he died in 483, the Buddha traveled about northern India, particularly Hindustan, preaching his message and eventually attracting thousands of converts. He made enemies, however, and survived a number of attempts on his life. He died of food poisoning around the age of eighty in a forest near Kushinagar (or Kusinagara), Nepal. His last words were reported to have been: "All compounded things are ephemeral; work diligently on your salvation."

Explanation and Analysis of the Document

The document begins by listing the steps of the Eightfold Path. These steps are divided into three categories. The first category, Wisdom, comprises the first two steps: Right Un-

"This is the Middle Path which the Perfect One has found out, which makes one both to see and to know, which leads to peace, to discernment, to enlightenment, to Nirvana. Free from pain and torture is this path, free from groaning and suffering; it is the perfect path."

"And what is the root of unwholesome karma? Greed is a root of unwholesome karma; Anger is a root of unwholesome karma; Delusion is a root of unwholesome karma."

"In this respect one may rightly say of me: that I teach annihilation, that I propound my doctrine for the purpose of annihilation, and that I herein train my disciples; for, certainly, I do teach annihilation—the annihilation, namely, of greed, anger and delusion, as well as of the manifold evil and unwholesome things."

"But, how does the disciple dwell in contemplation of the body? There, the disciple retires to the forest, to the foot of a tree, or to a solitary place, sits himself down, with legs crossed, body erect, and with attentiveness fixed before him. With attentive mind he breathes in, with attentive mind he breathes out."

"Whenever the disciple is dwelling in contemplation of body, feeling, mind and phenomena, strenuous, clearly conscious, attentive, after subduing worldly greed and grief—at such a time his attentiveness is undisturbed; and whenever his attentiveness is present and undisturbed, at such a time he has gained and is developing the Element of Enlightenment 'Attentiveness'; and thus this element of enlightenment reaches fullest perfection."

"And further: after the subsiding of verbal thought and rumination, and by the gaining of inward tranquility and oneness of mind, he enters into a state free from verbal thought and rumination, the second trance, which is born of Concentration, and filled with Rapture and Happiness."

derstanding and Right Mindedness. The second category, Morality, comprises the next three steps of the path: Right Speech, Right Action, and Right Living. Finally, the third category, Concentration, comprises Right Effort, Right Attentiveness, and Right Concentration. Taken together, the eight steps constitute the Middle Way, a path of moderation between the extremes of self-mortification and sensual indulgence—in other words, the path of wisdom. Each of the steps begins with the word *right*, which in the original language has connotations of "perfect" or "complete."

♦ First Step: Right Understanding

"Right understanding" can also be translated as "right view," "right perspective," or "right vision." The purpose of right understanding is to look at life, nature, and the world as they really are, with a view to clearing one's path of confusion, misunderstanding, and delusion. Right understanding explains the reasons for human existence, sickness, suffering, aging, and death, and the existence of greed, hatred, and delusion. Right understanding begins with knowledge, but through the practice of right concentration, it gradually transforms into wisdom, which can throw off the mind's fetters. Right understanding inspires people to lead virtuous lives.

According to the text, there are two types of right understanding. The first is "Mundane Right Understanding," which "yields worldly fruits and brings good results." This type has merit and is suitable for laypeople. The second type, though, is "Ultramundane Right Understanding," which leads to liberation and self-awakening and is usually more suitable for the monastic life.

To achieve Right Understanding, one must become aware of the reality of the law of karma. On a moral level, the law of karma says that every action, such as speech, has a karmic result or reaction; that is, "one experiences the fruits of this action, be it in this life, or the next life, or in some future life." However, the Buddha teaches "annihilation" of "greed, anger and delusion" and of evil and "unwholesome" things. The result will be the negation of suffering, for suffering is the result of craving; if craving is eliminated, so too will suffering.

♦ Second Step: Right Mindedness

Right Mindedness is also translated as "right thought," "right intention," "right resolve," "right conception," "right aspiration," or even "the exertion of the will to change." In this step, followers try to shed qualities in themselves they know to be immoral or destructive, such as lust and cruelty. Right mindedness is a form of renunciation, of "being holy, being turned away from the world, and conjoined with the path, the holy path being pursued." It is a quality of being harmless to other living beings.

♦ Third Step: Right Speech

The principle of Right Speech, the first principle of ethical conduct, is simple: "It is abstaining from lying; abstaining from tale-bearing; abstaining from harsh language; abstaining from vain talk." In the Buddha's view, ethical conduct is a guide to moral discipline, which in turn supports the other steps in the Eightfold Path. Speech is important in Buddhist ethics because words can be used to save lives or destroy them, to make friends or enemies, and even to make peace or launch a war. Thus, the Buddha urges his followers to avoid false speech, slander, and malicious speech; words that can hurt or offend others; and idle, inconsequential chatter.

♦ Fourth Step: Right Action

Again, the principle of Right Action, or "right conduct," is relatively simple and involves bodily actions: "It is abstaining from killing; abstaining from stealing; abstaining from unlawful sexual intercourse." The disciple who follows this step "is anxious for the welfare of all living beings." Actions that are unwholesome create unsound mental states. Accordingly, Buddha's followers are enjoined from harming sentient beings, taking things that do not belong to them, and engaging in sexual misconduct.

♦ Fifth Step: Right Living

Right Living, or "right livelihood," calls on followers to avoid occupations that might harm other people. Elsewhere, in the "Discourse on Blessings" and other text, the types of businesses that followers are to avoid are enumerated. They include trading in weapons used to kill other people; any form of trading in human beings, including prostitution and slavery; business in meat or intoxicants, and any form of trade in poisons or toxic agents designed to kill.

♦ Sixth Step: Right Effort

Right Effort, or "right endeavor," involves the effort to abandon all harmful thoughts, words, and deeds. The Buddha refers to "Four Great Efforts: the effort to avoid, the effort to overcome, the effort to develop, and the effort to maintain." Put differently, this means to *avoid* "demeritorious things," to *overcome* evil, to *develop* a state of solitude and detachment that leads to enlightenment, and to *maintain* meritorious conditions that lead to growth and maturity. Right Effort is a prerequisite, for without Right Effort, the other steps in the path cannot be taken, and nothing can be achieved. Mental energy drives Right Effort, just as mental energy can fuel lust, greed, envy, aggression, and other unwholesome behaviors.

♦ Seventh Step: Right Attentiveness

Right Attentiveness is also translated as "right mindedness," "right memory," or "right awareness." The Buddha characterizes Right Attentiveness as "the only way that leads to the attainment of purity, to the overcoming of sorrow and lamentation, to the end of pain and grief," and to the achievement of nirvana, or salvation through enlightenment. He then goes on to discuss the "Four Fundamentals of Attentiveness," which include focus on the body, feelings, the mind, and mental qualities. The excerpt includes discussion of "Contemplation of the Body," which involves the kind of physical relaxation and focus often associated in the modern world with yoga: "The disciple retires to the forest, to the foot of a tree, or to a solitary place, sits himself down, with legs crossed, body erect, and with attentiveness fixed before him." The disciple then engages in breathing exercises that calm the body, focus concentration, and sever his attachment to the world.

Here follows an extended discussion of how the practitioner can achieve a state of nirvana through breathing exercises. "Watching over In- and Outbreathing" can bring about more focused attentiveness, leading to "Wisdom and Deliverance to perfection." It clears the consciousness, subdues worldly grief and greed, fills one with energy, and leads to a state of "supersensuous rapture." One's "spiritual frame and his mind become tranquil," and the "element of enlightenment reaches fullest perfection."

◆ Eighth Step: Right Concentration

The eighth and final step in the Eightfold Path is Right Concentration. Through Right Concentration the practitioner develops a mental force that the document calls "fixing the mind to a single object" or "One-pointedness of mind." In this state, all of a person's mental faculties are unified and directed onto a single object. Buddhists develop right concentration through meditation, where the meditating mind enters a trancelike state and focuses on a selected object. The mind first directs itself to the object, then sustains and intensifies concentration.

The document describes the "four trances" through which a practitioner achieves Right Concentration. In the first, a person is "detached from sensual objects" and "unwholesome things" and enters a state of rumination filled with "Rapture" and "Happiness." The practitioner then escapes from the "5 Hindrances": Lust, Ill-will, Torpor and Dullness, Restlessness, and Mental Worry. The practitioner can then enter into the second trance, "free from verbal thought and rumination." In the third trance state, the practitioner can achieve "equanimity." Finally, the fourth trance state, a person has given up "pleasure and pain." He enters in "a state beyond pleasure and pain" to achieve a kind of purity.

Audience

The audience for the Noble Eightfold Path is nominally the followers of Theravadin Buddhism, who regard this and other texts in the Pali canon as recording the actual words of the Buddha. However, the text is not a dogmatic religious pronouncement intended for a limited audience. The Buddha himself preached to anyone who would listen to him, and over the centuries many Buddhist texts have attracted widespread audiences because they offer philosophical guidance on how to lead a better, more fulfilling, and more enlightened life. In the modern world, numerous editions of the Noble Eightfold Path are available and are widely read by people in the West as well as in the East as a source of wisdom.

Questions for Further Study

1. In what respect does the origin of the Noble Eightfold Path resemble that of the Hadith of Islam? For reference, see the entries Sahih al-Bukhari and Usul al-kafi.

2. In what way did the split between the Theravadins and the Mahayanas resemble the split between Catholicism and Protestantism, as explicated in the entry on Martin Luther's *Ninety-five Theses*? How did circumstances surrounding and motivations for the split differ?

3. What application do you think the Noble Eightfold Path might have for business leaders or people who form public policy? To what extent do you think today's business and political leaders practice the precepts of the Noble Eightfold Path?

4. In the modern world, Buddhism is closely identified with the practice of yoga as a form of relaxation and exercise. Many community centers, for example, conduct yoga classes as part of their efforts to provide members of the community with activities. Do you think that the Buddha would approve of yoga as it is practiced in the modern world in Western nations? Why or why not?

5. Why did some major religious leaders—Christ, Muhammad, the Buddha, the Bab—attract enemies who wanted to eliminate them and sometimes succeeded in doing so?

One specific impact of the Pali canon in general and the Noble Eightfold Path in particular had to do with Ashoka, one of the greatest rulers in Indian history, who reigned from 269 to 232 BCE. Ashoka was a member of the Maurya Dynasty, and he was largely responsible for uniting the numerous provinces of the Indian Subcontinent, including the regions of modern-day Bangladesh and Pakistan, into a coherent state. Having expanded the territory of his empire for several years, he turned his attention to the kingdom of Kalinga, located on the eastern coast of present-day India (corresponding roughly to today's Orissa). A key event in his reign was the Battle of Kalinga, fought in 261 BCE, which resulted in a victory for Ashoka's forces. But the death of about one hundred thousand people, the imprisonment of one hundred and fifty thousand, the displacement of many more, and the large-scale devastation resulting from the war moved Ashoka very much, and according to Buddhist tradition, he felt remorse and was converted to Buddhism by the monk Upagupta after the Kalinga War. As a patron of Buddhism, Ashoka changed the course of history not only on the Indian Subcontinent but also in the Far East and Southeast Asia. Abandoning his earlier adherence to Hinduism, Ashoka envisaged a new doctrine based in part on the Noble Eightfold Path. He propagated numerous moral precepts inspired in large part by Buddhism, and he may have sponsored the Third Buddhist Council in 250. Some scholars believe that it was around the time of the Third Council that the text of the Noble Eightfold Path began to coalesce.

Although Theravada was historically allied with early Buddhist traditions, since the 1960s the two branches of Buddhism have conducted conferences to emphasize what they have in common. Today, though, Theravada is still the dominant form of Buddhism as it is practiced not only in India but also in such countries as Cambodia, Laos, Myanmar, Sri Lanka, and Thailand. It is likewise practiced in Bangladesh, parts of China, and Vietnam, and it has experienced a revival in southern India. Through missionary activity, Theravada has spread throughout the world. The Noble Eightfold Path continues to influence modern thinkers. Some see affinities between the Noble Eightfold Path and the teachings of Jesus Christ. Some see it as a way of moving beyond the concern with terrorism prompted by such events as the attacks on the United States on September 11, 2001. Some apply the principles of the Noble Eightfold Path to business, others use it in such fields as public-policy analysis, and still others write "self-help" books intended to help people apply the Buddha's teachings to everyday life and the quest for contentment.

Further Reading

■ **Books**

Armstrong, Karen. *Buddha*. New York: Viking Penguin, 2001.

Chodron, Thubten. *Buddhism for Beginners*. Ithaca, N.Y.: Snow Lion Publications, 2001.

Nhát Hanh, Thich. *Heart of the Buddha's Teaching: Transforming Suffering into Peace, Joy, and Liberation: The Four Noble Truths, the Noble Eightfold Path, and Other Basic Buddhist Teachings*. Berkeley, Calif.: Parallax Press, 1998.

Sangharakshita. *Vision and Transformation: An Introduction to the Buddha's Noble Eightfold Path*. 2nd ed. Birmingham, U.K.: Windhorse Publications, 2009.

Smith, Jean. *The Beginner's Guide to Walking the Buddha's Eightfold Path*. New York: Random House, 2002.

■ **Web Sites**

Bodhi, Bhikku. "The Noble Eightfold Path: The Way to the End of Suffering."
http://www.accesstoinsight.org/lib/authors/bodhi/waytoend.html

—Michael J. O'Neal

Noble Eightfold Path

It is the Noble Eightfold Path, the way that leads to the extinction of suffering, namely:

1. Right Understanding,

2. Right Mindedness, which together are Wisdom.

3. Right Speech,

4. Right Action,

5. Right Living, which together are Morality.

6. Right Effort,

7. Right Attentiveness,

8. Right Concentration, which together are Concentration.

This is the Middle Path which the Perfect One has found out, which makes one both to see and to know, which leads to peace, to discernment, to enlightenment, to Nirvana. Free from pain and torture is this path, free from groaning and suffering; it is the perfect path. Truly, like this path there is no other path to the purity of insight. If you follow this path, you will put an end to suffering. But each one has to struggle for himself, the Perfect Ones have only pointed out the way. Give ear then, for the Immortal is found. I reveal, I set forth the Truth. As I reveal it to you, so act! And that supreme goal of the holy life, for the sake of which, sons of good families rightly go forth from home to the homeless state: this you will, in no long time, in this very life, make known to yourself, realize, and make your own.

First Step: Right Understanding

WHAT, now, is Right Understanding? It is understanding the Four Truths. To understand suffering; to understand the origin of suffering; to understand the extinction of suffering; to understand the path that leads to the extinction of suffering: This is called Right Understanding. Or, when the noble disciple under-

stands what is karmically wholesome, and the root of wholesome karma; what is karmically unwholesome, and the root of unwholesome karma, then he has Right Understanding. ["Karmically unwholesome" is every volitional act of body, speech, or mind which is rooted in greed, hatred, or delusion, and produces evil and painful results in this or any future form of existence.] What, now, is "karmically unwholesome?" In Bodily Action it is destruction of living beings; stealing; and unlawful sexual intercourse. In Verbal Action it is lying; tale-bearing; harsh language; and frivolous talk. In Mental Action it is covetousness; ill-will; and wrong views.

And what is the root of unwholesome karma? Greed is a root of unwholesome karma; Anger is a root of unwholesome karma; Delusion is a root of unwholesome karma. [The state of greed, as well as that of anger, is always accompanied by delusion; and delusion, ignorance, is the primary root of all evil.] Therefore, I say, these demeritorious actions are of three kinds: either due to greed, or due to anger, or due to delusion. What, now, is "karmically wholesome?" In Bodily Action it is to abstain from killing; to abstain from stealing; and to abstain from unlawful sexual intercourse. In Verbal Action it is to abstain from lying; to abstain from tale-bearing; to abstain from harsh language; and to abstain from frivolous talk. In Mental Action it is absence of covetousness; absence of ill-will; and right understanding. And what is the root of wholesome karma? Absence of greed (unselfishness) is a root of wholesome karma; absence of anger (benevolence) is a root of wholesome karma; absence of delusion (wisdom) is a root of wholesome karma. Or, when one understands that corporeality, feeling, perception, mental formation, and consciousness, are transient [subject to suffering, and without an Ego], also in that case one possesses Right Understanding. . . .

♦ The Two Understandings
Therefore, I say, Right Understanding is of two kinds:

1. The view that alms and offerings are not useless; that there is fruit and result, both of good and bad actions; that there are such things as this life, and the next life; that father and mother as spontaneously born beings (in the heavenly worlds) are no

mere words; that there are monks and priests who are spotless and perfect, who can explain this life and the next life, which they themselves have understood: this is called the "Mundane Right Understanding," which yields worldly fruits, and brings good results.

2. But whatsoever there is of wisdom, of penetration, of right understanding, conjoined with the Path—the mind being turned away from the world, and conjoined with the path, the holy path being turned away from the world, and conjoined with the path, the holy path being pursued;—this is called the "Ultramundane Right Understanding," which is not of the world, but is ultramundane, and conjoined with the Path. [Thus, there are two kinds of the Eightfold Path: the "mundane," practiced by the "worldling"; and the "ultramundane," practiced by the "Noble Ones."] Now, in understanding wrong understanding as wrong, and right understanding as right, one practices Right Understanding [1st step]; and in making efforts to overcome wrong understanding, and to arouse right understanding, one practices Right Effort [6th step]; and in overcoming wrong understanding with attentive mind, and dwelling with attentive mind in the possession of right understanding, one practices Right-Attentiveness [7th step]. Hence, there are three things that accompany and follow upon right understanding, namely: right understanding, right effort, and right attentiveness. . . .

♦ Karma: Rebirth—Producing and Barren

Verily, because beings, obstructed by Delusion, and ensnared by Craving, now here now there seek ever fresh delight, therefore such action comes to ever fresh Rebirth. And the action that is done out of greed, anger and delusion, that springs from them, has its source and origin there: this action ripens wherever one is reborn; and wherever this action ripens, there one experiences the fruits of this action, be it in this life, or the next life, or in some future life. However, through the fading away of delusion through the arising of wisdom, through the extinction of craving, no future rebirth takes place again. For the actions, which are not done out of greed, anger and delusion, which have not sprung from them, which have not their source and origin there—such actions are, through the absence of greed, anger and delusion, abandoned, rooted out, like a palm-tree torn out of the soil, destroyed, and not liable to spring up again.

In this respect one may rightly say of me: that I teach annihilation, that I propound my doctrine for the purpose of annihilation, and that I herein train

my disciples; for, certainly, I do teach annihilation—the annihilation, namely, of greed, anger and delusion, as well as of the manifold evil and unwholesome things. ["Dependent Origination" is the teaching of the strict conformity to law of everything that happens, whether in the realm of the physical, or the psychical. It shows how the totality of phenomena, physical and mental, the entire phenomenal world that depends wholly upon the six senses, together with all its suffering—and this is the vital point of the teaching is not the mere play of blind chance, but has an existence that is dependent upon conditions; and that, precisely with the removal of these conditions, those things that have arisen in dependence upon them—thus also all suffering—must perforce disappear and cease to be.]

Second Step: Right Mindedness

WHAT, now, is Right Mindedness? It is thoughts free from lust; thoughts free from ill-will; thoughts free from cruelty. This is called right mindedness. Now, Right Mindedness, let me tell you, is of two kinds: 1. Thoughts free from lust, from ill-will, and from cruelty:—this is called the "Mundane Right Mindedness," which yields worldly fruits and brings good results. 2. But, whatsoever there is of thinking, considering, reasoning, thought, ratiocination, application—the mind being holy, being turned away from the world, and conjoined with the path, the holy path being pursued—: these "Verbal Operations" of the mind are called the "Ultramundane Right Mindedness," which is not of the world, but is ultramundane, and conjoined with the paths.

Now, in understanding wrong-mindedness as wrong, and right-mindedness as right, one practices Right Understanding [1st step]; and in making efforts to overcome evil-mindedness, and to arouse right-mindedness, one practices Right Effort [6th step]; and in overcoming evil-mindedness with attentive mind, and dwelling with attentive mind in possession of right-mindedness, one practices Right Attentiveness [7th step]. Hence, there are three things that accompany and follow upon right-mindedness, namely: right understanding, right effort, and right attentiveness.

Third Step: Right Speech

WHAT, now, is Right Speech? It is abstaining from lying; abstaining from tale-bearing; abstaining from harsh language; abstaining from vain talk. There, someone avoids lying, and abstains from it. He speaks the truth, is devoted to the truth, reliable, worthy of confidence, is not a deceiver of men. Being at a meeting, or amongst people, or in the midst of his relatives, or in a society, or in the king's court, and called upon and asked as witness, to tell what he knows, he answers, if he knows nothing: "I know nothing"; and if he knows, he answers: "I know"; if he has seen nothing, he answers: "I have seen nothing," and if he has seen, he answers: "I have seen." Thus, he never knowingly speaks a lie, neither for the sake of his own advantage, nor for the sake of another person's advantage, nor for the sake of any advantage whatsoever. He avoids tale-bearing, and abstains from it. What he has heard here, he does not repeat there, so as to cause dissension there; and what he heard there, he does not repeat here, so as to cause dissension here. Thus he unites those that are divided; and those that are united, he encourages. Concord gladdens him, he delights and rejoices in concord, and it is concord that he spreads by his words. He avoids harsh language, and abstains from it. He speaks such words as are gentle, soothing to the ear, loving, going to the heart, courteous and dear, and agreeable to many.

. . . He avoids vain talk, and abstains from it. He speaks at the right time, in accordance with facts, speaks what is useful, speaks about the law and the discipline; his speech is like a treasure, at the right moment accompanied by arguments, moderate and full of sense. This is called right speech.

Now, right speech, let me tell you, is of two kinds: 1. Abstaining from lying, from tale-bearing, from harsh language, and from vain talk; this is called the "Mundane Right Speech," which yields worldly fruits and brings good results. 2. But the abhorrence of the practice of this four-fold wrong speech, the abstaining, withholding, refraining therefrom—the mind being holy, being turned away from the world, and conjoined with the path, the holy path being pursued—: this is called the "Ultramundane Right Speech," which is not of the world, but is ultramundane, and conjoined with the paths. Now, in understanding wrong speech as wrong, and right speech aright, one practices Right Understanding [1st step); and in making efforts to overcome evil speech and to arouse right speech, one practices Right Effort [6th step]; and in overcoming wrong speech with attentive mind, and dwelling with attentive mind in possession of right speech, one practices Right Attentiveness [7th step]. Hence,

there are three things that accompany and follow upon right attentiveness.

Fourth Step: Right Action

WHAT, now, is Right Action? It is abstaining from killing; abstaining from stealing; abstaining from unlawful sexual intercourse. There, someone avoids the killing of living beings, and abstains from it. Without stick or sword, conscientious, full of sympathy, he is anxious for the welfare of all living beings. He avoids stealing, and abstains from it; what another person possesses of goods and chattels in the village or in the wood, that he does not take away with thievish intent. He avoids unlawful sexual intercourse, and abstains from it. He has no intercourse with such persons as are still under the protection of father, mother, brother, sister or relatives, nor with married women, nor female convicts, nor, lastly, with betrothed girls. This is called Right Action.

Now, Right Action, let me tell you, is of two kinds: 1. Abstaining from killing, from stealing, and from unlawful sexual intercourse—this is called the "Mundane Right Action," which yields worldly fruits and brings good results. But the abhorrence of the practice of this three-fold wrong action, the abstaining, withholding, refraining therefrom—the mind being holy, being turned away from the world, and conjoined with the path, the holy path being pursued—: this is called the "Ultramundane Right Action," which is not of the world, but is ultramundane, and conjoined with the paths. Now, in understanding wrong action as wrong, and right action as right, one practices Right Understanding [1st step]; and in making efforts to overcome wrong action, and to arouse right action, one practices Right Effort [6th step]; and in overcoming wrong action with attentive mind, and dwelling with attentive mind in possession of right action, one practices Right Attentiveness [7th step]. Hence, there are three things that accompany and follow upon right action, namely: right understanding, right effort, and right attentiveness.

Fifth Step: Right Living

WHAT, now, is Right Living? When the noble disciple, avoiding a wrong way of living, gets his livelihood by a right way of living, this is called Right Living. Now, right living, let me tell you, is of two kinds: 1.When the noble disciple, avoiding wrong living, gets his livelihood by a right way of living—this is called the "Mundane Right Living," which yields worldly fruits and brings good results. 2. But the abhorrence of wrong living, the abstaining, withholding, refraining therefrom—the mind being holy, being turned away from the world, and conjoined with the path, the holy path being pursued—: this is called the "Ultramundane Right Living," which is not of the world, but is ultramundane, and conjoined with the paths.

Now, in understanding wrong living as wrong, and right living as right, one practices Right Understanding [1st step]; and in making efforts to overcome wrong living, to arouse right living, one practices Right Effort [6th step]; and in overcoming wrong living with attentive mind, and dwelling with attentive mind in possession of right living, one practices Right Attentiveness [7th step]. Hence, there are three things that accompany and follow upon right living, namely: right understanding, right effort, and right attentiveness.

Sixth Step: Right Effort

WHAT, now, is Right Effort? There are Four Great Efforts: the effort to avoid, the effort to overcome, the effort to develop, and the effort to maintain. What, now, is the effort to avoid? There, the disciple incites his mind to avoid the arising of evil, demeritorious things that have not yet arisen; and he strives, puts forth his energy, strains his mind and struggles. Thus, when he perceives a form with the eye, a sound with the ear, an odor with the nose, a taste with the tongue, a contact with the body, or an object with the mind, he neither adheres to the whole, nor to its parts. And he strives to ward off that through which evil and demeritorious things, greed and sorrow, would arise, if he remained with unguarded senses; and he watches over his senses, restrains his senses. Possessed of this noble "Control over the Senses," he experiences inwardly a feeling of joy, into which no evil thing can enter. This is called the effort to avoid.

What, now, is the effort to Overcome? There, the disciple incites his mind to overcome the evil, demeritorious things that have already arisen; and he strives, puts forth his energy, strains his mind and struggles. He does not retain any thought of sensual lust, ill-will, or grief, or any other evil and demeritorious states that may have arisen; he abandons them, dispels them, destroys them, causes them to disappear. . . .

What, now, is the effort to Develop? There the disciple incites his will to arouse meritorious conditions that have not yet arisen; and he strives, puts forth his

energy, strains his mind and struggles. Thus he develops the "Elements of Enlightenment," bent on solitude, on detachment, on extinction, and ending in deliverance, namely: Attentiveness, Investigation of the Law, Energy, Rapture, Tranquility, Concentration, and Equanimity. This is called the effort to develop.

What, now, is the effort to Maintain? There, the disciple incites his will to maintain the meritorious conditions that have already arisen, and not to let them disappear, but to bring them to growth, to maturity and to the full perfection of development; and he strives, puts forth his energy, strains his mind and struggles. Thus, for example, he keeps firmly in his mind a favorable object of concentration that has arisen, as the mental image of a skeleton, of a corpse infested by worms, of a corpse blue-black in color, of a festering corpse, of a corpse riddled with holes, of a corpse swollen up. This is called the effort to maintain. . . .

Seventh Step: Right Attentiveness

WHAT, now, is Right Attentiveness? The only way that leads to the attainment of purity, to the overcoming of sorrow and lamentation, to the end of pain and grief, to the entering upon the right path and the realization of Nirvana, is the "Four Fundamentals of Attentiveness." And which are these four? In them, the disciple dwells in contemplation of the Body, in contemplation of Feeling, in contemplation of the Mind, in contemplation of the Mind-objects, ardent, clearly conscious and attentive, after putting away worldly greed and grief.

♦ Contemplation of the Body

But, how does the disciple dwell in contemplation of the body? There, the disciple retires to the forest, to the foot of a tree, or to a solitary place, sits himself down, with legs crossed, body erect, and with attentiveness fixed before him. With attentive mind he breathes in, with attentive mind he breathes out. When making a long inhalation, he knows: "I make a long inhalation"; when making a long exhalation, he knows: "I make a long exhalation." When making a short inhalation, he knows: "I make a short inhalation"; when making a short exhalation, he knows: "I make a short exhalation." "Clearly perceiving the entire [breath]-body, I will breathe in": thus he trains himself; "clearly perceiving the entire [breath]-body, I will breathe out": thus he trains himself. "Calming this bodily function, I will breathe in": thus he trains himself; "calming this bodily function, I will breathe out": thus he trains himself.

Thus he dwells in contemplation of the body, either with regard to his own person, or to other persons, or to both. He beholds how the body arises; beholds how it passes away; beholds the arising and passing away of the body. . . . "A body is there, but no living being, no individual, no woman, no man, no self, and nothing that belongs to a self; neither a person, nor anything belonging to a person"—this clear consciousness is present in him, because of his knowledge and mindfulness, and he lives independent, unattached to anything in the world. Thus does the disciple dwell in contemplation of the body.

And further, whilst going, standing, sitting, or lying down, the disciple understands the expressions: "I go"; "I stand"; "I sit"; "I lie down"; he understands any position of the body. [The disciple understands that it is not a being, a real Ego, that goes, stands, etc., but that it is by a mere figure of speech that one says: "I go," "I stand," and so forth.]

And further, the disciple is clearly conscious in his going and coming; clearly conscious in looking forward and backward; clearly conscious in bending and stretching; clearly conscious in eating, drinking, chewing, and tasting; clearly conscious in discharging excrement and urine; clearly conscious in walking, standing, sitting, falling asleep and awakening; clearly conscious in speaking and in keeping silent. "In all the disciple is doing, he is clearly conscious: of his intention, of his advantage, of his duty, of the reality."

And further, the disciple contemplates this body from the sole of the foot upward, and from the top of the hair downward, with a skin stretched over it, and filled with manifold impurities: "This body consists of hairs, nails, teeth, skin, flesh, sinews, bones, marrow, kidneys, heart, liver, diaphragm, spleen, lungs, intestines, bowels, stomach, and excrement; of bile, phlegm, pus, blood, sweat, lymph, tears, semen, spittle, nasal mucus, oil of the joints, and urine." Just as if there were a sack, with openings at both ends, filled with all kinds of grain—with paddy, beans, sesamum and husked rice—and a man not blind opened it and examined its contents, thus: "That is paddy, these are beans, this is sesamum, this is husked rice": just so does the disciple investigate this body.

And further, the disciple contemplates this body with regard to the elements: "This body consists of the solid element, the liquid element, the heating element and the vibrating element." Just as a skilled butcher or butcher's apprentice, who has slaughtered a cow and divided it into separate portions, should sit down at the junction of four highroads: just so does the disciple contemplate this body with regard to the elements.

And further, just as if the disciple should see a corpse thrown into the burial-ground, one, two, or three days dead, swollen-up, blue-black in color, full of corruption he draws the conclusion as to his own body: "This my body also has this nature, has this destiny, and cannot escape it." And further, just as if the disciple should see a corpse thrown into the burial-ground, eaten by crows, hawks or vultures, by dogs or jackals, or gnawed by all kinds of worms—he draws the conclusion as to his own body: "This my body also has this nature, has this destiny, and cannot escape it."

And further, just as if the disciple should see a corpse thrown into the burial-ground, a framework of bones, flesh hanging from it, bespattered with blood, held together by the sinews; a framework of bones, stripped of flesh, bespattered with blood, held together by the sinews; a framework of bones, without flesh and blood, but still held together by the sinews; bones, disconnected and scattered in all directions, here a bone of the hand, there a bone of the foot, there a shin bone, there a thigh bone, there the pelvis, there the spine, there the skull—he draws the conclusion as to his own body: "This my body also has this nature, has this destiny, and cannot escape it."

And further, just as if the disciple should see bones lying in the burial ground, bleached and resembling shells; bones heaped together, after the lapse of years; bones weathered and crumbled to dust;—he draws the conclusion as to his own body: "This my body also has this nature, has this destiny, and cannot escape it." Thus he dwells in contemplation of the body, either with regard to his own person, or to other persons, or to both. He beholds how the body arises; beholds how it passes away; beholds the arising and passing of the body. "A body is there"—this clear consciousness is present in him, because of his knowledge and mindfulness; and he lives independent, unattached to anything in the world. Thus does the disciple dwell in contemplation of the body. . . .

♦ **Nirvana through Watching over Breathing**

"Watching over In- and Outbreathing" practiced and developed, brings the four Fundamentals of Attentiveness to perfection; the four fundamentals of attentiveness, practiced and developed bring the seven Elements of Enlightenment to perfection; the seven elements of enlightenment, practiced and developed, bring Wisdom and Deliverance to perfection.

But how does Watching over In- and Outbreathing, practiced and developed, bring the four Fundamentals of Attentiveness to perfection?

I. Whenever the disciple is conscious in making a long inhalation or exhalation, or in making a short inhalation or exhalation, or is training himself to inhale or exhale whilst feeling the whole [breath]-body, or whilst calming down this bodily function—at such a time the disciple is dwelling in "contemplation of the body," of energy, clearly conscious, attentive, after subduing worldly greed and grief. For, inhalation and exhalation I call one amongst the corporeal phenomena.

II. Whenever the disciple is training himself to inhale or exhale whilst feeling rapture, or joy, or the mental functions, or whilst calming down the mental functions—at such a time he is dwelling in "contemplation of the feelings," full of energy, clearly conscious, attentive, after subduing worldly greed and grief. For, the full awareness of In- and Outbreathing I call one amongst the feelings.

III. Whenever the disciple is training himself to inhale or exhale whilst feeling the mind, or whilst gladdening the mind or whilst concentrating the mind, or whilst setting the mind free—at such a time he is dwelling in "contemplation of the mind," full of energy, clearly conscious, attentive, after subduing worldly greed and grief. For, without attentiveness and clear consciousness, I say, there is no Watching over In- and Outbreathing.

IV. Whenever the disciple is training himself to inhale or exhale whilst contemplating impermanence, or the fading away of passion, or extinction, or detachment at such a time he is dwelling in "contemplation of the phenomena," full of energy, clearly conscious, attentive, after subduing worldly greed and grief. Watching over In- and Outbreathing, thus practiced and developed, brings the four Fundamentals of Attentiveness to perfection.

But how do the four Fundamentals of Attentiveness, practiced and developed, bring the seven Elements of Enlightenment to full perfection? Whenever the disciple is dwelling in contemplation of body, feeling, mind and phenomena, strenuous, clearly conscious, attentive, after subduing worldly greed and grief—at such a time his attentiveness is undisturbed; and whenever his attentiveness is present and undisturbed, at such a time he has gained and is developing the Element of Enlightenment "Attentiveness"; and thus this element of enlightenment reaches fullest perfection.

And whenever, whilst dwelling with attentive mind, he wisely investigates, examines and thinks over the Law—at such a time he has gained and is developing the Element of Enlightenment "Investigation of the Law"; and thus this element of enlightenment reaches fullest perfection. And whenever, whilst wisely investigating, examining and thinking over the law, his energy is firm and unshaken—at such a time he has gained and is developing the Element of Enlightenment "Energy"; and thus this element of enlightenment reaches fullest perfection.

And whenever in him, whilst firm in energy, arises supersensuous rapture—at such a time he has gained and is developing the Element of Enlightenment "Rapture"; and thus this element of enlightenment reaches fullest perfection.

And whenever, whilst enraptured in mind, his spiritual frame and his mind become tranquil—at such a time he has gained and is developing the Element of Enlightenment "Tranquility"; and thus this element of enlightenment reaches fullest perfection.

And whenever, whilst being tranquilized in his spiritual frame and happy, his mind becomes concentrated—at such a time he has gained and is developing the Element of Enlightenment "Concentration"; and thus this element of enlightenment reaches fullest perfection.

And whenever he thoroughly looks with indifference on his mind thus concentrated—at such a time he has gained and is developing the Element of Enlightenment "Equanimity."

The four fundamentals of attentiveness, thus practiced and developed, bring the seven elements of enlightenment to full perfection. But how do the seven elements of enlightenment, practiced and developed, bring Wisdom and Deliverance to full perfection? There, the disciple is developing the elements of enlightenment: Attentiveness, Investigation of the Law, Energy, Rapture, Tranquility, Concentration and Equanimity, bent on detachment, on absence of desire, on extinction and renunciation. Thus practiced and developed, do the seven elements of enlightenment bring wisdom and deliverance to full perfection.

Just as the elephant hunter drives a huge stake into the ground and chains the wild elephant to it by the neck, in order to drive out of him his wonted forest ways and wishes, his forest unruliness, obstinacy and violence, and to accustom him to the environment of the village, and to teach him such good behavior as is required amongst men: in like manner also has the noble disciple to fix his mind firmly to these four fundamentals of attentiveness, so that he may drive out of himself his wonted worldly ways and wishes, his wonted worldly unruliness, obstinacy and violence, and win to the True, and realize Nirvana.

Eighth Step: Right Concentration

WHAT, now, is Right Concentration? Fixing the mind to a single object ("One-pointedness of mind"): this is concentration. The four Fundamentals of Attentiveness (seventh step): these are the objects of concentration. The four Great Efforts (sixth step): these are the requisites for concentration. The practicing, developing and cultivating of these things: this is the "Development" of concentration.

[Right Concentration has two degrees of development: 1. "Neighborhood-Concentration," which approaches the first trance, without however attaining it; 2. "Attainment Concentration," which is the concentration present in the four trances. The attainment of the trances, however, is not a requisite for the realization of the Four Ultramundane Paths of Holiness; and neither Neighborhood-Concentration nor Attainment-Concentration, as such, in any way possesses the power of conferring entry into the Four Ultramundane Paths; hence, in them is really no power to free oneself permanently from evil things. The realization of the Four Ultramundane Paths is possible only at the moment of insight into the impermanency, miserable nature, and impersonality of phenomenal process of existence. This insight is attainable only during Neighborhood-Concentration, not during Attainment-Concentration. He who has realized one or other of the Four Ultramundane Paths without ever having attained the Trances, is called a "Dry-visioned One," or one whose passions are "dried up by Insight." He, however, who after cultivating the Trances has reached

one of the Ultramundane Paths, is called "one who has taken tranquility as his vehicle."]

♦ The Four Trances

Detached from sensual objects, detached from unwholesome things, the disciple enters into the first trance, which is accompanied by "Verbal Thought," and "Rumination," is born of "Detachment," and filled with "Rapture," and "Happiness." This first trance is free from five things, and five things are present. When the disciple enters the first trance, there have vanished [the 5 Hindrances]: Lust, Ill-will, Torpor and Dullness, Restlessness and Mental Worry, Doubts; and there are present: Verbal Thought, Rumination, Rapture, Happiness, and Concentration.

And further: after the subsiding of verbal thought and rumination, and by the gaining of inward tranquility and oneness of mind, he enters into a state free from verbal thought and rumination, the second trance, which is born of Concentration, and filled with Rapture and Happiness.

And further: after the fading away of rapture, he dwells in equanimity, attentive, clearly conscious; and he experiences in his person that feeling, of which the Noble Ones say: "Happy lives the man of equanimity and attentive mind"—thus he enters the third trance.

And further: after the giving up of pleasure and pain, and through the disappearance of previous joy and grief, he enters into a state beyond pleasure and pain, into the fourth trance, which is purified by equanimity and attentiveness.

[The four Trances may be obtained by means of Watching over In- and Outbreathing, as well as through the fourth sublime meditation, the "Meditation of Equanimity," and others. The three other Sublime Meditations of "Loving Kindness," "Compassion," and "Sympathetic Joy" may lead to the attainment of

Glossary

karma	the effects of a person's actions, which determine one's destiny in one's next incarnation
Middle Way	a path of moderation between the extremes of self-mortification and sensual indulgence
Nirvana	the state of being free from suffering
Perfect One	the Buddha (Siddhartha Gautama)
sesamum	a tropical herb and flowering plant, one variety of which is the source of sesame seeds
ultramundane	beyond mundane, or beyond ordinary; higher

the first three Trances. The "Cemetery Meditations," as well as the meditation "On Loathsomeness," will produce only the First Trance. The "Analysis of the Body," and the Contemplation on the Buddha, the Law, the Holy Brotherhood, Morality, etc., will only produce Neighborhood-Concentration.]

Develop your concentration: for he who has concentration understands things according to their reality. And what are these things? The arising and passing away of corporeality, of feeling, perception, mental formations and consciousness. Thus, these five Groups of Existence must be wisely penetrated; Delusion and Craving must be wisely abandoned; Tranquility and Insight must be wisely developed. This is the Middle Path which the Perfect One has discovered, which makes one both to see and to know, and which leads to peace, to discernment, to enlightenment, to Nirvana. And following upon this path, you will put an end to suffering.

Carved statue of Mahavira

(Carved statue of Mahavira from the Vimala Sha Temple [photo], Indian School / Mount Abu, Rajasthan, India / Dinodia / The Bridgeman Art Library International)

JAIN SUTRAS

"A wise man should neither be glad nor angry (about his lot): thou shouldst know and consider the happiness of living creatures."

Overview

Composed sometime between the fifth and third centuries BCE, the Jain Sutras represent the system of thought crystallized by the Indian ascetic and teacher Mahavira in the sixth century BCE. Also called the Angas, or "Limbs," this body of eleven works is one part of the Jain canon, collectively called the Agamas. The sutras are the most important part of the canon, which also includes texts that explain and comment upon the sutras; instructions on how Jain monks, nuns, and laypeople should behave; and miscellaneous works covering general knowledge, such as grammar, mathematics, and astronomy.

The Acaranga Sutra is probably the oldest of all the Jain Sutras and lays out a worldview based on an ancient doctrine of karma—the cycle of actions and consequences—that predates Mahavira and was shared by other major Indian schools of thought, like those of the Buddhists and the Brahmins. The theory of karma holds that existence is an endless cycle wherein all actions, good or bad, bring about consequences for the person who performs them and for the rest of the world. When people die, there are always outstanding consequences related to their actions that they did not experience, such that people are reincarnated in order to experience equivalent consequences. Although it draws on the same ideas as the Buddhist and Brahmin texts, the Acaranga Sutra gives a radically different solution to the problem of karma, distinguished by a heavy emphasis on ahimsa, or nonviolence. The Jains taught that every living thing has a soul and that to kill something with a soul is to commit a sin and acquire karmic debt. To avoid this, Jain monks went to great lengths, sweeping the ground in front of them so as not to step on any creatures and covering their mouths with cloths to avoid unintentionally swallowing flying insects.

Context

One of the earliest of the Jain Sutras, the Acaranga Sutra was compiled by unknown authors who based their text on the teachings of Mahavira, a Jain saint who had died several generations before, in 527 BCE. Jainism had long been present in India when Mahavira was born. But the age in which he lived, the middle of the first millennium BCE, saw sweeping religious, social, economic, and political changes that transformed Indian culture.

About a thousand years before Mahavira, around 1500 BCE, a group of nomadic cattle herders migrated into northwestern India from Central Asia, bringing with them a body of orally transmitted texts called the Vedas and a religion based on the regular performance of sacrifice. As the religion of the Vedas took hold, there arose a priestly class responsible for transmitting the sacred texts and performing the elaborate rituals they contained. This class, called the Brahmins, was at the top of a hereditary four-tier caste system that was ranked according to access to the all-important sacrifice. Below the Brahmins were the class of warriors and kings, then the class of farmers and craftsmen, and finally slaves. The Brahmins, whose religion is the basis of the Hindu tradition, worshipped a pantheon of deities related to the gods of ancient Greece and Scandinavia and held the Vedas up as the absolute authority on everything. Their knowledge of the texts and their exclusive right to perform the sacrifices kept the Brahmins in a position of privilege.

By the fifth century BCE the Brahmins had composed a vast body of commentary, called the Upanishads, about the secret meaning of the Vedas. Some of the Brahmins renounced the world and retreated into the wilderness to transmit their esoteric knowledge to students. They also began to see meditation and intense asceticism as ways to internalize sacrifice and gain great philosophical insights. Out of this movement of forest dwellers, the great traditions of Buddhism and Jainism were born. Mahavira and Siddhartha Gautama, the two most important figures in Jainism and Buddhism, respectfully, were born not into the Brahmin class but into the warrior class. Unlike the Brahmins, Buddhists and Jains rejected the sacrifice and the authority of the Vedas.

The Brahmins had thrived when Indian society was organized into small tribal chiefdoms, such that there were plenty of local rulers to support them. But when the great empires, especially the Maurya Empire, founded in 322 BCE, supplanted the authority of local rulers, the Brahmins began to lose their patronage. The ideas of Buddhism and Jainism,

CA. 850 –750 BCE	■ Parsvanatha, the purported founder of Jainism, is believed to have lived.
CA. 599 BCE	■ Mahavira is born into a warrior clan as Vardhamana in the village of Kundagrama, outside the city of Vaishali, in what is now the Indian state of Bihar.
CA. 569 BCE	■ Mahavira's parents die, and he leaves his wife and daughter to become a Jain monk.
CA. 557 BCE	■ Mahavira achieves enlightenment after twelve years of self-mortification and begins to preach.
CA. 527 BCE	■ Mahavira dies and attains ultimate liberation.
CA. 500 –200 BCE	■ The followers of Mahavira compile the Jain Sutras from oral transmissions of his teachings.
CA. 350 –300 BCE	■ The first Jain council is held at Pataliputra to determine the contents of the canon.
CA. 100 –200 CE	■ A schism occurs between Digambara and Svetambara Jains over whether or not an ascetic may wear clothing.
CA. 300 –400 CE	■ The second Jain council successfully agrees upon the canon at Vallabhi.

which appealed to non-Brahmins because they rejected the Brahmins' hierarchy, quickly spread throughout the subcontinent via merchants, who could travel freely because of the political stability created by the empires. The Acaranga Sutra came out of this period of sweeping change, offering a new worldview that declared the futility of the material power coveted by the Brahmins and outlined a new path to liberation based on asceticism and nonviolence.

About the Author

No one knows who actually composed the Jain Sutras, but according to tradition they were compiled several gen-

erations after Mahavira's death by disciples of his disciples. Jainism does not acknowledge any founder but does recognizes Mahavira as the last of a line of twenty-four Tirthankaras, or gurus, stretching back for millennia. Only the last two Tirthankaras, Mahavira and Parsvanatha, can be linked to historical figures. The rest are legendary.

Mahavira, originally named Vardhamana, was born into a powerful warrior clan called the Jnatas, and many of the metaphors used in the sutras come from battle terminology. For example, the first two chapters of the Acaranga Sutra are called "Knowledge of the Weapon" and "Conquest of the World." Likewise, the word *Jain* or *Jaina* itself refers to the follower of a *jina*, or "conqueror," and Vardhamana's adopted name of *Mahavira* means "Great Hero" or "Great Man." In Jain iconography, he is sometimes represented by a lion.

Like all Jain monks, Mahavira underwent severe austerities, such as prolonged periods of meditation, nakedness, and fasting. After he achieved enlightenment and began teaching, Mahavira remained faithful to his Jain tradition, though he did add a fifth vow, celibacy, to the traditional monastic vows of nonviolence, not having possessions, and refraining from lying and stealing. Mahavira had eleven disciples to whom he revealed his message and who, in turn, passed it on. He lived and taught for thirty years after his enlightenment; when he died in 527 BCE, according to Jain tradition, he was not reincarnated because he had escaped the cycle of death and rebirth.

Explanation and Analysis of the Document

Unlike the texts of the Brahmins, which were composed in the scholarly language of Sanskrit, and the Buddhist texts, composed in the related language of Pali, the Acaranga Sutra was written in Ardhamagadhi, one of the many vernacular tongues, called Prakrits, that common people used in ancient India. The Jain Sutras were written in numerous Prakrits, including several South Indian languages unrelated to Sanskrit. The fact that the texts were composed in commonly spoken, nonliturgical language made them easily accessible and popular with the merchant class that was quickly growing throughout the subcontinent, facilitating the spread of Jainist ideas. The following two lectures are the first of the twenty-four lectures that make up the Acaranga Sutra. The text is aimed at Jain monks and nuns and lays out the proper mind-set and actions for one who wishes to follow the path of asceticism. Parenthetical wording in the document text indicates passages where the translator has supplied contextual meaning that does not explicitly appear in the text.

♦ First Lecture: "Knowledge of the Weapon"

First Lesson: The text is organized systematically in a series of lectures that lay out what Mahavira sees as the diagnosis of the disease that is human existence. The text of each lecture is broken up into numbered verses. In this first lecture, the text makes clear that Mahavira's disciple Sudharman is relating one of the master's speeches to his

A group of Jain nuns
(A group of Jain nuns [photo], / Dinodia / The Bridgeman Art Library International)

own disciple, Gambusvamin. Thus, Mahavira may be effectively considered the speaker (though Sudharman refers to him within the text as "the Revered One"). In calling the lesson "Knowledge of the Weapon," Mahavira emphasizes the destructive aspects of actions performed by ignorant people who do not understand the consequences.

Before he introduces his theory on consequential action, Mahavira establishes the doctrine of reincarnation in verses 2–4. Whenever a being acquires karmic debt by causing some harm, time is added to his existence so that he can remain to suffer consequences. This was a common idea in ancient India, but Mahavira also taught that many who retreated into the woods and abstained from worldly life were false ascetics who were unintentionally acquiring karmic debt in ways they could not comprehend.

When Mahavira says in verse 5 that the wise man "believes in soul, believes in the world, believes in reward, believes in action," he takes aim at two of his rival sects. The first is a philosophical Brahmin sect called the Advaita, or "Non-dualists," who believe that the individual souls (atman) of beings are not individual at all but are parts of one universal, fundamental being called Brahmin. Thus, the Advaitas believe that there is no duality between the "soul" and the "world" and do not recognize the first two of the

four conditions Mahavira lists. The second sect Mahavira is arguing against is Buddhism, which teaches that there is no permanent "soul" at all but only a collection of karmic impressions that undergo constant rebirth.

Offering an alternative to what he considers false teachings, Mahavira lists some important tenets of Jainism: that a soul separate from the body undergoes reincarnation, that everything in the universe has some kind of soul, and that a relationship between actions in the world (*kriya*) and karmic debt ties beings to the cycle of rebirth. But, as Mahavira concludes, "He who, in the world, comprehends and renounces these causes of sin, is called a reward-knowing sage."

Second Lesson: Lest the reader be confused that the cycle of rebirth is somehow preferable to the complete extinction of the self, in the second lesson Mahavira hammers home his point that suffering and human existence are inextricably linked. In order to pursue the rigorous and austere Jain path, one must first be convinced that existence is suffering. In the ensuing verses, Mahavira explains what makes the Jain practice of nonviolence different from the practices of Brahmins, Buddhists, and other sects. The Jains believed that since everything in the universe has a soul, people are constantly harming things like soil, rocks, and the earth itself without realizing it as they go about their daily lives. Even Buddhist monks are still harming the earth in their daily lives and thus still laden with karmic debt.

Third Lesson: Having discussed the unintentional harm that false ascetics like the Buddhists do to the class of earthly beings, Mahavira moves on in the third lesson to the beings that live in water. But the lesson begins with a definition of the true ascetic as "he who acts rightly, who does pious work, who practises no deceit." All three of these ideals are also common to Buddhism, but as the lessons continue, Mahavira continues to expose what he sees as the ways in which Buddhists only believe they are following these ideals.

As in the previous two lessons, Mahavira connects each of these individual teachings about the souls that exist in water to a belief in the self. In verse 3, he iterates the formula "He who denies the world (of water-bodies), denies the self; and he who denies the self, denies the world of (water-bodies)." Mahavira is insisting here that the teachings of Jainism be taken together as a whole, rather than piecemeal; what he is presenting is a totalizing worldview. This held great appeal for the masses, since it presented a democratic type of religion with the same rules for everyone, as opposed to the hierarchy of Brahminism. But it also appealed to the would-be emperors who were beginning to extend their rule over large parts of South Asia and pull together disparate regions under their centralized control. A universalizing religion goes hand in hand with imperial domination. But eventually it was Buddhism, not Jainism, that spread across Asia with the conversion of the Mauryan emperor Ashoka in the third century BCE.

Jain thought, like other ancient Indian schools of thought, is very systematic in its approach. In keeping with this systematic way of thinking, Mahavira divides up the beings of the world into beings of earth, water, fire, air, and plants. He further subdivides each class of beings into three categories—sentient, insentient, and mixed. The insentient beings do not have souls, and one does not acquire karmic debt by harming them. But, long before science discovered microscopic organisms, Mahavira taught that there are more lives in the water than can be seen, leading him to declare in verse 7 that Jain monks, unlike their Buddhist counterparts, must strain water before they drink it or wash with it so that they will not accidentally kill anything.

Fourth Lesson: Having discussed the existence of earth beings and water beings, Mahavira moves on in lesson 4 to the class of fire beings. He also introduces what some scholars see as an early form of environmentalism in verse 3: "He who is unmindful of duty, and desiring of the qualities (i.e. of the pleasure and profit which may be derived from the elements) is called the torment (of living beings). Knowing this, a wise man (resolves): 'Now (I shall do) no more what I used to do wantonly before.'" Mahavira is arguing that those who seek to gain by exploiting earth, water, fire, and plant life without considering the harmful consequences of their actions are a torment to living beings. The word translated as "torment" is *danda*, which refers to a stick used to beat and punish wrongdoers.

Unlike earth beings, which live in the earth, and water beings, which live in the water, the fire beings discussed in this lesson seem not to be beings that live in fire but the insects that die as a result of carelessly built fires. In verse 6, Mahavira describes the fire beings as small insects and other creatures that live in the earth on which the fire is built, in the cow dung and wood used as fuel, and in the dry grass used as kindling, as well as the insects that may accidentally jump or fly into the fire.

Mahavira's condemnation of the violence of fire is an indictment against the Brahmin cult of sacrifice. The Vedic rituals of sacrifice all depended on the sacred fire, personified by the god Agni, and the ritual building of the fire pit and lighting of the flame were among the most solemn Brahmin rituals. In addition, Brahmin males were required to keep a sacred fire going in their homes at all times from the day of their entrance into manhood. When Mahavira attacks fire, he is attacking the Brahmin religion.

Fifth Lesson: In keeping with the systematic nature of the Acaranga Sutra, the discussions of earth beings, water beings, and fire beings would be followed by air beings in order to complete the sequence of the four classical elements. Contrary to expectation, the next class of beings discussed is not air beings but plants. The reason for this, according to later commentators on the text, was to strengthen the argument by moving on to a class of beings that everyone recognized. In ancient India, the place of air in the elements was not as well established as that of fire, water, and earth, since the latter are visible, but air or wind is not.

While many ancient Indian ascetic groups advocated vegetarianism and abstaining from killing animals, the Jains were unique in arguing that it is also sinful to kill plants. Mahavira points out the parallels between plant and human life in verse 6, noting that both are born and age over time, can suffer injury, need food, and utlimately die and decay. He argues that plants have sentience based on the fact that they know the proper times to bloom and to drop their leaves. Mahavira also picks up the argument against the exploitation of natural resources, begun in the previous chapter, in verses 2 and 3, where he equates the desire for the material benefits of the elements to a whirlpool that sucks men again and again into the cycle of rebirth.

Sixth Lesson: The sixth lesson deals with the subject of killing animals. Mahavira begins with an eightfold division of animals according to the ways in which they are born. The final class, those born by reincarnation, includes not only human beings but also gods and hell beings. Jains acknowledge that a life filled with good deeds may result in being reborn in a heaven as a god, while a life of evil deeds will result in being reborn in a hell; neither of these states are permanent, and beings always return to the cycle of rebirth.

Mahavira goes on to argue that all beings feel pain and terror and so killing them for any reason, including sacrifice, is a sinful act. Like the discussion of fire in the fourth

"Some know that their soul is born again and again, that it arrives in this or that direction, whatever direction that may be. He believes in soul, believes in the world, believes in reward, believes in action (acknowledged to be our own doing in such judgments as these): 'I did it'; 'I shall cause another to do it'; 'I shall allow another to do it.' In the world, these are all the causes of sin, which must be comprehended and renounced."

"The (living) world is afflicted, miserable, difficult to instruct, and without discrimination. In this world full of pain, suffering by their different acts, see the benighted ones cause great pain."

"Having well considered it, having well looked at it, I say thus: all beings, those with two, three, four senses, plants, those with five senses, and the rest of creation, (experience) individually pleasure or displeasure, pain, great terror, and unhappiness."

"Knowing pain and pleasure in all their variety, and seeing his life not yet decline, a wise man should know that to be the proper moment (for entering a religious life); while the perceptions of his ear, eye, organs of smelling, tasting, touching are not yet deteriorated, while all these perceptions are not yet deteriorated, man should prosecute the real end of his soul."

"'Frequently (I have been born) in a high family, frequently in a low one; I am not mean, nor noble, nor do I desire (social preferment).' Thus reflecting, who would brag about his family or about his glory, or for what should he long? Therefore a wise man should neither be glad nor angry (about his lot): thou shouldst know and consider the happiness of living creatures."

"Thus spake the hero: 'Be careful against this great delusion; the clever one should have done with carelessness by considering death in tranquillity, and that, the nature of which is decay (viz. the body); these (pleasures), look! will not satisfy (thee). Therefore have done with them!'"

lesson, Mahavira's condemnation of sacrifice is an argument aimed at his intellectual opponents, the Brahmins.

Seventh Lesson: The seventh lesson completes the elemental quartet with a discussion of wind beings; but the actual description of the wind beings in verse 4 is nothing more than a nearly word-for-word restatement of verse 6 in the lesson on fire beings. Mahavira makes the real point of this lesson in verses 6 and 7, when he says that those who consider themselves to be pious and ascetic but do not recognize the harm they do in their daily actions to the six kinds of beings described earlier are doomed to be reborn into the world of suffering.

♦ **Second Lecture: Conquest of the World**
First Lesson: Keeping with the martial theme, the second lecture of the Acaranga Sutra is called "Conquest of the World," which can be accomplished only through conquest of the self. In the Brahmin worldview, political power and spiritual authority are two separate domains, but Mahavira's message equates the warrior values of his martial clan with the virtues of the ascetic.

Having discussed the nature of violence, Mahavira uses the second lecture to introduce a nonviolent way of conquest through renunciation. He begins by arguing that the pursuit of worldly pleasure and attachment to things leads inexorably to sorrow and suffering. But when a man waits until he is old and his senses fail him to realize that material pursuits are worthless and turn to asceticism, it is already too late. In ancient India it was not uncommon for a householder of any caste to become an ascetic late in life, giving up his possessions and allowing his sons to inherit before his death. This practice of retirement ensured that the lands would always be tended by able-bodied men, while the old could live on the donations of others. Yet in verse 5, Mahavira recommends that a man should begin ascetic pursuits while he is still young and strong enough to enjoy the pleasures of life he is renouncing.

Second Lesson: After recommending that young men pursue the road of self-denial and discipline that comes with being "houseless"—that is, a wandering monk—Mahavira warns them against the danger of following false teachers, by which he means Buddhists, Brahmins, and Ajivikas, the followers of his rival, Gosala. Likening the cycle of rebirth to a wide and treacherous sea, Mahavira says that the wise will cross to the other side by completely renouncing desire. But the ignorant will become trapped in the pursuit of wealth and pleasure, which always entails violence, or fall under the spell of priests who convince them that sponsoring sacrifices will remove their sins.

Third Lesson: In the third lesson, Mahavira attacks the hereditary privilege of the Brahmin's caste system, writing in verse 1, "'Frequently (I have been born) in a high family, frequently in a low one; I am not mean, nor noble . . . .' Thus reflecting, who would brag about his family or about his glory?" Despite the fact that he was born into a powerful clan, Maha-

vira recognizes that over his multitude of past lives, he has taken the form of every type of being, from king to insect. And at all times he was equally trapped in the vicious cycle of rebirth because, as he says in verse 4, "there is nothing inaccessible for death."

For Mahavira, those who delight in their noble birth are as deluded as those who work to acquire wealth. In verse 5, he describes the man who abuses labor animals and natural resources to become rich, only to have his fortune divided among his heirs upon his death or taken away by misfortune during his lifetime. The money he makes will be gone, but the karmic debt he accrues in acquiring that money will still cause his soul to suffer.

Fourth Lesson: The fourth lesson continues Mahavira's portrayal of the ignorant man who seeks pleasure and enjoyment in the world, repeating the description of the uncertainties of wealth from the previous lesson. Like those of most Indian ascetics, Mahavira's teachings contain a deep suspicion of the female gender, treating them as objects of sexual temptation for his overwhelmingly male audience. Warning against involvement with women in verse 3, Mahavira declares that expecting happiness from them leads men "to pain, to delusion, to death, to hell, to birth as hell-beings or brute beasts." Returning to his martial metaphor in verse 4, Mahavira calls on Jain monks to be heroic in their resistance of the transitory pleasures of the world and steadfast in their adherence to strict self-denial and control of the passions.

Fifth Lesson: After describing the futility of clinging to the pleasures of this world in the third and fourth lessons, in the fifth lesson Mahavira proceeds to give monks some practical measures to adopt to avoid succumbing to desire and attachment. Beginning in verse 3, he lists the precepts for Jain monks to follow. They must not engage in commerce; they must not keep possessions, unless they are necessary items for their monastic practice, such as robes, walking sticks, and begging bowls; and they must accept donations and refusals to donate with the same indifference. The question of what is proper for a monk to keep was one of the points of contention that caused a rift between the Digambaras and the Svetambaras. Significantly, the Digambaras, who insisted upon nudity, rejected the legitimacy of this text, which says that monks may own robes.

In verse 5, Mahavira encourages monks to consider the loathsome nature of the body in order to quell their sexual desires and help them stop identifying themselves with their own physical shapes, which are impermanent. Finally, Mahavira warns again against trusting false teachers who profess to be able to alleviate desire.

Sixth Lesson: Those who understand the impermanence of the physical world and recognize the existence of the six kinds of beings listed in the first lecture, cautions Mahavira, have a higher level of responsibility than ignorant men. According to verse 1, if the wise man kills one kind of being, he will be as guilty as if he had killed all six kinds.

The Jain monk must accept good and bad with equanimity and reject the idea of property. Calling him "the hero," Mahavira proclaims in verse 3 that the Jain monk must not tolerate lust or discontent, must remain unattached to objects, must despise and mortify his physical body, and must eat only the simplest of food. In the last verses, he describes the Jain monk as one who refrains from killing, by which he means killing any of the six beings, and who preaches the Jain message to anyone who will listen.

Audience

Although the Jain tradition had mass appeal, the Acaranga Sutra is aimed at Jain monks and nuns and those aspiring to the monastic life. The laity were not expected to take on the severe austerities that the text describes. Their path, rather, was to attain merit by donating to monks and nuns. To the extent that Mahavira's followers were in constant debate with Brahmins, Buddhists, and others, the text is also intended for those rival sects, as a refutation of their central ideas.

The modern audience for the sutras may include both lay Jains, who take from the text the fundamental teaching of nonviolence, and contemporary monks and nuns who are following some version of the Jain ascetic path. As the oldest extant Jain literature, roughly contemporary with the early Buddhist scriptures, the Jain Sutras also give scholars

an idea of what kind of intellectual and social currents were running through India in the early centuries BCE.

Impact

Like his contemporary Siddhartha Gautama—who achieved enlightenment and became known as the Buddha—Mahavira preached his message to non-Brahmins and rejected the caste system altogether. But unlike the Buddha, he was not seen as the founder of a new tradition. Instead, he was simply the last great teacher of the Jain tradition, whose instructions were a refinement of what had been handed down by his predecessor, Parsvanatha. Contemporary Buddhist sources speak of the Jains as a rival sect whose members went naked, followed a teacher named Jnataputra ("Son of the Jnatas," an epithet for Mahavira), and were already well established when Buddhism first came into being.

By the early centuries of the Common Era, the Jain community founded on the teachings of Mahavira and Parsvanatha had splintered into two major divisions. One sect was known as the Digamabaras, or "Sky-clad," because they went around naked, believing that a monk should own nothing, not even clothes. The other sect was called the Svetambaras, or "White-clad," because of the white robes they wore. When the Acaranga Sutra, along with a whole list of other canonical Jain texts that had been lost or nearly

---

Questions for Further Study

1. What is the distinction between Buddhism and Jainism, especially given that the two religions share many characteristics (including reliance on sutras)?

2. What is "karmic debt," and what role does the concept play in the Jain faith?

3. Respond to the following statement: "The essence of Jainism is vegetarianism."

4. If, according to the Jain faith, existence is suffering, then in what fundamental ways, if any, does Jainism differ from the Judeo-Christian tradition as reflected in such texts as the biblical book of Genesis? How do Jains, Jews, and Christians deal with suffering in the earthly sphere?

4. Jains do not believe in a creator god. Rather, they believe that the universe and Jainism have always existed. To what extent, then, is Jainism as much a philosophy of life as a religion, as the word is generally understood in the West?

5. The word *Jain* is derived from the word *Jina,* which refers to the faith's great teachers. The word *Jina,* in turn, literally means "conqueror." Describe how and why Jains might regard themselves as "conquerors."

lost since the time of Mahavira, was "recovered" from the collective memory of the monks in the third century CE, the Digambaras refused to recognize its authority. As a result, the Digambara Jains still consider the text to be lost, while the Svetambaras continue to use the Acaranga Sutra as it is known today.

Further Reading

■ **Books**

Dundas, Paul. *The Jains*. London: Routledge, 1992.

Jaini, Padmanabh S. *The Jaina Path of Purification*. Berkeley: University of California Press, 1979.

Nyayavijayaji, Muni Shri. *Jaina Philosophy and Religion*, trans. Nagin J. Shah. Delhi: Motilal Banarsidass, 1998.

Sangave, Vilas A. *Jaina Religion and Community*. Long Beach, Calif.: Long Beach Publications, 1997.

Schubring, Walther. *The Doctrine of the Jainas: Described after the Old Sources*, trans. Wolfgang Beurlen. Delhi: Motilal Banarsidass, 1962.

Tatia, Nathmal. *Studies in Jaina Philosophy*. Varanasi, India: Jain Cultural Research Society, 1951.

—Brian Collins

Jain Sutras

Acaranga Sutra: First Book

♦ First Lecture: Knowledge of the Weapon

First Lesson: O long-lived (Gambûsvâmin)! I (Sudharman) have heard the following discourse from the venerable (Mahavira): (1) Here many do not remember whether they have descended in an eastern direction (when they were born in this world), or in a southern, or in a western, or in a northern direction, or in the direction from above, or in the direction from below, or in a direction intermediate (between the cardinal points), or in a direction intermediate between these (and the cardinal points). (2) Similarly, some do not know whether their soul is born again and again or not, nor what they were formerly, nor what they will become after having died and left this world. (3) Now this is what one should know, either by one's own knowledge or through the instruction of the highest (i.e. a Tirthakara), or having heard it from others: that he descended in an eastern direction, or in any other direction. Similarly, some know that their soul is born again and again, that it arrives in this or that direction, whatever direction that may be. (4) He believes in soul, believes in the world, believes in reward, believes in action (acknowledged to be our own doing in such judgments as these): "I did it"; "I shall cause another to do it"; "I shall allow another to do it." In the world, these are all the causes of sin, which must be comprehended and renounced. (5) A man that does not comprehend and renounce the causes of sin, descends in a cardinal or intermediate direction, wanders to all cardinal or intermediate directions, is born again and again in manifold births, experiences all painful feelings. (6) About this the Revered One has taught the truth (comprehension and renunciation). For the sake of the splendour, honour, and glory of this life, for the sake of birth, death, and final liberation, for the removal of pain, all these causes of sin are at work, which are to be comprehended and renounced in this world. He who, in the world, comprehends and renounces these causes of sin, is called a reward-knowing sage (muni). Thus I say. (7)

Second Lesson: The (living) world is afflicted, miserable, difficult to instruct, and without discrimination. In this world full of pain, suffering by their different acts, see the benighted ones cause great pain. (1) See! there are beings individually embodied (in earth; not one all-soul). See! there are men who control themselves, (whilst others only) pretend to be houseless (i.e. monks, such as the Bauddhas, whose conduct differs not from that of householders), because one destroys this (earth-body) by bad and injurious doings, and many other beings, besides, which he hurts by means of earth, through his doing acts relating to earth. (2) About this the Revered One has taught the truth: for the sake of the splendour, honour, and glory of this life, for the sake of birth, death, and final liberation, for the removal of pain, man acts sinfully towards earth, or causes others to act so, or allows others to act so. This deprives him of happiness and perfect wisdom. About this he is informed when he has understood or heard, either from the Revered One or from the monks, the faith to be coveted. (3) There are some who, of a truth, know this (i.e. injuring) to be the bondage, the delusion, the death, the hell. For this a man is longing when he destroys this (earth-body) by bad, injurious doings, and many other beings, besides, which he hurts by means of earth, through his doing acts relating to earth. Thus I say. (4)

As somebody may cut or strike a blind man (who cannot see the wound), as somebody may cut or strike the foot, the ankle, the knee, the thigh, the hip, the navel, the belly, the flank, the back, the bosom, the heart, the breast, the neck, the arm, the finger, the nail, the eye, the brow, the forehead, the head, as some kill (openly), as some extirpate (secretly), (thus the earth-bodies are cut, struck, and killed though their feeling is not manifest). (5)

He who injures these (earth-bodies) does not comprehend and renounce the sinful acts; he who does not injure these, comprehends and renounces the sinful acts. Knowing them, a wise man should not act sinfully towards earth, nor cause others to act so, nor allow others to act so. He who knows these causes of sin relating to earth, is called a reward-knowing sage. Thus I say. (6)

Third Lesson: (Thus I say): He who acts rightly, who does pious work, who practises no deceit, is called houseless. (1) One should, conquering the world, persevere in that (vigour of) faith which one had on the entrance in the order; the heroes (of faith), humbly bent, (should retain their belief in) the illustrious road (to final liberation) and in the world (of water-bodies); having rightly comprehended them through the instruction (of Mahavira), (they should retain) that which causes no danger (i.e. self-control). Thus I say. (2) A man should not (himself) deny the world of (water-bodies), nor should he deny the self. He who denies the world (of water-bodies), denies the self; and he who denies the self, denies the world of (water-bodies). (3)

See! there are men who control themselves; others pretend only to be houseless; for one destroys this (water-body) by bad, injurious doings, and many other beings, besides, which he hurts by means of water, through his doing acts relating to water. (4) About this the Revered One has taught the truth: for the sake of the splendour, honour, and glory of this life, for the sake of birth, death, and final liberation, for the removal of pain, man acts sinfully towards water, or causes others to act so, or allows others to act so. (5) This deprives him of happiness and perfect wisdom. About this he is informed when he has understood and heard from the Revered One, or from the monks, the faith to be coveted. There are some who, of a truth, know this (i.e. injuring) to be the bondage, the delusion, the death, the hell. For this a man is longing when he destroys this (water-body) by bad and injurious doings, and many other beings, besides, which he hurts by means of water, through his doing acts relating to water. Thus I say. (6)

There are beings living in water, many lives; of a truth, to the monks water has been declared to be living matter. See! considering the injuries (done to water-bodies), those acts (which are injuries, but must be done before the use of water, eg. straining) have been distinctly declared. Moreover he (who uses water which is not strained) takes away what has not been given (i.e. the bodies of water-lives). (A Bauddha will object): "We have permission, we have permission to drink it, or (to take it) for toilet purposes." Thus they destroy by various injuries (the water-bodies). But in this their doctrine is of no authority.

He who injures these (water-bodies) does not comprehend and renounce the sinful acts; he who does not injure these, comprehends and renounces the sinful acts. (7) Knowing them, a wise man should not act sinfully towards water, nor cause others to act so, nor allow others to act so. He who

knows these causes of sin relating to water, is called a reward-knowing sage. Thus I say. (8)

Fourth Lesson: (Thus I say): A man should not, of his own accord, deny the world (of fire-bodies), nor should he deny the self. He who denies the world (of fire-bodies), denies the self; and he who denies the self, denies the world (of fire-bodies). (1) He who knows that (viz. fire) through which injury is done to the long-living bodies (i.e. plants), knows also that which does no injury (i.e. control); and he who knows that which does no injury, knows also that through which no injury is done to the long-living bodies. (2) This has been seen by the heroes (of faith) who conquered ignorance; for they control themselves, always exert themselves, always mind their duty. He who is unmindful of duty, and desiring of the qualities (i.e. of the pleasure and profit which may be derived from the elements) is called the torment (of living beings). Knowing this, a wise man (resolves): "Now (I shall do) no more what I used to do wantonly before." (3) See! there are men who control themselves; others pretend only to be houseless; for one destroys this (fire-body) by bad and injurious doings, and many other beings, besides, which he hurts by means of fire, through his doing acts relating to fire. About this the Revered One has taught the truth: for the sake of the splendour, honour, and glory of this life, for the sake of birth, death, and final liberation, for the removal of pain, man acts sinfully towards fire, or causes others to act so, or allows others to act so. (4) This deprives him of happiness and perfect wisdom. About this he is informed when he has understood, or heard from the Revered One or from the monks, the faith to be coveted. There are some who, of a truth, know this (i.e. injuring) to be the bondage, the delusion, the death, the hell. For this a man is longing, when he destroys this (fire-body) by bad and injurious doings, and many other beings, besides, which he hurts by means of fire, through his doing acts relating to fire. Thus I say. (5)

There are beings living in the earth, living in grass, living on leaves, living in wood, living in cowdung, living in dust-heaps, jumping beings which coming near (fire) fall into it. Some, certainly, touched by fire, shrivel up; those which shrivel up there, lose their sense there; those which lose their sense there, die there. (6)

He who injures these (fire-bodies) does not comprehend and renounce the sinful acts; he who does not injure these, comprehends and renounces the sinful acts. Knowing them, a wise man should not act sinfully towards fire, nor cause others to act so, nor allow others to act so. He who knows the causes of sin relating to fire, is called a reward-knowing sage. Thus I say. (7)

Fifth Lesson: "I shall not do (acts relating to plants) after having entered the order, having recognised (the truth about these acts), and having conceived that which is free from danger (i.e. control)."

He who does no acts (relating to plants), has ceased from works; he who has ceased from them is called "houseless." (1) Quality is the whirlpool (avatta = samara), and the whirlpool is quality. Looking up, down, aside, eastward, he sees colours, hearing he hears sounds; (2) longing upwards, down, aside, eastward, he becomes attached to colours and sounds. That is called the world; not guarded against it, not obeying the law (of the Tirthakaras), relishing the qualities, conducting himself wrongly, he will wantonly live in a house (i.e. belong to the world). (3)

See! there are men who control themselves; others pretend only to be houseless, for one destroys this (body of a plant) by bad and injurious doings, and many other beings, besides, which he hurts by means of plants, through his doing acts relating to plants. (4) About this the Revered One has taught the truth: for the sake of the splendour, honour, and glory of this life, for the sake of birth, death, and final liberation, for the removal of pain, man acts sinfully towards plants, or causes others to act so, or allows others to act so. This deprives him of happiness and perfect wisdom. About this he is informed when he has understood, or heard from the Revered One or from the monks, the faith to be coveted. There are some who, of a truth, know this (i.e. injuring) to be the bondage, the delusion, the death, the hell. For this a man is longing when he destroys this (body of a plant) by bad and injurious doings, and many other beings, besides, which he hurts by means of plants, through his doing acts relating to plants. Thus I say. (5)

As the nature of this (i.e. men) is to be born and to grow old, so is the nature of that (i.e. plants) to be born and to grow old; as this has reason, so that has reason; as this falls sick when cut, so that falls sick when cut; as this needs food, so that needs food; as this will decay, so that will decay; as this is not eternal, so that is not eternal; as this takes increment, so that takes increment; as this is changing, so that is changing. (6) He who injures these (plants) does not comprehend and renounce the sinful acts; he who does not injure these, comprehends and renounces the sinful acts. Knowing them, a wise man should not act sinfully towards plants, nor cause others to act so, nor allow others to act so. He who knows these causes of sin relating to plants, is called a reward-knowing sage. Thus I say. (7)

Sixth Lesson: Thus I say: There are beings called the animate, viz. those who are produced 1. from eggs (birds, &c.), 2. from a fetus (as elephants, &c.), 3. from a fetus with an enveloping membrane (as cows, buffaloes, &c.), 4. from fluids (as worms, &c.), 5. from sweat (as bugs, lice, &c.), 6. by coagulation (as locusts, ants, &c.), 7. from sprouts (as butterflies, wagtails, &c.), 8. by regeneration (men, gods, hell-beings). This is called the Samsara (1) for the slow, for the ignorant. Having well considered it, having well looked at it, I say thus: all beings, those with two, three, four senses, plants, those with five senses, and the rest of creation, (experience) individually pleasure or displeasure, pain, great terror, and unhappiness. Beings are filled with alarm from all directions and in all directions. See! there the benighted ones cause great pain. See! there are beings individually embodied. (2)

See! there are men who control themselves; others pretend only to be houseless, for one destroys this (body of an animal) by bad and injurious doings, and many other beings, besides, which he hurts by means of animals, through his doing acts relating to animals. (3) About this the Revered One has taught the truth: for the sake of the splendour, honour, and glory of this life, for the sake of birth, death, and final liberation, for the removal of pain, man acts sinfully towards animals, or causes others to act so, or allows others to act so. This deprives him of happiness and perfect wisdom. About this he is informed, when he has understood, or heard from the Revered One or from the monks, the faith to be coveted. There are some who, of a truth, know this (i.e. injuring) to be the bondage, the delusion, the death, the hell. For this a man is longing, when he injures this (body of an animal) by bad and injurious doings, and many other beings, besides, which he hurts by means of animals, through acts relating to animals. Thus I say. (4)

Some slay (animals) for sacrificial purposes, some kill (animals) for the sake of their skin, some kill (them) for the sake of their flesh, some kill them for the sake of their blood; thus for the sake of their heart, their bile, the feathers of their tail, their tail, their big or small horns, their teeth, their tusks, their nails, their sinews, their bones; with a purpose or without a purpose. Some kill animals because they have been wounded by them, or are wounded, or will be wounded. (5)

He who injures these (animals) does not comprehend and renounce the sinful acts; he who does not injure these, comprehends and renounces the sinful acts. Knowing them, a wise man should not act sinfully towards animals, nor cause others to act so, nor allow others to act so. He who knows these causes of sin relating to animals, is called a reward-knowing sage. Thus I say. (6)

Seventh Lesson: He who is averse from (all actions relating to) wind, knows affliction. Knowing what is bad, he who knows it with regard to himself, knows it with regard to (the world) outside; and he who knows it with regard to (the world) outside, knows it with regard to himself: this reciprocity (between himself and) others (one should mind). Those who are appeased, who are free from passion, do not desire to live. (1)

See! there are men who control themselves; others pretend only to be houseless, for one destroys this (wind-body) by bad and injurious doings, and many other beings, besides, which he hurts by means of wind, through his doing acts relating to wind. (2) About this the Revered One has taught the truth: for the sake of the splendour, honour, and glory of this life, for the sake of birth, death, and final liberation, for the removal of pain, man acts sinfully towards wind, or causes others to act so, or allows others to act so. This deprives him of happiness and perfect wisdom. About this he is informed when he has understood, or heard from the Revered One or from the monks, the faith to be coveted. There are some who, of a truth, know this to be the bondage, the delusion, the death, the hell. For this a man is longing when he destroys this (wind-body) by bad and injurious acts, and many other beings, besides, which hurts by means of wind, through his doing acts relating to wind. Thus I say. (3) There are jumping beings which, coming near wind, fall into it. Some, certainly, touched by wind, shrivel up; those which shrivel up there, lose their sense there; those which lose their sense there, die there. (4)

He who injures these (wind-bodies) does not comprehend and renounce the sinful acts; he who does not injure these, comprehends and renounces the sinful acts. Knowing them, a wise man should not act sinfully towards wind, nor cause others to act so, nor allow others to act so. He who knows these causes of sin relating to wind, is called a reward-knowing sage. Thus I say. (5)

Be aware that about this (wind-body) too those are involved in sin who delight not in the right conduct, and, though doing acts, talk about religious discipline, who conducting themselves according to their own will, pursuing sensual pleasures, and engaging in acts, are addicted to worldliness. He who has the true knowledge about all things, will commit no sinful act, nor cause others to do so,

&c. (6) Knowing them, a wise man should not act sinfully towards the aggregate of six (kinds of) lives, nor cause others to act so, nor allow others to act so. He who knows these causes of sin relating to the aggregate of the six (kinds of) lives, is called a reward-knowing sage. Thus I say. (7)

End of the First Lecture, called Knowledge of the Weapon.

◆ Second Lecture: Conquest of the World

First Lesson: Quality is the seat of the root, and the seat of the root is quality. He who longs for the qualities, is overcome by great pain, and he is careless. (For he thinks) I have to provide for a mother, for a father, for a sister, for a wife, for sons, for daughters, for a daughter-in-law, for my friends, for near and remote relations, for my acquaintances, for different kinds of property, profit, meals, and clothes. Longing for these objects, people are careless, suffer day and night, work in the right and the wrong time, desire wealth and treasures, commit injuries and violent acts, direct the mind, again and again, upon these injurious doings (described in the preceding lecture). (1) (Doing so), the life of some mortals (which by destiny would have been long) is shortened. For when with the deterioration of the perceptions of the ear, eye, organs of smelling, tasting, touching, a man becomes aware of the decline of life, they after a time produce dotage. Or his kinsmen with whom he lives together will, after a time, first grumble at him, and he will afterwards grumble at them. They cannot help thee or protect thee, nor canst thou help them or protect them. (2) He is not fit for hilarity, playing, pleasure, show. Therefore, ah! proceeding to pilgrimage, and thinking that the present moment is favourable (for such intentions), he should be steadfast and not, even for an hour, carelessly conduct himself. His youth, his age, his life fade away.

A man who carelessly conducts himself; who killing, cutting, striking, destroying, chasing away, frightening (living beings) resolves to do what has not been done (by any one)—him his relations with whom he lived together, will first cherish, and he will afterwards cherish them. But they cannot help thee or protect thee, nor canst thou help them or protect them. (3)

Or he heaps up treasures for the benefit of some spendthrifts, by pinching himself. Then, after a time, he falls in sickness; those with whom he lives together will first leave him, and he will afterwards leave them. They cannot help thee or protect thee, nor canst thou help them or protect them. (4)

Knowing pain and pleasure in all their variety, and seeing his life not yet decline, a wise man should know that to be the proper moment (for entering a religious life); while the perceptions of his ear, eye, organs of smelling, tasting, touching are not yet deteriorated, while all these perceptions are not yet deteriorated, man should prosecute the real end of his soul. Thus I say. (5)

Second Lesson: A wise man should remove any aversion (to control); he will be liberated in the proper time. Some, following wrong instruction, turn away (from control). They are dull, wrapped in delusion. While they imitate the life of monks, (saying), "We shall be free from attachment," they enjoy the pleasures that offer themselves. Through wrong instruction the (would-be) sages trouble themselves (for pleasures); thus they sink deeper and deeper in delusion, (and cannot get) to this, nor to the opposite shore. Those who are freed (from attachment to the world and its pleasures), reach the opposite shore. Subduing desire by desirelessness, he does not enjoy the pleasures that offer themselves. Desireless, giving up the world, and ceasing to act, he knows, and sees, and has no wishes because of his discernment; he is called houseless. (1)

(But on the contrary) he suffers day and night, works in the right and the wrong time, desires wealth and treasures, commits injuries and violent acts, again and again directs his mind upon these injurious doings; for his own sake, to support or to be supported by his relations, friends, the ancestors, gods, the king, thieves, guests, paupers, Sramanas. (2)

Thus violence is done by these various acts, deliberately, out of fear, because they think "it is for the expiation of sins," or for some other hope. Knowing this, a wise man should neither himself commit violence by such acts, nor order others to commit violence by such acts, nor consent to the violence done by somebody else.

This road (to happiness) has been declared by the noble ones, that a clever man should not be defiled (by sin). Thus I say. (3)

Third Lesson: "Frequently (I have been born) in a high family, frequently in a low one; I am not mean, nor noble, nor do I desire (social preferment)." Thus reflecting, who would brag about his family or about his glory, or for what should he long? (1)

Therefore a wise man should neither be glad nor angry (about his lot): thou shouldst know and consider the happiness of living creatures. Carefully conducting himself, he should mind this: blindness, deafness, dumbness, one-eyedness, hunchbackedness, blackness, variety of colour (he will always experience); because of his carelessness he is born in many births, he experiences various feelings. (2)

Not enlightened (about the cause of these ills) he is afflicted (by them), always turns round (in the whirl of) birth and death. Life is dear to many who own fields and houses. Having acquired dyed and coloured (clothes), jewels, earrings, gold, and women, they become attached to these things. And a fool who longs for life, and worldly-minded, laments that (for these worldly goods) penance, self-restraint, and control do not avail, will ignorantly come to grief. (3)

Those who are of a steady conduct do not desire this (wealth). Knowing birth and death, one should firmly walk the path (i.e. right conduct), (and not wait for old age to commence a religious life),

For there is nothing inaccessible for death. All beings are fond of life, like pleasure, hate pain, shun destruction, like life, long to live. To all life is dear. (4)

Having acquired it (i.e. wealth), employing bipeds and quadrupeds, gathering riches in the three ways, whatever his portion will be, small or great, he will desire to enjoy it. Then at one time, his manifold savings are a large treasure. Then at another time, his heirs divide it, or those who are without a living steal it, or the king takes it away, or it is ruined in some way or other, or it is consumed by the conflagration of the house. Thus a fool doing cruel deeds which benefit another, will ignorantly come thereby to grief. (5)

This certainly has been declared by the sage. They do not cross the flood, nor can they cross it; they do not go to the next shore, nor can they go to it; they do not go to the opposite shore, nor can they go to it.

And though hearing the doctrine, he does not stand in the right place; but the clever one who adopts the true (faith), stands in the right place (i.e. control).

He who sees by himself, needs no instruction. But the miserable, afflicted fool who delights in pleasures, and whose miseries do not cease, is turned round in the whirl of pains. Thus I say. (6)

Fourth Lesson: Then, after a time, he falls in sickness: those with whom he lives together, first grumble at him, and he afterwards grumbles at them. But they cannot help thee or protect thee, nor canst thou help them or protect them. (1)

Knowing pleasure and pain separately, they trouble themselves about the enjoyment (of the external objects). For some men in this world have (such a character that) they will desire to enjoy their portion, whether it be large or small, in the three ways: Then, at one time, it will be sufficiently large, with many resources. Then, at another time, his heirs divide it, or those who have no living steal it, or the king takes it away, or it is ruined in some way or other, or it is consumed by the conflagration of the house. Thus a fool, doing cruel acts, comes ignorantly to grief. (2)

Wisely reject hope and desire, and extracting that thorn (i.e. pleasure) thou (shouldst act rightly). People who are enveloped by delusion do not understand this: he who (gathers wealth) will, perhaps, not have the benefit of it.

The world is greatly troubled by women. They (viz. men) forsooth say, "These are the vessels (of happiness)." But this leads them to pain, to delusion, to death, to hell, to birth as hell-beings or brute beasts. The fool never knows the law. (3)

Thus spake the hero: "Be careful against this great delusion; the clever one should have done with carelessness by considering death in tranquillity, and that, the nature of which is decay (viz. the body); these (pleasures), look! will not satisfy (thee). Therefore have done with them! Sage, look! this is the great danger, it should overcome none whomsoever. He is called a hero who is not vexed by (the hardships caused) by control. He should not be angry because the (householder) gives him little. If turned off, he should go. Thou shouldst conform to the conduct of the sages." Thus I say. (4)

Fifth Lesson: That for this (viz. pleasure) the wants of the world should be supplied by bad injurious doings: for one's own sons, daughters, daughters-in-law, kinsmen, nurses, kings, male and female slaves, male and female servants, for the sake of hospitality, of supper and breakfast, the accumulation of wealth is effected. (1)

(This is) here for the enjoyment of some men. (But a wise man) exerting himself, houseless, noble, of noble intellect, of noble perception recognises the proper moment (for all actions). He should not accept, nor cause others to accept, or permit them to accept anything unclean. Free from uncleanliness he should wander about. (2)

Being not seen in buying and selling, he should not buy, nor cause others to buy, nor consent to the buying of others. This mendicant who knows the time, the strength (of himself), the measure (of all things), the practice, the occasion (for begging, &c.), the conduct, the religious precepts, the true condition (of the donor or hearer), who disowns all things not requisite for religious purposes, who is under no obligations, he proceeds securely (on the road to final liberation) after having cut off both (love and hate). Clothes, almsbowls, blankets, brooms, property, straw mats, with regard to these things he should know (what is unclean). When he receives food he should know the quantity required. This has been declared by the Revered One: he should not rejoice in the receipt of a gift, nor be sorry when he gets nothing. Having got much, one should not store it away; one should abstain from things not requisite for religious purposes. With a mind different (from that of common people) a seer abandons (these things). This is the road taught by the noble ones, well acquainted with which one should not be defiled (by sin). Thus I say. (3) Pleasures are difficult to reject, life is difficult to prolong. That man, certainly, who loves pleasures, is afflicted (by their loss), is sorry in his heart, leaves his usual ways, is troubled, suffers pain. The farsighted one who knows the world, knows its inferior part (hell), its upper part (heaven), its sidelong part (the state of brute beasts). He who knows the relation (of human affairs, viz.) that he who desires for the world is always turned round (in the samsara), is called among mortals a hero, who liberates those who are fettered. (4)

As the interior (of the body is loathsome), so is the exterior; as the exterior, so is the interior. In the interior of the body he perceives the foul interior humours, he observes their several courses (or eruptions). A well-informed man knowing (and renouncing the body and pleasures), should not eat (his saliva); he should not oppose himself to the (current of knowledge). Certainly, that man who engages in worldly affairs, who practises many tricks, who is bewildered by his own doings, acts again and again on that desire which increases his unrighteousness. Hence the above has been said for the increase of this (life). (A man addicted to pleasures) acts as if immortal, and puts great faith (in pleasure); but when he perceives that this body sustains pains, he cries in his ignorance. Therefore keep in your mind what I say. (5) A heretic professes to cure (the love of pleasure), while he kills, cuts, strikes, destroys, chases away, resolves to do what has not been done before. To whom he applies the cure—enough of that fool's affection; or he who has (the cure) applied, is a fool. This does not apply to the houseless. Thus I say. (6)

Sixth Lesson: He who perfectly understands (what has been said in the preceding lesson) and follows the (faith) to be coveted, should therefore do no sinful act, nor cause others to do one. Perchance he meditates a sin (by an act against only) one (of the six aggregates of lives); but he will be guilty (of sin against) every one of the six, Desiring happiness and bewailing much, he comes ignorantly to grief through his own misfortune. (1) Through his own carelessness every one produces that phase of life in which the vital spirits are pained. Observing (the pain of mundane existence, one should) not (act) with violence. This is called the true knowledge (and renunciation). He who ceasing from acts relinquishes the idea of property, relinquishes property itself. That sage has seen the path (to final liberation) for whom there exists no property. Knowing this, a wise man, who knows the world and has cast off the idea of the world, should prudently conquer the obstructions to righteousness. Thus I say. (2)

The hero does not tolerate discontent,

The hero does not tolerate lust.

Because the hero is not careless,

The hero is not attached (to the objects of the senses).

Being indifferent against sounds (and the other) perceptions, detest the comfort of this life.

A sage adopting a life of wisdom, should treat his gross body roughly.

The heroes who have right intuition, use mean and rough food.

Such a man is said to have crossed the flood (of life), to be a sage, to have passed over (the samsara), to be liberated, to have ceased (from all activity). Thus I say. (3)

A sage is called unfit who does not follow the law and fails in his office. (But on the contrary) he is praised as a hero, he overcomes the connection with the world, he is called the guide (or the right way). What has been declared to be here the unhappiness of mortals, of that unhappiness the clever ones propound the knowledge. (4)

Thus understanding (and renouncing) acts, a man who recognises the truth, delights in nothing else; and he who delights only in the truth, recognises nothing else. As (the law) has been revealed for the full one, so for the empty one; as for the empty one, so for the full one. But he (to whom the faith is preached) will perhaps disrespectfully beat (the preacher). Yet know, there is no good in this (indiscriminate preaching). (But ascertain before) what sort of man he is, and whom he worships. He is called a hero who liberates the bound, above, below, and in the sideward directions. He always conforms to all knowledge (and renunciation); the hero is not polluted by the sin of killing. He is a wise man who perfectly knows the non-killing, who searches after the liberation of the bound. The clever one is neither bound nor liberated; he should do or leave undone (what the hero does or does not do); he should not do what (the hero) leaves undone:

Knowing (and renouncing) murder of any kind and worldly ideas in all respects.

He who sees himself, needs no instruction. But the miserable and afflicted fool who delights in pleasures and whose miseries do not cease, is turned round in the whirl of pains. Thus I say. (5)

End of the Second Lecture, called Conquest of the World.

Glossary

Bauddhas	followers of the Buddha
Gambusvamin	Sudharman's disciple
Gosala	Mahavira's rival
Mahavira	the founder, or "discoverer," of Jainism
Revered One	that is, Mahavira
Samsara	literally, "wandering on"; the concept of passing through states of birth, life, death, and rebirth
Sramanas	wandering ascetics who renounced the world
Sudharman	Mahavira's disciple
Tirthakara	also Tirthankara, one who has achieved enlightenment

Brahman stele depicting the Trimurti, or divine triad of Brahma, Vishnu, and Shiva

(Brahman stele depicting the Trimurti, 2nd - 7th century [sandstone], Cambodian / Musee Guimet, Paris, France / Giraudon / The Bridgeman Art Library International)

UPANISHADS

"The little space within the heart is as great as this vast universe. The heavens and the earth are there, and the sun, and the moon, and the stars."

Overview

The Upanishads are a collection of Hindu sacred texts that were recorded in Sanskrit over the course of some two thousand years, through the end of the Middle Ages. The majority were composed between 500 BCE and 200 CE but likely began earlier in an oral tradition. They are meant to be read in the form of instruction, teaching, or dialogue between guru and student. The term *Upanishad* comes from either of the roots *upasan* or *upa-na-shad*, which respectively mean to "draw near" and "sit down close to"; some see this as suggesting instruction or sitting at the foot of a master. At the heart of the Upanishads is a process for investigating ultimate truth, such that one might understand the nature of reality and the soul might become freed from the physical body. The texts are traditionally considered to be a further unfolding of the ancient Vedas, allowing those earliest teachings to persist as meaningful for subsequent generations. Approximately 108 of the traditional Upanishads have survived. Some scholars have expanded the literary category or collection to include over two hundred Upanishads, as technically they can still be composed.

The Upanishadic age likely began around 500 BCE, when the Brihadaranyaka and Chandogya Upanishads are believed to have been written. While there is some disagreement over the historical placement of this date (as some historians have traditionally stretched dates for oral composition back as far as three hundred years), the most recent scholarly trends reflect an estimate coinciding with the adult life of the Buddha (563–483 BCE) for the early usage and influence of the Upanishad texts. The Brihadaranyaka Upanishad is most certainly the oldest, while the Chandogya is quite long, with some 155 chapters; these two bodies of scripture would come to form the basis of what would be known as Vedantic ("end of the Vedas") literature.

In the centuries after the death of Siddhartha Gautama—known as the Buddha—the Mundaka, Aitareya, Prashna, Kaushitaki, Taittiriya, and Kathaka Upanishads were written, among which the Kaushitaki is the oldest. While there is again much disagreement over the dating of this group of scriptures, all of these middle-period texts have elements of Buddhist influence and likely could not have been composed before 400 BCE. The Kena, Mandukya, and Isa Upanishads date to a period after the first century of the Common Era. Early-twentieth-century discoveries of previously unknown ancient texts, like the Bashkala, Chhagaleya, Arsheya, and Saunaka Upanishads, have added to the canon. Several Upanishads that bear Islamic influences were composed in the late medieval period, and there are even some contemporary Upanishads, from the mid-twentieth century, that have been considered for canonical inclusion.

Context

The early Upanishads came out of a period when the eastern Ganges River valley, in the northeast of the Indian Subcontinent, was dominated by the great kingdoms of Koshala and Magadha. A series of trading towns connected by roads—with many from Koshala and Magadha leading to the great city of Varanasi (modern-day Benares), the capital of the Kashi kingdom—were the reason for the economic success of the region. In 543 BCE, King Bimbisara, of the Haryankan dynasty, conquered the Magadhan capital of Rajagriha and expanded the Magadha kingdom further east. Bimbisara's death in about 493 BCE precipitated a war between Koshala and Magadha. A marriage alliance between the royal families ended the conflict.

Through this period new ideas were spreading, and additional classes or subcastes were quickly developing. The Kshatriyan class's wealthy aristocrats and warriors were gaining power and beginning to challenge the authority of the Brahmins, the highest caste, that of priestly families. India had relied heavily upon the ritualistic Vedic tradition, which originated as early as the thirteenth century BCE but experienced some decline around the ninth century BCE. The Vedas, which were closely guarded by the Brahmin caste, began in oral tradition, as handed down through priestly families, and were later written in a rather difficult form of Sanskrit, such that only the most educated had access to them. By the eighth century BCE, new ideas were being reflected in religious literature. The Brahmanas, from the eighth or seventh century BCE, accentuated the impor-

Time Line

CA. 1500 –900 BCE	■ The Vedas, deriving from oral tradition, are composed.
CA. 800 –600 BCE	■ The Brahmanas, which attempt to remediate Vedic ritual and to contextualize the relationship between the human and animal world with reality beyond, are composed.
CA. 600 BCE	■ The golden age of the Koshala kingdom begins.
CA. 600 –500 BCE	■ The Aranyakas, centered on orthodox ritual, are composed.
CA. 543 BCE	■ The Magadha Empire is conquered by Bimbisara, and the capital is moved to Rajagriha.
CA. 520 BCE	■ The Persian Achaemenid Empire, led by Darius the Great, invades India.
CA. 500 BCE	■ The use of classical Sanskrit begins; the Shrauta Sutras, focused on spiritual consciousness, are composed, some in late Vedic Sanskrit and a few in classical Sanskrit.
CA. 500 –400 BCE	■ The Brihadaranyaka, Chandogya, and Kaushitaki Upanishads are written down.
CA. 483 BCE	■ Siddhartha Gautama, the founder of Buddhism, dies (though some scholars place his life more than half a century later).
CA. 468 BCE	■ Mahavira, the founder of Jainism, dies (though some scholars place his life half a century earlier).
CA. 400 BCE	■ Beginning around this time, the Mundaka, Aitareya, Prashna, Kaushitaki, Taittiriya, and Kathaka Upanishads are written down.
CA. 327 BCE	■ Alexander the Great leads the Greek invasion of India.

tance of priesthood and ritual activity but began to move toward increasingly creative and symbolic ways for spiritual energy to be transferred. In the later Brahmanas, there is even a move away from the traditionally literal interpretation of the gods. A more monistic conception of divinity, suggesting a unified force or source, began to emerge in some of the very late Brahmanic thought.

The Aranyakas were books of "wilderness rituals" or forest books, composed in late Vedic Sanskrit around the sixth century BCE and handed down through gurus (religious teachers) outside the context of formal Hindu worship. However "wild" they were, the texts were much concerned with an orthodox implementation of ritual. They may have appealed to the notion of returning to a simpler time and place, like that of the small rural village or town, as affluence and urban populations began to soar in India in the seventh through fifth centuries BCE. The Shrauta Sutras, composed in the sixth century BCE, may have been aimed at the new social groups emerging at this time. There is a focus on the notion of "consciousness" within the Shrauta texts. Spirituality was becoming more personalized and more individualistic as society moved away from cultic activity, in an environment that was becoming increasingly crowded and communal. The diverse social and political environment of this era may give some insight into why the Brahmins were willing to introduce a new religious literature like the Upanishads, which call for less ritualistic rigidity while associating new ideas with the textual traditions of the Vedas.

During the ensuing Upanishadic period, gurus operated as enlightened teachers who attempted to lead their followers toward the realm of spirit and truth. Although some may have had families, others renounced wealth and became ascetics—that is, persons who forsake worldly pleasures and live lives of self-denial. The early oral traditions of the Upanishads may have been spread by such gurus. Knowledge of ultimate reality not connected to the material world was believed to be their treasure, which would lead the gurus and their followers to *moksha*, or union with the Brahman—the universal soul, source, force, or ultimate essence—and release from this life. The doctrine of karma, as related to one's deeds or merit and morally earning one's way from the present life to the next reincarnation, was surely redirected by the commercial spirit of the day. Reaction to this can be seen in the Upanishads. Societal inclinations toward individual freedom and the rejection of caste came from emerging powerful clans who subscribed to the simple hierarchy of one high and one low class. Siddhartha Gautama, who became the Buddha, and Vardhamana, who in founding Jainism would be known as Mahavira (ca. 540–468 BCE), both came from the clan-dominated regions, not the major trading cities. (According to tradition, King Bimbisara was said to have been a contemporary of both the Buddha and Mahavira; he appears many times in both Jain and Buddhist texts.) Wandering ascetics, called *shramanas* or *sanyasins*, whether Hindu Brahmins, Kshatriyas, or others, became noticeable elements in the religious scene of the sixth and fifth centuries BCE. The second group of Upanishadic texts is particularly influenced by ideas from this period. The third group of Upanishads, written around 100 CE, move further toward incorporating dualistic ideas that make distinctions between matter and spirit. They also present notions foreshadowing later philosophical developments in the various schools of Yoga.

About the Author

Hindus have long maintained divine authorship of the Vedas. Since the Upanishads are often referred to as Vedanta (end of the Vedas), they, too, are seen by many adherents as a revelatory part of the class of texts known as shruti ("that which is heard"). Scholars have had difficulty pinpointing any exact authorship of the early Upanishads. In some sense, this gives the Upanishads an advantage over other scriptures that have had to endure the scrutiny of historical and critical scholarship linked to a particular author. The many Upanishads seem to have been the products of different groups, authors, or traditions, and initially they were not created to represent a unified philosophical whole. Rather, the Upanishads were each composed in a certain place at a particular time for a specific purpose.

There is some general agreement among most recent scholarship that the Upanishads began to be written down in northern India sometime around 500 bce. Historians have attempted to connect internal stories from particular Upanishadic texts to various teachers who have been described therein. According to one such tradition, the Chandogya Upanishad was composed in the Kuru-Panchala kingdom, in western India, at about the time that the Persian Achaemenid Empire was expanding into the region, by the sage and theologian Uddalaka Aruni, who is featured in stories from the Chandogya Upanishad (such as in part 6). Evidence for this view is that Aruni (known by either of his names) had been attacked in earlier Upanishads, but he is a prominent figure implicitly defended in the Chandogya Upanishad. He is also mentioned in the Mahabharata (in book 1, section 3) as a pupil of the great teacher Dhaumya Muni. Tradition suggests that he systematized the Vedic literature along with the early Upanishads. Uddalaka also appears in the Brihadaranyaka Upanishad (sometimes considered the seventh Brahmana) but there is treated with much less respect. Unfortunately, there is little historical context for this figure, other than the fact that he is repeatedly mentioned in a number of sacred texts and was reputed to be a great sage. Other general theories of authorship range from an unknown reform-minded Brahmin to someone from the Kshatriyan class to an individual outside the mainstream of traditional Hindu thought.

Explanation and Analysis of the Document

The Chandogya is one of the earliest and most important of the Upanishads. It was written primarily in the form of prose, possibly dating to the late sixth or early fifth century bce. It is often associated with the Sama Veda, which

Time Line

CA. 100 BCE

■ Around this time or later, the Kena, Mandukya, and Isa Upanishads are composed.

was written as a reaction and "updating" of the existing Vedic literature. Traditionally, the Chandogya Upanishad is divided into eight parts. The first five parts deal with *upansa*, or ritual worship primarily connected to meditation. The sixth part is a nondual Vedanta segment involving *tattvamasi* (literally, "thou art that" or "that you are," the connection of one's innermost self to the Brahman). The seventh part contains the doctrine of *bhuma* (infinity), and the eighth part concerns instruction regarding the atman, or individual soul as connected to the Universal Spirit. The original text of the combined Chandogya is 155 chapters long. A number of these chapters are quite short, while some are several pages long. Many of the subsequent Upanishads reiterate themes from the Chandogya.

♦ **Parts 1 and 2**

Parts 1 and 2 deal with creation. Infinite space here is aligned with the Sanskrit term *akasa*, which can also mean the Supreme Self; while the word "return" refers to the time of universal dissolution. Thus, the ultimate grounding of the universe is the Supreme Self. Prajapati, the Creator God, meditated and brought about the essence of the world. He meditated on his creation and on the sounds of the entities therein. As earth, air, and sky are the origins of the human realm, the sounds of those words resonated to produce the sound "om," the syllable and sound that induces all to meditate. As the stem of a plant holds its leaves together, so om is the symbol of the unity of the Brahman, ties the universe together, and is the essence of all. The three Vedas referred to here are the Rig, Sama, and Yajur Vedas.

♦ **Part 3**

Gayatri is a type of meter for the verses used in the Vedas. The *gayatri* contains four *padas* (also known as feet), with six letters (*aksara*)—each equivalent to a syllable—in each *pada*. It is the simplest and shortest of meters and is present within all the other meters of the Vedas. But "Gayatri" is also the name of one of the most sacred hymns in all of the Vedas. In chapter 13, Gayatri represents the epitome of all words; speech is one with Gayatri and leads to knowledge of the Brahman, the Universal Spirit. Three-quarters of its being resides in heaven; the other quarter covers the universe. Pure Brahman is greater than Gayatri and does not contain parts. Part of the glory of the Brahman—part of "his heaven"—is the notion that it is immortal and unchanging. Hindus believe in a variety of levels or layers in the heavens. In the highest heaven is the realm of Brahma, who is the primary creator, greatest

Milestone Documents

The Mughal emperor Akbar
(Akbar [1542-1605] [gouache on paper], Indian School, [17th century] /
Prince of Wales Museum, Mumbai, India / Giraudon / The Bridgeman Art
Library International)

The "Imperishable Treasure" of chapter 15 can be seen as the chest of the universe, the storehouse of all treasures. Inside it are all things, including the results of all actions as well as their material connections. This chapter is a meditation that is to be recited and refers to requests for blessings upon one's descendant (understood based on the Sanskrit to literally be a son), who may live long and prosper.

The sixteenth chapter of part 3 is a meditation on living a long life free of disease and ailments, in which (as is implied) one can enjoy the company of sons and earthly pleasure into old age. The sages began to see the individual as a combination of physical body, senses, drives, and so forth. It was believed that the Self could preserve the physical body through a series of mantras and meditations. The early or morning stages of one's life, the first twenty-four years, are identified with the twenty-four sounds of the Gayatri hymns and the libations of *soma* (an intoxicating ritual beverage) that should be offered in the morning to the Vasus—gods of this earth, usually a group of eight divinities. The forty-four years of midlife are equated with the midday offering of soma made through the Trishtubh, another Vedic meter type for hymns (with forty-four sounds), to the Rudras, a group of eleven gods often connected to Shiva, the "destroyer." The last forty-eight years of life are equated with the evening offering, in which prayers and offerings are made through the Jagati—another Vedic hymnal meter—to the Adityas, the twelve gods of light. One who is able to make these offerings throughout his life may live to 116 years (24 + 44 + 48).

♦ **Part 4**

The fourth chapter of part 4 deals with the story of Satyakama, who begins to see the divisions of the universe all as Brahman. He wishes to become a student of religion and study with a master. The story thus exhorts and legitimizes proper religious instruction. According to some contemporary interpreters of the tale, Satyakama's mother does not know his true heritage—that is, if in fact he was of the priestly Brahmin caste—perhaps because his father died before he was born and Satyakama should possibly be seen as illegitimate. When the master confronts Satyakama about his heritage, implicitly asking whether he is a Brahmin, the youth answers truthfully that he does not know. In that the story extols the notion that a true Brahmin never departs from the truth, Satyakama is thereby presumed to be Brahmin and is allowed to study with the master Gautama. This tale also might convey the idea that during this period the Brahmins did not have a monopoly on religious teaching or education, as reflected in Master Gautama's willingness to accept a student of uncertain lineage.

♦ **Part 6**

Part 6 presents the idea of nonduality through the tale of Svetaketu. At the age of twelve the young Brahmin, like all the male members of his family before him, is sent away to study the Vedas. The story in chapter 1 seems to imply that there were members of Brahmin families at that time who called themselves Brahmins but never bothered to un-

of the gods, and first entity of the supreme triad—Brahma, Vishnu, Shiva. Here, the phrase "beyond . . . the very highest heavens" refers to the entire universe. The "Light" is none other than the Brahman, that which should be the object of deepest meditation.

Part 3 continues by saying that the visible universe that humanity lives in comes from Brahman and remains one with him at all times. The fourteenth chapter is an exposition on meditation of the Brahman without using a symbol; rather, the individual is asked to meditate upon the nature of the Brahman within oneself. The word "faith," from *kratu* in Sanskrit, sometimes translated as "will," is used a number of times in chapter 14. Faith, will, or *kratu* is insight or determination that believes in an object or truth as one certain thing and nothing else. "Light," in the third stanza, might also be understood as consciousness. "Spirit" is used here to denote the Self, not as the individual self, or the "little" self, but as the Universal Self. "Spirit," then, is the greater Self or Spirit within, that which is linked to the Brahman yet longs for perfect and ultimate union. Sandilya was an ancient sage after which one of the great Brahmin families took its name.

"There is a Spirit that is mind and life, light and truth and vast spaces. He contains all works and desires and all perfumes and all tastes. He enfolds the whole universe, and in silence is loving to all. This is the Spirit that is in my heart."

"O my son, you cannot see the Spirit. But in truth he is here. An invisible and subtle essence is the Spirit of the whole universe. That is Reality. That is Truth. Thou art that."

"I am the whole universe. Atman is above and below, North and South and East and West. Atman is the whole universe. He who sees, knows, and understands this, who finds in Atman, the Spirit, his love and his pleasure and his union and his joy, becomes a Master of himself. His freedom then is infinite."

"OM. In the centre of the castle of Brahman, our own body, there is a small shrine in the form of a lotus-flower, and within can be found a small space. We should find who dwells there, and we should want to know him."

"The little space within the heart is as great as this vast universe. The heavens and the earth are there, and the sun, and the moon, and the stars; fire and lightning and winds are there; and all that now is and all that is not: for the whole universe is in Him and He dwells within our heart."

"There is a Spirit which is pure and which is beyond old age and death; and beyond hunger and thirst and sorrow. This is Atman, the Spirit in man. All the desires of this Spirit are Truth. It is this Spirit that we must find and know: man must find his own Soul. He who has found and knows his Soul has found all the worlds, has achieved all his desires."

dertake preparation for the priestly caste. When the young man returns from his training twelve years later, he appears very serious and haughty, even arrogant. Apparently he had learned many things. But in order to teach him good manners and to reorient him as to his place, the father—tradition says he is the famous sage Uddalaka Aruni—tests Svetaketu by seeing how much he had truly learned about

the Self (Atman) and about the Brahman. In this sense, the story may also be a critique on Brahmin education of the day. Svetaketu had learned about what was knowable, but what did he know about that which is unknowable? In this story, the father demonstrates that actions imparted on an object of a certain nature may have visible effects but do not alter its inherent quality; that is, its nature is nondualistic. By knowing the nature of a thing, one can know that there is but one nature. Other names and labels for things of the same nature only serve to show modifications that do not alter that nature. That which is present in all things of a similar nature—clay in vessels, gold in coins, and, by extension, Brahman in all—constitutes the only reality. Some commentators have asked why Uddalaka did not teach his own son the Vedic knowledge in the first place; one response is that he was perhaps a man who was transitioning from the old traditions into the new Upanishadic age.

Eleven chapters later, in chapters 12–14, Svetaketu is still being taught by his father. The question here is how the vast universes in which life resides could be produced from that "Spirit" which is nameless and formless in its purest state. Just as the trunk, branches, and fruit of a giant tree are produced from the essence of a tiny seed, so is the entire world produced from something that cannot be seen. The example of the salt dissolving in water shows that an object can be existent yet invisible, such that there are other ways of perceiving it. One might thus come to know the Brahman, the One True Spirit, through one's own atman, or individual spirit.

The narrative that closes part 6 concerns the way to self-knowledge. It imagines a man who, perhaps set upon and bound by thieves, is blindfolded and led to a "desert place" outside his home in the land of the Gandharas. At that time, Gandhara was a great trading kingdom along the Kabul River, to the north of India. The man in the story is conceived to be freed by one who finds him abandoned and to be directed to return to his home civilization by inquiring at the villages along the way. Just as a person whose deeds lead him away from the truth and leave him lost in the desert of bodily nature and appetites, ignorance of one's true nature keeps one removed from the realm of spirit. And just as the man may be found by a compassionate stranger, a teacher who is illuminated by self-awareness might lead a discriminating student to the Truth of Self, ultimately connecting one to the Universal Reality or Truth. The home of the soul is that of True Spirit. Yet no one is perfect, even after attaining such awareness of Truth. One continues to wander in one's earthly body in this world until death, when one can fully achieve such liberation.

♦ Part 7

Chapter 6 of part 7 indicates that no matter how much one knows about the greater world, it is meditation, not thought (or the quest for knowledge), that brings the greatest good. If one can see the contemplative aspects of nature and meditate upon them as extensions of the Brahman, one is on the path to spiritual greatness.

The opening portion of chapters 16–25 of part 7 presents a rhetorical chain that roots truth in knowledge, knowledge in thought, thought in faith, and so on, finally rooting joy, and by extension truth and everything else, in the Infinite. The latter half of this section elaborates on the notion that truth and the Infinite are everywhere—above, beyond, behind, in between, below, north, south, east, and west—to be found by those who seek them. It is suggested that truth is

greater than the self. When one begins to aspire to the truth, one leaves the phenomenological world and moves toward the Infinite. Understanding, reflection, faith, single-mindedness, and concentration on bliss can lead to truth, and, in turn, the Infinite is blissful. Meanwhile, all experiences of the finite, marked by differentiation between the physical reality and the spiritual foundation, are dual. The nondual reality is where one can see, hear, and understand only the Infinite. The Infinite is great but does not even need its own greatness, so to speak, because it is beyond such conceptions. For those who are ignorant, the notion of self is represented by the body and its achievements and acquisitions; for those enlightened, the Self is Atman. In the Infinite, one knows the Self (the higher self), and experiences freedom. Those in the finite world remain as unliberated slaves.

♦ Part 8

Expounding the notion that the Brahman is free from time, space, and the dualistic world, chapter 1 of part 8 presents the allegory of the Brahman as it dwells within humanity. The castle of Brahman is the body, while the shrine of the lotus flower is the heart. One might wonder if the Brahman is small, since it can dwell in a small place like the heart, but the analogy is used because the Upanishads see the Brahman as transcendental and not occupying physical space. Rather, as the Brahman occupies the Atman, it is greater than all the elements of the physical universe. The enlightened Spirit, once realized in one's inner consciousness, is free from death, free from age, and free from bodily desires and lives on after the physical body perishes.

Chapter 4 describes a bridge that separates the various elements of the physical and transcendent existences. The planes of reality, with their earthly limits, are regulated by cause and effect, good and evil, caste and life stages. Once one crosses the bridge, one leaves behind the vestiges of the phenomenological world and enters into the limitless realm of Spirit. The word *Atman* as used here may denote not merely the higher Self but the aspect of the Brahman into which the Self has the potential to cross. Some translations use the term "dam" instead of "bridge" to denote the separation.

Chapter 8 concerns itself with the problem of the Atman and the many impediments that befall earthly human bodies. Prajapati, the Creator God, warns of the perils of never fully realizing the Self. Indra, a king of the gods, and Virochana, a king of the demons, both go to Prajapati to learn of the Atman—intimating to the reader that knowledge of the Self is more important than the powers these entities already possessed. Arriving with "fuel in their hands" as an offering and sign of respect, the two live with the master Prajapati for thirty-two years. As students, they overcome any rivalry they might have had (one being a demon, the other a god), since they believe Prajapati's statement that those who come to know the Atman, the Self, can obtain all the worlds and all their desires. In that they are undertaking the rigors of spiritual and ascetic training, they are now fellow yogis. Prajapati tells them that the Atman can be seen as they look into another's eyes. This would not be strictly as one would visually see but as one would encounter the Spirit. The two are tested in seeing their reflections in a bowl of water and are led to believe, incorrectly, that the glory of the Self is in the body seen in the reflection. The Self to them is merely a shadow, and the body is the cause of it. In taking the body to be the Self, they fail to consider that the body is not immutable and is subject to change.

Virochana returns satisfied to the world of the demons and begins to preach what he thinks to be the truth. He believes the physical body to be the cause of the soul and focuses on the worldly self, which allows him to catch a glimpse (or shadow) of the Atman. For Virochana, the soul is dependent upon the body. It is said that the doctrine of the demons is still followed by people and can be seen in the way they treat their bodies both during life (in terms of adornment, vanity, and so on) and after life (in embalming and fancy burial). This is why Hindus cremate the deceased, believing that the quicker the body is eliminated, the sooner the soul will be free from the physical. Those who bury the body with food, nice clothing, elaborate coffins, and decorations are admitting a dependence of the soul on physical body.

Since Virochana remains deluded by the false doctrine about the glory of the Atman, only Indra returns to Prajapati unsatisfied. Realizing his ill conception, he once again asks to become a pupil, living with Prajapati for another thirty-two years. He is then directed to glorify the elements of a dreaming existence. Yet unsatisfied, a third time he returns for another thirty-two years of instruction, still unconvinced that he has been shown the True Self. After contemplating an existence in deep, undisturbed, dreamless slumber, he returns yet one more time, still unclear. Prajapati asks him this time to stay for five more years, for a total of 101 years; even Indra, who was already a significant spiritual being

(namely, a god), had to spend an incredible amount of time as a student to reach an understanding of the True Self, the incorporeal self, the Atman. Once the false notion of identity with a body is gone, only then is Indra free to move toward bliss, unconnected to duality, and able to attain pure form as Spirit. Thus did Indra learn about the Self from Prajapati and teach it to the other gods. Interestingly, while the Vedic gods are the main characters of this story, they reflect the antiritualistic sentiment of the Upanishadic age. The gods are not worshipped but rather are themselves involved in reflective and introspective activity.

Audience

The early Upanishads attempted not to eradicate the Vedic traditions but to modernize and expand their interpretation. There was a perceived need to move past the rigid ritualism of the Brahmins, the priestly class, in order to embrace emerging movements, including Buddhism, Jainism, and other branches of Hinduism. Thus, the Upanishads were possibly aimed at two major groups, the Brahmins and the *shramanas* (wandering ascetics, not all of whom were Hindu in the orthodox sense), who seemed to be at ideological odds with one another. Each of these audiences may have had different ways of understanding the Upanishads. Changes in the attitudes of the Brahmins likely stemmed from the contemporary social and religious influences within Indian society; but as the Upanishads began to be embraced by Hindu orthodoxy, the Brahmins took its spirituality to heart. Those who were aware of such tensions and were struggling to make sense of them might have been prime targets for this literature.

Questions for Further Study

1. What impact might intercaste conflict have played in the development of the Upanishads?

2. A common feature of early Hinduism was asceticism and self-denial. Why do you think this way of life was so important to Hindus at that time?

3. The entry discusses "clan-dominated regions" in opposition to the cities. What impact did the distinction between the two have on Hinduism, perceptions of caste, and the Upanishads?

4. What do you think might have motivated Thomas Jefferson, the third U.S. president, to learn Sanskrit and read the Upanishads?

5. In your own words, explicate the meaning of this passage from the Upanishads: "In the centre of the castle of Brahman, our own body, there is a small shrine in the form of a lotus-flower, and within can be found a small space. We should find who dwells there, and we should want to know him." What could this passage mean for people in modern life?

The Upanishads are written in a later Sanskrit that makes them grammatically much easier to read than the Vedas; this accessibility may have allowed them to be read by wider audiences. In modern India, the Upanishads retain their place as revered ancient texts, especially among more-educated Hindus and those who follow with interest the version of reformed Hinduism called Neo-Vedanta, which enfolds Western philosophical traditions and the findings of modern science in seeking to bring the message of Hinduism to the West.

Impact

Around the time that the Chandogya Upanishad was composed, the Brihadaranyaka Upanishad was also written. These two bodies of literature would form the basis for the Vedanta ideology and serve as links between the Vedic Age and the reforms to come. The initial impact of the Upanishads was not earth shattering, as there were contemporary movements that were also trying to reform Hinduism. Some modern scholars have even suggested that the Upanishads were ineffective in their own age, as they failed to eradicate or change the caste system and did not efficiently alter the moral order of the day. Part of the Upanishads' own philosophy was that "change" is merely an illusion. However, the enduring character of nonduality seems to be the text's strongest feature, a feature that would remain a part of Hindu identity through the centuries.

While interaction between India and Greece was going on long before Alexander the Great's fourth century BCE invasion, the Hellenization of the Persian Empire opened the door for further interaction between India and the West. The Upanishads have been considered by some modern scholars to be influential upon Greek philosophy, particularly the thought of certain fifth-century BCE monists and especially the work of Plato (ca. 428–348 BCE). Monism, which evolved in India as strongly influenced by nondual notions (unity with the Brahman) during the Upanishadic age, is the belief that some force, unity, universal being, or ultimate reality is tied or linked to all living things as well as to the universe itself.

Indian scholars have continually returned to the Upanishadic philosophies in post-classical Hinduism. Shankara (778–820) wrote famous commentaries on the Brihadaranyaka and Katha Upanishads, emphasizing knowledge of the Self, or the Brahman within. The nondual philosophy of Shankara—rejecting the Jain notion of two natures, the evil physical universe and the good realm of the spirit—draws heavily from the Chandogya Upanishad. According to Shankara, the merging of one's soul with the Nirguna Brahman, or the Brahman as conceived without form or characteristics, is the ultimate goal. The pivotal role of Shankara and his Advaita school in reviving monistic Hinduism cannot be overstated. The Mughal emperor Akbar (1542–1605) had the Upanishads translated into Persian, and his great-grandson Dara Shikoh (1615–1659) attempted to use the Upanishadic literature to forge a link between Hinduism and mystical Islam.

Translations of the Upanishads into Latin were made in the early 1800s by the French scholar Abraham-Hyacinthe Anquetil-Duperron. This set was followed by an English version in 1853 and another more lengthy and famous rendition in 1879 by Max Müller. The German philosopher Immanuel Kant (1724–1804) developed theories of transcendental idealism based upon these Eastern influences, and the Upanishads were embraced by the later German philosopher Arthur Schopenhauer (1788–1860), as reflected in his works *The World as Will and Representation* (1819) and *Parerga and Paralipomena* (1851). Thomas Jefferson learned Sanskrit and read the Upanishads in their original form. Growing criticisms of Christianity by European idealists spurred fresh interest in the spirituality inherent in the Upanishads. Writers like the Englishman Samuel Taylor Coleridge (1772–1834), the Frenchman Victor Cousin (1792-1867), and the Scotsman Thomas Carlyle (1795–1881) drew deep inspiration from Eastern philosophies. In a vein more familiar to Americans, the Transcendentalists of New England, like Ralph Waldo Emerson and Henry David Thoreau, built upon European inspirations delving into the mystical and naturalistic connections offered by the Upanishads. The Upanishads remain among the great classics of world religion and spirituality. Modern students of religion are continually attracted to the possibility of ultimate divine connectivity offered by these texts.

Further Reading

■ Books

Black, Brian. *The Character of the Self in Ancient India: Priests, Kings, and Women in the Early Upanisads*. Albany: State University of New York Press, 2007.

Doniger, Wendy. *The Hindus: An Alternative History*. New York: Penguin Press, 2009.

Flood, Gavin. *An Introduction to Hinduism*. Cambridge, U.K.: Cambridge University Press, 2004.

Nikhilananda, Swami. *The Upanishads*, Vol. 4: *Taittiriya and Chhandogya*. New York: Ramakrishna-Vivekananda Center, 1994.

Olivelle, Patrick. *The Early Upanisads: Annotated Text and Translation*. New York: Oxford University Press, 1998.

Sharma, Shubhra. *Life in the Upanishads*. New Delhi: Abhinav Publications, 1985.

■ Web Sites

"The Upanishads." Atma Jyoti Ashram "Spiritual Writings" Web site. http://www.atmajyoti.org/spirwrit_upanishad_intro.asp

—Tim Davis

UPANISHADS

Chandogya Upanishad

♦ Part 1: Chapter 9

Wherefrom do all these worlds come? They come from space. All beings arise from space, and into space they return: space is indeed their beginning, and space is their final end. . . .

♦ Part 2: Chapter 23

Prajapati, the Creator of all, rested in life-giving meditation over the worlds of his creation; and from them came the three *Vedas*. He rested in meditation and from those came the three sounds: bhur, bhuvas, svar, earth, air, and sky. He rested in meditation and from the three sounds came the sound om. Even as all leaves come from a stem, all words come from the sound om. om is the whole universe, om is in truth the whole universe. . . .

♦ Part 3: Chapter 12

Great is the Gayatri, the most sacred verse of the *Vedas*; but how much greater is the Infinity of Brahman! A quarter of his being is this whole vast universe: the other three quarters are his heaven of Immortality. . . .

♦ Part 3: Chapter 13

There is a Light that shines beyond all things on earth, beyond us all, beyond the heavens, beyond the highest, the very highest heavens. This is the Light that shines in our heart. . . .

♦ Part 3: Chapter 14

All this universe is in truth Brahman. He is the beginning and end and life of all. As such, in silence, give unto him adoration.

Man in truth is made of faith. As his faith is in this life, so he becomes in the beyond: with faith and vision let him work.

There is a Spirit that is mind and life, light and truth and vast spaces. He contains all works and desires and all perfumes and all tastes. He enfolds the whole universe, and in silence is loving to all.

This is the Spirit that is in my heart, smaller than a grain of rice, or a grain of barley, or a grain of mustard-seed, or a grain of canary-seed, or the kernel of a grain of canary-seed. This is the Spirit that is in my heart, greater than the earth, greater than the sky, greater than heaven itself, greater than all these worlds.

He contains all works and desires and all perfumes and all tastes. He enfolds the whole universe and in silence is loving to all. This is the Spirit that is in my heart, this is Brahman.

To him I shall come when I go beyond this life. And to him will come he who has faith and doubts not. Thus said Sandilya, thus said Sandilya. . . .

♦ Part 3: Chapter 15

I go to the Imperishable Treasure: by his grace, by his grace, by his grace.

I go to the Spirit of life: by his grace, by his grace, by his grace.

I go to the Spirit of the earth: by his grace, by his grace, by his grace.

I go to the Spirit of the air: by his grace, by his grace, by his grace.

I go to the Spirit of the heavens: by his grace, by his grace; by his grace. . . .

♦ Part 3: Chapter 16

A man is a living sacrifice. The first twenty-four years of his life are the morning offering of the Soma-wine; because the holy Gayatri has twenty-four sounds, and the chanting of the Gayatri is heard in the morning offering. The Vasus, the gods of the earth, rule this offering. If a man should be ill during that time, he should pray: "With the help of the Vasus, the powers of my life, may my morning offering last until my midday offering and may not my sacrifice perish whilst the Vasus are the powers of my life."

The next forty-four years of his life are the midday offering of the Soma-wine; because the holy Trishtubh has forty-four sounds, and the chanting of the Trishtubh is heard with the midday offering. The Rudras, the gods of the air, rule this offering. If a man should be ill during that time, he should pray: "With the help of the Rudras, the powers of my life, may my midday offering last until my evening offering, and may not my sacrifice perish whilst the Rudras are the powers of my life."

The next forty-eight years of his life are the evening offering; because the holy Jagati has forty-eight sounds, and the chanting of the Jagati is heard with the evening offering. The Adityas, the gods of light, rule this offering. If a man should be ill during that time, he should pray: "With the help of the Adityas, the powers of my life, let my evening offering last until the end of a long life; and may not my sacrifice perish whilst the Adityas are the powers of my life."

Mahidasa Aitareya knew this when he used to say: "Why should I suffer an illness when I am not going to die?" And he lived one hundred and sixteen years. . . .

♦ Part 4: Chapter 4

Once Satyakama went to his mother and said: "Mother, I wish to enter upon the life of a religious student. Of what family am I?"

To him she answered: "I do not know, my child, of what family thou art. In my youth, I was poor and served as a maid many masters, and then I had thee: I therefore do not know of what family thou art. My name is Jabala and thy name is Satyakama. Thou mayest call thyself Satyakama Jabala."

The boy went to the Master Haridrumata Gautama and said: "I want to become a student of sacred wisdom. May I come to you, Master?"

To him the Master asked: "Of what family art thou, my son?"

"I do not know of what family I am," answered Satyakama. "I asked my mother and she said: 'I do not know, my child, of what family thou art. In my youth, I was poor and served as a maid many masters, and then I had thee: I therefore do not know of what family thou art. My name is Jabala and thy name is Satyakama.' I am therefore Satyakama Jabala, Master."

To him Master Gautama said: "Thou art a Brahmin, since thou hast not gone away from truth. Come, my son, I will take thee as a student." . . .

♦ Part 6: Chapter 1

OM. There lived once a boy, Svetaketu Aruneya by name. One day his father spoke to him in this way: "Svetaketu, go and become a student of sacred wisdom. There is no one in our family who has not studied the holy *Vedas* and who might only be given the name of Brahman by courtesy."

The boy left at the age of twelve and, having learnt the *Vedas*, he returned home at the age of twenty-four, very proud of his learning and having a great opinion of himself.

His father, observing this, said to him: "Svetaketu, my boy, you seem to have a great opinion of yourself, you think you are learned, and you are proud. Have you asked for that knowledge whereby what is not heard is heard, what is not thought is thought, and what is not known is known?"

"What is that knowledge, father?" asked Svetaketu.

"Just as by knowing a lump of clay, my son, all that is clay can be known, since any differences are only words and the reality is clay;

Just as by knowing a piece of gold all that is gold can be known, since any differences are only words and the reality is only gold;

And just as by knowing a piece of iron all that is iron is known, since any differences are only words and the reality is only iron."

Svetaketu said: "Certainly my honoured masters knew not this themselves. If they had known, why would they not have told me? Explain this to me, father."

"So be it, my child." . . .

♦ Part 6: Chapters 12–14

"Bring me a fruit from this banyan tree."

"Here it is, father."

"Break it."

"It is broken, Sir."

"What do you see in it?"

"Very small seeds, Sir."

"Break one of them, my son."

"It is broken, Sir."

"What do you see in it?"

"Nothing at all, Sir."

Then his father spoke to him: "My son, from the very essence in the seed which you cannot see comes in truth this vast banyan tree. Believe me, my son, an invisible and subtle essence is the Spirit of the whole universe. That is Reality. That is Atman. Thou art that."

"Explain more to me, father," said Svetaketu.

"So be it, my son. Place this salt in water and come to me tomorrow morning."

Svetaketu did as he was commanded, and in the morning his father said to him: "Bring me the salt you put into the water last night."

Svetaketu looked into the water, but could not find it, for it had dissolved.

His father then said: "Taste the water from this side. How is it?"

"It is salt."

"Taste it from the middle. How is it?"

"It is salt."

"Taste it from that side. How is it?"

"It is salt."

"Look for the salt again and come again to me,"

The son did so, saying: "I cannot see the salt. I only see water."

His father then said: "In the same way, O my son, you cannot see the Spirit. But in truth he is here. An invisible and subtle essence is the Spirit of the whole universe. That is Reality. That is Truth. Thou art that."

"Explain more to me, father."

"So be it, my son. Even as a man, O my son, who had been led blindfolded from his land of the Gandharas and then left in a desert place, might wander to the East and North and South, because he had been taken blindfolded and left in an unknown place, but if a good man took off his bandage and told him "In that direction is the land of the Gandharas, go in that direction," then, if he were a wise man, he would go asking from village to village until he would have reached his land of the Gandharas; so it happens in this world to a man who has a Master to direct him to the land of the Spirit. Such a man can say: 'I shall wander in this world until I attain liberation; but then I shall go and reach my Home.'

This invisible and subtle essence is the Spirit of the whole universe. That is Reality. That is Truth. Thou art that." . . .

♦ **Part 7: Chapter 6**

Is there anything higher than thought?

Meditation is in truth higher than thought. The earth seems to rest in silent meditation; and the waters and the mountains and the sky and the heavens seem all to be in meditation. Whenever a man attains greatness on this earth, he has his reward according to his meditation. . . .

♦ **Part 7: Chapters 16–25**

When a man speaks words of truth he speaks words of greatness: know the nature of truth.

When a man knows, he can speak truth. He who does not know cannot speak truth: know the nature of knowledge.

When a man thinks then he can know. He who does not think does not know: know the nature of thought.

When a man has faith then he thinks. He who has not faith does not think: know the nature of faith.

Where there is progress one sees and has faith. Where there is no progress there is no faith: know the nature of progress.

Where there is creation there is progress. Where there is no creation there is no progress: know the nature of creation.

Where there is joy there is creation. Where there is no joy there is no creation: know the nature of joy.

Where there is the Infinite there is joy. There is no joy in the finite. Only in the Infinite there is joy: know the nature of the Infinite.

Where nothing else is seen, or heard, or known there is the Infinite. Where something else is seen, or heard, or known there is the finite. The Infinite is immortal; but the finite is mortal.

"Where does the Infinite rest?" On his own greatness, or not even on his own greatness.

In this world they call greatness the possession of cattle and horses, elephants and gold, servants and wives, lands and houses. But I do not call this greatness, for here one thing depends upon another.

But the Infinite is above and below, North and South and East and West. The Infinite is the whole universe.

I am above and below, North and South and East and West. I am the whole universe.

Atman is above and below, North and South and East and West. Atman is the whole universe.

He who sees, knows, and understands this, who finds in Atman, the Spirit, his love and his pleasure and his union and his joy, becomes a Master of himself. His freedom then is infinite.

But those who see not this become the servants of other masters and in the worlds that pass away attain not their liberation. . . .

♦ **Part 8: Chapter 1**

OM. In the centre of the castle of Brahman, our own body, there is a small shrine in the form of a lotus-flower, and within can be found a small space. We should find who dwells there, and we should want to know him.

And if anyone asks, "Who is he who dwells in a small shrine in the form of a lotus-flower in the centre of the castle of Brahman? Whom should we want to find and to know?" we can answer:

"The little space within the heart is as great as this vast universe. The heavens and the earth are there, and the sun, and the moon, and the stars; fire and lightning and winds are there; and all that now is and all that is not: for the whole universe is in Him and He dwells within our heart."

And if they should say, "If all things are in the castle of Brahman, all beings and all desires, what remains when old age overcomes the castle or when the life of the body is gone?" we can answer:

"The Spirit who is in the body does not grow old and does not die, and no one can ever kill the Spirit who is everlasting. This is the real castle of Brahman wherein dwells all the love of the universe. It is Atman, pure Spirit, beyond sorrow, old age, and death;

beyond evil and hunger and thirst. It is Atman whose love is Truth, whose thoughts are Truth.

Even as here on earth the attendants of a king obey their king, and are with him wherever he is and go with him wherever he goes, so all love which is Truth and all thoughts of Truth obey the Atman, the Spirit. And even as here on earth all work done in time ends in time, so in the worlds to come even the good works of the past pass away. Therefore those who leave this world and have not found their soul, and that love which is Truth, find not their freedom in other worlds. But those who leave this world and have found their soul and that love which is Truth, for them there is the liberty of the Spirit in this world and in the worlds to come." . . .

♦ **Part 8: Chapter 4**

There is a bridge between time and Eternity; and this bridge is Atman, the Spirit of man. Neither day nor night cross that bridge, nor old age, nor death nor sorrow.

Evil or sin cannot cross that bridge, because the world of the Spirit is pure. This is why when this bridge has been crossed, the eyes of the blind can see, the wounds of the wounded are healed, and the sick man becomes whole from his sickness.

To one who goes over that bridge, the night becomes like unto day; because in the worlds of the Spirit there is a Light which is everlasting. . . .

♦ **Part 8: Chapter 8**

"There is a Spirit which is pure and which is beyond old age and death; and beyond hunger and thirst and sorrow. This is Atman, the Spirit in man. All the desires of this Spirit are Truth. It is this Spirit that we must find and know: man must find his own Soul. He who has found and knows his Soul has found all the worlds, has achieved all his desires." Thus spoke Prajapati.

The gods and the devils heard these words and they said: "Come, let us go and find the Atman, let us find the Soul, so that we may obtain all our desires."

Then Indra amongst the gods and Virochana amongst the devils went without telling each other to see Prajapati, carrying fuel in their hands as a sign that they wanted to be his pupils.

And so for thirty-two years they both lived with Prajapati the life of religious students. At the end of that time Prajapati asked them: "Why have you been living the life of religious students?"

Indra and Virochana answered: "People say that you know the Atman, a Spirit which is pure and which is beyond old age and death, and beyond hun-

ger and thirst and sorrow, a Spirit whose desires are Truth and whose thoughts are Truth; and that you say that this Spirit must be found and known, because when he is found all the worlds are found and all desires are obtained. This is why we have been living here as your pupils."

Prajapati said to them: "What you see when you look into another person's eyes, that is the Atman, immortal, beyond fear, that is Brahman."

"And who is he whom we see when we look in water or in a mirror?" they asked.

"The same is seen in all," he answered. And then he said to them: "Go and look at yourselves in a bowl of water and ask me anything you want to know about the Atman, your own self."

The two went and looked in a bowl of water. "What do you see?" asked Prajapati.

"We see ourselves clearly from our hair down to our nails," they said.

"Adorn yourselves and dress in clothes of beauty," said Prajapati, "and look at yourselves again in a bowl of water."

They did so and looked again in the bowl of water. "What do you see?" asked Prajapati.

"We see ourselves as we are," they answered, "adorned and dressed in clothes of beauty."

"This is the Immortal beyond all fear: this is Brahman," said Prajapati.

Then they left with peace in their hearts.

Prajapati looked at them and said: "They have seen but they have not understood. They have not found the Atman, their soul. Anyone who holds their belief, be he god or devil, shall perish."

Then Virochana went to the devils full of self-satisfaction, and gave them this teaching: "We ourselves are our own bodies, and those must be made happy on earth. It is our bodies that should be in glory, and it is for them that we should have servants. He who makes his body happy, he who for his body has servants, he is well in this world and also in the world to come."

That is why when here on earth a man will not give any gifts, when a man has no faith and will not sacrifice, people say "This man is a devil"; for this is in truth their devilish doctrine. They dress their dead bodies with fine garments, and glorify them with perfumes and ornaments, thinking that thereby they will conquer the other world.

But before Indra had returned to the gods he saw the danger of this teaching and he thought: "If our self, our Atman, is the body, and is dressed in clothes of beauty when the body is, and is covered with ornaments when the body is, then when the body is blind the self is blind, and when the body is lame the self is lame; and when the body dies, our self dies. I cannot find any joy in this doctrine."

He therefore went back to Prajapati with fuel in hand as a sign that he wanted to be his pupil.

"Why have you returned, great Maghavan?" asked Prajapati. "You went away with Virochana with peace in your heart."

Indra replied: "Even as the Atman, the self, our soul, is dressed in clothes of beauty when the body is, and is covered with ornaments when the body is, when the body is blind the self is blind, and when the body is lame the self is lame, and when the body dies the self dies. I cannot find any joy in this doctrine."

"It is even so, Maghavan," said Prajapati. "I will teach you a higher doctrine, live with me for another thirty-two years."

Indra was with Prajapati for another thirty-two years, and then Prajapati said: "The spirit that wanders in joy in the land of dreams, that is the Atman, that is the Immortal beyond fear: that is Brahman."

Then Indra left with peace in his heart; but before he had returned to the gods he saw the danger of this teaching and he thought: "Even if in dreams when the body is blind the self is not blind, or when the body is lame the self is not lame, and does not indeed suffer the limitations of the body, so that when the body is killed the self is not killed; yet in dreams the self may seem to be killed and to suffer, and to feel much pain and weep. I cannot find any joy in this doctrine."

He therefore went with fuel in hand back to Prajapati, who said to him: "You left, Maghavan, with peace in your heart; why have you returned?"

Indra replied: "Even if in dreams when the body is blind the Atman is not blind, or when the body is lame the Atman is not lame, and indeed does not suffer the limitations of the body, so that when the body is killed the self is not killed; yet in dreams the self may seem to be killed and suffer, and to feel much pain and weep. I cannot find any joy in this doctrine."

"What you say is true, Maghavan," said Prajapati. "I will teach you a higher doctrine. Live with me for another thirty-two years."

Indra was with Prajapati another thirty-two years. And then Prajapati said:

"The spirit who is sleeping without dreams in the silent quietness of deep sleep, that is the Atman, that is the Immortal beyond fear: that is Brahman."

Then Indra left with peace in his heart, but before he had reached the gods he saw the danger of this teaching and he thought: "If a man is in deep sleep without dreams he cannot even say "I am" and he cannot know anything. He in truth falls into nothingness. I cannot find any joy in this doctrine." And he went again to Prajapati with fuel in hand.

"Why have you returned, Maghavan? You left with peace in your heart," asked Prajapati.

Indra replied: "If a man is in deep sleep without dreams he cannot even say 'I am' and he cannot know anything. He in truth falls into nothingness. I cannot find any joy in this doctrine."

"What you say is true, Maghavan," said Prajapati. "I will teach you a higher doctrine, the highest that can be taught. Live with me now for five years."

And Indra lived with Prajapati for five years. He lived with Prajapati a total of years one hundred and one. This is why people say: "Great Indra lived with Prajapati the life of chastity of a Brahmacharya spiritual student for one hundred and one years."

Prajapati then spoke to Indra:

"It is true that the body is mortal, that it is under the power of death; but it is also the dwelling of Atman, the Spirit of immortal life. The body, the house of the Spirit, is under the power of pleasure and pain; and if a man is ruled by his body then this man can never be free. But when a man is in the joy of the Spirit, in the Spirit which is ever free, then this man is free from all bondage, the bondage of pleasure and pain.

The wind has not a body, nor lightning, nor thunder, nor clouds; but when those rise into the higher spheres then they find their body of light. In the same way, when the soul is in silent quietness it arises and leaves the body, and reaching the Spirit Supreme finds there its body of light. It is the land of infinite liberty where, beyond its mortal body, the Spirit of man is free. There can he laugh and sing of his glory with ethereal women and friends. He enjoys ethereal chariots and forgets the cart of his body on earth. For as a beast is attached to a cart, so on earth the soul is attached to a body.

Know that when the eye looks into space it is the Spirit of man that sees: the eye is only the organ of sight. When one says 'I feel this perfume,' it is the Spirit that feels: he uses the organ of smell. When one says 'I am speaking,' it is the Spirit that speaks: the voice is the organ of speech. When one says 'I am hearing,' it is the Spirit that hears: the ear is the organ of hearing. And when one says 'I think,' it is the Spirit that thinks: the mind is the organ of thought. It is because of the light of the Spirit that the human mind can see, and can think, and enjoy this world.

All the gods in the heaven of Brahman adore in contemplation their Infinite Spirit Supreme. This is why they have all joy, and all the worlds and all desires. And the man who on this earth finds and knows Atman, his own Self, has all his holy desires and all the worlds and all joy."

Thus spoke Prajapati. Thus in truth spoke Prajapati.

Glossary

Atman	the self, the individual spirit
Brahman	the universal spirit; the original source of the cosmos
Gayatri	type of meter for the verses used in the Vedas
Indra	king of the gods
Jagati	type of meter for the verses used in the Vedas
land of the Gandharas	a trading kingdom along the Kabul River, to the north of India
Prajapati	creator god
Sandilya	an ancient sage
Soma	an intoxicating ritual beverage
Trishtubh	a Vedic meter type for hymns
Vedas	the oldest scriptures of Hinduism

Confucius

(Confucius, Tanyu, Kano [1602-74] / Private Collection / Peter Newark Pictures / The Bridgeman Art Library International)

CONFUCIUS: ANALECTS

"Learning without thought is labor lost; thought without learning is perilous."

Overview

The Analects (Lunyu) is presented as a discourse between Confucius and his disciples, and it reflects the ideas associated with Confucianism. More of a collection of aphorisms than a philosophical treatise, the Analects offers a guide to ethical behavior centered on the concepts of virtue, ritual (also translated as "propriety"), and benevolence; additionally, it emphasizes self-cultivation and a careful study of the teachings of the ancient sages as the means by which to understand and practice these ideas. Although it is sometimes characterized as a religion, Confucianism is secular in nature, enabling it to coexist peacefully with other religions. To be sure, references to heaven and the spirits appear in the Analects, but they reflect Confucius's acceptance of conventional beliefs rather than his proselytizing of a specific religious creed.

The belief that the ruler held the Mandate of Heaven, which had emerged during the Western Zhou Period (ca. 1027–771 BCE), greatly influenced Confucius's thinking. Despite its religious connotations, the Mandate of Heaven did not refer to a pantheon of gods who granted or revoked a ruler's right to rule at will. Understood more as a political concept, the Mandate of Heaven symbolized an impersonal cosmological force that legitimized dynastic authority as long as the emperor's rule brought harmony and prosperity to the empire. The emperor's actions, rather than divine will, determined whether he held or lost the Mandate of Heaven. The notion of the Mandate of Heaven convinced Confucius that individual actions held social and political consequences and were inextricably linked to the cosmic order. He believed that the "superior man," through his possession of virtue, attention to ritual and propriety, and benevolent attitude, understood best how to maintain a harmonious balance between the human and divine worlds. Confucius asserted that a morally upright ruler, aided by officials who had proved themselves to be superior men, was the most qualified person to restore order and bring harmony to China.

The Analects reflects Confucius's emphasis on moral education as the path to good government. Although his proposals were dismissed by the rulers of his day, his ideas took root, and over the course of several centuries the evolution of a philosophical tradition—one that bears his name—continued its path. By the second century BCE, Confucianism was well established as the official ideology of imperial China. Over the next two millennia, its influence grew and spread throughout East Asia and Southeast Asia. Despite its commitment to restoring the glory days of the ancient past, Confucianism has successfully met the unprecedented challenges of the present.

Context

During the Eastern Zhou Period (771–221 BCE), political turmoil was accompanied by an intellectual creativity evident in the emergence of "the hundred schools" of thought; consequently, some scholars labeled this era the "age of philosophers." Confucius lived during the first part of the Eastern Zhou, referred to as the Spring and Autumn Period (722–481 BCE). This era witnessed the decline of the Zhou rulers and the rise of powerful lords who would vie with one another to become the new ruler of China during the aptly named Warring States Period (403–221 BCE). The weakness of the Zhou Dynasty paved the way for the emergence of a multistate system dominated by expansion-minded hegemons (ba) who acknowledged the Zhou emperor as their overlord but acted autonomously, forming alliances and declaring war when it suited them. Internecine warfare reduced the number of states from about 170 during the Spring and Autumn Period to just seven during the Warring States Period.

In response to the warfare and instability surrounding them, a number of Chinese thinkers proposed reforms aimed at restoring peace and unity. Those whose ideas survived in written form are credited with founding the major philosophies of China: Mohism, Daoism, Legalism, and, of course, Confucianism. Personally experiencing the social dislocation and economic disruption that accompanied political disunity, educated Chinese men—Confucius among them—pondered questions such as these: What is the key to good governance? How should people treat one another? Are humans by nature good or evil? More than a philosophical

Time Line

CA. 1027 BCE	■ The Western Zhou Period, so named because the Zhou people established their capital in western China, begins and spans some 250 years.
771 BCE	■ The next half century, known as the Eastern Zhou Period, begins with the eastward relocation of the Zhou capital and witnesses the decline of Zhou power.
722–481 BCE	■ The first half of the Eastern Zhou Period is known as the Spring and Autumn Period.
CA. 551 BCE	■ Confucius is born in Shandong, China.
CA. 479 BCE	■ Confucius dies.
CA. 479–249 BCE	■ After Confucius's death, his disciples write down his ideas. Over the course of the next two centuries, the Analects assumes its present form.
478 BCE	■ The Temple of Confucius is built in what is today Qufu, in Shandong Province.
403–221 BCE	■ Armies grow, conflict worsens, and Chinese states are consolidated in what is referred to as the Warring States Period.
221–206 BCE	■ Confucianism declines in influence during the Qin Dynasty.
206 BCE –220 CE	■ Confucianism rises to prominence as the official ideology of the Han Dynasty.
618–907	■ The Confucian-based civil service examination system is established during the Tang Dynasty.
1127–1279	■ Neo-Confucianism emerges during the Southern Song Dynasty. It emphasizes a return to the original core of Confucian texts.

debate, such questions sought answers to the political crisis crippling China during these turbulent centuries. Many aspiring leaders attempted to gain an official post that would enable them to turn their ideas into policies—policies that would restore order and unify the country.

Confucius never found a receptive audience for his ideas among the powerholders of his day, although he enjoyed a large following of students, both during his lifetime and long after his death. Confucius's ideas form the core of the philosophy that bears his name, but the contributions of his followers helped to elaborate his precepts. Mencius (ca. 371–ca. 289 BCE) emphasized reciprocity over hierarchy, and Xunzi (ca. 312–ca. 230 BCE) argued that human nature was evil, although he believed in the transformative power of moral education. By the end of the Eastern Zhou Period, Confucianism was well poised to take its position at the center of Chinese civilization.

About the Author

Confucius was born in the small state of Lu, near present-day Qufu in Shandong, China, around 551 BCE. Born Kong Qiu, he later acquired the names Zhong Ni and Kong Fuzi (Master Kong); the latter was rendered into Latin as "Confucius" by Jesuit missionaries in the sixteenth century. Details about his life come from sources that postdate his death and reflect later generations' preoccupation with the ideas he left behind rather than the life he led. It is generally believed that his family, members of the lower ranks of the aristocracy, fell on hard times and that his father died when he was a young boy. As a young man, Confucius briefly engaged in farm labor and commerce. He married at the age of nineteen and had one son and two daughters.

Despite economically straitened circumstances, Confucius acquired an education that enabled him to pursue careers in government service and teaching. After some initial success in various administrative posts, he eventually became a target of political attack. Dismissed from office and driven into exile, Confucius traveled to neighboring states offering his services as a political adviser. But in the highly stratified society of the Spring and Autumn Period access to the top levels of government was reserved for the highest-ranking members of the nobility.

Convinced that morality provided the antidote to the widespread chaos endemic to his era, Confucius believed that a virtuous ruler—exemplified by the sage-kings of antiquity—could restore order and uphold a harmonious society. Met with disinterest, Confucius turned his attention to teaching in the hope of training the next generation of leaders in the virtues that he believed were key to successful governance. Ultimately, it was as a scholar-teacher that Confucius left his greatest legacy. Although he is not worshipped as a deity, Confucius is honored as a sage, an "uncrowned king," and even a prophet by his followers and admirers. It was only after his death, around 479 BCE, that Confucianism gained significance and that Confucius received the recognition that had eluded him all his life.

Explanation and Analysis of the Document

Compiled over the course of several centuries, the Analects reached their final form around the third century BCE. Although it is considered the authoritative source of Confucius's teachings, authorship is attributed to his many disciples, some of whom became teachers with their own disciples. The Analects presents moral lessons taught through maxims and brief conversations between master and disciple. By posing questions—many of them rhetorical—and presenting analogies, Confucius guides his students to the formation of the answers on their own. The division of the text into twenty chapters does not reflect any chronological order or serve any discernible pedagogical purpose; indeed, the same ideas are expressed throughout the text, whether told using different examples, or in some cases, repeated verbatim. Excerpts from nine of the twenty chapters—1–8 and 12—are discussed here.

♦ Chapters 1 and 2

Confucius begins with a series of rhetorical questions, the last one containing his main point. Assuming that his audience agrees with him—that diligence in study and the company of faraway friends bring joy—he concludes that the answer to the third question would also be affirmative: A virtuous man (also translated as superior man) does not seek glory or recognition; to have virtue is to know humility (1.1). The "man of complete virtue" also spurns gluttony, luxury, flattery, and ingratiating behavior; he acts sincerely and chooses his words wisely (1.3, 1.14). It is not enough, Confucius clarifies, to refrain from flattery or display humility; the superior man must be able to find joy in poverty and not let wealth blind him to propriety (1.15). "Propriety" refers to a complex set of rules that govern political, social, and family relationships based on class, age, and sex; when translated as "ritual," it denotes the intricate rites and ceremonies that shape all aspects of life.

Confucius acknowledges that being virtuous does not come naturally but requires constant vigilance and study. The superior man is expected to grasp the meaning of virtue through study and to practice it by examining his conduct in order to identify and eliminate his flaws; this is what is referred to as self-cultivation or what is translated here as "polite studies" (1.6) and "learning" (1.8). Notably, when Confucius advised against having "friends not equal to yourself" (1.8), he meant equal in terms of virtue, which is suggested in his advice to youth to "cultivate the friendship of the good" (1.6). They should seek the friendship of virtuous men, moral exemplars from whom they can learn and improve themselves. Not surprisingly, Confucius is held up by his disciples as a model to emulate. Following Confucius's example, one should be "benign" so that people do not feel threatened. One should be "upright" to earn their trust, "courteous" to earn their affection, "temperate" to make them feel comfortable, and "complaisant" so people will be as obliging in return. And last, one should be knowledgeable about the current political situation (1.10).

Time Line

1915–1925	■ The New Culture Movement (also referred to as the May Fourth Movement) attacks Confucianism.
1934	■ The New Life Movement, which witnesses the revival of Confucianism, is launched by Chiang Kai-shek, leader of the Guomindang (also referred to as the Nationalist Party).
1966	■ The Cultural Revolution begins, aiming to destroy the "Four Olds," which includes Confucianism.
1974	■ The Criticize Lin Biao and Confucius Movement is launched.

For Confucius, learning offered a path to enlightenment, as his chronology of his educational development suggests (2.4). As a youth, he was eager to learn. Through the education that he had acquired, he matured into a resolute and confident adult. In the last decades of his life, he came to understand the will of Heaven, to see the true nature of things, and to be one with morality, much as the sage-kings had been; for Confucians, this was the ultimate goal, but a goal limited to the superior man. Confucius describes the superior man as a man of action whose words match his deeds (2.13). What is probably being described here is the setting of precedent: Only after the superior man takes an action and presumably deems it worthy of repetition does he then declare that action a precedent. Learning is what distinguishes the superior man from the mean man; the former's active pursuit of knowledge expands his horizons, while the latter's lack of education blinds him to the world outside his insulated community (2.14). Yet although the superior man is an avid learner, he is not a know-it-all. True knowledge, as Confucius points out, comes from the ability to distinguish between what one knows and what one does not know (2.17). Confucius also encouraged active learning through a critical engagement with the subjects of study, and he believed that the production of new knowledge should be based upon a sound understanding of past scholarship (2.15). This emphasis on critical interpretation can be seen in the prolific production of commentaries on the Confucian classics in later generations. However, not all knowledge is beneficial, as his warning of the dangers of heterodox ideas suggests, a warning that later rulers took seriously (2.16). After its adoption as the official ideology during the Han Dynasty (206 BCE–220 CE), any doctrine that challenged the political influence of Confucianism was labeled heterodox and targeted by the state for elimination.

A propaganda poster of Mao leading the people

(Long Live the thoughts of Chairman Mao, September 1969 [colour litho], Chinese School, [20th century] / Private Collection / © The Chambers Gallery, London / The Bridgeman Art Library International)

"If the people be led by laws, and uniformity sought to be given them by punishments, they will try to avoid the punishment, but have no sense of shame. If they be led by virtue, and uniformity sought to be given them by the rules of propriety, they will have the sense of shame, and moreover will become good."

"Learning without thought is labor lost; thought without learning is perilous."

"Yu, shall I teach you what knowledge is? When you know a thing, to hold that you know it; and when you do not know a thing, to allow that you do not know it; this is knowledge."

"What I do not wish men to do to me, I also wish not to do to men."

"The relation between superiors and inferiors is like that between the wind and the grass. The grass must bend, when the wind blows across it."

The philosopher Yu explains virtue in terms of filial piety and fraternal submission (1.2). To be filial is to honor and obey one's parents without question and to sacrifice everything—including one's life if circumstances demanded—for one's parents. Despite the egalitarian connotations attached to "fraternal," the emphasis is on obedience, as suggested by the phrase "fraternal submission" in the second paragraph. Simply stated, the first paragraph explains that those who are "filial and fraternal" obey their superiors and hence do not cause trouble. This, then, is the heart of the matter—the "radical" to which the second paragraph refers (the Chinese term translated here as "radical" also has the meaning of "root" or "source"). The superior man, then, must understand the importance of inculcating these values, particularly in the general population. A filial and submissive populace is one that does not rebel. Consequently, as the rhetorical question posed at the end suggests, their superiors' actions will be motivated by benevolence, a cardinal virtue in the Confucian moral code.

Continuing with the same theme, the statement by the philosopher Tsang attributes the "virtue of the people" to the fulfillment of filial obligations and the proper performance of ritual, hinting at the sociopolitical implications of individual acts (1.9). Adult children were expected to shoulder their parents' burdens, provide their elders with the best that they could afford, and support their parents in their old age, but only those who performed all these acts with sincerity and reverence were considered filial (2.7, 2.8). Parents were expected to care for their children, suggesting some degree of reciprocity in the relationship between parents and children (2.6). One's filial duties did not end with the death of parents; they merely changed. Descendants were expected to observe in proper sequence and with due respect the elaborate mourning and burial rites appropriate to their station and to make offerings to their ancestors on specific days of the year (1.9, 2.5). It was believed that ritual connected the human world to heaven and that its proper completion maintained cosmic harmony, which was reflected in the human world. Conversely, disregarding ritual or failing to carry it out in the prescribed manner invited divine wrath, which expressed itself in political tumult, social disorder, and natural disasters. As Tsang's conclusion makes clear, Confucianism held that ritual, diligently carried out, ensured that the people would be virtuous, which in this context meant loyal and obedient. In this way, ritual was a means to legitimize political authority and maintain social harmony; the ruler, by carefully conducting the appropriate rituals, could regularly reaffirm his claim to the Mandate of Heaven and pacify the people.

Like ritual, propriety maintained the delicate balance between the human and divine realms. It was believed that the sage-kings who had once ruled over a unified and prosperous China best mediated the relationship between the human and divine worlds, so Confucians looked to these "ancient kings" for inspiration and guidance (1.12). Those who strictly observed the rules of propriety were also acceptable "guides and masters" (1.13). Confucius had in mind learned scholars like himself, who had studied the ways of the ancient sage-kings.

More than a code of ethics for individuals to follow, the Analects presents a vision of a government based on moral leadership. A morally upright ruler who led by example could better govern the people than a ruler with an army. By comparing the virtuous ruler to the north polar star (2.1), Confucius wishes to emphasize the qualities of the ideal king: a superior man of unshakable moral integrity who serves as a moral compass for others. In response to some of his contemporaries who advocated a position that came to be labeled Legalist, Confucius argues that the power of morality—acquired by being virtuous—works better to secure the people's compliance than force, regulations, or punishment. Confucius elaborates this point in the next statement when he compares the roles of law and virtue in governing the people (2.3). A ruler who uses laws and the threat of punishment relies on fear to control the people; in contrast, a ruler who teaches the people virtue and propriety by his own example instills in them a sense of shame that acts as a more effective check on errant behavior precisely because it is internally generated rather than externally imposed. It should be noted that Confucius does not oppose the use of law in governing, but he believes that law should be based upon the rules of propriety; for Confucius, law and morality are inseparable.

Confucius offers specific advice to rulers on how to lead by virtue. When people see that the ruler rewards virtue, they will support him; however, when they see that he rewards vice, they will resist. That being the case, to secure the cooperation of the people, the ruler must promote only those of good moral character (2.19). One cannot help but wonder how much of this reflects Confucius's personal feelings about being pushed aside by his obsequious and opportunistic contemporaries in the struggle for an official appointment. Although he is far from democratic, Confucius does believe that the best government is one supported by the people. To that end, a ruler must take his responsibilities seriously, be benevolent but stern and impartial, and promote those who excelled at their jobs and help those who struggled (2.20).

♦ **Chapters 3–6**

The proper maintenance of relationships, Confucius believes, ensures harmony and order. Consequently, a prince should treat his ministers with propriety, and his ministers should be loyal to their prince (3.19). Emphasizing a point made in earlier chapters, Confucius implies that a prince would best be able to rule if he enjoys the acquiescence of his subjects, which he could secure by adhering to the rules of propriety (4.13). There seems to be a hint of reciprocity in these two statements that later disciples, most notably

Mencius, would emphasize. In both, the prince is expected to act in accordance with propriety, and in return he will receive the "faithfulness" of his ministers and the "complaisance" of the subjects in his kingdom. If the prince fails to properly carry out his role, however, then chaos would prevail. In the example of Ning Wu, Confucius describes a prince who rules in accordance with propriety as "a wise man" and characterizes a ruler who does not rule in this way as "a stupid man"; the country of the former is in "good order," while that of the latter is "in disorder" (5.20).

The notion of reciprocity, however, does not govern family relationships, as Confucius's description of a son's relationship with his parents suggests (4.18). From the outset, it is clear that a son's duty is to serve his parents. He is allowed to criticize them if he feels that they are in the wrong, but, ever mindful of his subordinate position, he can do so only "gently." Confucius exhorts the son to persist even if his parents rebuff him but cautions the son to display even greater deference to his parents to offset what may be misinterpreted as disobedience. Failing to persuade his parents and earning their wrath, the son should accept whatever punishment his parents mete out without complaint. Confucius's encouragement of the son to persevere suggests two things: The son is in the right, and a filial son should always look out for the best interests of his parents, even at the risk of punishment. Indeed, the punishment serves as a reminder of his filial piety. If it turns out later that the son was right, then the parents cannot blame him for not trying hard enough to warn them.

The remaining statements underscore the central role virtue played in Confucianism. Confucius's belief that only the virtuous could endure suffering or remain in a state of joy depicts virtue as having almost supernatural powers (4.2). Although it is difficult to attain, virtue is within reach if one sets one's mind to it, for Confucius believed that everyone has the potential to live a virtuous life (4.4, 4.6). All it takes is a strong resolve to rectify one's bad habits and a daily commitment to live virtuously.

While everyone may have the potential to be virtuous, only the superior man truly achieves that state. Echoing earlier descriptions, the superior man is a humble man who acts with proper decorum: respectful toward his superiors and kind and just toward the people (5.15). He is ever mindful of the "Constant Mean" (also known as the Golden Mean): to treat others the way you would want to be treated (5.11, 6.27, 12.2). Above all, the superior man is distinguished by his dedication to learning and adherence to propriety; that being the case, Confucius concludes, the superior man does not take sides and will always do the right thing, implying that he follows an absolute standard of morality (4.10, 6.25). For Confucius, the weight of scholarship and the rules of propriety represent the cornerstones of morality.

Throughout the Analects, the superior man is contrasted to the mean (also translated as "small") man. Where the superior man aspires to live a virtuous life and obeys the law, the mean man seeks a comfortable life and acts only to his advantage, angering others (4.11, 4.12, 4.16).

Where the superior man worries about whether he has the merit to deserve a position, the mean man laments the lack of a position; where the superior man devotes his energy to activities that will make him "worthy to be known," the mean man bewails his lack of fame (4.14). The superior man represents the "men of worth" that one should aspire to, while the mean man belongs to the category of "men of contrary character" who exemplify all that one ought not to be (4.17). Confucius believes that both offer important lessons: From the superior man, one should learn how to be virtuous; from the mean man, one should conduct a critical self-examination and eliminate any flaws that resemble the qualities of the mean man.

♦ **Chapters 7, 8, and 12**

Confucius highlights two points about education in this section: the importance of the past and the building of good moral character. Earlier passages had already acknowledged the contributions of the teachings of the ancient sage-kings and had emphasized the importance of learning from them (1.13, 1.15). When Confucius states that he is "not one who was born in the possession of knowledge," he means two things (7.18). First, he distinguishes between intuition and knowledge; the former comes naturally while the latter has to be learned. Confucius believes that real knowledge comes only from arduous and diligent study and, as his statement suggests, dismisses as "knowledge" what comes instinctively. The second meaning refers to knowledge as a body of scholarship that originated in the age of the sage-kings. References to antiquity in the Analects and by Confucian scholars invariably hark back to what is considered China's golden age, a period when wise and virtuous rulers reigned over a harmonious polity. Yet being "fond of antiquity" was more than just about being nostalgic; Confucian scholars looked to the past for inspiration and guidance in resolving the crises of the present. This reverence for the past has contributed to widely held views of Confucianism as a conservative political philosophy that stifled innovation and creativity.

Learning not only instills in one a greater appreciation of the past but also improves one's moral character, as suggested in Confucius's prediction that after three years of study a man will "be good" (8.12). In many respects, the Analects carry out the task of moral education. By studying the lessons imparted by Confucius and his disciples in the text, the reader can understand how to become a good person. Of course, the assumption is that the processes of reading, understanding, and practicing form part of a seamless and coherent whole; Confucius takes for granted that once people understand what it means to be good they will be good. This was the fundamental premise of the civil service examination system that became institutionalized during the Tang Dynasty (618–907 CE). Candidates for political office were selected based on their performance on the exams, which tested understanding of the Confucian classics. Success on the exams presumably indicated one's moral superiority, which in the Confucian-inspired political system, qualified one for an official post.

The discussion on propriety and virtue in this section repeats points made in earlier chapters. For Confucius, propriety is what gives actions meaning and worth. When propriety guides conduct, a display of respect holds great significance, the exercise of caution indicates prudence, a daring act signals courage, and a candid response shows honesty. However, in the absence of propriety, a kowtow becomes a meaningless routine, hesitation leads to a lack of action, audacity turns into an act of defiance, and bluntness becomes offensive (8.2). The second paragraph suggests the sociopolitical implications of acting in accordance with the rules of propriety. The Chinese characters translated here as "those who are in high stations" can also be rendered as the "superior man"; for Confucius, the superior man exemplified the qualities of a good leader. When the people in power "perform well all their duties to their relations" by following the rules of propriety in fulfilling their filial obligations, then "the people are aroused to virtue"; because they all aspire to be good subjects, they will be easy to rule, and peace and order will prevail. Likewise, when officials nurture their long-standing friendships, the people will learn by example how to be true (8.2). In all the references to "the people" in the Analects, they are always depicted as followers, the "grass" that bends to the "wind" (12.19). As Confucius notes, the people may be taught to act in a certain way, but they lack the capacity to comprehend the meaning of their actions (8.9).

One of the most important ideas in Confucianism is what is generally called the "rectification of names," which refers to the correspondence between the title of a person and the actions of that person. When Confucius explains that government obtains when "the prince is prince," "the minister is minister," "the father is father," and "the son is son," he means that a government is worthy of the name when everyone fulfills the duty appropriate to their station (12.11). Previous passages have already explained how people in each of these roles were to conduct themselves. In short, a prince should rule with benevolent sternness, a minister should be loyal to the prince, a father should be caring but authoritative, and a son should be filial. If people do not act according to their prescribed roles, then although the government may continue to function (as suggested by the duke's statement that taxes would still be collected), Confucians would not regard it as a successful government. In this regard, this was Confucius's diagnosis for the problems crippling the governments of his day.

Audience

The original audience of the words recorded in the Analects was made up of Confucius's disciples, who passed down their master's teachings to their own disciples, who in turn wrote them down in what eventually became the Analects. The book was used as an instructional manual to inculcate in future generations the moral values Confucius believed were critical for political leadership. In written form, Confucius's teachings reached a wider audience, going well beyond the circle of its intended readers—rulers, officials, and aspiring "superior men." By the second century BCE, the Han Dynasty's adoption of Confucianism as the official ideology increased the readership of the Analects, and by the seventh century, the institutionalization of the civil service examination system based on the Confucian classics made the Analects required reading for schoolboys. Today, the Analects is used as a primer for classical Chinese; it is also read (often in translation) by students of Chinese philosophy and history.

Impact

The significance of Confucianism is indisputable, as its continuing influence in China, Japan, Korea, and Vietnam attest. As a purported record of Confucius's words, the Analects enjoys a privileged place in the Confucian canon. A return to the original core of Confucian writings during the Southern Song Dynasty in the twelfth century led to the creation of Neo-Confucianism and renewed scholarly interest in the Analects. While the political and philosophical ideas discussed in Confucian texts like the Analects legitimized dynastic rule and directed intellectual activiity, their ethical precepts shaped family and social relations. By the early twentieth century, however, the widespread appeal of Western notions of freedom, equality, and individualism challenged the Confucian emphasis on obedience, hierarchy, and community. During the New Culture Movement (also referred to as the May Fourth

Movement), reform-minded intellectuals attacked Confucianism, identifying it with the "backwardness" of China and blaming it for China's subordinate position on the world stage of politics.

In the mid-1930s, Confucianism enjoyed a brief revival under the state-sponsored New Life Movement. The ascendancy of the Chinese Communist Party, which established the People's Republic of China in 1949, witnessed the decline of Confucianism in official circles if not in the popular imagination. In fact, the hold of Confucianism over Chinese society was perceived as so strong that Mao Zedong, the leader of the People's Republic of China until his death in 1976, launched an anti-Confucius campaign to eliminate what were then considered to be "feudal remnants." As part of the Cultural Revolution initiated by Mao to create a new Socialist culture and oust leaders who he felt betrayed the commitment to Communism, the campaign against Confucius was a thinly disguised attempt to topple Lin Biao, who had been the second-in-command until he fell out of favor with Mao.

Widely known, if not widely read anymore, the Analects conveys a set of ideas that have left a deep and lasting imprint on East Asia. In recent years, Confucius's popularity has resurfaced in China, reflecting the continuing importance attached to filial piety and education. While few people today have read the Analects, most are familiar with many of its sayings, which often appear in books of proverbs and sometimes even inside fortune cookies.

Questions for Further Study

1. Based on your reading of Chapters 1 and 2, explain why some people regard Confucianism not as a religion but rather as a life philosophy. On what basis might others disagree with that view?

2. Explain why Confucius presented his teachings in the form of a dialogue with students and followers. What purpose did the dialogue form serve?

3. Summarize Confucius's view of filial piety, and explain why this virtue was so important to him.

4. What is the Mandate of Heaven, and why was it important during the Western Zhou Period and later in Chinese history?

5. The entry states that "the widespread appeal of Western notions of freedom, equality, and individualism challenged the Confucian emphasis on obedience, hierarchy, and community." Explain this statement and give examples of how Confucianism differs from the point of view generally adopted by people in Western nations.

Further Reading

■ Books

Nivison, David S. "The Classical Philosophical Writings." In *The Cambridge History of Ancient China: From the Origins of Civilization to 221 BC*, ed. Michael Loewe and Edward L. Shaughnessy. Cambridge, U.K.: Cambridge University Press, 1999.

Schwartz, Benjamin. *The World of Thought in Ancient China*. Cambridge, Mass.: Belknap Press of Harvard University Press, 1985.

Tu, Wei-ming. *Humanity and Self-Cultivation: Essays in Confucian Thought*. Berkeley, Calif.: Asian Humanities Press, 1979.

Van Norden, Bryan W., ed. *Confucius and the Analects: New Essays*. Oxford, U.K.: Oxford University Press, 2002.

■ Journals

Shuo Dongfang, Hongcheng Lin, and Deyuan Huang. "Separation of Politics and Morality: A Commentary on Analects of Confucius." *Frontiers of Philosophy in China* 1, no. 3 (September 2006): 401–417.

Kieschnick, John. "Analects 12.1 and the Commentarial Tradition." *Journal of the American Oriental Society* 112, no. 4 (October–December 1992): 567–576.

—Lisa Tran

CONFUCIUS: ANALECTS

♦ Chapter 1

1. The Master said, "Is it not pleasant to learn with a constant perseverance and application?

"Is it not delightful to have friends coming from distant quarters?

"Is he not a man of complete virtue, who feels no discomposure though men may take no note of him?"

2. The philosopher Yu said, "They are few who, being filial and fraternal, are fond of offending against their superiors. There have been none, who, not liking to offend against their superiors, have been fond of stirring up confusion.

"The superior man bends his attention to what is radical. That being established, all practical courses naturally grow up. Filial piety and fraternal submission—are they not the root of all benevolent actions?"

3. The Master said, "Fine words and an insinuating appearance are seldom associated with true virtue."

4. The philosopher Tsang said, "I daily examine myself on three points: whether, in transacting business for others, I may have been not faithful; whether, in intercourse with friends, I may have been not sincere; whether I may have not mastered and practiced the instructions of my teacher." . . .

6. The Master said, "A youth, when at home, should be filial, and, abroad, respectful to his elders. He should be earnest and truthful. He should overflow in love to all, and cultivate the friendship of the good. When he has time and opportunity, after the performance of these things, he should employ them in polite studies."

7. Tsze-hsia said, "If a man withdraws his mind from the love of beauty, and applies it as sincerely to the love of the virtuous; if, in serving his parents, he can exert his utmost strength; if, in serving his prince, he can devote his life; if, in his intercourse with his friends, his words are sincere: although men say that he has not learned, I will certainly say that he has."

8. The Master said, "If the scholar be not grave, he will not call forth any veneration, and his learning will not be solid.

"Hold faithfulness and sincerity as first principles.

"Have no friends not equal to yourself.

"When you have faults, do not fear to abandon them."

9. The philosopher Tsang said, "Let there be a careful attention to perform the funeral rites to parents, and let them be followed when long gone with the ceremonies of sacrifice; then the virtue of the people will resume its proper excellence."

10. Tsze-ch'in asked Tsze-kung saying, "When our master comes to any country, he does not fail to learn all about its government. Does he ask his information? Or is it given to him?"

Tsze-kung said, "Our master is benign, upright, courteous, temperate, and complaisant and thus he gets his information. The master's mode of asking information—is it not different from that of other men?" . . .

12. The philosopher Yu said, "In practicing the rules of propriety, a natural ease is to be prized. In the ways prescribed by the ancient kings, this is the excellent quality, and in things small and great we follow them.

"Yet it is not to be observed in all cases. If one, knowing how such ease should be prized, manifests it, without regulating it by the rules of propriety, this likewise is not to be done."

13. The philosopher Yu said, "When agreements are made according to what is right, what is spoken

can be made good. When respect is shown according to what is proper, one keeps far from shame and disgrace. When the parties upon whom a man leans are proper persons to be intimate with, he can make them his guides and masters."

14. The Master said, "He who aims to be a man of complete virtue in his food does not seek to gratify his appetite, nor in his dwelling place does he seek the appliances of ease; he is earnest in what he is doing, and careful in his speech; he frequents the company of men of principle that he may be rectified: such a person may be said indeed to love to learn."

15. Tsze-kung said, "What do you pronounce concerning the poor man who yet does not flatter, and the rich man who is not proud?" The Master replied, "They will do; but they are not equal to him, who, though poor, is yet cheerful, and to him, who, though rich, loves the rules of propriety." . . .

♦ **Chapter 2**

1. The Master said, "He who exercises government by means of his virtue may be compared to the north polar star, which keeps its place and all the stars turn towards it." . . .

3. The Master said, "If the people be led by laws, and uniformity sought to be given them by punishments, they will try to avoid the punishment, but have no sense of shame.

"If they be led by virtue, and uniformity sought to be given them by the rules of propriety, they will have the sense of shame, and moreover will become good."

4. The Master said, "At fifteen, I had my mind bent on learning. "At thirty, I stood firm. "At forty, I had no doubts. "At fifty, I knew the decrees of Heaven. "At sixty, my ear was an obedient organ for the reception of truth. "At seventy, I could follow what my heart desired, without transgressing what was right."

5. Mang I asked what filial piety was. The Master said, "It is not being disobedient."

Soon after, as Fan Ch'ih was driving him, the Master told him, saying, "Mang-sun asked me what filial piety was, and I answered him, 'not being disobedient.'"

Fan Ch'ih said, "What did you mean?" The Master replied, "That parents, when alive, be served according to propriety; that, when dead, they should be buried according to propriety; and that they should be sacrificed to according to propriety."

6. Mang Wu asked what filial piety was. The Master said, "Parents are anxious lest their children should be sick."

7. Tsze-yu asked what filial piety was. The Master said, "The filial piety nowadays means the support of one's parents. But dogs and horses likewise are able to do something in the way of support; without reverence, what is there to distinguish the one support given from the other?"

8. Tsze-hsia asked what filial piety was. The Master said, "The difficulty is with the countenance. If, when their elders have any troublesome affairs, the young take the toil of them, and if, when the young have wine and food, they set them before their elders, is THIS to be considered filial piety?" . . .

13. Tsze-kung asked what constituted the superior man. The Master said, "He acts before he speaks, and afterwards speaks according to his actions."

14. The Master said, "The superior man is catholic and not partisan. The mean man is partisan and not catholic."

15. The Master said, "Learning without thought is labor lost; thought without learning is perilous."

16. The Master said, "The study of strange doctrines is injurious indeed!"

17. The Master said, "Yu, shall I teach you what knowledge is? When you know a thing, to hold that you know it; and when you do not know a thing, to allow that you do not know it; this is knowledge." . . .

19. The Duke Ai asked, saying, "What should be done in order to secure the submission of the people?" Confucius replied, "Advance the upright and set aside the crooked, then the people will submit. Advance the crooked and set aside the upright, then the people will not submit."

20. Chi K'ang asked how to cause the people to reverence their ruler, to be faithful to him, and to go on to nerve themselves to virtue. The Master said, "Let him preside over them with gravity; then they will reverence him. Let him be final and kind to all; then they will be faithful to him. Let him advance the good and teach the incompetent; then they will eagerly seek to be virtuous." . . .

♦ **Chapter 3**

. . .

19. The Duke Ting asked how a prince should employ his ministers, and how ministers should serve their prince. Confucius replied, "A prince should employ his minister according to the rules of propriety; ministers should serve their prince with faithfulness." . . .

♦ **Chapter 4**

. . .

2. The Master said, "Those who are without virtue cannot abide long either in a condition of poverty and hardship, or in a condition of enjoyment. The virtuous rest in virtue; the wise desire virtue." . . .

4. The Master said, "If the will be set on virtue, there will be no practice of wickedness." . . .

6. The Master said, "I have not seen a person who loved virtue, or one who hated what was not virtuous. He who loved virtue would esteem nothing above it. He who hated what is not virtuous, would practice virtue in such a way that he would not allow anything that is not virtuous to approach his person.

"Is any one able for one day to apply his strength to virtue? I have not seen the case in which his strength would be insufficient.

"Should there possibly be any such case, I have not seen it." . . .

10. The Master said, "The superior man, in the world, does not set his mind either for anything, or against anything; what is right he will follow."

11. The Master said, "The superior man thinks of virtue; the small man thinks of comfort. The superior man thinks of the sanctions of law; the small man thinks of favors which he may receive."

12. The Master said: "He who acts with a constant view to his own advantage will be much murmured against."

13. The Master said, "If a prince is able to govern his kingdom with the complaisance proper to the rules of propriety, what difficulty will he have? If he cannot govern it with that complaisance, what has he to do with the rules of propriety?"

14. The Master said, "A man should say, I am not concerned that I have no place, I am concerned how I may fit myself for one. I am not concerned that I am not known, I seek to be worthy to be known." . . .

16. The Master said, "The mind of the superior man is conversant with righteousness; the mind of the mean man is conversant with gain."

17. The Master said, "When we see men of worth, we should think of equaling them; when we see men of a contrary character, we should turn inwards and examine ourselves."

18. The Master said, "In serving his parents, a son may remonstrate with them, but gently; when he sees that they do not incline to follow his advice, he shows an increased degree of reverence, but does not abandon his purpose; and should they punish him, he does not allow himself to murmur." . . .

♦ **Chapter 5**

. . .

11. Tsze-kung said, "What I do not wish men to do to me, I also wish not to do to men." The Master said, "Ts'ze, you have not attained to that." . . .

15. The Master said of Tsze-ch'an that he had four of the characteristics of a superior man—in his conduct of himself, he was humble; in serving his superior, he was respectful; in nourishing the people, he was kind; in ordering the people, he was just." . . .

20. The Master said, "When good order prevailed in his country, Ning Wu acted the part of a wise

man. When his country was in disorder, he acted the part of a stupid man. Others may equal his wisdom, but they cannot equal his stupidity." . . .

♦ **Chapter 6**

. . .

25. The Master said, "The superior man, extensively studying all learning, and keeping himself under the restraint of the rules of propriety, may thus likewise not overstep what is right." . . .

27. The Master said, "Perfect is the virtue which is according to the Constant Mean! Rare for a long time has been its practice among the people." . . .

♦ **Chapter 7**

. . .

18. The Master said, "I am not one who was born in the possession of knowledge; I am one who is fond of antiquity, and earnest in seeking it there." . . .

♦ **Chapter 8**

. . .

2. The Master said, "Respectfulness, without the rules of propriety, becomes laborious bustle; carefulness, without the rules of propriety, becomes timidity; boldness, without the rules of propriety, becomes insubordination; straightforwardness, without the rules of propriety, becomes rudeness.

"When those who are in high stations perform well all their duties to their relations, the people are aroused to virtue. When old friends are not neglected by them, the people are preserved from meanness." . . .

9. The Master said, "The people may be made to follow a path of action, but they may not be made to understand it." . . .

12. The Master said, "It is not easy to find a man who has learned for three years without coming to be good." . . .

♦ **Chapter 12**

. . .

2. Chung-kung asked about perfect virtue. The Master said, "It is, when you go abroad, to behave to every one as if you were receiving a great guest; to employ the people as if you were assisting at a great sacrifice; not to do to others as you would not wish done to yourself; to have no murmuring against you in the country, and none in the family." Chung-kung said, "Though I am deficient in intelligence and vigor, I will make it my business to practice this lesson." . . .

11. The Duke Ching, of Ch'i, asked Confucius about government.

Confucius replied, "There is government, when the prince is prince, and the minister is minister; when the father is father, and the son is son."

"Good!" said the duke; "if, indeed, the prince be not prince, the minister not minister, the father not father, and the son not son, although I have my revenue, can I enjoy it?" . . .

19. Chi K'ang asked Confucius about government, saying, "What do you say to killing the unprincipled for the good of the principled?" Confucius replied, "Sir, in carrying on your government, why should you use killing at all? Let your evinced desires be for what is good, and the people will be good. The relation between superiors and inferiors is like that between the wind and the grass. The grass must bend, when the wind blows across it."

Glossary

catholic	here, broad in sympathies, interests, or tastes
Duke Ai	a duke of the state of Lu
Duke Ting	a duke of the state of Lu
Yu	Yu the Great (2276–2177 BCE), founder of the Xia Dynasty

Mosaic depiction of Orpheus

(Orpheus Charming the Animals [mosaic], Roman, [2nd century AD] / Musee Archeologique, Saint-Roman-en-Gal, France / Giraudon / The Bridgeman Art Library International)

ORPHIC TABLETS AND HYMNS

"Happy and blessed one, you shall be a god instead of a mortal."

Overview

Orpheus is one the most familiar figures from Greek mythology but also one of the most mysterious. His priests were denounced as charlatans by the philosopher Plato in classical Greece, yet the figure of Orpheus was used as a bulwark against the threat Christianity posed to the last followers of traditional Greek religion in the Roman Empire. Orpheus is the hero of a large body of myths, ranging from his invention of music to his descent to and return from the underworld. Less well known is Orpheus's role as the mythical founder of religious initiations that constitute a secret aspect of ancient Greek religion and the credit granted to him as the pseudepigraphic author of a vast body of poetry. Poems and hymns stretching from the origins of Greek civilization to the beginning of the Middle Ages in the Byzantine Empire have been attributed to the mythical figure of Orpheus. A sampling of these texts are examined here—the verses from the golden tablets that were buried in the graves of Orphic initiates and a corpus of Orphic hymns from the Roman Empire. Both sets of texts attest to the development of the Orphic cult throughout Greco-Roman history.

Context

In the archaic period, between about 750 and 550 BCE, Greek civilization underwent a period of dynamic economic and cultural expansion. Small farming villages were organized into cities, national institutions were created, and overseas trade brought the benefit of contact with older, more civilized cultures. Besides integrating many new features of life in Greece—among them, the use of money and the development of writing—the forces consolidating the urban centers had to choose which parts of tradition to keep and which to abandon, or at least try to abandon. This went on in religion as well as every other aspect of life. The new cities kept what was useful for the common good. The centers of places like Athens and Corinth were crowded with temples to the patron divinities of the cities (such as Athena at Athens), the ancestors of Greece (Heracles), the gods who made it rain (Zeus) so that crops could grow (Demeter), and the other familiar Olympians who made the new industry (Hephaestus) and commerce (Poseidon) of the cities possible. The gods communicated their will through great oracular shrines, such as the ancient sanctuaries at Delphi and Dodona, which were acknowledged by the whole Greek world, and Greek unity was celebrated with festivals at Olympia and Isthmia. All of the apparatus of this new state religion concerned what was good for cities and what was good for Greece. The notion of doing what was good for a single Greek, perhaps at the expense of other Greeks, was something the cities wanted to leave behind. But not everyone in Greece felt this way, even if Plato and other philosophers were anxious to legitimize their new discipline by joining forces with civic institutions.

Thus, private religion was left to another world, one outside the official world of the city. The private priests who practiced older kinds of rituals forgotten by the cities took Orpheus as their patron, a representative of the kind of religious and magical powers that they claimed for themselves. Their beliefs and practices went far back into Greek as well as Indo-European antiquity. The magical practice of Orpheus and his priests were shamanic. The shamans of traditional cultures the world over are believed to enter a trance state that releases their souls from their bodies to wander throughout this world and the next, empowering their words to become real. This is why Orpheus's spells were thought to reverse nature, even going so far as saving the dead from the underworld. The belief in reincarnation, a central part of Orphic practice, also stretches far back into the early history of the Indo-European peoples. These primitive and mysterious beliefs compose the religious current that flows through the figure of Orpheus. But shamanic magic, by its very nature, cannot be constrained by an ordered society, so it had to be excluded from the Greek world, dismissed as magic and superstition. In Plato's view (as put forward in his dialogue on justice, the *Republic*), the Orphic priests were frauds and magicians who manipulated their clients with fear and lies and did not represent legitimate religious tradition; accordingly, Orphism became a tradition rejected by the civic and intellectual guardians of Greek culture.

Time Line

CA. 1200 BCE	■ According to myth, Orpheus lived at about this time.
CA. 500 BCE	■ The original of the Derveni papyrus is composed.
CA. 400 BCE	■ The earliest golden tablet is buried at the Greek colony of Hipponion.
CA. 25 BCE	■ The latest golden tablet is buried in Crete.
CA. 200 −300 CE	■ The Orphic hymns are composed.
CA. 500	■ The *Orphic Lithika* and the *Orphic Argonautica* are composed.
1834	■ The first Orphic tablets discovered in modern times are put up for sale by Neapolitan tomb robbers.

Each Orphic work has its own context in the particular place and time in which it was created. The oldest Orphic poetry (virtually all Orphic writing is in verse) was created in the archaic and classical periods (before 400 BCE) by itinerant priests who offered initiations into the worship of the Greek god of wine and festivity, Dionysus, in the name of Orpheus. Very little of this survives. An important document related to this literature, however, is the Derveni papyrus, which was discovered in the grave of a nobleman in Hellenistic Macedonia. A commentary on an old Orphic poem, the text of the Derveni papyrus attempts to find philosophical doctrines in Orphic poems by allegorical interpretation (reading religious language as if it had a philosophical or even scientific meaning). Interestingly, the scroll on which the text was written was burned at the time the tomb was sealed, though the fire went out before any irreparable damage was done. This might suggest that the manuscript was supposed to accompany its owner into the next world, as the gold tablets of Orpheus were intended to do. The gold tablets that are examined here originated throughout the Greek world in locations extending from the Black Sea to Sicily and come from a later time, between 400 and 1 BCE; still, they reflect an initiatory practice, since they are, as it were, tokens of earlier imitations buried with the initiates. After the turn of the Common Era, such initiations seem to lapse, and no more tablets are found.

The cultural height of the Roman Empire after 100 CE produced a new Orphic literature. Two collections of poems are known from this time: One remains lost but was extensively quoted by Neoplatonic philosophers between 300 and 500 CE, and the other—the extant collection of Orphic hymns—are thought never to have been quoted by another ancient author. Nothing whatsoever is known about the context of the Orphic hymns, but a great deal can be surmised. They were most likely written between 200 and 300. There can be little question that the hymns belong to the culture movement called the Second Sophistic, by which Greeks living in the eastern half of the Roman Empire in the second and third centuries tried to redefine their identity; the term *Sophist* refers to a class of experts in Greek culture who in philosophical matters sometimes used deceptive reasoning. The overwhelmingly Homeric style of the hymns and their many references to Greek philosophy, without taking the limited position of a single school, point to the Second Sophistic. The Second Sophistic was especially concerned with defending the superiority of Greek culture over various rivals, such as the dominant Roman political establishment and emerging Christianity, and so would naturally turn to ancient traditions like those of Orpheus for their subject matter (though many of the eighty-eight hymns have very little that is distinctly Orphic). The hymns clearly are meant to help establish an identity based on Greek tradition. They also indulge in the typically Sophistic delight in obscure subject matter and esoteric meanings. In the same time period, Orpheus was certainly used as an emblem of Greek culture, as can be seen from the frequent appearance of Orpheus himself in the mosaic floors of aristocratic houses from Antioch to Britain. But any solid evidence for the actual practice of Orphic initiations or mysteries in the later period, after the gold tablets ceased to be buried, is completely lacking. Ultimately, it is impossible to determine whether the Orphic hymns were composed entirely as a literary exercise or actually functioned in a religious setting, as the texts themselves claim.

About the Author

Although he is considered historical by the ancient Greeks, Orpheus is a legendary figure: The story of his life and deeds is fictitious. Information about him, as is most often the case with anything in the ancient world, comes from a bewildering profusion of brief references in ancient sources, the most useful ones frequently quoting fragments from older works that are now lost. The best single continuous account of Orpheus comes from the poetry of books 10 and 11 of Ovid's *Metamorphoses*. To briefly summarize the key points of his myth: Orpheus was not Greek but a Thracian, from a tribal culture situated to the northeast of Greece. He invented the lyre and probably music as well. His music had magical powers and could not only tame wild animals but also make trees and rocks dance and rivers reverse their courses.

Orpheus sailed on the *Argo* with a crew of other ancient Greek heroes under the leadership of Jason. The purpose of the voyage, whose story was already widely known through the Homeric tradition manifested in the *Iliad*, was to recov-

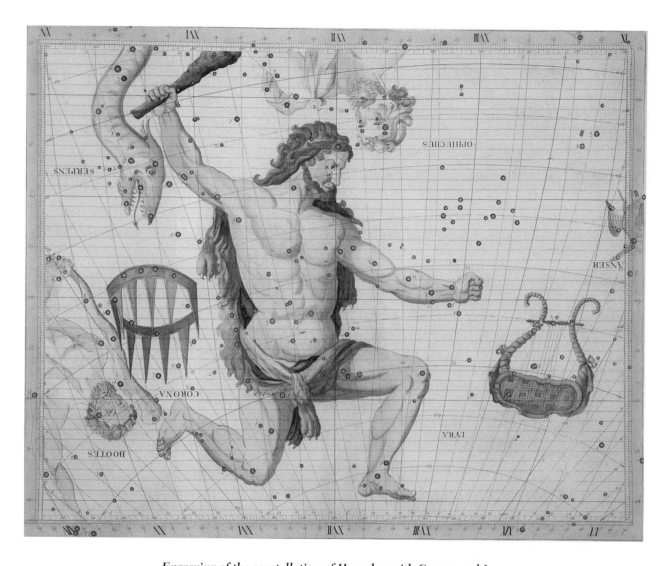

Engraving of the constellation of Hercules, with Corona and Lyra

(Constellation of Hercules with Corona and Lyra, plate 21 from 'Atlas Coelestis', by John Flamsteed, published in 1729, Thornhill, Sir James [1675-1734]

[after] / Private Collection / The Stapleton Collection / The Bridgeman Art Library International)

er the magical Golden Fleece, which was tied to the legitimate succession to the throne of Iolkhos, forming a sort of backstory for the hero Achilles. According to the myth, Orpheus saved the expedition by outsinging the Sirens, nymphs whose songs drew sailors to crash on rocks and drown.

Later, Orpheus fell in love with Eurydice, who was killed by the bite of a snake on their wedding day. Overcome with grief, Orpheus descended to the underworld, the place of the dead in Greek thought, to bring her back to life. His singing cast its spell on Persephone, the queen of the dead, and she interceded with her husband, Hades, to allow Eurydice to go with Orpheus back up to the world of the living—on one condition: Orpheus had to let Eurydice follow him without looking back at her. Just as he reached the surface of the land of the living and saw the light of the sun, however, he could not help but turn to see her; tragically, she immediately went back down to the underworld.

Desolate over his loss of Eurydice for a second time, Orpheus wandered blindly through the countryside and was fallen upon by a band of maenads, female worshippers of Dionysus. In an ecstatic frenzy, the maenads mistook Orpheus for an animal and tore him apart. His head did not die, however, but gained the power to speak prophecy. It was found by nymphs and sent floating over the sea to the island of Lesbos, where, as the legend goes, it was kept as an oracle until just before historic times. The gods honored Orpheus by transforming his lyre into the constellation Lyra.

The individual texts of the gold tablets of Orpheus were part of a tradition of initiatory literature written by itinerant priests who offered initiation into mysteries of salvation in Orpheus's name. Whatever hymns, prayers, and spells they used, of which the texts on the tablets were only a small sample, were attributed to Orpheus. The texts mention some rather obscure gods (Mise, Hipta, and Melinoe) local to Asia Minor, which suggests that the author of the Orphic hymns was living in the Greek city of Pergamum.

"A I am dry with thirst and am perishing. / B Come, drink, I pray, from the ever-flowing spring on the right, where the cypress is. Who are you, and whence? / A I am the son of Earth and starry Heaven."

"I come from the pure, O pure Queen of the earthly ones, Euclês, Eubouleus, and ye other immortal gods! I too claim to be of your blessed race, but Fate and other immortal gods conquered me, (and sent) the star-smiting thunder."

"Happy and blessed one, you shall be a god instead of a mortal."

"O Mighty Titans, who from heav'n and earth / Derive your noble and illustrious birth, / Our fathers fires, in Tartarus profound / Who dwell, deep merg'd beneath the solid ground: / Fountains and principles, from whom began / Th' afflicted, miserable, race of man."

Explanation and Analysis of the Document

The readings presented here come from two discrete fields of Orphic literature. The Orphic gold tablets are texts that were buried in the graves of initiates in Italy and the eastern Mediterranean region between the fourth and first centuries BCE. The Orphic hymns come from a later period but recall the earliest Orphic literature, which is otherwise lost.

♦ Orphic Tablets

The Orphic tablets are very mysterious objects, unlike anything that exists in the modern world. They are small pieces of gold foil about the size of a large Post-it Note, written on by using a stylus to dent the surface of the thin metal. The tablets were unearthed from graves and so were buried with the dead, seemingly offering instructions for what the soul of the deceased should do upon reaching the next world. The tablet from Rome, for instance, makes it clear that the soul is being reminded of something it learned in life: "And I have this gift of Memory prized by men." The Orphic tablets warn the soul of a trap that awaits at the entrance to the underworld, where gatekeepers will try to direct it to drink from a spring on the right next to a white cypress tree. This is what most souls, lacking the golden ticket, will do. If they drink from the spring, such souls will forget everything about their lives and then be punished (if they had been particularly wicked) or else reincarnated into a new body.

The tablet from Eleutherna actually gives a script of the conversation the soul must have with the gatekeeper in order to avoid this common fate: "A I am dry with thirst and am perishing. / B Come, drink, I pray, from the ever-flowing spring on the right, where the cypress is. Who are you, and whence? / A I am the son of Earth and starry Heaven." The soul must resist the impulse to drink, and instead tell the gatekeeper that it is a god, born of the same parents as the gods: Heaven and Earth. One of the tablets from Thurii assures the soul that it will be accepted as the guardians reply: "Happy and blessed one, you shall be a god instead of a mortal." The soul will go on to the same eternal paradise that Greek belief normally reserved for heroes (human beings favored by the gods with a blessed afterlife): "the holy meadow and groves of Persephone."

The tablets evoke a number of underworld deities. Persephone is the wife of Hades, the ruler of the underworld. As described in the Homeric "Hymn to Demeter," Persephone—the daughter of Demeter, the goddess of agriculture—was kidnapped by and married to her uncle Hades. Zeus reconciles Hades and Demeter over the marriage, so that Persephone dwells in the underworld half the year and, during the growing season, on the earth's surface with her mother. On one of the tablets from Thurii, Demeter is referred to by the name of her barbarian counterpart, Cybele. The same group of tablets mentions Euboleus. Originally a god of plowing (his name means the "good glebe," *glebe* being a term for cultivated land), in the Homeric hymn he becomes a swineherd who witnesses Persephone's abduction. His role may be connected to the piglets sacrificed by initiates. The common name Eucles may have been chosen merely because it sounds well with Euboleus.

The tablet from Rome gives the name of the person for whom it was written, Caecillia Secundina. She is otherwise unknown but was probably aristocratic, as she was interested in Greek culture and able to pay for initiation. The Roman name could conceal Greek ancestry, however.

The gold tablets acted as reminders to the souls of the deceased, telling the souls to recall what they had learned when they were alive and initiated into the mysteries that Plato speaks of. There is some reason to think that the actual performance of the mysteries for the initiate may have been a dramatic "run-through" of the scene expected to come in the underworld. The oldest Orphic poetry (of which barely a trace survives quoted by later writers) describes the relationship of the soul to the body, as well as what the other world is like and what the soul has to do there. Legend tells us that Orpheus and the Orphic priests knew these secrets because they had been to that world when, as shamans, they sent their own souls forth from their bodies. Modern-day readers are fortunate the gold tablets waited patiently in the ground for two millennia to initiate us into their forgotten world.

♦ Orphic Hymns

The closest thing mainstream Greek religion had to a scriptural text was Hesiod's poetry, namely his poems the *Theogony* ("Generation of the Gods") and the *Works and Days*. These works tell the story of the successive generations of the divine family from the first gods Uranus and Gê (sky and earth); their children the Titans, including Cronus and Rhea; and finally the Olympian gods ruled by Zeus. They move on to the creation of human beings and describe the character of their lives. This story incorporates much that was traditional within Greek culture but also much mythology from the Near East that had the authority and glamor of more ancient civilizations. The priests of Orpheus wrote their own poems, which treated precisely the same subject matter as Hesiod but in myths that were different in detail. Almost nothing of these poems remains to be read today, but it seems that the author of the Orphic hymns was able to read at least some of them and incorporated myths and ideas from them into his own work.

Each hymn addresses a god or group of gods and praises them by telling their myths. The texts of the hymns suggest that they functioned in a cultic setting, since each one begins with instructions on what fumigation, or burnt offering, to make to the god. The Orphic myths are referred to allusively, so it is not always clear what the text means. Another problem is that there was more than one Orphic theogony (account of the origin of the gods), each one different from the others. It is obvious that the Orphic myths stay to a degree within a Hesiodic framework. In the gold tablets, for instance, the divine soul of the initiate identifies itself as a child of the earth and sky, just as the gods were in Hesiod. But the Orphic theogonies are much more

elaborate and call on more, or at least other, Near Eastern myths as their points of reference. The hymn "To Protogonus, or the First-born" mentions Protogonus and Phanes, obscure representatives of two generations of an Orphic theogony. Phanes, who is addressed by the still-more obscure title Ericapaeus, may be a sort of Orphic creator. The Protogonus (the name may be a metaphorical reference to Dionysus) is said to have been born from an egg, which is a reference to the myths taught at the Egyptian city of Hermopolis. This hymn also addresses Priapus, who stands for the divine power of generation. So the Orphic myths, just like Hesiod's, drew on material from the Near East, equating wisdom with what was unfamiliar to most Greeks.

The hymn "To Rhea" fits this familiar goddess into the Orphic framework. To Hesiod, Rhea, like the other Titans, was a child of Gê and Uranus. In Hesiod she is the wife of Cronus (Saturn in Latin). But the Orphics change the genealogy. Rhea is the daughter of the mysterious Protogonus and is herself called the mother of earth and heaven. The mention of the frenzied music of her worshippers shows that Rhea is being identified with the Phrygian goddess Cybele, whose cult title was Mother of the Gods. Both goddess are for all intents and purposes merely other names for Demeter in this context.

"To Thundering Jove" (that is, Zeus) treats its subject in a highly allegorical manner. It is true that Zeus is present as an anthropomorphic personality as in Homer or Hesiod, but he is also an "all-devouring force, entire and strong, / Horrid, untam'd." This is a force or nature or cosmic principle that goes far beyond any anthropomorphic conception. It is not hard to recognize this description as an allegory of the element of fire, which Greek philosophers considered the first and most perfect of the four elements, the other three being air, earth, and water. Undoubtedly, the author of the hymns has in mind here ideas about fire derived from the Hellenistic philosophy of Stoicism, namely, that it is a pure creative force. But the Stoic conception of fire, in turn, originated in Orphic speculation, as the philosophical text in the Derveni papyrus makes clear.

"To Proserpine" (that is, Persephone) addresses the queen of the underworld, the wife of Pluto (that is, Hades), whom Orpheus's spells enchanted, allowing the return of the dead Eurydice to life (or almost to life). The hymn alludes to the fact that the Orphic initiates could hope for a blissful afterlife. It names Persephone as the mother of Dionysus (in "To Bacchus"), something quite contrary to the normal run of Greek myth, which makes him the son of the mortal woman Semele. The epithet "thrice-begotten" might say something about his complex genealogy in Orphic myth. Dionysus, or Bacchus, the god of wine and festivity, is the most important god of Orphic myth. He is perhaps to be identified with the firstborn principle of creation and is ultimately responsible for saving human souls (he has influence with his mother, Persephone). The story of his birth is also associated with perhaps the most important Orphic myth, the one that explains why souls need saving at all.

When Dionysus was an infant, he was protected by the Curetes (whom the translator of the hymns, Taylor, glosses as Corybantes and Salians, dancing religious orders he hoped his readers would find familiar), who danced and shouted to cover the noise of his crying. But the Titans, the older gods who see the younger Olympians as a threat, nevertheless kidnapped him, luring him away with toys. They killed, butchered, cooked, and ate him in the manner of a sacrificial animal. Only his heart was saved by the goddess Athena, and Zeus used it either to reassemble or to recreate his body, resurrecting him (there are elements here of the Egyptian myth of Isis and Osiris). Zeus punished the Titans by blasting them with his thunderbolt, reducing them to ashes. Zeus then proceeded to create the first human beings from those ashes. So, in "To the Titans," it is they "from whom began / Th' afflicted, miserable, race of man." The souls of human beings are in need of salvation because they have inherited the evil nature of the Titans, and Dionysus is the only one who can save them because only he can forgive them for their inherited crime. This myth, too, has its origins in the Near East. In the Babylonian national epic, Enuma Elish, the god Marduk makes human beings out of the blood of an executed rebel god, and for that reason they are doomed to a life of toil and suffering in service to the gods.

This Bacchic myth, perhaps because of its Near Eastern origin, is similar to Christian myth. The idea of salvation perhaps attracted early Christians to use Orpheus as a symbol of their own faith. In addition, it most certainly attracted defenders of Greek culture—such as the author of the hymns and the later Neoplatonist philosophers—to Orpheus as the foundation for a religion of salvation that could be opposed to Christianity, however ultimately unsuccessful their efforts were.

Audience

In the most literal sense, the audience for the Orphic gold tablets comprised the souls of the dead in whose graves the tablets were buried, since these are the only entities ever meant to see them. They were to be read as a reminder that certain things had to be done in the underworld, and these things could be accomplished only with knowledge learned during a ceremony of initiation. Therefore, the tablets contained information that was kept secret within the community of Orphic priests and initiates, and indeed they seem to contain teachings that are unknown in detail to any surviving ancient writers from outside the circle of Orphic cultists.

It is impossible to determine whether the Orphic hymns were also intended for use in private religious ceremonies, or if they were merely literary exercises. Consequently, it is not known if the audience included Orphic worshippers of Dionysus and the other gods addressed in the hymns or the class of educated Greek aristocrats at large. One thing that can be said is that no ancient author mentions the hymns, so the many late antique authors who write about Orpheus and quote Orphic literature likely did not know of them or did not think them important. The Orphic hymns were very popular among Byzantine scholars, however, who had

a lively interest in everything related to Orpheus. No fewer than forty copies of the hymns (of which thirty-six still survive) were transported to Italy in the early fifteenth century by Byzantine monks who were fleeing the impending Turkish destruction of Constantinople. In Italy, they found a receptive audience of humanists eager to read any Greek text, especially those related to the famous Orpheus. The hymns are of interest to modern scholars mainly as conveyers of Orphic traditions, offering access to earlier branches of Orphic thought consulted by the author or authors but now no longer in existence.

Impact

The Orphic gold tablets have been at the heart of scholarly controversy since they began to be discovered by archaeologists in the 1870s. On the one hand, some scholars wanted to show that Orphism was a flourishing ancient religion that was tremendously influential in the formation of Christianity. At a time when rationalism and secularism conflicted with a resurgent Catholic Church in Europe, historicizing Christianity as something that might have developed from Orphism would weaken the Church's claim to be a legitimate social authority. To this day, an argument for Orphic influence on Christianity has to be treated with caution, although a great deal of suggestive evidence exists, for example the frequent use of scenes of Orpheus charming the beasts in Christian burial places (most famously the Catacomb of Domatilla, a woman executed as a Christian by the first-century emperor Domitian despite being a relative of his). This perception naturally led to a reaction among later scholars such as Germany's Günther Zuntz, who wished to minimize Orphism into anything but a religion. Only in the last generation, after new archaeological finds have clearly linked the tablets to wider Orphic literature, have scholars come to a more balanced view of the historical extent to which Orphic cults were an important and widespread phenomenon in the Greek world. The tablets should be viewed, therefore, as only one element of Orphic tradition, without amounting to an organized religion in any modern sense. It remains necessary to speak of Orphic cults and Orphic texts, rather than a single monolithic Orphism.

The Orphic hymns are part of the revival of Orphic literature in the Roman Empire. Eventually, this revival led the Neoplatonist philosophers of late antiquity to try to create an Orphic religion out of older Orphic texts and practices. There can be little doubt that this phenomenon came about in reaction to the pressure of Christianity. The leaders of the Greek cultural world tried to compete directly with Christianity by reinventing what Orphic material they had access to as a revealed religion of salvation that could match Christianity point for point in its appeal of granting its followers a beatific afterlife. Orpheus was not the only figure reinterpreted in this way. Efforts were also made to turn figures like the pre-Socratic philosopher Pythagoras and the first-century Neopythagorean philosopher (and purported magician) Apollonius of Tyana into wonderworkers after the fashion of Jesus. Orpheus's claim to bring the dead back to life and to save the soul in the underworld made him a logical alternative to Jesus; the early Christians even used him as a symbol for Jesus, as evidenced by his frequent appearance in early Christian art. Their efforts, however, were ultimately unsuccessful and could not slow the whole Greco-Roman world from becoming a new Christian world. Scholars of the Christian Byzantine Empire, however, did not lose any enthusiasm for Orpheus and continued to compose new works in his name, including books of magic like the *Orphic Lithika* (on magical gems) and the *Orphic Argonautica*, a retelling of the adventure to recover the Golden Fleece.

Orpheus's fame endured through the Renaissance, when he was the subject of the first opera, Claudio Monteverdi's *L'Orfeo* (1607). Orpheus continues to be reinvented by modern artists in works ranging from Gustave Moreau's 1865 painting *Orpheus* to such films as the Orphic Trilogy of Jean Cocteau—*Blood of a Poet* (1930), *Orpheus* (1950), and *The Testament of Orpheus* (1959)—to Marcel Camus' *Black Orpheus* (1950) and Denise Levertov's 1968 poem "A Tree Telling of Orpheus." But these center on the myth of Orpheus. The quasi-religious Orphic cult, with its mysteries and secrets, remains largely unknown in popular culture.

Further Reading

■ Books

Alderink, L. J. *Creation and Salvation in Ancient Orphism.* Chico, Calif.: Scholars Press, 1981.

Athanassakis, Apostolos N. *The Orphic Hymns: Text, Translation, and Notes.* Missoula, Mont.: Scholars Press, 1977.

Betegh, Gábor. *The Derveni Papyrus: Cosmology, Theology, and Interpretation.* Cambridge, U.K.: Cambridge University Press, 2004.

Burkert, Walter. *Ancient Mystery Cults.* Cambridge, Mass.: Harvard University Press, 1987.

Detienne, Marcel. *The Writings of Orpheus,* trans. Janet Lloyd. Baltimore, Md.: Johns Hopkins University Press, 2002.

Eliade, Mircea. *Shamanism: Archaic Techniques of Ecstasy,* trans. W. R. Transk. New York, Pantheon, 1964.

Graf, Fritz, and Sarah Iles Johnston. *Ritual Texts for the Afterlife: Orpheus and the Bacchic Gold Tablets.* London, U.K.: Routledge, 2007.

Questions for Further Study

1. What impact did urbanization in ancient Greece have on the preservation of the hymns to Orpheus?

2. Ancient Greece was characterized by a split between "official" and "unofficial" sets of religious beliefs. What interest did the state have in sanctioning official religion, and why did some citizens of Greece maintain their more traditional, unofficial religious beliefs?

3. In the modern world, numerous people lay claim to being able to function much like the shamans of ancient Greece; that is, they claim to be able to have contact with the nonmaterial world and to practice various forms of magic. To what extent does the belief system of these modern "shamans" stretch back to ancient Greece? Do you believe, as Plato probably would have, that this type of religion is superstitious and that its practitioners are charlatans?

4. What do the contents of the Orphic tablets have in common with ancient Egyptian burial practices, as reflected in the "Great Hymn to the Aten" and the Egyptian Book of the Dead? What do the similarities and differences tell you about ancient attitudes to death and the afterlife?

5. What connection, if any, exists between the cult of Orpheus and Christianity? Do you think the cult might have influenced the development of early Christianity?

Kotansky, Roy. "Incantations and Prayers for Salvation on Inscribed Greek Amulets." In *Magika Hiera: Ancient Greek Magic and Religion*, ed. Christopher A. Faraone and Dirk Obbink. Oxford, U.K.: Oxford University Press, 1991.

Plato. *The Dialogues of Plato*, trans. Benjamin Jowett. New York: Macmillan, 1892.

Swain, Simon. *Hellenism and Empire: Language, Classicism, and Power in the Greek World 50–250*. Oxford, U.K.: Clarendon, 1996.

West, M. L. *The Orphic Poems*. Oxford, U.K.: Clarendon Press, 1983.

Zuntz, Günther. *Persephone: Three Essays on Religion and Thought in Magna Graecia*. Oxford, U.K.: Clarendon Press, 1971.

■ **Journals**

Nilsson, M. "Early Orphism and Kindred Religious Movements." *Harvard Theological Review* 28 (1935): 181–230.

—Bradley A. Skeen

ORPHIC TABLETS AND HYMNS

Orphic Tablets

◆ Gold tablet from Petelia (ca. 350 BCE)

You will find a spring on the left of the halls of Hades, and beside it a white cypress growing. Do not even go near this spring. And you will find another, from the Lake of Memory, flowing forth with cold water. In front of it are guards. You must say, "I am the child of Gê (Earth) and of starry Ouranos (Heaven); this you yourselves also know. I am dry with thirst and am perishing. Come, give me at once cold water flowing forth from the Lake of Memory." And they themselves will give you to drink from the divine spring, and then thereafter you shall reign with the other heroes.

◆ Gold tablet from Eleutherna (ca. 150 BCE)

A I am dry with thirst and am perishing.

B Come, drink, I pray, from the ever-flowing spring on the right, where the cypress is. Who are you, and whence?

A I am the son of Earth and starry Heaven.

◆ Gold tablet from Thurii (ca. 350 BCE)

I come from the pure, O pure Queen of the earthly ones, Euclês, Eubouleus, and ye other immortal gods! I too claim to be of your blessed race, but Fate and other immortal gods conquered me, (and sent) the star-smiting thunder. And I flew out from the hard and deeply-grievous circle, and stepped on to the crown with my swift feet, and slipped into the bosom of the Mistress, the Queen of the Underworld. And I stepped out from the crown with my swift feet.

"Happy and blessed one, you shall be a god instead of a mortal."

I have fallen as a kid into milk.

◆ Gold tablet from Thurii (ca. 350 BCE)

I come pure from the pure, Queen of the Underworld, Euclês, Eubouleus and all other gods! For I too claim to be of your race. And I have paid the penalty for unjust deeds, whether Fate conquered me . . . with the thunderbolt and the lightning flash. Now a [female] suppliant I come to noble Persephone, that she may be kind and send me to the seats of the pure.

◆ Gold tablet from Rome (ca. 200 BCE)

I come pure from the pure, Queen of the Underworld, Euclês, Eubouleus, noble child of Zeus! And I have this gift of Memory prized by men.

"Caecilia Secundina, come, made divine by the Law!"

◆ Gold tablet from Thurii (ca. 350 BCE)

But whenever a soul leaves the light of the sun—enter on the right where one must if one has kept all (the laws) well and truly. Rejoice at the experience! This you have never before experienced: you have become a god instead of a man. You have fallen as a kid into milk. Hail, hail, as you travel on the right, through the holy meadow and groves of Persephone!

◆ Gold tablet from Thurii (ca. 350 BCE)

To Earth, first-born Mother, Cybelian Korê said: . . . Of Demeter . . . All-seeing Zeus.

O Sun, Fire, you went through all towns, when you appeared with the Victories and Fortunes and all-wise Fate, where you increase the brightness of the festival with your lordship, O glorious deity! By you are all things subdued, all things overpowered, all things smitten! The decrees of Fate must everywhere be endured. O Fire, lead me to the Mother, if the fast can endure, to fast for seven nights and days! For there was a seven-day fast, O Olympian Zeus and all-seeing Sun.

Orphic Hymns

◆ "To Protogonus, or the First-born"
The fumigation from myrrh.

O Mighty first-begotten, hear my pray'r,
Two-fold, egg-born, and wand'ring thro' the air,
Bull-roarer, glorying in thy golden wings,
From whom the race of Gods and mortals springs.
Ericapaeus, celebrated pow'r,
Ineffable, occult, all shining flow'r.
From eyes obscure thou wip'st the gloom of night,
All-spreading splendour, pure and holy light
Hence Phanes call'd, the glory of the sky,
On waving pinions thro' the world you fly.

Priapus, dark-ey'd splendour, thee I sing,
Genial, all-prudent, ever-blessed king,
With joyful aspect on our rights divine
And holy sacrifice propitious shine.

♦ **"To Rhea"**
The fumigation from aromatics.

Daughter of great Protogonus, divine,
Illustrious Rhea, to my pray'r incline,
Who driv'st thy holy car with speed along,
Drawn by fierce lions, terrible and strong.
Mother of Jove, whose mighty arm can wield
Th' avenging bolt, and shake the dreadful shield.
Drum-beating, frantic, of a splendid mien,
Brass-sounding, honor'd, Saturn's blessed queen.
Thou joy'st in mountains and tumultuous fight,
And mankind's horrid howlings, thee delight.
War's parent, mighty, of majestic frame,
Deceitful saviour, liberating dame.
Mother of Gods and men, from whom the earth
And lofty heav'ns derive their glorious birth;
Th' aetherial gales, the deeply spreading sea
Goddess aerial form'd, proceed from thee.
Come, pleas'd with wand'rings, blessed and divine,
With peace attended on our labours shine;

Bring rich abundance, and wherever found
Drive dire disease, to earth's remotest bound.

♦ **"To Thundering Jove"**
The fumigation from storax.

O Father Jove, who shak'st with fiery light
The world deep-sounding from thy lofty height:
From thee, proceeds th' aetherial lightning's blaze,
Flashing around intolerable rays.
Thy sacred thunders shake the blest abodes,
The shining regions of th' immortal Gods:
Thy pow'r divine, the flaming lightning shrouds,
With dark investiture, in fluid clouds.
'Tis thine to brandish thunders strong and dire,
To scatter storms, and dreadful darts of fire;
With roaring flames involving all around,
And bolts of thunder of tremendous sound.
Thy rapid dart can raise the hair upright,
And shake the heart of man with wild afright.
Sudden, unconquer'd, holy, thund'ring God,
With noise unbounded, flying all abroad;
With all-devouring force, entire and strong,
Horrid, untam'd, thou roll'st the flames along.
Rapid, aetherial bolt, descending fire,
The earth all-parent, trembles at thy ire;

Glossary

Bacchus	the Roman name for Dionysius, the Greek god of wine
Caecilia Secundina	the name of the woman for whom the tablet was written
Corybantes	a dancing religious order that worshipped the Phrygian goddess Cybele with drumming and dancing and whose members made up the nine dancers who venerated Rhea
Curetes	also Corybantes, a dancing religious order
Demeter	the goddess of agriculture and the mother of Persephone
Dionysus	the god of wine and festivity
Euboleus	originally a god of plowing; he becomes a swineherd who witnesses Persephone's abduction
Euclês	a common Greek name that may have been chosen for its euphony in the context
frankincense	an aromatic resin used in perfumes and incense
Hades	either the underworld itself or the god of the underworld
Jove	Zeus
Mars	the god of war
myrrh	an aromatic resin, at times more valuable than gold

The sea all-shining; and each beast that hears
The sound terrific, with dread horror fears:
When Nature's face is bright with flashing fire,
And in the heavens resound thy thunders dire.
Thy thunders white, the azure garments tear,
And burst the veil of all surrounding air.
O Jove, all-blessed, may thy wrath severe,
Hurl'd in the bosom of the deep appear,
And on the tops of mountains be reveal'd,
For thy strong arm is not from us conceal'd.
Propitious to these sacred rites incline,
And crown my wishes with a life divine:
Add royal health, and gentle peace beside,
With equal reason, for my constant guide.

♦ **"To Proserpine"**

Daughter of Jove, almighty and divine,
Come, blessed queen, and to these rites incline:
Only-begotten, Pluto's honor'd wife,
O venerable Goddess, source of life:
'Tis thine in earth's profundities to dwell,
Fast by the wide and dismal gates of hell:
Jove's holy offspring, of a beauteous mien,
Fatal, with lovely locks, infernal queen:

Source of the furies, whose blest frame proceeds
From Jove's ineffable and secret seeds:
Mother of Bacchus, Sonorous, divine,
And many-form'd, the parent of the vine:
The dancing Hours attend thee, essence bright,
All-ruling virgin, bearing heav'nly light:
Illustrious, horned, of a bounteous mind,
Alone desir'd by those of mortal kind.
O, vernal queen, whom grassy plains delight,
Sweet to the smell, and pleasing to the sight:
Whose holy form in budding fruits we view,
Earth's vig'rous offspring of a various hue:
Espous'd in Autumn: life and death alone
To wretched mortals from thy power is known:
For thine the task according to thy will,
Life to produce, and all that lives to kill.
Hear, blessed Goddess, send a rich increase
Of various fruits from earth, with lovely Peace;
Send Health with gentle hand, and crown my life
With blest abundance, free from noisy strife;
Last in extreme old age the prey of Death,
Dismiss we willing to the realms beneath,
To thy fair palace, and the blissful plains
Where happy spirits dwell, and Pluto reigns.

Glossary

Persephone	the wife of Hades
Phanes	a mystic god of procreation
Pluto	that is, the god Hades
Priapus	the fertility god
Proserpine	that is, Persephone
Protogonus	identified with Phanes, a mystic god of procreation
Queen of the Underworld	Persephone, the wife of Hades
Rhea	in Orphic cosmology, the daughter of Protogonus and the mother of earth and heaven
Samothracia	an island in the Aegean Sea
Saturn	a god of agriculture and the harvest
storax	a resinous secretion of sweetgum, used in incense
Thundering Jove	Zeus
Titans	the older gods, who existed before the Olympians
Zeus	the "father of gods and men" and the ruler of the gods on Mount Olympus

♦ **"To Bacchus"**
The fumigation from storax.

Bacchus I call, loud-sounding and divine,
Fanatic God, a two-fold shape is thine:
Thy various names and attributes I sing,
O, first-born, thrice-begotten, Bacchic king:
Rural, ineffable, two-form'd, obscure,
Two-horn'd, with ivy crown'd, euion, pure.
Bull-fac'd, and martial, bearer of the vine,
Endu'd with counsel prudent and divine:
Triennial, whom the leaves of vines adorn,
Of Jove and Proserpine, occultly born.
Immortal daemon, hear my suppliant voice,
Give me in blameless plenty to rejoice;
And listen gracious to my mystic pray'r,
Surrounded with thy choir of nurses fair.

♦ **"To the Curetes"**
A hymn.

Leaping Curetes, who with dancing feet
And circling measures, armed footsteps beat:
Whose bosom's mad, fanatic transports fire,
Who move in rythm to the founding lyre:
Who traces deaf when lightly leaping tread,
Arm bearers, strong defenders, rulers dread:
Propitious omens, guards of Proserpine,
Preserving rites, mysterious and divine
Come, and benevolent my words attend,
(In herds rejoicing), and my life defend.

♦ **"To the Curetes"**
The fumigation from frankincense.

Brass-beating Salians, ministers of Mars,
Who guard his arms the instruments of wars
Whose blessed frames, heav'n, earth, and sea compose,
And from whose breath all animals arose:
Who dwell in Samothracia's sacred ground,
Defending mortals thro' the sea profound.
Deathless Curetes, by your pow'r alone,
Initial rites to men at first were shewn:
Who shake old Ocean thund'ring to the sky,

And stubborn oaks with branches waving high.
'Tis your's in glittering arms the earth to beat,
With lightly-leaping, rapid, sounding feet;
Then every beast the noise terrific flies,
And the loud tumult wanders thro' the skies:
The dust your feet excites with matchless force,
Flies to the clouds amidst their whirling course;
And ev'ry flower of variegated hue,
Grows in the dancing motion form'd by you.
Immortal daemons, to your pow'rs consign'd
The talk to nourish, and destroy mankind.
When rushing furious with loud tumult dire,
O'erwhelm'd, they perish in your dreadful ire;
And live replenish'd with the balmy air,
The food of life, committed to your care.
When shook by you, the seas, with wild uproar,
Wide-spreading, and profoundly whirling, roar:
The concave heav'ns, with Echo's voice resound,
When leaves with ruffling noise bestrew the ground.
Curetes, Corybantes, ruling kings,
Whose praise the land of Samothracia sings:
From Jove descended; whose immortal breath
Sustains the soul, and wafts her back from death;
Aerial-form'd, much-fam'd, in heav'n ye shine
Two-fold, in heav'n all-lucid and divine:
Blowing, serene, from whom abundance springs,
Nurses of seasons, fruit-producing kings.

♦ **"To the Titans"**
The fumigation from frankincense.

O Mighty Titans, who from heav'n and earth
Derive your noble and illustrious birth,
Our fathers fires, in Tartarus profound
Who dwell, deep merg'd beneath the solid ground:
Fountains and principles, from whom began
Th' afflicted, miserable, race of man:
Who not alone in earth's retreats abide,
But in the ocean and the air reside;
Since ev'ry species from your nature flows,
Which all prolific, nothing barren knows:
Avert your rage, if from th' infernal seats
One of your tribe should visit our retreats.

Laozi

(Lao-Tzu [c.604-531 BC], illustration from 'Myths and Legends of China', by Edward T.C. Werner / Private Collection / The Bridgeman Art Library International)

Dao De Jing

"A thousand-mile journey begins with a single step."

Overview

The Dao De Jing (also called Tao Te Ching) is by far the most important text of the immense Daoist canon, known as the Daozang. The significance of this text was recognized by both philosophical and religious schools within Daoism, each offering a great variety of interpretations of its content. Attributed to the legendary sage Laozi (also known as Lao-tzu), an older contemporary of Confucius, but probably compiled during the late fourth and third centuries BCE, the Dao De Jing expresses in a highly compressed style the basic religious, philosophical, and political beliefs of this ancient tradition centered on the concepts of the Dao ("the Way") and De ("power" or "virtue").

Interpreted as a religious text, the Dao De Jing contains teachings on the nature of the Absolute, human relations toward the Absolute, practical lessons for everyday life, the ideal of human existence (the ideal of a sage), and hints on immortality as the ultimate goal of a sage. Its succinct, aphoristic language and generous use of metaphors make it fertile ground for diverse interpretations, ranging from the reading of the text as a secret instruction manual for prolonging life to reading it as the earliest manifesto of environmentalism, particularly pertinent for today's world. This richness of content combined with extreme economy of language make the Dao De Jing a unique document in the vast collection of religious scriptures, whose influence on arts, literature, and philosophy long surpassed the boundaries of any single religious tradition or geographical area. The more widely accepted pinyin system of transliteration of Chinese words is used here, while the older Wade-Giles system is used in the source document itself.

Context

The content of the Dao De Jing was influenced by the political and philosophical realities of the Warring States period in Chinese history (ca. 475–221 BCE). The author or authors of the text implicitly juxtapose their worldview with at least two other competing ideologies of the day,

Confucianism (influential from the fifth century BCE onward), and Legalism (influential from 400 to 200 BCE). Several passages in the text (chapters 18 and 19, for instance) downplay the importance of central Confucian virtues, such as benevolence and filial piety, and elsewhere the author expresses his doubts about the effectiveness of repressive laws for establishment of social order (as in chapter 57). The latter criticism is apparently aimed at the position of Legalists in ancient China, who, not unlike the English political philosopher Thomas Hobbes many centuries later, held a rather pessimistic view of human nature, emphasizing the importance of centralized coercive power.

The political realities of the time period when the Dao De Jing was most likely composed were characterized by further fragmentation of China into a number of autonomous states, frequent wars, and social upheavals, which would last up to the time of unification of China under the Qin Dynasty (221–206 BCE). The character of a traveling sage, who would offer his advice and guidance to a local ruler in a time of trouble, is well known at least since the time of Confucius. Such employment was often short-lived and dangerous, but thanks to the profusion of independent and semi-independent states, one could always find a suitable patron. It is likely, then, that the Dao De Jing is at least partly the product of a certain school of political advisers, who would blend practical suggestions for state policy with a heavy dose of mysticism, deeply rooted in China's indigenous religious traditions.

About the Author

According to orthodox Daoist tradition, the author of the Dao De Jing is Laozi, whose name literally means "Old Master" or, alternatively, "Old Child." Our primary source of information about this obscure figure is the famous Chinese historian Sima Qian (ca. 145 or 135–87 BCE) who in his *Shi Ji*, or *Records of the Grand Historian*, introduces a short biography of Laozi. But even for Sima Qian, Laozi was already a semimythical person, and very few solid facts were known about him. The author places Laozi in late sixth century BCE, mentioning his occupation in the royal city of Lo-yang (Luoyang) as a state archivist or a librarian. He endorses the myth of Laozi's conversations with Confu-

Time Line	
CA. 604 BCE	■ The legendary Laozi, claimed author of the Dao De Jing, is said to be born and lives until ca. 520 BCE.
CA. 551 BCE	■ Confucius is thought to be born and lives until ca. 479 BCE.
CA. 475 BCE	■ The Warring States period begins in China, ending in 221 BCE.
CA. 300 –200 BCE	■ The Dao De Jing is most likely created.
1972	■ The Mawangdui Silk Texts, containing the oldest nearly complete version of the Dao De Jing (dated ca. 190 BCE), is discovered.
1993	■ The Guodian Chu Slips, containing the oldest fragments of the Dao De Jing (about one-third of the standard text), dated prior to 300 BCE, is discovered.

cius and relates a story of how Laozi, frustrated with government corruption, left his position and rode an ox to the western frontier of China. Before leaving the country forever and after being pressed by the keeper of the Western Gates, Laozi put to writing his thoughts on various metaphysical and social issues into a collection of sayings that today is known as the Dao De Jing. Later sources, which appeared at the time of gradual deification of Laozi (Laojun or Lord Lao) in the second to fifth centuries CE, supply many more details of his life. Among the most curious are the stories of his conception by a shooting star, his having been born as an elderly man eighty-one years of age, his philosophical discussions with the Buddha in India after traveling west, his eventual return to China, and his later ascension into the sky.

Most contemporary scholars agree, however, that the earliest layers of the Dao De Jing could not have been written prior to the middle of the fourth century BCE, and the final version of the book was completed in the third century BCE. This leaves us with several possibilities regarding the identity of Laozi. First, if the name refers to a historical personage who lived during sixth and fifth centuries BCE, then he could not have been the author of the Dao De Jing in its present form. Second, if Laozi ever existed and indeed contributed to some of the sayings of the Dao De Jing, then we should place him much later on the time line. Finally, there was never a single person uniquely corresponding to

the author of the Dao De Jing, and the name Laozi ("Old Master") is an abstraction, a later personification of "the elders"—the anonymous authors of a long oral tradition.

Explanation and Analysis of the Document

The present entry is a complete version of the Dao De Jing, traditionally consisting of eighty-one chapters, or paragraphs. In the original Chinese, the Dao De Jing is written with rhythmic prose and rhyming verses, features that are lost in most translations. The breakdown of the text into eighty-one verses is the product of the first centuries of the Common Era (the Han Dynasty) and is often arbitrary. The number 81 is of special significance to Chinese numerology—the number 9 stands for the yang principle, and 9 × 9 (81) yields a perfect or complete yang. The number of chapters is also likely connected with later legends about Laozi's miraculous birth at the age of eighty-one. The earliest known full version of the Dao De Jing, the recently discovered copy of the text at the tombs of Mawangdui, dates to the year 190 BCE and has a different arrangement, with fewer paragraphs. Indeed, the Mawangdui version reverses the usual order of presentation, with the text corresponding to (our) chapters 38–81 coming before the first half of the book. Among the transmitted editions of the Dao De Jing, the three primary ones are named for early commentators: the scholar Yan Zun (fl. 80 BCE–10 CE), the legendary sage Heshang Gong (202–157 BCE), and the philosopher Wang Bi (226–249 CE). Most contemporary translations follow the edition of the Dao De Jing that dates to the third century CE (the Wang Bi version) and divide the text into two parts—Book I: The Book of Dao (Dao Jing) (chapters 1–37) and Book II: The Book of De (De Jing) (chapters 38–81).

♦ Book 1: The Book of Dao

Chapters 1–6: The opening chapters of the Dao De Jing introduce the Dao as the central notion of this important text. The initial difficulty presents itself in a form of a paradox in the first chapter—the Dao in its primeval form exceeds all linguistic categories, and we lose its essence the moment we try to capture it by means of a concept (a name). Yet the ineffable, transcendent, nameless Dao (later correlated with "Heaven's Dao") is contrasted here with the Dao of immanence, which admits naming and categorization as reflecting a more immediate principle of generation and is referred to as "the mother of ten thousand things." Such descriptions of Dao as "the Valley Spirit," "the Mysterious Female," "the mother," "Bottomless," and "the Ancestor" refer to the Dao of immanence and emphasize its generative powers as well as "feminine" (yin) characteristics.

The selection continues by presenting the underlying dialectic in the way the Dao operates. The opposites in all aspects of existence (aesthetics, morals, physical properties of objects, and so on) depend on each other and are born from each other, which is illustrated by a series of seemingly paradoxical statements, such as "Recognize good and

Symbol representing the principles of yin and yang

(Taijitu, traditional symbol representing the principles of Yin and Yang [colour litho], Chinese School [20th Century] / Bibliotheque Nationale, Paris, France /

Archives Charmet / The Bridgeman Art Library International)

evil is born; / Is and Isn't produce each other." An important character, the Sage, is introduced at this point, as the person who understands the inner workings of Dao and who is capable of drawing practical lessons from these abstract underlying principles. The most important practical lesson turns out to be the lesson of nonaction (*wu-wei*). Wu-wei is a crucial notion in the Daoist worldview and is variously translated as effortlessness, spontaneous action, nonag- gression, or nonmeddlesome action. The ideal of wu-wei in the Dao De Jing and in later Daoist literature (for example, the Zhuangzi) connotes the attitude of passive reception of Dao's creative energy, without presumptuously imposing one's own order upon self, nature, or society. By adopting wu-wei as his guide, the Sage imitates the Dao itself and is later characterized in terms of softness, apparent weakness, and flexibility through his unassuming posture.

"Best to be like water, which benefits the ten thousand things and does not contend. It pools where humans disdain to dwell, close to the Tao. Live in a good place. Keep your mind deep. Treat others well. Stand by your word. Make fair rules. Do the right thing. Work when it's time. Only do not contend, and you will not go wrong."

"Tao engenders One, One engenders Two, Two engenders Three, Three engenders the ten thousand things. The ten thousand things carry shade and embrace sunlight. Shade and sunlight, yin and yang, breath blending into harmony. . . . We gain by losing, lose by gaining. What others teach, I also teach: 'A violent man does not die a natural death.'"

"The more prohibitions and rules, the poorer people become. The sharper people's weapons, the more they riot. . . . The more elaborate the laws, the more they commit crimes. Therefore the Sage says, I do nothing and people transform themselves. I enjoy serenity and people govern themselves. I cultivate emptinessand people become prosperous."

"A tree too big to embrace is born from a slender shoot. A nine-story rises from a pile of earth. A thousand-mile journey begins with a single step."

"Humans are born soft and weak. They die stiff and strong. The ten thousand plants and trees are born soft and tender, and die withered and sere. The stiff and strong are Death's companions; the soft and weak are Life's companions."

*Chapters 7–13:*The next section is concerned with further exploring the lessons of the Dao and showing how the Sage puts into practice the qualities of the Dao that he is able to discern. Following the Dao, the Sage achieves prominence by withdrawing and secures his interest by denying the self. Concrete recommendations begin to appear in chapter 8, which can be taken as the earliest short summary of Daoist ethics. Simple moral rules like "Treat others well" and "Stand by your word" are contrasted with the vice of contention. Contention or, alternatively, competitiveness that leads to conflict is a recurrent antivalue in the Dao De Jing, and it can be seen as the normative antipode of the wu-wei ideal.

Two important metaphors appear for the first time in these chapters—the metaphors of water and infant. Certain char-

acteristics of water make it perhaps the most fitting metaphor for the Dao and for the Sage, who imitates Dao. Nurturing all living things, naturally flowing to low places, being soft and malleable and yet extremely powerful, having hidden depth beyond the surface—these are some of the features of water that most impressed the author of the Dao De Jing. Direct and indirect references to water appear often in the text. The second metaphor, the metaphor of an infant or a baby (or "baby in the womb," in chapter 20), has a dual significance in the Dao De Jing. First, a baby is seen as a being with unlimited (because not yet dissipated) life force (vital energy, or qi), and, in this respect, the Sage must learn to become like a baby by constantly increasing his qi. Second, a baby represents the state of unlimited potentiality; it has not yet "hardened" into certain form and may thus illustrate the nature of the Dao itself as the ultimate undifferentiated source of the "ten thousand things."

The word *De* (chapter 10) in different translations is variously rendered as "mysterious quality," "the Dao's power," or "virtue" or is simply left untranslated. It appears in the title and is arguably one of the most difficult notions to grasp. Here are several examples of how this concept functions throughout the text, which may indicate the range of its rich meaning: We are told that De flows from the Dao and that just like the Dao itself it is qualified as "great" (chapter 21). A person may be high or low in De (chapter 38). It is advisable to be filled with De "like a baby," since it makes one invulnerable (chapter 55). Displaying one's De is a proper response to hatred (chapter 63). De signifies the wisdom that is necessary for the actions of a Sage and a ruler (chapters 10 and 65). It is indeed difficult to find a single English equivalent that would suit all these contexts, but at the very least it connotes both an active power, emanating from the Dao, and a desirable human quality. It is the Dao's power as it is concretely embodied in the individual. A person, then, is filled with De to the extent that he or she approaches the Dao's character. The expression "dark Te [De]" at the end of chapter 10 refers to the De's unknown, hidden, or mysterious aspect and is not a moral evaluation.

Emptiness is another important Daoist category and first appears in chapter 11 of the Dao De Jing. The importance of emptiness is illustrated by a wheel, a pot and a room—the usefulness of these objects essentially depends on the "unfilled" parts of the design, that is, on empty space between walls or spokes. The category of emptiness is conceptually connected with the notion of wu-wei. But whereas nonaction primarily qualifies human behavior, emptiness appears as the mark of the Dao in all existing things. The Dao lacks determination; it is not a particular *thing* but rather the absolute absence of a determinate form ("uncarved wood"), and herein is the source of its generative power. Later theorists would correlate Daoist emptiness with the Buddhist notion of *shunyata* (emptiness, vacuity).

Chapters 14–25: This selection starts with one of the more mystical descriptions of the Dao as the primeval beginning of the universe. The Dao has none of the ordinary attributes of physical objects; it is invisible, inaudible, and intangible. It enjoys ultimate unity and is described as "dark, wondrous, profound, penetrating" (chapter 15). It eludes human grasp, but at the same time it is found everywhere. Stillness, gentleness, and softness are the qualities of the ancient Sages, followers of the Dao. Dao cannot be actively pursued; rather, an attitude of quiet passive reception is the precondition for penetrating into this mystery: "Calm the muddy water / It becomes clear" (chapter 15). One is reminded that calming the water requires abstaining from any activity—a nonaction.

The doctrine of eternal reversion is at the root of the Daoist worldview, and we can see it mentioned in chapter 16 of the Dao De Jing: "The ten thousand things stir about; / I only watch for their going back. Things grow and grow, / But each goes back to its root." There is an invariable law in things—activity turns into inactivity, and any movement that goes to its extreme of development necessarily becomes its opposite. "Go-

ing far means returning," keenly observes the author (chapter 25), as if he has the spherical shape of our earth in mind. This dynamic movement from one opposite to another—inherent in Dao's nature and exhibited in the natural order of things—excludes the notion of decline or deterioration. Things and qualities transform into their opposites: The interplay of the yin and yang forces is ever present, but the Sage sees an orderly pattern in this apparent chaos. Ultimately, death does not signify an end but is rather a moment of the cycle of eternal recurrence and is not to be feared: "Tao endures. / Your body dies. / There is no danger" (chapter 16). Indeed, as the author states later, "Reversal is Tao's movement" (chapter 40).

Criticism of core Confucian values (chapters 18–20) provides an interesting background against which we can better appreciate the Daoist perspective. The author takes a deeper look and observes that a preoccupation with virtues (for example, benevolence and filial piety) is a symptom of a disorderly society where "the Great Tao[is] rejected." It is important to observe that the moral ideal of Confucianism is contrasted here not with an alternative system of morality but with a preferred pre-moral state of being: "Banish benevolence, discard righteousness: / People will return to duty and compassion" (chapter 19). These chapters can also be interpreted as an attack on "civilization" in general.

The selection ends with the proclamation of the strict cosmic hierarchy: "Humans follow earth. / Earth follows heaven. / Heaven follows Tao. / Tao follows its own nature" (chapter 25). Following its own nature or spontaneity, the Dao has no external guiding principle and appears as the only unlimited reality in the universe. This self-sufficiency of Dao should not be understood in terms of its omnipotence (after all, the Dao is not a personal God); rather, it connotes its boundless raw potential, the full wealth of yet-unrealized possibilities.

Chapters 26–37: The remaining chapters of Book I reiterate themes mentioned earlier and also introduce a new topic, the theory of government, which is central to the second part of the Dao De Jing. Chapter 28 provides an important transition from the abstract metaphysics of the Dao to "applied" aspects of Daoist philosophy. The three slogans "Return to infancy," "Return to the uncarved block," and "Return to simplicity" are now aimed at the Sage "as high official," that is, as a ruler of the land. It is noteworthy that the Sage as ruler is expected to maintain the yin character throughout, which is referred to in the text as "female," "black," and "the valley of the world."

Unsurprisingly, the wu-wei attitude in private life is extended to government affairs as well. "The most fruitful outcome / Does not depend on force" (chapter 30) is the essence of the author's pacifistic worldview. One should note, however, that rejection of violence and humility are justified in a utilitarian manner as the most efficient strategies for achieving one's goals in the long run. On the other hand, "Those who rejoice in killing people / Cannot achieve their purpose in this world" (chapter 31).

♦ **Book II: The Book of De**

Chapters 38–56: Most modern editions start Book II of the Dao De Jing from chapter 38, even though the oldest known version of the text (the Mawangdui version) places these final forty-four chapters before the first half of the text. The initial selection contains some of the most profound verses of the whole book, but only few leading themes can be accentuated here.

"Tao engenders One, / One engenders Two, / Two engenders Three, / Three engenders the ten thousand things" (chapter 42) is the essence of Daoist cosmology. The gradual differentiation proceeds from the "nameless" Dao to the Dao of immanence (the One), which is bifurcated into cosmic forces of yin and yang, then further divides into three realms (water, earth, heaven), and finally multiplies into all existing things. Religious Daoism takes as its goal the reversal of this primordial movement and, starting with the "ten thousand things," seeks gradually to achieve the original unity in the Dao (chapter 56).

Chapter 47 advocates an intensive rather than an extensive model of knowledge. The familiar everydayness is where true wisdom is hidden. Since the Dao is present in all of nature as its underlying pattern of development, the Sage will be able to discern the Way by observing the most ordinary things (for example, water). "The further you travel, / The less you know" should not be understood as the author's preference for a sedentary lifestyle or his dislike of foreign lands (after all, Laozi is known for his travels); rather, it is a warning against philosophical speculations that are too detached from common human experience.

The subsequent development of Daoist religion and its applied aspect, alchemy, with its quest for physical immortality, often found inspiration in the Dao De Jing, especially in chapters 50 and 55. Invulnerability, imperviousness to harm, having "no mortal spot"—these are the characteristics of a Daoist Sage, who manages to be "like a baby" and whose vital essence (qi) is complete. Enhancing and nurturing this life force (qi), either through specially prepared elixirs (external alchemy) or through intense meditation, physical exercises, and regulation of breathing (internal alchemy) became the main practical goal of later Daoism.

Chapters 57–81: This section of the text requires comparatively less interpretation. Recommendations for domestic and foreign governmental policies, methods of waging war and the ways of keeping the population in submission are typically not relevant topics for religion, although this practical theme might have been the main reason behind composing the book. Practical application of Daoist philosophy to politics is occasionally contrasted with Legalist methods of "prohibitions and rules" (chapter 57), and, in general, the quietist approach to worldly matters is juxtaposed to the active stand of Confucianism. One can find support in the text for the libertarian model of a government that does not intrude on the lives of citizens (chapters 58 and 75), an introduction of the ideal of a small, self-sufficient city-state with a bare minimum of technical sophistication (chapter 80), as well as a much more controversial advice for keeping people ignorant and dull lest they revolt against their rulers (chapter 65). The latter advice reiterates the point made at the very beginning of the book where the Sage is said to rule "by emptying hearts and filling bellies [of the people]" (chap-

ter 3). It is true, however, that most of these claims were interpreted metaphorically by later readers, and one can understand the "ignorance" and "emptiness of hearts" elevated here as the real wisdom of a Daoist Sage, wrongly perceived as ignorance by the Confucian literati.

This final selection also contains some of the most frequently quoted aphorisms as well the most memorable imagery of softness and apparent weakness triumphing over strength and stiffness. Water and infancy are again the primary examples here: "Nothing in the world is soft and weak as water. / But when attacking the hard and strong / nothing can conquer so easily" (chapter 78). A metaphysical conclusion drawn from observing the ordinary things (for example, a newborn) links softness with life and strength with death and is quite in line with the overall direction of Daoist philosophy, which prizes humbleness, social withdrawal, and nonaction above "active" virtues.

Audience

We do not know for sure who the intended audience of this treatise was, but we may make some conjectures based on the content of the Dao De Jing. Given the likely period of its compilation and the numerous recommendations regarding the proper way of conducting both foreign and domestic policy, we may surmise that the treatise was partly aimed at the regional warlords of the Warring States period in China, where it would have figured as a solution to the seemingly unending confrontation between states and the civil unrest within states. If this is the case, the treatise can be seen as an alternative to the Confucian and Legalist models of social justice. Needless to say, the text soon appealed to a much wider group of intellectuals, initially in China, but eventually in the rest of the world, and, if it failed to convert the rulers and to initiate a radical political reform, it surely left a lasting imprint on many other areas.

Impact

It is hard to overestimate the impact of this short treatise to Chinese and world cultures. For more than two thousand years after its compilation, the text's influence was confined to East Asia, and translations of the Dao De Jing into European languages have become widely available only since the nineteenth century. In China a particular esoteric interpretation of the text played a role in the development of Daoist alchemy in the early centuries of the Common Era, justifying its quest for the elixir of immortality. Zhang Daoling (34–156 CE), the founder of Tianshi Dao, or the Heavenly Masters School, one of the major surviving Daoist religious sects, claimed to have received his spiritual authority directly from Laozi during one of the latter's appearances on the earth. Naturally, the Dao De Jing became the primary scripture of that tradition. One can also find numerous examples of the Dao De Jing's influence on Chinese poetry, literature, painting, and calligraphy.

The number of Laozi's readers increased tremendously in the past two hundred years, once first renderings of it appeared in Western languages. Christian missionaries in China were the first to encounter Daoism, and they were naturally attracted to the transcendent nature of the Dao (which they would interpret as God) as well as to the central virtues of Daoism, such as noncontention, humbleness, and nonaction. Both Western literature and philosophy of the past 150 years often found inspiration in this ancient text, and one can find quotes from the Dao De Jing in such writers as Lev Tolstoy and such philosophers as Martin Heidegger. It is also not unusual to encounter environmentalists appealing to Laozi's ideal of harmony between nature and humans and citing his advocacy of a simple lifestyle and what we would call a sustainable local economy. "A thousand-mile journey begins with a single step" is perhaps the most recognizable line from the Dao De Jing, with many people using it as an old proverb, not realizing its origin.

Today the Dao De Jing is the second most widely translated text in the world after the Bible, with at least 112 English translations available at the moment. The discovery of the ancient Mawangdui versions of the text in 1970s has renewed interest in this masterpiece and has given impetus to a number of new editions that take into account the specifics of the oldest known edition.

Further Reading

■ Books

Ames, Roger T. *The Art of Rulership: A Study of Ancient Chinese Political Thought.* Albany: State University of New York, 1994.

Fowler, Jeaneane. *An Introduction to the Philosophy and Religion of Taoism.* Portland, Ore.: Sussex Academic Press, 2005.

Kohn, Livia. *Daoism and Chinese Culture.* Cambridge, Mass.: Three Pines Press, 2001.

Robinet, Isabelle. *Taoism: Growth of a Religion,* trans. Phyllis Brooks. Stanford: Stanford University Press, 1997.

Slingerland, Edward. *Effortless Action: Wu-wei as a Conceptual Metaphor and Spiritual Ideal in Early China.* New York: Oxford University Press, 2003.

Yutang, Lin. *The Wisdom of Laotse.* Westport, Conn.: Greenwood Press, 1979.

■ Journals

Kirkland, J. Russell. "The Historical Contours of Taoism in China: Thoughts on Issues of Classification and Terminology." *Journal of Chinese Religions* 25 (1997): 57–82.

Olles, Volker. "Lord Lao's Mountain: From Celestial Master Daoism to Contemporary Daoist Practice." *Journal of Daoist Studies* 2 (2009): 109–136.

■ Web Sites

Center for Daoist Studies Web site.
   http://www.daoistcenter.org

Das Tao Te King von Lao Tse Web site.
   http://home.pages.at/onkellotus/TTK/_IndexTTK.html

—Andrei G. Zavaliy

Questions for Further Study

1. Respond to the point of view that Daoism as reflected in the Dao De Jing is not a religion but a philosophy of life.

2. Using Daoism and the Dao De Jing as an example, explain how certain types of religious beliefs can emerge as a response to social disorder and other historical circumstances.

3. Explain why the Dao De Jing is open to widely different translations and interpretations. What challenges does this present to the modern student of religion and to translators?

4. Describe ways in which you think Daoism might be having an impact on thinking in the Western world.

5. The Dao De Jing relies heavily on metaphors. Select one such metaphor and be prepared to explain its significance in the text.

DAO DE JING

1

Tao called Tao is not Tao.
Names can name no lasting name.
Nameless: the origin of heaven and earth.
Naming: the mother of ten thousand things.
Empty of desire, perceive mystery.
Filled with desire, perceive manifestations.
These have the same source, but different names.
Call them both deep—
Deep and again deep:
the gateway to all mystery.

2

Recognize beauty and ugliness is born.
Recognize good and evil is born.
Is and Isn't produce each other.
Hard depends on easy,
Long is tested by short,
High is determined by low,
Sound is harmonized by voice,
After is followed by before.
Therefore the Sage is devoted to non-action,
Moves without teaching,
Creates ten thousand things without instruction,
Lives but does not own,
Acts but does not presume,
Accomplishes without taking credit.
When no credit is taken,
Accomplishment endures.

3

Don't glorify heroes,
And people will not contend.
Don't treasure rare objects,
And no one will steal.
Don't display what people desire,
And their hearts will not be disturbed.
Therefore, the Sage rules
By emptying hearts and filling bellies,
By weakening ambitions and strengthening bones;
Leads people
Away from knowing and wanting;
Deters those who know too much

From going too far:
Practices non-action
And the natural order is not disrupted.

4

Tao is empty—
Its use never exhausted.
Bottomless—
The origin of all things.
It blunts sharp edges,
Unties knots, Softens glare,
Becomes one with the dusty world.
Deeply subsistent—
I don't know whose child it is.
It is older than the Ancestor.

5

Heaven and Earth are not kind:
The ten thousand things are straw dogs to them.
The Sage is not kind:
People are straw dogs to him.
Yet Heaven and Earth
And all the space between
Are like a bellows:
Empty but inexhaustible,
Always producing more.
Longwinded speech is exhausting.
Better to stay centered.

6

The Valley Spirit never dies.
It is called the Mysterious Female.
The entrance to the Mysterious Female
Is called the root of Heaven and Earth.
Endless flow
Of inexhaustible energy.

7

Heaven is long, Earth enduring.
Long and enduring
Because they do not exist for themselves.
Therefore the Sage

Steps back, but is always in front,
Stays outside, but is always within.
No self-interest?
Self is fulfilled.

8

Best to be like water,
Which benefits the ten thousand things
And does not contend.
It pools where humans disdain to dwell,
Close to the Tao.
Live in a good place.
Keep your mind deep.
Treat others well.
Stand by your word.
Make fair rules.
Do the right thing.
Work when it's time.
Only do not contend,
And you will not go wrong.

9

Hold and fill it—
Not as good as stopping in time.
Measure and pound it—
It will not long survive.
When gold and jade fill the hall,
They cannot be guarded.
Riches and pride
Bequeath error.
Withdrawing when work is done:
Heaven's Tao.

10

Can you balance your life force
And embrace the One
Without separation?
Can you control your breath
Gently
Like a baby?
Can you clarify
Your dark vision
Without blemish?
Can you love people
And govern the country
Without knowledge?
Can you open and close
The gate of heaven
Without clinging to earth?

Can you brighten
The four directions
Without action?
Give birth and cultivate.
Give birth and do not possess.
Act without dependence.
Excel but do not rule.
This is called the dark Te.

11

Thirty spokes join one hub.
The wheel's use comes from emptiness.
Clay is fired to make a pot.
The pot's use comes from emptiness.
Windows and doors are cut to make a room.
The room's use comes from emptiness.
Therefore, Having leads to profit,
Not having leads to use.

12

Five colors darken the eyes.
Five tones darken the ears.
Five tastes jade the palate.
Hunting and racing madden the heart.
Exotic goods ensnarl human lives.
Therefore the Sage
Takes care of the belly, not the eye,
Chooses one, rejects the other.

13

Favour and disgrace are like fear.
Honour and distress are like the self.
What does this mean?
Favour debases us.
Afraid when we get it,
Afraid when we lose it.
The self embodies distress.
No self,
No distress.
Respect the world as your self:
The world can be your lodging.
Love the world as your self:
The world can be your trust.

14

Seeing but not seeing, we call it dim.
Listening but not hearing, we call it faint.
Groping but not touching, we call it subtle.

These three cannot be fully grasped.
Therefore they become one.
Rising, it is not bright; setting it is not dark.
It moves all things back to where there is nothing
Meeting it there is no front,
Following it there is no back.
Live in the ancient Tao,
Master the existing present,
Understand the source of all things.
This is called the record of Tao.

15

The ancients who followed Tao:
Dark, wondrous, profound, penetrating.
Deep beyond knowing.
Because they cannot be known,
They can only be described.
Cautious,
Like crossing a winter stream.
Hesitant,
Like respecting one's neighbours.
Polite,
Like a guest.
Yielding,
Like ice about to melt;
Blank,
Like uncarved wood.
Open,
Like a valley.
Mixing freely,
Like muddy water.
Calm the muddy water,
It becomes clear.
Move the inert,
It comes to life.
Those who sustain Tao
Do not wish to be full.
Because they do not wish to be full
They can fade away
Without further effort.

16

Attain complete emptiness,
Hold fast to stillness.
The ten thousand things stir about;
I only watch for their going back.
Things grow and grow,
But each goes back to its root.
Going back to the root is stillness.
This means returning to what is.

Returning to what is
Means going back to the ordinary.
Understanding the ordinary:
Enlightenment.
Not understanding the ordinary:
Blindness creates evil.
Understanding the ordinary:
Mind opens.
Mind opening leads to compassion,
Compassion to nobility,
Nobility to heavenliness,
Heavenliness to Tao.
Tao endures.
Your body dies.
There is no danger.

17

Great rising and falling—
People only know it exists.
Next they see and praise.
Soon they fear.
Finally they despise.
Without fundamental trust
There is no trust at all.
Be careful in valuing words.
When the work is done,
Everyone says
We just acted naturally.

18

Great Tao rejected:
Benevolence and righteousness appear.
Learning and knowledge professed:
Great Hypocrites spring up.
Family relations forgotten:
Filial piety and affection arise.
The nation disordered:
Patriots come forth.

19

Banish learning, discard knowledge:
People will gain a hundredfold.
Banish benevolence, discard righteousness:
People will return to duty and compassion.
Banish skill, discard profit:
There will be no more thieves.
These three statements are not enough.
One more step is necessary.
Look at plain silk; hold uncarved wood.

The self dwindles; desires fade.

20

Banish learning, no more grief.
Between Yes and No
How much difference?
Between good and evil
How much difference?
What others fear I must fear—
How pointless!
People are wreathed in smiles
As if at a carnival banquet.
I alone am passive, giving no sign,
Like an infant who has not yet smiles.
Forlorn as if I had no home.
Others have enough and more,
I alone am left out.
I have the mind of a fool,
Confused, confused.
Others are bright and intelligent,
I alone and dull, dull,
Drifting on the ocean,
Blown about endlessly.
Others have plans,
I alone am wayward and stubborn,
I alone am different from others,
Like a baby in the womb.

21

Great Te appears
Flowing from Tao.
Tao in action—
Only vague and intangible.
Intangible and vague,
But within it are images.
Vague and intangible;
Within are entities.
Shadowy and obscure;
Within there is life,
Life so real,
That within it there is trust.
From the beginning its name is not lost
But reappears through multiple origins.
How do I know these origins?
Like this.

22

Crippled become whole,
Crooked becomes straight,

Hollow becomes full,
Worn becomes new,
Little becomes more,
Much becomes delusion.
Therefore the Sages cling to the One
And take care of this world;
Do not display themselves
And therefore shine.
Do not assert themselves and therefore stand out.
Do not praise themselves
And therefore succeed.
Do not contend
And therefore no one under heaven
Can contend with them.
The old saying
Crippled becomes whole
Is not empty words.
It becomes whole and returns.

23

Spare words; nature's way.
Violent winds do not blow all morning.
Sudden rain cannot pour all day.
What causes these things? Heaven and Earth.
If Heaven and Earth do not blow and pour for long,
How much less should humans?
Therefore in following Tao:
Those on the way become the way,
Those who gain become the gain,
Those who lose become the loss.
All within the Tao:
The wayfarer, welcome upon the way,
Those who gain, welcome within gain,
Those who lose, welcome within loss.
Without trust in this,
There is no trust at all.

24

Upon tiptoe: no way to stand.
Clambering: no way to walk.
Self-display: no way to shine.
Self-assertion: no way to succeed.
Self-praise: no way to flourish.
Complacency: no way to endure.
According to Tao,
Excessive food,
Extraneous activity
Inspire disgust.
Therefore the follower of Tao
Moves on.

25

Something unformed and complete
Before heaven and Earth were born,
Solitary and silent,
Stands alone and unchanging.
Pervading all things without limit.
It is like the mother of all things under heaven,
But I don't know its name—
Better call it Tao.
Better call it great.
Great means passing on.
Passing on means going far.
Going far means returning.
Therefore Tao is great,
And heaven,
And earth,
And humans.
Four great things in the world.
Aren't humans one of them?
Humans follow earth.
Earth follows heaven.
Heaven follows Tao.
Tao follows its own nature.

26

Gravity is the root of lightness,
Stillness the master of passion.
The Sage travels all day
But does not leave the baggage-cart;
When surrounded by magnificent scenery
Remains calm and still.
When a lord of ten thousand chariots
Behaves lightly in this world,
Lightness loses its root,
Passion loses its master.

27

Good travelers leave no tracks.
Good words leave no trace.
Good counting needs no markers.
Good doors have no bolts
Yet cannot be forced.
Good knots have no rope
But cannot be untied.
In this way the Sage
Always helps people
And rejects none,
Always helps all beings,
And rejects none.

This is called practicing brightness.
Therefore the good person
Is the bad person's teacher,
And the bad person
Is the good person's resource.
Not to value the teacher,
Not to love the resource,
Causes great confusion even for the intelligent.
This is called the vital secret.

28

Know the male, maintain the female,
Become the channel of the world,
And Te will endure.
Return to infancy.
Know the white, sustain the black,
Become the pattern of the world,
And Te will not falter.
Return to the uncarved block.
Know honour, sustain disgrace,
Become the valley of the world,
And Te will prevail.
Return to simplicity.
Simplicity divided becomes utensils
That are used by the Sage as high official.
But great governing does not carve up.

29

Trying to control the world?
I see you won't succeed.
The world is a spiritual vessel
And cannot be controlled.
Those who control, fail.
Those who grasp, lose.
Some go forth, some are led,
Some weep, some blow flutes,
Some become strong, some superfluous,
Some oppress, some are destroyed.
Therefore the Sage
Casts off extremes,
Casts off excess,
Casts off Extravagance.

30

Use Tao to help rule people.
This world has no need for weapons,
Which soon turn on themselves.
Where armies camp, nettles grow.
After each war, years of famine.

The most fruitful outcome
Does not depend on force,
But succeeds without arrogance
Without hostility
Without Pride
Without resistance
Without violence.
If these things prosper and grow old,
This is called not-Tao.
Not-Tao soon ends.

31

Fine weapons are ill-omened tools.
They are hated.
Therefore the old Tao ignores them.
At home, honour the left.
In war, honor the right.
Good omens honour the left.
Bad omens honour the right.
The lieutenant on the left,
The general on the right
As in funeral ceremonies.
Weapons are ill-omened,
Not proper instruments.
When their use can't be avoided,
Calm restraint is best.
Don't think they are beautiful.
Those who think they are beautiful
Rejoice in killing people.
Those who rejoice in killing people
Cannot achieve their purpose in this world.
When many people are killed
We feel sorrow and grief.
A great victory
Is a funeral ceremony.

32

Tao endures without a name.
Though simple and slight,
No one under heaven can master it.
If kings and lords could posses it,
All beings would become their guests.
Heaven and earth together
Would drip sweet dew
Equally on all people
Without regulation.
Begin to make order and names arise.
Names lead to more names—
And to knowing when to stop.
Tao's presence in this world

Is like valley streams
Flowing into rivers and seas.

33

Knowing others is intelligent.
Knowing yourself is enlightened.
Conquering others takes force.
Conquering yourself is true strength.
Knowing what is enough is wealth.
Forging ahead shows inner resolve.
Hold your ground and you will last long.
Die without perishing and your life will endure.

34

Great Tao overflows.
To the left
To the right.
All beings owe their life to it
And do not depart from it.
It acts without a name.
It clothes and nourishes all beings
But does not become their master.
Enduring without desires,
It may be called slight.
All beings return to it,
But it does not become their master.
It may be called immense.
By not making itself great,
It can do great things.

35

Hold the great elephant—
The great image—
And the world moves.
Moves without danger in safety and peace.
Music and sweets
Make passing guests pause.
But the Tao emerges
Flavourless and bland.
Look—you won't see it.
Listen—
You won't hear it.
Use it—
You will never use it up.

36

To collect, first scatter.
To Weaken, first strengthen.

To abolish, first establish.
To conclude, first initiate.
This is called subtle illumination.
Soft and weak overcome stiff and strong.
Fish cannot escape the deep pool.
A country's sharpest weapons
Cannot be displayed.

37

Tao endures without a name,
Yet nothing is left undone.
If kings and lords could possess it,
All beings would transform themselves.
Transformed, they desire to create;
I quiet them through nameless simplicity.
Then there is no desire.
No desire is serenity,
And the world settles of itself.

38

High Te? No Te!
That's what Te is.
Low Te doesn't lack Te;
That's what Te is not.
Those highest in Te take no action
And don't need to act.
Those lowest in Te take action
And do need to act.
Those highest in benevolence take action
But don't need to act.
Those highest in righteousness take action
And do need to act.
Those highest in propriety take action
And if people don't reciprocate
Roll up their sleeves and throw them out.
Therefore
Lose Tao
And Te follows.
Lose Te
And benevolence follows.
Lose benevolence
And righteousness follows.
Lose righteousness
And propriety follows.
Propriety dilutes loyalty and sincerity:
Confusion begins.
Foreknowledge glorifies the Tao:
Stupidity sets in.
And so the ideal person dwells
In substance, not dilution,

In reality, not glory,
Accepts one, rejects the other.

39

Of old, these attained the One:
Heaven attaining the One
Became clear.
Earth attaining the One
Became stable.
Spirits attaining the One
Became sacred.
Valleys attaining the One
Became bountiful.
Myriad beings attaining the One
Became fertile.
Lords and kings attaining the One
Purified the world.
If Heaven were not clear
It might split.
If Earth were not stable
It might erupt.
If spirits were not sacred
They might fade.
If valleys were not bountiful
They might wither.
If myriad beings were not fertile,
They might perish.
If rulers and lords were not noble,
They might stumble.
Therefore,
Noble has humble as its root,
High has low as its foundation.
Rulers and lords call themselves
Poor and lonely orphans.
Isn't this using humility as a root?
They use many carriages
But have no carriage;
They do not desire to glisten like jade
But drop like a stone.

40

Reversal is Tao's movement.
Yielding is Tao's practice.
All things originate from being.
Being originates from non-being.

41

The great scholar hearing the Tao
Tries to practice it.

The middling scholar hearing the Tao,
Sometimes has it, sometimes not.
The lesser scholar hearing the Tao
Has a good laugh.
Without that laughter
It wouldn't be Tao.
Therefore these sayings:
The bright road seems dark,
The road forward sees to retreat,
The level road seems rough.
Great Te seems hollow.
Great purity seems sullied.
Pervasive Te seems deficient.
Established Te seems furtive.
Simple truths seem to change.
The great square has no corners.
The great vessel is finished late.
The great sound is scarcely voiced.
The great image has no form.
Tao hides, no name.
Yet Tao alone gets things done.

42

Tao engenders One,
One engenders Two,
Two engenders Three,
Three engenders the ten thousand things.
The ten thousand things carry shade
And embrace sunlight.
Shade and sunlight, yin and yang,
Breath blending into harmony.
Humans hate
To be alone, poor, and hungry.
Yet kings and princes
Use these words as titles.
We gain by losing,
Lose by gaining.
What others teach, I also teach:
"A violent man does not die a natural death."
This is the basis of my teaching.

43

The softest thing in the world
Rides roughshod over the strongest.
No-thing enters no-space.
This teaches me the benefits of no-action.
Teaching without words
Benefit without action—
Few in this world can attain this.

44

Name or body: which is closer?
Body or possessions: which means more?
Gain or loss: which one hurts?
Extreme love exacts a great price.
Many possessions entail a heavy loss.
Know what is enough—
Abuse nothing.
Know when to stop—Harm nothing.
This is how to last for a long time.

45

Great accomplishment seems unfinished
But its use is continuous.
Great fullness seems empty
But in use is inexhaustible.
Great straightness seems bent,
Great skill seems clumsy,
Great eloquence seems mute.
Exertion overcomes cold.
Calm overcomes heat.
Pure calm is the norm under heaven.

46

With Tao under heaven
Stray horses fertilize the fields.
Without Tao under heaven
Warhorses are bred at the frontier.
There is no greater calamity
Than not knowing what is enough.
There is no greater fault
Than desire for success.
Therefore,
Knowing that enough is enough
Is always
Enough.

47

Without going out the door,
Know the world.
Without peeping through the window,
See heaven's Tao.
The further you travel,
The less you know.
This is why the Sage
Knows without budging,
Identifies without looking,
Does without trying.

48

Pursue knowledge, gain daily.
Pursue Tao, lose daily.
Lose and again lose,
Arrive at non-doing.
Non-doing—and nothing not done.
Take the entire world as nothing.
Make the least effort,
And the world escapes you.

49

The Sage has no set heart.
Ordinary people's hearts
Become the Sage's heart.
People who are good
I treat well.
People who are not good
I also treat well:
Te as goodness.
Trustworthy people
I trust. Untrustworthy people
I also trust.
Te as trust.
Sages create harmony under heaven
Blending their hearts with the world.
Ordinary people fix their eyes and ears upon them,
But Sages become the world's children.

50

Emerge into life, enter death,
Life is only the thirteen body parts.
Death is only the thirteen body parts.
Human life, moving towards death,
Is the same thirteen.
Why is this?
Because life gives life to substance.
You have heard of people
Good at holding on to life.
Walking overland they don't avoid
Rhinos and tigers.
In battle they don't arm themselves.
The rhino's horn find nothing to gore;
The tiger's claws find nothing to flay,
Weapons find nothing to pierce.
Why is this?
They have no mortal spot.

51

Tao bears them
Te nurses them
Events form them
Energy completes them.
Therefore the ten thousand beings
Honour Tao and respect Te.
Tao is honoured
Te is respected
Because they do not give orders
But endure in their own nature.
Therefore,
Tao bears them and Te nurses them,
Rears them,
Raises them,
Shelters them,
Nurtures them,
Supports them,
Protects them.
Bears them without owning them,
Helps them without coddling them,
Rears them without ruling them.
This is called original Te.

52

The world has a source: the world's mother.
Once you have the mother,
You know the children.
Once you know the children,
Return to the mother.
Your body dies.
There is no danger.
Block the passage,
Bolt the gate:
No strain
Until your life ends.
Open the passage,
Take charge of things
No relief
Until your life ends.
Seeing the small is called brightness
Maintaining gentleness is called strength.
Use this brightness to return to brightness.
Don't cling to your body's woes.
Then you can learn endurance.

53

Having some knowledge
When walking the Great Tao

Only brings fear.
The Great Tao is very smooth,
But people like rough trails.
The government is divided,
Fields are overgrown,
Granaries are empty.
But the nobles' clothes are gorgeous,
Their belts show off swords,
And they are glutted with food and drink.
Personal wealth is excessive.
This is called thieves' endowment,
But it is not Tao.

54

Well planted, not uprooted.
Well embraced, never lost.
Descendants will continue
The ancestral rituals.
Maintain oneself:
Te becomes real.
Maintain the family:
Te becomes abundant.
Maintain the community:
Te becomes extensive.
Maintain the country:
Te becomes public.
Maintain the world:
Te becomes omnipresent.
Therefore,
Through self contemplate self,
Through family contemplate family,
Through community contemplate community,
Through country contemplate country,
Through world contemplate world.
How do I know the world?
Like this!

55

Be filled with Te,
Like a baby:
Wasps, scorpions and vipers
Do not sting it.
Fierce tigers do not stalk it.
Birds of prey do not attack it.
Bones weak, muscles soft,
But its grasp is tight.
It does not yet know
Union of male and female,
But its sex is formed,
Its vital essence complete.

It can scream all day and not get hoarse,
Its harmony is complete.
Knowing harmony is called endurance.
Knowing endurance is called illumination.
Increasing life is called fortune.
Mind controlling energy is called power.
When beings prosper and grow old,
Call them not-Tao.
Not-Tao soon ends.

56

Those who know don't talk.
Those who talk don't know.
Block the passage
Bolt the gate
Blunt the sharp
Untie the knot
Blend with the light
Become one with the dust

This is called original unity.
It can't be embraced
It can't be escaped,
It can't be helped
It can't be harmed,
It can't be exalted
It can't be despised,
Therefore it is revered under Heaven.

57

Use the unexpected to govern the country,
Use surprise to wage war,
Use non-action to win the world.
How do I know?
Like this!
The more prohibitions and rules,
The poorer people become.
The sharper people's weapons,
The more they riot.
The more skilled their techniques,
The more grotesque their works.
The more elaborate the laws,
The more they commit crimes.
Therefore the Sage says,
I do nothing
And people transform themselves.
I enjoy serenity
And people govern themselves.
I cultivate emptiness
And people become prosperous.

I have no desires
And people simplify themselves.

58

If government is muted and muffled
People are cool and refreshed.
If government investigates and intrudes,
People are worn down and hopeless.
Bad fortune rests upon good fortune.
Good luck hides within bad luck.
Who knows how it will end?
If there is no principle
Principle reverts to disorder,
Good reverts to calamity,
People's confusion hardens and lingers on.
Therefore the Sage squares without cutting,
Corners without dividing,
Straightens without extending,
Shines without dazzling.

59

Governing people and serving heaven
Is like living off the land.
Living sparingly and responding quickly
Means accumulating Te.
There is nothing that cannot be overcome.
There is no limit.
You can become the country
And the country's mother, and nourish and extend it.
This is called deep roots, firm base.
This is the Tao of living long and seeing far.

60

Govern big countries
Like you cook a little fish.
When Tao harmonizes the world,
Demons lose their power.
Not that demons lose their power,
But their power does not harm people.
Not that their power does not harm people,
But the Sage does not harm people.
If neither does harm,
Then Te flows and returns.

61

A great nation flows down
To be the world's pool,
The female under heaven

In stillness
The female constantly overcomes the male,
In stillness
Takes the low place.
Therefore a great nation
Lowers itself
And wins over a small one.
A small nation keeps itself low
And wins over a great one.
Sometimes becoming low wins,
Sometimes staying low wins.
A great nation desires nothing more
Than to unite and protect people.
A small nation desires nothing more
Than to enter the service of people.
When both get what they wish
The great one should be low.

62

Tao is the mysterious center of all things,
A treasure for those who are good,
A refuge for those who are not.
Beautiful words can be traded,
Noble deeds can enhance reputations,
But if people lack them,
Why should they be rejected?
When the Son of Heaven is enthroned
And the Three Ministers installed,
Presenting jade discs
And four-horse chariots
Cannot compare to sitting still
And offering the Tao.
The ancients honoured this Tao.
Didn't they say:
Through it seekers find,
Through it the guilty escape?
This is why Tao is honoured under Heaven.

63

Act without acting.
Serve without serving.
Taste without tasting.
Big, little,
Many, few,
Repay hatred with Te.
Map difficult with easy
Approach great through narrow.
The most difficult things in the world
Must be accomplished through the easiest.
The greatest things in the world

Must be accomplished through the smallest.
Therefore the Sage
Never attempts great things and so accomplishes
    them.
Quick promises
Mean little trust.
Everything easy
Means great difficulty.
Thus for the Sage everything is difficult,
And so in the end
Nothing is difficult.

64

At rest is easy to hold.
Not yet impossible is easy to plan.
Brittle is easy to break.
Fine is easy to scatter.
Create before it exists.
Lead before it goes astray.
A tree too big to embrace
Is born from a slender shoot.
A nine-story rises from a pile of earth.
A thousand-mile journey
Begins with a single step.
Act and you ruin it.
Grasp and you lose it.
Therefore the Sage
Does not act
And so does not ruin.
Does not grasp
And so does not lose.
People commonly ruin their work
When they are near success.
Proceed at the end as at the beginning
And your work won't be ruined.
Therefore the Sage
Desires no desires
Prizes no prizes
Studies no studies
And returns
To what others pass by.
The Sage
Helps all beings find their nature,
But does not presume to act.

65

Taoist rulers of old
Did not enlighten people
But left them dull.
People are difficult to govern

Because they are very clever.
Therefore,
Ruling through cleverness leads to rebellion.
Not leading through cleverness
Brings good fortune.
Know these two things
And understanding the enduring pattern.
Understand the enduring pattern:
This is called original Te.
Original Te goes deep and far.
All things reverse
Return
And reach the great headwaters.

66

Rivers and seas
Can rule the hundred valleys
Because they are good at lying low
They are lords of the valleys.
Therefore those who would be above
Must speak as if they are below
Those who would lead
Must speak as if they are behind.
In this way the Sage dwells above
And the people are not burdened.
Dwells in front
And they are not hindered.
Therefore the whole world
Is delighted and unwearied.
Since the Sage does not contend
No one can contend with the Sage.

67

Everyone under heaven calls my Tao great,
And unlike anything else.
It is great only because
It is unlike anything else.
If it were like anything else
It would stretch and become thin.
I have three treasures to maintain and conserve:
The first is compassion.
The second is frugality.
The third is not presuming
To be first under heaven.
Compassion leads to courage.
Frugality allows generosity.
Not presuming to be first
Creates a lasting instrument.
Nowadays, People reject compassion
But want to be brave,

Reject frugality
But want to be generous,
Reject humility
And want to come first.
This is death.
Compassion:
Attack with it and win.
Defend with it and stand firm.
Heaven aids and protects
Through compassion.

68

The accomplished person is not aggressive.
The good soldier is not hot-tempered.
The best conqueror does not engage the enemy.
The most effective leader takes the lowest place.
This is called the Te of not contending.
This is called the power of the leader.
This is called matching Heaven's ancient ideal.

69

There is a saying in the army:
I do not presume to be the master,
But become the guest.
I do not dare advance an inch,
But retreat a foot.
This is called moving without moving,
Rolling up sleeves without showing your arms,
Repelling without opposing,
Wielding without a weapon.
There is no disaster greater than
Contempt for the enemy.
Contempt for the enemy—
What a treasure is lost!
Therefore,
When the fighting gets hot,
Those who grieve will conquer.

70

My words are very easy to understand,
Very easy to practice.
No one under heaven can understand them,
No one can practice them.
Words have ancestors,
Deeds have masters.
If people don't understand this,
They don't understand me.
Few understand me,
And that is my value.

Therefore the Sage wears rough clothing
And carries Jade inside.

71

Know not-knowing: supreme.
Not know knowing: faulty
Only faulting faults is faultless.
The Sage is faultless
By faulting faults,
And so is without fault.

72

When people are not in awe of power,
Power becomes great.
Do not intrude into their homes,
Do not make their lives weary.
If you do not weary them,
They will not become weary of you.
Therefore the Sage
Has self-knowledge without self-display,
Self-love without personal pride,
Rejects one, accepts the other.

73

Courage to dare kills,
Courage not to dare saves.
One brings profit, one brings harm.
Of these two, one is good, and one is harmful.
Some are not favored by heaven.
Who knows why?
Even the wise consider it a difficult question.
Heaven hates what it hates—
Who knows why!
Even the Sage finds it difficult.
Heaven's Tao does not contend
But prevails,
Does not speak,
But responds,
Is not summoned,
But arrives,
Is utterly still,
But plans all actions.
Heaven's net is wide, wide,
Loose—
But nothing slips through.

74

If people do not fear death,

How dare you threaten them with death?
But if people with a normal fear of death
Are about to do something vicious,
And I could seize and execute them,
Who would dare?
There is always an official executioner.
Trying to take the executioner's place,
Is like trying to replace a master woodworker—
Few would not slice their own hands.

75

People are hungry.
When rulers tax grain
People are hungry.
People are rebellious.
When rulers are active
People are rebellious.
People ignore death.
When searching only for life's bounty
People ignore death.
Only those who do not strive after life
Truly respect life.

76

Humans are born soft and weak.
They die stiff and strong.
The ten thousand plants and trees
Are born soft and tender,
And die withered and sere.
The stiff and strong
Are Death's companions
The soft and weak
Are Life's companions.
Therefore the strongest armies do not conquer,
The greatest trees are cut down.
The strong and great sink down.
The soft and weak rise up.

77

Heaven's Tao
Is a stretched bow,
Pulling down on the top
Pulling up on the bottom.
If it's too much, cut.
If it's not enough,
Add on to it:
Heaven's
Tao.
The Human Route

Is not like this,
Depriving the poor,
Offering to the rich.
Who has a surplus
And still offers it to the world?
Only those with Tao.
Therefore the Sage
Acts and expects nothing,
Accomplishes and does not linger,
Has no desire to seem worthy.

78

Nothing in the world is soft and weak as water.
But when attacking the hard and strong
Nothing can conquer so easily.
Weak overcomes strong,
Soft overcomes hard.
Everyone knows this,
No one attains it.
Therefore the Sage says:
Accept a country's filth
And become master of its sacred soil.
Accepts country's ill fortune
And become king under heaven.
True words resemble their opposites.

79

Appease great hatred
And hatred will remain.
How can this be good?
Therefore the Sage
Holds the tally
But does not judge people.
Those who have Te
Control the tally.
Those who lack Te
Collect their due.
Heaven has no favourites
But endures in good people.

80

Small country, few people—
Hundreds of devices,
But none are used.
People ponder on death
And don't travel far.
They have carriages and boats,
But no one goes on board;
Weapons and armour,

But no one brandishes them.
They use knotted cords for counting.
Sweet is their food,
Beautiful their clothes,
Peaceful their homes,
Delightful their customs.
Neighboring countries are so close
You can hear their chickens and dogs.
But people grow old and die
Without needing to come and go.

81

Sincere words are not pretty.
Pretty words are not sincere.

Good people do not quarrel.
Quarrelsome people are not good.
The wise are not learned.
The learned are not wise.
The Sage is not acquisitive—
Has enough
By doing for others,
Has even more
By giving to others.
Heaven's Tao Benefits and does not harm.
The Sage's Tao
Acts and does not contend.

Glossary

jade	a semiprecious gemstone, usually greenish
Sage	wise person
Tao	a variant of *dao*, or "the way"
Te	a variant of *de*, loosely translated as "virtue"
Valley Spirit	another name for the "mother," the principle of generation and the feminine spirit

The angel Azazel, head of the fallen angels

(The Angel Azazel [pen & ink with w/c heightened with bodycolour], Stanhope, John Roddam Spencer [1829-1908] / Private Collection / Photo © The Maas Gallery, London / The Bridgeman Art Library International)

BOOK OF ENOCH

"And now, the giants, who are produced from the spirits and flesh, shall be called evil spirits upon the earth, and on the earth shall be their dwelling."

Overview

The book of Enoch is an ancient religious work that presents esoteric wisdom and examines the origin of sin, blending ancient Jewish history and Christian-like views. It was probably written in either Hebrew or Aramaic and perhaps in both languages. It survives, however, in an Ethiopic language called Ge'ez, while fragments of the book exist in Greek and Latin. Scholars agree that the five portions of the book were written over a period of perhaps two centuries, from 300 to 100 BCE, most probably in or around Jerusalem by the Essenes, a Jewish sect. These texts were then compiled into a single work, often referred to today as 1 Enoch, to distinguish it from 2 Enoch, which survives only in the Old Slavonic language, and 3 Enoch, which was written in about the fifth or sixth century CE.

The book of Enoch is one of the apocryphal books of the Bible. *Apocrypha,* a Greek word meaning "hidden," "esoteric," or "of questionable authenticity," refers to books that were never included in the official Bible because they were not considered divinely inspired or because they were of spurious or unknown origin. Additionally, biblical scholars refer to the book of Enoch as *pseudepigraphical,* meaning that although the book is ascribed to a Hebrew patriarch—in this case, Enoch—scholars generally agree that the book's five sections were each written by different authors.

The book is significant because it is one of the most extended early examples of apocalyptic literature. The word *apocalyptic* in modern times is generally taken to refer to catastrophic end-of-the-world events, but in biblical studies the word refers to literature that presumably reveals ancient, secret, mysterious wisdom, often about the future but sometimes about past events. The book of Enoch looks back to take as its reference point the story of Noah's Flood, as recounted in the book of Genesis, and explores such issues as the fall of the angels, the origin of sin in the world, judgment, and the nature of heaven and hell. In this way it resembles, for example, Revelation (the last book of the New Testament) rather than a more historical book such as any of the Gospels or Genesis itself, in the Old Testament.

It is believed that the book of Enoch was held in high regard for at least five hundred years, revered by the Jews and early Christians, but that it lost this status among some Hebrew and Christian theologians because of its controversial discussion of the fallen angels as the origin of sin. It was thus excluded from the official Christian canon at the Council of Laodicea in about 364 CE. Consequently, the book of Enoch was lost for a thousand years, until it was discovered in 1773 by the Scottish explorer James Bruce in Ethiopia, where it had been saved and kept alongside other books of the Bible.

Context

The historical context in which the book of Enoch was written is referred to as Second Temple Judaism. This period began with the rebuilding of the Temple in Jerusalem in 520–516 BCE (the First Temple having been destroyed by the Babylonians in 586 BCE) and ended with the destruction of the Second Temple in 70 CE. This was a time of important changes in Judaism. In particular, it was during this period that the Hebrew Bible was assembled. As such, it marked the roots of what came to be called rabbinic Judaism, which originated in the teachings of the Pharisees, who stressed the need for critical interpretation of the Jewish Torah, the first five books of the Old Testament. This form of Judaism emphasizes the study of the Talmud—the record of rabbinic discussions of law, philosophy, customs, traditions, and ethics—and debate regarding the theological and legal issues it raises.

The Second Temple period was also a time of considerable turmoil in Jerusalem and the Middle East. After Alexander the Great died in 323 BCE, the Greek empire broke into three regions: the Syrian portion, ruled by the Seleucid Dynasty; the Egyptian portion, ruled by the Ptolemaic Dynasty; and Greece proper, including Athens, Sparta, and other city-states. Jerusalem fell under the Ptolemies of Egypt. Matters changed, however, in 198 BCE, when the Seleucids, led by King Antiochus III, defeated the Ptolemies and assumed control of Palestine. His successor, Antiochus IV, felt that the Seleucid position was weak; the Ptolemies were a continuing threat, as was the Roman

520–516 BCE	■ The Second Temple is built in Jerusalem.
323 BCE	■ Alexander the Great dies, leaving the Roman Empire to break into three competing regions.
CA. 300 –200 BCE	■ The Hebrew Torah is translated into Greek.
CA. 300 –100 BCE	■ The book of Enoch is written.
198 BCE	■ The Seleucids, led by King Antiochus III, defeat the Ptolemies and assume control of Palestine.
167 BCE	■ Antiochus IV begins persecution of the Jews in Palestine.
165 BCE	■ The Second Temple is rededicated after the success of the Maccabean revolt.
CA. 364 CE	■ The book of Enoch is excluded from the Christian Bible by the Council of Laodicea.
1773	■ James Bruce, a famous Scottish traveler, obtains copies of the book of Enoch in Ethiopia and takes the copies to Europe.
1947 –1956	■ Fragments of the book of Enoch are found among the Dead Sea Scrolls.

translation. Jewish culture and the Hellenic culture of the Greeks were becoming intertwined.

Matters were complicated by divisions among the Jews. On the one hand, some Jews in the empire became entirely Hellenized—that is, they adopted the dominant Greek culture. They spoke Greek, sent their children to Greek schools, and adopted Greek customs and traditions. In contrast stood traditional Jews, who maintained their religious beliefs as well as the culture and traditions they had inherited from the time of the patriarchs. But making matters tenser, beginning in the third century BCE a division emerged within the group of traditional religious Jews. On one side of this division were the Sadducees, who did not accept the divinity of the oral Torah, or the religious revelations Moses had acquired on Mount Sinai that were not written down. The Sadducees accepted only the written Torah, which they interpreted literally, even when the laws of the written Torah were obscure, even incomprehensible. They believed that God has no concern with the activities of humans and, in particular, has no concern about whether any human activity is evil. They regarded any choice between good and evil as a choice made by humans. They did not believe in the immortality of the soul or in punishment or rewards in an afterlife. On the other side of the division were the Pharisees, who followed traditional, orthodox teachings and accepted the truth of the oral Torah. The Greek overlords in Palestine found the "modern-thinking" Sadducees more compatible than the stodgy Pharisees.

Matters worsened again in the late second century BCE when the Hellenized Jews enlisted the support of Antiochus IV in an effort to Hellenize all Jews in the empire—in effect, to destroy traditional Judaism. What followed was a kind of reign of terror (as described in the biblical book of Maccabees). Antiochus seized control of the Temple; tried to eliminate the Jewish calendar; forbade the observance of the Sabbath, Passover, Rosh Hashanah, Yom Kippur, and other major Jewish holy days; and outlawed studying the Torah and keeping the Old Testament's kosher dietary laws. Copies of the Torah were burned, and the Temple was defiled by pagan sacrifices. Antiochus also forbade the practice of circumcision. Jews were forced to eat pork, and those who refused were tortured. Altars to the Greek god Zeus were constructed in the villages. Being a high priest at the Temple became a political appointment, and because the Sadducees were more Greek than Jewish, they were appointed to the highest positions in the priestly class—and accordingly became corrupt.

Ultimately, mainstream Jews—that is, the traditional Jews and Pharisees who were not Hellenized and did not have any rapport with the Greeks—revolted. A rebel army called the Maccabees seized control of parts of Palestine, reasserted their traditions, and reduced the influence of the Greeks. After Judas Maccabee's victory in the revolt, the Jews rededicated the Temple in 165 BCE, an event celebrated in Jewish tradition as the festival of Hanukkah. It is in this historical context that the book of Enoch examines the origin of sin and comments obliquely on the corruption of the priestly class.

Empire. Further, he believed that the Jews of Palestine were resistant to the imposition of Greek culture. In fact, to the Greeks, the Jews were an alien culture, particularly because the Jews were monotheistic, meaning that they believed in a single deity; in contrast, the Greeks were polytheistic, meaning that they believed in a panoply of gods and goddesses. For their part, however, the Jews of Palestine admired the Greeks, particularly the value they placed on education and intellectual pursuits. The Hebrew Torah was translated into Greek in the third century BCE, and this Greek version came to be called the Septuagint, named after the seventy rabbis who carried out the

About the Author

As noted, the book of Enoch is one of the most prominent pseudepigraphical books. Although it was ascribed to Enoch, it was most likely written by several unknown authors over a two-century period. The scrolls are traditionally identified with the ancient Jewish sect called the Essenes, though some recent interpretations have challenged this association and argue that the scrolls were penned by priests, Zadokites (Sadducees), or other unknown Jewish groups. The Essenes lived throughout Palestine in their own communities, and they are believed to have founded a small community in Khirbat Qumran, just off the northwestern coast of the Dead Sea. They are considered to be responsible for the Dead Sea Scrolls. The attribution of the book to Enoch at the time was likely intended to place the book within the patriarchal tradition and thus give it more credence and weight. The Enoch of the Bible supposedly lived approximately seven hundred years before the Flood, when, according to the Old Testament, most of earth's physical features had not been formed—so the mention of mountains tends to disprove that Enoch wrote the book.

Nevertheless, the book is attributed to the Hebrew patriarch Enoch, whose biography is found in the Bible in Genesis 5:21–24. Enoch was the seventh descendant from Adam. His father was Jared, and at the age of sixty-five he became the father of Methuselah, the oldest man to live on earth. He was also the great-grandfather of Noah, the only man who lived among a wicked generation and was saved from the flood that destroyed the earth. Enoch lived on earth for 365 years and did not die like his predecessors but was taken up to heaven.

The story of Enoch in the Bible is very short, consisting of only three verses, but reference is made to him in two other books of the New Testament. In Hebrews 11:5 he is mentioned among the fathers of the faith, and he is quoted as referring to God's judgment of "ungodly sinners" in the one-chapter book of Jude, verses 14–15. The question raised by this quotation is whether Enoch actually left a book behind or whether the quote is from some other source such as oral tradition. From the very short story of Enoch in the Bible and the tribute to him in Hebrews, it is understood that Enoch lived a righteous life and God rewarded him by taking him into heaven.

Explanation and Analysis of the Document

The book of Enoch consists of five parts: "Book of the Watchers," "Book of Parables" (or the "Similitudes of Enoch"), "Astronomical Book" (or the "Book of the Heavenly Luminaries"), "Book of Dream Visions" (or just "Book of Dreams"), and "Epistle of Enoch." The section reproduced here is the "Book of the Watchers," beginning with Chapter VI. These thirty chapters describe the fall from heaven of the two hundred angels known as Watchers, so called because they were to watch over human affairs without interfering. These angels each make a decision to take

James Bruce

(James Bruce of Kinnaird, 1762 [oil on canvas], Batoni, Pompeo Girolamo [1708-87] / Scottish National Portrait Gallery, Edinburgh, Scotland / The Bridgeman Art Library International)

wives from the daughters of men on earth because these daughters are beautiful. Their resolve is to defile these women and have children by them. After taking an oath on Mount Hermon, they carry out their plan, but this action is to spell doom temporarily for the earth and permanently for the fallen angels. Enoch, considered righteous by God and the holy angels, is sent to tell the Watchers of their fate. During this assignment, he has visions in which he is spoken to by God, and he is later shown many places and secrets by the holy angels.

There is no single authoritative text of the book of Enoch. The most complete version is the one found in Ethiopia in the eighteenth century. Additionally, there exist fragments of the book in Greek and Latin. The passage reproduced here is an edited version that collates the texts. In some passages, editors have provided missing words in parentheses. Other passages remain garbled and obscure.

♦ Chapters VI–VII

These chapters deal with the fall of the angels, the "Watchers." The angels, the "children of heaven," lust after the "beautiful and comely" daughters on earth. The angels commune with one another to choose wives from these daughters and have children from them. Their leader is Semjaza, who urges the Watchers to take responsibility for the action they are about to embark upon, implying that he is aware that what they are about to do is sinful. Semjaza's fellow angels—two hundred in all—take an oath on Mount Hermon to go ahead with the plan. Having sworn this oath, the two hundred angels take for themselves wives and begin to defile themselves with them.

Biblical scholars have tried to interpret these chapters in light of traditional biblical history. They argue that the "angels" were not really angels but rather the male descendants of Seth, the third son of Adam and Eve, while the daughters were the female descendants of Cain. Hence, these sons of Seth defiled themselves by marrying unbelievers, resulting in corruption and moral decadence. Additionally, these chapters suggest an origin for sin in the world: the intermixing of angels and humans, or spirit and flesh. It was for this reason that the book of Enoch was regarded as noncanonical, for traditional Judeo-Christian theology holds that sin comes from breaking the law—specifically, from the fall of humankind in the Garden of Eden, when Adam and Eve violated God's law.

The Watchers teach these wives all sort of charms and enchantments and the "cutting of roots," and they make their wives acquainted with plants. The meaning of this passage is obscure but could refer to the acquisition of divine secrets not intended for humankind. The union of the fallen angels and their wives results in the birth of giants, the Nephilim, each of whose height is three hundred ells (an ell is a unit of measure about the length of the forearm, related etymologically to the word *elbow*). These giants cannot be sustained by the "acquisitions of men," so they consume humankind, animals, and, finally, one another's flesh and blood. Perhaps the immense size of the Nephilim signifies the enormity of the evil that has spread through the earth.

♦ **Chapters VIII–XI**

The Watchers teach their wives about metalworking, enchantments, and astrology, resulting in godlessness and fornication. This suggests that there is a catalog of knowledge and wisdom about the stars, planets, and elements that perhaps was not intended for humans. People are led astray, becoming completely corrupt and subsequently perishing. However, in their perishing, their souls cry out and go up to heaven and are heard by the angels of God: Michael, Uriel, Raphael, and Gabriel. The angels bring the petition of the souls of men to God, giving details of what the angels who descended from heaven have taught the men of the world.

God, the "Most High," responds to the angels' petition by giving each one of them specific assignments concerning punishments due to the fallen angels, their wives, and their children. In addition, they are sent to heal the earth. Uriel, whose name means "Light of God" and who is one of the angels prominently mentioned in esoteric texts, is sent to Noah, instructing him to hide himself and his offspring to preserve the generations of the world. Uriel also reveals to Noah God's plan to destroy the earth by flood. Additionally, God instructs the angel Michael to "destroy all the spirits of the reprobate and the children of the Watchers, because they have wronged mankind. Destroy all wrong from the face of the earth and let every evil work come to an end."

In an extended metaphor, the spreading of righteousness is described in terms of the sowing of seeds and planting.

♦ **Chapters XII–XIV**

While these events are taking place, Enoch's family is unaware of his whereabouts. What readers gather from Chapter XII is that Enoch has been hidden because of the activities of the Watchers and is with the holy angels. The holy angels, considering Enoch's righteousness, send him to the Watchers to tell them of the impending destruction of their children. Enoch carries out the assignment, telling the fallen angels of the great coming punishment; this causes fear among the fallen Watchers, who ask Enoch to petition the Lord for forgiveness. Enoch acquiesces to their request and writes out petitions concerning their forgiveness. He reads them until he falls asleep at the waters of Dan. Here, he dreams of having visions of chastisement, with a voice bidding him to reprimand the sons of heaven. Enoch tells the fallen Watchers that God will not grant their petition, and from thenceforth they will no longer ascend into heaven and on the earth they would be in bonds. In Chapter XIV, Enoch describes in allegorical detail his vision of heaven.

♦ **Chapters XV–XVI**

In these chapters, Enoch describes in further detail the visions he had at the waters of Dan. He first records the words of God to him concerning the fallen Watchers. God began by telling Enoch to tell the Watchers that angels were meant to intercede for men and not men for angels; the suggestion is that evil in the world is a kind of inversion of the natural order. He told Enoch that because of their sin, the children born to them, a product of spirit and flesh, would be called evil spirits; hence their dwelling would be on earth, causing much affliction, oppression, destruction, and war. God reemphasized that the giants would be destroyed. Finally, he sent Enoch to tell the Watchers that all the mysteries they made known to the women were worthless, as all the mysteries had not yet been revealed to them in heaven before they left.

♦ **Chapters XVII–XIX**

These chapters describe Enoch's first journey through the earth and Sheol—a place of darkness to which all dead souls go and where they are denied the light of God. The spirits of the dead will reside here until the death and Resurrection of the Messiah allow the righteous spirits to depart to Paradise; likewise, the wicked spirits of men are cast in Sheol, where they await judgment. Here, Enoch sees the luminaries (celestial or heavenly bodies), the treasures of the stars, thunder, lightning, and rivers. Finally, he is taken to a place at the end of heaven and earth that became "a prison for the stars and the host of heaven." In this place the fallen angels will stand until the Day of Judgment; similarly, judgment will be pronounced on the women they have sinned with and who are described as sirens, or seducers. This punishment could be seen as a curse upon these women, who were to live their lives leading men astray. Enoch remarks that these visions were seen by him alone and that no other man was to see

"And it came to pass when the children of men had multiplied that in those days were born unto them beautiful and comely daughters. And the angels, the children of the heaven, saw and lusted after them, and said to one another: 'Come, let us choose us wives from among the children of men and beget us children.'"

"And all the others together with them took unto themselves wives, and each chose for himself one, and they began to go in unto them and to defile themselves with them, and they taught them charms and enchantments, and the cutting of roots, and made them acquainted with plants. And they became pregnant, and they bare great giants, whose height was three thousand ells."

"Then said the Most High, the Holy and Great One spake, and sent Uriel to the son of Lamech, and said to him: 'Go to Noah and . . . reveal to him the end that is approaching: that the whole earth will be destroyed, and a deluge is about to come upon the whole earth, and will destroy all that is on it. And now instruct him that he may escape and his seed may be preserved for all the generations of the world.'"

"Before these things Enoch was hidden, and no one of the children of men knew where he was hidden, and where he abode, and what had become of him. And his activities had to do with the Watchers, and his days were with the holy ones."

"And now, the giants, who are produced from the spirits and flesh, shall be called evil spirits upon the earth, and on the earth shall be their dwelling."

"And I, Enoch, alone saw the vision, the ends of all things: and no man shall see as I have seen."

what he had seen. Again, the theology of the book of Enoch involves revelations of the secrets of the cosmos—secrets that the Watchers should not have shared with their earthly wives. The book of Enoch was thus an early manifestation of esoteric wisdom. In this respect it contrasted sharply with the didactic, or instructional, wisdom of the canonical books of the Hebrew scripture.

♦ **Chapter XX–XXV**

Chapter XX gives the names and functions of the seven archangels in heaven. These archangels serve as guides and escorts to Enoch in his second journey through the earth and Sheol, interpreting for him the places he comes across and things he sees. Chapters XXI–XXV focus on Enoch's second journey through the earth and the underworld. Chapter XXI describes the beginning and final place of punishment of the fallen angels. In the next chapter, Enoch gives an account of Sheol, which he describes as being divided into sections. Raphael, his guide, explains to him that the four divisions have been made to separate the spirits of the dead. From here, Enoch is transported to the west ends of the earth, where he sees more visions. He sees seven magnificent mountains; one of them is isolated and resembles the seat of a throne with fragrant trees encircling it. Among these trees is one noteworthy for its fragrance and beauty. Michael explains that no mortal is permitted to touch it till the great judgment, when God will take vengeance on all. The fruits of the tree will be food for the righteous and holy, and it will be transplanted to the holy place, to the temple of the Lord. The allusion to the Tree of the Knowledge of Good and Evil in the Genesis account of the Garden of Eden is clear.

♦ **Chapters XXVI–XXXVI**

Enoch goes to the middle of the earth and marvels at a blessed place with trees, mountains, ravines, and streams; this place signifies the holy city of Jerusalem. In this same place, Enoch beholds an accursed valley, which Uriel explains is the valley for those who have uttered unsuitable words against the Lord. At the end of the thirty-second chapter, Enoch sees a very beautiful tree, which the angel Raphael explains is the tree of wisdom from which his old father and aged mother ate and learned wisdom. These parents are Adam and Eve, who were deceived into eating fruit of the Tree of the Knowledge of Good and Evil against God's instruction. Enoch's journey takes him to the ends of the earth and then the north, west, and south, and he blesses the Lord for his glorious wonders.

Audience

It is impossible to cite a specific audience for the book of Enoch in its time. It is not known who wrote its various parts, nor is it known specifically when they were written. Because the work is built around revelations of secret wisdom, it would have been of interest to Jewish mystics and others who regarded orthodox Hebrew scripture as incomplete. The book was read by early church fathers, who found it instructive but were not prepared to regard it as divinely inspired scripture. The book, however, is considered canonical by the Ethiopian Orthodox Church—and indeed it was not discovered in the West until the eighteenth century, when it was imported from Ethiopia to western Eu-

---

Questions for Further Study

1. The book of Enoch is referred to as an example of "apocalyptic" literature. What does this term mean in biblical studies? In what way is the book similar to the biblical book of Revelation, and how does it differ?

2. During the early years of the Christian Church, both Christianity and Judaism were in a state of turmoil, as new sects developed, heresies emerged, and contention arose about biblical books and which were canonical. What part did the book of Enoch and the events surrounding its production play in this turmoil? Why was this book not accepted as canonical, despite being admired by early church fathers and occupying a place in the canon of the Ethiopian Orthodox Church?

3. Imagine that you are an archeologist with a particular interest in religious history and that you discovered a new biblical text, perhaps one stored in an ancient monastery or museum. The text purports to have been written by one of Judas Maccabee's followers, and it excites you because it presents a widely differing version of events during this period in Jewish history. What would you do with the text? How would you authenticate it? Try to recreate the process of studying lost ancient texts from the standpoint of a historian or archeologist.

4. The book of "Enoch" almost certainly was not written by the biblical figure Enoch. Why, then, is it called the book of Enoch? More important, does the authorship of the book make any difference in the matter of its authority?

5. It is highly likely that most Christians have heard of such groups as the Pharisees and the Sadducees, whose names appear in readings from the Gospels at church services. It is also highly likely that most laypeople have only a vague understanding of who these groups were. Based on your reading of the entry, who were the Pharisees and Sadducees, and why was the distinction between the two groups important?

---

rope. It is not entirely surprising that the Christian Church in Ethiopia would retain the book of Enoch in its canon, for Ethiopian Orthodox Christianity is a blend of Christian and Jewish practices. For example, every Ethiopian Christian male is circumcised, the Sabbath (Saturday) is kept as holy, an ark (representing the Ark of the Covenant) is a key part of every church, and priests make sacrifices of goats and lambs for the sick. The peculiar blend of ancient Jewish history and Christian-like views in the book of Enoch makes the book appealing to the strain of Christianity adhered to by Ethiopian Christians.

Impact

The book of Enoch was read for about five hundred years and found approval among such early church theologians as Clement of Alexandria, Tertullian, Origen, and Saint Augustine. It was regarded as particularly valuable because it provided an explanation for some puzzling verses found in the book of Genesis. In Genesis 6, just before the exposition involving Noah and the Flood, readers are informed that "when men began to multiply on the face of the ground, and daughters were born to them, the sons of God saw that the daughters of men were fair; and they took to wife such of them as they chose." The passage goes on:

> Then the Lord said, "My spirit shall not abide in man for ever, for he is flesh, but his days shall be a hundred and twenty years." The Nephilim were on the earth in those days, and also afterward, when the sons of God came in to the daughters of men, and they bore children to them. These were the mighty men that were of old, the men of renown.

The passage continues by referring to the "wickedness of man" and men's "evil." The passage states that God was sorry that he had created human beings and concludes that he will "blot out man." Only Noah, who had "found favor in the eyes of the Lord," would be spared.

The book of Enoch, though, was considered heretical by the early Church. At the Council of Laodicea in about 364, it was not included in the official biblical canon, although the passage from the council's proceedings that lists the officially recognized books of the Bible is of somewhat doubtful authenticity. Thus, the attitude of the Church to the book of Enoch is shrouded in some mystery. What is known is that the book essentially disappeared in the West for over a thousand years.

Modern biblical scholars have taken renewed interest in the book of Enoch, for in many respects it bears similarities to the New Testament. For example, it espouses the reality of the Kingdom of God and the need for repentance. It also discusses such matters as the Messiah, the end of the world, and final judgment. But although early theologians held the book in high esteem, it was never referred to by Jesus Christ or the apostles and is not thought of as scriptural. Rather, it provides insights into the thinking of Jewish writers in the centuries immediately before the advent of the Christian age, when Judaism was changing and conflict over historical teachings divided the Jewish community.

Further Reading

■ Books

Baigent, Michael, and Richard Leigh. *The Dead Sea Scrolls Deception*. London: Corgi, 1992.

Black, Matthew, James C. VanderKam, and Otto Neugebauer. *The Book of Enoch; or, I Enoch: A New English Edition*. Leiden, Netherlands: Brill, 1985.

Henry, Matthew. *Commentary on the Whole Bible, Complete and Unabridged*. Peabody, Mass.: Hendrickson, 2003.

Humphreys, David. *The Lost Book of Enoch*. London: Janus Publishing, 2005.

Knibb, Michael A. *Essays on the Book of Enoch and Other Early Jewish Texts and Traditions*. Leiden, Netherlands: Brill, 2009.

Ladd, John D. *Commentary on the Book of Enoch*. Longwood, Fla.: Xulon Press, 2008.

Reed, Annette Yoshiko. *Fallen Angels and the History of Judaism and Christianity: The Reception of Enochic Literature*. Cambridge, U.K.: Cambridge University Press, 2005.

VanderKam, James C. *Enoch and the Growth of an Apocalyptic Tradition*. Washington, D.C.: Catholic Biblical Association of America, 1984.

VanderKam, James C. *Enoch: A Man for All Generations*. Columbia: University of South Carolina Press, 1995.

■ Web Sites

Suter, David W. "Enoch as Precursor: The Role of the Enochic Manuscripts in the Qumran Literature." University of St. Andrews School of Divinity Web site.
http://www.st-andrews.ac.uk/divinity/rt/dss/guestlectures/suter

—Mary A. Afolabi

BOOK OF ENOCH

CHAPTER VI.

1. And it came to pass when the children of men had multiplied that in those days were born unto them beautiful and comely daughters. 2. And the angels, the children of the heaven, saw and lusted after them, and said to one another: "Come, let us choose us wives from among the children of men and beget us children." 3. And Semjaza, who was their leader, said unto them: "I fear ye will not indeed agree to do this deed, and I alone shall have to pay the penalty of a great sin." 4. And they all answered him and said: "Let us all swear an oath, and all bind ourselves by mutual imprecations not to abandon this plan but to do this thing." 5. Then sware they all together and bound themselves by mutual imprecations upon it. 6. And they were in all two hundred; who descended in the days of Jared on the summit of Mount Hermon, and they called it Mount Hermon, because they had sworn and bound themselves by mutual imprecations upon it. 7. And these are the names of their leaders: Semiazaz, their leader, Arakiba, Rameel, Kokabiel, Tamiel, Ramiel, Danel, Ezeqeel, Baraqijal, Asael, Armaros, Batarel, Ananel, Zaqiel, Samsapeel, Satarel, Turel, Jomjael, Sariel. 8. These are their chiefs of tens.

CHAPTER VII.

1. And all the others together with them took unto themselves wives, and each chose for himself one, and they began to go in unto them and to defile themselves with them, and they taught them charms and enchantments, and the cutting of roots, and made them acquainted with plants. 2. And they became pregnant, and they bare great giants, whose height was three thousand ells: 3. Who consumed all the acquisitions of men. And when men could no longer sustain them, 4. the giants turned against them and devoured mankind. 5. And they began to sin against birds, and beasts, and reptiles, and fish, and to devour one another's flesh, and drink the blood. 6. Then the earth laid accusation against the lawless ones.

CHAPTER VIII.

1. And Azazel taught men to make swords, and knives, and shields, and breastplates, and made known to them the metals of the earth and the art of working them, and bracelets, and ornaments, and the use of antimony, and the beautifying of the eyelids, and all kinds of costly stones, and all colouring tinctures. 2. And there arose much godlessness, and they committed fornication, and they were led astray, and became corrupt in all their ways. Semjaza taught enchantments, and root-cuttings, Armaros the resolving of enchantments, Baraqijal, (taught) astrology, Kokabel the constellations, Ezeqeel the knowledge of the clouds, Araqiel the signs of the earth, Shamsiel the signs of the sun, and Sariel the course of the moon. And as men perished, they cried, and their cry went up to heaven. . . .

CHAPTER IX.

1. And then Michael, Uriel, Raphael, and Gabriel looked down from heaven and saw much blood being shed upon the earth, and all lawlessness being wrought upon the earth. 2. And they said one to another: "The earth made without inhabitant cries the voice of their crying up to the gates of heaven. 3. And now to you, the holy ones of heaven, the souls of men make their suit, saying, 'Bring our cause before the Most High.'" 4. And they said to the Lord of the ages: "Lord of lords, God of gods, King of kings, and God of the ages, the throne of Thy glory (standeth) unto all the generations of the ages, and Thy name holy and glorious and blessed unto all the ages! 5. Thou hast made all things, and power over all things hast Thou: and all things are naked and open in Thy sight, and Thou seest all things, and nothing can hide itself from Thee. 6. Thou seest what Azazel hath done, who hath taught all unrighteousness on earth and revealed the eternal secrets which were (preserved) in heaven, which men were striving to learn: 7. And Semjaza, to whom Thou hast given authority to bear rule over his associates. 8. And they have gone to the daughters of men upon the earth, and have slept with the women, and have defiled themselves, and revealed to them

all kinds of sins. 9. And the women have borne giants, and the whole earth has thereby been filled with blood and unrighteousness. 10. And now, behold, the souls of those who have died are crying and making their suit to the gates of heaven, and their lamentations have ascended: and cannot cease because of the lawless deeds which are wrought on the earth. 11. And Thou knowest all things before they come to pass, and Thou seest these things and Thou dost suffer them, and Thou dost not say to us what we are to do to them in regard to these."

CHAPTER X.

1. Then said the Most High, the Holy and Great One spake, and sent Uriel to the son of Lamech, and said to him: 2. "Go to Noah and tell him in my name 'Hide thyself!' and reveal to him the end that is approaching: that the whole earth will be destroyed, and a deluge is about to come upon the whole earth, and will destroy all that is on it. 3. And now instruct him that he may escape and his seed may be preserved for all the generations of the world." 4. And again the Lord said to Raphael: "Bind Azazel hand and foot, and cast him into the darkness: and make an opening in the desert, which is in Dudael, and cast him therein. 5. And place upon him rough and jagged rocks, and cover him with darkness, and let him abide there for ever, and cover his face that he may not see light. 6. And on the day of the great judgement he shall be cast into the fire. And heal the earth which the angels have corrupted, and proclaim the healing of the earth, that they may heal the plague, and that all the children of men may not perish through all the secret things that the Watchers have disclosed and have taught their sons. 8. And the whole earth has been corrupted through the works that were taught by Azazel: to him ascribe all sin." 9. And to Gabriel said the Lord: "Proceed against the bastards and the reprobates, and against the children of fornication: and destroy the children of fornication and the children of the Watchers from amongst men and cause them to go forth: send them one against the other that they may destroy each other in battle: for length of days shall they not have. 10. And no request that they (their fathers) make of thee shall be granted unto their fathers on their behalf; for they hope to live an eternal life, and that each one of them will live five hundred years." 11. And the Lord said unto Michael: "Go, bind Semjaza and his associates who have united themselves with women so as to have de-

filed themselves with them in all their uncleanness. 12. And when their sons have slain one another, and they have seen the destruction of their beloved ones, bind them fast for seventy generations in the valleys of the earth, till the day of their judgement and of their consummation, till the judgement that is for ever and ever is consummated. 13. In those days they shall be led off to the abyss of fire: and to the torment and the prison in which they shall be confined for ever. And whosoever shall be condemned and destroyed will from thenceforth be bound together with them to the end of all generations. 15. And destroy all the spirits of the reprobate and the children of the Watchers, because they have wronged mankind. 16. Destroy all wrong from the face of the earth and let every evil work come to an end: and let the plant of righteousness and truth appear: and it shall prove a blessing; the works of righteousness and truth shall be planted in truth and joy for evermore. 17. And then shall all the righteous escape, And shall live till they beget thousands of children, And all the days of their youth and their old age Shall they complete in peace. 18. And then shall the whole earth be tilled in righteousness, and shall all be planted with trees and be full of blessing. 19. And all desirable trees shall be planted on it, and they shall plant vines on it: and the vine which they plant thereon shall yield wine in abundance, and as for all the seed which is sown thereon each measure (of it) shall bear a thousand, and each measure of olives shall yield ten presses of oil. 20. And cleanse thou the earth from all oppression, and from all unrighteousness, and from all sin, and from all godlessness: and all the uncleanness that is wrought upon the earth destroy from off the earth. 21. And all the children of men shall become righteous, and all nations shall offer adoration and shall praise Me, and all shall worship Me. And the earth shall be cleansed from all defilement, and from all sin, and from all punishment, and from all torment, and I will never again send (them) upon it from generation to generation and for ever.

CHAPTER XI.

1. And in those days I will open the store chambers of blessing which are in the heaven, so as to send them down upon the earth over the work and labour of the children of men. 2. And truth and peace shall be associated together throughout all the days of the world and throughout all the generations of men."

CHAPTER XII.

1. Before these things Enoch was hidden, and no one of the children of men knew where he was hidden, and where he abode, and what had become of him. 2. And his activities had to do with the Watchers, and his days were with the holy ones. 3. And I, Enoch was blessing the Lord of majesty and the King of the ages, and lo! the Watchers called me—Enoch the scribe—and said to me: 4. "Enoch, thou scribe of righteousness, go, declare to the Watchers of the heaven who have left the high heaven, the holy eternal place, and have defiled themselves with women, and have done as the children of earth do, and have taken unto themselves wives: 'Ye have wrought great destruction on the earth: 5. And ye shall have no peace nor forgiveness of sin: and inasmuch as they delight themselves in their children, 6. The murder of their beloved ones shall they see, and over the destruction of their children shall they lament, and shall make supplication unto eternity, but mercy and peace shall ye not attain.'"

CHAPTER XIII.

1. And Enoch went and said: "Azazel, thou shalt have no peace: a severe sentence has gone forth against thee to put thee in bonds: 2. And thou shalt not have toleration nor request granted to thee, because of the unrighteousness which thou hast taught, and because of all the works of godlessness and unrighteousness and sin which thou hast shown to men." 3. Then I went and spoke to them all together, and they were all afraid, and fear and trembling seized them. 4. And they besought me to draw up a petition for them that they might find forgiveness, and to read their petition in the presence of the Lord of heaven. 5. For from thenceforward they could not speak (with Him) nor lift up their eyes to heaven for shame of their sins for which they had been condemned. 6. Then I wrote out their petition, and the prayer in regard to their spirits and their deeds individually and in regard to their requests that they should have forgiveness and length of days. 7. And I went off and sat down at the waters of Dan, in the land of Dan, to the south of the west of Hermon: I read their petition till I fell asleep. 8. And behold a dream came to me, and visions fell down upon me, and I saw visions of chastisement, and a voice came bidding (me) I to tell it to the sons of heaven, and reprimand them. 9. And when I awaked, I came unto them, and they were all sitting gathered together, weeping in 'Abelsjail, which is between Lebanon and Seneser, with their faces covered. 10. And I recounted before them all the visions which I had seen in sleep, and I began to speak the words of righteousness, and to reprimand the heavenly Watchers.

CHAPTER XIV.

1. The book of the words of righteousness, and of the reprimand of the eternal Watchers in accordance with the command of the Holy Great One in that vision. 2. I saw in my sleep what I will now say with a tongue of flesh and with the breath of my mouth: which the Great One has given to men to converse therewith and understand with the heart. 3. As He has created and given to man the power of understanding the word of wisdom, so hath He created me also and given me the power of reprimanding the Watchers, the children of heaven. 4. I wrote out your petition, and in my vision it appeared thus, that your petition will not be granted unto you throughout all the days of eternity, and that judgement has been finally passed upon you: yea (your petition) will not be granted unto you. 5. And from henceforth you shall not ascend into heaven unto all eternity, and in bonds of the earth the decree has gone forth to bind you for all the days of the world. 6. And (that) previously you shall have seen the destruction of your beloved sons and ye shall have no pleasure in them, but they shall fall before you by the sword. 7. And your petition on their behalf shall not be granted, nor yet on your own: even though you weep and pray and speak all the words contained in the writing which I have written. 8. And the vision was shown to me thus: Behold, in the vision clouds invited me and a mist summoned me, and the course of the stars and the lightnings sped and hastened me, and the winds in the vision caused me to fly and lifted me upward, and bore me into heaven. 9. And I went in till I drew nigh to a wall which is built of crystals and surrounded by tongues of fire: and it began to affright me. And I went into the tongues of fire and drew nigh to a large house which was built of crystals: and the walls of the house were like a tesselated floor (made) of crystals, and its groundwork was of crystal. 11. Its ceiling was like the path of the stars and the lightnings, and between them were fiery cherubim, and their heaven was (clear as) water. 12. A flaming fire surrounded the walls, and its portals blazed with fire. 13. And I entered into that house, and it was hot as fire and

cold as ice: there were no delights of life therein: fear covered me, and trembling got hold upon me. 14. And as I quaked and trembled, I fell upon my face. 15. And I beheld a vision, And lo! there was a second house, greater than the former, and the entire portal stood open before me, and it was built of flames of fire. 16. And in every respect it so excelled in splendour and magnificence and extent that I cannot describe to you its splendour and its extent. 17. And its floor was of fire, and above it were lightnings and the path of the stars, and its ceiling also was flaming fire. 18. And I looked and saw therein a lofty throne: its appearance was as crystal, and the wheels thereof as the shining sun, and there was the vision of cherubim. 19. And from underneath the throne came streams of flaming fire so that I could not look thereon. 20. And the Great Glory sat thereon, and His raiment shone more brightly than the sun and was whiter than any snow. 21. None of the angels could enter and could behold His face by reason of the magnificence and glory and no flesh could behold Him. 22. The flaming fire was round about Him, and a great fire stood before Him, and none around could draw nigh Him: ten thousand times ten thousand (stood) before Him, yet He needed no counselor. 23. And the most holy ones who were nigh to Him did not leave by night nor depart from Him. 24. And until then I had been prostrate on my face, trembling: and the Lord called me with His own mouth, and said to me: "Come hither, Enoch, and hear my word." 25. And one of the holy ones came to me and waked me, and He made me rise up and approach the door: and I bowed my face downwards.

CHAPTER XV.

1. And He answered and said to me, and I heard His voice: "Fear not, Enoch, thou righteous man and scribe of righteousness: approach hither and hear my voice. 2. And go, say to the Watchers of heaven, who have sent thee to intercede for them: 'You should intercede for men, and not men for you: 3. Wherefore have ye left the high, holy, and eternal heaven, and lain with women, and defiled yourselves with the daughters of men and taken to yourselves wives, and done like the children of earth, and begotten giants (as your) sons? 4. And though ye were holy, spiritual, living the eternal life, you have defiled yourselves with the blood of women, and have begotten (children) with the blood of flesh, and, as the children of men, have lusted after flesh and blood as those

also do who die and perish. 5. Therefore have I given them wives also that they might impregnate them, and beget children by them, that thus nothing might be wanting to them on earth. 6. But you were formerly spiritual, living the eternal life, and immortal for all generations of the world. 7. And therefore I have not appointed wives for you; for as for the spiritual ones of the heaven, in heaven is their dwelling. 8. And now, the giants, who are produced from the spirits and flesh, shall be called evil spirits upon the earth, and on the earth shall be their dwelling. 9. Evil spirits have proceeded from their bodies; because they are born from men, and from the holy Watchers is their beginning and primal origin; they shall be evil spirits on earth, and evil spirits shall they be called. 10. As for the spirits of heaven, in heaven shall be their dwelling, but as for the spirits of the earth which were born upon the earth, on the earth shall be their dwelling. 11. And the spirits of the giants afflict, oppress, destroy, attack, do battle, and work destruction on the earth, and cause trouble: they take no food, but nevertheless hunger and thirst, and cause offences. And these spirits shall rise up against the children of men and against the women, because they have proceeded from them.

CHAPTER XVI.

1. From the days of the slaughter and destruction and death of the giants, from the souls of whose flesh the spirits, having gone forth, shall destroy without incurring judgement—thus shall they destroy until the day of the consummation, the great judgement in which the age shall be consummated, over the Watchers and the godless, yea, shall be wholly consummated.' 2. And now as to the Watchers who have sent thee to intercede for them, who had been aforetime in heaven, (say to them): 'You have been in heaven, but all the mysteries had not yet been revealed to you, and you knew worthless ones, and these in the hardness of your hearts you have made known to the women, and through these mysteries women and men work much evil on earth.' 4. Say to them therefore: 'You have no peace.'"

CHAPTER XVII.

1. And they took and brought me to a place in which those who were there were like flaming fire, and, when they wished, they appeared as men. 2.

And they brought me to the place of darkness, and to a mountain the point of whose summit reached to heaven. 3. And I saw the places of the luminaries and the treasuries of the stars and of the thunder and in the uttermost depths, where were a fiery bow and arrows and their quiver, and a fiery sword and all the lightnings. 4. And they took me to the living waters, and to the fire of the west, which receives every setting of the sun. 5. And I came to a river of fire in which the fire flows like water and discharges itself into the great sea towards the west. 6. I saw the great rivers and came to the great river and to the great darkness, and went to the place where no flesh walks. 7. I saw the mountains of the darkness of winter and the place whence all the waters of the deep flow. 8. I saw the mouths of all the rivers of the earth and the mouth of the deep.

CHAPTER XVIII.

1. I saw the treasuries of all the winds: I saw how He had furnished with them the whole creation and the firm foundations of the earth. 2. And I saw the corner-stone of the earth: I saw the four winds which bear the earth and the firmament of the heaven. 3. And I saw how the winds stretch out the vaults of heaven, and have their station between heaven and earth: these are the pillars of the heaven. 4. I saw the winds of heaven which turn and bring the circumference of the sun and all the stars to their setting. 5. I saw the winds on the earth carrying the clouds: I saw the paths of the angels. I saw at the end of the earth the firmament of the heaven above. And I proceeded and saw a place which burns day and night, where there are seven mountains of magnificent stones, three towards the east, and three towards the south. 7. And as for those towards the east, one was of coloured stone, and one of pearl, and one of jacinth, and those towards the south of red stone. 8. But the middle one reached to heaven like the throne of God, of alabaster, and the summit of the throne was of sapphire. 9. And I saw a flaming fire. And beyond these mountains 10. is a region the end of the great earth: there the heavens were completed. 11. And I saw a deep abyss, with columns of heavenly fire, and among them I saw columns of fire fall, which were beyond measure alike towards the height and towards the depth. 12. And beyond that abyss I saw a place which had no firmament of the heaven above, and no firmly founded earth beneath it: there was no water upon it, and no birds, but it was a waste and horrible place.

13. I saw there seven stars like great burning mountains, and to me, when I inquired regarding them, 14. The angel said: "This place is the end of heaven and earth: this has become a prison for the stars and the host of heaven. 15. And the stars which roll over the fire are they which have transgressed the commandment of the Lord in the beginning of their rising, because they did not come forth at their appointed times. 16. And He was wroth with them, and bound them till the time when their guilt should be consummated (even) for ten thousand years."

CHAPTER XIX.

1. And Uriel said to me: "Here shall stand the angels who have connected themselves with women, and their spirits assuming many different forms are defiling mankind and shall lead them astray into sacrificing to demons as gods, (here shall they stand,) till the day of the great judgement in which they shall be judged till they are made an end of. 2. And the women also of the angels who went astray shall become sirens." 3. And I, Enoch, alone saw the vision, the ends of all things: and no man shall see as I have seen.

CHAPTER XX.

1. And these are the names of the holy angels who watch. 2. Uriel, one of the holy angels, who is over the world and over Tartarus. 3. Raphael, one of the holy angels, who is over the spirits of men. 4. Raguel, one of the holy angels who takes vengeance on the world of the luminaries. 5. Michael, one of the holy angels, to wit, he that is set over the best part of mankind and over chaos. 6. Saraqael, one of the holy angels, who is set over the spirits, who sin in the spirit. 7. Gabriel, one of the holy angels, who is over Paradise and the serpents and the Cherubim. 8. Remiel, one of the holy angels, whom God set over those who rise.

CHAPTER XXI.

1. And I proceeded to where things were chaotic. 2. And I saw there something horrible: I saw neither a heaven above nor a firmly founded earth, but a place chaotic and horrible. 3. And there I saw seven stars of the heaven bound together in it, like great mountains and burning with fire. 4. Then I said: "For what sin are

they bound, and on what account have they been cast in hither?" 5. Then said Uriel, one of the holy angels, who was with me, and was chief over them, and said: "Enoch, why dost thou ask, and why art thou eager for the truth? 6. These are of the number of the stars of heaven, which have transgressed the commandment of the Lord, and are bound here till ten thousand years, the time entailed by their sins, are consummated." 7. And from thence I went to another place, which was still more horrible than the former, and I saw a horrible thing: a great fire there which burnt and blazed, and the place was cleft as far as the abyss, being full of great descending columns of fire: neither its extent or magnitude could I see, nor could I conjecture. 8. Then I said: "How fearful is the place and how terrible to look upon!" 9. Then Uriel answered me, one of the holy angels who was with me, and said unto me: "Enoch, why hast thou such fear and affright?" And I answered: "Because of this fearful place, and because of the spectacle of the pain." 10. And he said unto me: "This place is the prison of the angels, and here they will be imprisoned for ever."

CHAPTER XXII.

1. And thence I went to another place, and he showed me in the west another great and high mountain and of hard rock.

E [Ethiopean] 2. And there was in it four hollow places, deep and wide and very smooth. How smooth are the hollow places and deep and dark to look at.

Gg [Greek] 2. And there were four hollow places in it, deep and very smooth: three of them were dark and one bright; and there was a fountain of water in its midst. And I said: "How smooth are these hollow places, and deep and dark to view."

3. Then Raphael answered, one of the holy angels who was with me, and said unto me: "These hollow places have been created for this very purpose, that the spirits of the souls of the dead should assemble therein, yea that all the souls of the children of men should assemble here. And these places have been made to receive them till the day of their judgement and till their appointed period till the period appointed, till the great judgement (comes) upon them."

E 5. I saw the spirits of the children of men who were dead, and their voice went forth to heaven and made suit. 6. Then I asked Raphael the angel who was with me, and I said unto him: "This spirit— whose is it whose voice goeth forth and maketh suit?"

Gg 5. I saw (the spirit of) a dead man making suit, and his voice went forth to heaven and made suit. 6. And I asked Raphael the angel who was with me, and I said unto him: "This spirit which maketh suit, whose is it, whose voice goeth forth and maketh suit to heaven?"

7. And he answered me saying: "This is the spirit which went forth from Abel, whom his brother Cain slew, and he makes his suit against him till his seed is destroyed from the face of the earth, and his seed is annihilated from amongst the seed of men."

E 8. Then I asked regarding it, and regarding all the hollow places: "Why as one separated from the other?"

Gg 8. Then I asked regarding all the hollow places: "Why is one separated from the other?"

E 9. And he answered me and said unto me: "These three have been made that the spirits of the dead might be separated. And such a division has been made for the spirits of the righteous, in which there as the bright spring of water. 10. And such has been made for sinners when they die and are buried in the earth and judgement has not been executed on them in their lifetime. 11. Here their spirits shall be set apart in this great pain till the great day of judgement and punishment and torment of those who curse for ever, and retribution for their spirits. There He shall bind them for ever. 12. And such a division has been made for the spirits of those who make their suit, who make disclosures concerning their destruction, when they were slain in the days of the sinners. 13. Such has been made for the spirits of men who were not righteous but sinners, who were complete in transgression, and of the transgressors. they shall be companions: but their spirits shall not be slain in the day of judgement nor shall they be raised from thence." 14. Then I blessed the Lord of glory and said: "Blessed be my Lord, the Lord of righteousness, who ruleth for ever."

Gg 9. And he answered me saying: "These three have been made that the spirits of the dead might be separated. And this division has been made for the spirits of the righteous, in which there is the bright spring of water. 10. And this has been made for sinners when they die and are buried in the earth and judgement has not been executed upon them in their lifetime. 11. Here their spirits shall be set apart in this great pain, till the great day of judgement, scourgings, and torments of the accursed for ever, so that (there may be) retribution for their spirits. There He shall bind them for ever. 12. And this division has been made for the spirits of those who make their suit, who make disclosures concerning their destruction, when they were slain in the days of the sinners. 13. And this has been made for the spirits of men who shall not be righteous but sinners, who are godless, and of the lawless they shall be companions: but their spirits shall not be punished in the day of judgement nor shall they be raised from thence." 14. Then I blessed the Lord of Glory and said: "Blessed art Thou, Lord of righteousness, who rulest over the world."

CHAPTER XXIII.

1. From thence I went to another place to the west of the ends of the earth. 2. And I saw a burning fire which ran without resting, and paused not from its course day or night but (ran) regularly. 3. And I asked saying: "What is this which rests not?" 4. Then Raguel, one of the holy angels who was with me, answered me and said unto me: "This course of fire which thou hast seen is the fire in the west which persecutes all the luminaries of heaven.

CHAPTER XXIV.

1. And from thence I went to another place of the earth, and he showed me a mountain range of fire which burnt day and night. 2. And I went beyond it and saw seven magnificent mountains all differing each from the other, and the stones (thereof) were magnificent and beautiful, magnificent as a whole, of glorious appearance and fair exterior: three towards the east, one founded on the other, and three towards the south, one upon the other, and deep rough ravines, no one of which joined with any other. 3. And the seventh mountain was in the midst of these, and it excelled them in height, resembling the seat of a throne: and fragrant

trees encircled the throne. 4. And amongst them was a tree such as I had never yet smelt, neither was any amongst them nor were others like it: it had a fragrance beyond all fragrance, and its leaves and blooms and wood wither not for ever: and its fruit is beautiful, and its fruit resembles the dates of a palm. 5. Then I said: "How beautiful is this tree, and fragrant, and its leaves are fair, and its blooms very delightful in appearance." 6. Then answered Michael, one of the holy and honoured angels who was with me, and was their leader.

CHAPTER XXV.

1. And he said unto me: "Enoch, why dost thou ask me regarding the fragrance of the tree, and why dost thou wish to learn the truth?" Then I answered him saying: "I wish to know about everything, but especially about this tree." And he answered saying: "This high mountain which thou hast seen, whose summit is like the throne of God, is His throne, where the Holy Great One, the Lord of Glory, the Eternal King, will sit, when He shall come down to visit the earth with goodness. 4. And as for this fragrant tree no mortal is permitted to touch it till the great judgement, when He shall take vengeance on all and bring (everything) to its consummation for ever. It shall then be given to the righteous and holy. 5. Its fruit shall be for food to the elect: it shall be transplanted to the holy place, to the temple of the Lord, the Eternal King.

6. Then shall they rejoice with joy and be glad,
And into the holy place shall they enter;
And its fragrance shall be in their bones,
And they shall live a long life on earth,
Such as thy fathers lived:

Glossary

t

Abel . . . Cain	the sons of Adam and Eve
antimony	a chemical element, a silvery gray metal
Azazel	a mysterious supernatural being in Jewish mythology, regarded as an outcast or as having characteristics of Satan
chiefs of tens	that is, each of the leaders listed led ten other Watchers; there were two hundred Watchers, but only nineteen leaders listed, an inconsistency that has no explanation
cutting of roots	possibly an indication that the wives were provided with secret wisdom
Dan	a biblical city, the northernmost city in Israel, belonging to the Israelite tribe of Dan
Dudael	the place of imprisonment for Azazel

And in their days shall no sorrow or plague
Or torment or calamity touch them."

7. Then blessed I the God of Glory, the Eternal King, who hath prepared such things for the righteous, and hath created them and promised to give to them.

CHAPTER XXVI.

1. And I went from thence to the middle of the earth, and I saw a blessed place in which there were trees with branches abiding and blooming of a dismembered tree. 2. And there I saw a holy mountain, and underneath the mountain to the east there was a stream and it flowed towards the south. 3. And I saw towards the east another mountain higher than this, and between them a deep and narrow ravine: in it also ran a stream underneath the mountain. 4. And to the west thereof there was another mountain, lower than the former and of small elevation, and a ravine deep and dry between them: and another deep and dry ravine was at the extremities of the three mountains. 5. And all the ravines were deep and narrow, (being formed) of hard rock, and trees were not planted upon them. 6. And I marveled at the rocks, and I marveled at the ravine, yea, I marveled very much.

CHAPTER XXVII.

1. Then said I: "For what object is this blessed land, which is entirely filled with trees, and this accursed valley between?" 2. Then Uriel, one of the holy angels who was with me, answered and said: "This accursed valley is for those who are accursed for ever: Here shall all the accursed be gathered together who utter with their lips against the Lord unseemly words and of His glory speak hard things.

E 3. Here shall they be gathered together, and here shall be their place of judgement. In the last days there shall be upon them the spectacle of righteous judgement in the presence of the righteous for ever: here shall the merciful bless the Lord of glory, the Eternal King.

Gg 3. Here shall they be gathered together, and here shall be the place of their habitation. 3. In the last times, in the days of the true judgement in the presence of the righteous for ever: here shall the godly bless the Lord of Glory, the Eternal King.

4. In the days of judgement over the former, they shall bless Him for the mercy in accordance with which He has assigned them (their lot)." 5. Then I blessed the Lord of Glory and set forth His glory and lauded Him gloriously.

CHAPTER XXVIII

1. And thence I went towards the east, into the midst of the mountain range of the desert, and I saw a wilderness and it was solitary, full of trees and plants. 2. And water gushed forth from above. 3. Rushing like a copious watercourse which flowed towards the northwest it caused clouds and dew to ascend on every side.

Glossary

Erythraean sea	a name used to refer variously to the Red Sea, the Persian Gulf, and portions of the Indian Ocean
frankincense	an aromatic resin used in perfumes and incense
mastic	here, a plant resin
Michael, Uriel, Raphael, and Gabriel	the angels of God
Mount Hermon	a mountain on the border between Syria and Lebanon
myrrh	an aromatic resin, at times more valuable than gold
son of Lamech	that is, Noah
Tartarus	the underworld; hell

CHAPTER XXIX.

1. And thence I went to another place in the desert, and approached to the east of this mountain range. 2. And there I saw aromatic trees exhaling the fragrance of frankincense and myrrh, and the trees also were similar to the almond tree.

CHAPTER XXX.

1. And beyond these, I went afar to the east, and I saw another place, a valley (full) of water. 2. And therein there was a tree, the colour of fragrant trees such as the mastic. 3. And on the sides of those valleys I saw fragrant cinnamon. And beyond these I proceeded to the east.

CHAPTER XXXI.

1. And I saw other mountains, and amongst them were groves of trees, and there flowed forth from them nectar, which is named sarara and galbanum. 2. And beyond these mountains I saw another mountain to the east of the ends of the earth, whereon were aloe trees, and all the trees were full of stacte, being like almond-trees. 3. And when one burnt it, it smelt sweeter than any fragrant odour.

CHAPTER XXXII.

E 1. And after these fragrant odours, as I looked towards the north over the mountains I saw seven mountains full of choice nard and fragrant trees and cinnamon and pepper.

Gg 1. To the north-east I beheld seven mountains full of choice nard and mastic and cinnamon and pepper.

2. And thence I went over the summits of all these mountains, far towards the east of the earth, and passed above the Erythraean sea and went far from it, and passed over the angel Zotiel.

E 3. And I came to the Garden of Righteousness, and saw beyond those trees many large trees growing there and of goodly fragrance, large, very beautiful and glorious, and the tree of wisdom whereof they eat and know great wisdom.

Gg 3. And I came to the Garden of Righteousness, and from afar off trees more numerous than these trees and great—two trees there, very great, beautiful, and glorious, and magnificent, and the tree of knowledge, whose holy fruit they eat and know great wisdom.

4. That tree is in height like the fir, and its leaves are like (those of) the Carob tree: and its fruit is like the clusters of the vine, very beautiful: and the fragrance of the tree penetrates afar. 5. Then I said: "How beautiful is the tree, and how attractive is its look!" 6. Then Raphael the holy angel, who was with me, answered me and said: "This is the tree of wisdom, of which thy father old (in years) and thy aged mother, who were before thee, have eaten, and they learnt wisdom and their eyes were opened, and they knew that they were naked and they were driven out of the garden."

CHAPTER XXXIII.

1. And from thence I went to the ends of the earth and saw there great beasts, and each differed from the other; and (I saw) birds also differing in appearance and beauty and voice, the one differing from the other. 2. And to the east of those beasts I saw the ends of the earth whereon the heaven rests, and the portals of the heaven open. 3. And I saw how the stars of heaven come forth, and I counted the portals out of which they proceed, and wrote down all their outlets, of each individual star by itself, according to their number and their names, their courses and their positions, and their times and their months, as Uriel the holy angel who was with me showed me. 4. He showed all things to me and wrote them down for me: also their names he wrote for me, and their laws and their companies.

CHAPTER XXXIV.

1. And from thence I went towards the north to the ends of the earth, and there I saw a great and glorious device at the ends of the whole earth. 2. And here I saw three portals of heaven open in the heaven: through each of them proceed north winds: when they blow there is cold, hail, frost, snow, dew, and rain. 3. And out of one portal they blow for good: but when they blow through the other two portals, it is with violence and affliction on the earth, and they blow with violence.

CHAPTER XXXV.

1. And from thence I went towards the west to the ends of the earth, and saw there three portals of the heaven open such as I had seen in the east, the same number of portals, and the same number of outlets.

CHAPTER XXXVI.

1. And from thence I went to the south to the ends of the earth, and saw there three open portals of the heaven: and thence there come dew, rain, and wind. 2. And from thence I went to the east to the ends of the heaven, and saw here the three eastern portals of heaven open and small portals above them. 3. Through each of these small portals pass the stars of heaven and run their course to the west on the path which is shown to them. 4. And as often as I saw I blessed always the Lord of Glory, and I continued to bless the Lord of Glory who has wrought great and glorious wonders, to show the greatness of His work to the angels and to spirits and to men, that they might praise His work and all His creation: that they might see the work of His might and praise the great work of His hands and bless Him for ever.

Zeus on his throne

(Statue of Olympian Zeus on his throne inside his temple at Olympus, 1814 [colour litho], French School [19th century] / Private Collection / Archives
Charmet / The Bridgeman Art Library International)

Cleanthes: "Hymn to Zeus"

"For nothing can be better for gods or men / Than to adore with hymns the Universal King."

Overview

Cleanthes' "Hymn to Zeus" is both a religious and a philosophical record of the attitudes of ancient Greek thinkers of the early Stoic school. As the only nearly complete piece of early Stoic writing that has survived intact, it offers a unique insight into the Stoic theological and cosmological worldview of the early third century BCE. It is remarkable for its ability to straddle multiple purposes. It is at the same time a lyric "hymn," in the style of the popular prayers of the period, and a philosophical treatise. It also contains divergent and seemingly incongruous ideas: Within its lines, Zeus, ruling god of the Greek pantheon, is depicted as both a conscious, "knowable" god and an impersonal, pantheistic force of nature. This is a theological standpoint particular to Stoicism.

Cleanthes' "Hymn to Zeus" has been analyzed and debated by thinkers throughout history, its precise purpose, whether it was primarily poetic or didactic, obscured by time. What is known is that its author, a prolific philosophical writer, also dabbled in poetry; the "Hymn to Zeus" most likely served to express early Stoic views on the cosmos and humanity's place within it in a pleasing context. Whether or not the hymn was regularly sung by the average Greek, or even by the students of Cleanthes and his successors, is unknown, though it seems likely that it was meant to be performed in public, perhaps before a meeting of the Stoic school or for a general audience or at some private occasion such as a wedding or a symposium—a gathering designed for the participants to drink wine together and discuss various academic subjects in an informal setting. Regardless, it seems highly likely that its preservation resulted from its considerable aesthetic attributes and not just its philosophical content.

In his "Hymn to Zeus," Cleanthes discusses one of the most important themes in Stoic theology. Diverging from the doctrines of his predecessor and teacher, Zeno of Citium, Cleanthes presents a theological view that would come to characterize the early Stoics. It depicts a God knowable yet austere, who directs the actions of both the cosmos and the human being, while allowing room for the ability of humankind to exercise free will. The tension of this seeming contradiction resonates throughout the poem and foreshadows the religious debates of later philosophers and theologians—Greek, Christian, and contemporary—many of whom have been attracted to the austerity and spirituality of the Stoic worldview.

Context

The context of Cleanthes' "Hymn to Zeus" lies within the fecund period of Greek thought that existed in the fifth through third centuries BCE. Within these three centuries, nearly all of what would grow to become the most prominent Greek schools of philosophical thought were established in Athens—the Skeptics, Pythagoreans, Platonists, Aristotelians, and Stoics. Throughout this period, floods of young men, looking to study philosophy or rhetoric, poured into Athens to study under a specific, often widely renowned, philosopher or school of thought.

Greek philosophical schools can be envisioned as the "graduate education" of their day, with numerous varieties to choose from, all promising intellectual and moral advantages to their training. This was the atmosphere of Athens when Zeno of Citium, founder of the Stoic school, came to the city in 313 BCE. Purportedly he studied with both the Cynics and the Platonists but was primarily influenced by the former school and its emphasis on living in accordance with Nature. Zeno took that doctrine to demand the deliberate eschewing of the pettiness that dominates most "civilized" behavior and the pursuit instead of simply being "good." It is atop this simple, organic substratum that the ideas that formed the framework of Stoicism would form.

Zeno and other Cynics of his time saw that being "good" meant pursuing a life akin to that lived by the Athenian sage Socrates (469–399 BCE)—one unfettered by societal expectations of wealth, status, or public decorum. In many ways, Zeno's ideas become a blend of Platonism, focused on the "good," with the self-denial and simplicity of the Cynics. Fusing the Cynic "way of living" with his interest in cosmology and logic, Zeno eventually graduated to teaching his own mode of philosophy and founded a school, labeled for the place where his ideas were taught. The Stoa Poikile, literally the "Painted Colonnade," was a fixture of the great central square of Ath-

Time Line

CA. 347 BCE	■ Plato, a disciple of Socrates and teacher of Aristotle, dies in his early eighties.
CA. 335 BCE	■ Zeno is born in Citium (modern-day Cyprus).
CA. 331 BCE	■ Cleanthes is born in Assos, on the Aegean coast of Asia Minor (present-day Behramköy, Turkey).
CA. 322 BCE	■ Aristotle dies in his early sixties.
CA. 313 BCE	■ Zeno arrives in Athens, to study under Cynic and Socratic philosophers.
CA. 301 BCE	■ Zeno begins teaching at the Stoa Poikile in the Athenian Agora.
CA. 280 –276 BCE	■ Cleanthes composes his "Hymn to Zeus."
CA. 263 BCE	■ Cleanthes is named successor to Zeno and becomes head of the Stoic school.
CA. 232 BCE	■ Cleanthes dies and is succeeded by Chrysippus.

ens, the Agora. (A stoa was simply a roofed portico.) Although it was a public place, this is where Zeno and his follows chose to meet, and his followers came to bear the name "the men from the Stoa," or "Stoics." It was into this inchoate "school" that Cleanthes arrived near the end of the fourth century BCE.

About the Author

Cleanthes, son of Phanias, was born in about 331 BCE in the town of Assos on the Aegean coast (present-day Behramköy, Turkey). Information on his early life is restricted to only a few sources, though the consensus is that he followed the profession of a boxer. He arrived in Athens at the end of the fourth century with few resources and ultimately found his way to the study of philosophy. After listening to lectures given by adherents of the various philosophical schools, he became a pupil of the famous Zeno of Citium, founder of Stoicism.

Cleanthes was known for his hard work and industry, if not his intellectual prowess. Owing to his modest station,

he was forced to support himself through physical labor, often working as a "water bearer" for gardeners, an activity that would gain him the nickname "Well-Water Bringer." It is said that he spent nineteen years as Zeno's pupil, sustaining himself by his nightly toils while studying and writing during the day. Though his mind was not known for extraordinary swiftness—another nickname was "the Ass"—his responses always seemed to stress the persevering spirit of his nature and discipline. Diogenes Laertius, a biographer of the third century BCE, reports that Cleanthes' response to these comments was that he "did not mind" this criticism, since "he alone was strong enough to carry the load of Zeno" and his teachings.

Through his hard work and dedication and his personification of the moral ideals of the Stoic doctrine, Cleanthes was chosen to succeed Zeno as the head of the school upon the founder's death in 263, a post he would retain until his own death in 232. Dozens of works have been attributed to him, on a wide range of topics, though his importance for Greek thought rests primarily on his discussions of physics and cosmology. Fragments of many treatises survive as quotations in other ancient authors, but it is his "Hymn to Zeus" that provides the most complete picture of his religious and philosophical thought.

Explanation and Analysis of the Document

The existing version of Cleanthes' "Hymn to Zeus," as presented to modern readers, is nearly complete. However, there are apparent gaps in the text from the extant copies used to formulate modern translations. While the narrative and content of the hymn are not obscured by these small gaps, a particularly large one has obscured half of a verse in line 26. It has accordingly been reconstructed by scholars in order to complete the sense of the line and those portions are indicated by brackets. The remainder of the text can be assumed to be complete, owing to the hymn's close structural correlation with similar pieces of ancient Greek religious writing, moving from invocation, argument, and, finally, to praise.

♦ **Lines 1–6**

Cleanthes diverges from the standard format of Greek religious hymns in his first line: Rather than firmly name the god being praised, he begins by rolling off various religious epithets. The tension built in the first line is relieved by the use of Zeus's name in the beginning of the second. To cite Zeus as the god who can be termed "greatest" of the gods is also of interest on a philosophical level. Though Zeus occupied the supreme position in the Greek pantheon, he was also considered a god capable of having "many names." Some scholars interpret this to mean that he is a figure capable of representing more than just one figure among the Greek pantheon, while remaining synonymous with the active principle of the universe or "God" in a theistic sense.

Calling Zeus the "origin of Nature" (line 2) is a noteworthy choice as well: The "Hymn to Zeus" is the earliest known use of this particular descriptor. Stoic doctrine is evinced here, since the idea of acting in accordance with "Nature" as the primary good for human beings is a central tenet of Stoic philosophy. Many scholars believe that all mention of divinity or deity in Stoic theology or cosmology is purely pantheistic. However, interpreters of Cleanthes and the later Stoics contest that view. An image of a God who acts with volition in the world has been strongly supported by analysis of subsequent Stoic writings. In Cleanthes' text, Zeus as representing the "universal force" envisioned by the Stoics is combined with a figure that is capable of acting in the world. That is, far from being a passive principle as posited by other Greek philosophical systems, the Zeus invoked here takes part in worldly actions. He is "knowable" and personal, a departure from other Stoic representations of divinity. This provides the rationale for Cleanthes' earnest entreaties for him to "guard men from sad error" in line 29 and "dispel the clouds of the soul" in line 30.

Lines 4–6 focus on a theme that is not specifically Stoic, though it accords with an overall understanding of the importance of Zeus in Greek religion and the concomitant human obligation to praise him. Cleanthes' reason is that humans alone have been granted the power of "imitative speech." The subtext here is that speech alone is not the reason for humanity's gratitude; rather, those who are capable of reasoned speech, and they alone, can offer *meaningful* praise in the form of songs or hymns. This idea is traditional in Greek religion and in line with the overall tone of the hymn's introductory lines. Human beings, being the sole possessors of reason in the natural world, need to thank the gods for their unique gift.

◆ **Lines 7–14**

The first line here has a phrase that may seem innocuous at first reading: "Thee the wide heaven, which surrounds the earth, obeys." Other translations replace "surround" with "spins about," making this line state that the heavens indeed turn about the earth and not vice versa, as other contemporary thinkers had asserted. Cleanthes wants to have the earth, the cornerstone of the cosmos for Greek religious thought of this time, retain its primacy, and here he displays simultaneously his conservatism and his piety.

Perhaps the most important aspect of this portion of the hymn is the device by which Zeus rules—his thunderbolt. The adjectives "flaming" and "immortal" hold special meanings within a Stoic philosophical construct. "Flaming" recalls the idea that of the four classical elements (earth, air, fire, and water), fire is the most primal. In orthodox Stoic cosmology, the first stage of the creation of the cosmos culminated in the universe being converted entirely into flame. It was after the end of this conflagration that the other three elements slowly coalesced. Stoics further believed that at the end of the universe, fire would consume all, with everything reverting to the most basic element. It is unsurprising, then, that the weapon Zeus chooses to rule is "flaming," representing that primordial force that rules all others. Additionally, the concept of heat in ancient thought was considered to be the active principle behind all life and motion in the universe. That Zeus's symbol of governance

Portrait bust of Zeno of Citium, founder of the Stoic school of thought

(Bust of Zeno of Citium [c.335-c.264 BC] [stone] [b/w photo], Greek / Museo Archeologico Nazionale, Naples, Italy / Alinari / The Bridgeman Art Library International)

is associated with that force underscores his responsibility for the creation and sustenance of the cosmos. The epithet "immortal," used in conjunction with "flaming," emphasizes these aspects of the latter term. For a thunderbolt to be everlasting or "immortal" seems a paradox, in light of its transient nature. Yet Cleanthes here asserts that Zeus's thunderbolt is more than just a weapon, being also an extension of his rule. It shares in his omnipotence and becomes an object through which he can direct and guide, as evinced by the next line.

The reference to Zeus ruling "in the common reason" which "appears mingled in all things" and is the "king of all existences" deserves note as well. "Common reason" here translates the Greek *Logos*, a ubiquitous term in Greek thought and one that is capable of many interpretations. It can mean the faculty of reason, a spoken utterance or thought, or even a principle or law. Here it has a dual meaning, being both a plan or course of action and a dynamic process, a thing that is occurring and continues to occur. Zeus rules both according to this common Logos and through it, thus exhibiting the Stoics' dual conception of deity as both existing within nature and also directing it.

◆ **Lines 15–21**

The next three lines set up a situation that many Stoic thinkers address. Lines 15 and 16 acknowledge that nothing can happen without Zeus's involvement and direction—nothing except "the evil preferred by the senseless wicked." But if Zeus is omnipotent and all-directing, how is it possible that humans are able to choose to go so wrongly? This is the paradox of a cosmos that is both deterministic, because human beings have no choice but to follow the dictates of the heavens, and also free, because rational choice remains possible. This apparent conflict had been reconciled by previous Stoic thinkers such as Zeno, and their synthesis would be expanded upon by Cleanthes' successor, Chrysippus, in the famous "dog comparison." Simply put, the situation of human beings is akin to that of a dog tied to a cart. If it wills to go along with the cart, then there is no tension and it is pulled along. If it does not wish to follow, it is dragged by force. Either way, the dog has some volition, though ultimately its fate is dictated by the direction of the cart. Therefore, though Zeus is in all and directs all, the "wicked" may still choose to disobey, but to their certain consternation.

Indeed, the next few lines of the hymn inform the reader of what will occur if this happens, since Zeus is also "able to bring to order that which is chaotic" (including the rebelling human spirit) and make "good out of evil." The reader is thus reminded that there is "one great law" (the Logos) throughout nature that exists as a guiding principle and active force.

♦ **Lines 22–27**

The next few lines expand on the fate of the "wicked" in more detail. A full treatment of the problem of evil is not possible here, but instead we are given a description of how the foolish go afield from the Logos described earlier in the poem. The Stoic conception of morality posits a universal "law" or "reason" with which human beings can align themselves and describes evil as an aberration from that law. Thus Cleanthes labels as "Poor fools!" those who will not hear that universal law or reason and who act in disharmony with the "divine commands." The hymn reaffirms that only Zeus's ability to make the "discordant" right again can rescue them from their errors.

The description of how the wicked fall away draws upon terminology common to ancient Greek moral thought. Mentions of blindness, straying away, or fleeing from moral prescriptions are common in the early Stoics and other Greek thinkers. The straying away from the universal reason mentioned in line 25 is seen as the opposite of the intent to "follow" mentioned in line 30, which Cleanthes and Zeno posit as the greatest good—living in accordance with Nature, here deemed synonymous with the figure of Zeus.

Lines 26 and 27 list the ways by which these wicked fall away from this universal reason—by "thirst of glory" or "avarice" or "pleasures sensual"—all common charges against the wicked (or those uninitiated into the moral system being espoused). The criticism here belongs to the tradition (dating back to Plato, Socrates, and earlier Greek philosophers) of the sage who eschews worldly things in order to focus on that which is truly important. From other writings by Cleanthes, we know that among the things he considered good were piety, self-control, patience, and austerity;

he mentions little about the pursuit of pleasure or fame or any other of the more common pursuits of his time. Cleanthes has been labeled as an "antihedonist" in that he felt that physical pleasure, whether sexual or otherwise, had almost no real value. Sextus Empiricus, a philosopher and physician of the second century CE, attributes to Cleanthes the view that pleasure is akin to a "cosmetic"—a trifle that contributes little to one's daily life.

There is, however, a debate as to whether the Stoics generally considered these things—worldly pursuits, including pleasure—to be "evils." One reading of Stoic thought posits that the wicked chase after these objectives instead of pursuing the universal reason and that this poor choice of focus is their fault. Their flaw is inconstancy and blindness, not simply a love of pleasure or fame. The latter can be seen as positive, if inconsequential, parts of "living in accordance with Nature" and not as intrinsically evil. This distinction is an important one. It places Stoicism at the boundary line between systems of religious or philosophical thought that renounce the worldly, such as Cynicism, and those that embrace it, such as Epicureanism.

♦ **Lines 28–35**

The hymn closes with what is traditionally referred to as the prayer, the petitionary portion that serves as the ultimate purpose for the hymn itself. The previous portions invoked and described the powers of Zeus and the plight of men; now a request is made for deliverance. It begins, mirroring the opening, with a list of epithets: Zeus as "all-bestower," "cloud-compeller," "ruler of thunder." Most of these terms are traditionally characteristic of Zeus, though the first deserves comment. Zeus is not usually described as the force that gives or grants all things. "All-bestower" is not a traditional epithet and should be seen here as Cleanthes' reassertion of the Stoic Zeus—the force synonymous with fate, destiny, and divine will.

Zeus, addressed as "Father," a common epithet deriving from his high-ranking place in the Greek pantheon, is asked to "dispel the clouds of the soul" in line 30, a phrase typical of Greek poetry that here references the Stoic notion of evil or wickedness as lack of foresight or lack of the ability to act in accordance with nature. The petition asks Zeus to allow humanity "to follow" his reign, a theme reiterated throughout the hymn.

The concluding lines revert to a general praise of Zeus the god. "That we may be honored, let us honor thee again," a common formula in Greek religious thought. Prayers and hymns often revolved around reciprocity between gods and men. The gods are due honor and praise for any benefits granted. Cleanthes does not deviate from this custom, acknowledging that "nothing can be better" than for "gods or men" than to sing the praises and adore the "Universal King." Interestingly, this line, drawing on a traditional understanding of the diverse Greek pantheon, indicates that both "gods" and humans ought to praise Zeus. Although Stoic theology placed Zeus as the primary deity, synonymous with Nature or "God," there was room for lesser divinities as well.

"Zeus, origin of Nature, governing the universe by law, / All hail! For it is right for mortals to address thee."

"Thou holdest at thy service, in thy mighty hands, / The two-edged, flaming, immortal thunderbolt, / Before whose flash all nature trembles."

"Nor without thee, Oh Deity, does anything happen in the world, / From the divine ethereal pole to the great ocean, / Except only the evil preferred by the senseless wicked."

"Thus throughout nature is one great law / Which only the wicked seek to disobey, / Poor fools! who long for happiness, / But will not see nor hear the divine commands."

"For nothing can be better for gods or men / Than to adore with hymns the Universal King."

Audience

The audience for the "Hymn to Zeus" would have been primarily those students studying with Cleanthes or, later, students associated with the Stoic school in Athens, although there is no direct evidence for how or in what context it was performed. As can be gathered from his other writings, Cleanthes' attitude toward fame and striving for recognition in posterity mimics that of many other Stoic thinkers: to desire recognition from without goes against the teaching of inner dependence that resides at the core of the Stoic system. It is therefore unlikely that the hymn was written with the purpose of being widely distributed. However, Aristotle and other philosophic writers of the time also composed works written in a "hymnical" style, many of which were performed at public or semipublic events. It has been argued that the "Hymn to Zeus" was a "table prayer" intended to inaugurate a meeting or symposium devoted to religious or philosophical discussion. As such, it may have been performed with musical accompaniment, most typically a lyre, and sung by a soloist. It also could have served as a model prayer or "invocation"—a preface to a series of talks or speeches on philosophy. Regardless, the primary audience of the poem would have been students of philosophy or at least those interested in Stoic ideas. In later years, the hymn was certainly read and discussed, but only as part of greater discussions of Stoic cosmology—and even such interest fell by the wayside after the Roman Stoics of the early few centuries CE expanded on and, in many ways, supplanted the Greek Stoics' teachings.

Impact

The poetic power of Cleanthes' "Hymn to Zeus" helped ensure its survival, almost intact, to the present day. It is the only nearly complete piece of early Greek Stoic writing to survive and the text that has received the most commentary. Ancient Greeks, later Roman Stoics such as Seneca (the Younger), Epictetus, and Marcus Aurelius, and even Christian figures writing centuries after its composition would read Cleanthes' philosophical and religious ideas as a summary or perhaps introduction to the cosmological view of Stoic philosophy.

While the direct impact of this particular poem is hard to trace, the persistence of Stoic philosophy is not. Stoic ideas unquestionably penetrated much later thought. The Neoplatonist school that would attain dominance over ancient philosophy prior to the advent of Christianity was deeply permeated by the Stoic concept of self-possession—that human beings cannot be made unhappy by outside influences unless they themselves allow it. Plotinus, a leading figure of the Neoplatonist school in the third century CE, upheld this view in his famous *Enneads*, and other Neoplatonist figures, including the Roman emperor Marcus Aurelius (d. 180 CE), would blend Stoicism and Aristotelianism with the viewpoints of Plato.

The Stoic influence did not end with the closing of the great philosophical schools by the Christian emperor Justinian in 529 CE. It continued well into the Christian era, when Stoicism, unlike Aristotelian and other philosophical systems, was never officially outlawed. The fact that Stoicism was both a philosophy and a "way of living," focused on correcting and improving behavior, gave it a particular advantage; it never conflicted with the teachings of Christianity, a fact that thus allowed many of the early Christian writers, such as Clement of Alexandria (d. before 216), Gregory of Nyssa (d. 395), and Origen (d. 254/255), to study and incorporate some of the Stoic writings and teachings into their theology. It is unsurprising, then, that Cleanthes' poem, at once literature, philosophy, and theology, would be copied and recopied by the generations of clergy before being taken up again by Renaissance and Enlightenment scholars.

Stoicism's influence has ebbed and waned throughout the centuries that followed, attaining a high degree of popularity during the sixteenth and seventeenth centuries, when its pantheism and antimaterialism appealed to those unsatisfied with the religious temperament of the time. Writers such as the French Michel de Montaigne (1533–1592) and the Flemish Justus Lipsius (1547–1606) helped bring about the foundation of what would be termed Neostoicism, a seventeenth-century movement that flourished only briefly but that commanded responses from prominent seventeenth-century intellectuals like Blaise Pascal and Nicolas Malebranche.

As philosophy slowly took on its present academic form, Stoicism would be supported, debated, denounced, and rediscovered continuously for the next three hundred years. Its ideas, and the ideas of Cleanthes himself, find reference in the correspondence of the American president John Adams and the twentieth-century philosophers Bertrand Russell and Gilles Deleuze. Therefore, the impact of Stoicism and the influence of Cleanthes' "Hymn to Zeus" as an entryway into this religious and philosophical system have been omnipresent and yet diffuse, very much like the almighty "Ruler of thunder" that it depicts.

Further Reading

■ Books

Diogenes Laertius. *Lives of Eminent Philosophers*, trans. R. D. Hicks., vol. 2. Cambridge, Mass.: Harvard University Press, 2000.

Johansen, Karsten Friis. *A History of Ancient Philosophy: From the Beginnings to Augustine*, trans. Henrik Rosenmeier. London: Routledge, 1998.

Questions for Further Study

1. The entry states that the "Hymn to Zeus" "depicts a God knowable yet austere, who directs the actions of both the cosmos and the human being, while allowing room for the ability of humankind to exercise free will." In what ways, if any, does this conception of God differ from that of Christianity or Judaism? Would this statement serve as a more or less accurate description of God as conceived in monotheistic religions? Explain.

2. In the modern world, the words *stoic* and *stoicism* refer to a person's ability to put up with pain or hardship without complaining. To what extent, if any, does this use of the words reflect the philosophy of the Stoics of ancient Greece?

3. Another classical view of God and creation is contained in *On the Nature of Things* by the Roman writer Lucretius. Read that entry and compare it with the "Hymn to Zeus." What differing conceptions of the role of the deity do they present?

4. Do you see any similarities between Zeus and Vishnu, as reflected in the Hindu document Vishnu Purana? Explain.

5. Stoicism is described as both a philosophy and a way of living. Indeed, many religious/philosophical systems are concerned primarily with instructing people how to lead better lives; a good example would be the Noble Eightfold Path by Siddhartha Gautama, better known as the Buddha. In what respect do these works help people lead better lives, or at least try to?

Meijer, P. A. *Stoic Theology: Proofs for the Existence of the Cosmic God and of the Traditional Gods; Including a Commentary on Cleanthes' Hymn on Zeus*. Delft, Netherlands: Eburon, 2007.

Sandbach, F. H. *The Stoics*. London: Chatto and Windus, 1975.

Sellars, John. *Stoicism*. Berkeley: University of California Press, 2006.

Thom, Johan C. *Cleanthes' Hymn to Zeus: Text, Translation, and Commentary*. Tübingen, Germany: Mohr Siebeck, 2005.

Verbeke, Gérard. *The Presence of Stoicism in Medieval Thought*. Washington, D.C.: Catholic University of America Press, 1983.

—Eric May

CLEANTHES: "HYMN TO ZEUS"

Greatest of the gods, God with many names, God
  ever-ruling, and ruling all things!
Zeus, origin of Nature, governing the universe by law,
All hail! For it is right for mortals to address thee;
For we are thy offspring, and we alone of all
That live and creep on earth have the power of imita-
  tive speech.
Therefore will I praise thee, and hymn forever thy power.
Thee the wide heaven, which surrounds the earth,
  obeys:
Following where thou wilt, willingly obeying thy law.
Thou holdest at thy service, in thy mighty hands,
The two-edged, flaming, immortal thunderbolt,
Before whose flash all nature trembles.
Thou rulest in the common reason, which goes
  through all,
And appears mingled in all things, great or small,
Which filling all nature, is king of all existences.
Nor without thee, Oh Deity, does anything happen in
  the world,
From the divine ethereal pole to the great ocean,
Except only the evil preferred by the senseless wicked.

But thou also art able to bring to order that which
  is chaotic,
Giving form to what is formless, and making the dis-
  cordant friendly;
So reducing all variety to unity, and even making
  good out of evil.
Thus throughout nature is one great law
Which only the wicked seek to disobey,
Poor fools! who long for happiness,
But will not see nor hear the divine commands.

[In frenzy blind they stray away from good,]
By thirst of glory tempted, or sordid avarice,
Or pleasures sensual and joys that fall.
But do thou, Oh Zeus, all-bestower, cloud-compeller!
Ruler of thunder! guard men from sad error.
Father! dispel the clouds of the soul, and let us follow
The laws of thy great and just reign!
That we may be honored, let us honor thee again,
Chanting thy great deeds, as is proper for mortals,
For nothing can be better for gods or men
Than to adore with hymns the Universal King.

HAN FEIZI

"Circumstances change according to the age, and ways of dealing with them change with the circumstances."

Overview

Han Fei was an ancient Chinese writer credited with the work that bears his name, the *Han Feizi*, which is generally translated as *The Writings of Master Han Fei*. Completed around 230 BCE and divided into fifty-five chapters, the *Han Feizi* is considered to be the best synthesis of the ideas of Legalism, also referred to as the School of Law. Elements of Legalist thought date to as early as the fourth century BCE, with some accounts tracing them to as far back as the seventh century BCE. Although little is known about the philosophies of earlier thinkers like Shang Yang (d. 338 BCE) and Shen Buhai (d. 337 BCE), their influence in the *Han Feizi* is widely noted. Scholars also acknowledge the contributions of other Legalist thinkers but credit Han Fei with combining Legalist ideas into a compendium.

Generally regarded as a political treatise rather than a religious text, the *Han Feizi* is concerned above all with state power. Written in reaction to the widespread political turmoil during the aptly named Warring States Period, the *Han Feizi* diagnoses sources of political weakness and offers a pragmatic program to build and strengthen state power. In contrast to the Confucian view, with which Han Fei was intimately familiar owing to his Confucian education, the Legalist view holds that morality has no place in politics and, in fact, hinders the pursuit of power. The *Han Feizi* rejects the Confucian notion of leadership by moral example and advocates instead a uniform system of laws, rewards, and punishments as the most effective means to strengthen the state and control the people. Legalists believe that people—even the ruler—are inherently selfish and that only by appealing to their self-interest and instilling fear in them can a state maintain order. Legalism enjoyed imperial patronage during the Qin Dynasty (221–206 BCE). Although its prestige declined after the fall of the Qin, Legalism has continued to influence Chinese intellectuals up to the present day.

Context

The Eastern Zhou Dynasty (771–221 BCE), which is roughly divided into two periods—the Spring and Autumn Period (722–481 BCE) and the Warring States Period (403–221 BCE)—was an era of endemic political disorder. During the Warring States Period, the states struggling for supremacy, which had numbered well over a hundred during the Spring and Autumn Period, had dwindled to about half a dozen. Although wars declined in frequency during this era (no doubt owing to the reduced number of contenders), they grew longer, at times lasting up to five years. Advances in military weaponry such as the crossbow also made warfare deadlier than before. Moreover, the preoccupation with war created armies that were larger in size and more diverse in social composition, reflecting the broader trend toward greater social mobility. The decisive victory of the Qin state and the inauguration of the Qin Dynasty brought to an end centuries of internecine warfare and allowed for the ascendancy of Legalism.

The Eastern Zhou Dynasty represents a formative moment in Chinese intellectual history, often described as the "age of philosophers" in recognition of the so-called hundred schools of thought that proliferated during this time. In response to the warfare and instability surrounding them, a number of Chinese thinkers proposed reforms aimed at restoring peace and unity. Those whose ideas survived in written form are associated with the major intellectual traditions of China: Confucianism, Mohism, Daoism, and Legalism. Personally experiencing the social dislocation and economic disruption that accompanied political turbulence, educated Chinese men like Han Fei pondered such questions as these: How does a state increase its power? What are the keys to effective governance? Are humans by nature good or evil? Constituting more than a philosophical debate, such questions aimed to find a viable solution to the political crises crippling China during these turbulent centuries, and many educated men aspired to official posts that would enable them to turn their ideas into policies that would restore order and unify the country.

Although Han Fei received a Confucian education, he came to reject what his teacher, Xunzi, had taught him, with one notable exception. He agreed with Xunzi's theory that human nature was inherently bad. But whereas Xunzi placed faith in the redemptive potential of moral education to teach people to be good, Han Fei was less optimistic, relying instead on laws viewed as infallible, a position widely held within the Legalist

Time Line

771 BCE	■ The Eastern Zhou Dynasty begins, during which the "hundred schools of thought" contend.
403 BCE	■ The Warring States Period begins, with a handful of states vying for political dominance.
CA. 280 BCE	■ Han Fei is born in the state of Han.
CA. 264 BCE	■ The Confucian master Xunzi begins teaching at the Jixia Academy in the state of Qi. Han Fei most likely studied under Xunzi at this time.
CA. 234 BCE	■ Han Fei travels to Qin to plead on behalf of the Han state and is believed to have taken a position in the Qin court.
234 BCE	■ The Qin state invades Han Fei's home state of Han.
CA. 233 BCE	■ Han Fei completes "The Difficulties of Persuasion"; he dies of poisoning the same year.
CA. 230 BCE	■ The *Han Feizi* is completed.
221 BCE	■ The Warring States Period comes to an end; with the inception of the Qin Dynasty, Legalism is adopted as the official ideology.
206 BCE	■ Legalism is displaced by Confucianism as the official ideology in the Han Dynasty, which is to last until 220 CE.

About the Author

As a descendant of the royal Han family that ruled over the state by the same name, Han Fei (ca. 280–233 BCE) not only held a keen interest in the political developments of his time but also had a personal stake in the outcome. He allegedly stuttered, which placed him at a serious disadvantage against his more eloquent rivals. Turning to writing to communicate his ideas, Han Fei composed a series of memorials to his relatives advising them on how to strengthen the Han state, with the ultimate goal of conquering their neighbors, who were for the most part larger and more powerful.

Although they were ignored by his own kin, Han Fei's writings caught the attention of Li Si, a minister in the Qin state, who presented Han Fei's ideas to the Qin ruler. Li Si and Han Fei had both studied under the Confucian master Xunzi, who had held that human nature was inherently bad. But whereas Xunzi had emphasized moral education as a corrective measure, Han Fei and Li Si concluded that law and punishment were the only ways to curb the evil tendencies in humanity. Finding an eager audience for his proposals, Han Fei is believed to have taken a position in the Qin court.

In an ironic twist of events, Han Fei's proposals to save his own state were used by its enemies to destroy it; in 234 BCE, the Qin state launched a successful military campaign against the small Han state. Prior to the invasion, the Han ruler, whether in an act of desperation or in recognition of Han Fei's political acumen, turned to Han Fei for assistance. Although Han Fei's Legalist ideas were well received by the Qin ruler, his pleas on behalf of his home state were not. Whether motivated by jealousy or mistrust, Li Si advised the Qin ruler to execute Han Fei. Before his death by poison, Han Fei composed his last work, "The Difficulties of Persuasion." Shortly after his death, Han Fei's writings were collected in a volume that bears his name. Completed around 230 BCE, the *Han Feizi* also reflects the thoughts and writings of other Legalist thinkers, though little is known about these other contributors or the compiler of the *Han Feizi*. As is often the case with texts from the Warring States Period, authorship is difficult to determine with any degree of certainty, for the individuals whose names are synonymous with the title of a work cannot always be assumed to be the authors.

Explanation and Analysis of the Document

Although some doubts remain about whether Han Fei authored the book that bears his name, the *Han Feizi* is widely accepted as an accurate reflection of his ideas as well as an authoritative and systematic exposition of Legalist thought. The *Han Feizi* builds its argument by using historical examples and refuting Confucian views on government and human nature. Organized into fifty-five chapters, the text offers perhaps the most coherent synthesis of Legalist ideas, which had already been in circulation for several centuries.

school. Legalist thinkers believed that most people were selfish and that the only way they could be taught to serve the public interest was through rewards for activities that furthered it and punishments for activities that injured it. Laws, simply written so that people could easily understand them, communicated to the people what the public interest was and spelled out the specific consequences for particular actions. Although Han Fei was not alone—nor the first—in voicing these opinions, the synthesis of Legalist ideas in the book that bears his name, the *Han Feizi*, makes him the most well-known Legalist thinker.

Perhaps the most famous chapter is chapter 49, which is discussed here. It sums up well the main principles of Legalism: the role of law in governance and the use of rewards and punishments to regulate the people. The chapter closes with a discussion of the "five vermin" mentioned in the chapter title; Han Fei blames these groups for the current state of disorder. Identified as scholars, speechmakers, wayward "swordsmen," cowards, and merchants and artisans (which are lumped together), these "five vermin," if not eliminated, will bring about the utter destruction of any state that tolerates their presence. Han Fei's designation of these groups as vermin also shows his disdain for intellectual debate—which he dismissed as pedantic sophistry and empty rhetoric—his emphasis on loyal military service to the state, and his privileging of agriculture over commerce.

♦ **Paragraphs 1–5**

The story of the farmer who hopes that another rabbit will run into the stump in his field is meant as a criticism of Confucianism, for its insistence that the solutions to the problems of the day lay in the ancient past, a point made explicit in the last sentence. Confucians revered the sage-kings who ruled during the golden age, a reference to the period that led to the emergence of the legendary Xia Dynasty sometime before the first documented dynasty, the Shang (ca. 1600–1050 BCE). While lack of evidence places the existence of the Xia in question, stories passed down from generation to generation provided a link to this mythical past. Inspired by those stories, Confucians held that a government modeled after "the ways of the ancient kings" could restore the political unity and social harmony enjoyed in the distant past. By comparing Confucians to the farmer, Han Fei illustrates the error in the Confucian logic. The rabbit running into the tree stump was an accident; since the event is not indicative of a broader pattern, there is no guarantee that another rabbit will run into the same tree stump. Just as the farmer waiting in vain for another rabbit to die in the same way in the same location is considered foolish, so, too, is the Confucian belief that another morally upright ruler will appear to usher in another golden age of peace and prosperity.

The next paragraphs explain why methods that worked in the past are no longer effective in the present. Yao and Yu, along with Shun, were the ancient sage-kings extolled by Confucians for their moral perfection. Han Fei compares Yao's life as a ruler to that of "a lowly gatekeeper" and Yu's life as a ruler to that of "a slave taken prisoner in the wars" to set up his argument that the past and the present are fundamentally different. In the present, even the office of the magistrate, the lowest-ranking official, brings with it privileges and wealth that his descendants will continue to enjoy. In contrast to Yao and Yu, who in handing over their position as "Son of Heaven" were "merely forsaking the life of a gatekeeper and escaping from the toil of a slave," even the lowly magistrate occupies a post considered a "prize."

Thus, while Yao and Yu easily surrendered their thrones, magistrates fight to retain their positions. Han Fei drives his point home with the conclusion that "this is

During the Qin Dynasty, Li Si oversaw the suppression of speech and writings in the form of book burnings and executions.

(Burning the Books, illustration from 'Hutchinsons History of the Nations', c.1910 (litho), Burton, H.M. (20th century) / Private Collection / The Bridgeman Art Library International)

because of the difference in the actual benefits received." Because of the much-sought-after entitlements attached to political office in Han Fei's time, officials were driven by greed. If this were true for the magistrate, one is left wondering how much more this would have been the case for the ruler of a state. As in the previous paragraph, Han Fei implies that Confucians are naive to expect a ruler to be inspired by benevolence and altruism to make morally upright choices; in current times, rulers are motivated by self-interest. Even if a ruler were to "lightly relinquish the position of Son of Heaven" in the pattern of the ancient sage-kings, Han Fei continues in the next paragraph, it would not be a reflection of his moral uprightness but would be owing to the lack of benefits attached to the royal title. The quest for power, he concludes, is what drives the competition for political office.

In his efforts to discredit Confucianism, Han Fei questions the moral superiority of the sage-kings, but he does not abandon the model of the sage as a ruler. Han Fei depicts the sage-king as a pragmatist, concerned more with economic than moral issues, as suggested by the sage's preoccupation with "the quantity of things" as they relate

"Circumstances change according to the age, and ways of dealing with them change with the circumstances."

"Past and present have different customs; new and old adopt different measures."

"People by nature grow proud on love, but they listen to authority."

"The best rewards are those that are generous and predictable, so that the people may profit by them. The best penalties are those that are severe and inescapable, so that the people will fear them. The best laws are those that are uniform and inflexible, so that the people can understand them."

"The ruler occupies a position whereby he may impose his will upon others, and he has the whole wealth of the nation at his disposal; he may dispense lavish rewards and severe penalties and, by wielding these two handles, may illuminate all things through his wise policies."

to "scarcity and plenty." Han Fei's sage metes out punishments in accordance with current customs. Consequently, a light penalty should not be misconstrued as a reflection of his "compassion," as Confucians are wont to do, in much the same way that a harsh sentence should not be misread as cruelty. Han Fei's sage adapts to changing times, ruling in accordance with what the present situation dictates rather than trying to impose outdated ideas in a futile effort to re-create a past long gone.

Han Fei uses a simile here to reinforce his point. The people are compared to a "runaway horse," and the "reins" and "whip" symbolize laws and punishments. Just as it is impossible to control a wild horse without "reins or whip," so is the Confucian prescription of "generous and lenient government" ineffective in ruling the people. Or, put another way, just as reins and a whip can be used to control the horse, so, too, can laws and punishments be used to rule the people. Rulers in this "critical age" face unprecedented challenges, and traditional Confucian reforms are no longer up to the task. As Han Fei sums up, "Past and present have different customs; new and old adopt different measures." The Confucians' "ignorance" stems from their refusal to recognize that the present no longer resembles the past; their insistence on using old methods to confront new problems, Han Fei predicts, can only bring "misfortune."

♦ Paragraphs 6–10

Since Han Fei believes that people are driven by self-interest, he rejects the Confucian idea of benevolence and the Mohist belief that people can be taught to view the interests of others as their own. Paragraph 6 presents the Confucian and Mohist case; paragraph 7 counters the argument. As evidence of the "universal love" held by the ancient kings toward the world, Confucians and Mohists point out that these rulers felt saddened whenever a penalty was carried out, reacting as if their own children had been punished or executed. Confucians and Mohists hold that as long as rulers regard their subjects in the same way as fathers treat their sons, then order will prevail. In his rebuttal, Han Fei identifies two conditions that must be true for their argument to prevail: first, all fathers have to be kind and loving caretakers, and, second, all children have to be dutiful and deferential. However, the existence of "an unruly father or son" disrupts the Confucian and Mohist premise. Using the example of the unruly son, Han Fei reasons that even if the first condition is met, as "all parents may show love for their children," the second condition does not follow, for "the children are not always well behaved." Therein lies the flaw of the Confucian and Mohist logic regarding the effectiveness of "universal love." Han Fei concludes with a rhetorical question: If the affection that parents shower on their children cannot guarantee that the children will be respectful, then how can a ruler's love for his subjects be expected to produce an obedient populace?

The only way to secure the obedience of the people, Han Fei continues, is through a system of laws and punishments applied universally and enforced uniformly. Even the ancient sage-kings subscribed to this view. Although their "humaneness" may have made them "shed tears and be reluctant to apply penalties," they recognized that "penalties must be applied" and upheld the law. When forced to make a choice, they "allowed law to be supreme." Although the Legalist advocacy of the supremacy of the law should not be conflated with contemporary understandings of the "rule of law," there are obvious similarities. Revising the Confucian interpretation of the sage-kings, Han Fei attributes the peace and order of ancient times to the sage-kings' reliance on laws and punishments, not to their benevolent morality.

In paragraph 9, Han Fei returns to the example of the unruly son—here described as "a young man of bad character"—to reiterate his point that the sharp sting of the law works more effectively than the gentle guidance of morality to remold behavior. As Han Fei explains at the end, "people by nature grow proud on love, but they listen to authority." The symbols of love—parents, neighbors, and teachers—have no effect on this young man's behavior; their loving concern only makes him more arrogant. But the agents of authority—the magistrate and soldiers—fill him with terror and motivate him to change his ways.

Paragraph 10 sums up well the Legalist position: good governance depends on rewards, penalties, and laws. Since people are motivated by "profit" and "fear," a system of rewards and punishments provides the best means to encourage desired behavior and curb unwanted conduct. The more appealing the rewards for a particular action, the more people will participate in that activity. Likewise, the harsher the penalty, the less they will engage in that activity. Lest there be any confusion about what the state considers to be bad conduct, laws should be clearly communicated to the people. Han Fei's criteria for the "best" of things within the Legalist system reflect his concern with standardization: predictable rewards, inescapable penalties, and uniform and inflexible laws. The emphasis on uniformity in particular has led some scholars to credit the Legalists with the concept of equality under the law.

♦ Paragraphs 11–15

Legalists disagree with the Confucian emphasis on moral education as the cornerstone of good government. The Confucian political ideal is a virtuous ruler who leads by moral example and is assisted by a retinue of scholar-officials. Han Fei, however, sees fundamental conflicts of interest between morality and power and between scholarly learning and government administration. To illustrate his point, he first tells the story of Honest Gong from Chu, who in turning his father in to the magistrate for stealing a sheep, served his king but betrayed his father; for this he was executed. Confucius, too, acknowledges the potential conflict between loyalty to the ruler and filial piety to the father, and he privileges the latter, as indicated in the second story of the man from Lu, who chose to fulfill his filial

obligation to his ailing father over his military service to his king, a decision Confucius rewarded with a promotion.

But for Han Fei, these scenarios present an irreconcilable conflict in Confucianism, one that undermines the ability of the state to effectively govern. In paragraph 13 he brings the two stories together to drive home his point. When the magistrate of Chu executed Honest Gong for turning in his father, the magistrate presumably did not punish the father for stealing the sheep, as suggested by Han Fei's comment that "the felonies of the state were never reported to the authorities." And when Confucius rewarded the man from Lu who elected to be filial to his father rather than loyal to his king, the people learned that it was acceptable to shirk their military duties. Both cases privileged filial piety; the former punished Honest Gong for not being filial, and the latter rewarded the man from Lu for being filial. But in both cases, the state lost; in the former, a crime against the state went unreported and unpunished, and in the latter, people learned to ignore the state's call to service. Private interests are inherently at odds with state goals, Han Fei concludes, since a ruler cannot praise "the private individual" for acts of filial piety without jeopardizing "the state's altars of the soil and grain," or the needs to defend the state's territory and to ensure agricultural production.

Han Fei turns to etymology to reinforce his point that "public and private are mutually opposed." The ideogram for "public" is, in fact, composed of two units, one meaning "opposed to" and the other meaning "private"; where the character for "public" means "opposed to private," the senses of the terms follow suit. If privacy connotes "self-centeredness," then it can never be "identical in interest" to that of the collective.

Next, Han Fei elaborates the point he made in paragraph 10 about the importance of promulgating laws that the people can easily understand. In contrast to Confucians, who hold that laws should be based on ritual and propriety, which only the learned truly grasp, Legalists see no need to link laws to abstruse philosophical abstractions. In their defense, Confucians do not think that the people need to understand "the doctrines of the wise men"; Confucius is reputed to have said that people can be made to act in specific ways even if they cannot be made to understand why.

♦ Paragraphs 16–19

Legalists question the Confucian emphasis on moral integrity as a basis for government on philosophical and practical grounds. Confucians view "integrity and good faith" as prerequisites for public service, but Han Fei sees no place for these qualities in politics. Only the weak, Han Fei argues, value "integrity and good faith" because they "have no means to protect themselves from deceit." To illustrate his point, he compares commoners to the ruler. Most people seek honest friends because, lacking the wealth and authority to influence others, they are unable to protect themselves from deceit. The ruler, on the other hand, has access to the entire country's wealth and holds the power to reward or punish as he sees fit; this is what enables him to rule effectively and to keep dishonest officials in line. A ruler should rely on wealth and power to help him govern, rather than waiting for the assistance of men of strong moral character as the Confucians suggest.

In the next paragraph, Han Fei explains why the Confucian suggestion is unrealistic. Han Fei does concede that there are "men of true integrity and good faith" to be found and that they would make good officials. However, such men are too few in number to staff all the positions in government. Thus, instead of relying on "wise men," rulers should turn to laws. As suggested by their names, Legalists place greater faith in laws than in men to govern. Men of good character come and go, but well-constructed laws remain forever.

Paragraph 18 can be summed up with the axiom "Actions speak louder than words." In another subtle barb at Confucians, Han Fei criticizes people who read about and discuss politics, agriculture, and warfare but do nothing. He advises rulers to "make use of men's strength" and "reward their accomplishments" as ways to gain the devotion of their subjects. Paragraph 19 offers specific suggestions. Farmers should be well paid for their crops, to motivate them to continue with the arduous labor necessary to maintain the state's wealth. Soldiers should be honored for their service, to encourage citizens to make sacrifices for the state's security. If learning and oratory instead are to be rewarded, as the Confucians suggest, then Han Fei predicts "the age will become disordered," as most people will forgo "hard work" and "the danger of battle" to gain wealth and fame through the unproductive pursuit of learning.

♦ Paragraphs 20–22

The remaining paragraphs should be read together. Paragraph 20 describes "the state of an enlightened ruler," which stands in stark contrast to the "disordered state" detailed in paragraph 21. The last paragraph concludes with predictions of the dire consequences that will result if Han Fei's suggestions are not followed. In paragraph 20, Han Fei makes clear his disdain for learning. Laws, not books, are all that need to be read. The words of current officials, not of former kings, should guide actions. Military skill, not book learning, should be cultivated. Fighting should occur only on the part of those in the army against a common enemy. All actions should have practical, utilitarian purposes. According to Han Fei, any state that follows these prescriptions will acquire wealth and power.

Not surprisingly, "the customs of a disordered state" are the complete opposite of those in the "enlightened" state. The disordered state's "scholars" are blamed for invoking the ancient sage-kings and manipulating rhetoric to undermine current laws and confuse the ruler. Han Fei targets this state's "speechmakers" for pursuing their own interests and defrauding the state. He castigates its "swordsmen" for caring only about gaining fame for themselves and defying the state, prompting people to look for ways to shirk military service. Its "merchants and artisans" care only about maximizing their profits and contribute nothing useful to society. These are the five groups identified by Han Fei in the last paragraph as "the vermin of the state" that rulers must eliminate in order to save their state and their dynasty.

Audience

Han Fei's audience consisted of the rulers of his day, who he hoped would enlist him as a political adviser. The ruler of the Qin state took notice of Han Fei's ideas, and although he sent Han Fei to his death instead of retaining him for political service, the Qin ruler did adopt many Legalist precepts. Thinkers from other philosophical tradi-

Questions for Further Study

1. What was Legalism, and what did the doctrines and beliefs of Legalists have to do with religion?

2. The entry explains that the document arose from the turmoil surrounding the Warring States Period. Compare this with the political turmoil surrounding Martin Luther's *Ninety-five Theses* and the Canons and Decrees of the Council of Trent. In what ways did the documents' authors write in a political context?

3. In what ways did the Legalist philosophy differ from traditional Confucianism? Why were these differences important? For comparative purposes, see the entry on the Analects of Confucius.

4. To what extent, if any, do you believe that the contemporary United States embodies elements of a Legalist philosophy? Explain.

5. What, in Han Fei's view, are the characteristics of an enlightened ruler? To what extent do you believe that contemporary presidents, premiers, prime ministers, and the like should adopt a philosophy similar to Han Fei's?

tions, most notably Confucianism, also read the *Han Feizi* and were harsh critics of Legalist views on political authority and human nature. Given the prominence of Confucianism beginning in the second century BCE, the readership of the *Han Feizi* declined, although it continued to be read for its political ideas as well as for its rhetoric.

In recent times the *Han Feizi* has gained a more receptive and wider audience, both within and outside China. Students of comparative political philosophy, Chinese philosophy, and Chinese history have appreciated its contributions to political theory and rhetorical style. Often read in conjunction with Confucian texts like the Analects, the *Han Feizi* continues the millennia-long debate on the nature of political power.

Impact

The adoption of Legalist ideas during the short-lived Qin Dynasty saw the meteoric rise of Legalism but ironically also caused its fall, in name if not in form. Although recent scholarship has done much to rehabilitate the image of the Qin, it is still generally regarded as an authoritarian state notorious for its ruthlessness. Because of its association with the Qin, Legalism's contribution to Chinese civilization has not been given the attention it deserves. Given that much of what is known about the Qin and Legalism comes from the Han—the dynasty that followed the Qin and which formally adopted Confucianism as its official ideology—the negative connotations attached to both are not surprising. Yet the continuing influence of Legalism can be discerned in the long tradition of legal codification promoted by Han Fei and other Legalist philosophers.

Despite the denunciation of Legalism by Confucian scholars, the rulers of the Han Dynasty, which endorsed Confucianism, recognized the practical value of Legalist ideas. For all their philosophical differences, history has proved that Confucianism and Legalism can coexist, as reflected in what has been described as the "Confucianization" of Chinese law. The Tang Code, which dates to the seventh century, is the earliest extant legal code, traceable in large part to its reproduction in the codes of subsequent dynasties. The punitive tone of all imperial legal codes re-flects the Legalist emphasis on punishment as a means to curb criminal behavior.

The *Han Feizi* is also recognized for its contributions to political theory. Often compared to the Italian philosopher Niccolò Machiavelli's 1513 treatise *Il principe* (*The Prince*), the *Han Feizi* is above all concerned with power—how to acquire it, maintain it, and expand it. Its explicit rejection of moral governance, a reflection of its criticism of Confucianism, has been construed as advocating amorality at best or justifying immorality at worst. In recent years, Legalism has garnered greater attention as China reforms its legal system and laws. Some who wish to emphasize the longevity of the legal tradition in Chinese history hold Legalism up as evidence that the concepts of equality before the law and the rule of law have long existed in China.

Further Reading

■ Books

Han Fei. *Han Feizi: Basic Writings*, trans. Burton Watson. New York: Columbia University Press, 2003.

Head, John W., and Yanping Wang. *Law Codes in Dynastic China: A Synopsis of Chinese Legal History in the Thirty Centuries from Zhou to Qing*. Durham, N.C.: Carolina Academic Press, 2005.

Qu Tongzu. *Law and Society in Traditional China*. Paris: Mouton, 1961.

■ Journals

Han Fei Tzu and W. K. Liao. "Learned Celebrities: A Criticism of the Confucians and the Moists." *Harvard Journal of Asiatic Studies* 3, no. 2 (July 1938): 161–171.

Hulsewé, A. F. P. "Fragments of Han Law." *T'oung Pao* 76, nos. 4/5 (1990): 208–233.

Rubin, Vitali. "Shen Tao and Fa-Chia." *Journal of the American Oriental Society* 94, no. 3 (July–September 1974): 337–346

—Lisa Tran

HAN FEIZI

♦ **"The Five Vermin"**

There was a farmer of Song who tilled the land, and in his field was a stump. One day a rabbit, racing across the field, bumped into the stump, broke its neck, and died. Thereupon the farmer laid aside his plow and took up watch beside the stump, hoping that he would get another rabbit in the same way. But he got no more rabbits, and instead became the laughingstock of Song. Those who think they can take the ways of the ancient kings and use them to govern the people of today all belong in the category of stump-watchers! . . .

When Yao ruled the world, he left the thatch of his roof untrimmed, and the raw timber of his beams was left unplaned. He ate coarse millet and a soup of greens, wore deerskin in the winter days and rough fiber robes in summer. Even a lowly gatekeeper was no worse clothed and provided for than he. When Yu ruled the world, he took plow and spade in hand to lead his people, working until there was no more down on his thighs or hair on his shins. Even the toil of a slave taken prisoner in the wars was no bitterer than his. Therefore those men in ancient times who abdicated and relinquished the rule of the world were, in a manner of speaking, merely forsaking the life of a gatekeeper and escaping from the toil of a slave. Therefore they thought little of handing over the rule of the world to someone else. Nowadays, however, the magistrate of a district dies and his sons and grandsons are able to go riding about in carriages for generations after. Therefore people prize such offices. In the matter of relinquishing things, people thought nothing of stepping down from the position of Son of Heaven in ancient times, yet they are very reluctant to give up the post of district magistrate today; this is because of the difference in the actual benefits received. . . .

When men lightly relinquish the position of Son of Heaven, it is not because they are high-minded but because the advantages of the post are slight; when men strive for sinecures in the government, it is not because they are base but because the power they will acquire is great.

When the sage rules, he takes into consideration the quantity of things and deliberates on scarcity and plenty. Though his punishments may be light, this is not due to his compassion; though his penalties may be severe, this is not because he is cruel; he simply follows the custom appropriate to the time. Circumstances change according to the age, and ways of dealing with them change with the circumstances. . . .

Past and present have different customs; new and old adopt different measures. To try to use the ways of a generous and lenient government to rule the people of a critical age is like trying to drive a runaway horse without using reins or whip. This is the misfortune that ignorance invites.

Now the Confucians and the Mohists all praise the ancient kings for their universal love of the world, saying that they looked after the people as parents look after a beloved child. And how do they prove this contention? They say, "Whenever the minister of justice administered some punishment, the ruler would purposely cancel all musical performances; and whenever the ruler learned that the death sentence had been passed on someone, he would shed tears." For this reason they praise the ancient kings.

Now if ruler and subject must become like father and son before there can be order, then we must suppose that there is no such thing as an unruly father or son. Among human affections none takes priority over the love of parents for their children. But though all parents may show love for their children, the children are not always well behaved. ... And if such love cannot prevent children from becoming unruly, then how can it bring the people to order? . . .

Humaneness may make one shed tears and be reluctant to apply penalties, but law makes it clear that such penalties must be applied. The ancient kings allowed law to be supreme and did not give in to their tearful longings. Hence it is obvious that humaneness cannot be used to achieve order in the state. . . .

Now here is a young man of bad character. His parents rail at him, but he does not reform; the neighbors scold, but he is unmoved; his teachers instruct him, but he refuses to change his ways. Thus, although three fine influences are brought to bear on him—the love of his parents, the efforts of the neighbors, the wisdom of his teachers—yet he remains unmoved and refuses to change so much as a hair on his shin. But let the district magistrate send out the government soldiers to enforce the law and search for evildoers, and then he is filled with terror, reforms his conduct, and changes his ways. Thus the love of parents is not enough to make children learn what is right, but must be backed up by the strict penalties of the local officials; for people by nature grow proud on love, but they listen to authority. . . .

The best rewards are those that are generous and predictable, so that the people may profit by them. The best penalties are those that are severe and inescapable, so that the people will fear them. The best laws are those that are uniform and inflexible, so that the people can understand them. . . .

Those who practice humaneness and rightness should not be praised, for to praise them is to cast aspersion on military achievements; men of literary accomplishment should not be employed in the government, for to employ them is to bring confusion to the law. In the state of Chu there was a man named Honest Gong. When his father stole a sheep, he reported the theft to the authorities. But the local magistrate, considering that the man was honest in the service of his sovereign but a villain to his own father, replied, "Put him to death!" and the man was accordingly sentenced and executed. Thus we see that a man who is an honest subject of his sovereign may be an infamous son to his father.

There was a man of Lu who accompanied his sovereign to war. Three times he went into battle, and three times he ran away. When Confucius asked him the reason, he replied, "I have an aged father, and if I should die, there would be no one to take care of him." Confucius, considering the man filial, recommended him and had him promoted to a post in the government. Thus we see that a man who is a filial son to his father may be a traitorous subject to his lord.

The magistrate of Chu executed a man, and as a result the felonies of the state were never reported to the authorities; Confucius rewarded a man, and as a result the people of Lu thought nothing of surrendering or running away in battle. Since the interests of superior and inferior are as disparate as all this, it is hopeless for the ruler to praise the actions of the private individual and at the same time try to ensure blessing to the state's altars of the soil and grain.

In ancient times when Cang Jie created the system of writing, he used the character for "private" to express the idea of self-centeredness, and combined the elements for "private" and "opposed to" to form the character for "public." The fact that public and private are mutually opposed was already well understood at the time of Cang Jie. To regard the two as being identical in interest is a disaster that comes from lack of consideration. . . .

The world calls worthy those whose conduct is marked by integrity and good faith, and wise those whose words are subtle and mysterious. But even the wisest man has difficulty understanding words that are subtle and mysterious. Now if you want to set up laws for the masses and you try to base them on doctrines that even the wisest men have difficulty in understanding, how can the common people comprehend them? ... Now in administering your rule and dealing with the people, if you do not speak in terms that any man or woman can plainly understand, but long to apply the doctrines of the wise men, then you will defeat your own efforts at rule. Subtle and mysterious words are no business of the people.

If people regard those who act with integrity and good faith as worthy, it must be because they value men who have no deceit, and they value men of no deceit because they themselves have no means to protect themselves from deceit. The common people in selecting their friends, for example, have no wealth by which to win others over, and no authority by which to intimidate others. For that reason they seek for men who are without deceit to be their friends. But the ruler occupies a position whereby he may impose his will upon others, and he has the whole wealth of the nation at his disposal; he may dispense lavish rewards and severe penalties and, by wielding these two handles, may illuminate all things through his wise policies. In that case, even traitorous ministers like Tian Chang and Zihan would not dare to deceive him. Why should he have to wait for men who are by nature not deceitful?

Hardly ten men of true integrity and good faith can be found today, and yet the offices of the state number in the hundreds. If they must be filled by men of integrity and good faith, then there will never be enough men to go around; and if the offices are left unfilled, then those whose business it is to govern will dwindle in numbers while disorderly men increase. Therefore the way of the enlightened ruler is to unify the laws instead of seeking for wise men, to lay down firm policies instead of longing for men of good faith. Hence his laws never fail him, and there is no felony or deceit among his officials. . . .

Now the people of the state all discuss good government, and everyone has a copy of the works on law by Shang Yang and Guan Zhong in his house, and yet the state gets poorer and poorer, for though many people talk about farming, very few put their hands to a plow. The people of the state all discuss military affairs, and everyone has a copy of the works of Sun Wu and Wu Qi in his house, and yet the armies grow weaker and weaker, for though many people talk about war, few buckle on armor. Therefore an enlightened ruler will make use of men's strength but will not heed their words, will reward their accomplishments but will prohibit useless activities. Then the people will be willing to exert themselves to the point of death in the service of their sovereign.

Farming requires a lot of hard work, but people will do it because they say, "This way we can get rich." War is a dangerous undertaking, but people will take part in it because they say, "This way we can become eminent." Now if men who devote themselves to literature or study the art of persuasive speaking are able to get the fruits of wealth without the hard work of the farmer and can gain the advantages of eminence without the danger of battle, then who will not take up such pursuits? So for every man who works with his hands there will be a hundred devoting themselves to the pursuit of wisdom. If those who pursue wisdom are numerous, the laws will be defeated, and if those who labor with their hands are few, the state will grow poor. Hence the age will become disordered.

Therefore, in the state of an enlightened ruler there are no books written on bamboo slips; law supplies the only instruction. There are no sermons on the former kings; the officials serve as the only teachers. There are no fierce feuds of private swordsmen; cutting off the heads of the enemy is the only deed of valor. Hence, when the people of such a state make a speech, they say

nothing that is in contradiction to the law; when they act, it is in some way that will bring useful results; and when they do brave deeds, they do them in the army. Therefore, in times of peace the state is rich, and in times of trouble its armies are strong. . . .

These are the customs of a disordered state: Its scholars praise the ways of the former kings and imitate their humaneness and rightness, put on a fair appearance and speak in elegant phrases, thus casting doubt upon the laws of the time and causing the ruler to be of two minds. Its speechmakers propound false schemes and borrow influence from abroad, furthering their private interests and forgetting the welfare of the state's altars of the soil and grain. Its swordsmen gather bands of followers about them and perform deeds of honor, making a fine name for themselves and violating the prohibitions of the five government bureaus. Those of its people who are worried about military service flock to the gates of private individuals and pour out their wealth in bribes to influential men who will plead for them, in this way escaping the hardship of battle. Its merchants and artisans spend their time making articles of no practical use and gathering stores of luxury goods, accumulating riches, waiting for the best time to sell, and exploiting the farmers.

These five groups are the vermin of the state. If the rulers do not wipe out such vermin, and in their place encourage men of integrity and public spirit, then they should not be surprised, when they look about the area within the four seas, to see states perish and ruling houses wane and die.

Glossary

Cang Jie	the legendary creator of the Chinese writing system
Mohists	members of an influential philosophical, social, and religious movement that flourished during the Warring States Period
Shang Yang and Guan Zhong	well-known legal scholars; Shang Yang was the author of *The Book of Lord Shang*, and Guan Zhong was an administrator and reformist
Song	a reference to a ruling dynasty in China
Sun Wu	a military general during the Spring and Autumn Period
Wu Qi	a Chinese military leader during the Warring States Period
Yu	the legendary founder of the Xia Dynasty in China

Krishna instructing Arjuna

(Krishna instructing Arjuna, illustration from 'Myths of the Hindus and Buddhists' / Private Collection / The Stapleton Collection / The Bridgeman Art Library International)

ca. 200 BCE –200 CE

"A man should not hate any living creature. Let him be friendly and compassionate to all."

Overview

The Bhagavad Gita is a small part (eighteen chapters) of an epic Indian poem called the Mahabharata. The epic narrates events surrounding a historic war so ancient that it is difficult to prove it actually happened. The Bhagavad Gita narrates an interlude prior to a great battle in that war, during which the hero-warrior Arjuna questions Lord Krishna about the best path to spiritual enlightenment, the nature of God and reality, and the purpose of life. Although it is located within the sixth book of the Mahabharata, the Bhagavad Gita can stand alone and is often read independently of the larger epic. It provides a guide for those seeking the right way to live and the purpose of life and answers to other fundamental questions. The title Bhagavad Gita means "Song of God." As the title implies, it consists almost entirely of a message from God, which is conveyed by Lord Krishna, an avatar (incarnation) of Vishnu, the god of preservation. His message speaks of duty, order, enlightenment, the means to enlightenment, and the nature of God, humanity, and the universe.

The Gita has served as inspiration and support for a wide variety of thinkers and spiritual seekers in India and in the Western world. It has been the subject of discourse since the very early stages; there are hundreds of commentaries, subcommentaries, and translations in existence. It contains a condensed and wide-ranging description of Hindu beliefs and practices. Some refer to it as the Hindu Bible, but its impact goes far beyond India and Hindus. It has been widely read in numerous countries and languages and had significant influence in the West. The Gita's authors are unknown, and its date composition, roughly between 200 BCE and 200 CE, can only be estimated.

Context

In the Bhagavad Gita, one finds acceptance of many spiritual paths. The myriad gods and goddesses found within and outside Hinduism are viewed as representatives of the one eternal, unmanifest God, Brahman; worship of any of these gods is considered spiritually appropriate. Also, according to the Gita, such worship is not the only path to spiritual progress. There are many paths, some more effective than others, but all are acceptable to God, as represented in the Gita by Lord Krishna. This acceptance of religious and spiritual diversity helps explain the importance the Gita holds and has held in India for centuries. Hinduism is a mix of many colors; it is a term that covers all of the religions and spiritual paths of an incredibly diverse culture. All of these find acceptance in the Bhagavad Gita.

The Gita discusses philosophy and yoga in ways that encompass the wide range of Hindu spiritual thought and practice, but perhaps most important is its discussion of the path of devotion, or bhakti yoga. In this "Song of God," Krishna explains how to become one with God, to "dwell in" the Lord, and that selfless devotion to any of the multitudinous deities will lead one to him. This emphasis on devotion to God was not always central to the religion of India.

The Gita has its foundation in the Vedas, the earliest scriptures of Indian religion. Although they are accessible today, the Vedas were for millennia passed on orally only to specially trained students of the upper class. The Vedas are based on the religion of the Aryans, or Indo-Europeans, who came out of Central Asia into India around 1500 BCE and include the Rig Veda, Sama Veda, and Yajur Veda, with a fourth, the Atharva Veda, added later. In Vedism, the fire sacrifice was (and still is) performed, using exact formulas, chants, and hymns. The purposes of these rites were to control the gods in order to obtain material favor and to adjust the cosmic order to produce good fortune.

But the meaning of sacrifice eventually changed. Still the province of the priestly class, the sacrifice came to be located within as well as without. Now, the person was also the cosmos where, through the asceticism of fasting and concentration, one could build up interior heat, creating a fire sacrifice within the body in order to attain power or gain cosmic vision. Rather than making adjustments to an outer cosmos through the fire sacrifice and its precise formulas, the person became both the sacrifice and the one sacrificed to. These ideas are best articulated in the Upanishads, the latest of the Vedic commentaries, which were composed around 800–500 BCE. Here, the doctrines of reincarnation and karma and the concept of Brahman as the supreme reality, which are seen in the Bhagavad Gita, are

Time Line

CA. 1500— 800 BCE	■ The Vedas are composed and passed down orally. Religion centers on formulaic rituals of sacrifice to personified nature deities.
CA. 800— 500 BCE	■ The Upanishads are composed, articulating doctrines of reincarnation, karma, the concept of Brahman as the supreme reality, and the idea that Atman is Brahman.
CA. 500 BCE	■ Devotional Hinduism begins to develop, a process that continues to the present day.
CA. 200 BCE —200 CE	■ The Mahabharata, of which the Bhagavad Gita is part, is composed.

clearly articulated for the first time. Of particular relevance to the Gita is the idea of the Atman, which is seen in the Upanishads as "Thou art That," meaning that the self (Atman) is really Brahman, the Only Being, the One Existent, the One Mind.

While the Vedas and Vedic commentaries, including the Bramanas, Aranyakas, and Upanishads, were restricted to advanced upper-caste students, indigenous religion persisted, with its varied spiritual and philosophic cultures. Beginning around 500 BCE, wandering teachers, holy men who begged for food, traveled from village to village offering spiritual instruction. Their teachings varied, but many advocated self-denial and self-control. One such teacher was Siddhartha Gautama, the founder of Buddhism, who taught the middle way between extreme asceticism and indulgence. Hinduism rose to the challenge of competition from this new popular religion with varied responses and alternatives and ultimately superseded Buddhism in India. The new Hinduism offered liberation as well as social organization and plural spiritual paths and stages. Devotional Hinduism also became important, according to which the individual relates to the mystical presence of the unknowable god through love for a personal deity. All of these trends are brought together in the Bhagavad Gita.

About the Author

The Mahabharata is a classic of Indian culture, basically a narrative of war. The original is in Sanskrit, and its author or authors are unknown. However, tradition holds that a legendary sage, Vyasa, dictated the Mahabharata, including the Bhagavad Gita, to the divine scribe Ganesha. Vyasa was

grandfather to both families whose war with each other is narrated in the epic. In addition, the text of the Gita consists primarily of a message from Lord Krishna, an incarnation of Vishnu, the Hindu god of preservation. Thus, it has the authority of God by tradition, though it was heard and written down by a human being.

Among language and literature scholars in both India and the West, opinions vary about the date of the Gita's composition, but current scholarship places it between 200 BCE and 200 CE. It was almost certainly part of India's oral tradition long before it was written down. As such, it would have been recited by traveling singers with great variety of detail and style; the original written text is composed in a metrical form of poetry that is traditionally chanted. Although the Gita is included in the Mahabharata, some believe it to be a later addition to the epic. Note that although the original Gita is entirely in verse, this translation includes both verse and prose.

Explanation and Analysis of the Document

The Bhagavad Gita begins with a dilemma. In the first chapter, as two armies prepare for battle, Arjuna, a warrior of the Pandavas, moves to a position between his army and that of his enemies, the Kauravas. There he sees relatives and teachers on both sides. Overwhelmed at the thought of killing his kin, Arjuna drops his weapon and says he will not fight. The rest of the book is a dialogue between Arjuna and Krishna, Arjuna's dear friend, his chariot driver, and an incarnation of the supreme God, Vishnu.

Arjuna's dilemma is clear: Killing his kin would be wrong, but so would failing in his duty to fight a righteous war. Thus, he is torn between the choice to act and not to act. His concern is with the sinfulness of shedding the blood of his relations. Will this not result in bad karma, leading away from the path of enlightenment and liberation from the cycle of rebirth? Krishna's response, which takes up most of the book, explains reincarnation, karma as the cause of rebirth, and paths to liberation from the cycle of birth and death.

Multiple beliefs and practices are discussed. Each leads to success, according to Krishna, but only renunciation or loss of the ego-self will yield the ultimate reward—release from the cycle of birth and death. Although the three main yogas he discusses, the yogas of knowledge (jnana yoga), action (karma yoga), and devotion (bhakti yoga), differ in method, each entails selflessness. Karma yoga is action dedicated to God and performed without attachment to results, jnana yoga is discriminative knowledge of and absorption in God through meditation and withdrawal from the world, and bhakti yoga is total devotion and surrender to God. Krishna also discusses the nature of God and God's relation to the human self and the larger universe, and he says that all prayers go to him, no matter which god one worships.

Krishna dancing

(Kaliya Krishna [bronze], Indian School [12th century] / Government Museum and National Art Gallery, Madras, India / Giraudon / The Bridgeman Art Library International)

"The world is imprisoned in its own activity, except when actions are performed as worship of God. Therefore you must perform every action sacramentally, and be free from all attachments to results."

"When you have reached enlightenment, ignorance will delude you no longer. In the light of that knowledge you will see the entire creation within your own Atman and in me. / And though you were the foulest of sinners, / This knowledge alone would carry you / Like a raft, over all your sin. / The blazing fire turns wood to ashes: / The fire of knowledge turns all karmas to ashes."

"Brahman is the ritual, / Brahman is the offering, / Brahman is he who offers / To the fire that is Brahman."

"When senses touch objects / The pleasures therefrom / Are like wombs that bear sorrow. / They begin, they are ended: / They bring no delight to the wise."

"A man should not hate any living creature. Let him be friendly and compassionate to all. He must free himself from the delusion of 'I' and 'mine.' He must accept pleasure and pain with equal tranquility. He must be forgiving, ever-contented, self-controlled, united constantly with me in his meditation. His resolve must be unshakable. He must be dedicated to me in intellect and in mind. Such a devotee is dear to me."

♦ **The Yoga of Knowledge**

Krishna begins his response to the question posed in the previous chapter. He admonishes Arjuna; as a member of the warrior caste, it is Arjuna's duty to maintain order and protect the kingdom. The battle is between good and evil, with Arjuna on the side of good. Arjuna's cousins, the Kauravas, have usurped the throne and created disarray and corruption in the kingdom. Since justice demands impartiality, Arjuna should fight; had nonrelations committed such evil deeds, Arjuna would not fail to fight.

Arjuna asks how to recognize one who is illumined. Krishna responds that the illumined are free from the things of desire. Having renounced cravings—such as fear, anger, and lust—they experience "bliss in the Atman," the true self or soul within each person, which is also identified with Brahman. This bliss is happiness beyond worldly pleasure and pain, gained through experience of the Atman within.

Those who practice the yoga of knowledge withdraw from the world, renounce all worldly desires, and become absorbed in God through meditation. They control the senses and are unaffected by them. They fix their thoughts on Brahman, or God, as the impersonal absolute, and seek happiness only through him. Freedom from worldly desires leads one to remain calm, whether faced with fortune or adversity. But those who merely abstain from the things of desire are only running away. Even though they do not act on their desires, they are still tortured by them. The true yogi leaves desire behind. The true yogi knows that the self is Atman and that desire keeps one within the cycle of birth and death. Even one who knows this, however, can have difficulty; the senses are strong and easily delude people.

It takes practice to control the senses and focus attention on God. Merely thinking about sense objects is a slippery slope leading away from the path of enlightenment. When one is confused, one loses the ability to discriminate, or to see the Atman within.

Lust and hatred together contain the whole of human sense attachment. Lust represents all that a person might desire and become attached to, while hatred represents all that one might be averse to. It is only by letting go of these feelings that one can find true peace and happiness. Desire and hatred make it impossible to concentrate on the Atman within. The Atman is the true self, and this is referred to as the light. The senses are illusory, and these are referred to as the dark. Because the senses delude us, we can see the truth only when the senses are put to rest. The Atman is the true light, but it is invisible to the ignorant, who think light comes from the senses. Thus light and dark are referred to as truth and illusion. Although all embodied beings have desires, desire flows through the enlightened without affecting them. Thus, they know peace and are free of ego and pride. This is the "state of enlightenment in Brahman."

◆ Karma Yoga

Arjuna says he is confused. While Krishna has said that renouncing the world leads to release from rebirth, he has also told Arjuna to continue his dutiful actions. Krishna responds, explaining the nature of karma and release from karma. Karma refers to the law of karma, which says that for every action there is a reaction. Thus, action attached to the physical self leads to reaction that keeps one within the physical world through reincarnation. When one dies, the soul is born again in a new body. Karma also simply means action, and karma yoga is the path of liberation through dedicated action. By dedicating one's actions to God and renouncing the desire for results, one acts selflessly, without attachment.

But, Arjuna wonders, since actions bind us to reincarnation through the law of karma, is not renunciation of the world the only way to release? Krishna affirms both paths, saying the yoga of knowledge is for those of a contemplative nature and the yoga of action is for those of an active nature, like Arjuna. Besides, no one can be free of activity—that is the nature of life in the body. Even jnana yogis are not free of action; they practice mental activity.

The conditioned physical world consists of the three *gunas*—*sattwa*, *rajas*, and *tamas*. These dispose us toward certain traits or activities, such as knowledge (*sattwa*), action (*rajas*), or stupor (*tamas*). What binds us to the wheel of life and death is not action but attachment to the results of one's acts. When doing work, for example, if one seeks status and power, one will fear failure and desire success. Such attachment to the results of acts binds people to the cycle of birth and death. Even if one refrains from all actions but continues to think about the things of desire, one remains bound. Krishna says that Arjuna should continue in his duties but without attachment to results and that he should dedicate all his actions to God. One who does this engages in the yoga of action. The world is conditioned by action and reaction—thus imprisoned within

its activity. But actions performed as sacrifices to God do not keep one imprisoned.

Krishna explains that each person is given duties by the Lord of Creation, and such duties involve sacrifice, by which humans flourish. These gods have power and live a very long time, but they too eventually die and are reborn. Those who perform their assigned duties of ritual sacrifice to the *devas* and who pray to the *devas* have their prayers answered by the *devas*. Giving thanks to the *devas* for what they give is also a duty. The *devas* are gods of heavenly realms that are also part of the conditioned world. Brahman ordained that people should perform these acts of sacrifice and thanks; one who fails to do so sins. These rites are revealed in the scriptures (the Vedas). But the yogi who knows bliss in the Atman is no longer bound to perform any action or ritual because he or she does not desire anything that can be attained through these acts. Instead, the yogi offers sacrifice of a different kind, which leads to a different reward.

Krishna says Arjuna should continue in his duties but without attachment to the results. Rather than concern for results, he should perform duties out of concern for others. By continuing in his duties even though he desires nothing that will result from this, Arjuna will set a proper example to others who are less enlightened. Krishna then uses himself as an example: As God, Krishna already possesses everything, yet he continues to work because whatever he does, others will follow. If he did not work, those who look to his example would fail to perform their duties, society would become disordered, and the world would be destroyed.

Krishna compares the ignorant and the wise. The former work for results while the latter work as an example to others. He says the wise should lead by example, showing the ignorant that work dedicated to God is holy. People are not the doers of actions, although egoism leads them to think they are. Actions consist of senses attaching themselves to objects. If Arjuna were to take his weapon and fight, this would not mean that he, Arjuna, acted. Instead, it would mean that *gunas* attached to other *gunas*. The true self is the Atman, which is eternal, unchanging, and unmoved; it does not act nor is it acted upon. The actor is the physical self.

Knowledge of this is obscured, and humans are deluded into thinking they are mind and matter rather than the Atman. This delusion makes them subject to the *gunas*. Since they identify themselves with the physical (and mental) self, they bind themselves to it. The wise know that acts are performed by the *gunas* and do not become attached to the results of these acts. Krishna tells Arjuna to go ahead and fight but to dedicate all actions to God. He also tells Arjuna to renounce the ego, focus on the Atman, and be detached from the results. This is the nature of right action, which leads to union with God rather than to worldly rewards. This teaching, if followed with complete faith, will lead to release from the bondage of karma.

◆ Renunciation through Knowledge

Krishna names sages who lived thousands of years ago and says he taught this yoga to them. (Note that "Foe-consumer" refers to Arjuna.) This confuses Arjuna, who sees

Krishna as a young man like himself. Arjuna knows Krishna is God incarnate, but he sometimes forgets, since this knowledge weighs heavily on him. Krishna replies that all are born and reborn over and over. Owing to the power of *Prakriti*, mortals do not remember their past lives. *Prakriti* is the power that brings the physical world into being and is the cause of illusion. (Note that *Maya* and *Prakriti* are interchangeable terms.) Since Krishna is not mortal but God incarnate, he is not subject to this illusion; he therefore remembers his past lives.

Krishna is one of many avatars of Vishnu, the god of preservation. He comes into the world to reestablish order whenever disorder increases. Knowledge of this truth ensures freedom from rebirth, and upon death the knower is united with God. One who takes refuge in Krishna gains freedom from desire, fear, and anger and is cleansed of sin. (Note that karma, which binds one to rebirth, is often referred to as sin or impurity.) Those who worship Krishna will have their wishes granted; whatever path they choose in seeking God, they will find him. Those who seek material success will attain it.

The four castes are Brahmins (scholars, priests), Kshatriyas (warriors, kings), Vaishyas (merchants, farmers), and Shudras (servants). These castes are said to correspond to the *gunas* as well. Although God authored this system, he is beyond it; God has no desires and so is not bound by the *gunas*, nor do any of his actions result in karmic reaction. Action without karmic reaction can also be engaged in by those who seek liberation if they act without desire for results.

Knowledge of action and inaction liberates one from attachment and the karma that results from it. Acting with desire creates karmic reaction, binding one to the *gunas* and to reincarnation. But one who is without desire is free of the binding effects of his or her acts. Free of the ego sense of "I" and "mine," such a person's acts do not result in karmic reaction. Desiring nothing, the person feels neither happiness when things are pleasant nor sorrow when there is loss but is simply contented with whatever comes. Such a person will be freed from all past karma and from future karma as well, as every action is made as a sacrifice to Brahman. When actions are dedicated to Brahman, Brahman is in the ritual, the offering, the one who offers, and the one who receives the offering; that is, Brahman is in all. Those who worship the *devas* in search of worldly rewards find what they seek, but those who renounce the self and make sacrifice to Brahman will find him.

Krishna lists many of the ways of renunciation, calling each a sacrifice. Each of these ways leads to union with Brahman/God. Each is a form of sacrificial worship that frees one from karma and rebirth. The scriptures prescribe all of these ways and more, and each involves action. Unlike ritual sacrifice of material offerings (to the *devas*), which leads only to material rewards, worship of Brahman with internal sacrifices leads to spiritual rewards.

The author supports the tradition of subordinating oneself to a guru for spiritual instruction. The enlightened see the whole world within the Atman and within God. This knowledge alone is enough to cleanse one of all past karma, even the worst. Devotion to God and mastery of the senses lead to enlightenment and knowledge of Brahman and union with God. This knowledge comes to those who master the senses through yoga practice. One who acts selflessly and knows Brahman through experience in the Atman is not bound by karma.

Krishna says Arjuna still has doubts and that delusion is the cause. He tells Arjuna to use his faculty of discrimination to destroy his doubts. Discrimination is a faculty of the higher intellect through which one can recognize that there is no "I" or "mine," only the Atman.

♦ **The Yoga of Renunciation**

Arjuna asks for a definite answer as to whether acting or renouncing action is better. Krishna replies that both are better than abstaining from action. One who renounces desire and aversion is on the path to true knowledge. Those who say jnana yoga and karma yoga differ are ignorant, for both lead to the same end, freedom from rebirth. The jnana yogi must also act rightly. Right action is action dedicated to God. The jnana yogi finds Brahman quickly when he or she is purified by the yoga of action.

Awake to the Atman, the yogi knows that he or she is one with all creatures; all share the same soul, and all exist within Brahman. One who is enlightened does not identify the self with the senses and therefore knows that he or she is not the doer of any act. The body senses and moves, eats, breathes, and excretes. But the true "I" is not the body; it is the Atman. Desiring nothing, the yogi offers all acts as a sacrifice to Brahman, and hence no karma results. The karma yogi knows the self that acts is simply an instrument. Knowing this, his actions do not create reactions, and his past karma eventually wears off ("his heart grows pure"). One who is joined with Brahman through knowledge of true Reality, who renounces desire for results, and who performs his own duties is free of karmic reaction. He finds peace. But those who desire results are slaves to action and reaction.

Discrimination is that higher faculty that enables one to recognize the Atman. The city of nine gates is the body (two eyes, two ears, and so forth). One who is enlightened is happy knowing that his or her Atman is unaffected by action and that he or she does nothing to affect the karma of others. The ignorant dream that they are the body and that they are the doers. This illusion is created by Maya; God does not create this illusion. God is perfect, God is everywhere. God has no desire one way or the other. We dream this illusion because darkness deludes us.

Atman is Brahman. Knowledge of Atman drives out the darkness, and the true self, Brahman, is revealed. To know and dwell with God/Brahman always is the true aim of the enlightened. Find God in your heart, dwell with God always, and you become free of sin from past deeds and thoughts. You will not be reborn. The enlightened see everything the same—all dwell in Brahman, and Atman is within all. Note that *Brahmin* refers to persons of the priestly class and not to God/Brahman.

Brahman never changes and is forever untouched by karma. Constant devotion to Brahman leads one beyond the limitations of physical life even while living in the body. Those who dwell in Brahman are unaffected by things pleasant or unpleasant. They are affected only by Brahman; their reward is happiness forever. Sensual pleasures result only in sorrow. Such pleasures are transient. The person who masters every impulse that derives from desire or anger will know Brahman and be happy, even while residing in the body. One whose only happiness derives from bliss in the Atman will unite with Brahman and finally know ultimate and eternal bliss after death. Such a person has complete faith and total mastery of the senses, acts only for the benefit of others, and desires nothing. Imperfections and past sins are washed away. Nirvana is to be found in this life and after death by those self-controlled, free of desire, and with knowledge of the Atman. The yogi who withdraws from the senses; sets aside desire, fear, and anger; and focuses on the Atman through meditation practice will find eternal freedom.

Here, Krishna identifies himself with Brahman, saying one who finds Brahman through concentration on Atman finds him. Krishna also says he is the "author of every offering and all austerity." Thus, Krishna identifies himself with each devotee as well. Note that "son of Kunti" is a reference to Arjuna, whose mother was Kunti.

◆ The Yoga of Devotion

In the chapter before "The Yoga of Devotion," Krishna has revealed himself fully to Arjuna. This is an extraordinary passage, in which Arjuna experiences a theophany, or vision of God. The vision is so magnificent and terrifying that Arjuna asks Krishna to retake the comfortable human form he previously knew. "The Yoga of Devotion" follows the theophany with Krishna's discourse on the third path to liberation, the yoga of devotion to God. Arjuna asks whether worshipping Krishna as a personal god versus worshipping Brahman as the impersonal absolute leads to greater understanding of yoga. Krishna says it is the former.

Devotees of the impersonal absolute will also unite with God, he says, but this is the harder task for embodied souls to attain. Those who offer selfless devotion to Krishna, offering every action as a sacrifice to him, take the easier and faster path to union with God. Krishna says he will save those who love him from repeated births and deaths. Krishna tells Arjuna to put his thoughts steadily on him, and, if Arjuna cannot do this, to seek God in meditation. If he cannot do this, he should surrender the self completely to God.

Concentration on God with wisdom is better than mechanical ritual or prayer, but devoting oneself to worship of God day and night is even better. Better still is renouncing the self by surrendering to God; it brings instant peace. Renunciation, then, is the quickest means to union with God. Krishna names the ways to endear oneself to him, such as not hating any living being; being a compassionate, forgiving friend to all; letting go of belief in "I" and "mine"; and so forth. He says the true wisdom of these words will lead to freedom from the cycle of life and death.

Audience

The Mahabharata has been sung or recited orally to all classes in India for many centuries and continues to be retold today in the popular Indian media. The Gita, however, is often read independently of the epic in India and more and more across the world. Its original intended audience was Hindus and likely included yoga practitioners, devotees of Krishna, and other seekers of truth about God, reality, and enlightenment. Today the Gita remains popular among the Indian masses and across the world. In India, it is read or recited by devotees of Krishna and other Hindu gods and may be read by anyone from childhood to old age as a guide to right living. In the West, it is also popular with a wide variety of audiences, from religious seekers to academics, social activists, and yoga practitioners, who may profess to any or no religious faith.

Impact

The impact of the Bhagavad Gita within and outside India can hardly be overestimated. From the Indian philosopher Adi Shankara, of the eighth century CE, to Ramanuja in the eleventh century and Madhva in the thirteenth, the meaning of the Gita has been variously interpreted to support nondualist, theistic, and mystical philosophies, among others. In the nineteenth century, it became a symbol of Hindu nationalism, and in the twentieth, the Indian political and spiritual leader Mohandas Gandhi, viewing the Gita as allegory rather than history, used it as both a political and a moral guide.

The Gita's message of action in the world for the welfare of others supports an activist element within Indian nationalism, but the book also supports renunciatory views of withdrawal from the world in the quest for liberation. The former was seen especially in connections between social and political action and the Gita's message about karma yoga. Bal Gangadhar Tilak, the first leader of Indian independence, felt that the Gita taught that action could not be avoided and was necessary for the welfare of the world and therefore the book's importance lay in its promotion of dedicated action. Gandhi saw the Gita as a work offering comfort, wisdom, and guidance. Interpreting the martial setting of the book allegorically, he believed the Gita taught prayer, devotion, and selfless action that should be nonviolent. He believed the Gita set out the principles of Hinduism more clearly than any other Hindu scripture and rejected the idea that it taught withdrawal from the world. Rather, he believed it taught the merging of religion with everyday life.

In the West, the Gita was first translated into English in 1785, followed by translations into French, Latin, and German. In the nineteenth century, the Gita influenced American transcendentalists Ralph Waldo Emerson and Henry David Thoreau and was the subject of lectures by Swami Vivekenanda to Western audiences. In the twentieth century, the Gita has helped spread Hinduism through such important figures as Swami Bhaktivedanta, founder of the International Society for Krishna Consciousness; Paramahansa Yogananda, founder of Self-Realization Fellowship; and Maharishi Mahesh Yogi, who introduced Transcendental Meditation.

The Gita continues to be highly influential and inspirational to many audiences today. It is a truly international book of spiritual, moral, political, and artistic import. Beyond India, it is often read in the West by those at various levels of involvement with Hindu-inspired movements such as Vedanta, Self-Realization, and Transcendental Meditation. The message of dedicated action, in particular, has been taken as an ideal for political action by influential persons such as Thoreau, Gandhi, and the American civil rights activist Martin Luther King, each of whom worked toward nonviolent resistance to tyranny and oppression and was inspired in goals and methods by the Gita.

Further Reading

■ Books

Brockington, J. L. *The Sacred Thread: Hinduism in Its Continuity and Diversity*. Edinburgh: Edinburgh University Press, 1981.

Buck, William. *Mahabharata*. Berkeley: University of California Press, 2000.

Daniélou, Alain. *Hindu Polytheism*. New York: Pantheon Books, 1964.

Desai, Mahadev H., ed. *The Gospel of Selfless Action; or, The Gita according to Gandhi*. Roseville, Calif.: Dry Bones Press, 2000.

Flood, Gavin. *An Introduction to Hinduism*. Cambridge, U.K.: Cambridge University Press, 2004.

Lipner, Julius, ed. *The Fruits of Our Desiring: An Enquiry into the Ethics of the Bhagavadgita for Our Times*. Calgary, Canada: Bayeux, 1997.

Robinson, Catherine A. *Interpretations of the Bhagavad-Gita and Images of the Hindu Tradition: The Song of the Lord*. London: Routledge, 2006.

Roebuck, Valerie J., trans. *The Upanishads*. London: Penguin Books, 2003.

Sharpe, Eric J. *The Universal Gita*. LaSalle, Ill.: Open Court, 1985.

■ Web Sites

"Bhagavad-Gita: The Book of Life." Atma Jyoti Ashram Web site.
   http://www.atmajyoti.org/gi_bhagavad_gita_intro.asp

"The Bhagavad-Gita Home Page." Hindu Web site.
   http://www.hinduwebsite.com/gitaindex.asp

"Indian Philosophies." Advaita Vedanta Web site.
   http://www.advaita-vedanta.org/avhp/ind-phil.html

—Susan de Gaia

Questions for Further Study

1. In the West, yoga is practiced by many people as a form of physical exercise and relaxation. Based on your reading of the Bhagavad Gita, how do you think a Hindu would define the word *yoga?*

2. Similarly, the word *karma* is often used in the West, often casually to meaning something like "good vibes" or "bad vibes." Again, based on your reading of the Bhagavad Gita, how do you think a Hindu would define the word *karma?*

3. Hindus accept a passage from the Rig Veda that says, "The truth is One, but different sages [wise people] call it by different names." To what extent do you think this philosophy is embodied in the Bhagavad Gita?

4. The Bhagavad Gita repeatedly refers to Brahman as God, or the impersonal absolute. Yet Hinduism is a polytheistic religion. How would you explain what appears on the surface to be an inconsistency?

5. What is dualism, and what does the Bhagavad Gita say or imply about the dualist view of the universe?

BHAGAVAD GITA

◆ The Yoga of Knowledge

Arjuna:

Krishna, how can one identify a man who is firmly established and absorbed in Brahman? In what manner does an illumined soul speak? How does he sit?
How does he walk?

Sri Krishna:

He knows bliss in the Atman
And wants nothing else.
Cravings torment the heart:
He renounces cravings.
I call him illumined.

Not shaken by adversity,
Not hankering after happiness:
Free from fear, free from anger,
Free from the things of desire.
I call him a seer, and illumined.

The bonds of his flesh are broken.
He is lucky, and does not rejoice:
He is unlucky, and does not weep.
I call him illumined.

The tortoise can draw in its legs:
The seer can draw in his senses.
I call him illumined.

The abstinent run away from what they desire
But carry their desires with them:
When a man enters Reality,
He leaves his desires behind him.

Even a mind that knows the path
Can be dragged from the path:
The senses are so unruly.
But he controls the senses
And recollects the mind
And fixes it on me.
I call him illumined.

Thinking about sense-objects

Will attach you to sense-objects;
Grow attached, and you become addicted;
Thwart your addiction, it turns to anger;
Be angry, and you confuse your mind;
Confuse your mind, you forget the lesson of experience;
Forget experience, you lose discrimination;
Lose discrimination, and you miss life's only purpose.

When he has no lust, no hatred,
A man walks safely among the things of lust and hatred.
To obey the Atman
Is his peaceful joy;
Sorrow melts
Into that clear peace:
His quiet mind
Is soon established in peace.

The uncontrolled mind
Does not guess that the Atman is present:
How can it meditate?
Without meditation, where is peace?
Without peace, where is happiness?

The wind turns a ship
From its course upon the waters:
The wandering winds of the senses
Cast man's mind adrift
And turn his better judgment from its course.

When a man can still the senses
I call him illumined.
The recollected mind is awake
In the knowledge of the Atman
Which is dark night to the ignorant:
The ignorant are awake in their sense-life
Which they think is daylight:
To the seer it is darkness.

Water flows continually into the ocean
But the ocean is never disturbed:
Desire flows into the mind of the seer
But he is never disturbed.
The seer knows peace:
The man who stirs up his own lusts
Can never know peace.
He knows peace who has forgotten desire.

He lives without craving:
Free from ego, free from pride.

This is the state of enlightenment in Brahman:
A man does not fall back from it
Into delusion.
Even at the moment of death
He is alive in that enlightenment:
Brahman and he are one.

♦ **Karma Yoga**

Arjuna:

BUT, KRISHNA, if you consider knowledge of Brahman superior to any sort of action, why are you telling me to do these terrible deeds?

Your statements seem to contradict each other. They confuse my mind. Tell me one definite way of reaching the highest good.

Sri Krishna:

I have already told you that, in this world, aspirants may find enlightenment by two different paths. For the contemplative is the path of knowledge: for the active is the path of selfless action.

Freedom from activity is never achieved by abstaining from action. Nobody can become perfect by merely ceasing to act. In fact, nobody can ever rest from his activity even for a moment. All are helplessly forced to act, by the gunas.

A man who renounces certain physical actions but still lets his mind dwell on the objects of his sensual desire, is deceiving himself. He can only be called a hypocrite. The truly admirable man controls his senses by the power of his will. All his actions are disinterested. All are directed along the path to union with Brahman.

Activity is better than inertia. Act, but with self-control. If you are lazy, you cannot even sustain your own body.

The world is imprisoned in its own activity, except when actions are performed as worship of God. Therefore you must perform every action sacramentally, and be free from all attachments to results.

In the beginning
The Lord of beings
Created all men,
To each his duty.
"Do this," He said,
"And you shall prosper.
Duty well done
Fulfills desire
Like Kamadhenu
The wish-fulfiller."

"Doing of duty
Honors the devas:
To you the devas
In turn will be gracious:
Each honoring other,
Man reaches the Highest.
Please the devas:
Your prayer will be granted."
But he who enjoys the devas' bounty
Showing no thanks,
He thieves from the devas.

Pious men eat
What the gods leave over
After the offering:
Thus they are sinless.
But those ungodly
Cooking good food
For the greed of their stomachs
Sin as they eat it.
Food quickens the life-sperm:
Food grows from the rainfall
Called down out of heaven
By sacrifice offered:
Sacrifice speaks
Through the act of the ritual.

This is the ritual
Taught by the sacred
Scriptures that spring
From the lips of the Changeless:
Know therefore that Brahman
The all-pervading
Is dwelling for ever
Within this ritual.
If a man plays no part
In the acts thus appointed
His living is evil
His joy is in lusting.
Know this, O Prince:
His life is for nothing.

But when a man has found delight and satisfaction and peace in the Atman, then he is no longer obliged to perform any kind of action. He has nothing to gain in this world by action, and nothing to lose by refraining from action. He is independent of everybody and everything. Do your duty, always; but without attachment. That is how a man reaches the ultimate Truth; by working without anxiety about results. In fact, Janaka and many others reached enlightenment, simply because they did their duty in this spirit. Your motive in working should be to set others, by your example, on the path of duty.

Whatever a great man does, ordinary people will imitate; they follow his example. Consider me: I am not bound by any sort of duty. There is nothing, in all the three worlds, which I do not already possess; nothing I have yet to acquire. But I go on working, nevertheless. If I did not continue to work untiringly as I do, mankind would still follow me, no matter where I led them. Suppose I were to stop? They would all be lost. The result would be caste-mixture and universal destruction.

The ignorant work
For the fruit of their action:
The wise must work also
Without desire
Pointing man's feet
To the path of his duty.
Let the wise beware
Lest they bewilder
The minds of the ignorant
Hungry for action:
Let them show by example
How work is holy
When the heart of the worker
Is fixed on the Highest.

Every action is really performed by the gunas. Man, deluded by his egoism, thinks: "I am the doer." But he who has the true insight into the operations of the gunas and their various functions, knows that when senses attach themselves to objects, gunas are merely attaching themselves to gunas. Knowing this, he does not become attached to his actions.

The illumined soul must not create confusion in the minds of the ignorant by refraining from work. The ignorant, in their delusion, identify the At-

man with the gunas. They become tied to the senses and the action of the senses.

Shake off this fever of ignorance. Stop hoping for worldly rewards. Fix your mind on the Atman. Be free from the sense of ego. Dedicate all your actions to me. Then go forward and fight. . . .

♦ **Renunciation through Knowledge**

Sri Krishna:

Foe-consumer,
Now I have shown you
Yoga that leads
To the truth undying.

I taught this yoga
First to Vivaswat,
Vivaswat taught it
In turn to Manu,
Next Ikshvaku
Learnt it from Manu,
And so the sages
In royal succession
Carried it onward
From teacher to teacher,
Till at length it was lost,
Throughout ages forgotten.

Arjuna:

Vivaswat was born long before you. How am I to believe that you were the first to teach this yoga?

Sri Krishna:

You and I, Arjuna,
Have lived many lives.
I remember them all:
You do not remember.

I am the birthless, the deathless,
Lord of all that breathes.
I seem to be born:
It is only seeming,
Only my Maya.
I am still master
Of my Prakriti,
The power that makes me.

When goodness grows weak,
When evil increases,

I make myself a body.

In every age I come back
To deliver the holy,
To destroy the sin of the sinner,
To establish righteousness.

He who knows the nature
Of my task and my holy birth
Is not reborn
When he leaves this body:
He comes to me.

Flying from fear,
From lust and anger,
He hides in me
His refuge, his safety:
Burnt clean in the blaze of my being,
In me many find home.

Whatever wish men bring me in worship,
That wish I grant them.
Whatever path men travel
Is my path:
No matter where they walk
It leads to me.

Most men worship the gods because they want success in their worldly undertakings. This kind of material success can be gained very quickly here on earth.

I established the four castes, which correspond to the different types of guna and karma. I am their author; nevertheless, you must realize that I am beyond action and changeless. Action does not contaminate me. I have no desire at all for the fruits of action. A man who understands my nature in this respect will never become the slave of his own activity. Because they understood this, the ancient seekers for liberation could safely engage in action. You, too, must do your work in the spirit of those early seers.

What is action? What is inaction? Even the wise are puzzled by this question. Therefore, I will tell you what action is. When you know that, you will be free from all impurity. You must learn what kind of work to do, what kind of work to avoid, and how to reach a state of calm detachment from your work. The real nature of action is hard to understand.

He who sees the inaction that is in action, and the action that is in inaction, is wise indeed. Even

when he is engaged in action he remains poised in the tranquility of the Atman.

The seers say truly
That he is wise
Who acts without lust or scheming
For the fruit of the act:
His act falls from him,
Its chain is broken,
Melted in the flame of my knowledge.
Turning his face from the fruit,
He needs nothing:
The Atman is enough.
He acts, and is beyond action.

Not hoping, not lusting,
Bridling body and mind,
He calls nothing his own:
He acts, and earns no evil.

What God's Will gives
He takes, and is contented.
Pain follows pleasure,
He is not troubled:
Gain follows loss,
He is indifferent:
Of whom should he be jealous?
He acts, and is not bound by his action.

When the bonds are broken
His illumined heart
Beats in Brahman:
His every action
Is worship of Brahman:
Can such acts bring evil?
Brahman is the ritual,
Brahman is the offering,
Brahman is he who offers
To the fire that is Brahman.
If a man sees Brahman
In every action,
He will find Brahman.

Some yogis merely worship the devas. Others are able, by the grace of the Atman, to meditate on the identity of the Atman with Brahman. For these, the Atman is the offering, and Brahman the sacrificial fire into which It is offered.

Some withdraw all their senses from contact with exterior sense-objects. For these, hearing and other senses are the offering, and self-discipline the sacrificial fire. Others allow their minds and senses to wander unchecked, and try to see Brahman within all exterior sense-objects. For these, sound and the other sense-objects are the offering, and sense-enjoyment the sacrificial fire.

Some renounce all the actions of the senses, and all the functions of the vital force. For these, such actions and functions are the offering, and the practice of self-control is the sacrificial fire, kindled by knowledge of the Atman.

Then there are others whose way of worship is to renounce sense-objects and material possessions. Others set themselves austerities and spiritual disciplines: that is their way of worship. Others worship through the practice of Raja Yoga.

Others who are earnest seekers for perfection and men of strict vows, study and meditate on the truths of the scriptures. That is their way of worship.

Others are intent on controlling the vital energy; so they practice breathing exercises—inhalation, exhalation, and the stoppage of the breath. Others mortify their flesh by fasting, to weaken their sensual desires, and thus achieve self-control.

All these understand the meaning of sacrificial worship. Through worship, their sins are consumed away. They eat the food which has been blessed in the sacrifice. Thus they obtain immortality and reach eternal Brahman. He who does not worship God cannot be happy even in this world. What, then, can he expect from any other?

All these, and many other forms of worship are prescribed by the scriptures.

All of them involve the doing of some kind of action. When you fully understand this, you will be made free in Brahman

The form of worship which consists in contemplating Brahman is superior to ritualistic worship with material offerings

The reward of all action is to be found in enlightenment.

Those illumined souls who have realized the Truth will instruct you in the knowledge of Brahman, if you will prostrate yourself before them, question them and serve them as a disciple.

When you have reached enlightenment, ignorance will delude you no longer. In the light of that knowledge you will see the entire creation within your own Atman and in me.

And though you were the foulest of sinners,
This knowledge alone would carry you
Like a raft, over all your sin.

The blazing fire turns wood to ashes:
The fire of knowledge turns all karmas to ashes.

On earth there is no purifier
As great as this knowledge,
When a man is made perfect in yoga,
He knows its truth within his heart.
The man of faith,
Whose heart is devoted,
Whose senses are mastered:
He finds Brahman.
Enlightened, he passes
At once to the highest,
The peace beyond passion.

The ignorant, the faithless, the doubter
Goes to his destruction.
How shall he enjoy
This world, or the next,
Or any happiness?

When a man can act without desire,
Through practice of yoga;
When his doubts are torn to shreds,
Because he knows Brahman;
When his heart is poised
In the being of the Atman
No bonds can bind him.

Still I can see it:
A doubt that lingers
Deep in your heart
Brought forth by delusion.
You doubt the truth
Of the living Atman.

Where is your sword
Discrimination?

Draw it and slash
Delusion to pieces.
Then arise
O son of Bharata:
Take your stand
In Karma Yoga.

◆ **The Yoga of Renunciation**
Arjuna:

YOU SPEAK SO HIGHLY of the renunciation of ac-
    tion; yet you ask me to follow the yoga of action.
    Now tell me definitely: which of these is better?

Sri Krishna:

Action rightly renounced brings freedom:
Action rightly performed brings freedom:
Both are better
Than mere shunning of action.

When a man lacks lust and hatred,
His renunciation does not waver.
He neither longs for one thing
Nor loathes its opposite:
The chains of his delusion
Are soon cast off.

The yoga of action, say the ignorant,
Is different from the yoga of the knowledge of Brah-
    man.
The wise see knowledge and action as one:
They see truly.
Take either path
And tread it to the end:
The end is the same.
There the followers of action
Meet the seekers after knowledge
In equal freedom.

It is hard to renounce action
Without following the yoga of action.
This yoga purifies
The man of meditation,
Bringing him soon to Brahman.

When the heart is made pure by that yoga,
When the body is obedient,
When the senses are mastered,
When man knows that his Atman
Is the Atman in all creatures,
Then let him act,

Untainted by action.

The illumined soul
Whose heart is Brahman's heart
Thinks always: "I am doing nothing."
No matter what he sees,
Hears, touches, smells, eats;
No matter whether he is moving,
Sleeping, breathing, speaking,
Excreting, or grasping something with his hand,
Or opening his eyes,
Or closing his eyes:
This he knows always:
"I am not seeing, I am not hearing:
It is the senses that see and hear
And touch the things of the senses."

He puts aside desire,
Offering the act to Brahman.
The lotus leaf rests unwetted on water:
He rests on action, untouched by action.

To the follower of the yoga of action,
The body and the mind,
The sense-organs and the intellect
Are instruments only:
He knows himself other than the instrument
And thus his heart grows pure.

United with Brahman,
Cut free from the fruit of the act,
A man finds peace
In the work of the spirit.
Without Brahman,
Man is a prisoner,
Enslaved by action,
Dragged onward by desire.

Happy is that dweller
In the city of nine gates
Whose discrimination
Has cut him free from his act:
He is not involved in action,
He does not involve others.

Do not say:
"God gave us this delusion."
You dream you are the doer,
You dream that action is done,
You dream that action bears fruit.
It is your ignorance,
It is the world's delusion

That gives you these dreams.

The Lord is everywhere
And always perfect:
What does He care for man's sin
Or the righteousness of man?

The Atman is the light:
The light is covered by darkness:
This darkness is delusion:
That is why we dream.

When the light of the Atman
Drives out our darkness
That light shines forth from us,
A sun in splendor,
The revealed Brahman.

The devoted dwell with Him,
They know Him always
There in the heart,
Where action is not.
He is all their aim.
Made free by His Knowledge
From past uncleanness
Of deed or of thought,
They find the place of freedom,
The place of no return.

Seeing all things equal,
The enlightened may look
On the Brahmin, learned and gentle,
On the cow, on the elephant,
On the dog, on the eater of dogs.

Absorbed in Brahman
He overcomes the world
Even here, alive in the world.
Brahman is one,
Changeless, untouched by evil:
What home have we but Him?

The enlightened, the Brahman-abiding,
Calm-hearted, unbewildered,
Is neither elated by the pleasant
Nor saddened by the unpleasant.

His mind is dead
To the touch of the external:
It is alive
To the bliss of the Atman.
Because his heart knows Brahman

His happiness is for ever.

When senses touch objects
The pleasures therefrom
Are like wombs that bear sorrow.
They begin, they are ended:
They bring no delight to the wise.

Already, here on earth,
Before his departure,
Let man be the master
Of every impulse
Lust-begotten
Or fathered by anger:
Thus he finds Brahman,
Thus he is happy.

Only that yogi
Whose joy is inward,
Inward his peace,
And his vision inward
Shall come to Brahman
And know Nirvana.

All consumed
Are their imperfections,
Doubts are dispelled,
Their senses mastered,
Their every action
Is wed to the welfare
Of fellow-creatures:
Such are the seers
Who enter Brahman
And know Nirvana.

Self-controlled,
Cut free from desire,
Curbing the heart
And knowing the Atman,
Man finds Nirvana
That is in Brahman,
Here and hereafter.

Shutting off sense
From what is outward,
Fixing the gaze
At the root of the eyebrows,
Checking the breath-stream
In and outgoing
Within the nostrils,
Holding the senses,
Holding the intellect,

Holding the mind fast,
He who seeks freedom,
Thrusts fear aside,
Thrusts aside anger
And puts off desire:
Truly that man
Is made free for ever.

When thus he knows me
The end, the author
Of every offering
And all austerity,
Lord of the worlds
And the friend of all men:
O son of Kunti
Shall he not enter
The peace of my presence? . . .

♦ **The Yoga of Devotion**

Arjuna:

SOME WORSHIP you with steadfast love. Others worship God the unmanifest and changeless. Which kind of devotee has the greater understanding of yoga?

Sri Krishna:

Those whose minds are fixed on me in steadfast love, worshipping me with absolute faith, I consider them to have the greater understanding of yoga.

As for those others, the devotees of God the unmanifest, indefinable and changeless, they worship that which is omnipresent, constant, eternal, beyond thought's compass, never to be moved. They

hold all the senses in check. They are tranquil-minded, and devoted to the welfare of humanity. They see the Atman in every creature. They also will certainly come to me.

But the devotees of the unmanifest have a harder task, because the unmanifest is very difficult for embodied souls to realize.

Quickly I come
To those who offer me
Every action,
Worship me only,
Their dearest delight,
With devotion undaunted.

Because they love me
These are my bondsmen
And I shall save them
From mortal sorrow
And all the waves
Of Life's deathly ocean.

Be absorbed in me,
Lodge your mind in me:
Thus you shall dwell in me,
Do not doubt it,
Here and hereafter.

If you cannot become absorbed in me, then try to reach me by repeated concentration. If you lack the strength to concentrate, then devote yourself to works which will please me. For, by working for my sake only, you will achieve perfection. If you cannot even do this, then surrender yourself to me altogether. Control the

Glossary

Atman	the human soul
Brahman	an unmanifest Hindu deity that represents the unity of reality
city of nine gates	the human body, with its nine openings
devas	the "shining ones," benevolent supernatural beings
gunas	three states in the physical world: knowledge, action, and stupor
Ikshvaku	the founder and first king of an ancient Indian dynasty
Janaka	a line of ancient kings in India
Kamadhenu	in Hindu mythology, divine cow believed to be the mother of all cows

lusts of your heart, and renounce the fruits of every action.

Concentration which is practiced with discernment is certainly better than the mechanical repetition of a ritual or a prayer. Absorption in God—to live with Him and be one with Him always—is even better than concentration. But renunciation brings instant peace to the spirit.

A man should not hate any living creature. Let him be friendly and compassionate to all. He must free himself from the delusion of "I" and "mine." He must accept pleasure and pain with equal tranquility. He must be forgiving, ever-contented, self-controlled, united constantly with me in his meditation. His resolve must be unshakable. He must be dedicated to me in intellect and in mind. Such a devotee is dear to me.

He neither molests his fellow men, nor allows himself to become disturbed by the world. He is no longer swayed by joy and envy, anxiety and fear. Therefore he is dear to me.

He is pure, and independent of the body's desire. He is able to deal with the unexpected: prepared for everything, unperturbed by anything. He is neither vain nor anxious about the results of his actions. Such a devotee is dear to me.

He does not desire or rejoice in what is pleasant. He does not dread what is unpleasant, or grieve over it. He remains unmoved by good or evil fortune. Such a devotee is dear to me.

His attitude is the same toward friend and foe. He is indifferent to honor and insult, heat and cold, pleasure and pain. He is free from attachment. He values praise and blame equally. He can control his speech. He is content with whatever he gets. His home is everywhere and nowhere. His mind is fixed upon me, and his heart is full of devotion. He is dear to me.

This true wisdom I have taught will lead you to immortality. The faithful practice it with devotion, taking me for their highest aim. To me they surrender heart and mind. They are exceedingly dear to me.

Glossary

Karma Yoga	a form of yoga based on the principle of selfless action
Krishna	the preserver god, also called Vishnu
Manu	the progenitor of humankind and the world's first king
Nirvana	the escape from the cycle of birth, life, death, and rebirth to achieve salvation
Prakriti	nature, matter, the physical being
Raja Yoga	a form of yoga concerned primarily with cultivation of the mind through meditation
Sri	an honorific title associated with holiness
Vivaswat	essentially, the sun—the "brilliant" or "shining" one

蒲輪徵賢

Emperor Wu Ti, welcoming a man of letters

(Emperor Wu Ti [156-87 BC, r. 141-87 BC] welcoming a man of letters, from a history of Chinese emperors (colour on silk), Chinese School, [17th century] / Bibliotheque Nationale, Paris, France / Giraudon / The Bridgeman Art Library International)

"Pride should not be allowed to grow; the desires should not be indulged; the will should not be gratified to the full; pleasure should not be carried to excess."

Overview

The Book of Rites, sometimes called Ritual Record or Classic of Rites, is one of the Five Classics (Wujing) of Confucianism, a series of books first brought together as a collection in the second century BCE. In addition to the Book of Rites, the Five Classics include the Book of Changes, the Book of Odes, the Book of History, and the Spring and Autumn Annals; a sixth book, the Book of Music, is lost. These texts, including the Book of Rites, were written between 200 and 100 BCE and are collectively referred to as the Confucian classics because of their influence on Confucianism, a philosophy and religion originating in China. Traditionally, the Book of Rites was attributed to the teacher-scholar Confucius, but it is now known that the core ideas of all of the Five Classics predate Confucius. The Book of Rites was required reading for all educated people and was included on the governmental examinations for employment.

The Five Classics are part of the central canon of Confucianism. Scholars chose these five specifically because their topics include such matters as morality, divination, and history to help all humans to follow the correct path and be righteous. The Book of Rites examines social forms, governmental systems, and ancient ceremonial rites. Scholars also believed that by reading the Book of Rites and the other classics, the meaning of life and the universe could be found if the reader reflected on the words. The texts had different readings and interpretations based on the scholar and the social and political environment in which he lived. Their interpretations, called commentaries, were read by future scholars and included as addendums or "wings" of the Classics. The Book of Rites was and is a living document with a long history of discussion and debate.

Context

The Book of Rites was not written as part of a set; rather, the Five Classics were separate books written at different times by various authors, though all are attributed to Confucius. The Book of Rites was written during the Zhou Dy-

nasty (ca. 1150–256 BCE), so named because it was led by members of the Zhou clan. The Zhou Dynasty was wracked by ongoing warfare, as various states within the region that is now modern China vied for supremacy. This state of warfare was particularly intense during the Warring States Period, which ran from about 475 BCE to 221 BCE. Contributing to the prevalence of war were advances in military technology, particularly the development of weapons for individual foot soldiers. Prior to this time, war was conducted by the ruling elites and aristocrats in chariots. But advances in metallurgy gave an advantage to states that had the economic wherewithal to manufacture weapons to equip a much larger percentage of the population—that is, to create armies. These advances in military technology made it inevitable that the smaller Chinese states would become consolidated as a result of conquest.

The name Warring States Period suggests a time of brutality and chaos. To some extent this is true, but the later centuries of the Zhou Dynasty were also a time of great intellectual ferment. Prominent Confucian scholars, including Mencius (Meng-tzu; ca. 372?–289? BCE) and Xun Zi (Hsun-tzu; ca. 312–230 BCE) wrote during this period. Furthermore, the dynasty was developing administrative systems that enabled it to maintain control over its territories. During the fourth and third centuries BCE, however, the powerful kingdom of Qin in northwestern China gained ascendancy, partly through military might and partly by playing the other warring kingdoms off against one another. After the death of the last Zhou ruler in 256, states continued to vie for power. Qin conquered the southeastern kingdom of Chu in 223 BCE. The last opponent, the kingdom of Qi, was conquered two years later, in 221 BCE, thus creating the empire of Qin, a unified China.

During the Warring States Period (and before), major social and political changes took place, as the old ways of thinking were being discarded. New philosophies were emerging to find answers to ending war and chaos. The different philosophies created their own branches of learning, collectively known as the Hundred Schools of Thought. Each school believed that the sages of ancient China were superior intellectuals and that their works would provide direction and answers. One of these schools was under the guidance of the teacher-philosopher (or sage) Confucius.

Time Line

1150 BCE	■ The Zhou Dynasty is founded.
551 BCE	■ Confucius is born.
400s BCE	■ Confucianism arises as a foremost philosophy within the Hundred Schools of Thought.
479 BCE	■ Confucius dies.
256– 221 BCE	■ After the last Zhou ruler dies, states vie for power until the Qin Dynasty begins, bringing the unification of China.
213 BCE	■ The Burning of the Books and burying of scholars takes place under the Qin Dynasty.
206 BCE	■ The Qin Dynasty ends, and the Han Dynasty begins.
191 BCE	■ The ban on philosophy and historical works is lifted.
100s BCE	■ Restoration of Confucian works, including the Book of Rites, is undertaken to create the Five Classics.
136 BCE	■ The Five Erudites of the Five Classics is started at the Han court.
51 BCE	■ Confucianism becomes the state religion of China.
175 CE	■ A government-approved version of the Five Classics is carved into stone tablets and erected in Chang'an (modern-day Xi'an).

His ideas were informed by the reading of ancient texts, and his followers continued to read and interpret those texts for the next few hundred years.

After the fall of the Zhou Dynasty and the rise of the short-lived Qin Dynasty (221–206 BCE), classical books and other Confucian works were threatened with destruction. The Qin emperor Shi Huangdi, who had united all of China after years of warfare, was a follower of Legalism, a pro-military philosophy that stood in opposition to Confucianism and other religions. To eradicate the other schools of thought, in 213 BCE he ordered the burning of all non-Legalist books in an event called the Burning of the Books. He also decreed that any scholars who opposed him would be buried alive. In defiance, some Confucian scholars hid copies of the classical texts or memorized them.

The ban on Confucianism ended when the Qin Dynasty fell as a result of rebellion in 206 BCE. The newly formed Han Dynasty (206 BCE–220 CE) was more sympathetic to Confucianism, possibly because Confucianism was a philosophy that addressed politicians' and rulers' roles and morals. Confucianism also provided a mechanism to determine who the chosen righteous rulers of China must be. This mechanism, called the Mandate of Heaven, stated that rulers who were chosen by heaven must be compassionate and righteous, or they would lose the right to rule China. The Han elite realized that this was a powerful way to legitimize their own right to rule, so they supported Confucian doctrine.

When the Han government lifted the ban on the scholars in 191 BCE, Confucian scholars were able to rewrite books from memory or pull out hidden copies, and they decided that a core set of books should be brought together as their canon. They chose five books, including the Book of Rites, as the Five Classics, the ancient works that were to them the repositories of truth and the words of the great sages. In 136 BCE, the Han Emperor Wu Ti formed the five Erudites or Scholarships of the Five Classics and set it up as a state school. Here, the first debates, edits, and commentaries on the Five Classics began. The commentaries were used as study aids and are still read along with the Five Classics. The students of the Erudites became government officials, who believed in the precepts of Confucian rituals and morals and put many into law. The supremacy of the Five Classics was absolute over China: In 175 CE the government-approved version of the books was carved into stone and set in the capital Chang'an (modern-day Xi'an).

The Book of Rites (in transliterated Chinese, Liji, Liki, or Li Ch'i) is actually a collection of several books on philosophy, rituals, and etiquette for any event and role in life. The Book of Rites' central precept is *li*, or proper behavior. Confucius lived in a time of ongoing warfare, and, in his opinion, unjust rulers did not follow the right path. He stated that humanity needed rites, ceremonies, and rules of conduct so that people could fulfill their responsibilities to society and to each other.

About the Author

Traditionally, the author of the Book of Rites has been regarded as one of a group of sages or unknown philosophers who set down this and other works to guide humankind. One such sage, Confucius (551–479 BCE), was popularly believed to be one of the writers or editors of the Book of Rites. Confucius was born in the state of Lu (now Shandong Province). His father was a member of the warrior class but died when Confucius was young. Although he and his mother lived in poverty, Confucius had the support and encouragement of his mother to study. He excelled in school and wanted to become a politician but never won an appointment. Instead, he became a teacher and gained a strong following of students. His followers wrote down some of his teaching in the Analects. With respect to the Five Classics generally and the Book of Rites in particular, however, there is little evidence that he wrote or edited any of the text. It is held that his teachings influenced society and culture at large and thus influenced future compilers and discourse on these ancient writings.

Explanation and Analysis of the Document

The primary emphasis of Confucian teachings is on the ethics of social relationships, particularly between parents and children but also all human relationships at all levels, including the ruler's relationship to his subjects. If ethics and morals were followed, an orderly hierarchical society would exist, which would be characterized by altruism, humanism, and personal integrity. To bring about this society, humans needed to focus on correct actions and thoughts and be virtuous. The four keys to proper conduct are to demonstrate benevolence, righteousness, propriety, and understanding. All these aspects of conduct are addressed in the Book of Rites. Parenthetical words are the translator's interpolations for the sake of clarity.

◆ Book I: Summary of the Rules of Propriety

This section of the Book of Rites outlines the Confucian meaning of propriety—that is, conforming to established standards of good or proper behavior or manners, in all circumstances. This section also deals with specific habits or tendencies incompatible with propriety, gives instances of propriety in superior men, and offers directions for certain cases. It calls for reverence in speech, for example, especially by an authority figure, and cautions that pride is not a virtue and all desires should not be fulfilled. Paragraph 3 encourages open-mindedness, stating that a person can love someone while acknowledging that people can have evil tendencies. The author also calls on readers to recognize that wealth should be shared with the needy. Paragraph 5 urges the reader not to make positive affirmations when he has doubts about a matter. Paragraphs 6 and 7 focus on rules for sitting and standing and suggest how to act during a mission to another state. If the rules of propriety are followed, there will be no suspicion or doubt about one's actions. The phrase "personator of the deceased" refers to the role undertaken by an individual serving as a representative of the dead, who always sat and who always bore himself with gravity.

Paragraphs 8–11 set forth the idea that propriety is indispensable for the regulation of the individual and society and that it is what makes a gentleman worthy of the name. A virtuous man does not try always to please others, merely saying what others wish to hear, and he does not impose on others or behave in too familiar a way with them. If a virtuous man conducts himself well and his words reflect his vir-

Terra-cotta sculptures of warriors, from the mausoleum of Emperor Shi Huangdi

(View over the Terracotta Army, 210 BC [photo], Chinese School, [3rd century BC] / Tomb of Qin shi Huang Di, Xianyang, China / Bildarchiv Steffens Leo F. Postl / The Bridgeman Art Library International)

tue as well, then the rules of propriety are being fulfilled. A man should be a model to other people but not set himself as superior, for doing so exhibits pride.

Paragraphs 13–18 explain that propriety is necessary for men to act in the name of virtue, benevolence, and righteousness. Exhibiting manners and courtesy, clearing up quarrels and making decisions, maintaining the duties between the four relationships ("ruler and minister, high and low, father and son, elder brother and younger"), showing reverence for teachers (on the part of students), discharging official duties, and adhering to the law all require propriety.

Paragraphs 19 and 20 address the spiritual aspects of Confucianism. Confucius himself did not mention the spiritual world. However, the pre-Confucian shamanistic religions, such as Daoism, did deal with the otherworld, spirits, and gods. Because the Book of Rites contains ideas that are older than Confucianism, it is infused with traditional spirit worship, instructions about offerings to the earth and heaven, and prayers. These spiritual concerns were assumed by the follow-

"Pride should not be allowed to grow; the desires should not be indulged; the will should not be gratified to the full; pleasure should not be carried to excess."

"To cultivate one's person and fulfill one's words is called good conduct. When the conduct is (thus) ordered, and the words are accordant with the (right) course, we have the substance of the rules of propriety."

"While the parents are both alive, at their regular meals, morning and evening, the (eldest) son and his wife will encourage them to eat everything, and what is left after all, they will themselves eat. When the father is dead, and the mother still alive, the eldest son should wait upon her at her meals; and the wives of the other sons will do with what is left as in the former case."

"The jade uncut will not form a vessel for use; and if men do not learn, they do not know the way (in which they should go). On this account the ancient kings, when establishing states and governing the people, made instruction and schools a primary object;—as it is said in the Charge to Yueh, 'The thoughts from first to last should be fixed on learning.'"

"The respect, the caution, the importance, the attention to secure correctness in all the details, and then (the pledge of) mutual affection,— these were the great points in the ceremony, and served to establish the distinction to be observed between man and woman, and the righteousness to be maintained between husband and wife."

ers of Confucianism, including the emperor, who was understood to rule by the Mandate of Heaven and was required to pray to and make offerings to heaven in return.

The final paragraphs of book I, 21 and 22, delineate what separates humans from other animals such as parrots or apes. Other animals can also "speak," so that characteristic has scant meaning: Humans, in fact, are not far removed from their brutish nature, so they must follow the rules of propriety or else there is little to distinguish them from lower beasts.

♦ Book X: The Pattern of the Family

Book X begins by stating that these rules of conduct in the family are being passed along as a decree from the em-

peror, thus giving weight and legitimacy to the content of this section. The focus of book X is on filial piety—that is, on the right actions to take with parents. In traditional China, married couples went to live with the husband's family, and it was expected that the household would be multigenerational. Respect for parents and the elderly is still a core value in China and other Confucian societies, on the premise that parents have made great sacrifices for the welfare of their children, and reciprocation is needed, especially as parents or any elder relative ages. This means that children, including sons' wives, should be clean in the presence of their elders; hence there are all the details on appearance and dress in line 2. In line 3 details about the appearance of wives and their tools for the day are listed.

These sections suggest that sons and their wives are to be prepared for all situations that may arise during the day. Further, sons and daughters-in-law should show decorum and kindness to parents—all done with ease and calm to show that they are pleased to help their parents.

Directions are also given to young unmarried sons ("youths who have not yet been capped") and daughters ("maidens who have not yet assumed the hair-pin") in paragraph 5. They also have to pay attention to personal hygiene and present themselves to assist their older siblings in attending to their parents. Paragraph 6 states that the household inside and out must be carefully maintained, by whoever is charged with that duty—perhaps servants in large, rich households but otherwise mostly the younger women of the house. Paragraphs 7 and 8 give directions for sharing a household when the son has attained his own position and work as an official, and paragraph 8 addresses the manner in which older parents should be attended to and made comfortable. Being considerate of parents' comfort was seen as part of being a kind person. Paragraph 9 notes that sons and their wives should not move the personal articles of parents, for they do not own the parents' objects and should show reverence for these objects. This instruction includes leaving their food containers alone as well.

Paragraph 10 provides a hint of how an older woman's treatment in the home changes if her husband dies. When the parents are both alive, then the oldest son and his wife will serve them both and wait until they have eaten. However, when the father dies, the eldest son will wait on his mother, but his wife and the other members of the family can begin. While still revered, the mother is no longer seen as part of a unit and is treated differently as an individual.

♦ Book XVI: Record on the Subject of Education

In Confucianism, education is the hallmark of a moral man, and all people needed to be educated to be virtuous. The only way to be moral and virtuous was to study, with tireless effort. Confucius argued that real understanding of any subject comes only from long and careful study, not natural talent. In paragraph 1, rulers are given the duty of educating and thereby transforming their subjects to perfect their manners and customs. In paragraph 2, the writer mentions the "Charge to Yueh" from the Analects, which refers to the student Yueh and the charge or call to action from his teachers, such as Confucius: "The thoughts from first to last should be fixed on learning." The relationship between student and teacher must be one of mutual benefit, paragraph 3 says further: A teacher and student should have a close relationship, where both have an understanding of the other's situation and each can assist the other in fulfilling their duties.

Paragraphs 4–6 focus on the systems of teaching that existed in ancient China. Only sons in elite families could have a tutor or be sent to school, which was usually set up by the family to instruct the children. Girls were educated at home, usually by their female relatives. Only boys who showed great aptitude could attend the colleges in the capitals of each state. What was expected of the students and teachers

was very strict, as outlined in paragraphs 5 and 6. Offerings were made to the ancient sages, the writers of the Five Classics. After many years of study, the students could sit for the examinations for positions in the government.

Paragraphs 7–9 deal with the responsibilities of the student to study at home and give himself wholly to his studies—at the same time maintaining balance in his life. The student is required to be attentive to his teacher and his friends, enjoy the arts, and cultivate morality, not just work to be a brilliant scholar. This ideal situation, however, is contrasted in paragraph 10 by a complaint about the failures of the system of teaching at the time that this text was written. The paragraph describes teachers of the day as being insincere and contrary, which distresses the student, who then resents his teachers and gives up on his studies.

The remedy for these defects in education is the proper conduct of teachers. Paragraphs 11–19 give direct instructions about how teachers can be more skillful and more effective for their students. Only when the teacher acts as a ruler, as an imparter of great knowledge and proper morals, will his students respect him. A skillful teacher encourages reverence and receives it from his students. By contrast, the duties of a skillful learner are to focus on the work and use the teacher as a resource. The analogy in paragraph 18 is that the teacher is like a bell, waiting to be "struck" by the student with the correct question. If the student asks small, meaningless questions, then a small answer is given. If the question is about a concept that is too big, a large, overwhelming answer will be given. The best question to ask is one that is proper to the level of discussion and will produce an excellent sound—that is, the correct answer. However the teacher needs to answer in a clear way and not ask students questions beyond their own learning, so they will not become discouraged.

Paragraphs 20–22 deal with the scholar and his improved ability to learn if his knowledge and morals are superior. Paragraph 20 states that a superior man can instruct himself in any trade because he has developed a method for learning. Paragraph 21 makes an analogy about learning by comparing it to a drum or to water: The drum has no musical pitch, but it helps harmonize notes. Water has no color, but it is useful for displaying color. Learning itself is not a sense, but it organizes our understanding of the experience of the senses. Paragraph 22 closes the book by reminding that the value of learning applies to any office and that knowledge or virtuous conduct should not be limited to any one area of life.

♦ Book XLI: The Meaning of the Marriage Ceremony

Paragraph 1 reflects the Confucianism belief that marriage is absolutely necessary and that it cultivates virtue for both men and women. In Confucian thought, marriage should be founded on love and bring two families together. The families were to be of different clans with different surnames, as a way of avoiding intermarriage, which was considered not only immoral but also not politically advantageous. Further, the ancestors were to be an important part of the ceremonies. Ancestral worship predated Confucianism, but Confucians continued the practice by making offerings and prayers in order to secure their deceased relatives' support for the marriage.

Because of the emphasis on a marriage that was advantageous to both families, marriages were arranged, and introduction ceremonies were conducted, as outlined in paragraph 2. With his father's permission, symbolized by the passing of a cup, the son would go by himself to meet his future father-in-law and present him with gifts, including a goose. This was part of the bride price, or dowry, the groom needed to pay. The groom would then escort the bride to a carriage and drive around her home three times to symbolize that she was leaving her natal home and joining his family. Eating the same food was a further symbol, which meant that the couple was now officially married. Not only were they one body and pledged to mutual affection, they were also equal in rank, meaning that whoever's family had title and political importance now passed it to the lower-ranked partner. The elevation of rank was extremely important to the families, as their rank would increase by association.

Paragraphs 3 and 4 deal with the importance of the marriage as a correct or righteous act that brings two people together. Mutual affection and respect are seen as a foundation for the marriage, which began the minute the couple shared their first meal. The nature of their union would affect their children: Confucian belief was that a happy home meant the children would grow up well. Domestic happiness would improve society as a whole, positively affecting all other relationships, including those with ministers and the ruler. Therefore, marriage was seen as so important that

it was ranked above all other ceremonies, including funerals and state ceremonies.

The wife's and husband's roles are detailed in paragraphs 5–10. When a woman left her parents' home to marry, the departure was for good. Rarely would she return to her own parents' house, even to visit. Her obedience to her new parents was demonstrated the morning after the marriage, when she brought food to them. They, in turn, showed their approval of her with the presentation of a pig prepared for the table. The next day they would all drink from a single cup, then leave by separate stairs. This ritual marked the changing of position for the parents and the new wife; she was to take over the position of female head of the household. Her duties would include having children—especially sons to carry on the family name—and managing all affairs of the household, including making clothes and maintaining the storehouses. She was then taught the family's history and how to conduct offerings to her husband's ancestors. These duties were almost universal for all classes, elite and poor women alike.

Paragraphs 11–12 recount Confucian mythology about how the roles and responsibilities of people were made in heaven in ancient times: Each woman was given certain responsibilities and assigned a level or grade. Women in large, elite households were given roles based on their social standing. For example, the first wife of an official would rank highest in the household, over any other wives or concubines he later took. If each woman knew her own roles and position, harmony would reign in the household. The outside world was the male domain, but the internal world was the woman's. Because of this, women were the key pro-

Questions for Further Study

1. The Book of Rites is attributed to Confucius (though this is a matter of debate). In what sense does the Book of Rites resemble the Islamic Hadith, or sayings attributed to Muhammad? (For reference, see the entry Sahih al-Bukhari.) How does it differ?

2. What impact did the events surrounding the Warring States Period have on the Five Classics in general and the Book of Rites in particular?

3. What factors might have motivated the Han Dynasty to be more sympathetic to Confucianism, in contrast to the preceding Qin Dynasty?

4. If, as the entry states, "the primary emphasis of Confucian teachings is on the ethics of social relationships, particularly between parents and children but also all human relationships at all levels, including the ruler's relationship to his subjects," in what sense is the Book of Rites a religious document?

5. Although both the Book of Rites and Gerald Gardner's *Book of Shadows* focus on "rites," how do the two documents reflect entirely different cultural values and ways of looking at the world?

viders of moral education to everyone in the household. If these roles were not fulfilled, the effect was destructive. As symbolized in the moon and the sun, women's and men's roles in their respective spheres of influence needed to be maintained to make a harmonious heaven and household.

Audience

The Book of Rites was written and compiled for and by men of its era and those who would come after. Women are spoken of in the text and directed as to how to comport themselves, but the understanding of the book's writers was that all learning and governance were dominated by men. Women who were literate would perhaps read the Book of Rites, and, if they could not, their mothers and husbands might educate them, but the intended audience was mainly elite scholars, statesmen, and literati—all male positions that had great power and influence in Chinese society. A specific targeted group was that made up of gentlemen-scholars, who would serve and improve society. Such men would form a class of educated gentry at the top of the social hierarchy. Throughout the Book of Rites, various more specific audiences were addressed, depending on the topic under discussion; these audiences included rulers and ministers, students, and the sons and daughters of households.

Impact

The impact on Chinese society of the Five Classics, in general, and the Book of Rites, in particular, was profound and continues to this day. Confucian beliefs were founded on morals and ethics that shaped Chinese society for centuries. Confucianism was adopted as the state religion during the Han Dynasty and spread to all corners of China. Its ideas elevated the importance of scholars and officials as moral leaders, and, indeed, men who sat for civil service examinations were expected to know and be able to interpret the Book of Rites and the other Confucian classics. Moreover, the text's central ideal of filial piety and obedience to the family continued throughout China's history into the twenty-first century. As China grew and expanded, it exported the philosophy of Confucianism to other nations, such as Korea and Japan. Its adoption may be due to the inclusiveness of Confucianism: Because it elevated no specific gods, it was not in direct conflict with other religious beliefs. Many people could and do practice Confucianism along with other religions, such as Buddhism and Christianity.

Further Reading

■ Books

Berthrong, John H., and Evelyn Nagai-Berthrong. *Confucianism: A Short Introduction*. Oxford, U.K.: Oneworld, 2000.

Ebrey, Patricia Buckley. *The Inner Quarters: Marriage and the Lives of Chinese Women in the Sung Period*. Berkeley: University of California Press, 1993.

Legge, James. *The Chinese Classics*. 5 vols. London: Trubner, 1861–1872.

Minford, John, and Joseph S. M. Lau, eds. *Classical Chinese Literature: An Anthology of Translations*. Vol. 1: *From Antiquity to the Tang Dynasty*. New York: Columbia University Press and the Chinese University of Hong Kong, 2000.

Nylan, Michael. *The Five Confucian Classics*. New Haven, Conn.: Yale University Press, 2001.

Oldstone-Moore, Jennifer. *Confucianism: Origins, Beliefs, Practices, Holy Texts, Sacred Places*. Oxford, U.K.: Oxford University Press, 2002.

Yao, Xinzhong. *An Introduction to Confucianism*. Cambridge, U.K.: Cambridge University Press, 2000.

■ Web Sites

"Confucius." *Stanford Encyclopedia of Philosophy*. http://plato.stanford.edu/entries/confucius.

—Tereasa Maille

BOOK OF RITES

Book I: Summary of the Rules of Propriety

1. The Summary of the Rules of Propriety says:—Always and in everything let there be reverence; with the deportment grave as when one is thinking (deeply), and with speech composed and definite. This will make the people tranquil.

2. Pride should not be allowed to grow; the desires should not be indulged; the will should not be gratified to the full; pleasure should not be carried to excess.

3. Men of talents and virtue can be familiar with others and yet respect them; can stand in awe of others and yet love them. They love others and yet acknowledge the evil that is in them. They accumulate (wealth) and yet are able to part with it (to help the needy); they rest in what gives them satisfaction and yet can seek satisfaction elsewhere (when it is desirable to do so).

4. When you find wealth within your reach, do not (try to) get it by improper means; when you meet with calamity, do not (try to) escape from it by improper means. Do not seek for victory in small contentions; do not seek for more than your proper share.

5. Do not positively affirm what you have doubts about; and (when you have no doubts), do not let what you say appear (simply) as your own view.

6. If a man be sitting, let him do so as a personator of the deceased; if he be standing, let him do so (reverently), as in sacrificing.

7. In (observing) the rules of propriety, what is right (for the time and in the circumstances) should be followed. In discharging a mission (to another state), its customs are to be observed.

8. They are the rules of propriety, that furnish the means of determining (the observances towards) relatives, as near and remote; of settling points which may cause suspicion or doubt; of distinguishing where there should be agreement, and where difference; and of making clear what is right and what is wrong.

9. According to those rules, one should not (seek to) please others in an improper way, nor be lavish of his words.

10. According to them, one does not go beyond the definite measure, nor encroach on or despise others, nor is fond of (presuming) familiarities.

11. To cultivate one's person and fulfill one's words is called good conduct. When the conduct is (thus) ordered, and the words are accordant with the (right) course, we have the substance of the rules of propriety.

12. I have heard that it is in accordance with those rules that one should be chosen by others (as their model); I have not heard of his choosing them (to take him as such). I have heard in the same way of (scholars) coming to learn; I have not heard of (the master) going to teach.

13. The course (of duty), virtue, benevolence, and righteousness cannot be fully carried out without the rules of propriety;

14. nor are training and oral lessons for the rectification of manners complete;

15. nor can the clearing up of quarrels and discriminating in disputes be accomplished;

16. nor can (the duties between) ruler and minister, high and low, father and son, elder brother and younger, be determined;

17. nor can students for office and (other) learners, in serving their masters, have an attachment for them;

18. nor can majesty and dignity be shown in assigning the different places at court, in the government of the armies, and in discharging the duties of office so as to secure the operation of the laws;

19. nor can there be the (proper) sincerity and gravity in presenting the offerings to spiritual Beings on occasions of supplication, thanksgiving, and the various sacrifices.

20. Therefore the superior man is respectful and reverent, assiduous in his duties and not going beyond them, retiring and yielding;—thus illustrating (the principle of) propriety.

21. The parrot can speak, and yet is nothing more than a bird; the ape can speak, and yet is nothing more than a beast. Here now is a man who observes no rules of propriety; is not his heart that of a beast? But if (men were as) beasts, and without (the principle of) propriety, father and son might have the same mate.

22. Therefore, when the sages arose, they framed the rules of propriety in order to teach men, and cause them, by their possession of them, to make a distinction between themselves and brutes. . . .

Book X: The Pattern of the Family

1. The sovereign and king orders the chief minister to send down his (lessons of) virtue to the millions of the people.

2. Sons, in serving their parents, on the first crowing of the cock, should all wash their hands and rinse their mouths, comb their hair, draw over it the covering of silk, fix this with the hair-pin, bind the hair at the roots with the fillet, brush the dust from that which is left free, and then put on their caps, leaving the ends of the strings hanging down. They should then put on their squarely made black jackets, knee-covers, and girdles, fixing in the last their tablets. From the left and right of the girdle they should hang their articles for use:—on the left side, the duster and handkerchief, the knife and whetstone, the small spike, and the metal speculum for getting fire from the sun; on the right, the archer's thimble for the thumb and the armlet, the tube for writing instruments, the knife-case, the larger spike, and the borer for getting fire from wood. They should put on their leggings, and adjust their shoe-strings.

3. (Sons') wives should serve their parents-in-law as they served their own. At the first crowing of the cock, they should wash their hands, and rinse their mouths; comb their hair, draw over it the covering of silk, fix this with the hair-pin, and tie the hair at the roots with the fillet. They should then put on the jacket, and over it the sash. On the left side they should hang the duster and handkerchief, the knife and whetstone, the small spike, and the metal speculum to get fire with; and on the right, the needle-case, thread, and floss, all bestowed in the satchel, the great spike, and the borer to get fire with from wood. They will also fasten on their necklaces, and adjust their shoe-strings.

4. Thus dressed, they should go to their parents and parents-in-law. On getting to where they are, with bated breath and gentle voice, they should ask if their clothes are (too) warm or (too) cold, whether they are ill or pained, or uncomfortable in any part; and if they be so, they should proceed reverently to stroke and scratch the place. They should in the same way, going before or following after, help and support their parents in quitting or entering (the apartment). In bringing in the basin for them to wash, the younger will carry the stand and the elder the water; they will beg to be allowed to pour out the water, and when the washing is concluded, they will hand the towel. They will ask whether they want anything, and then respectfully bring it. All this they will do with an appearance of pleasure to make their parents feel at ease. (They should bring) gruel, thick or thin, spirits or must, soup with vegetables, beans, wheat, spinach, rice, millet, maize, and glutinous millet,—whatever they wish, in fact; with dates, chestnuts, sugar and honey, to sweeten their dishes; with the ordinary or the large-leaved violets, leaves of elm-trees, fresh or dry, and the most soothing rice-water to lubricate them; and with fat and oil to enrich them. The parents will be sure to taste them, and when they have done so, the young people should withdraw.

5. Youths who have not yet been capped, and maidens who have not yet assumed the hair-pin, at the first crowing of the cock, should wash their hands, rinse their mouths, comb their hair, draw over it the covering of silk, brush the dust from that which is left free, bind it up in the shape of a horn, and put on their necklaces. They should all bang at their girdles the ornamental (bags of) perfume; and as soon as it is daybreak, they should (go to) pay their respects (to their parents) and ask

what they will eat and drink. If they have eaten already, they should retire; if they have not eaten, they will (remain to) assist their elder (brothers and sisters) and see what has been prepared.

6. All charged with the care of the inner and outer parts (of the house), at the first crowing of the cock, should wash their hands and mouths, gather up their pillows and fine mats, sprinkle and sweep out the apartments, hall, and courtyard, and spread the mats, each doing his proper work. The children go earlier to bed, and get up later, according to their pleasure. There is no fixed time for their meals.

7. From the time that sons receive an official appointment, they and their father occupy different parts of their residence. But at the dawn, the son will pay his respects, and express his affection by (the offer of) pleasant delicacies. At sunrise he will retire, and he and his father will attend to their different duties. At sundown, the son will pay his evening visit in the same way.

8. When the parents wish to sit (anywhere), the sons and their wives should carry their mats, and ask in what direction they shall lay them. When they wish to lie down, the eldest among them should carry the mats, and ask where they wish to place their feet, while the youngest will carry a (small) bench for them to lean on while they stretch out their legs. (At the same time) an attendant will place a stool by them. They should take up the mat on which they had been lying and the fine mat over it, bang up the coverlet, put the pillow in its case, and roll up the fine mat and put it in its cover.

9. (Sons and their wives) should not move the clothes, coverlets, fine mats, or undermats, pillows, and stools of their parents; they should reverently regard their staffs and shoes, but not presume to approach them; they should not presume to use their vessels for grain, liquor, and water, unless some of the contents be left in them; nor to eat or drink any of their ordinary food or drink, unless in the same case.

10. While the parents are both alive, at their regular meals, morning and evening, the (eldest) son and his wife will encourage them to eat everything, and what is left after all, they will themselves eat. When the father is dead, and the mother still alive, the eldest son should wait upon her at her meals; and the wives of the other sons will do with what is left as in the former case. The children should have the sweet, soft, and unctuous things that are left. . . .

Book XVI: Record on the Subject of Education

1. When a ruler is concerned that his measures should be in accordance with law, and seeks for the (assistance of the) good and upright, this is sufficient to secure him a considerable reputation, but not to move the multitudes.

When he cultivates the society of the worthy, and tries to embody the views of those who are remote (from the court), this is sufficient to move the multitudes, but not to transform the people.

If he wish to transform the people and to perfect their manners and customs, must he not start from the lessons of the school?

2. The jade uncut will not form a vessel for use; and if men do not learn, they do not know the way (in which they should go). On this account the ancient kings, when establishing states and governing the people, made instruction and schools a primary object;—as it is said in the Charge to Yueh, "The thoughts from first to last should be fixed on learning."

3. However fine the viands be, if one do not eat, he does not know their taste; however perfect the course may be, if one do not learn it, he does not know its goodness. Therefore when he learns, one knows his own deficiencies; when he teaches, he knows the difficulties of learning. After he knows his deficiencies, one is able to turn round and examine himself; after he knows the difficulties, he is able to stimulate himself to effort. Hence it is said, "Teaching and learning help each other;" as it is said in the Charge to Yueh, "Teaching is the half of learning."

4. According to the system of ancient teaching, for the families of (a hamlet) there was the village school; for a neighborhood there was the hsiang; for the larger districts there was the hsu; and in the capitals there was the college.

5. Every year some entered the college, and every second year there was a comparative examination. In the first year it was seen whether they could read the texts intelligently, and what was the meaning of each; in the third year, whether they were reverently attentive to their work, and what companionship was most pleasant to them; in the fifth year, how they extended their studies and sought the company of their teachers; in the seventh year, how they could discuss the subjects of their studies and select their friends. They were now said to have made some small attainments. In the ninth year, when they knew the different classes of subjects and had gained a general intelligence, were firmly established and would not fall back, they were said to have made grand attainments. After this the training was sufficient to transform the people, and to change (anything bad in) manners and customs. Those who lived near at hand submitted with delight, and those who were far off thought (of the teaching) with longing desire. Such was the method of the Great learning; as is said in the Record, "The little ant continually exercises the art (of amassing)."

6. At the commencement of the teaching in the Great college, (the masters) in their skin caps presented the offerings of vegetables (to the ancient sages), to show their pupils the principle of reverence for them; and made them sing (at the same time) the (first) three pieces of the Minor Odes of the Kingdom, as their first lesson in the duties of officers. When they entered the college, the drum was beaten and the satchels were produced, that they might begin their work reverently. The cane and the thorns were there to secure in them a proper awe. It was not till the time for the summer sacrifice was divined for, that the testing examination was held;—to give composure to their minds. They were continually under inspection, but not spoken to,—to keep their minds undisturbed. They listened, but they did not ask questions; and they could not transgress the order of study (imposed on them). These seven things were the chief regulations in the teaching. As it is expressed in the Record, "In all learning, for him who would be an officer the first thing is (the knowledge of) business; for scholars the first thing is the directing of the mind."

7. In the system of teaching at the Great college, every season had its appropriate subject; and when the pupils withdrew, and gave up their lessons (for the day), they were required to continue their study at home.

8. If a student do not learn (at college) to play in tune, he cannot quietly enjoy his lutes; if he do not learn extensively the figures of poetry, he cannot quietly enjoy the odes; if he do not learn the varieties of dress, he cannot quietly take part in the different ceremonies; if he do not acquire the various accomplishments, he cannot take delight in learning.

9. Therefore a student of talents and virtue pursues his studies, withdrawn in college from all besides, and devoted to their cultivation, or occupied with them when retired from it, and enjoying himself. Having attained to this, he rests quietly in his studies and seeks the company of his teachers; he finds pleasure in his friends, and has all confidence in their course. Although he should be separated from his teachers and helpers, he will not act contrary to the course;—as it is said in the Charge to Yueh, "Maintain a reverent humility, and strive to be constantly earnest. In such a case the cultivation will surely come."

10. According to the system of teaching now-a-days, (the masters) hum over the tablets which they see before them, multiplying their questions. They speak of the learners' making rapid advances, and pay no regard to their reposing (in what they have acquired). In what they lay on their learners they are not sincere, nor do they put forth all their ability in teaching them. What they inculcate is contrary to what is right, and the learners are disappointed in what they seek for. In such a case, the latter are distressed by their studies and hate their masters; they are embittered by the difficulties, and do not find any advantage from their (labor). They may seem to finish their work, but they quickly give up its lessons. That no results are seen from their instructions:—is it not owing to these defects?

11. The rules aimed at in the Great college were the prevention of evil before it was manifested; the timeliness of instruction just when it was required; the suitability of the lessons in adaptation to circumstances; and the good influence of example to parties observing one another. It was from these four things that the teaching was so effectual and flourishing.

12. Prohibition of evil after it has been manifested meets with opposition, and is not successful. Instruction given after the time for it is past is done with toil, and carried out with difficulty. The communication of lessons in an undiscriminating manner and without suitability produces injury and disorder, and fails in its object. Learning alone and without friends makes one feel solitary and uncultivated, with but little information. Friendships of festivity lead to opposition to one's master. Friendships with the dissolute lead to the neglect of one's learning. These six things all tend to make teaching vain.

13. When a superior man knows the causes which make instruction successful, and those which make it of no effect, he can become a teacher of others. Thus in his teaching, he leads and does not drag; he strengthens and does not discourage; he opens the way but does not conduct to the end (without the learner's own efforts). Leading and not dragging produces harmony. Strengthening and not discouraging makes attainment easy. Opening the way and not conducting to the end makes (the learner) thoughtful. He who produces such harmony, easy attainment, and thoughtfulness may be pronounced a skilful teacher.

14. Among learners there are four defects with which the teacher must make himself acquainted. Some err in the multitude of their studies; some, in their fewness; some, in the feeling of ease (with which they proceed); and some, in the readiness with which they stop. These four defects arise from the difference of their minds. When a teacher knows the character of his mind, he can save the learner from the defect to which he is liable. Teaching should be directed to develop that in which the pupil excels, and correct the defects to which he is prone.

15. The good singer makes men (able) to continue his notes, and (so) the good teacher make them able to carry out his ideas. His words are brief, but far-reaching; unpretentious, but deep; with few illustrations, but instructive. In this way he may be said to perpetuate his ideas.

16. When a man of talents and virtue knows the difficulty (on the one hand) and the facility (on the other) in the attainment of learning, and knows (also) the good and the bad qualities (of his pu-

pils), he can vary his methods of teaching. When he can vary his methods of teaching, he can be a master indeed. When he can be a teacher indeed, he can be the Head (of an official department). When he can be such a Head, he can be the Ruler (of a state). Hence it is from the teacher indeed, that one learns to be a ruler, and the choice of a teacher demands the greatest care; as it is said in the Record, "The three kings and the four dynasties were what they were by their teachers."

17. In pursuing the course of learning, the difficulty is in securing the proper reverence for the master. When that is done, the course (which he inculcates) is regarded with honor. When that is done, the people know how to respect learning. Thus it is that there are two among his subjects whom the ruler does not treat as subjects. When one is personating (his ancestor), he does not treat him as such, nor does he treat his master as such. According to the rules of the Great college, the master, though communicating anything to the son of Heaven, did not stand with his face to the north. This was the way in which honor was done to him.

18. The skilful learner, while the master seems indifferent, yet makes double the attainments of another, and in the sequel ascribes the merit (to the master). The unskillful learner, while the master is diligent with him, yet makes (only) half the attainments (of the former), and in the sequel is dissatisfied with the master. The skilful questioner is like a workman addressing himself to deal with a hard tree. First he attacks the easy parts, and then the knotty. After a long time, the pupil and master talk together, and the subject is explained. The unskillful questioner takes the opposite course. The master who skillfully waits to be questioned, may be compared to a bell when it is struck. Struck with a small hammer, it gives a small sound. Struck with a great one, it gives a great sound. But let it be struck leisurely and properly, and it gives out all the sound of which it is capable. He who is not skilful in replying to questions is the opposite of this. This all describes the method of making progress in learning.

19. He who gives (only) the learning supplied by his memory in conversations is not fit to be a master. Is it not necessary that he should hear the questions (of his pupils)? Yes, but if they are not able to put questions, he should put subjects before

them. If he do so, and then they do not show any knowledge of the subjects, he may let them alone.

20. The son of a good founder is sure to learn how to make a fur-robe. The son of a good maker of bows is sure to learn how to make a sieve. Those who first yoke a (young) horse place it behind, with the carriage going on in front of it. The superior man who examines these cases can by them instruct himself in (the method of) learning.

21. The ancients in prosecuting their learning compared different things and traced the analogies between them. The drum has no special relation to any of the musical notes; but without it they cannot be harmonized. Water has no particular relation to any of the five colours; but without it they cannot be displayed. Learning has no particular relation to any of the five senses; but without it they cannot be regulated. A teacher has no special relation to the five degrees of mourning; but without his help they cannot be worn as they ought to be.

22. A wise man has said, "The Great virtue need not be confined to one office; Great power of method need not be restricted to the production of one article; Great truth need not be limited to the confirmation of oaths; Great seasonableness accomplishes all things, and each in its proper time." By examining these four cases, we are taught to direct our aims to what is fundamental.

Book XLI: The Meaning of the Marriage Ceremony

1. The ceremony of marriage was intended to be a bond of love between two (families of different) surnames, with a view, in its retrospective character, to secure the services in the ancestral temple, and in its prospective character, to secure the continuance of the family line. Therefore the superior men, (the ancient rulers), set a great value upon it. Hence, in regard to the various (introductory) ceremonies, the proposal with its accompanying gift; the inquiries about the (lady's) name; the intimation of the approving divination; the receiving the special offerings; and the request to fix the day: these all were received by the principal party (on the lady's side), as he rested on his mat or leaning-stool in the ancestral temple, (When they arrived), he met the messenger, and greeted him outside the gate, giving place to him as he entered, after which

they ascended to the hall. Thus were the instructions received in the ancestral temple, and in this way was the ceremony respected, and watched over, while its importance was exhibited and care taken that all its details should be correct.

2. The father gave himself the special cup to his son, and ordered him to go and meet the bride; it being proper that the male should take the first step (in all the arrangements). The son, having received the order, proceeded to meet his bride. Her father, who had been resting on his mat and leaning-stool in the temple, met him outside the gate and received him with a bow, and then the son-in-law entered, carrying a wild goose. After the (customary) bows and yielding of precedence, they went up to the hall, when the bridegroom bowed twice and put down the wild goose. Then and in this way he received the bride from her parents.

After this they went down, and he went out and took the reins of the horses of her carriage, which he drove for three revolutions of the wheels, having handed the strap to assist her in mounting. He then went before, and waited outside his gate. When she arrived, he bowed to her as she entered. They ate together of the same animal, and joined in sipping from the cups made of the same melon; thus showing that they now formed one body, were of equal rank, and pledged to mutual affection.

3. The respect, the caution, the importance, the attention to secure correctness in all the details, and then (the pledge of) mutual affection,—these were the great points in the ceremony, and served to establish the distinction to be observed between man and woman, and the righteousness to be maintained between husband and wife. From the distinction between man and woman came the righteousness between husband and wife. From that righteousness came the affection between father and son; and from that affection, the rectitude between ruler and minister. Whence it is said, 'The ceremony of marriage is the root of the other ceremonial observances.'

4. Ceremonies (might be said to) commence with the capping; to have their root in marriage; to be most important in the rites of mourning and sacrifice; to confer the greatest honor in audiences at the royal court and in the interchange of visits at the

feudal courts; and to be most promotive of harmony in the country festivals and celebrations of archery. These were the greatest occasions of ceremony, and the principal points in them.

5. Rising early (the morning after marriage), the young wife washed her head and bathed her person, and waited to be presented (to her husband's parents), which was done by the directrix, as soon as it was bright day. She appeared before them, bearing a basket with dates, chestnuts, and slices of dried spiced meat. The directrix set before her a cup of sweet liquor, and she offered in sacrifice some of the dried meat and also of the liquor, thus performing the ceremony which declared her their son's wife.

6. The father and mother-in-law then entered their apartment, where she set before them a single dressed pig, thus showing the obedient duty of (their son's) wife.

7. Next day, the parents united in entertaining the young wife, and when the ceremonies of their severally pledging her in a single cup, and her pledging them in return, had been performed, they descended by the steps on the west, and she by those on the east, thus showing that she would take the mother's place in the family.

8. Thus the ceremony establishing the young wife in her position; (followed by) that showing her obedient service (of her husband's parents); and both succeeded by that showing how she now occupied the position of continuing the family line: all served to impress her with a sense of the deferential duty proper to her. When she was thus deferential, she was obedient to her parents-in-law, and harmonious with all the occupants of the women's apartments; she was the fitting partner of her husband, and could carry on all the work in silk and linen, making cloth and silken fabrics, and maintaining a watchful care over the various stores and depositories (of the household).

9. In this way when the deferential obedience of the wife was complete, the internal harmony was secured; and when the internal harmony was secured, the long continuance of the family could be calculated on. Therefore the ancient kings attached such importance (to the marriage ceremonies).

10. Therefore, anciently, for three months before the marriage of a young lady, if the temple of the high ancestor (of her surname) were still standing (and she had admission to it), she was taught in it, as the public hall (of the members of her surname); if it were no longer standing (for her), she was taught in the public hall of the Head of that branch of the surname to which she belonged; she was taught there the virtue, the speech, the carriage, and the work of a wife. When the teaching was accomplished, she offered a sacrifice (to the ancestor), using fish for the victim, and soups made of duckweed and pondweed. So was she trained to the obedience of a wife.

11. Anciently, the queen of the son of Heaven divided the harem into six palace-halls, (occupied) by the 3 ladies called fu-zan, the 9 pin, the 27 shih-fu, and the 81 yu-khi. These were instructed in the domestic and private rule which should prevail throughout the kingdom, and how the deferential obedience of the wife should be illustrated; and thus internal harmony was everywhere secured, and families were regulated. (In the same way) the son of Heaven established six official departments, in which were distributed the 3 kung, the 9 khing, the 27 ta fu, and the 81 sze of the highest grade. These were instructed in all that concerned the public and external government of the kingdom, and how the lessons for the man should be illustrated; and thus harmony was secured in all external affairs, and the states were properly governed.

It is therefore said, 'From the son of Heaven there were learned the lessons for men; and from the queen, the obedience proper to women.' The son of Heaven directed the course to be pursued by the masculine energies, and the queen regulated the virtues to be cultivated by the feminine receptivity. The son of Heaven guided in all that affected the external administration (of affairs); and the queen, in all that concerned the internal regulation (of the family). The teachings (of the one) and the obedience (inculcated by the other) perfected the manners and ways (of the people); abroad and at home harmony and natural order prevailed; the states and the families were ruled according to their requirements:—this was what is called 'the condition of complete virtue.'

12. Therefore when the lessons for men are not cultivated, the masculine phenomena in nature do

not proceed regularly;—as seen in the heavens, we have the sun eclipsed. When the obedience proper to women is not cultivated, the feminine phenomena in nature do not proceed regularly; as seen in the heavens, we have the moon eclipsed. Hence on an eclipse of the sun, the son of Heaven put on plain white robes, and proceeded to repair what was wrong in the duties of the six official departments, purifying everything that belonged to the masculine sphere throughout the kingdom; and on an eclipse of the moon, the queen dressed herself in plain white robes, and proceeded to repair what was wrong in the duties of the six palace-halls, purifying everything that belonged to the feminine sphere throughout the kingdom. The son of Heaven is to the queen what the sun is to the moon, or the masculine energy of nature to the feminine. They are necessary to each other, and by their interdependence they fulfill their functions.

Glossary

Charge to Yueh	from the Analects of Confucius
fillet	a headband
girdle	here, a belt or sash
Minor Odes of the Kingdom	a section from the book of Music
queen of the son of Heaven	that is, the queen, whose husband, the king, was the "son of Heaven"
Record	probably a reference to *Records of the Grand Historian* by Sima Qian
son of Heaven	the king
speculum	here, a mirror

A Geringer.   Lith. de Marlet,C.ᵉ r.du Boulai Nº 49

Brama.

Brahma

(Brahma, engraved by de Marlet [colour litho], Geringer, A. [19th century] [after] / Private Collection / The Stapleton Collection / The Bridgeman Art Library International)

LAWS OF MANU

"A man who knows the true meaning of the vedic treatise, in whatever order of life he may live, becomes fit for becoming Brahman while he is still in this world."

Overview

Known by many names—Manavadharmashastra, Manu Smriti, and the Law Codes of Manu—the Laws of Manu is both a legal and a religious text that elaborates on the basic Hindu tenets while providing a window into the religion, culture, and society of ancient India. It covers topics ranging from the role of women to the definition of sin to an explanation of the caste system and its utility in the maintenance of the universe. The Laws of Manu probably dates to between the second century BCE and the second century CE, most likely during the end of the Maurya Dynasty (324–180 BCE).

The Laws of Manu is part of the set of early post-Vedic texts—that is, texts written after the ancient Hindu Vedas (ca. 1200–900 BCE)—known as the Dharma Shastras, which further develop the concept of dharma. While a clear, authoritative definition of Hinduism continues to elude scholars, who debate whether Hinduism is a religion or a way of life, the concepts of dharma, karma, and *moksha* are constants. Hindus believe that all living things exist in a cycle of life and death wherein the individual's collective actions, or karma, determine how one will be reborn into the world. The ultimate goal is *moksha*, escape or release from this cycle of rebirth. To achieve *moksha*, the individual should follow his or her dharma, or one's duty or responsibility, as assigned to each person at birth in accord with cosmic laws and order. By living one's life by dharma, the individual accumulates good karma, to be reborn as a higher form and eventually achieve *moksha*. The Laws of Manu, comprising 2,685 verses divided into twelve chapters, or lessons, clarifies the concepts of dharma, karma, and *moksha* by explaining the creation of the world; the source of dharma; the dharma for the four *varnas*, or castes; and, finally, how dharma is linked to karma, rebirth, and the ultimate goal of liberation.

While there are many subsequent Hindu texts that define the laws of Hindu society and further explicate dharma, all refer back to the authority of the Laws of Manu. Although the text was thus important to the development of the Hindu tradition, much is still unknown about the Laws of Manu. In particular, both its date of composition

and its authorship remain uncertain. Despite the shroud of mystery surrounding the text, scholars agree that it was written during a period of religious and social change in northern India, probably during the Maurya Dynasty, for an audience of Brahmins (the priestly caste) and Kshatriyas (the warrior and royalty caste). With each generation of scholars contributing to debate as well as activists utilizing the text for various causes, the Laws of Manu persists as an important and relevant text in India and in Hindu communities abroad.

Context

One may only speculate as to the historical context in which the Laws of Manu was composed, since there is no agreed-upon dating of the text. Problems with dating are common with Hindu sacred texts, which scholars generally date in relation to other Sanskrit texts by comparing the use of verses and words. Content details are also considered; for example, ethnic groups mentioned in the Laws of Manu may point to an approximate date. Such scholars as Patrick Olivelle and Wendy Doniger propose that the Laws of Manu was composed between the second century BCE and the second century CE. Within this time frame, the Indian Subcontinent witnessed the dissolution of the Maurya Empire and the rise of the Shunga Empire.

The Maurya Empire, one of the largest empires of the subcontinent, is known for its religious freedom and tolerance. Prior to this period, Brahmins occupied a privileged space within society, but they lost this privileged status as Maurya emperors investigated other religious traditions in the area, such as Buddhism and Jainism. For example, Emperor Candragupta was drawn to Jainism, while Emperor Ashoka embraced Buddhism. Hinduism at this time began to incorporate Jain and Buddhist ideas into its practice while moving away from the rigidness of the caste system. The caste system divided society into four castes, or classes: Brahmins (priests), Kshatriyas (rulers and warriors), Vaishyas (farmers and merchants) and Shudras, or Untouchables (all other professions). The individual is born into a caste and must live by the caste's restrictions. For example a Shudra would never rule a kingdom and was

CA. 324 BCE	■ The Maurya Dynasty begins with the reign of Candragupta, who will later abdicate his throne to become a Jain monk.
CA. 272 −242 BCE	■ The Mauryan ruler Ashoka, a patron of Buddhism, reigns.
CA. 200 BCE −200 CE	■ The Laws of Manu are thought to have been composed.
CA. 185 BCE	■ The last Mauryan ruler, Brihadratha, is assassinated by Pushyamitra, who becomes the first ruler of the Shunga Empire.
CA. 75 BCE	■ The Shunga Dynasty is succeeded by the Kanva Dynasty, which is to last almost fifty years.
CA. 26 BCE	■ The Kanva Dynasty, which leaves little historical record, comes to a close, after which few if any major dynasties appear for several centuries.
1794	■ Sir William Jones publishes the first English translation of the Laws of Manu.
1927	■ **December** Dr. Bhimrao Ambedkar, a Shudra (Untouchable) leader in preindependence India, burns a copy of the Laws of Manu in Maharashtra State, in central India, in protest against the continued mistreatment of the Shudra caste.
2000	■ **March 25** Copies of the Laws of Manu are burned in protest against the erection of a statue of Manu in front of a courthouse in the Indian state of Rajasthan.

have prompted the assassination of the last Mauryan emperor, Brihadratha, by his commander in chief, Pushyamitra, a Brahmin who became the first ruler of the Shunga Empire around 180 BCE. Pushyamitra's reign became what the historian John Keay has described as an "orthodox brahmanical backlash" during which Buddhists were persecuted. It was in this context that the Laws of Manu was probably composed, such that the text could be seen as a treatise to reestablish Brahmins' power as the leaders of society.

The empire amassed by the Maurya Dynasty disintegrated during the 110 years of the Shunga Dynasty. Little is known about the following dynasties that reigned in northern India during the remaining probable time frame of the composition of the Laws of Manu. The Kanva Dynasty, which immediately followed the Shunga, lasted almost fifty years but left minimal archaeological records. Otherwise, no major dynasties existed in this region of India after the Kanvas until the emergence of the Guptas around 320 CE.

About the Author

Even less is known about the possible author of the text. The Laws of Manu begins with a group of seers asking Manu to explain the laws of the social classes. It is this Manu, the first human being and son of the "Self-existent One," or the Creator of the world, who is credited with the authorship of the text. But who was the writer behind this mythical Manu? Scholars lack access to any information that could identify him or how his socioeconomic status, religion, and geographic location influenced the composition of the text.

The text was duly credited to Manu until Georg Bühler's translation of 1886, at which point scholars generally began arguing that either a single other author or a group of authors composed the text. Like many ancient Hindu texts—such as the Mahabharata, the great Hindu verse epic that chronicles a feuding royal family to illustrate how dharma and karma operate—the Laws of Manu is widely believed to have been compiled over time, with additions and edits from a variety of authors. Some scholars go so far as to question the text's originality by arguing that it is merely a compilation of earlier proverbs and laws into a single volume. However, when one considers the overarching tone, with the majority of the text supporting a specific vision of Hindu society, Olivelle's argument for a single author proves convincing. While the true author or compiler (or authors or compilers) of the Laws of Manu may never be known, he was most likely an educated Brahmin who was an innovative writer. The Laws of Manu was one of the first Indian texts to be composed entirely in *shlokas*—a type of Sanskrit verse composed of two lines of sixteen syllables each, as used in Hindu epics such as the Mahabharata—and to utilize a conversation-based style of writing. The entire text reads as a dialogue between a teacher and a group of students.

restricted from entering certain temples, while a Brahmin occupied the highest rung of society, with his guidance and services sought by all. No individual, not even a king, could perform a religious ritual without a Brahmin.

Buddhism and Jainism do not impose such caste restrictions on individuals, and they flourished during the Maurya Empire because of royal patronage. The orthodox Brahmins' resentment of this type of patronage might

Explanation and Analysis of the Document

The present excerpts from the Laws of Manu are the beginning and ending chapters of the text, which introduce the idea of dharma, or duty, and its moral implications, the philosophical framework that underlies the entire text. These chapters explain the reasons and motivations for following the rules set out in the middle sections of the text.

♦ Chapter 1

Prologue: The text begins with a group of seers asking a meditating Manu to explain the laws that organize society. This initial set of verses establishes the style of the entire text. The rest of the text is the answering of the seers' request. This beginning half of chapter 1 is only part of the text where Manu answers this plea directly.

Creation: To explain the rules of the social classes, Manu begins by explaining creation. If one understands the creation of the world, one will understand what dharma is. According to Manu, originally nothing existed in the world except a dark state of slumber. The world as it is now known was born from the Creator, or the Self-existent Lord. This Creator is beyond description but exists in everything. As Manu describes it, the Creator meditated to create the diversity within the world. He created first water and then a golden egg from which he was physically born as Brahma. This idea that the Creator emerged from a golden egg mirrors a similar story in the Rig Veda, another Hindu sacred text that was composed around 1200 BCE and describes many Hindu deities. From the halves of the egg, Brahma created the heavens and earth as well as the eight directions. To structure where each creature exists within society and how it functions, Brahma developed the concepts of dharma (right) and *adharma* (wrong). These binary opposites will exist in each living thing to help organize the world away from chaos; each creature will be driven by these opposites to perform a specific function, as assigned by Brahma upon the creature's inception. The castes that divide Hindu society are derived from Brahma's body: The Brahmin is the head, the Kshatriya is the arm, the Vaishya is the thighs, and the Shudra is the feet. As a body cannot function properly if its parts do not act in concert, society will descend into chaos if each caste does not perform its appropriate function.

As the first lawgiver, Manu describes his own birth in the "Second Account of Creation." Brahma divides his body in half to make a man and a woman. With that woman, Brahma created Viraj, who meditated Manu into existence. Through this episode, the reader becomes aware of the duality in Brahma. This Brahma is both male and female, both existent and nonexistent. This duality mirrors the binary opposition between dharma and *adharma*. As the Brahma essentially begot Manu, Manu begot the ten great lords of creatures, who in turn brought the creation of the pantheon gods, heavenly creatures, animals, and humans. Manu concludes this description with the statement that all these creatures were created through "ascetic toil" and at his command.

Sir William Jones

(Sir William Jones (engraving), English School, (18th century) / Edinburgh University Library, Scotland / With kind permission of the University of Edinburgh / The Bridgeman Art Library International)

Manu then proceeds to explain the hierarchy of creatures (in "Classification of Flora and Fauna"), where Brahma is the zenith. Creatures are situated within the hierarchy in relation to their method of birth. Placenta births—that is, humans—occupy a higher position within the hierarchy than those hatched from eggs or grown from sprouts; the lowest forms are such plants as shrubs. Like humans, even these lower levels of creation are capable of feeling both pain and pleasure. Additionally each creature is assigned a certain task, which Manu does not elaborate upon in this chapter. He alludes to the idea of rebirth, whereby a creature's past deeds affect its position within this hierarchy. While he does not further explicate this concept in this chapter, it is elaborated in chapter 12, after all the rules have been enumerated.

Manu concludes his explanation of the creation of existence with a brief discussion titled "Cosmic Cycles." In this section, Manu reveals that this world will not exist forever. Just as the individual lives through cycles of rebirth, so does existence as a whole. Existence depends on the Creator: When he is awake the world is full of the action of creation, but eventually he falls back to sleep, and all creation dissolves back into his body, and his own body dissolves into nothing. Then the darkness that existed prior to creation returns again.

Having explained creation, Manu reveals (in "Transmission of the Law") the source of his knowledge, as he was told about creation from Brahma. Manu has already shared

"Together with the perishable atomic particles of the five elements given in tradition, this whole world comes into being in an orderly sequence. . . . Each creature follows on its own the very activity assigned to it in the beginning by the Lord. Violence or non-violence, gentleness or cruelty, righteousness [dharma] and unrighteousness [adharma], truthfulness or untruthfulness—whichever he assigned to each at the time of creation, it stuck automatically to that creature."

"Proper conduct is the highest Law, as well as what is declared in the Veda and given in traditional texts. Applying himself always to this treatise, therefore, let a twice-born man remain constantly self-possessed. When a Brahmin has fallen away from proper conduct, he does not reap the fruit of the Veda; but when he holds fast to proper conduct, tradition says, he enjoys its full reward."

"The rod of speech, the rod of mind, and the rod of action—a man in whose intellect these are kept under control is said to be 'triple-rodded.' When a man has laid down these rods with respect to all creatures and brought lust and anger under control, he thereby secures success."

"Among all these splendid activities, a particular activity has been declared as the best means for a man here to secure the supreme good. Among all these, tradition holds the knowledge of the self to be the highest; it is, indeed, the foremost of all sciences, for by it one attains immortality."

"A man who knows the true meaning of the vedic treatise, in whatever order of life he may live, becomes fit for becoming Brahman while he is still in this world."

"Some call him Fire, some Manu the Prajapati, others Indra, still others Breath, and yet others the eternal Brahman. This one, pervading all beings by means of the five forms, makes them go around like a wheel through birth, growth, and death. When a man thus sees by the self all beings as the self, he becomes equal towards all and reaches Brahman, the highest state."

the story of creation and his knowledge with his students, including Bhrigu. Since a student who has gained knowledge from a teacher should himself become a teacher and pass this knowledge on, Manu, sufficiently testifying to Bhrigu's capabilities, assigns Bhrigu the task of enumerating and explaining the laws for the remainder of the text. The motivations for this switch in narrator/teacher are unknown. The reader may assume it to be a call to echo this action and teach the laws to a larger audience.

Bhrigu begins his teachings (in "Time and Cosmology") with a brief recounting of Manu's lineage. Each progeny of Manu gave rise to his own epoch of existence. Bhrigu does not further explain how Manu's progeny came to be or how each one created and managed his epoch. Instead, he moves to a discussion of time. For both humans and divine beings, rest should be taken at night, whereas all activities should be completed during the day. However, the definition of a day differs. For living humans, a day is defined by the rising and setting of the sun, but a year constitutes a day for gods. While this section's aim is to highlight the insignificance of human time compared with time for the Supreme Lord, Bhrigu also points out that each age requires a different set of laws and that the human life span reduces with each successive age.

Bhrigu shifts to introduce the appropriate tasks for each of the four castes (in "Occupations of Social Classes"). Brahmins should focus their efforts on the teaching of the Vedas, while the Kshatriyas should learn the Vedas and protect their kingdoms but not become attached to worldly things. Vaishyas, too, should learn the Vedas but perform other occupations than the Kshatriyas—that is, farming and trade. The Shudra were assigned only one activity: to serve the other castes.

As related in "Excellence of the Brahmin," among the creatures and castes, Brahmins occupy the highest, most privileged position because they originated from the head of the Creator and are the eldest of all the castes. Bhrigu further explains the logic of his reasoning by presenting another hierarchy of creation in which intelligent living beings occupy a high rung, with Brahmins well educated in the Vedas occupying the highest rung. Bhrigu concludes this section by highlighting Brahmins' direct connection with the Creator. He is laying the foundation for the prevailing argument of the text: "This whole world—whatever there is on earth—is the property of the Brahmin."

Several terms used in this text bear phonetic similarities but have substantially different meanings. *Brahma* is the name of the Creator, while *Brahmin* is the caste of priestly individuals. Neither term should be confused with *Brahman*, which has various connotations: the essence of ritual, the essence of the universe, and also essence of the self, or atman. The individual who becomes Brahman realizes the essence of all things and will achieve *moksha*.

Bhrigu next explains (in "Treatise of Manu") the origins of the laws he will recite to the seers. These laws were passed down to Manu by the Creator, to explain how each social class should act and to clarify actions each class should avoid. This set of laws should be taught only by a Brahmin and should be studied attentively to ensure its preservation.

♦ Chapter 12

Action: Having finished explaining the rules that each caste should observe (in chapters 2–11, not included here), Bhrigu concludes his recitation of the Laws of Manu by explaining the results of rightly and wrongly observing these laws. Every action, physical or mental, results in either good karma or bad karma. A bad action, like telling a lie or stealing, will lead to returning to this world in a lesser form. Bhrigu describes three kinds of bad action: mental, verbal, and bodily. As he explains, a bad bodily action will result in reincarnation as an immobile creature, a bad verbal action will result in reincarnation as an animal, and a bad mental action will result in rebirth as an individual of the lowest caste. An individual who controls himself and does not succumb to bad action is successful in life.

Bhrigu continues to explain the process of rebirth. What happens to an individual after death depends on how one lived one's life. If an individual lives poorly, in that he performs bad acts, he is reborn in a body designed to punish him for these transgressions. After suffering for the sins, the individual is judged by his actions. If he acts rightly most of the time, he may continue to heaven, while if he acts mostly sinful, he will suffer additional punishments until his *jiva* (the internal self that exhibits the type of karma one incurs) is cleansed of these wrong acts.

One must appreciate that each individual has three attributes—goodness, vigor, and darkness, which manifest in the three respective forms of knowledge, passion and hatred, and ignorance. An individual should strive toward goodness. By knowing these three attributes and how they manifest, one can assess what kind of karma will be accumulated in performing an action. Bhrigu then explicates how one's actions affect rebirth by explaining how individuals driven by darkness become animals, by vigor become humans, and by goodness become gods. He further discusses the reincarnated forms the individual may assume, mirroring Manu's earlier explanation of the hierarchy of creation in chapter 1. Bhrigu groups creatures together according to which attribute they relate to.

Bhrigu continues to elucidate how bad karma affects the way in which one is reborn by providing examples of sin and the probable reincarnation the sinner will take after suffering through the hell referenced earlier. These descriptions of punishments are reminiscent of Dante Alighieri's *Inferno* (ca. 1314), with each type of infraction having an appropriate consequence. From Bhrigu's examples the reader observes that Brahmins fall the farthest by sinning. Another interesting observation is that gender appears to be a constant. When explaining what happens to a woman who steals, Bhrigu states that the female thief becomes the wife of the appropriate reincarnated creature as assigned for that type of theft.

Having explained the repercussions of bad actions, Bhrigu shifts the teaching (in "Actions Leading to the Supreme Good") toward the rewards of acting righteously or properly according to the Laws of Manu. Stating that the highest good is achieved through knowing oneself, he argues that this is made possible by following the rules laid out by the Vedas. According to the Vedas there are two kinds of actions: advancing actions, which are promoted by desire, and arresting actions, which transcend desire and are performed for the greater good. Bhrigu maintains through this section the primacy and authority of the Vedas, a collection of Hindu religious texts that had been in existence since 1200 BCE. The Vedas established the caste system as well as other elements of Hindu life. Bhrigu concludes this section with the argument that the ultimate power lies in a true understanding of the Vedas.

The penultimate section, titled "Secret Teaching," presents an interesting postscript to the overall text. While the laws enumerated in the text appear to cover all foreseeable issues, this section supports the authority of the Brahmins if a problem not addressed in the text should arise. Bhrigu goes even further by arguing that a "cultured" Brahmin should be consulted if such an occasion should arise. He defines a "cultured" Brahmin as one who has read the Vedas and its commentaries and demonstrates an ability to infer effectively. This is an interesting addition to the text that might suggest that the author is calling for the Brahmin caste to be more accountable to the responsibilities they are born into. Regardless, this section confirms again the probable goal of the text: to reestablish the authority and power of the Brahmin caste.

Conclusion: Bhrigu closes his teaching of the seers by reiterating the divine nature of these laws in again explaining the source of the teachings. He reminds the seers of the might of the Self-Existent Lord, who is unimaginable. The individual should strive to see himself in all creation and abide by the laws described in this text. If he lives his life in such a manner, he will reach Brahman, the highest state, and escape the cycle of reincarnation.

Audience

Most scholars agree that the author of this text had a clear agenda to protect the rights and privileges of the Brahmins while reestablishing the former alliance between the Brahmins and the Kshatriyas. The audience consisted of individuals who were probably educated and possibly conservative Brahmins. However, some scholars argue that the text can be understood as one written for the ruling class as a sort of propaganda to reelevate the Brahmin class. With the text's focus on individuals' occupying a specific place in society and performing their required roles correctly, the reader can sense that the author is attempting to persuade the ruling class to respect the Brahmin class.

Questions for Further Study

1. The creation account in the Laws of Manu invites comparison with other creation accounts. Compare this document with the creation account in the biblical book of Genesis or the creation myth explicated in the entry Yengishiki. What commonalities do you see in these creation accounts? What might account for these similarities?

2. The Laws of Manu provides a fundamental justification for the Indian caste system. Why, in your opinion, was the division of society into castes such an ingrained feature of life in India? What social, economic, historical, or geographical conditions might have led to the caste system?

3. The Laws of Manu are structured around the concept of duality: male/female, good/evil, dharma/*adharma*. What factors do you think might have prompted early cultures to conceive of creation and existence as a duality, as paired opposites?

4. Although the Laws of Manu is a religious text, it was probably written with political considerations in mind. What were these political considerations and how did the document contribute to the maintenance of the social status quo? Why does it continue to have political ramifications in the modern world?

5. The notion of rebirth is endemic to Hinduism, yet many people in the modern world claim to have been reincarnated, including non-Hindus. What is your position on reincarnation? Do you believe that reincarnation is a reality or merely a fiction? On what do you base your opinion?

Impact

The centuries following the composition of the Laws of Manu brought at least nine commentaries that declare the text's authority. The text is also referred to in other ancient texts. For example, significant portions of the Laws of Manu appear in the Mahabharata.

The authority and pervasiveness of the Laws of Manu extend well beyond the scope of ancient India. While Hindu society has changed significantly since the time when the code was probably composed, it has remained a text of much interest. When the British arrived in India, the colonial government utilized the Laws of Manu to guide their governing of the newly colonized Indian people. In fact, the text has the honor of being one of the first Sanskrit documents on dharma to be translated into English (in 1794), making non-European law and religion known for the first time to a broader Western audience. The text has been translated many times since. Georg Bühler's translation, first published in 1886, has remained the standard, but more recent translations by Wendy Doniger (1991) and Patrick Olivelle (2004) are more successful at capturing the essence of the original Sanskrit while preserving the use of verses.

The Laws of Manu remains a source of controversy within modern Indian society. While the text's modern audience is diverse in terms of caste, class, gender, and religion, the text has become a symbol of oppression and a rallying point for different social movements. Hindutva (or Hindu Right) organizations such as the Vishwa Hindu Parishad use the text to support their ideology by claiming the text was a Muslim creation. The official stance, published on their Web site, disowns the caste system described as Hindu in the Laws of Manu, going so far as to claim that the caste system was created to punish individuals unwilling to convert to Islam. Meanwhile, social activists attack the Laws of Manu for propagating injustices, seeing the text as the source of the gender and caste oppression in India. Before independence, the activist Dr. Bhimrao R. Ambedkar burned a copy of the text to represent his contempt for the oppression of lower-caste individuals. Such acts of burning the laws still occur. A recent significant occurrence happened in March 2000, when activists burned a copy after the Rajasthan High Court decided to erect a statue to Manu. However, as Madhu Kishwar, a women's rights activist, has pointed out, the modern audience does not remember the context in which the Laws of Manu and other texts were written. She argues that the public fails to consider that the authors of these texts would probably defer to the needs and conventions of the present rather than the authority of any text composed at a specific time in the past. Considering this history, the Laws of Manu will probably remain relevant to India and the Hindu tradition.

Further Reading

■ Books

Bhattacharyya, Parnasabari. *Conceptualizations in the Manusmrti.* New Delhi: Manohar, 1996.

Flood, Gavin. *An Introduction to Hinduism.* Cambridge, Mass.: Cambridge University Press, 1996.

Hopkins, Thomas J. *The Hindu Religious Tradition.* Belmont, Calif.: Wadsworth, 1971.

Keay, John. *India: A History.* New York: Atlantic Monthly Press, 2000.

Knipe, David M. *Hinduism: Experiments in the Sacred.* Long Grove: Waveland Press, 1991.

Manu. *The Law Code of Manu,* trans. Patrick Olivelle. New York: Oxford University Press, 2004.

Manu. *The Laws of Manu,* trans. Wendy Doniger and Brian K. Smith. Harmondsworth, U.K.: Penguin, 1991.

Olivelle, Patrick. *Manu's Code of Law: A Critical Edition and Translation of the Manava-Dharmasastra.* Oxford, U.K.: Oxford University Press, 2005.

Rocher, Ludo. "The Dharmasastras." In *The Blackwell Companion to Hinduism,* ed. Gavin Flood. Malden, Mass.: Blackwell, 2003.

■ Journals

Kishwar, Madhu. "Manu and the Brits." *Hinduism Today* (January–February 2001): 56–59.

■ Web Sites

Kishwar, Madhu. "From Manusmriti to Madhusmriti: Flagellating a Mythical Enemy." Educational Council on Indic Traditions Web site.
    http://www.infinityfoundation.com/ECITmythicalframeset.htm

—Rupa Pillai

LAWS OF MANU

CHAPTER 1

♦ PROLOGUE

Manu was seated, absorbed in contemplation, when the great seers came up to him, paid homage to him in the appropriate manner, and addressed him in these words: "Please, Lord, tell us precisely and in the proper order the Laws of all the social classes, as well as of those born in between; for you alone, Master, know the true meaning of the duties contained in this entire ordinance of the Self-existent One, an ordinance beyond the powers of thought or cognition."

So questioned in the proper manner by those noble ones, that Being of boundless might paid honour to all those great seers and replied: "Listen!"

♦ CREATION

"There was this world—pitch-dark, indiscernible, without distinguishing marks, unthinkable, incomprehensible, in a kind of deep sleep all Over. Then the Self-existent Lord appeared—the Unmanifest manifesting this world beginning with the elements, projecting his might, and dispelling the darkness. That One—who is beyond the range of senses; who cannot be grasped; who is subtle, unmanifest, and eternal; who contains all beings; and who transcends thought—it is he who shone forth on his own.

"As he focused his thought with the desire of bringing forth diverse creatures from his own body, it was the waters that he first brought forth; and into them he poured forth his semen. That became a golden egg, as bright as the sun; and in it he himself took birth as Brahma, the grandfather of all the worlds.

"The waters are called 'Nara'; the waters, clearly, are the off-spring of Nara. Because his first sojourn was in them, tradition calls him 'Narayana.' That cause which is unmanifest and eternal, which has the nature of both the existent and the non-existent—the Male produced from it is celebrated in the world as Brahma.

"After residing in that egg for a full year, that Lord on his own split the egg in two by brooding on his own body. From those two halves, he formed the sky and the earth, and between them the mid-space, the eight directions, and the eternal place of the waters.

"From his body, moreover, he drew out the mind having the nature of both the existent and the non-existent; and from the mind, the ego—producer of self-awareness and ruler—as also the great self, all things composed of the three attributes, and gradually the five sensory organs that grasp the sense objects. By merging the subtle parts of these six possessing boundless might into particles of his own body, moreover, he formed all beings. Because the six parts of his physical frame become attached to these beings, the wise call his physical frame 'body.' The great elements enter it accompanied by their activities, as also the mind, the imperishable producer of all beings, accompanied by its subtle particles.

"From the subtle particles of the physical frames of these seven males of great might, this world comes into being, the perishable from the imperishable. Of these, each succeeding element acquires the quality specific to each preceding. Thus, each element, tradition tells us, possesses the same number of qualities as the number of its position in the series. In the beginning through the words of the Veda alone, he fashioned for all of them specific names and activities, as also specific stations.

"The Lord brought forth the group of gods who are endowed with breath and whose nature is to act, the subtle group of Sadhyas, and the eternal sacrifice. From fire, wind, and sun, he squeezed out the eternal triple Veda characterized by the Rig verses, the Yajus formulas, and the Saman chants, for the purpose of carrying out the sacrifice. Time, divisions of time, constellations, planets, rivers, oceans, mountains, flat and rough terrain, austerity, speech, sexual pleasure, desire, and anger—he brought forth this creation in his wish to bring forth these creatures.

"To establish distinctions among activities, moreover, he distinguished the Right [*dharma*] from the Wrong [*adharma*] and afflicted these creatures with the pairs of opposites such as pleasure and pain. Together with the perishable atomic particles of the five elements given in tradition, this whole world comes into being in an orderly sequence. As they are brought forth again and again, each creature follows on its own the very activity assigned to it in the beginning by the Lord. Violence or non-violence, gentleness or cruelty, righteousness [*dharma*] or unrighteousness [*adharma*], truthfulness or untruthfulness—whichever he assigned to each at the time of creation, it stuck automatically to that creature. As at the change of seasons each season automatically adopts its own distinctive marks, so do embodied beings adopt their own distinctive acts.

"For the growth of these worlds, moreover, he produced from his mouth, arms, thighs, and feet, the Brahmin, the Kshatriya, the Vaishya, and the Shudra."

Excursus: *Second Account of Creation*: "Dividing his body into two, he became a man with one half and a woman with the other. By that woman the Lord brought forth Viraj.

"By heating himself with ascetic toil, that man, Viraj, brought forth a being by himself—know, you best of the twice-born, that I am that being, the creator of this whole world.

"Desiring to bring forth creatures, I heated myself with the most arduous ascetic toil and brought forth in the beginning the ten great seers, the lords of creatures: Marici, Atri, Angiras, Pulastya, Pulaha, Kratu, Pracetas Vasistha, Bhrigu, and Narada. They, in turn, brought forth seven other Manus of immense energy; the gods and the classes of gods; and the great sages of boundless might; Yaksas, Raksasas, Pisacas, Gandharvas, Apsarases, Asuras, Nagas, Sarpas, and Suparnas; the different groups of ancestors; lightnings, thunderbolts, clouds, rainbow streaks, rainbows, meteors, storms, comets, and the manifold heavenly lights; pseudo-humans, monkeys, fish, birds of various kind, farm animals, wild animals, humans, predatory animals, and animals with incisors in both jaws; worms, insects, moths, lice, flies, bugs, all creatures that sting and bite, and immobile creatures of various kind.

"In this manner through ascetic toil, those noble ones brought forth at my command this whole world, the mobile and the immobile, each creature in accordance with its activity."

Excursus: *Classification of Fauna and Flora*: "I will now explain to you exactly which type of activity is ascribed here to which type of creature, and also their relative order with respect to birth. Those born from placentas are farm animals, wild animals, predatory animals, animals with incisors in both jaws, Raksasas, Pisacas, and humans.

"Those born from eggs are birds, snakes, crocodiles, fish, and turtles, as well as other similar land and aquatic animals.

"Those born from warm moisture are creatures that sting and bite; lice, flies, and bugs; those born through heat; as well as other similar creatures.

"Those born from sprouts are all flora propagated through seeds or cuttings. Those that bear copious

flowers and fruits and die after their fruits mature are 'plants'; those that bear fruits without flowers, tradition calls 'forest lords'; and those that bear both flowers and fruits, tradition calls 'trees.' Various kinds of shrubs and thickets and different types of grasses, as also creepers and vines—all these also grow from either seeds or cuttings. Wrapped in a manifold darkness caused by their past deeds, these come into being with inner awareness, able to feel pleasure and pain. In this dreadful trans-migratory cycle of beings, a cycle that rolls on inexorably for ever, these are said to represent the lowest condition, and Brahma the highest.

Excursus: *Cosmic Cycles*: "After bringing forth in this manner this whole world and me, that One of inconceivable prowess once again disappeared into his own body, striking down time with time. When that god is awake, then this creation is astir; but when he is asleep in deep repose, then the whole world lies dormant. When he is soundly asleep, embodied beings, whose nature is to act, withdraw from their respective activities, and their minds become languid. When they dissolve together into that One of immense body, then he, whose body contains all beings, sleeps tranquil and at ease. Plunging himself into darkness, he lingers there for a long time together with his sense organs and ceases to perform his own activities. Then he emerges from that bodily frame. When, after becoming a minute particle, he enters, conjoined, the seminal form of mobile and immobile beings, then he discharges the bodily frame.

"In this manner, by waking and sleeping, that Imperishable One incessantly brings to life and tears down this whole world, both the mobile and the immobile."

Transmission of the Law: "After composing this treatise, he himself in the beginning imparted it according to rule to me alone; and I, in turn, to Marici and the other sages. Bhrigu here will relate that treatise to you completely, for this sage has learnt the whole treatise in its entirety from me."

When Manu had spoken to him in this manner, the great sage Bhrigu was delighted. He then said to all those seers: "Listen!"

Excursus: *Time and Cosmology*: There are six further Manus in the lineage of this Manu, the son of the Self-existent One: Svarocisa, Auttami, Tamasa, Raivata, Caksusa, of great energy, and the son of Vivasvat. Possessing great nobility and might, they each have brought forth their own progeny.

These seven Manus of immense energy, with the son of the Self-existent One at their head, gave rise to and secured this whole world, the mobile and the immobile, each in his own Epoch.

Eighteen Nimesas ("winks") make a Kastha ("second"), thirty Kasthas a Kala ("minute"), thirty Kalas a Muhurta ("hour"), and thirty Muhurtas a day-and-night. The sun divides the day and the night, both the human and the divine. The night is meant for creatures to sleep, and the day to engage in activities.

For ancestors, a month constitutes a day and a night, divided into the two fortnights. The dark fortnight is the day for engaging in activities, and the bright fortnight is the night for sleeping. For gods, a year is a day and a night and their division is this: the day is the northward passage of the sun, and the night is its southward passage.

Listen now to a concise account of the duration of a day-and-night of Brahma and of each Age in proper sequence. The Krta Age is said to last 4,000 years. It is preceded by a twilight lasting 400 years and followed by a twilight of the same length. For each of the three subsequent Ages, as also for the twilights that precede and follow them, the first number of the thousands and the hundreds is progressively diminished by one. These four Ages, computed at the very beginning as lasting 12,000 years, are said to constitute a single Age of the gods. The sum total of 1,000 divine Ages should be regarded as a single day of Brahma, and his night as having the very same duration. Those who know this propitious day of Brahma lasting 1,000 Ages, as also his night with the same duration—they are people who truly know day and night.

At the end of that day-and-night, he awakens from his sleep; and when he has woken up, he brings forth the mind, which is both existent and non-existent. The mind, driven by the desire to create, transmutes the creation. From the mind is born ether, whose distinctive quality is said to be sound. From ether, as it is being transmuted, is born wind—powerful, pure, and bearing all odours—whose distinctive quality is thought to be touch. From the wind, as it is being transmuted, is produced light—shining, brilliant, and dispelling darkness—whose distinctive quality, tradition says, is visible appearance. From light, as it is being transmuted, comes water, with taste as its distinctive quality; and from water, earth, with smell as its distinctive quality. That is how this creation was at the beginning.

The divine Age mentioned previously as lasting 12,000 years—that multiplied 71 times is here referred to as an "Epoch of a Manu". The countless Epochs of Manu, as also creation and dissolution—the Supreme Lord does this again and again as a kind of sport.

In the Krta Age, the Law is whole, possessing all four feet; and so is truth. People never acquire any property through unlawful means. By acquiring such property, however, the Law is stripped of one foot in each of the subsequent Ages; through theft, falsehood, and fraud, the Law disappears a foot at a time.

In the Krta Age, people are free from sickness, succeed in all their pursuits, and have a life span of 400 years. In the Treta and each of the subsequent Ages, however, their life span is shortened by a quarter. The life span of mortals given in the Veda, the benefits of rites, and the power of embodied beings—they all come to fruition in the world in conformity with each Age.

There is one set of Laws for men in the Krta Age, another in the Treta, still another in the Dvapara, and a different set in the Kali, in keeping with the progressive shortening taking place in each Age.

Ascetic toil, they say, is supreme in the Krta Age; knowledge in Treta; sacrifice in Dvapara; and gift-giving alone in Kali.

Excursus: *Occupations of Social Classes*: For the protection of this whole creation, that One of dazzling brilliance assigned separate activities for those born from the mouth, arms, thighs, and feet. To Brahmins, he assigned reciting and teaching the Veda, offering and officiating at sacrifices, and receiving and giving gifts. To the Kshatriya, he allotted protecting the subjects, giving gifts, offering sacrifices, reciting the Veda, and avoiding attachment to sensory objects; and to the Vaishya, looking after animals, giving gifts, offering sacrifices, reciting the Veda, trade, moneylending, and agriculture. A single activity did the Lord allot to the Shudra, however: the ungrudging service of those very social classes.

Excursus: *Excellence of the Brahmin*: A man is said to be purer above the navel. Therefore, the Self-existent One has declared, the mouth is his purest part. Because he arose from the loftiest part of the body, because he is the eldest, and because he retains the Veda, the Brahmin is by Law the lord of this whole creation. For, in the beginning, the Self-existent One heated himself with ascetic toil and brought him forth from his own mouth to convey divine oblations and ancestral offerings and to protect this whole world. What creature can surpass him through whose mouth the denizens of the triple heaven always eat their oblations, and the forefathers their offerings?

Among creatures, living beings are the best; among living beings, those who subsist by intelligence; among those who subsist by intelligence, human beings; and among human beings, Brahmins—so the tradition declares. Among Brahmins, the learned are the best; among the learned, those who have made the resolve; among those who have made the resolve, the doers; and among doers, the Vedic savants.

A Brahmin's birth alone represents the everlasting physical frame of the Law; for, born on account of the Law, he is fit for becoming Brahman. For when a Brahmin is born, a pre-eminent birth takes place on earth—a ruler of all creatures to guard the storehouse of Laws. This whole world—whatever there is on earth—is the property of the Brahmin. Because of his eminence and high birth, the Brahmin has a clear right to this whole world. The Brahmin eats only what belongs to him, wears what belongs to him, and gives what belongs to him; it is by the kindness of the Brahmin that other people eat.

Excursus: *Treatise of Manu*: To determine which activities are proper to him and which to the remaining classes in their proper order, Manu, the wise son of the Self-existent, composed this treatise. It should be studied diligently and taught to his pupils properly by a learned Brahmin, and by no one else.

When a Brahmin who keeps to his vows studies this treatise, he is never sullied by faults arising from mental, oral, or physical activities; he purifies those alongside whom he eats, as also seven generations of his lineage before him and seven after him; he alone, moreover, has a right to this entire earth.

This treatise is the best good-luck incantation; it expands the intellect; it procures everlasting fame; and it is the ultimate bliss. In this, the Law has been set forth in full—the good and the bad qualities of actions and the timeless norms of proper conduct—for all four social classes.

Proper conduct is the highest Law, as well as what is declared in the Veda and given in traditional texts. Applying himself always to this treatise, therefore, let a twice-born man remain constantly self-possessed. When a Brahmin has fallen away from proper conduct, he does not reap the fruit of the Veda; but when he holds fast to proper conduct, tradition says, he enjoys its full reward. Seeing thus that the Law proceeds from proper conduct, the sages understood proper conduct to be the ultimate root of all ascetic toil. . . .

CHAPTER 12

"You have described this Law for the four classes in its entirety, O Sinless One! Teach us accurately the ultimate consummation of the fruits of actions."

Bhrigu, the son of Manu and the very embodiment of the Law, said to those great seers, "Listen to the determination with respect to engagement in action."

♦ ACTION

The Fruits of Action: Action produces good and bad results and originates from the mind, speech, and the body. Action produces the human conditions—the highest, the middling, and the lowest.

One should understand that the action of the embodied self—action that in this world is of three kinds, has three bases, and contains ten characteristics—is set in motion by the mind.

Coveting the property of others, reflecting on undesirable things in one's mind, and adhering to false doctrines are the three kinds of mental action. Harshness, falsehood, slander of every sort, and idle chatter are the four kinds of verbal action. Taking what has not been given, unsanctioned killing, and sex with another's wife are given in tradition as the three kinds of bodily action.

A man experiences the good and bad results of mental actions in his mind alone; those of verbal actions, in his speech; and those of bodily actions, in his body alone. On account of faults resulting from bodily actions, a man becomes an immobile creature; on account of faults resulting from verbal actions, he becomes a bird or an animal; and on account of faults resulting from mental actions, he becomes a man of the lowest caste.

The rod of speech, the rod of mind, and the rod of action—a man in whose intellect these are kept under control is said to be "triple-rodded." When a man has laid down these rods with respect to all creatures and brought lust and anger under control, he thereby secures success.

The Inner Selves: The one who makes this body act is called Ksetrajna, "the knower of the field"; the one who does the actions, on the other hand, the wise call Bhutatman, "the elemental self." Another inner self innate to all embodied beings bears the name Jiva, "the individual self," by whom are experienced all the pleasures and pains in succeeding births.

These two—Mahat, "the Great", and Ksetrajna, "the knower of the field"—united with the elements, remain pervading the one who abides in creatures both great and small. From his body innumerable forms stream forth, which constantly set in motion the creatures both great and small.

The Process of Rebirth: When evil men die, another firm body is produced for them from the same five elemental particles, a body designed to suffer torments. After experiencing there the torments of Yama with that body, they merge into those very elemental particles, each into its corresponding particle.

After paying for the sins resulting from attachment to sensory objects, sins that lead to misery, he is freed from taint and approaches the same two beings of great power. Unwearied, these two jointly examine his merits and sins, linked to which one secures happiness or suffering here and in the hereafter.

If he acts righteously for the most part and unrighteously to a small degree, enveloped in those very elements, he enjoys happiness in heaven. If, on the other hand, he acts unrighteously for the most part and righteously to a small degree, abandoned by those elements, he suffers the torments of Yama. After enduring the torments of Yama, Jiva, "the individual self", becomes freed from taint and enters those same five elements, each into its corresponding particle.

Seeing with his own intellect those transitions of this Jiva, "the individual self," resulting from righteous and unrighteous conduct, let him always set his mind on righteous conduct.

The Three Attributes: One should understand Goodness, Vigour, and Darkness as the three attributes of the body, attributes by which Mahat, "the Great," remains pervading all these existences completely.

When one of these attributes thoroughly suffuses the body, it makes the embodied self dominant in that attribute. Goodness is knowledge, tradition tells us; Darkness is ignorance; and Vigour is passion and hatred. These are their pervasive forms that inhere in all beings.

Among these—when someone perceives within himself a condition full of joy, a sort of pure and tranquil light, he should recognize it as Goodness; when it is full of pain and causing anguish to himself, he should understand that it is Vigour, irresistible and constantly drawing embodied beings; when it is full of confusion, with an unclear object, unfathomable by argument, and indiscernible, he should recognize it as Darkness. I will explain to you completely the fruits arising from all these three attributes—the highest, the middling, and the lowest fruits.

Vedic recitation, ascetic toil, knowledge, purification, the control of the organs, righteous activity, and contemplation of the self—these mark the attribute of Goodness. Delight in undertaking activities, resolve, taking up improper tasks, and constant indulgence in sensual pleasures—these mark the attribute of Vigour. Greed, sloth, lack of resolve, cruelty, infidelity, deviation from proper conduct, habitual begging, and carelessness—these mark the attribute of Darkness.

These, in brief and in the proper order, should be known as the marks of all these three attributes located in the three times. An act about which a man is ashamed after he has committed it, while he is committing it, and when he is about to commit it—a learned man should recognize all that as the mark of the attribute of Darkness. An act by which a man seeks to win wide fame in the world and is not disappointed when he fails to win it—one should recognize it as the mark of the attribute of Vigour. What a man seeks to know with all his heart and is not ashamed to perform, at which his inner being rejoices—that is the mark of the attribute of Goodness.

Pleasure is said to be the mark of Darkness; Profit, of Vigour; and Law, of Goodness. Each later one is superior to each preceding. Which of these attributes leads to which types of cyclical existence—I will briefly state them in due order with respect to this entire world.

Those who possess Goodness become gods; those who possess Vigour become humans; and those who possess Darkness always become animals—that is the threefold course. One should recognize, however, that this triple course based on attributes is itself threefold, namely, lowest, middle, and highest, depending on the specific type of action and knowledge within each.

Immobile creatures, worms and insects, fish, snakes, creeping animals, farm animals, and jackals—these constitute the lowest course related to Darkness. Elephants, horses, Sudras, despised foreigners, lions, tigers, and boars—these constitute the middle course related to Darkness. Caranas, Suparnas, hypocritical men, fiends, and ghouls—these constitute the highest among the courses related to Darkness.

Jhallas, Mallas, Natas, men who live by vile occupations, and people addicted to gambling and drinking—these constitute the first course related to Vigour. Kings, Ksatriyas, royal chaplains, and professional debaters and soldiers—these constitute the middle course related to Vigour. Gandharvas, Guhyakas, Yaksas, divine attendants, and all the Apsarases—these constitute the highest among the courses related to Vigour.

Hermits, ascetics, Brahmins, divine hosts in celestial chariots, asterisms, and Daityas—these constitute the first course related to Goodness. Sacrificers, seers, gods, Vedas, celestial lights, years, ancestors, and Sadhyas—these constitute the second course related to Goodness. Brahma, creators of the universe, Law, Mahat and the Unmanifest—the wise call this the highest course related to Goodness. I have declared above everything coming from the three kinds of action—the entire transmigratory cycle affecting all beings, a threefold cycle which contains a further threefold division.

Vile and ignorant men attain evil transmigratory paths by their attachment to the senses and by their failure to follow the Law. Which kind of womb this Jiva, the "individual self", attains in due order within this world through which kind of action—listen to all of that.

Sin and Rebirth: Those who commit grievous sins causing loss of caste first go to dreadful hells during large spans of years; upon the expiration of that, they reach the following transmigratory states.

A murderer of a Brahmin enters the wombs of a dog, a pig, a donkey, a camel, a cow, a goat, a sheep, a deer, a bird, a Candala, and a Pulkasa.

A Brahmin who drinks liquor enters the wombs of worms, insects, moths, birds that feed on excrement, and vicious animals.

A Brahmin who steals enters thousands of times the wombs of spiders, snakes, lizards, aquatic animals, and vicious ghouls.

A man who has sex with an elder's wife enters hundred of times the wombs of grasses, shrubs, creepers, carnivorous animals, fanged animals, and creatures that commit cruel deeds.

Vicious individuals become carnivorous animals; those who eat forbidden food become worms; thieves become cannibals; and those who have sex with lowest-born women become ghosts.

A man who forges links with outcastes, has sex with someone else's wife, or steals what belongs to a Brahmin becomes a Brahmin fiend.

A man who steals gems, pearls, corals, or any of the various precious substances out of greed is born among goldsmiths. By stealing grain, one becomes a rat; by stealing bronze, a ruddy goose; by stealing water, a Plava coot; by stealing honey, a gnat; by stealing milk, a crow; by stealing sweets, a dog; by stealing ghee, a mongoose; by stealing meat, a vulture; by stealing fat, a Madgu cormorant; by stealing oil, a cockroach; by stealing salt, a cricket; by stealing curd, a Balaka flamingo; by stealing silk, a partridge; by stealing linen, a frog; by stealing cotton cloth, a Krauñca crane; by stealing a cow, a monitor lizard; by stealing molasses, a flying fox; by stealing fine perfumes, a muskrat; by stealing leafy vegetables, a peacock; by stealing various kinds of cooked food, a porcupine; by stealing uncooked food, a hedgehog; by stealing fire, a Baka heron; by stealing household utensils, a mason-wasp; by stealing dyed clothes, a francolin partridge; by stealing a deer or an elephant, a wolf; by stealing a horse, a tiger; by stealing fruits or flowers, a monkey; by stealing a woman, a bear; by stealing water, a cuckoo; by stealing vehicles, a camel; and by stealing farm animals, a goat. If a man steals anything at all belonging to some one else by

force or eats an oblation before the offering has been completed, he inevitably becomes an animal.

Women also, when they steal in the above manner, incur guilt; they become the wives of the very same creatures.

When people belonging to the social classes deviate from their respective occupations outside a time of adversity, they go through evil cyclical existences and end up as servants of the Dasyu people. When a Brahmin deviates, he will become an Ulkamukha ghost eating vomit; a Ksatriya will become a Kataputana ghost eating filth and corpses; a Vaisya will become a Maitraksajyotika ghost feeding on pus; and a Shudra who deviates from the Law proper to him will become a Cailasaka ghost.

The more that people addicted to sensual pleasures indulge in sensual pleasures, the more their proclivity to them grows. By repeatedly engaging in these sinful actions, these men of little understanding undergo torments here in various births—tossing about in dreadful hells such as Tamisra; the hell Asipatravana and the like; being tied up and cut up; various kinds of torture; being eaten by crows and owls; being burnt by hot sand-gruel; the unbearable tortures of being boiled in vats; taking birth constantly in evil wombs full of suffering; being assailed by cold and heat; terrors of various kinds; repeated residence in different wombs; being born agonizingly; being wrapped up in painful ways; doing servile work for others; being separated from relatives and loved ones; having to live in the company of evil people; earning and losing wealth; winning friends and enemies; old age, against which there is no remedy; being assailed by illnesses; various afflictions; and death itself, which is impossible to overcome.

When a man engages in any act with a certain inner disposition, he reaps its fruits with a body corresponding to that disposition. I have declared to you above all the fruits arising from actions. Listen now to these rules of action for a Brahmin, rules that secure the supreme good.

Actions Leading to the Supreme Good: Vedic recitation, ascetic toil, knowledge, controlling the senses, refraining from causing injury, and service of the teacher—these are the highest means of securing the supreme good. Among all these splendid activities, a particular activity has been declared as the best means for a man here to secure the supreme good. Among all these, tradition holds the knowledge of the self to be the highest; it is, indeed, the foremost of all sciences, for by it one attains immortality.

One should understand that acts prescribed by the Veda are always a more effective means of securing the highest good both here and in the hereafter than the above six activities. All these activities without exception are included within the scheme of the acts prescribed by the Veda, each in proper order within the rules of a corresponding act.

Acts prescribed by the Veda are of two kinds: advancing, which procures the enhancement of happiness; and arresting, which procures the supreme good. An action performed to obtain a desire here or in the hereafter is called an "advancing act", whereas an action performed without desire and prompted by knowledge is said to be an "arresting act". By engaging in advancing acts, a man attains equality with the gods; by engaging in arresting acts, on the other hand, he transcends the five elements.

A man who offers sacrifices within himself attains absolute sovereignty when he sees equally himself in all beings and all beings in himself. Leaving behind even the acts prescribed above, a Brahmin should apply himself vigorously to the knowledge of the self, to inner tranquillity, and to vedic recitation. This, indeed, is the consummation of one's existence, especially for a Brahmin; for only by achieving this does a twice-born accomplish all he has to do, and never otherwise.

The Veda is the eternal eyesight for ancestors, gods, and humans; for vedic teaching is beyond the powers of logic or cognition—that is the settled rule. The scriptures that are outside the Veda, as well as every kind of fallacious doctrine—all these bear no fruit after death, for tradition takes them to be founded on Darkness. All those different from the Veda that spring up and then flounder—they are false and bear no fruit, because they belong to recent times.

The four social classes, the three worlds, and the four orders of life, the past, the present and the future—all these are individually established by the Veda. Sound, touch, visible appearance, taste, and, the fifth, smell, are established by the Veda alone; their origin is according to attribute and action. The eternal vedic treatise bears on all beings; it is the means of success for these creatures; therefore, I consider it supreme.

A man who knows the vedic treatise is entitled to become the chief of the army, the king, the arbiter of punishment, and the ruler of the whole world. As a fire, when it has picked up strength, burns up even green trees, so a man who knows the Veda burns up his taints resulting from action. A man who knows the true meaning of the vedic treatise, in whatever order of life he may live, becomes fit for becoming Brahman while he is still in this world.

Those who rely on books are better than the ignorant; those who carry them in their memory are better than those who simply rely on books; those who understand are better than those who simply carry them in their memory; and those who resolutely follow them are better than those who only understand.

For a Brahmin, ascetic toil and knowledge are the highest means of securing the supreme good; by ascetic toil he destroys impurity and by knowledge he attains immortality.

Perception, inference, and treatises coming from diverse sources—a man who seeks accuracy with respect to the Law must have a complete understanding of these three. The man who scrutinizes the record of the seers and the teachings of the Law by means of logical reasoning not inconsistent with the vedic treatise—he alone knows the Law, and no one else.

This is the totality of activities leading to the supreme good as prescribed. The secret doctrine of this Treatise of Manu will now be taught.

Excursus: *Secret Teaching*: If it be asked: what happens in cases where specific Laws have not been laid down? What "cultured" Brahmins state is the undisputed Law. Those Brahmins who have studied the Veda together with its supplements in accordance with the Law and are knowledgeable in scripture, perception, and inference, should be recognized as "cultured."

Alternatively, when a legal assembly with a minimum of ten members, or with a minimum of three members firm in their conduct, determines a point of Law, no one must question that Law. A man who knows the three Vedas, a logician, a hermeneut, an etymologist, a specialist in Law, and three individuals belonging to the first three orders of life—these constitute a legal assembly with a minimum of ten members. A man who knows the Rig Veda, a man who knows the Yajurveda, and a man who knows the Samaveda—these should be recognized as constituting a legal assembly with a minimum of three members for settling doubts regarding the Law. When even a single Brahmin who knows the Veda determines something as the Law, it should be recognized as the highest Law, and not something uttered by myriads of ignorant men. Even if thousands of men who fail to follow the observances, who are unacquainted with the Veda, and who merely use their caste to earn a living, come together, they do not constitute a legal assembly. When fools enveloped by Darkness declare something as the Law, though they are ignorant of it—that sin, increased a hundredfold, stalks those who declare it.

I have explained to you above all the best means of securing the supreme good. A Brahmin who does not deviate from them obtains the highest state.

♦ CONCLUSION

Excursus: *Summation*:

In this manner, the blessed god, desiring to do what is beneficial for the people, revealed to me in its entirety this highest secret of the Law.

With a collected mind, a man should see in the self everything, both the existent and the non-existent; for when he sees everything in the self, he will not turn his mind to what is contrary to the Law. All the deities are simply the self, the whole world abides within the self; for the self gives rise to engagement in action on the part of these embodied beings.

Let him deposit space within his spaces; the wind within his motion and touch; the highest fire within his digestive organ and eyes; water within his fluids; earth within his physical form; the moon in his mind; directions in his ears; Vishnu in his stride; Hari in his strength; Fire in his speech; Mitra in his organ of evacuation; and Prajapati in his organ of procreation.

The ruler of all, more minute than even an atom, resplendent like gold, and to be grasped by the sleeping mind—he should know him as the supreme Person. Some call him Fire, some Manu the Prajapati, others Indra, still others Breath, and yet others the eternal Brahman. This one, pervading all beings by means of the five forms, makes them go around like a wheel through birth, growth, and death. When a man thus sees by the self all beings as the self, he becomes equal towards all and reaches Brahman, the highest state.

When a twice-born recites this Treatise of Manu proclaimed by Bhrigu, he will always follow the proper conduct and obtain whatever state he desires.

Glossary

Bhrigu	a mythological Hindu sage
Brahma	the Hindu creator god
Brahmin, the Kshatriya, the Vaishya, and the Shudra	the four castes, respectively, priests; warriors; merchants, artisans, and cattle herders; and unskilled laborers, the untouchables
Candala	a reference to outcasts
Hari	another name for Vishnu
Mahat	"point," "seed," "source"
Marici	possibly one of the seven sons of Brahma
Mitra	a Hindu sun god, responsible for preserving the physical and moral order of the universe
Prajapati	the "Lord of Creatures" that presided over procreation
Pulkasa	a person of low caste

Construction of the Tower of Babel

(The Tower of Babel, from the Atrium, detail of builders [mosaic], Veneto-Byzantine School [13th century] / Basilica di San Marco, Venice, Italy / Giraudon / The Bridgeman Art Library International)

All the souls of men will gnash their teeth, burning in a river, and brimstone and a rush of fire in a fiery plain, and ashes will cover all."

Overview

The Pseudo-Sibylline Oracles are a collection of twelve books in which the divine messages of a Sibyl are recorded. In ancient Greece, Sibyls were women who, in moments of ecstasy, were thought to utter predictions, often of woes and disasters, directly from the gods. Although this was a pagan phenomenon, both Jews and Christians living in the Greco-Roman world adapted it in order to place their own religious sentiments in a more widely accepted and familiar mode. The Pseudo-Sibylline Oracles represent this adaptation, hence their designation as "pseudo." As such, they were written in Greek poetic hexameters but are full of such Judeo-Christian markers as Old and New Testament references, polemics against idolatry, and praises of the one God.

Although various books appear together in the earliest manuscripts of the Oracles (dating from the fourteenth through the sixteenth century CE), each of the twelve books actually has a different date, provenance, and authorship. Based on specific historical references in the Oracles, it can be surmised that they were written over a span of more than eight hundred years, from the mid-second century BCE to the seventh century CE and in places throughout the Near East, from Egypt to Syria. The exact authorship is unknown; additions made over time to individual books have rendered the existing books a conglomeration of the work of different groups. At best, we can say that their authors were either Jews or Christians living in late antiquity.

The Oracles remained theologically important and continued to be quoted by early church fathers, from the first through the fifth centuries, reaching the height of their religious prominence in the medieval period (roughly 500–1500). Although their use in the church began to decline after the Middle Ages, scholars from the mid-sixteenth century onward started to recognize that an alternative significance lay in their unique mixture of traditions, or syncretism. The Oracles' portrayal of Jewish and Christian thought within a traditionally pagan framework not only gives us a glimpse into the diversity of religious thinking in the ancient world but also provides evidence of the degree to which people interacted with and borrowed from one another.

Context

Although the name "Sibyl" refers to one woman, beginning in the fourth century BCE a number of cities from Italy to Asia Minor are recorded as having their own Sibyls. Rome housed the most famous collection of Sibylline Oracles. Legend has it that the Sibyl from Cumae (near Naples) in Italy offered to sell the Roman king Tarquin the Elder (616–579 BCE) nine books of her verses. Tarquin initially refused, and she destroyed six books before he finally accepted them. Afterward these books were protected by special guardians and consulted only in times of political crisis and then only by command of the Roman Senate. They burned with the destruction of the Temple of Jupiter in 83 BCE. Eventually more were gathered and housed by Augustus in the Temple of Apollo on the Palatine Hill, where they remained until they were destroyed in the fifth century CE.

Only fragments of the Roman and other pagan Sibylline Oracles remain. Since the Sibyl often dealt with wars and political upheavals that would befall different nations (other predictions often centering on natural disasters such as earthquakes), these fragments were preserved in the works of later authors when they referenced such events. Given the very public nature of the Roman Sibylline collection, the Sibyl would have been a familiar phenomenon to Jews living in the Greco-Roman world. Since the Oracles have obvious similarities with prophecy as found in the Hebrew Bible (or Old Testament; see the Oracles against the nations in Amos 1.3–2.5), it is not surprising that as early as the second century BCE Jews began to adopt the Sibyl as their own, identifying her (in book 3) as the "daughter-in-law of Noah" and as "a prophetess of the high God" and thus fully assimilating her into the biblical tradition.

The last centuries before the Common Era in the Mediterranean world—called the Hellenistic Period on account of the pervasive Greek (Hellenic) influence—were a time of changing imperial rule. After the death of Alexander the Great in 323 BCE, his empire was divided among his generals, leading to a near-constant competition between the Syrian Seleucid and the Egyptian Ptolemaic empires for control of the Near East, especially Israel. Simultaneously, Rome was growing in power, eventually seizing control of

CA. 750 –675 BCE	■ The early Greek poet Hesiod writes his accounts of the gods.
CA. 616 –579 BCE	■ According to legend, the Sibyl delivers to King Tarquin the Elder of Rome a set of oracles, which became known as the Roman Sibylline Oracles.
83 BCE	■ The Roman Sibylline Oracles are destroyed in a fire.
64 BCE	■ Rome seizes control of Syria.
63 BCE	■ Rome seizes control of Judaea.
30 BCE	■ Rome seizes control of Egypt.
70 CE	■ Romans destroy the Jerusalem Temple.
CA. 240 –320 CE	■ The Christian author Lactantius quotes books 1 and 2, giving us a time before which the Sibylline Oracles were written (*terminus ante quem*).
500–600	■ The prologue to the Oracles is written, explaining why the author collected them.
1300–1600	■ Three manuscript traditions emerge for a unified collection of the Oracles.
1545	■ The first printed edition of Pseudo-Sibylline Oracles is published by Xystus Betuleius at Basel, Switzerland.

books were finally gathered together in the sixth century CE and an anonymous prologue added to the collection by a Christian who saw their importance in their ability to demonstrate how even a pagan oracle was bound to testify that history had led up to the truth of Jesus Christ.

About the Author

The Pseudo-Sibylline Oracles have no identifiable authors. While the words are ostensibly those of a Sibyl, in actuality they represent the concerns of various Jewish and Christian communities in late antiquity. Scholars have surmised, though not with absolute certainty, that books 3, 5, and 11–14 were produced in Egypt; books 4, 6, and 7 come from Syria; and books 1 and 2 are from Asia Minor. (Books 9 and 10 replicate material found in the first eight books.) The provenance of book 8 is obscure, but most likely it is also in the Near East. These designations are based on internal references in the texts. For example, in book 1 there is a lengthy section devoted to the location of Noah's ark, here said to be in Phrygia. Based on the prominence of this reference, scholars have assumed that the oracle originates here, an area in west-central Asia Minor (modern-day Turkey).

Furthermore, the authors of the various books are known to have lived and learned in multicultural settings. They had to be in close contact with Greeks and Romans in order to know about Sibyls, and they also had to be sufficiently educated in the Greek language to be able to read classical Greek authors and emulate Sibylline poetics. There are also numerous references to classical literature that would necessitate a broad education; in addition to Greek myths like that of the Titans, there are also allusions to the ancient Greek poets Homer (eighth or seventh century BCE) and, in particular, Hesiod (ca. 750–675 BCE). Hesiod, the father of Greek didactic poetry, is known for one of the earliest examples of the concept of universal history, *Works and Days*, which traces history from its beginning to the present, and for his collection of a multitude of Greek myths, *Theogony*. Taken together, Hesiod's works provide a Greek understanding of both the human and the divine. Beyond their educated backgrounds, the authors of the Oracles had to have both a commitment to their particular religious communities, ones that were in the minority and were sometimes persecuted, and an ability to disguise their Jewish or Christian identity in order to appeal to the larger majority audience.

Explanation and Analysis of the Document

Books 1 and 2 constitute one unit in the medieval manuscripts and so are best treated together. They represent an original Jewish text with notable Christian additions, but the extent of these additions is hard to determine. These two books are mostly concerned with ethics and eschatology (the end of the world) and less with historical events. The dearth of historical references in comparison with the

Syria (64 BCE), Israel (63 BCE), and Egypt (30 BCE). Not surprisingly, the common thread throughout the Jewish Pseudo-Sibylline Oracles is a Jewish reaction to these foreign elements, whether to their religion, their rule, or their history. The Sibyl, then, was the perfect tool for criticizing pagans, because the criticism was cloaked in an anonymous pagan voice.

It was the need of Jews to react to the changing, and often violent, world around them, therefore, that gave rise to the Jewish Oracles. A similar motivation also lay behind the creation of the Christian books among the Oracles. These

other books makes the text difficult to date. However, the Christian author Lactantius quoted the books in the mid-third century, providing us with a time before which it must have existed (*terminus ante quem*). The provenance, or place of origin, is most likely Asia Minor.

♦ Book 1

The Sibyl's Introduction: As with many of the other Sibylline Oracles, this book begins with the Sibyl identifying herself and her task. Like prophecy in the Old Testament, the Sibyl not only focuses heavily on the future but also devotes attention to the past and present.

The Creation—The Fall: The Sibyl makes clear that she speaks on behalf of God, not herself. Her first task is to recount the world's creation. Although the basis of the creation account is that of the Bible, there are also marked differences. She does attribute creation to God's words "let it come to be" (Genesis 1:3) and includes similar aspects of creation, such as light, heaven, sea, stars, earth, plants, birds, beasts, and creeping things. But here the Sibyl adds additional elements such as clouds, rivers, and winds and does not divide these acts of creation into separate days. This may be because her stated intent is not to depict the creation in detail, but rather to illustrate its majesty in such a way that it serves to highlight God's power and, in turn, promote religious adherence.

Our first glimpse of Greek influence appears with the mention of Tartarus, which is used in Greek literature to refer to the deepest place in the underworld, where the foes of Zeus reside. Here it seems to refer to the formless "abyss" of Genesis 1:2.

Following creation, the Sibyl retells the stories of Adam and Eve. Her version represents an early form of biblical interpretation. Genesis contains two accounts of the creation of animals and human beings; the day-by-day creation (1:1–2:4) and the creation in the Garden of Eden (2:5–25). It appears that the Sibyl's author has attempted to make sense of these two separate accounts by molding them into one. Thus, we see elements of the first (for example, man and woman created in God's image) combined with those of the second (for example, woman created from man's rib).

The Sibyl also lessens the impact of Adam and Eve's disobedience in the garden. After eating from the forbidden fruit, they are expelled (Genesis 3:23–24), but instead of curses (hard labor and difficult childbirth, as in Genesis 3:16–19), they receive blessing to be fruitful and multiply (Genesis 1:28). Thus, we can see that the Sibyl's author felt license to delete and rearrange biblical material to create a softer story.

The First Five Generations: This section of the text introduces the first five of ten generations of humanity. History's division into finite periods has parallels both in other of the Oracles (for instance, book 4) and, most notably, in Hesiod's *Works and Days*. The first generation mirrors Hesiod's notion of a golden age in which people enjoyed long life spans and freedom from suffering. In both the Oracle and in Hesiod, following this age, human beings continue to deteriorate and grow more violent. Much of the

Michelangelo's Cumaean Sibyl from the Sistine Chapel
(Sistine Chapel Ceiling: Cumaean Sibyl, 1510 [fresco] [post restoration], Buonarroti, Michelangelo (1475-1564) / Vatican Museums and Galleries, Vatican City, Italy / The Bridgeman Art Library International)

deterioration is the result of the Watchers, divine beings who taught humans various skills, a concept that appears elsewhere in early Jewish literature (for example, 1 Enoch 6–11), and who mated with human women to produce giants. (The Hebrew Bible accepted as canonical by Jews and Christians includes a few references to such giants, as in Genesis 6:4.) Thus, we can see that the Sibyl's author has grafted biblical stories onto a Greek periodization of history.

Noah and the Flood: The ensuing sections recount the biblical story of Noah and the Flood, derived from Genesis 6–8. The Sibyl's version of the Flood narrative does differ from that of Genesis in one respect: Whereas the biblical Noah never speaks to the sinful human beings, the Sibyl's patriarch takes the opportunity to admonish the people and entreat them to repent, because they are "abandoning modesty, desiring shamelessness, tyrants in fickleness and violent sinners, liars, sated with faithlessness, evildoers, truthful in nothing, adulterers, ingenious at pouring out slander." This exhortation, which is characteristic of books 1–2, is made all the more powerful in the face of the Flood's impending worldwide destruction. The Sibyl's author, therefore, places this story exactly halfway through the ten generations and allots it an enormous amount of space, both of which serve to highlight its distinct ethical focus.

The Sixth and Seventh Generations: The Titans: The Sibyl again speaks in the first person and implicitly identi-

"Beginning from the first generation of articulate men down to the last, I will prophesy all in turn, such things as were before, as are, and as will come upon the world through the impiety of men."

"But he being alone in the luxuriant plantation of the garden desired conversation, and prayed to behold another form like his own. God himself indeed took a bone from his flank and made Eve, a wonderful maidenly spouse, whom he gave to this man to live with him in the garden. And he, when he saw her, was suddenly greatly amazed in spirit, rejoicing, such a corresponding copy did he see."

"Then again there will be a great contest for entry to the heavenly city. It will be universal for all men, holding the glory of immortality. Then every people will strive for the immortal prizes of most noble victory."

"Give a hand to one who has fallen. Save a solitary man. All have a common lot, the wheel of life, unstable prosperity. If you have wealth, stretch out your hand to the poor. The things which God gave you, give of them to one in need."

"All the souls of men will gnash their teeth, burning in a river, and brimstone and a rush of fire in a fiery plain, and ashes will cover all."

fies herself as the daughter-in-law of Noah. Thus, as she continues to recount the sixth and seventh generations, her words claim the legitimacy of an eyewitness account. The sixth generation emulates the first, because it occurs after the world has been created anew following the Flood. As with the first generation, the sixth will also live long without disease. But, like the five antediluvian (pre-Flood) generations, this blessed generation quickly deteriorates. The seventh generation of Titans "will fight in opposition against the starry heaven." This account is a melding of the biblical story of the Tower of Babel (Genesis 11) with Hesiod's depiction in his *Theogony* of the Titans, who, in Greek mythology, were the elder deities born of Heaven and Earth who clashed with their own offspring, led by Zeus, for control. While the Sibyl's author has turned the Titans into men with one language, as in the biblical story, the tower building has become an attack on heaven, as in the Greek story. It would seem, therefore, that, the Sibyl's author viewed the haughty desire of the Bible's tower builders

to make a name for themselves (Genesis 11:4) as an aggressive move for divine control.

Christian Passage on the Incarnation and Life of Christ: A Christ-focused section abruptly interrupts the counting of the remaining ten generations. This insertion is the basis for the scholarly position that there is both an original Jewish oracle and a later Christian redaction of it. The riddle of Jesus's name echoes the riddle on God's name that occurs earlier in book 1. These riddles have proved confusing to scholars, but they both might be a reflection of the Jewish penchant for *gematria*, the belief that each letter in the Hebrew alphabet corresponds to a number, such that when the letters of a given word are added together, the word's total numerical value can be compared to the values of other words, thereby signifying deeper spiritual meanings.

This section depicts the entirety of Christ's life; it begins with his birth and then quickly moves on to his ministry. There are familiar elements, such as walking on water, exorcising demons, feeding the multitudes, and curing the sick. The section concludes with the Passion and, finally, the Resurrection, melding together the accounts of the four Christian particular interest is the fact that the Oracle explicitly blames the Jews ("Hebrews") for killing Christ ("son of the heavenly God"), clearly indicating that this is a Christian addition.

Prophecy of Dispersion of the Jews: Given book 1's lack of historical references, its concluding section stands out for the specific allusion to the Roman suppression of the Jewish revolt in 70 CE and, in particular, Roman destruction of the Temple. It is unclear whether this is a Christian addition or not. On the one hand, its date is clearly late enough to have been inserted by a Christian. On the other hand, while the Jews meet with much misfortune in this section, there is no mention of its being a direct punishment for killing Jesus and also no hint of Christians superseding them.

♦ **Book 2**

The Inspiration of the Sibyl—Prophecy of Disasters: The first five lines of book 2 are commonly viewed as a transitional segment, an attempt to explain why the ten-generation scheme was interrupted; God himself caused her to pause. The Sibyl resumes with the generations, and thus we can consider this part of the original Jewish text. However, she has skipped from the seventh to the tenth. It seems safe to assume that there were originally eighth and ninth generations but that in the merging of the two books with their Christian revisions, they were somehow lost.

Disasters loom large for this tenth generation, which mirrors the fifth generation and its inevitable end in the destructive Flood. Here, however, many natural disasters and threats—earthquakes, lightning, wild animals, barren lands—presage an impending final disaster. The eschatological (that is, end-of-the-world) focus and reference to a coming savior (or messiah) accord with both Jewish and Christian thought at the beginning of the Common Era. Christian influence on this passage is possible but uncertain.

The Heavenly Contest: The next section, however, is very clearly Christian in nature. This serves as the introduction for a contest in order to gain entry into heaven. Aside from the explicit mention of Christ, there are also common Christian figures, such as martyrs and virgins who are esteemed by God and will be assured of success in the contest.

On Justice and Other Virtues—Conclusion of the Contest: Just as the impending Flood during the fifth generation offered an opportunity for the Sibyl's author to insert an ethical exhortation into Noah's mouth, so too does the doom of the tenth generation present a chance for further ethical warnings. This rather large section, then, focuses on a multitude of values and actions worthy of emulation. They range from the general—"Dispense all things justly"—to the specific—"Pity the shipwrecked, for the voyage is uncertain." Two things, in particular, are important to note about this passage. First, it is an excerpt from Pseudo-Phocylides, an Alexandrian Jew who wrote sometime between the first century BCE and the first century CE. He, in turn, was imitating a Greek poet of the sixth century BCE who wrote practical advice for everyday living. (Pseudepigraphy,

the attribution of writings to earlier authorities, was a common practice of the age.) What is notable about Pseudo-Phocylides and, therefore, his text's inclusion in book 2, is that the exhortations are generic and not specific to Jews. The admonition to "honor God, then your parents" is not cited as one of the Ten Commandments. This appears to be an example of the Sibyl author's attempt to make the text palatable to non-Jewish readers. Parentheses surrounding text in these passages indicate that the Sibylline author is adding something new to the work of Pseudo-Phocylides.

Signs of the End—Eschatological Rule of the Hebrews: More signs of the impending end of times are revealed. First there are general calamities that befall people, such as famines, pestilence, and wars, but gradually the universal shifts to the religious as prophecy is replaced with lies and holy and faithful men are confused. This occurs under the reign of Beliar (or Belial), a Satan-like figure frequently referred to in postbiblical Jewish literature such as the Dead Sea Scrolls (150 BCE–68 CE). Next the Jews, "the Hebrews," will rule and Elijah (called "the Thesbite" after his birthplace) will come. The tradition that Elijah will act as the forerunner of the messianic period is found in the Bible's Malachi 4:5, which reads, "Lo, I will send the prophet Elijah to you before the coming of the awesome, fearful day of the Lord." Because there is no specific mention of Jesus, it is hard to determine whether this section is from the book's Jewish or Christian strata.

Destruction by Fire: The next section brings the final, worldwide destruction that book 2 has been leading up to. It should be noted that in book 1, the Sibyl's author left out any reference to Genesis 8:21, in which the Lord tells Noah, "I will never again destroy every living being, as I have done." This resolves any possible indication that God does not keep his word; instead, this second destruction is legitimized.

As has been emphasized, the tenth generation is in many regards parallel to the fifth. The same is true with respect to this section: The fifth generation was destroyed by water; the tenth is destroyed by fire, water's opposite. However, it is also a more expansive destruction. Noah managed to save animals and his family, but now "all the elements of the world will be bereft."

The Judgment—Resurrection of the Dead: What happens after the fiery destruction is unclear. It seems that after humanity has perished, souls are brought to judgment by four angels. Before the judgment can take place, the dead are resurrected. Among them are those, like the Giants, who were destroyed in the fifth generation. The judgment scene has direct parallels with the biblical book of Daniel, chapter 7, where God sits as a judge on a throne in the midst of fire. The accusation that the Jews killed their own prophets is also a clear Christian interpolation.

Distinction of Righteous and Wicked—Punishment of the Wicked—Rewards of the Righteous: The judgment is simple: The righteous will be saved, and the wicked will perish. The list of the wicked is an abbreviated version of the material from Pseudo-Phocylides; clearly these are the people who did not heed the Sibyl's words. They will be thrown into Gehenna, which in Jewish tradition is a place of punishment after death. Interestingly, here it is paralleled with the Greek Tartarus, mentioned in book 1. The righteous, in contrast, will be rewarded with a life with God. This too is equated with a Greek concept, that of the Elysian plain (or fields), the resting place of heroes in Greek mythology .

Confession of the Sibyl: Book 2 ends with the Sibyl speaking once more about herself. Despite her ability to prophesy, she emphasizes her humanity and her "shameless [that is, shameful] deeds," for which she knows that she, too, will be judged. She concludes with a prayer for salvation.

Audience

As with authorship, the actual audience of books 1 and 2 is difficult to determine with any precision. It is certain, however, that the author(s) anticipated a Greek-speaking audience that would recognize the Sibyl's divine authority and understand allusions to both Greek mythology and the Bible. The repeated emphasis on how an individual should act would seem to indicate that the author wanted the Oracles to serve as a reforming tool. We can imagine that the author hoped that someone who encountered the oracle might be persuaded to stop committing any one of the number of sins listed. It is unclear, however, whether these Oracles were aimed at Jews, Christians, or pagans. As mentioned, the individual morality presented in Pseudo-Phocylides is not specifically Jewish or Christian in nature and would have been applicable to most listeners. Thus,

it seems possible that books 1–2 were for a general audience—both those Jews and Christians who were acculturated into Greek society and those pagans who needed to be convinced of the commonalities they shared with Jews and Christians. In contrast, those who read them today do not do so for the moral admonitions but for what the Oracles can teach us about early Jews and Christians.

Impact

While it is difficult to say what, if any, impact the Jewish books among the Pseudo-Sibylline Oracles had on contemporary Jewish audiences, it is clear that they were sufficiently well known for Christian authors to select them for adaptation. It is this Christian attention, in turn, that ensured this collection's preservation while so many other Sibylline oracles were lost. Christians continued to view them as important for what they had to say about Christ, and thus at least twenty-two different texts written by early church fathers contain verses from these Sibylline Oracles. For example, Clement of Alexandria (ca. 150–211 CE) in his *Stromateis* placed in the mouth of the apostle Paul the message to "take also the Greek books, get to know from the Sibyl how she revealed one God and the things to come." The first Christian Roman emperor, Constantine (r. 306–337), even made mention of them in one of his speeches, "Ad sanctorum coetum" ("Oration for the Saints"), recorded by Eusebius in *Life of Constantine*. In support of the Sibyl, the

Questions for Further Study

1. What does the mere fact of the existence of the Pseudo-Sibylline Oracles tell modern historians about the interaction and intermingling of religious groups in late antiquity? Of what interest is this interaction?

2. The ancient Greeks were "pagan" and polytheistic. Judaism and Christianity were (and are) monotheistic. Why, then, did the Pseudo-Sibylline Oracles become assimilated into Judaism and Christianity?

3. Compare this entry with the entry on the Book of Enoch. What do the two works have to say about the "Watchers" and their role in human affairs? Further, the entry on the Book of Enoch discusses "Hellenized Jews." Who were the Hellenized Jews, and what importance did they have both for the Book of Enoch and the Pseudo-Sibylline Oracles?

4. Most religious traditions have an account of creation. Compare the creation account in this document with one from another tradition. Possible documents to consult include Genesis, the Popol Vuh, or the Sefer Yetzirah.

5. Why do you think that the Judeo-Christian tradition ultimately rejected the vision of God and creation contained in the Pseudo-Sibylline Oracles?

emperor quotes thirty-three verses from book 8 about the life of Jesus and declares, "For my part I regard as blessed, whom the Savior selected as a prophetess of his forethought for us." Perhaps the two most striking uses of the Sibylline Oracles are Dante's use of book 2's vision of punishment for his *Inferno* and Michelangelo's painting of five Sibyls amid biblical prophets in the Sistine Chapel. Thus, the Sibylline Oracles continued to be a pertinent theme amid religious art well into the Renaissance.

The modern reception, however, is far more ambiguous. The Oracles have received little scholarly attention, most likely because the text does not fit into a clear field. On the one hand, its Greek language, incorporation of classical sources, and poetics make it difficult for scholars of Judaism or Christianity, while, on the other hand, its Judeo-Christian subject matter, biblical allusions and interpretations, and subtle references to postbiblical literature make it difficult for classicists. Furthermore, the Oracles do not stem from one historical period or from one geographical region, having been created throughout the Hellenistic era and into the medieval period and all over the Mediterranean region. Thus, the study of the Oracles necessitates a familiarity with more than one religious tradition as well as a wide range of literature, history, and languages.

Those scholars who study the Oracles, however, emphasize the importance of their manifold nature. They represent a centuries-long process of religious accretion, as their authors pulled from Greco-Roman, Jewish, and Christian sources. Furthermore, for the historian, while the Oracles do not provide enough concrete factual data to enhance historical knowledge, the ways in which they refer to historical events and people provide examples of how these moments in history were perceived.

Further Reading

■ Books

Bartlett, John R. "The Sibylline Oracles." In his *Jews in the Hellenistic World: Josephus, Aristeas, the Sibylline Oracles, Eupolemus.* Cambridge, U.K.: Cambridge University Press, 1985.

Collins, J. J. *The Sibylline Oracles of Egyptian Judaism.* Missoula, Mont.: Society of Biblical Literature, 1974.

Collins, J. J. "The Sibylline Oracles." In *Jewish Writings of the Second Temple Period: Apocrypha, Pseudepigrapha, Qumran Sectarian Writings, Philo, Josephus,* ed. Michael E. Stone. Philadelphia: Fortress Press, 1984.

Collins, J. J. "Sibylline Oracles." In *The Old Testament Pseudepigrapha.* Vol. 1: *Apocalyptic Literature and Testaments,* ed. James H. Charlesworth. Peabody, Mass.: Hendrickson Publishers, 2009.

Lightfoot, J. L. *The Sibylline Oracles with Introduction, Translation, and Commentary on the First and Second Books.* Oxford, U.K.: Oxford University Press, 2007.

Parke, H. W. *Sibyls and Sibylline Prophecy in Classical Antiquity,* ed. B. C. McGing. New York: Routledge, 1988.

■ Journals

Potter, D. S. "Sibyls in the Greek and Roman World." *Journal of Roman Archaeology* 3 (1990): 471–483.

—Alexandria Frisch

PSEUDO-SIBYLLINE ORACLES

Book 1

◆ The Sibyl's Introduction

Beginning from the first generation of articulate men down to the last, I will prophesy all in turn, such things as were before, as are, and as will come upon the world through the impiety of men.

◆ The Creation

First God bids me tell truly how the world came to be. But you, devious mortal, so that you may never neglect my commands, attentively make known the most high king. It was he who created the whole world, saying, "let it come to be" and it came to be. For he established the earth, draping it around with Tartarus, and he himself gave sweet light. He elevated heaven, and stretched out the gleaming sea, and he crowned the vault of heaven amply with bright-shining stars and decorated the earth with plants. He mixed the sea with rivers, pouring them in, and with the air he mingled fragrances, and dewy clouds. He placed another species, fish, in the seas, and gave birds to the winds; to the woods, also, shaggy wild beasts, and creeping serpents to the earth; and all things which now are seen. He himself made these things with a word, and all came to be, swiftly and truly. For he is self-begotten looking down from heaven. Under him the world has been brought to completion. And then later he again fashioned an animate object, making a copy from his own image, youthful man, beautiful, wonderful. He bade him live in an ambrosial garden, so that he might be concerned with beautiful works. But he being alone in the luxuriant plantation of the garden desired conversation, and prayed to behold another form like his own. God himself indeed took a bone from his flank and made Eve, a wonderful maidenly spouse, whom he gave to this man to live with him in the garden. And he, when he saw her, was suddenly greatly amazed in spirit, rejoicing, such a corresponding copy did he see. They conversed with wise words which flowed spontaneously, for God had taken care of everything. For they neither covered their minds with licentiousness nor felt shame, but were far removed from evil heart; and they walked like wild beasts with uncovered limbs.

◆ The Fall

To these did God then address commands and instruct them not to touch the tree. But a very horrible snake craftily deceived them to go to the fate of death and receive knowledge of good and evil. But the woman first became a betrayer to him. She gave, and persuaded him to sin in his ignorance. He was persuaded by the woman's words, forgot about his immortal creator, and neglected clear commands. Therefore, instead of good they received evil, as they had done. And then they sewed the leaves of the sweet fig tree and made clothes and put them on each other. They concealed their plans, because shame had come upon them. The Immortal became angry with them and expelled them from the place of immortals. For it had been decreed that they remain in a mortal place, since they had not kept the command of the great immortal God, and attended to it. But they, immediately, going out on the fruitful earth wept with tears and groans. Then the immortal God himself spoke to them for the better: "Increase, multiply, and work on earth with skill, so that by sweat you may have your fill of food." Thus he spoke, but he made the serpent, cause of the deceit, press the earth with belly and flank, having bitterly driven him out. He aroused a dire enmity between them. The one guards his head to save it, the other his heel, for death is at hand in the proximity of men and malignant poisonous snakes.

◆ The First Generation

And then the race multiplied as the universal ruler himself commanded, and innumerable peoples grew one after another. They constructed all sorts of houses and also made cities and walls, well and with understanding. To these he granted a lengthy day for a very lovely life. For they did not die worn out with troubles, but as if overcome by sleep. Blessed were the great-hearted mortals, whom the immortal savior king, God, loved. But they also sinned, smitten with folly. For they shamelessly ridiculed their fathers and dishonored their mothers. Plotters against their brothers, they did not know their familiar friends. They were polluted, sated with the blood of people, and they made wars. Upon them came a final ruin, cast from heaven, which removed them, terrible ones, from life. But Hades received them. They called it Hades, since Adam first went (there) having tasted death, and earth covered him. Therefore all men who are born on earth are said to go to the House of Hades. But all these, even when they went to Hades, had honor, since they were the first race.

♦ The Second Generation

But when it had received these, he fashioned again another very diverse second race from the most righteous men who were left. These were concerned with fair deeds, noble pursuits, proud honor, and shrewd wisdom. They practiced skills of all kinds, discovering inventions by their needs. One discovered how to till the earth with plows, another, carpentry, another was concerned with sailing, another, astronomy and divination by birds, another, medicine, again another, magic. Different ones devised that with which they were each concerned, enterprising Watchers, who received this appellation because they had a sleepless mind in their hearts and an insatiable personality. They were mighty, of great form, but nevertheless they went under the dread house of Tartarus guarded by unbreakable bonds, to make retribution, to Gehenna of terrible, raging, undying fire.

♦ The Third Generation

After these again a third race, mighty in spirit, of overbearing terrible men appeared, who performed many evils among themselves. Wars, slaughters, and battles destroyed these continually, men of proud heart.

♦ The Fourth Generation

After these things, in succession came another race of men, late of fulfilment, the youngest, bloodthirsty, indiscriminate, in the fourth generation. They shed much blood, neither fearing God nor respecting men. For a raging wrath and grievous impiety was indeed inflicted on them. Wars and slaughters and battles cast some to the netherworld, though they were miserable impious men. Others the heavenly God himself later removed from his world in wrath, draping them around with great Tartarus, under the base of the earth.

♦ The Fifth Generation

Again he made afterward another far inferior race of men, for whom thereafter immortal God fashioned no good, since they suffered many evils. For they were insolent, much more than those Giants, crooked ones, abominably pouring forth slander.

♦ Noah Bidden Prepare for the Flood

Noah alone among all was most upright and true, a most trustworthy man, concerned for noble deeds. To him God himself spoke as follows from heaven: "Noah, embolden yourself, and proclaim repentance to all the peoples, so that all may be saved. But if they do not heed, since they have a shameless spirit, I will destroy the entire race with great floods of waters. But I bid you to construct quickly an imperishable wooden house, flourishing with unthirsting roots. I will place a mind in your breast, and crafty skill, and (will put) measures in your lap; I will take care of everything so that you and as many as live with you will be saved.

♦ A Riddle on the Name of God

I am the one who is, but you consider in your heart: I am robed with heaven, draped around with sea, the earth is the support of my feet, around my body is poured the air, the entire chorus of stars revolves around me. I have nine letters, I am of four syllables. Consider me. The first three have two letters each. The last has the rest, and five are consonants. The entire number is: twice eight plus three hundred, three tens and seven. If you know who I am you will not be uninitiated in my wisdom.

♦ Noah Preaches Repentance

Thus he spoke, but an immeasurable fear seized the man, such a thing did he hear. And then, having craftily devised all in turn, he entreated the peoples and began to speak in words like these: "Men sated with faithlessness, smitten with a great madness, what you did will not escape the notice of God, for he knows all things, the immortal savior, who oversees everything, who commanded me to announce to you, so that you may not be destroyed by your hearts. Be sober, cut off evils, and stop fighting violently with each other, having a bloodthirsty heart, drenching much earth with human blood. Mortals, stand in awe of the exceedingly great, fearless heavenly creator, imperishable God, who inhabits the vault of heaven, and entreat him, all of you—for he is good—for life, cities, and the whole world, four-footed animals and birds, so that he will be gracious to all. For the time will come when the whole immense world of men perishing by waters will wail with a dread refrain. Suddenly you will find the air in confusion and the wrath of the great God will come upon you from heaven. It will truly come to pass that the immortal savior will cast forth upon men ... unless you propitiate God and repent as from now, and no longer anyone do anything ill-tempered or evil, lawlessly against one another but be guarded in holy life." When they heard him they sneered at him, each one, calling him demented, a man gone mad. Then again Noah cried out a refrain: "O very wretched, evil-hearted fickle men, abandoning modesty, desiring shamelessness, tyrants in fickleness and violent sinners, liars, sated with faithlessness, evildoers, truthful in nothing, adulterers, ingenious at pouring out slander, not fearing the anger of the most high God, you who were preserved till the fifth generation to make retribution. You do not bewail each other, cruel ones, but laugh. You will laugh with a bitter smile when this comes to pass, I say, the terrible and strange water of God. Whenever the abominable race of Rheia, a perennial shoot on the earth, flourishing with un-thirsting roots, disappears root and all in a single night, and the earth-shaking land-quaker will scatter cities complete with their inhabitants, and the hiding places of the earth and will undo walls, then also the entire world of innumerable men will die. But as for me, how much will I lament, how much will I weep in my wooden house, how many tears will I mingle with the waves? For if this water commanded by God comes on, earth will swim, mountains will swim, even the sky will swim. All will be water and all things will perish in water. Winds will stop, and there will be a second age. O Phrygia, you will emerge first from the surface of the water. You, first, will nourish another generation of men as it begins again. You will be nurse for all."

♦ Noah Enters the Ark

But when he had spoken these things in vain to a lawless generation the Most High appeared. He again cried out and spoke. "Now the time is at hand, Noah, (to say all in turn), to do to the immense world everything which on that day I promised and indicated to you, as much as the myriad evils generations did previously, on account of a faithless people. But quickly go on board with your sons and wife and daughters-in-law. Call as many as I bid you to address, species of four-footed animals, and serpents and birds. I will subsequently put in the breasts of as many as I apportion life to go willingly." Thus he spoke. But the man went, cried out loudly and spoke and then his spouse and sons and daughters-in-law entered the wooden house. But then the other creatures went in turn, as many as God wished to save. But when the joining bolt was about the shutter, fitted to a side in the polished wall, then indeed the plan of the heavenly God was accomplished.

♦ The Flood

He threw clouds together and hid the brightly gleaming disk. Having covered the moon, together with the stars, and the crown of heaven all around, he thundered loudly, a terror to mortals, sending out hurricanes. All the storm winds were gathered together and all the springs of waters were released as the great cataracts were opened from heaven, and from the recesses of the earth and the endless abyss measureless waters appeared and the entire immense earth was covered. The wondrous house itself swam on the flood. Battered by many raging waves and swimming under the impact of the winds, it surged terribly. The keel cut immense foam as the rushing waters were moved. But when God had deluged the entire world with rains then Noah considered that he might look on the counsel of the immortal, and see the Hades of Nereus. He quickly opened the shutter from the polished wall, fixed as it was skillfully with fastenings opposite each other. Beholding the great mass of limitless waters, Noah was struck with terror to see with his eyes only death on all sides, and he quivered greatly at heart. And then the air drew back a little, since it had labored many days drenching the whole world, and showed then the great vault of heaven at evening, as it were bloodied, greenish-yellow, and the brightly gleaming disk hard pressed. Noah barely maintained his courage. And then taking one dove aside, he cast it out, so that he might know in his heart whether firm land had yet appeared. But she, laboring with her wings, having flown all over, returned again; for the water was not receding, but rather it had filled everything. But he waited again some days and sent a dove once more, so that he might know if the great waters had ceased. But she, flying, winged her way and went on the land. Having rested herself a little on the damp land, she returned to Noah again, bringing an olive twig, a great sign of her message. Courage and great joy seized them all because they were hoping to see land. And then afterward he sent out quickly another black-winged bird. But this one, trusting in his wings, flew prudently, and when he came to the land he stayed there. And Noah knew that land was near, closer by. But when the heavenly craft had swum to and fro on the dashing waves, by the billows of the sea, it was fastened on a small beach and made fast.

♦ The Ark Lands in Phrygia

There is a certain tall lofty mountain on the dark mainland of Phrygia. It is called Ararat. When all were about to be saved on it, thereupon there was a great heartfelt longing. There the springs of the great river Marsyos had sprung up. In this place the Ark remained on lofty summits when the waters had subsided. Then again from heaven the wondrous voice of the great God cried out as follows: "Noah, trustworthy righteous man who has been preserved, go forth boldly with your sons and wife and three daughters-in-law and fill the whole earth increasing and multiplying, dealing justly with each other, to generations of generations, until the whole race of men comes to trial, when there will be judgment for all." Thus the heavenly voice spoke. But Noah took courage and jumped to the land from the Ark, and his sons with him and his wife, and daughters-in-law and serpents and birds, the species of four-footed animals and all the other creatures together went out of the wooden house into one place. And then Noah, most righteous of men, came out eighth, having fulfilled forty-one dawns on the waters, through the counsels of the great God.

◆ The Sixth Generation

Then again a new generation of life dawned, the first golden, excellent one, which is the sixth since the time of the first formed man. Its name is "heavenly," for God will take care of everything. O the first race of the sixth generation! O great joy! in which I later shared, when I escaped dire destruction, having been much buffeted by waves, suffering terrible things with my husband and brothers-in-law, and father-in-law and mother-in-law, and fellow brides. I will tell exactly. There will be a multicolored flower on the fig tree. Time will be at its midpoint. There will be a royal scepter-bearing rule. For three great-spirited kings, most righteous men, will destroy the fates and will rule for a period of many years, administering justice to men. They will be concerned with labor, and fair deeds. The earth will rejoice, sprouting with many spontaneous fruits, overladen with offspring. Those who give nourishment will be ageless, always. Free from hard raging diseases they will die, smitten by sleep, and will go away to Acheron in the halls of Hades, and there they will have honor, since they were a race of blessed ones, happy men, to whom Sabaoth gave a noble mind. To these also he always confided his counsels. But they will be blessed, even entering Hades.

◆ The Seventh Generation: The Titans

Then thereafter another grievous, mighty second race of earthborn men (will arise), the Titans. Each individual will have a similar form, appearance, and size; there will be one nature and one language, as God previously put in their breasts, from the first generation. But they also will have a proud heart and finally rushing toward destruction will plot to fight in opposition against the starry heaven. And then the rushing of the mighty ocean of raging waters will be among them. But the great Sabaoth in anger will shut them out, preventing them, because he promised not to make a flood again against evil-spirited men. But when he will make the immense billow of many waters of a wave surging this way and that, to cease from anger, the great loud thundering God will reduce the depths of the sea to other measures, having defined it around the land with harbors and rough shores.

◆ Christian Passage on the Incarnation and Life of Christ

Then indeed the son of the great God will come, incarnate, likened to mortal men on earth, bearing four vowels, and the consonants in him are two. I will state explicitly the entire number for you. For eight units, and equal number of tens in addition to these, and eight hundreds will reveal the name to men who are sated with faithlessness. But you, consider in your heart Christ, the son of the most high, immortal God. He will fulfill the law of God—he will not destroy it— bearing a likeness which corresponds to types, and he will teach everything. Priests will bring gifts to him, bringing forward gold, myrrh, and incense. For he will also do all these things. But when a certain voice will come through the desert land bringing tidings to mortals, and will cry out to all to make the paths straight and cast away evils from the heart, and that every human person be illumined by waters, so that, being born from above they may no longer in any respect at all transgress justice—but a man with barbarous mind, enslaved to dances will cut out this voice and give it as a reward—then there will suddenly be a sign to mortals when a beautiful stone which has been preserved will come from the land of Egypt. Against this the people of the Hebrews will stumble. But the gentiles will be gathered under his leadership. For they will also recognize God who rules on high on account of this man's path in common light. For he will show eternal life to chosen men but will bring the fire upon the lawless for (all) ages. Then indeed he will cure the sick and all who are blemished, as many as put faith in him. The blind will see, and the lame will walk. The deaf will hear; those who cannot speak will speak. He will drive out demons, there will be a resurrection of the dead; he will walk the waves, and in a desert place he will satisfy five thousand from five loaves and a fish of the sea, and the leftovers of these will fill twelve baskets for the hope of the peoples. And then Israel, intoxicated, will not perceive nor yet will she hear, afflicted with weak ears. But when the raging wrath of the Most High comes upon the Hebrews it will also take faith away from them, because they did harm to the son of the heavenly God. Then indeed Israel, with abominable lips and poisonous spittings, will give this man blows. For food they will give him gall and for drink unmixed vinegar, impiously, smitten in breast and heart with an evil craze, not seeing with their eyes more blind than blind rats, more terrible than poisonous creeping beasts, shackled with heavy sleep. But when he will stretch out his hands and measure all, and bear the crown of thorns—and they will stab his side with reeds—on account of this, for three hours there will be monstrous dark night in midday. And then indeed the temple of Solomon will effect a great sign for men, when he goes to the house of Adonis announcing the resurrection to the dead. But when he comes to light again in three days and shows a model to men and teaches all things, he will mount on clouds and journey to the house of heaven leaving to the world the account of the gospel. Named after him, a new shoot will sprout from the nations, of those who follow the law of the Great One. But also after these things there will be wise leaders, and then there will be thereafter a cessation of prophets.

♦ **Prophecy of Dispersion of the Jews**

Then when the Hebrews reap the bad harvest, a Roman king will ravage much gold and silver. Thereafter there will be other kingdoms continuously, as kingdoms perish, and they will afflict mortals. But there will be a great fall for those men when they launch on unjust haughtiness. But when the temple of Solomon falls in the illustrious land cast down by men of barbarian speech with bronze breastplates, the Hebrews will be driven from their land; wandering, being slaughtered, they will mix much darnel in their wheat. There will be evil strife for all men; and the cities, violated in turn, will weep for each other on receiving the wrath of the great God in their bosom, since they committed an evil deed.

Book 2

♦ **The Inspiration of the Sibyl**

When indeed God stopped my most perfectly wise song as I prayed many things, he also again placed in my breast a delightful utterance of wondrous words. I will speak the following with my whole person in ecstasy, for I do not know what I say, but God bids me utter each thing.

♦ **Prophecy of Disasters in the Tenth Generation**

But when on earth there are raging earthquakes and thunderbolts, thunders, and lightnings ... and mildew of the land and frenzy of jackals and wolves, and slaughters and destructions of men and bellowing oxen, f our-footed cattle and laboring mules and goats and sheep, then much farmland will be left barren through neglect, and fruits will fail. Selling of free men into slavery will be practiced among very many people, and robbing of temples. Then indeed the tenth generation of men will also appear after these things, when the earth-shaking lightning-giver will break the glory of idols and shake the people of seven-hilled Rome. Great wealth will perish, burned in a great fire by the flame of Hephaestus. Then there will be bloody precipitation from heaven ... but the entire world of innumerable men will kill each other in madness. In the tumult God will impose famines and pestilence and thunderbolts on men who adjudicate without justice. There will be a scarcity of men throughout the whole world so that if one were to see a man's footprint on the ground, one would wonder. Then further, the great God who lives in the sky will be a savior of pious men in all respects. Then also there will be deep peace and understanding, and the fruitful earth will again bear more numerous fruits, being neither divided nor in servitude any longer. Every harbor, every port will be free for men as it was before, and shamelessness will perish. And then again God will perform a great sign, for a star will shine like a resplendent crown, resplendent, gleaming from the radiant heaven for no small number of days. For then he will show from heaven a crown to men who strive in contest.

♦ **The Heavenly Contest**

Then again there will be a great contest for entry to the heavenly city. It will be universal for all men, holding the glory of immortality. Then every people will strive for the immortal prizes of most noble victory. For no one there can shamelessly buy a crown for silver. For holy Christ will make just awards to these and crown the worthy. But to martyrs he will give an immortal treasure, to those who pursue the contest even to death. He will give an imperishable prize from the treasure to virgins who run well and to all men who perform justice and to diverse nations who live piously and acknowledge one God, who love marriage and refrain from adultery. He will give rich gifts and eternal hope to these also. For every soul of mortals is a gracious gift of God and it is not lawful for men to defile it with any grievous things.

[Extract from Pseudo-Phocylides:]

♦ On Justice

Do not gain wealth unjustly, but live from legitimate things. Be satisfied with what is available, and refrain from what belongs to others. Do not tell lies, but preserve all truths. (Do not revere idols, to no good purpose, but always the imperishable one.) First, honor God, then your parents. Dispense all things justly, and do not come to an unjust judgment. Do not unjustly cast down poverty. Do not be partial in judgment. If you judge badly, God will judge you later. Avoid false witness. Adjudicate justly. Guard that which is deposited with you. Preserve love in all things. Give just measures, but an overmeasure to all is good. Do not cheat in measuring, but weigh evenly. Do not commit perjury either in ignorance or willingly. God detests a perjurer, whatever one swears. (Never accept in your hand a gift which derives from unjust deeds.) Do not steal seeds. Whoever takes for himself is accursed (to generations of generations, to the scattering of life. Do not practice homosexuality, do not betray information, do not murder.) Give one who has labored his wage. Do not oppress a poor man. Take heed of your speech. Keep a secret matter in your heart. (Make provision for orphans and widows and those in need.) Do not be willing to act unjustly, and therefore do not give leave to one who is acting unjustly.

♦ On Mercy

Give to the poor at once and do not tell them to come tomorrow. (With perspiring hand give a portion of corn to one who is in need. Whoever gives alms knows that he is lending to God. Mercy saves from death when judgment comes. God wants not sacrifice but mercy instead of sacrifice. Therefore clothe the naked. Give the hungry a share of your bread.) Receive the homeless into your house and lead the blind. Pity the shipwrecked, for the voyage is uncertain. Give a hand to one who has fallen. Save a solitary man. All have a common lot, the wheel of life, unstable prosperity. If you have wealth, stretch out your hand to the poor. The things which God gave you, give of them to one in need. Every life of men is common, but falls out unequally. (When you see a poor man, never mock

him with words and do not verbally abuse a person who is at fault. Life is assessed in death. Whether one acted lawlessly or righteously will be distinguished when one comes to judgment.

♦ On Moderation

Do not damage your mind with wine or drink to excess.) Do not eat blood. Abstain from what is sacrificed to idols. Gird on the sword, not for killing but for defense. May you not use it either lawlessly or righteously. For even if you kill an enemy, you defile your own hand. Keep off a neighboring field. Do not trespass. (Every boundary is just; but trespass is grievous.) The acquisition of legitimate things is profitable, but that of unjust things is bad. Do not damage any fruit of the soil when it is growing. Let strangers have equal honor among citizens, for all will experience exile of many hardships (as guests of each other. But no one will be a stranger among you since you are all mortals of one blood), and a country has no secure place for men.

♦ On Money

(Neither wish to be wealthy nor pray for it. But pray for this: to live on a little, having nothing unjust.) The love of money is mother of all evil. (Have no desire for gold or silver. Also in these there will be double-edged iron which destroys the spirit.) Gold and silver are always a deception for men. Life-destroying gold, originator of evils, crushing all things, would that you were not a desired affliction for men, for because of you are battles, plunderings, murders, children hostile to their parents and brothers to their kindred.

♦ On Honesty and Moderation

(Do not weave plots, and do not arm your heart against a friend.) Do not hide one thought in your heart while you say another. Do not change in your place like a many-footed creature which clings to rock. Be straightforward with all. Speak what comes from your soul. Whoever deliberately does injustice is an evil man. As for one who acts under compulsion, I will not pronounce his end. But let the counsel of each man be straight. Do not boast of wisdom or strength or wealth. There is One, God, at once wise, powerful, and rich. Do not wear out your heart with passing evils for that which has happened can no longer be undone. Be not precipitous to the hand. Bridle wild anger, for often one who struck a blow unintentionally committed murder. Let your passions be normal, neither great nor excessive. Abundant profit is not a good thing for mortals. Much luxury draws toward inordinate desires. Great wealth is proud, and it fosters arrogance. Ire, when it takes the initiative, fashions a destructive frenzy. Anger is a propensity, but wrath goes to excess. The zeal of the good is noble, but that of the bad is bad. The daring of the wicked is destructive, but that of the good brings glory. Love of virtue is revered, but that of Aphrodite augments disgrace. A man who is too simple is called a fool among the citizens. Eat, drink, and discourse in moderation. Of all things, moderation is best, but excess is grievous. (Be not envious or faithless or a slanderer or of evil mind, or an inordinate deceiver.) Practice temperance. Refrain from base deeds. Do not imitate evil but leave vengeance to justice, for persuasion is a profit, but strife engenders strife in turn. Do not trust quickly, before you see the end with certainty.

[End of passage from Pseudo-Phocylides]

♦ **Conclusion of the Contest**

This is the contest, these are the prizes, these the awards. This is the gate of life and entry to immortality which the heavenly God appointed as reward of victory for most righteous men. But they, when they receive the crown, will pass through this in glory.

♦ **Signs of the End**

But whenever this sign appears throughout the world, children born with gray temples from birth, afflictions of men, famines, pestilence, and wars, change of times, lamentations, many tears; alas, how many people's children in the countries will feed on their parents, with piteous lamentations. They will place their flesh in cloaks and bury them in the ground, mother of peoples, defiled with blood and dust. O very wretched dread evildoers of the last generation, infantile, who do not understand that when the species of females does not give birth, the harvest of articulate men has come. The gathering together is near when some deceivers, in place of prophets, approach, speaking on earth. Beliar also will come and will do many signs for men. Then indeed there will be confusion of holy chosen and faithful men, and there will be a plundering of these and of the Hebrews. A terrible wrath will come upon them when a people of ten tribes will come from the east to seek the people, which the shoot of Assyria destroyed, of their fellow Hebrews. Nations will perish after these things.

♦ **Eschatological Rule of the Hebrews**

Later the faithful chosen Hebrews will rule over exceedingly mighty men, having subjected them as of old, since power will never fail. The Most High, who oversees all, living in the sky, will spread sleep over men, having closed their eyes. O blessed servants, as many as the master, when he comes, finds awake; for they have all stayed awake all the time looking expectantly with sleepless eyes. For he will come, at dawn, or evening, or midday. He will certainly come, and it will be as I say. It will come to pass for future generations, when from the starry heaven all the stars appear in midday to all, with the two luminaries, as time presses on.

♦ **Coming of Elijah and Other Signs**

Then the Thesbite, driving a heavenly chariot at full stretch from heaven, will come on earth and then display three signs to the whole world, as life perishes. Alas, for as many as are found bearing in the womb on that day, for as many as suckle infant children, for as many as dwell upon the wave; alas, for as many as will see that day. For a dark mist will cover the boundless world east and west and south and north.

♦ **Destruction by Fire**

And then a great river of blazing fire will flow from heaven, and will consume every place, land and great ocean and gleaming sea, lakes and rivers, springs and implacable Hades and the heavenly vault. But the heavenly luminaries will crash together, also into an utterly desolate form. For all the stars will fall together from heaven on the sea. All the souls of men will gnash their teeth, burning in a river, and brimstone and a rush of fire in a fiery plain, and ashes will cover all. And then all the elements of the world will be bereft—air, land, sea, light, vault of heaven, days, nights. No longer will innumerable birds fly in the air. Swimming creatures will no longer swim the sea at all. No laden ship will voyage on the waves. No guiding oxen will plow the soil. No sound of trees under the winds. But at once all will melt into one and separate into clear air.

♦ **The Judgment**

Then the imperishable angels of immortal God, Michael, Gabriel, Raphael, and Uriel, who know what evils anyone did previously, lead all the souls of men from the murky dark to judgment, to the tribunal of the great immortal God. For one alone is imperishable, the universal ruler, himself, who will be judge of mortals.

♦ **Resurrection of the Dead**

Then the heavenly one will give souls and breath and voice to the dead and bones fastened with all kinds of joinings ... flesh and sinews and veins and skin about the flesh, and the former hairs. Bodies of humans, made solid in heavenly manner, breathing and set in motion, will be raised on a single day. Then Uriel, the great angel, will break the gigantic bolts, of unyielding and unbreakable steel, of the gates of Hades, not forged of metal; he will throw them wide open and will lead all the mournful forms to judgment, especially those of ancient phantoms, Titans and the Giants and such as the Flood destroyed. Also those whom the wave of the sea destroyed in the oceans, and as many as wild beasts and serpents and birds devoured; all these he will call to the tribunal. Again, those whom the flesh-devouring fire destroyed by flame, these also he will gather and set at the tribunal of God. When Sabaoth Adonai, who thunders on high, dissolves fate and raises the dead, and takes his seat on a heavenly throne, and establishes a great pillar, Christ, imperishable himself, will come in glory on a cloud toward the imperishable one with the blameless angels. He will sit on the right of the Great One, judging at the tribunal the life of pious men and the way of impious men. Moses, the great friend of the Most High, also will come, having put on flesh. Great Abraham himself will come, Isaac and Jacob, Joshua, Daniel and Elijah, Habbakuk and Jonah, and those whom the Hebrews killed. He will destroy all the Hebrews after Jeremiah, judged on the tribunal, so that they may receive and make appropriate retribution for as much as anyone did in mortal life.

♦ **Distinction of Righteous and Wicked**

And then all will pass through the blazing river and the unquenchable flame. All the righteous will be saved, but the impious will then be destroyed for all ages, as many as formerly did evil or committed murders, and as many as are accomplices, liars, and crafty thieves, and dread destroyers of houses, parasites, and adulterers, who pour out slander, terrible violent men, and lawless ones, and idol worshipers; as many as abandoned the great immortal God and became blasphemers and ravagers of the pious, breakers of faith and murderers of the righteous men, and as many elders and reverend deacons as, by crafty and shameless duplicity regard ... judge with respect, dealing unjustly with others, trusting in deceitful statements ... More destructive than leopards and wolves, and most wicked; or as many as are very arrogant or are usurers, who gather interest upon interest in their homes and harm in each case orphans and widows, or as many as give to widows and orphans what derives from unjust deeds, and as many as make reproach when they give

from the fruit of their own labors; as many as abandoned their parents in old age, not making return at all, not providing nourishment to their parents in turn. Also as many as disobeyed or answered back an unruly word to their parents, or as many as denied pledges they had taken, and such servants as turned against their masters. Again, those who defiled the flesh by licentiousness, or as many as undid the girdle of virginity by secret intercourse, as many as aborted what they carried in the womb, as many as cast forth their offspring unlawfully.

♦ **Punishment of the Wicked**

These and the sorcerers and sorceresses in addition to them will the anger of the heavenly imperishable God also bring near to the pillar, around which an undying fiery river flows in a circle. All these at once the angels of the immortal, everlasting God will punish terribly from above with whips of flame, having bound them around with fiery chains and unbreakable bonds. Then, in the dead of night, they will be thrown under many terrible infernal beasts in Gehenna, where there is immeasurable darkness. But when they have inflicted many punishments on all whose heart was evil, then later a fiery wheel from the great river will press them hard all around, because they were concerned with wicked deeds. Then they will wail here and there at a distance in most piteous fate, fathers and infant children, mothers and weeping children at the breast. They will not have their fill of tears, nor will their voice be heard as they lament piteously here and there, but in distress they will shout at length below dark, dank Tartarus. In places unholy they will repay threefold what evil deed they committed, burning in much fire. They will all gnash their teeth, wasting away with thirst and raging violence. They will call death fair, and it will evade them. No longer will death or night give these rest. Often they will request God, who rules on high in vain, and then he will manifestly turn away his face from them. For he gave seven days of ages to erring men for repentance through the intercession of the holy virgin.

♦ **Rewards of the Righteous**

But as for the others, as many as were concerned with justice and noble deeds, and piety and most righteous thoughts, angels will lift them through the blazing river and bring them to light and to life without care, in which is the immortal path of the great God and three springs of wine, honey, and milk. The earth will belong equally to all, undivided by walls or fences. It will then bear more abundant fruits spontaneously. Lives will be in common and wealth will have no division. For there will be no poor man there, no rich, and no tyrant, no slave. Further, no one will be either great or small anymore. No kings, no leaders. All will be on a par together. No longer will anyone say at all "night has come" or "tomorrow" or "it happened yesterday," or worry about many days. No spring, no summer, no winter, no autumn, no marriage, no death, no sales, no purchases, no sunset, no sunrise. For he will make a long day. To these pious ones imperishable God, the universal ruler, will also give another thing. Whenever they ask the imperishable God to save men from the raging fire and deathless gnashing he will grant it, and he will do this. For he will pick them out again from the undying fire and set them elsewhere and send them on account of his own people to another eternal life with the immortals in the Elysian plain where he has the long waves of the deep perennial Acherusian lake.

♦ **Confession of the Sibyl**

Alas for me, wretched one. What will become of me on that day in return for what I sinned, ill-minded one, busying myself about everything but caring neither for marriage nor for reasons? But also in my dwelling, which was that of a very wealthy man, I shut out those in need; and formerly I committed lawless deeds knowingly. But you, savior, rescue me, a brazen one, from my scourges, though I have done shameless deeds. I beseech you to give me a little rest from the refrain, holy giver of manna, king of a great kingdom.

Glossary

Acheron	a river in northwestern Greece, but in Greek mythology a river associated with pain and the underworld
Acherusian lake	the lake into which the Acheron flows, where souls come after death and, after a period of time, are sent back to earth as living creatures
Adonis	a figure in Greek mythology associated with rebirth and vegetation
Aphrodite	the Greek goddess of love, beauty, and sexuality
Elysian plain	or Elysian Fields; usually plural, the final resting places of the souls of the heroic and the virtuous at the western edge of the world
Gehenna	the place where children were sacrificed to the god Moloch
Hades	both the underworld itself and the god of the underworld; the brother of Zeus
Hephaestus	the god of fire; Zeus's son
Moses . . . Abraham . . .	a list of the Old Testament patriarchs of the Hebrews
Phrygia	a kingdom in what is modern-day Turkey
Rheia	the wife of the evil and devious Kronos (also Cronus; leader of the Titans) and a mother to the Olympians
Sabaoth	meaning "host" or "army" in Hebrew, a name associated with the divine majesty of God, the "Lord of Hosts"; also Sabaoth Adonai
Tartarus	the underworld in Greek mythology
temple of Solomon	here, the "First Temple," built by Solomon, the king of the Israelites, in Jerusalem early in the first millennium BCE
Thesbite	roughly, "prophet"
Titans	a race of powerful gods during the Greek golden age

Shakyamuni Buddha (Shakyamuni Buddha, Ming Dynasty, Xuande Period [1426-65] [gilt bronze], Chinese School, [15th century] / Museum of
Fine Arts, Boston, Massachusetts, USA / Gift of Miss Lucy T. Aldrich / The Bridgeman Art Library International)

LOTUS SUTRA

ca. 100 BCE –200 CE

"All the living beings who escape the threefold world are given the enjoyments of buddhas — meditation, liberation, and so forth."

Overview

The Sutra on the White Lotus of the Sublime Dharma (in Sanskrit, Saddharmapundarika-sutra; in Chinese, Miaofa lianhua jing; in Japanese, Myoho renge kyo), commonly known as the Lotus Sutra and believed to have been composed between the first century BCE and the second century CE, is arguably the most revered and influential sutra of Mahayana Buddhism and certainly one of the most significant sacred texts in eastern Asia. Through the medium of parables and short stories, the twenty-eight chapters of the Lotus Sutra present a number of core doctrines of early Mahayana Buddhism. This school first emerged in India and western Asia roughly five centuries after the death of the historical Buddha, Siddhartha Gautama (ca. 563–483 BCE), and would eventually come to dominate East Asian Buddhism. The Lotus Sutra's insistence on faith in the sutra as a revealed text of extraordinary power, combined with its promise of universal buddhahood for all beings, lends it an air of sacred authority that is unusual if not unique to Buddhist scriptures.

The Lotus Sutra is a devotional text—that is, one intended to work on the level of the emotions and the senses rather than the intellect. As such, it has been employed throughout East Asian history as a focus for devotion and also as an inspiration for art, literature, and political reform. In this respect, it plays a role equivalent to the Bible in Europe or the Qur'an in the Middle East. The Lotus Sutra is often paired with two shorter texts, the Sutra of Innumerable Meanings (in Sanskrit, Amitartha-sutra; in Chinese, Wuliangyi jing; in Japanese, Muryogi kyo) and the Sutra of Meditation on the Bodhisattva Universal Worthy (in Chinese, Puxian jing; in Japanese, Fugen kyo or Zange kyo), which serve as "prologue" and "epilogue," respectively. Together, these form the Threefold Lotus Sutra.

Context

At least some parts of the Lotus Sutra were likely composed in a local Indian or Central Asian dialect, which was then translated into a form of Sanskrit (known as Buddhist Hybrid Sanskrit) in order to lend it an air of authority and to allow the teachings to be shared with others. The Lotus Sutra's self-referential claims to transcendent authority and its insistence on the "one vehicle" of dharma—that is, of Buddhist law and teachings—are indicative of some of the disputes and transformations that were taking place within Indian Buddhism at the time of its creation. Between the first century BCE and the second century CE, a diffuse movement was developing that would come to be known as the Mahayana, or "great vehicle."

Mahayana Buddhists generally reject the traditional Buddhist pursuit of individual nirvana (literally, "extinction"), which implies both a release from worldly suffering during life and liberation from the endless cycle of rebirth (samsara) upon one's death. While Mahayana Buddhists continued to understand nirvana in terms of a release from suffering, they centralized the virtue of compassion and further emphasized the necessity of releasing others from suffering as well as oneself. Mahayana Buddhists utilize the term *bodhisattva* to refer specifically to beings who put aside all personal hopes for liberation in order to "save" other beings. This goal is contrasted with the traditional Buddhist goal of the arhat—enlightenment—which was perceived by Mahayanists as being somewhat "selfish." Given this context, it is not difficult to read the Lotus Sutra as part of a larger polemic by monks affiliated with the broader Mahayana movement to establish their credentials vis-à-vis more traditional monks. And yet, whatever its polemical or sectarian intent, the success of the Lotus Sutra as an inspirational and transformative text throughout East Asian history can hardly be reduced to this aspect alone.

Whatever its Indian (or possibly West Asian) origins, the oldest extant versions of the Lotus Sutra are in Chinese, and these Chinese translations—particularly that of the Indo-Kuchan monk-translator Kumarajiva (344–413)—became the standard versions of the text as it spread throughout East Asia. The Lotus Sutra would eventually serve as the primary text for two important East Asian Buddhist sects: the sixth-century Tiantai (in Japanese, Tendai) sect, often called the first indigenous Chinese Buddhist school, and the thirteenth-century Nichiren (also known as Hokke) sect, which can make a similar claim to being the first indigenous Japanese Buddhist sect. For followers of

Time Line

Date	Event
CA. 563 –483 BCE	■ Siddhartha Gautama, the Buddha, is alive.
CA. 100 BCE –200 CE	■ The Lotus Sutra is compiled in northwestern India (or West Asia).
286 CE	■ Dharmaraksa translates the Lotus Sutra into Chinese.
406 CE	■ Kumarajiva translates the Lotus Sutra into Chinese.
587–593	■ The Chinese Tiantai sect founder Zhiyi writes two commentaries on the Lotus Sutra, *Fahua wenju* and *Fahua xuanyi*, interpreting the Lotus Sutra as the pinnacle of Buddhist teachings and as a basis for meditative practice.
802	■ The Japanese Tendai sect founder Saicho lectures on the Lotus Sutra before the Japanese imperial court.
1260	■ The Nichiren sect founder Nichiren writes *Rissho ankoku ron*, which correlates a realm's devotion to the Lotus Sutra with its protection and pacification.
1852	■ The first translation of the Lotus Sutra in a Western language (French) appears: Eugène Burnouf's *Le lotus de la bonne loi*, based on medieval Sanskrit manuscripts.
1884	■ The first English translation of the Lotus Sutra appears: Hendrik Kern's *Saddharmapundarika; or, The Lotus of the True Law*, based on medieval Sanskrit manuscripts.
1930	■ Makiguchi Tsunesaburo establishes the lay Buddhist organization Soka Kyoiku Gakkai, based on the teachings of Nichiren and the Lotus Sutra.
1938	■ Niwano Nikkyo and Naganuma Myoko establish the lay Buddhist organization Rissho Kosei Kai, based on the Lotus Sutra.

both these traditions, the Lotus Sutra contains the highest stage of the teachings of Shakyamuni, the historical Buddha, also known as Siddhartha Gautama. In turn, all earlier teachings—that is, the texts and doctrines of the so-called Hinayana (a pejorative term meaning "lesser vehicle")—are considered provisional stages on the path toward the highest truth as revealed in the Lotus Sutra. For all this, the Lotus Sutra is notoriously vague about the actual content of this highest truth or highest law, to the extent that it has been called (and criticized as) an "empty text." Moreover, despite the fact that the text—like many other early Mahayana sutras—revels in complex visualizations and otherworldly splendor, it has often been employed as a vehicle for this-worldly sociopolitical critique and religious reform. Indeed, in terms of its usage, the Lotus Sutra is the most "political" of all Buddhist scriptures.

About the Author

Nothing is known about the authors of the Lotus Sutra. Given the content of the text, however, scholars assume that they were monks associated with the Mahayana Buddhist movement. The Lotus Sutra as it is known today is a pastiche of several distinct works, written at different times by different people for different purposes over a period of several centuries.

Explanation and Analysis of the Document

Within its spectacular scenes and various parables, the Lotus Sutra presents the following four core ideas of Mahayana Buddhism: the doctrine of *upaya*, or "skillful means," as the way in which buddhas and advanced bodhisattvas teach the dharma to less-advanced beings; perfect awakening, or buddhahood, as a realizable goal for all beings; the practice of compassion and the way of the bodhisattva as the highest goals of Buddhism; and the eternal and transcendent character of the Buddha. Although they are less immediately apparent, other significant Mahayana doctrines—such as emptiness, buddha nature, and the three bodies of Buddha—have also been read into the text by later exegetes.

The Lotus Sutra is made up of twenty-eight chapters of varying length. Each chapter contains a mix of straight narrative and verse, with the poetry generally repeating and reinforcing the prose (though most scholars believe that the verse portions are older). Like all Buddhist sutras, the Lotus claims to be a record of the words of the historical Buddha, Shakyamuni (meaning "Sage of the Shakyas," the people of his kingdom)—though it also asserts that this Buddha, like all buddhas, is considerably more than simply a historical teacher.

Four chapters are addressed here: chapter 2, "Skillful Means"; chapter 3, "A Parable"; chapter 12, "Devadatta"; and chapter 16, "The Lifetime of the Tathagata." The introductory chapter (not reproduced here), a later addition, sets the scene and provides a justification for the teachings that follow. Toward the end of his life, we are informed, Shakyamuni preached the Lotus Sutra at Mount Gridhra-kuta (Holy Eagle Peak) near the city of Rajagriha in northern India. While this is historically plausible, realism quickly breaks down as the reader is introduced to an astonishing cosmic tableau in which space and time extend in infinite directions and where buddhas from other realms travel to listen to Shakyamuni preach the Lotus. What the modern reader might take as pure fantasy or even science fiction is intended to unsettle one's usual habits of perception and understanding and to alert one to the power of the Buddha and the significance of what he is about to say.

The central message of the introductory chapter is that there is in fact only "one vehicle" for followers of dharma, namely, the path to perfect understanding or buddhahood, rather than three paths (those of *shravaka*, *pratyekabuddha*, and *bodhisattva*), as was traditionally understood and as the Buddha himself had previously taught. In the Mahayana understanding, a *shravaka* (literally, "hearer") is a disciple of the Buddha who has accepted the Buddha's teaching (dharma) and is committed to personal awakening; the term is often synonymous with the term *arhat*. A *pratyekabuddha* (or "solitary buddha") is one who achieves awakening on his or her own, without reliance on the words or teachings of others; this is considered a higher stage than the *shravaka*. Finally, the *bodhisattva* (or "buddha-to-be") is a being who is dedicated to the liberation of all beings and is thus an embodiment of compassion. Within the Mahayana, the bodhisattva represents the highest stage of awakening and the ideal for all followers of dharma.

♦ **2. Skillful Means**

This discussion leads to the introduction in the second chapter of the doctrine of *upaya*, or "skillful means," which most interpreters see as the heart and soul of the Lotus Sutra. After an initial section in which the Buddha asserts the "profound and immeasurable" wisdom of buddhas as well as the connection of each and every buddha to innumerable buddhas in the past, he claims to have employed a variety of parables and expedient measures in order to inspire his followers, who were not yet prepared for the higher, unifying wisdom of the Lotus Sutra. The assembly, including twelve hundred *shravakas*, monks, nuns, laymen, and laywomen, are confused, and the Buddha's disciple Shariputra asks the Buddha to clarify his meaning. After some hesitation, based on the fear that "the worlds' heavenly beings as well as human beings will be startled and perplexed," the Buddha finally agrees.

The Buddha's fears seem justified, as upon his saying this, five thousand monks, nuns, laymen, and laywomen immediately get up and leave the assembly, because "their roots of sin were so deep and they were so utterly arrogant that they imagined themselves to have already attained and born witness to what they had not actually attained." The Buddha goes on to explain that buddhas of all time periods have only one goal: to use a variety of methods to preach to all living beings "so that they might attain the complete

The Bodhisattva Manjushri riding on a lion

(The Bodhisattva Manjushri riding on a lion, illustration after a kakemono of the eleventh century from the temple of Kozan-Ji at Yamashiro, published in *The Kokka* magazine, May 1904, / Bibliotheque des Arts Decoratifs, Paris, France / Archives Charmet / The Bridgeman Art Library International)

wisdom of the One Buddha-Vehicle." The text also notes that buddhas appear in the world during times of chaos and pollution, an idea that would have a profound effect on the way later East Asian followers of the Lotus Sutra, such as Nichiren, would interpret its message as a call to radical personal and collective transformation in a time of *mappo*, the "end of the law." There is debate among scholars as to the precise implications of the doctrine of *upaya*—specifically with regard to how far the notion of "expedient means" extends, that is, whether it has metaphysical and ontological implications in addition to its more obvious pedagogical ones. However, there is no question that it has been taken by some followers to mean that, in exceptional circumstances, extreme measures may be justified in order to spread the dharma for the purpose of saving beings and transforming this world into a buddha land.

From a sociological or sectarian standpoint, this chapter may be understood as an attempt by the authors to give authenticity to what was clearly a belated set of teachings and to address the fact that many Buddhists would disapprove of the Lotus Sutra's message (as was indeed the case). This line of reasoning is common to the Mahayana movement more generally: We may be late to appear, but we are in possession of the highest, definitive teachings, which supersede all that has gone before. Also of note here is the fact that, despite this criticism of those who reject the Lotus (such as those who leave the assembly), the Lotus Sutra does not deny the validity of the earlier Buddhist texts and teachings but rather absorbs them as necessary but provisional stages toward the highest law of the Lotus. Thus, the primary disciples of the Buddha, arhats such as Shariputra and Mahakashyapa (who appears in chapter 6), are depicted in the Lotus as inquisitive *shravakas* struggling to comprehend the deeper Buddhist truths. Though they are less than fully enlightened, they are not mocked as in some other Mahayana sutras—in fact, they are depicted here as being joyously receptive to the Buddha's promise that they, too, will one day achieve full buddhahood.

♦ 3. A Parable

The third chapter, "A Parable," opens with Shariputra's expression of ecstatic joy upon hearing the promise of universal buddhahood for all. Shakyamuni responds with a promise that Shariputra himself will in the distant future assuredly become a buddha called Flower Light, and he goes on to provide an elaborate description of the paradisiacal realm over which Shariputra will preside. This is followed by what amounts to a giant heavenly party by the assembly, which is overwhelmed with joy at the news of Shariputra's future buddhahood, complete with a heavenly announcement that "the Dharma wheel" is once more being turned—that is, that the Buddha has introduced a new and more advanced set of teachings.

The second half of the third chapter expands upon the doctrine of *upaya* via the parable of the burning house, perhaps the most famous story of the Lotus Sutra. The reader is introduced to a wealthy man who discovers one day that his house—spacious but in a state of disrepair—is on fire, with his several dozen children playing inside unaware. In order to get them to escape the fire through the sole, narrow gate, he promises them a variety of splendid carriages—each drawn by sheep or goats or oxen—if they come outside. Delighted to finally obtain things they had long desired, they come running out of the house, only to discover not the promised carriages but rather a set of even more spectacular ox-driven carriages, one for each child. On one level, the meaning of the story is clear: Whereas the Buddha had previously taught three different paths to awakening, these three are, in fact, provisional means to-

ward the one vehicle, embodied in the quest for perfect buddhahood. Still, there is some confusion in the text as to whether this all-encompassing one vehicle is the same as or distinct from the bodhisattva path (the third of the three carriages) and, if distinct, what exactly it entails. Finally, the question is raised, not for the last time in the Lotus Sutra, as to whether the father in employing *upaya* was "guilty of falsehood." No, the reader is told; he simply employed the most effective strategy to serve his compassionate purposes. So, too, does the Buddha use *upaya* to save all living beings, by giving them, in the one-vehicle teaching of the Lotus Sutra, "something they had never had before and never expected to have."

♦ 12. Devadatta

Although it is considered a relatively late addition to the Lotus Sutra, the twelfth chapter, "Devadatta," is a dense chapter with significant historical impact, particularly in its presentation of the concept of the universality of buddhahood for all beings. The chapter opens with the Buddha telling the assembly that at one time in the distant past, he had been a king who sought "unexcelled awakening." One day he met a seer, who introduced the king to the Mahayana teachings as embodied in the Lotus Sutra. This wise seer, whom the king served faithfully for a thousand years and who was instrumental in leading the king toward full buddhahood, was reportedly none other than Shakyamuni's cousin Devadatta. Shakyamuni completes this short tale with a declaration to the assembly that Devadatta, too, will one day become a buddha. Although the text does not make note of this, Devadatta was a figure notorious to early Buddhists as the epitome of evil. Though he was a cousin and disciple of the Buddha, his jealousy led him to challenge the Buddha's authority, foment schism in the *sangha* (monastic community), and even make several attempts on the Buddha's life. The first part of this chapter, then, can be taken as a classic example of Mahayana shock tactics and contrarianism; the choice of Devadatta as an exemplary teacher and future buddha seems deliberately provocative, yet it also drives home the point of the universality of buddhahood raised here and throughout the Lotus.

The second half of the chapter provides another well-known example of an unlikely buddha, in this case one who has already achieved full awakening. Here the tale is told by Manjushri, the bodhisattva of wisdom, to a sceptical bodhisattva called Accumulated Wisdom. Manjushri has just arrived from the palace of Sagara, the dragon king, where he claims to have successfully converted innumerable beings via the teachings of the Lotus Sutra. Manjushri provides the remarkable example of the daughter of the dragon king, who, at just eight years old, achieved full buddhahood "in an instant." Accumulated Wisdom (as with, one might expect, most hearers or readers of the text) finds this unbelievable, given the countless eons it took Shakyamuni to achieve this same goal. The dragon princess duly appears before the assembly, and, in response to further skeptical and denigrating remarks by Shariputra, immediately transforms herself into: a male, a bodhisattva in a distant

"Shariputra, ever since I became a buddha, I have used a variety of causal explanations and a variety of parables to teach and preach, and countless skillful means to lead living beings, enabling them to give up their attachments. Why? Because the Tathagata has attained full use of skillful means and practice of insight."

"All the living beings who escape the threefold world are given the enjoyments of buddhas—meditation, liberation, and so forth. All are of one character and one type, praised by sages and capable of producing pure, wonderful, supreme happiness."

"Then the entire congregation saw the dragon girl instantly transformed into a male, take up bodhisattva practice, and immediately go to the world named Spotless, in the southern region, where, sitting on a precious lotus blossom, she attained impartial, proper awakening. With the thirty-two characteristics and eighty different attractive features she proclaimed the wonderful Dharma to all living beings everywhere in the universe."

"You should all listen carefully to hear about the Tathagata's secret and divine powers. In all the worlds, the humans, heavenly beings, and asuras think that the present Shakyamuni Buddha left the palace of the Shakya clan, sat at the place of the Way not far from the city of Gaya, and attained supreme awakening. But . . . in fact there have been innumerable, unlimited hundreds of thousands of billions of myriads of eons since I became a buddha."

realm called Spotless, and then a fully-awakened buddha, proclaiming the dharma to all living beings. The entire assembly, including Accumulated Wisdom and Shariputra, "silently believed and accepted this."

Once again, as with the example of Devadatta, the choice of the dragon princess as a fully awakened buddha undercuts traditional Buddhist understandings of the necessary conditions for awakening, including the various hindrances associated with being a child, a female, and a nonhuman. Later exegetes would interpret this chapter and similar promises of buddhahood in the Lotus in terms of the later Mahayana doctrine of "buddha nature," whereby all beings are possessed of a "spark" or "seed" of buddhahood. Contemporary feminist readers have mixed feelings

about this tale's message for women: on one hand, it seems liberatory, given that the dragon princess is able to attain full buddhahood, and yet in order to do so she has had to transform herself, even if only for an instant, into a male.

♦ 16. The Lifetime of the Tathagata

Contemporary scholars divide the text of the Lotus Sutra into several parts, with chapters 10–22, along with the introductory chapter but excluding chapter 12, representing a later group of writings. These chapters focus on the transcendent powers of the Buddha (and of buddhas more generally), one of the most significant innovations in Mahayana thought. This is vividly expressed in the sixteenth chapter, "The Lifetime of the Tathagata." The chapter follows a scene in which the bodhisattva Maitreya shows confusion as to how the Buddha could have possibly converted innumerable bodhisattvas, as he claims to have done, in the short span (roughly forty years) since his initial awakening under the bodhi tree. Here Shakyamuni answers Maitreya's question, in the process effectively reinterpreting the very concept of buddhahood by way of the doctrine of skillful means. The reader is informed that the Buddha, in fact, achieved awakening many eons in the past and has spent an inconceivably long time since then leading other beings to nirvana. Thus, the biography of the "historical" Buddha—including his birth, renunciation of wealth and family, awakening, and "final" nirvana—are revealed as expedient means employed by the (virtually) eternal and transcendent fully awakened Buddha to most effectively teach the dharma.

To make this point clear, the Buddha relates the parable of the medicinal herbs, in which a doctor finds to his distress that his sons—"ten, twenty, even a hundred"—have ingested poison. He gives them medicinal herbs to cure them, but some refuse to take the medicine, having already "lost their minds." In order to save these sons, the doctor fakes his own death, which prompts them to realize that they cannot simply depend on him anymore, and forthwith they consume the medicine. Once they are recovered, the father reveals himself to them. Again, as with the parable of the burning house, it is said that the father cannot be accused of "lying," since his intention was to liberate his sons from suffering.

Beyond the reiteration of the importance of skillful means, one implication of this chapter is that the Buddha remains "in the world" out of boundless compassion for the suffering of living beings. But he also does so as an extraordinarily powerful being, one who is able to control space and time at will. Here the early Buddhist understanding of *nirvana* as "extinction" is overturned—a move that would have significant implications for East Asian Buddhist doctrine and practice. This teaching of the "primordial" or "eternal buddha" would find more elaborate expression in the Chinese interpolation of the so-called three bodies of buddha (that is, living being, spirit, and truth itself), in the doctrinal formulations of the Tiantai founder Zhiyi, and in the development of original enlightenment thought in Japan, which suggests that not only buddhas but all living beings and even nonsentient things are always already awakened. Also of note in this chapter is a repetition of the trope of the Buddha as a "father" to those he teaches, a concept that some have argued is fundamental to understanding the transformation brought about by the early Mahayana sutras in general. This conception may also help account for the success of the Lotus Sutra in East Asia, where culturally embedded notions of family and filial piety would seem to otherwise work against Indian Buddhist traditions of monasticism and asceticism.

Audience

As with all Buddhist scriptures, the Lotus Sutra was initially compiled for the benefit of monastics. Over time, however, owing in no small part to the sutra's claims to universal salvific power, devotion to the Lotus spread beyond the *sangha* to lay Buddhists, both literate elites and nonliterate commoners.

The extent to which the Lotus Sutra was intended to "convert" audiences to a particular kind of Buddhism is uncertain. It is clear from the content that the Lotus Sutra is aligned with the Mayahana perspective and that its intention is to persuade its hearers or readers to follow the Mahayana-oriented teachings it provides. But most scholars now believe that there was no such thing as a coherent "Mahayana" movement until centuries after the Lotus Sutra was written, which means that its initial compilers and readers may have not even been thinking of conversion, per se, since the lines between "Mahayana" and "traditional" Buddhists remained vague. (Many scholars believe that they inhabited the same monasteries and engaged in many of the same practices for the first several centuries.) In short, the Lotus Sutra is understood to predate Mahayana but was adopted as a key text in some later Mahayana schools, especially those emerging in China and Japan. Thus, it is probably most accurate to assert that the Lotus Sutra attempts to convert its readers or hearers to the Lotus Sutra, rather than to any group or community called Mahayana.

Although the term *Mahayana* implies "Great Vehicle" or "Larger Vehicle," it is unlikely that the monks associated with Mahayana ever constituted a majority of Buddhists until the school began to grow and spread in China and perhaps some parts of West Asia. Schools with clearly Mahayana orientations emerged in China, such as the Tiantai/Tendai and Huayan/Kegon, in the fourth and fifth centuries CE. Through that era, Mahayana triumphed in China, and these schools would provide the basis for East Asian Buddhism in Vietnam, Korea, and Japan. Today, Mahayana Buddhism is the dominant—indeed, nearly exclusive—form in these countries, while Theravada, the only surviving major non-Mahayana school, dominates Buddhism in South and Southeast Asia, including Sri Lanka, Thailand, Burma, Cambodia, and Laos. A third school, Vajrayana, or tantric Buddhism, is the dominant form in the Himalayan regions of Tibet and Nepal and in parts of Siberia and Mongolia. In all, some 60 percent of the world's Buddhists follow traditions now associated with the Mahayana, while roughly 35 percent follow Theravada traditions and 5 percent Vajrayana.

Impact

The Lotus Sutra appears to have had little impact upon Indian Buddhism. Similarly, its influence within Tibetan and related forms of Buddhism has been marginal. The text first flourished in China, owing to the various Chinese translations from the third through fifth centuries and its adoption by the Tiantai sect—one of the foremost Mahayana branches—and then spread to Korea and Japan. Although Dharmaraksa's third-century translation may be the earliest Chinese version, it was the translation in 406 by Kumarajiva that proved most successful as the Lotus

Sutra spread throughout East Asia. Kumarajiva's work was furthered in the late sixth century by the Tiantai patriarch Zhiyi, who wrote several works extolling the power and significance of the Lotus Sutra. In addition, beginning in medieval China and extending to Japan, a number of so-called miracle tales focusing on the power of the Lotus Sutra began to circulate. Although these tales were not necessarily intended for a popular audience, they no doubt contributed to the spread of devotion to the Lotus among the nonliterate population in both countries. The story of the medicine king, in which a bodhisattva burns himself to death as an offering to the Buddha, inspired a tradition of self-immolation among certain Chinese and, more recently, Vietnamese monks. In addition, the Lotus Sutra played a role in spreading the cult of the bodhisattva Guanyin, the most popular Buddhist figure in East Asia. Finally, though its impact on politics and society is less pronounced in China than in Japan, images and scenes from the Lotus can be seen throughout medieval Chinese art and literature, including many of the spectacular Buddhist murals adorning caves along the Silk Road.

In Japan, from an early period, the Lotus Sutra was understood as a spiritual protector of the imperial family and the realm. One of the earliest commentaries is attributed to Shotoku Taishi (573–621), the semilegendary regent of Japan and "father of Japanese Buddhism." From the early medieval period, monasteries were constructed throughout the nation with the express purpose of reciting the Lotus Sutra. As noted, the Lotus Sutra was central to the Japanese Tendai sect, founded by Saicho, which would dominate Japanese Buddhism for several centuries and give birth to the various new Buddhist movements of the Kamakura Period (1185–1333). Saicho lectured on the Lotus Sutra before the Japanese emperor and court. Whereas Tendai embraced devotion to the Lotus Sutra as one path among many, Nichiren broke

from Tendai eclecticism by insisting that the sole effective path to buddhahood ran through the Lotus Sutra and that this could be achieved simply by chanting its title in good faith and with pure heart in a prayer known as the *daimoku*. For Nichiren and his followers, this prayer—*Namu myoho renge kyo*, or "devotion to the Sutra of the Lotus Flower of the Wonderful Dharma"—encapsulates all the teachings contained within the Lotus Sutra and thus, by extension, all the practices and merit accumulated by Shakyamuni Buddha through countless eons, which can then be transferred to the believer via the act of chanting. While this practice remains central to Nichiren Buddhism, some contemporary Nichirenists question the idea that the *daimoku* is sufficient for liberation in and of itself.

In modern times, the Lotus Sutra has played a role in a variety of Buddhist reform and activist movements in Japan, China, and Taiwan. This is due to the fact that the Lotus is often understood as giving primary importance to the very world in which humans dwell, an interpretation that runs from Zhiyi through Nichiren down to modern lay-Buddhist movements. Nichiren, in particular, interpreted the message of the Lotus Sutra in a political and eschatological fashion, teaching in works like *Rissho ankoku ron* (Treatise on Spreading Peace throughout the Country by Establishing the True Dharma, 1260) that widespread devotion to the Lotus in an age of decline could transform this world into an ideal "buddha land" and that, contrariwise, a refusal to embrace the text would bring disaster upon the realm.

This perceived message of the Lotus, combined with the inherent vagueness of the sutra itself, has allowed for manifold political interpretations. In prewar Japan, the Lotus inspired figures as diverse as Seno'o Giro (1881–1961), founder of the Socialist Youth League for Revitalizing Buddhism; the left-leaning poet, agronomist, and activist Miyazawa Kenji (1896–1933); Ishiwara Kanji (1889–1949),

Questions for Further Study

1. What is a sutra? Literally, in Sanskrit, the word means "a thread that holds things together." To what extent does this describe the Lotus Sutra? Explain.

2. Why is the Lotus Sutra "the most "political" of all Buddhist scriptures?

3. Buddhism, as reflected in the Lotus Sutra, places considerable emphasis on concepts such as enlightenment, wisdom, liberation, buddhahood, and awakening. To what extent, if any, do you think that the concepts found in the Lotus Sutra are valuable to ordinary people going about their ordinary busy lives? Do you find the concepts too vague and impractical, or do you think they would provide something valuable for, say, a construction worker, an insurance salesperson, or a high school student?

4. The entry states that the Lotus Sutra plays a role somewhat similar to that of the Bible among Western Christians and Jews and the Qur'an among Muslims. To what extent, if any, do you think this is true? Provide examples.

the Imperial Army general famous for his role in fomenting the 1931 Manchurian Incident, in which Japanese militarists dynamited a section of railroad in southern Manchuria and blamed the Chinese as a pretext for engaging China in all-out war; and Inoue Nissho (1886–1967), founder of the Ketsumeidan, or Blood Pledge Corps, a terrorist group that would embark on a wave of assassinations of prominent political figures and business leaders in the 1930s. In the radically changed circumstances of the postwar period, several new religious movements associated with Nichiren Buddhism began to flourish. Soka Kyoiku Gakkai, now known as Soka Gakkai or Soka Gakkai International, is a popular lay Buddhist movement that first emerged in the 1930s and, after surviving persecution during World War II, gained a massive following in Japan during the 1950s and 1960s, eventually spreading its activities to the United States. Its teachings are rooted in Nichirenist conceptions of the interconnectedness of personal and social transformation. Though it is somewhat less popular than Soka Gakkai, Rissho Koseikai, also founded in the 1930s, is rooted in similar Nichirenist assumptions as well as in the conviction of the continuing relevance of the Lotus Sutra.

In the West, the Lotus Sutra has had less direct impact, though Western-language translations have appeared since the mid-nineteenth century. The first was Eugène Burnouf's French version, *Le lotus de la bonne loi* (1852). This was followed several decades later by Hendrik Kern's *Saddharmapundarika; or, The Lotus of the True Law* (1884), the first translation into English. The number of English and Western-language translations of the Lotus Sutra has exploded through the end of the twentieth century, as Western scholars and lay Buddhists have begun to take a greater interest in this seminal East Asian sacred text.

Further Reading

■ Books

Cole, Alan. *Text as Father: Paternal Seductions in Early Mahayana Buddhist Literature.* Berkeley: University of California Press, 2005.

Leighton, Taigen Dan. *Visions of Awakening Space and Time: Dogen and the Lotus Sutra.* New York: Oxford University Press, 2007.

Niwano Nikkyo. *Buddhism for Today: A Modern Interpretation of the Threefold Lotus Sutra*, trans Kojiro Miyasaka. Tokyo: Kosei, 1976.

Pye, Michael. *Skilful Means: A Concept in Mahayana Buddhism.* 2nd ed. London: Routledge, 2003.

Reeves, Gene, ed. *A Buddhist Kaleidoscope: Essays on the Lotus Sutra.* Tokyo: Kosei, 2002.

Tanabe, George J., Jr., and Willa Jane Tanabe, eds. *The Lotus Sutra in Japanese Culture.* Honolulu: University of Hawaii Press, 1989.

Tanabe, Willa Jane. *Paintings of the Lotus Sutra.* New York: Weatherhill, 1988.

Teiser, Stephen F., and Jacqueline I. Stone, eds. *Readings of the Lotus Sutra.* New York: Columbia University Press, 2009.

Wang, Eugene Y. *Shaping the Lotus Sutra: Buddhist Visual Culture in Medieval China.* Seattle: University of Washington Press, 2007.

—James Mark Shields

LOTUS SUTRA

2. Skillful Means

At that time the World-Honored One rose calmly from concentration and said to Shariputra: "The wisdom of buddhas is both profound and immeasurable, and the gateways to this wisdom are hard to understand and hard to enter. No shravaka or pratyekabuddha can apprehend it.

"Why is this? It is because every buddha has been closely associated with hundreds of thousands of billions of buddhas in the past, fully practicing the way of the immeasurable Dharma of all the buddhas. Boldly and diligently working, they have become famous everywhere, fulfilling the very profound, unprecedented Dharma and teaching it wherever opportunities arose. Yet their intention is difficult to grasp.

"Shariputra, ever since I became a buddha, I have used a variety of causal explanations and a variety of parables to teach and preach, and countless skillful means to lead living beings, enabling them to give up their attachments. Why? Because the Tathagata has attained full use of skillful means and practice of insight. . . .

"In sum, Shariputra, the Buddha has fulfilled the whole Dharma—innumerable, unlimited, unprecedented teachings.

"But this is enough Shariputra. No more needs to be said. Why? Because what the Buddha has achieved is most rare and difficult to understand. Only among buddhas can the true character of all things be fathomed. This is because every existing thing has such characteristics, such a nature, such an embodiment, such powers, such actions, such causes, such conditions, such effects, such rewards and retributions, and yet such a complete fundamental coherence." . . .

At that time in the great assembly there were shravakas, arhats without faults, Ajnata-Kaundinya and others, twelve hundred in all. And there were various monks and nuns, laymen and laywomen who had vowed to become shravakas and pratyekabuddhas. They all thought: "Why does the World-Honored One speak so enthusiastically about skillful means? Why does he say that the Buddha's Dharma is so profound and so difficult to comprehend, and that what he says is so difficult that not even shravakas and pratyekabuddhas can understand it? And yet at the same time he has said that there is only one principle of libera-

tion, so that we too, with this Dharma, will attain nirvana. But now we do not know where this leads."

Then Shariputra, seeing the doubts in the minds of the four groups and not having fully understood everything himself, spoke to the Buddha: "World-Honored One, what are the reasons for you to praise so enthusiastically the buddhas' principle of skillful means and the very profound, fine, and wonderful Dharma, which is so hard to understand? Never before have I heard such teaching from the Buddha! Now these four groups are full of doubt. Will the World-Honored One please explain why you have so enthusiastically praised this very profound, fine, and wonderful Dharma, which is so difficult to comprehend?" . . .

Then the Buddha said to Shariputra: "Stop, stop! There is no need to say more. If I explain this matter, all of the worlds' heavenly beings as well as human beings will be startled and perplexed."

Again Shariputra said to the Buddha: "World-Honored One, please explain it. Please explain it! Why? Because in this gathering there are countless hundreds of thousands of billions of living beings who have already seen buddhas. Their faculties are excellent and their wisdom is clear. If they hear the Buddha preach, they will be able to believe respectfully." . . .

But the Buddha again said: "Stop, Shariputra! If I explained this, all the worlds of human and heavenly beings and asuras would be startled and perplexed, and extremely arrogant monks might fall into the great pit." . . .

Then Shariputra once again said to the Buddha; "World-Honored One, please explain it. Please explain it! In this meeting there are hundreds of thousands of billions of beings like me who in previous lives followed buddhas and were transformed. Certainly they can respect and believe what you say, and thereby enjoy great peace of mind throughout the long night of time and gain abundant benefits of various kinds." . . .

Then the World-Honored One said to Shariputra: "Since you have now earnestly repeated your request three times, how can I refuse you? Now listen carefully, ponder over what I will say and remember it, for I will explain it for you clearly."

When he had said this, immediately some five thousand monks and nuns, laymen and laywomen, got up and, bowing to the Buddha, left the meeting. Why? Because their roots of sin were so deep and they were so utterly arrogant that they imagined themselves to have already attained and born witness to what they had not actually attained. Having such faults, they could not stay. The World-Honored One kept silent and did not stop them.

Then the Buddha said to Shariputra: "Now the congregation no longer has useless branches and leaves, but only firm, good fruit. It is good, Shariputra, that such utterly arrogant ones have gone. So listen carefully now. I am ready to explain it for you."

And Shariputra said: "Very well, World-Honored One, I am eager to hear you."

The Buddha said to Shariputra: "Such a wonderful Dharma as this is taught by the buddha-tathagatas only on very rare occasions, just as the udumbara blossom is seen only very rarely. You should believe me, Shariputra, in the teachings of the buddhas nothing is empty or false.

"Shariputra, the meaning of the Dharma that buddhas preach as appropriate to the occasion is difficult to understand. Why? Because we use a variety of skillful means, causal explanations, and parables to teach. This Dharma cannot be well understood through calculation or analysis. Only a buddha can really grasp it. Why is this? Because it is for this great cause alone that buddhas, the world-honored ones, appear in the world.

"What do I mean by saying it is for this one great cause alone that buddhas, the world-honored ones, appear in the world? The buddhas, the world-honored ones, appear in the world because they want living beings to open a way to the buddhas' insight, and thus become pure. They appear in the world because they want to demonstrate the buddhas' insight to living beings. They appear in the world because they want living beings to apprehend things with the buddhas' insight. They appear in the world because they want living beings to enter into the way of the buddhas' insight. This alone is the one great cause, Shariputra, for which buddhas appear in the world." . . .

"Shariputra, I too am like those buddhas. Knowing that living beings have various desires and things to which they are deeply attached, I have taught the Dharma according to their basic nature, using a variety of causal explanations, parables, other kinds of expression, and the power of skillful means. Shariputra, this is so that they might attain the complete wisdom of the One Buddha-Vehicle.

"Shariputra, in the entire universe, there are not even two such vehicles, much less three!

"Shariputra, the buddhas appear in an evil world of five pollutions—the pollution of the age, the pollution from afflictions, the pollution of living beings, the pollution of views, and the pollution of life. When the age is in chaos, the stains run deep, and greedy and jealous living beings acquire unhealthy roots. For this reason, Shariputra, with their powers of skillful means, the buddhas have distinguished three ways within the One Buddha-Vehicle.

"Yet if any disciples of mine, Shariputra, thinking themselves to be arhats or pratyekabuddhas, neither hear nor know of these matters that the buddhas, the tathagatas, use only to teach and transform bodhisattvas, they are not true disciples of the Buddha, and not really arhats or pratyekabuddhas. Again, Shariputra, if such monks and nuns say to themselves: 'I have already become an arhat. This is my last body. I have already attained final nirvana!' And if they no longer vow to seek supreme awakening, you should know that they are extremely arrogant. Why? Because it is impossible that a monk who has already become an arhat would not believe this Dharma.

"There is only one exception—after a buddha has passed into extinction and there is no buddha present. Why? Because after a buddha's extinction it will be difficult to find people who can receive, embrace, read, recite, and understand a sutra such as this. But if they meet another buddha, they will receive decisive teachings about this Dharma.

"Shariputra, all of you should believe, understand, and embrace the words of the Buddha with all your hearts, for in the words of the buddhas, the tathagatas, there is nothing empty or false. There are no other vehicles. There is only the One Buddha-Vehicle."

3. A Parable

. . . at that time Shariputra, ecstatic with joy, stood up, put his palms together, reverently looked up at the face of the Honorable One and said to him: "Hearing this sound of the Dharma from the World-Honored One, I am filled with ecstasy, something I have never experienced before. Why? When we heard such a Dharma from the Buddha before, we saw that bodhisattvas were assured of becoming buddhas, but not that we ourselves were. And we were very distressed at never being able to have a tathagata's immeasurable insight.

"World-Honored One, whenever I was alone under the trees in a mountain forest, whether sitting or walking, I was occupied with this thought: 'We have all equally entered Dharma-nature. Why does the Tathagata offer us salvation only by the Dharma of a small vehicle?' This is our own fault, not the fault of the World-Honored One. Why? Because had we waited to hear you teach how to attain supreme awakening, we would certainly have been saved by the Great Vehicle. But, not understanding your way of preaching by skillful means according to what is appropriate, when we first heard the Buddha-dharma we only passively believed and accepted it, pondered it, and were informed by it.

"World-Honored One, ever since then I have spent whole days and nights blaming myself. But now, hearing from the Buddha the unprecedented Dharma that I have never heard before, all my doubts and regrets are over. I am mentally and physically at ease, and happily at peace. Today, having received my share of Buddha-dharma, I realize that I really am a child of the Buddha, born from the Buddha's mouth and transformed by the Dharma." . . .

Then the Buddha said to Shariputra: "Now in this great assembly of human and heavenly beings, mendicants, brahmans, and others, I say this: In the past, in the presence of two trillion buddhas, for the sake of the unexcelled way, I always taught and transformed you. And throughout long days and nights you have followed me and accepted my teaching. Since I used skillful means to guide you, you have been born into my Dharma.

"Shariputra, in the past I led you to aspire and vow to follow the Buddha way. But now you have entirely forgotten this, and therefore suppose that you have already attained extinction. Now, wanting you to recollect the way that you originally vowed to follow, for all the shravakas I teach this Great Vehicle sutra called the Lotus Flower of the Wonderful Dharma, by which bodhisattvas are taught and which buddhas watch over and keep in mind.

"Shariputra, in a future life, after innumerable, unlimited, and inconceivable eons, when you have served some ten million billion buddhas, maintained the true Dharma, and perfected the way of bodhisattva practice, you will be able to become a buddha whose name will be Flower Light Tathagata, one worthy of offerings, truly awakened, fully clear in conduct, well gone, understanding the world, unexcelled leader, trainer of men, teacher of heavenly beings and people, buddha, world-honored one.

"Your land will be called Free of Dirt. It will be level and smooth, pure and beautifully decorated, peaceful and prosperous. Both human and heavenly beings will flourish there. It will have lapis lazuli for its earth, with eight intersecting roads with golden cords marking their boundaries. Beside each road will be a row of trees of the seven precious materials, which will always be filled with flowers and fruit. Using the three vehicles, Flower Light Tathagata will teach and transform living beings. . . .

When all of the four groups, namely monks, nuns, laymen and laywomen, and the gods, dragons, satyrs, centaurs, asuras, griffins, chimeras, pythons, and others—the entire great assembly—saw that Shariputra had received his assurance of supreme awakening from the Buddha, their hearts overflowed with joy and danced in ecstasy. Each took off the outer robes they were wearing and presented them as offerings to the Buddha. Indra Devendra and Brahma, the king of heaven, as well as others, with countless children of heaven, also made offerings to the Buddha with their wonderful heavenly robes, mandarava and great mandarava flowers from heaven, and so on. The heavenly robes they had scattered remained in the sky, whirling around and around by themselves. With hundreds of billions of kinds of heavenly musical instruments, these heavenly beings made music together in the sky. And, raining down numerous flowers from heaven, they spoke these words: "In the past at Varanasi the Buddha first turned the Dharma wheel, and now he rolls the wheel again—the unexcelled, greatest Dharma wheel!" . . .

Then Shariputra said to the Buddha: "World-Honored One, I now have no more doubts or regrets. I personally have received assurance of supreme awakening from the Buddha. But these twelve hundred who are mentally free, while they were at the learning stage in the past, were always taught by the Buddha, who said: 'My Dharma can free you from birth, old age, disease, and death and enable you finally to attain nirvana.' These people, some still in training and some no longer in training, being free from views of self and about 'existence' or 'nonexistence,' thought they had attained nirvana. But now, hearing something they have never heard before from the World-Honored One, they have fallen into doubt.

"Thus, World-Honored One, I beg you to give causal explanations to the four groups so that they may be free from doubt and regret."

Then the Buddha said to Shariputra: "Did I not tell you before that when the buddhas, the world-honored ones, by using causal explanations, parables, and other kinds of expression, teach the Dharma by skillful means, it is all for the purpose of supreme awakening? All these teachings are for the purpose of transforming people into bodhisattvas. But, Shariputra, let me once again make this meaning still more clear through a parable, for intelligent people can understand through parables.

"Shariputra, suppose in a village or city in a certain kingdom there was a great elder. He had many fields, houses, and servants. His house was large and spacious but had only one gateway. Many people lived in the house, one hundred, two hundred, or even five hundred in all. Its halls and rooms were old and decaying, its walls crumbling, its pillars rotting at the base, its beams and rafters failing down and dangerous.

"All over the house, at the same moment, fire suddenly broke out, engulfing the house in flames. The children of the elder, say ten, twenty, or even thirty, were in this house. The elder, seeing this great fire spring up on every side, was very alarmed and thought: 'Though I can get out safely through the flaming gateway, my children are in the burning house enjoying themselves engrossed in play, without awareness, knowledge, alarm, or fear. Fire is closing in on them. Pain and suffering threaten, but they do not care or become frightened, and have no thought of trying to escape.'

"Shariputra, this elder said to himself: 'My body and arms are strong. I can wrap the children in some robes and put them on a palette or bench and carry them out of the house.' But then he thought again: 'This house has only one gateway, and it is narrow and small. My children are young. Knowing nothing as yet of the danger, they are absorbed in their play. Probably they will be burned up in the fire. I must tell them why I am alarmed, and warn them that the house is burning and that they must get out quickly or be burned up in the fire.' In accord with this line of thought, he called to his children: 'Get out quickly, all of you!'

"Although the father was sympathetic and tried to persuade them with kind words, the children, absorbed in their play, were unwilling to believe him and were neither alarmed nor frightened. They didn't even think about trying to escape. What's more, they did not understand what he meant by the fire, or the house, or losing their lives. They only kept running around playing, barely glancing at their father.

"Then the elder thought: 'This house is already going up in a great blaze. If my children and I do not get out at once, we will certainly be burned alive. Now I have to find some skillful means to get my children to escape from this disaster.'

"Knowing what his children always liked, and all the various rare and attractive playthings and curiosities that would please them, the father said to them: 'The things you like to play with are rare and hard to find. If you do not get them when you can, you will be sorry later. A variety of goat carriages, deer carriages, and ox carriages are now outside the gate for you to play with. You must get out of this burning house quickly, and I will give you whatever ones you want.'

"When they heard about the rare and attractive playthings described by their father, which were just what they wanted, all of the children, eagerly pushing and racing with each other, came scrambling out of the burning house.

"Then the elder, seeing that his children had safely escaped and were all sitting in the open square and no longer in danger, was very relieved and ecstatic with joy. Then each of the children said to their father: 'Those playthings you promised us, the goat carriages, deer carriages, and ox carriages, please give them to us now!'

"Shariputra, then the elder gave each of his children equally a great carriage. They were tall and spacious, and decorated with many jewels. They had railings around them, with bells hanging on all four sides. Each was covered with a canopy, which was also splendidly decorated with various rare and precious jewels. Around each was a string of precious stones and garlands of flowers. Inside were beautiful mats and rose-colored pillows. Pulling each of them was a handsome, very powerful white ox with a pure hide, capable of walking with a smooth gait and fast as the speed of the wind. Each also had many servants and followers to guard and take care of them.

"Why was this? Because this great elder's wealth was so inexhaustible, his many storehouses so full of treasures, he thought: 'There is no limit to my wealth. I should not give inferior carriages to my children. They are all my children and I cherish them equally. I have countless numbers of these large carriages with the seven precious materials. I should give one to each of the children without discrimination. I have so many large carriages I could give one to everyone in the land without running out. Surely I can give them to my own children.'

"Then the children rode on their great carriages, having received something they had never had before and never expected to have.

"Shariputra, what do you think about this? Is that elder, in giving equally the rare treasure of great carriages to his children, guilty of falsehood or not?"

Shariputra said: "No, World-Honored One. That elder only made it possible for his children to escape the disaster of the fire and preserve their lives. He committed no falsehood. Why do I say this? By saving their lives he has already given them a kind of plaything. How much more so when by skillful means he saved them from that burning house. World-Honored One, even if that elder had not given them one of the smallest of carriages, he would not be guilty of falsehood. Why? Because the elder, from the beginning, had intended to use some skillful means to enable his children to escape. That is the reason why he is not guilty of falsehood. How much less so, when knowing his own immeasurable wealth and wanting to benefit his children abundantly, he gave them equally great carriages!"

The Buddha said to Shariputra: "Good, good. It is just as you say, Shariputra. The Tathagata is also like this, for he is a father to the whole world. He has long ago completely gotten rid of all fear, distress, anxiety, ignorance, and blindness; has attained immeasurable insight, powers, and freedom from fear; and has gained great spiritual power and wisdom. He has fully mastered skillful means and the practice of wisdom. His great mercy and compassion never stop. He always seeks the good, whatever will enrich all beings.

"He was born into this threefold world, an old decaying burning house, in order to save living beings from the fires of birth, old age, disease, death, anxiety, sorrow, suffering, agony, folly, blindness, and the three poisons, and to teach and transform them, enabling them to reach supreme awakening. . . .

"Shariputra, the elder, seeing his children safely out of the burning house and no longer threatened, thought about his immeasurable wealth and gave each of his children a great carriage. The Tathagata does the same. He is the father of all living beings. He sees innumerable thousands of millions of beings escape from the suffering of the threefold world, from the fearful and perilous path, through the gateway of teachings of the Buddha, and thus gain the joys of nirvana. Then the Tathagata thinks: 'I have Dharma storehouses of buddhas, with immeasurable, unlimited wisdom, power, and freedom from fear. All these living beings are my children. I will give the Great Vehicle to them equally, so that no one will reach extinction individually, but all gain the same extinction as the Tathagata.'

"All the living beings who escape the threefold world are given the enjoyments of buddhas—meditation, liberation, and so forth. All are of one character and one type, praised by sages and capable of producing pure, wonderful, supreme happiness.

"Shariputra, the elder at first attracted his children with the three carriages and afterward gave them just one great carriage decorated with jewels, which was the safest and most comfortable carriage. Yet the man is not guilty of lying. The Tathagata does

the same. There is no falsehood in teaching three vehicles first, to attract living beings, and afterward using just the Great Vehicle to save them. Why? Because the Tathagata has Dharma storehouses of immeasurable wisdom, power, and freedom from fear. He can give all living beings the Great Vehicle Dharma. But not all are able to receive it. For this reason, Shariputra, you should understand that the buddhas use the power of skillful means, thus making distinctions within the One Buddha-Vehicle and teaching the three." . . .

12. Devadatta

At that time the Buddha addressed the bodhisattvas, the human and heavenly beings, and the four groups, saying: "Through innumerable eons in the past, I tirelessly sought the Dharma Flower Sutra. Throughout those many eons I was a king who vowed to seek unexcelled awakening. Never faltering, and wanting to become fully developed in the six transcendental practices, the king diligently and unstintingly gave alms—elephants, horses, the seven rare things, countries, cities, wives, children, male and female servants, attendants, and even his own head, eyes, marrow, brain, flesh, hands, and feet—not sparing his body or life.

"At that time a person's lifetime was beyond measure. For the sake of the Dharma, he gave up his kingdom and throne, left the government to the crown prince, sounded drums and sent proclamations in all directions, seeking the Dharma, and saying: 'For the rest of my life, I will be the provider and servant for anyone who can teach me the Great Vehicle.'

"Then a seer came to the king and said: 'I have a Great Vehicle sutra named the Lotus Flower of the Wonderful Dharma. If you will obey me, I will explain it for you.' Hearing what the seer said, the king became ecstatic with joy and immediately went with him, providing for his needs, gathering fruit, drawing water, collecting firewood, laying out his food, even offering his body as a seat and bed, yet never feeling tired physically or emotionally. During this period of service, all for the sake of the Dharma, a thousand years passed in which he diligently provided for the seer so he would lack nothing." . . .

The Buddha said to all the monks: "The king at that time was me and the seer was the present Devadatta. Because Devadatta was a good friend to me I was able to become fully developed in the six transcendental practices, in kindness, compassion, joy, and impartiality, in the thirty-two characteristics, the eighty different attractive features, the deep gold color, the ten powers, the four kinds of freedom from fear, the four social teachings, the eighteen kinds of uniqueness, and the powers of the divine way. That I have attained impartial, proper awakening and saved many of the living is due to my good friend Devadatta."

"I declare to all four groups that after innumerable eons have passed Devadatta will become a buddha whose name will be Heavenly King Tathagata, one worthy of offerings, truly awakened, fully clear in conduct, well done, understanding the world, unexcelled leader, trainer of men, teacher of heavenly beings and people, buddha, world-honored one. His world will be named Heaven's Way. At that time Heavenly King Buddha will live in the world for twenty intermediate eons, teaching the wonderful Dharma everywhere for the sake of all the living. Living beings as numerous as the sands of the Ganges will enjoy being arhats; innumerable beings will aspire to be pratyekabuddhas; and living beings as numerous as the sands of the Ganges, aspiring to the unexcelled way, will attain assurance of not being reborn and the stage of never backsliding. After the complete nirvana of Heavenly King Buddha, the true Dharma will dwell in his world for twenty intermediate eons. The remains of his entire body will be put in a stupa of the seven precious materials sixty leagues high and forty leagues in length and width. All the human and heavenly beings, with various flowers, powdered incense, incense for burning, paste incense, robes, garlands, banners, flags, jeweled canopies, and music and song, will respectfully greet and make offerings to the wonderful stupa of the seven precious materials. Innumerable living beings will enjoy being arhats; incalculable numbers of living beings will become awakened as pratyekabuddhas; and inconceivable numbers of the living will aspire to become awakened and reach the stage of never backsliding."

The Buddha then said to the monks: "In the future, if there are any good sons or good daughters who, hearing this Devadatta chapter of the Wonderful Dharma Flower Sutra, faithfully respect it with pure hearts and are free from doubt, they will not fall into a purgatory or become a hungry spirit or a beast, but will be born into the presence of the buddhas of the ten directions. Wherever they are born they will always hear this sutra. If they are born among human or heavenly beings, they will enjoy marvelous delights. And if they are reborn in the presence of a buddha, they will be born by transformation from lotus flowers."

Then a bodhisattva from a lower region, named Accumulated Wisdom, an attendant of Abundant Treasures, the World-Honored One, said to Abundant Treasures Buddha: "Let us return to our homeland."

But Shakyamuni Buddha said to Accumulated Wisdom: "Good man, wait a while. There is a bodhisattva here named Manjushri. You should meet him and discuss the wonderful Dharma with him, and then return to your homeland."

Then Manjushri, sitting on a thousand-petaled lotus flower as large as a carriage wheel, accompanied by bodhisattvas who had come with him also sitting on treasured lotus flowers, emerged naturally from the palace of Sagara Dragon King in the great ocean. Suspended in the air, he went to Holy Eagle Peak, got down from his lotus flower, went before the Buddha, and reverently prostrated himself at the feet of the two world-honored ones. When he had expressed his respect he went over to Accumulated Wisdom, and after they had exchanged greetings, they withdrew and sat to one side. Accumulated Wisdom Bodhisattva asked Manjushri: "When you were at the dragon palace, how many beings did you convert?"

Manjushri responded: "The number of them is innumerable, incalculable. It cannot be expressed in words or fathomed by the mind. Just wait a moment and there will be proof." And before he had finished speaking innumerable bodhisattvas sitting on treasured lotus flowers emerged from the ocean and went to Holy Eagle Peak, where they were suspended in the air. All these bodhisattvas had been transformed and delivered by Manjushri. They had done bodhisattva practice and together discussed the six transcendental practices. Those in the air, originally shravakas, taught shravaka practices, even though they were now all practicing the Great Vehicle principle of emptiness. Then Manjushri said to Accumulated Wisdom: "This is the result of my teaching and converting in the ocean." . . .

Manjushri replied: "What I always proclaimed when I was in the ocean was only the Wonderful Dharma Flower Sutra."

Accumulated Wisdom Bodhisattva asked Manjushri: "This sutra is very profound, fine and wonderful, the jewel of all the sutras, a rare thing in the world. Is there any living being who, diligently and devotedly practicing this sutra, can quickly become a buddha?"

Manjushri replied: "There is the daughter of the dragon king Sagara. Just eight years old, she is wise and has sharp faculties, and is well acquainted with the faculties and actions of living beings. She has mastered incantations. She has been able to receive and embrace all the profound inner core treasures preached by the buddhas. She has entered deeply into meditation and gained an understanding of all things. Within a moment, she aspired to become awakened and reached the stage of never backsliding. Her eloquence knows no bounds, and she has compassion for all the living as if they were her own children. She is full of blessings, and the thoughts in her mind and the explanations from her mouth are both subtle and great. Compassionate and respectful of others, kind and gentle, she is able to attain awakening."

Accumulated Wisdom Bodhisattva said: "I have seen how Shakyamuni Tathagata carried out arduous and difficult practices for innumerable eons, accumulating blessings and piling up virtue by following the way of the bodhisattva without resting. I have observed that in the three-thousand great thousandfold world there is not even a spot as small as a mustard seed where he has not laid down body and life as a bodhisattva for the sake of the living. Only after that did he attain the path of the awakened. It is unbelievable that this girl, in an instant, can become truly awakened."

But before he had finished talking, the daughter of the dragon king suddenly appeared and, after reverently prostrating herself at the Buddha's feet, withdrew to one side, praising him in verse:

Profound in insight into the nature of good and evil,
He illuminates the universe.
His fine and wonderful pure Dharma body
Has the thirty-two characteristics.
The eighty different attractive features adorn his
    Dharma body.
Human and heavenly beings look up to him,
Dragons and gods revere him,
And all kinds of living beings hold him in reverence.
Having heard him, I can become awakened
Only the Buddha can bear witness to this.
I will reveal the teaching of the Great Vehicle
To save living beings from suffering.

Then Shariputra said to the dragon girl: "You think that in no time at all you will attain the unexcelled way. This is hard to believe. Why? Because the body of a woman is filthy and impure, not a vessel for the Dharma. How could you attain unexcelled awakening? The Buddha way is long and extensive. Only after innumerable eons of enduring hardship, accumulating good works, and thoroughly carrying out all the practices can it be reached. Moreover, a woman's body has five hindrances: first, she cannot

become a king of a Brahma heaven; second she cannot become king Indra; third, she cannot become a devil king; fourth she cannot become a wheel-turning saintly king; and fifth she cannot have the body of a buddha. How then could you, in a woman's body, so quickly become a buddha?"

Then the dragon girl took a precious jewel that she had with her, worth as much as a three-thousand great thousandfold world, and presented it to the Buddha. The Buddha immediately accepted it. The dragon girl then said to Accumulated Wisdom Bodhisattva and the Venerable Shariputra: "I presented my precious jewel and the World-Honored One accepted it—was that not done quickly?" "Most quickly," they answered. The daughter told them: "Use your holy powers to watch me become a buddha even more quickly than that!"

Then the entire congregation saw the dragon girl instantly transformed into a male, take up bodhisattva practice, and immediately go to the world named Spotless, in the southern region, where, sitting on a precious lotus blossom, she attained impartial, proper awakening. With the thirty-two characteristics and eighty different attractive features she proclaimed the wonderful Dharma to all living beings everywhere in the universe.

Then from afar the bodhisattvas, shravakas, gods, dragons, the eightfold assembly, humans, and non-humans in this world watched the dragon girl become a buddha and teach the Dharma to all the gods and people in the assembly. Their hearts filled with great joy, they paid their respects from afar. Hearing the Dharma, countless living beings were able to understand it and reach the stage of never backsliding. The countless multitude also received assurance of attaining the Way. The world Spotless trembled and shook in six ways. Three thousand living beings in this world reached the stage of never backsliding, while three thousand living beings aspired to become awakened and obtained assurance of doing so.

Accumulated Wisdom Bodhisattva and Shariputra and the whole congregation silently believed and accepted this. . . .

16. The Lifetime of the Tathagata

At that time the Buddha said to the bodhisattvas and to all the great assembly: "Have faith in and understand, all you good sons, the truthful words of the Tathagata." . . .

"You should all listen carefully to hear about the Tathagata's secret and divine powers. In all the worlds, the humans, heavenly beings, and asuras think that the present Shakyamuni Buddha left the palace of the Shakya clan, sat at the place of the Way not far from the city of Gaya, and attained supreme awakening. But, my good sons, in fact there have been innumerable, unlimited hundreds of thousands of billions of myriads of eons since I became a buddha.

"Suppose someone were to take five hundred thousand billions of myriads of countless three-thousand great thousandfold worlds and grind them into dust. Then, after going east through five hundred thousand billions of myriads of innumerable lands, one of those specks of dust was deposited. And suppose he continued eastward until he had used up all those specks. What do you think, my good sons? Is it possible to imagine or calculate the number of all those worlds?" . . .

Then the Buddha said to all those bodhisattva great ones: "Good sons, now I will speak to you clearly. Suppose you took all those worlds, where a speck of dust has been deposited and where none has been deposited, and reduced them to dust. Let one speck be equal to an eon. The time that has passed since I became a buddha exceeds these by hundreds of thousands of billions of myriads of countless eons. Since that time I have constantly been in this world—preaching, teaching, and transforming. And in other places, in hundreds of thousands of billions of myriads of countless other lands, I have led and enriched living beings.

"Good sons, during this time I have talked about the Buddha Burning Light and others, and have told of their entering nirvana. In all of this I used skillful means to analyze things. . . .

"Thus, since I became Buddha a very long time has passed, a lifetime of innumerable countless eons of constantly living here and never entering extinction. Good sons, from the beginning I have practiced

Glossary

Ajnata-Kaundinya	one of the five ascetics who were companions of the Buddha
arhat	personal awakening
bodhisattva	or "buddha-to-be," one who is dedicated to the liberation of all beings and is thus an embodiment of compassion
Brahma	the Hindu god of creation
Devadatta	Shakyamuni's (the Buddha's) cousin
Dharma	a complex concept that can refer to the basic principles of the cosmos or to a person's duty to follow a virtuous path
Indra Devendra	title given to the Hindu god Indra
Maitreya	a bodhisattva who is to appear on the earth, achieve complete enlightenment, and teach the pure dharma
Manjushri	the bodhisattva of wisdom
nirvana	the extinction of suffering and escape from the cycle of reincarnation
pratyekabuddha	a "solitary Buddha," or one who achieves awakening on his or her own, without reliance on the words or teachings of others
Sagara	a dragon king
Shakyamuni	Siddhartha Gautama, or the historical Buddha
Shariputra	one of the Buddha's principal disciples
shravaka	literally, "hearer," a disciple of the Buddha who has accepted the Buddha's teaching
Tathagata	the name the Buddha used to refer to himself; literally, "one who has thus come" and "one who has thus gone"
Varanasi	a holy city on the banks of the River Ganges in India

the bodhisattva way, and that life is not yet finished, but will be twice as long as what has already passed. Even now, though I will not actually enter extinction, I announce that I will adopt the way of extinction. By using such skillful means, the Tathagata teaches and transforms living beings.

"Why is this? If the Buddha lives for a long time in this world, people of little virtue will not plant roots of goodness, and those who are poor and of humble origins will become attached to the five desires and be caught in a net of assumptions and false views. If they see that the Tathagata is always alive and never extinct, they will become arrogant and selfish or discouraged and neglectful. Unable to realize how difficult it is to meet him, they will not have a respectful attitude toward him.

"Therefore the Tathagata teaches by using skillful means, saying: 'Monks, you should know that it is difficult to meet a buddha who has come into the world.' Why is this? In the course of countless hundreds of thousands of billions of eons, some people of little virtue may see a buddha while others may never see one. For this reason I say this: 'Monks, it is difficult to see a tathagata.' Living beings, hearing such words, surely will realize that it is difficult to meet a buddha. They will yearn for one. Then they will cultivate roots of goodness. This is why the Tathagata announces his extinction even though he does not in reality become extinct.

"Good sons, the teachings of all the buddha-tathagatas are all like this. They are for the sake of liberating all the living. They are true and not empty.

"Suppose, for instance, there is a fine physician who is wise and clever and knows how to make medicines for curing all sorts of disease. He has many sons—say, ten, twenty, even a hundred. To take care of some business he goes off to a distant land. After he leaves, his children drink some poisonous drugs, which drives them into deliriums of agony and leaves them writhing on the ground.

"At this point their father comes back home to find the sons have drunk the poison. Some have lost their minds, others have not. Seeing their father in the distance, they are all very happy. Kneeling to greet him, they say: 'How good it is that you have returned safely! Foolishly we have taken some poison by mistake. Please heal us and give us back our lives.'

"The father sees his children in such suffering and agony and, following various formulas, looks for good medicinal herbs, perfect in color, fragrance, and flavor. Then he pounds, sifts, and mixes them

and gives them to his children, telling them: 'This excellent medicine is perfect in color, fragrance, and flavor. Take it and you will quickly be rid of your suffering and agony, and be free from the illness.'

"Those children who have not lost their minds, seeing this excellent medicine of good color and fragrance, take it immediately and are completely cured of their illness. The others, who have lost their minds, are also happy to see their father return and ask him to heal their illness. Yet when the medicine is given to them, they refuse to take it. Why? Because the poison has penetrated deeply into them and they have lost their minds. Even though this medicine has good color and fragrance, they think it is no good.

"The father thinks to himself: 'These poor children. Because of the poison in them, their minds are completely unbalanced. Though they are glad to see me and ask to be healed, they refuse to take this good medicine. Now I have to use some skillful means to get them to take this medicine,' Then he says to them: 'You should know that I am now worn out with old age, and the time for me to die has now arrived. I will leave this excellent medicine here. You should take it and not worry that it will not make you better.' After instructing them in this way, he leaves again for another land, from which he sends back a messenger to inform them: 'Your father is dead.'

"Now, when those children hear that their father has died and left them behind, they become very distressed and think to themselves: 'If our father were alive he would have been kind to us, and would have saved us. But now he has abandoned us and died in a distant land. We think of ourselves as orphans, with no one to rely on.'

"This continuous grief brings them to their senses. They recognize that the medicine is excellent in color, fragrance, and flavor, and they take it and are fully healed of the poison. The father, hearing that the children have all recovered, returns home immediately, so that they all see him again.

"Good sons, what do you think? Can anyone say that this fine physician is lying?"

"No, World-Honored One."

The Buddha said: "I too am like this. Since I became Buddha, innumerable, unlimited hundreds of thousands of billions of myriads of countless eons have passed. For the sake of living beings, I use the power of skillful means and say that I will take the way of extinction. Yet, taking the circumstances into account, no one can accuse me of being guilty of lying."

Calliope, the Greek muse of epic poetry (AP/Wide World Photos)

LUCRETIUS: ON THE NATURE OF THINGS

"Hence too it comes that Nature all dissolves / Into their primal bodies again, and naught / Perishes ever to annihilation."

Overview

Lucretius was a classical Roman writer whose only surviving work is *De rerum natura*. Usually the title is translated from the Latin as *On the Nature of Things*. Sometimes the title is translated as *On the Nature of the Universe*, for the work, an epic poem divided into six books, is a wide-ranging exploration of physics, the nature of the soul and mind, sensation and thought, the origins and evolution of the world, and a variety of natural phenomena such as lightning, thunder, earthquakes, heat and cold, and volcanoes.

Although it is not strictly a religious text, *On the Nature of Things* implicitly and explicitly examines a range of issues that are normally thought of as the province of religion and theology. That it does so is not surprising, for it was written in an age when science and religion often merged in the field of philosophy as philosophers tried to understand the nature of creation, the existence and role of deities, and the place of humans in the natural and spiritual order. *On the Nature of Things* espouses the theory of atomism, the belief that the universe is made up of two fundamental substances. One is atoms, conceived as the fundamental, indivisible, eternal building blocks of matter that can be neither created nor destroyed. The other is the void, or the infinite space between atoms where atoms continuously move about and combine, shift, dissipate, and recombine in an ongoing process of creation and destruction. The result of the atomist view was a philosophical determinism, which denied the role of deities in human affairs and stated that what people experience through their senses is the result of chance. Further, Lucretius argues that the soul, like all of creation, is made of up these atoms, which disperse when a person dies. While gods exist, they did not create the universe, nor do they involve themselves in human affairs. These views were the product of ideas Lucretius absorbed from the Greek philosopher Epicurus, who had lived some two and a half centuries earlier. Lucretius was an avid champion of the philosophical school to which Epicurus gave his name, Epicureanism. In *On the Nature of Things*, Lucretius argues that Epicurus's greatest achievement was the conquest of *religio*, usually translated as "religion" but, in the Greek, implying more of a "binding down" or "submission."

Context

Lucretius's life was coincident with a time of social and economic chaos in Rome. During his lifetime, Lucretius witnessed an almost nonstop parade of revolts, assassinations, rioting, political intrigue, civil war, mass executions, and overseas wars. In 100 BCE, the year before his birth, Rome was the scene of rioting and the murder of public officials. The rioting in large part was the result of a controversial bill that granted land to non-Roman soldiers but also the result of the enormous number of slaves being brought into Rome, leaving many Roman workers unemployed and indigent, In 98 BCE, a revolt erupted in Lusitania, the Roman colony that corresponds roughly to modern-day Portugal. In 91 BCE the so-called Social War pitted Rome against its Italian allies; this war lasted until 88 BCE. From 89 to 85 BCE Rome was at war with Mithridates VI of Pontus (a Greek colony in modern-day Turkey) to thwart his territorial ambitions, and war with Mithridates would break out again in 83 BCE and yet again in 73 BCE. Meanwhile, in 88 BCE, a renegade army commander, Lucius Cornelius Sulla, marched on Rome and seized it. By 82 BCE he was dictator, consolidating his power by arresting and executing some four thousand of Rome's leading citizens, including forty senators. In 73 BCE the famous slave revolt led by Spartacus erupted, lasting until 71 BCE. The massive revolt, involving some ninety thousand slaves and outlaws, was put down by Marcus Lucinius Crassus and Gnaeus Pompeius Magnus (usually called Pompey). Six thousand rebels were crucified along the Appian Way. In 65 BCE, Lucius Sergius Catilina, known in English as Catiline, was implicated in the First Catilinarian Conspiracy, an attempted coup whose goal was in part the assassination of Roman consuls. Later, in 63 BCE, Catiline was demonstrably at the center of the Second Catilinarian Conspiracy, another attempt at a military coup. By the time of his death in 62 BCE, Catiline's name was virtually synonymous with intrigue, scandal, conspiracy, and vaulting ambition. Rome was again at war in 58 BCE, when Julius Caesar launched the Gallic Wars, which lasted until 51 BCE. The campaign in Gaul, roughly equivalent to modern-day France, did not always go smoothly, for revolts, including one led by a tribal chieftain named Vercingetorix, led to heavy Roman losses.

Time Line

341 BCE	■ Epicurus is born on the island of Samos.
306 BCE	■ Epicurus founds the Garden, a philosophical community and school, in Athens.
CA. 99 BCE	■ Lucretius is born.
91 BCE	■ The Social War pits Rome against its Italian allies; the war ends in 88 BCE.
89 BCE	■ Rome is at war with Mithridates VI of Pontus; war with Mithridates would erupt again in 83 and 73 BCE.
88 BCE	■ Lucius Cornelius Sulla seizes Rome and later becomes dictator.
73 BCE	■ A massive slave revolt led by Spartacus erupts.
65 BCE	■ Lucius Sergius Catilina, or Catiline, is implicated in the First Catilinarian Conspiracy, an attempted military coup.
63 BCE	■ Catiline is at the center of the Second Catilinarian Conspiracy, another attempted military coup.
CA. 59 BCE	■ Lucretius begins composition of *On the Nature of Things*.
58 BCE	■ Julius Caesar launches his campaigns against the Gauls; the Gallic Wars end in 51 BCE.
CA. 55 BCE	■ Lucretius dies; the first copies of *On the Nature of Things* circulate.
44 BCE	■ Julius Caesar is named dictator in perpetuity but is assassinated on March 15.
1417	■ Two surviving ninth-century manuscripts of *On the Nature of Things* are discovered in a monastery by the Italian humanist Poggio Bracciolini.

None of these events had a direct effect on *On the Nature of Things*. Their indirect effect, however, was considerable, for throughout his life Lucretius was surrounded by turmoil and bloodshed. Little wonder, then, that he was attracted to the philosophical views of Epicurus, called Epicureanism, which form the heart of *On the Nature of Things*. Epicurus, a Greek, was born in 341 BCE on the island of Samos. The philosophical school he founded, Epicureanism, was a materialist philosophy based on its founder's belief that people were driven by fears and anxieties produced by their lack of understanding of the material world. Epicurus tried to offer a comprehensive theory of the origin, development, and workings of the universe, believing that once people understood these matters, they would be relieved of their fears and lead a life of greater tranquility and pleasure.

By all accounts Epicurus wrote extensively, but very little of his work survives. His principal book, *On Nature*, encompassed physics, including the atomistic theory discussed earlier. In the view of Epicurus, the world was in constant flux, an ongoing binding and unbinding of atoms. The mind and body are just examples of atoms in motion. These atoms are indestructible, and after death they dissipate and recombine to form new entities in an ongoing process of creation. Epicurus's work also examined sensation and perception, taking the position that physical sensation is the only avenue to truth. In the realm of ethics, Epicurus argued that intellectual pleasures, rather than the pleasures of the flesh, are the highest good, for they are the most permanent. Sometimes his name has been associated with a hedonistic way of life. In modern life, the word *epicurean* is often used to describe a fastidious person or a bon vivant who indulges in sensual pleasure, especially fine food and wine. While Epicurus believed that the highest good for humans was the pursuit of pleasure, "pleasure" was identified with tranquility and freedom from fear. The Epicureans of ancient Greece and Rome elevated intellectual pleasures and tranquility as a counterweight to social strife and irrational fears, particularly the fear of death. Epicurus himself was a strong advocate of a spartan life, one of simplicity, moral discipline, and self-denial.

In about 306 BCE, Epicurus moved to Athens, where he founded a school and philosophical community called the Garden. His views competed successfully with other philosophical views such as Stoicism, and in time communities of Epicureans sprang up and flourished. These communities survived into the first century BCE, including a vibrant Epicurean community around the Bay of Naples led by Philodemus during Lucretius's lifetime. *On the Nature of Things* remains significant not only for its lofty poetry but also because it is one of the major documents that preserves the views of Epicurus and his followers.

About the Author

Little is known about the life of Lucretius. Much of what is known is based on hints provided in *On the Nature of Things*, but modern scholars know less about his life than they do of most other classical Roman writers whose work has survived.

The legions of Julius Caesar in battle (AP/Wide World Photos)

Titus Lucretius Carus was born at the beginning of the first century BCE, probably in 99 BCE. Nothing is known of his early life, and it is unclear whether he was born into affluence or humble circumstances. He may have been a member of an aristocratic clan called the Lucretii, but it is equally possible that he was a family slave who was then freed and retained the family name. His poem demonstrates that he received an extensive education, for he was knowledgeable about Greek and Latin literature and, although he was a Roman, was fluent in Greek. Also, he had a fondness for using political and legal figures of speech in his poem, suggesting that he was educated for a life in politics or the law.

The poem suggests that Lucretius spent much of his life in Rome, for he makes reference to events he witnessed, such as military exercises, theatrical performances, and horse races. At the same time, the poem indicates that he spent considerable time in the countryside and may perhaps have owned a country villa. The poem is replete with sensitive depictions of nature, including forests, streams, wild animals, and mountains, as well as the activities of domesticated animals such as cattle. One line in the poem hints that he was married, and in fact literary tradition has endowed him with a wife, Lucilla; otherwise nothing is known of his domestic life. The poem is addressed to a friend, a Roman aristocrat named Gaius Memmius, thought to have

been Lucretius's patron, and he probably knew the Roman poet Catullus as well as Catullus's less-famous patron, Helvius Cinna. Otherwise, classicists can only guess as to whether he knew or was acquainted with other Epicurean philosophers such as Siro and Philodemus; writers such as Amafinius, Catius, and Rabirius, who did much to popularize the Epicurean philosophy on the Italian Peninsula; and possibly even Julius Caesar and one of Caesar's assassins, Cassius (Gaius Cassius Longinus), both of whom were sympathetic to the Epicurean philosophy.

On the Nature of Things is Lucretius's only surviving work. He began composing it in about 59 BCE and worked on it until his death, probably in 55 BCE. Glancing references to contemporary events have allowed classicists to date the composition of the work with some accuracy. Although the work was largely finished, some evidence suggests that Lucretius likely planned to make revisions to eliminate duplications, smooth abrupt transitions, and take up topics that he promised in the text as it exists to address but that are not included. After his death, minor corrections were probably made to the poem, though who made them is unclear. Four centuries later, Saint Jerome, an early church father, wrote that the poet Cicero prepared the work for publication, but scholars dispute this claim because Cicero was hostile to the Epicurean philosophy and would prob-

"Meantime, when once we know from nothing still / Nothing can be create, we shall divine / More clearly what we seek: those elements / From which alone all things created are, / And how accomplished by no tool of Gods."

"Hence too it comes that Nature all dissolves / Into their primal bodies again, and naught / Perishes ever to annihilation."

"Death is, then, to us / Much less—if there can be a less than that / Which is itself a nothing: for there comes / Hard upon death a scattering more great / Of the throng of matter, and no man wakes up / On whom once falls the icy pause of life."

"Therefore, O man, by living on, fulfil / As many generations as thou may: / Eternal death shall there be waiting still; / And he who died with light of yesterday / Shall be no briefer time in death's No-more / Than he who perished months or years before."

ably have had no interest in promulgating it. Some argue that Cicero's friend Atticus, himself an Epicurean and the owner of a publishing business, is the more likely candidate. Incidentally, Saint Jerome also wrote that Lucretius went insane after drinking a love potion, wrote during intermittent periods of lucidity, and ultimately committed suicide. While some scholars have claimed to find evidence of a morbid temperament in *On the Nature of Things*, no firm evidence supports Jerome's statements. Scholars note that during the early Christian period, the Catholic Church deliberately tried to expunge Lucretius from history and literary tradition because of his materialist "blasphemies," explaining Jerome's attempt to discredit him.

Explanation and Analysis of the Document

In the original Latin, *On the Nature of Things* is written in dactylic hexameters, a metrical form in which each line has six metrical feet (the hexameter), each consisting of a stressed syllable followed by two unstressed syllables (the dactyl), although considerable variation is allowed in the makeup of the metrical feet. This metrical form was commonly used in classical epic poems in both Greek and Latin, including those by Homer and Virgil, so the meter is

often called the heroic hexameter. Overall, Lucretius's work is divided into six books. The first two books examine the smallest elements of the universe: atoms and the void. The second two books study humans, particularly the nature of the human soul. The third pair of books moves to the cosmos as a whole and an examination of cosmic phenomena. The first excerpt, "Substance Is Eternal," is from Book I; the second, "Folly of the Fear of Death," is from Book III.

♦ Book I: Substance Is Eternal

The title of this section encompasses in three words the atomistic view of the universe. Lucretius begins by pointing to the terror, the "darkness of the mind," that afflicts humans. He responds by saying that nature's law teaches us that "Nothing from nothing ever yet was born." People are fearful because they do not understand the physical universe, believing that "Divinities are working there." Lucretius opposes this view, saying that the elements from which things are created are "no tool of Gods." To illustrate his point, he notes that each form of creation—men, cattle, wild animals, fruits, crops—emerges "from its own stuff, from its own primal bodies." If things emerged from "naught," or nothing, they would "spring abroad / Suddenly, unforeseen, in alien months." In Lucretius's view, the world is regular and predictable "because for all begotten things abides / The changeless stuff, and what from that may spring / Is fixed for-evermore." Not only are there "primordial germs," or "seeds," for all things, but also, in the ongoing process of creation and destruction, "naught from nothing can become" and all things in nature dissolve "Into their primal bodies again, and naught / Perishes ever to annihilation."

Lucretius continues by noting how the earth replenishes itself. Springs and rivers, for example, replenish the oceans. If matter were destructible, time and age would "eat" all things away. A mere "touch" might cause destruction if things were not of "imperishable stock." But because the "fastenings of primordial parts" combine and recombine, "Nothing returns to naught"; everything returns to "primal forms of stuff." As an example, Lucretius cites the rains, which "perish" when they fall to earth but then nourish the food that in turn nourishes cattle, people, and cities in an ongoing process of re-creation. Nature thus "upbuilds" one thing from another, allowing nothing "to come to birth but through some other's death."

Having established the permanence of creation's building blocks, Lucretius in the next subsection turns to the issue of atoms. He notes that our eyes cannot perceive the primal germs, for they are invisible—but so are the winds, whose effects can be witnessed, just as the effects of a body of water such as a wave or mighty river can be witnessed. As another example Lucretius cites smells, which again we perceive but cannot see. Like heat and cold, these phenomena "must be corporeal . . . / Since thus they smite the senses." In this respect, Lucretius is expressing the Epicurean view that all truth is obtained through sense perception. Continuing with the example of water, he notes that water soaks into the earth and then dries away by heat. Water is "dispersed about in bits / Too small for eyes to see." He cites other examples of things that imperceptibly disappear or shrink, such as the flesh of a finger under a ring, stone that is pummeled by water under the eaves of a house, the iron of a plow blade, and the pavement of a highway. Things dissolve in "motes," or tiny bits, but people cannot see the process taking place, just as they cannot see the growth of things by the imperceptible addition of tiny bits of matter. Yet people can perceive the effects of these phenomena over time, so it is clear that the processes are taking place. The essential point for Lucretius is that the universe is in an ongoing state of flux and change, with matter combining, dissolving, and recombining in new ways but in ways that are consistent with the fundamental nature of things. These changes are the result of natural processes, not the result of the activities of deities. When people understand these fundamental principles and that "naught / Perishes ever to annihilation," they can be less fearful of change, including the major form of change people experience, death.

♦ **Book III: Folly of the Fear of Death**

Death, then, is the subject of "Folly of the Fear of Death" from Book III. Lucretius begins with a bold statement: "Therefore death to us / Is nothing, nor concerns us in the least." Lucretius's central point is that before their birth, people "felt no touch of ill" during catastrophes.

He embellishes the point by reference to the Carthaginians, or the people of Carthage whom Rome fought in the three Punic Wars from 264 to 146 BCE. Those times were "shaken," and the heavens "Shuddered and trembled." Humankind thought that the empire ("empery") would fall. In the same vein, after death, nothing can "move our senses." A person's "mind" and "energy of soul" will dissipate, to be recombined into another entity, and even if the "matter of our frames" should be recollected again "in place as now," the succession of our senses would have been broken so that death would hold no fears. People do not concern themselves with what they were "aforetime" and so suffer no distress, for they cannot recall to consciousness their earlier existence. Thus, Lucretius concludes, "Nothing for us there is to dread in death, / No wretchedness for him who is no more." In death, people simply return to the state they were in before they were born.

In the next subsection, Lucretius elaborates the point. He suggests that people grieve over death because they believe that some "remainder" is left behind. When they envision their death, they fail to see that their essence is not the same as their body. Lucretius continues with the theme of grieving in the next subsection. Grief is based on the notion that all of life's joys are snatched from them by death, but "no longer unto thee / Remains a remnant of desire for them." Again the goal of Epicurean philosophy is tranquility and freedom from fear. Lucretius tries to allay fears not by holding out the promise of an afterlife but by seeing death as a "scattering" of the "throng of matter" that releases people from anxieties.

In the following sections Lucretius continues the argument. He imagines men lamenting the brevity of life, but then he imagines the response that nature would make. Nature would urge men to leave life with "mind content" to take their "unafflicted rest." He makes an ingenious argument in asking men why, if they lament that death means the end of their enjoyments, they want to add to life, additions that also will "perish foully." He notes that people lament the prospect of their death in youth, but then once again he imagines nature responding to the fears of those "riper in years and elder." Nature would call such a person a "buffoon" for craving what is "not at hand" and refusing to yield to a new generation of "sons." No man, Lucretius says, is ever consigned to the "abyss / Of Tartarus," that is, the underworld of classical mythology. Then follows one of the legal metaphors common in *On the Nature of Things*. Lucretius says that people are not given life in "fee-simple," a term that refers to unrestricted ownership of property. Rather, the atomistic nature of the universe means that people are given life in "usufruct," meaning that they can use the property only during their lifetime.

Lucretius goes on to make a number of further references to classical mythology and historical persons and events, as always with a view to dispelling his readers' fear of gods and death. The Acheron is a river across which Charon was said to ferry the dead to the underworld. Tantalus was a figure in Greek mythology who was condemned to stand in water beneath the branches of a fruit tree. Whenever he reached for a piece of fruit, the branches of the tree would rise out of his reach; whenever he stooped to drink, the water would recede. Tantalus is thus the source of the English word *tantalize*, referring to temptation without satisfaction. Tityus (or Tityos) was a mythological figure who was condemned to eternal punishment by being stretched out and having vultures feed on his liver. Sisyphus was a mythological figure who was condemned eternally to push a boulder up a hill, only to see it roll back down as he reached the top. Ancus is a reference to Ancus Marcius, who lived in the seventh century BCE and was the fourth king of Rome. Scipio is a reference to Publius Cornelius Scipio Africanus, a prominent Roman general who defeated Hannibal in the Second Punic War. The "Heliconian dames" were the Muses, a source of inspiration for Homer, who were thought to reside on Mount Helicon in Greece. Democritus, the "laughing philosopher," lived from about 460 to about 370 BCE and was an influential figure in the development of the atomistic philosophy. Predictably, Lucretius also makes mention of Epicurus. The purpose of all these references is to place in historical context the belief that death is not something to be feared. In death, people can lay down their burdens. Further, the atomistic nature of the universe means that the presumed tortures of the afterlife are myth rather than reality.

In the final two sections, Lucretius paints a picture of discontent and lack of tranquility. He envisions a man who "sickens of his home" and flees, trying to find amusement and distraction. Soon, though, he becomes bored and bustles about as though fleeing from himself. Lucretius's view is that rather than seeking distraction, men should "study to divine / The nature of things." People long for things they cannot achieve. Prolonging life provides no new pleasures and barely diminishes the eons during which people remain dead.

Audience

The poem is addressed to Gaius Memmius, a Roman aristocrat. Memmius was an orator, poet, and tribune, that is, an elected official of the Roman Republic. In the early decades of the first century BCE, he was deeply involved with Rome's intrigues and political disputes. At first, for example, he supported Pompey in the latter's struggle with Julius Caesar over control of the Republic. He quarreled with Pompey, however, and cast his support to Caesar. When he ran for consul in 54 BCE, he lost Caesar's support because of a scandal and was accused of election fraud. He retired to Athens and then to the Greek island of Lesbos before his death in 49 BCE. It is unclear what the relationship between Lucretius and Memmius was, though it is highly likely that Memmius was the poet's patron. It is generally agreed that Lucretius wrote *On the Nature of Things* in an effort to persuade Memmius and his circle of friends to adopt the philosophy of Epicurus as a way of escaping the political turmoil and intrigue that surrounded them.

Impact

Because the works of Epicurus exist only in fragments, *On the Nature of Things* is the most significant source for what is known about ancient Epicurean thought. It is unknown what, if any, specific impact the work had on Memmius or any other Romans in the first century BCE. In the early Christian era, the work was essentially lost, and Lucretius fell into oblivion. This is hardly surprising, for after the spread of Christianity and its establishment as the official religion of the Roman Empire, Christian officials would have wanted to expunge the "pagan" philosophies of people like Epicurus and Lucretius. *On the Nature of Things* was rediscovered during the European Renaissance when Poggio Bracciolini, an Italian humanist, found manuscripts of the poem in a monastery in 1417. Later, an earlier copy of the poem was found in the ruins at Herculaneum, one of the towns (along with Pompeii), that was buried by the volcanic eruption of Mount Vesuvius in 79 CE.

After the fifteenth century, the influence of Lucretius was considerable. Poets such as John Milton, Walt Whitman, Percy Bysshe Shelley, and William Wordsworth, who themselves wrote epic poems with cosmological significance, owed a debt to Lucretius. Lucretius won the admiration of poets and critics versed in Latin who found *On the Nature of Things* not only a profound philosophical work but also a magnificent poem. In the nineteenth century, the British poet Alfred Lord Tennyson wrote a poem titled "Lucretius" in which he used the poet and his views as a vehicle for commenting on contemporary religious issues. These issues arose in the context of burgeoning evolutionary theory, including the views of French scientist Jean-Baptiste Lamarck, who in the early decades of the nineteenth century propounded a theory of evolution according to natural laws. His views were followed by those of Charles Darwin, who shook the foundations of traditional religion when he published *On the Origin of Species* in 1859.

From a philosophical and scientific standpoint, Lucretius had a marked impact on a wide range of thought. During the Renaissance, the atomistic theory he propounded formed an important part of the philosophical and scientific backdrop out of which Newtonian physics arose. In 1649 a French Catholic priest, Pierre Gassendi, published *Syntagma philosophiae Epicuri* ("Treatise on Epicurean Philosophy"), which refined and elaborated the views of Epicurean science and reconciled Lucretius's materialistic views with his own spirituality. In the modern world, readers of *On the Nature of Things* cannot help but be struck by similarities between Lucretius's views and some of the findings of modern science, including those having to do with evolution and the search for the fundamental particles that make up the physical universe; the very word *atom* comes from the Greek word *atomos*, meaning "indivisible" or, more literally, "uncuttable." Lucretius would likely take interest in the modern search for the elusive Higgs boson, the subatomic particle often referred to as the "God particle" because it is thought to be the fundamental unit of matter in the universe.

Numerous modern philosophers owe a debt, directly or indirectly, to Lucretius. Henri Bergson, in his 1907 book *Creative Evolution* (in French, *L'Evolution créatrice*), described what he called the élan vital, a kind of life force that underlies human evolution; the élan vital can be seen as similar to Venus, whom Lucretius invokes at the beginning the poem as the motive force for the teeming universe. Alfred North Whitehead's "process philosophy," which identifies reality with change and dynamism, owes much to Epicurean philosophy and the work of Lucretius. Similarly, in his 1955 book *The Phenomenon of Man* (in French, *Le phénomène humain*), Pierre Teilhard de Chardin discusses the material development of the universe, from primordial particles to humans. In his view, the universe is in a continual process of evolving toward higher complexity and consciousness, ultimately leading to what he called the Omega Point, a time in the future when human consciousness will reach its highest plane of development. Again, these and other theories do not descend directly from Lucretius's views in *On the Nature of Things*, but in a larger sense Lucretius began a discussion of fundamental questions of the universe that continues two thousand years later.

Further Reading

■ Books

Bergson, Henri. *Philosophy of Poetry: The Genius of Lucretius,* trans. Wade Baskin. New York: Philosophical Library, 1959.

Clay, Diskin. *Lucretius and Epicurus.* Ithaca, N.Y.: Cornell University Press, 1983.

Gale, Monica. *Myth and Poetry in Lucretius.* New York: Cambridge University Press, 1994.

Gillespie, Stuart, and Philip Hardie, eds. *The Cambridge Companion to Lucretius.* New York: Cambridge University Press, 2007.

Godwin, John. *Lucretius.* London: Bristol Classical Press, 2004.

Johnson, W. R. *Lucretius and the Modern World.* London: Duckworth, 2000.

Jones, Howard. *The Epicurean Tradition.* New York: Routledge, 1989.

Segal, Charles P. *Lucretius on Death and Anxiety: Poetry and Philosophy in De Rerum Natura.* Princeton, N.J.: Princeton University Press, 1990.

■ Journals

Reinhardt, Tobias. "The Speech of Nature in Lucretius' De Rerum Natura 3.931–71." *Classical Quarterly* 52 (2002): 291–304.

■ Web Sites

Harris, William. "Lucretius: The Roman Epicurean Scientist." William Harris's Humanities and the Liberal Arts Web site.

http://community.middlebury.edu/~harris/LatinAuthors/Lucretius.html

Hutcheon, Pat Duffy. "What Lucretius Wrought." Humanists.net Web site.

http://www.humanists.net/pdhutcheon/humanist%20articles/lucritus.htm

—Michael J. O'Neal

Questions for Further Study

1. What is the relationship between the views Lucretius expressed and the philosophical school called Epicureanism?

2. Describe ways in which the views of Lucretius about matter are consistent with the findings of modern science.

3. In what ways did the political turmoil during the time Lucretius lived contribute to his philosophical views?

4. Why did the Christian Church find the views of Lucretius objectionable? How were those views inconsistent with Church teaching?

5. Lucretius was motivated in part by a desire to make people more accepting of death. How effective do you think his arguments are? Do you believe that his arguments would provide consolation to a person faced with death? Explain.

LUCRETIUS:
ON THE NATURE OF THINGS

Book I

♦ Substance Is Eternal

This terror, then, this darkness of the mind,
Not sunrise with its flaring spokes of light,
Nor glittering arrows of morning can disperse,
But only Nature's aspect and her law,
Which, teaching us, hath this exordium:
Nothing from nothing ever yet was born.
Fear holds dominion over mortality
Only because, seeing in land and sky
So much the cause whereof no wise they know,
Men think Divinities are working there.
Meantime, when once we know from nothing still
Nothing can be create, we shall divine
More clearly what we seek: those elements
From which alone all things created are,
And how accomplished by no tool of Gods.
Suppose all sprang from all things: any kind
Might take its origin from any thing,
No fixed seed required. Men from the sea
Might rise, and from the land the scaly breed,
And, fowl full fledged come bursting from the sky;
The horned cattle, the herds and all the wild
Would haunt with varying offspring tilth and waste;
Nor would the same fruits keep their olden trees,
But each might grow from any stock or limb
By chance and change. Indeed, and were there not
For each its procreant atoms, could things have
Each its unalterable mother old?
But, since produced from fixed seeds are all,
Each birth goes forth upon the shores of light
From its own stuff, from its own primal bodies.
And all from all cannot become, because
In each resides a secret power its own.
Again, why see we lavished o'er the lands
At spring the rose, at summer heat the corn,
The vines that mellow when the autumn lures,
If not because the fixed seeds of things
At their own season must together stream,
And new creations only be revealed
When the due times arrive and pregnant earth
Safely may give unto the shores of light
Her tender progenies? But if from naught
Were their becoming, they would spring abroad
Suddenly, unforeseen, in alien months,

With no primordial germs, to be preserved
From procreant unions at an adverse hour.
Nor on the mingling of the living seeds
Would space be needed for the growth of things
Were life an increment of nothing: then
The tiny babe forthwith would walk a man,
And from the turf would leap a branching tree—
Wonders unheard of; for, by Nature, each
Slowly increases from its lawful seed,
And through that increase shall conserve its kind.
Whence take the proof that things enlarge and feed
From out their proper matter. Thus it comes
That earth, without her seasons of fixed rains,
Could bear no produce such as makes us glad,
And whatsoever lives, if shut from food,
Prolongs its kind and guards its life no more.
Thus easier 'tis to hold that many things
Have primal bodies in common (as we see
The single letters common to many words)
Than aught exists without its origins.
Moreover, why should Nature not prepare
Men of a bulk to ford the seas afoot,
Or rend the mighty mountains with their hands,
Or conquer Time with length of days, if not
Because for all begotten things abides
The changeless stuff, and what from that may spring
Is fixed forevermore? Lastly we see
How far the tilled surpass the fields untilled
And to the labour of our hands return
Their more abounding crops; there are indeed
Within the earth primordial germs of things,
Which, as the ploughshare turns the fruitful clods
And kneads the mould, we quicken into birth.
Else would ye mark, without all toil of ours,
Spontaneous generations, fairer forms.
Confess then, naught from nothing can become,
Since all must have their seeds, wherefrom to grow,
Wherefrom to reach the gentle fields of air.
Hence too it comes that Nature all dissolves
Into their primal bodies again, and naught
Perishes ever to annihilation.
For, were aught mortal in its every part,
Before our eyes it might be snatched away
Unto destruction; since no force were needed
To sunder its members and undo its bands.
Whereas, of truth, because all things exist,

With seed imperishable, Nature allows
Destruction nor collapse of aught, until
Some outward force may shatter by a blow,
Or inward craft, entering its hollow cells,
Dissolve it down. And more than this, if Time,
That wastes with eld the works along the world,
Destroy entire, consuming matter all,
Whence then may Venus back to light of life
Restore the generations kind by kind?
Or how, when thus restored, may daedal Earth
Foster and plenish with her ancient food,
Which, kind by kind, she offers unto each?
Whence may the water-springs, beneath the sea,
Or inland rivers, far and wide away,
Keep the unfathomable ocean full?
And out of what does Ether feed the stars?
For lapsed years and infinite age must else
Have eat all shapes of mortal stock away:
But be it the Long Ago contained those germs,
By which this sum of things recruited lives,
Those same infallibly can never die,
Nor nothing to nothing evermore return.
And, too, the selfsame power might end alike
All things, were they not still together held
By matter eternal, shackled through its parts,
Now more, now less. A touch might be enough
To cause destruction. For the slightest force
Would loose the weft of things wherein no part
Were of imperishable stock. But now
Because the fastenings of primordial parts
Are put together diversely and stuff
Is everlasting, things abide the same
Unhurt and sure, until some power comes on
Strong to destroy the warp and woof of each:
Nothing returns to naught; but all return
At their collapse to primal forms of stuff.
Lo, the rains perish which Ether-father throws
Down to the bosom of Earth-mother; but then
Upsprings the shining grain, and boughs are green
Amid the trees, and trees themselves wax big
And lade themselves with fruits; and hence in turn
The race of man and all the wild are fed;
Hence joyful cities thrive with boys and girls;
And leafy woodlands echo with new birds;
Hence cattle, fat and drowsy, lay their bulk
Along the joyous pastures whilst the drops
Of white ooze trickle from distended bags;
Hence the young scamper on their weakling joints
Along the tender herbs, fresh hearts afrisk
With warm new milk. Thus naught of what so seems
Perishes utterly, since Nature ever
Upbuilds one thing from other, suffering naught

To come to birth but through some other's death.

And now, since I have taught that things cannot
Be born from nothing, nor the same, when born,
To nothing be recalled, doubt not my words,
Because our eyes no primal germs perceive;
For mark those bodies which, though known to be
In this our world, are yet invisible:
The winds infuriate lash our face and frame,
Unseen, and swamp huge ships and rend the clouds,
Or, eddying wildly down, bestrew the plains
With mighty trees, or scour the mountain tops
With forest-crackling blasts. Thus on they rave
With uproar shrill and ominous moan. The winds,
'Tis clear, are sightless bodies sweeping through
The sea, the lands, the clouds along the sky,
Vexing and whirling and seizing all amain;
And forth they flow and pile destruction round,
Even as the water's soft and supple bulk
Becoming a river of abounding floods,
Which a wide downpour from the lofty hills
Swells with big showers, dashes headlong down
Fragments of woodland and whole branching trees;
Nor can the solid bridges bide the shock
As on the waters whelm: the turbulent stream,
Strong with a hundred rains, beats round the piers,
Crashes with havoc, and rolls beneath its waves
Down-toppled masonry and ponderous stone,
Hurling away whatever would oppose.
Even so must move the blasts of all the winds,
Which, when they spread, like to a mighty flood,
Hither or thither, drive things on before
And hurl to ground with still renewed assault,
Or sometimes in their circling vortex seize
And bear in cones of whirlwind down the world:
The winds are sightless bodies and naught else—
Since both in works and ways they rival well
The mighty rivers, the visible in form.
Then too we know the varied smells of things
Yet never to our nostrils see them come;
With eyes we view not burning heats, nor cold,
Nor are we wont men's voices to behold.
Yet these must be corporeal at the base,
Since thus they smite the senses: naught there is
Save body, having property of touch.
And raiment, hung by surf-beat shore, grows moist,
The same, spread out before the sun, will dry;
Yet no one saw how sank the moisture in,
Nor how by heat off-driven. Thus we know,
That moisture is dispersed about in bits
Too small for eyes to see. Another case:
A ring upon the finger thins away

Along the under side, with years and suns;
The drippings from the eaves will scoop the stone;
The hooked ploughshare, though of iron, wastes
Amid the fields insidiously. We view
The rock-paved highways worn by many feet;
And at the gates the brazen statues show
Their right hands leaner from the frequent touch
Of wayfarers innumerable who greet.
We see how wearing-down hath minished these,
But just what motes depart at any time,
The envious nature of vision bars our sight.
Lastly whatever days and nature add
Little by little, constraining things to grow
In due proportion, no gaze however keen
Of these our eyes hath watched and known. No more
Can we observe what's lost at any time,
When things wax old with eld and foul decay,
Or when salt seas eat under beetling crags.
Thus Nature ever by unseen bodies works. . . .

Book III

♦ Folly of the Fear of Death

Therefore death to us
Is nothing, nor concerns us in the least,
Since nature of mind is mortal evermore.
And just as in the ages gone before
We felt no touch of ill, when all sides round
To battle came the Carthaginian host,
And the times, shaken by tumultuous war,
Under the aery coasts of arching heaven
Shuddered and trembled, and all humankind
Doubted to which the empery should fall
By land and sea, thus when we are no more,
When comes that sundering of our body and soul
Through which we're fashioned to a single state,
Verily naught to us, us then no more,
Can come to pass, naught move our senses then—
No, not if earth confounded were with sea,
And sea with heaven. But if indeed do feel
The nature of mind and energy of soul,
After their severance from this body of ours,
Yet nothing 'tis to us who in the bonds
And wedlock of the soul and body live,
Through which we're fashioned to a single state.
And, even if time collected after death
The matter of our frames and set it all
Again in place as now, and if again
To us the light of life were given, O yet
That process too would not concern us aught,
When once the self-succession of our sense

Has been asunder broken. And now and here,
Little enough we're busied with the selves
We were aforetime, nor, concerning them,
Suffer a sore distress. For shouldst thou gaze
Backwards across all yesterdays of time
The immeasurable, thinking how manifold
The motions of matter are, then couldst thou well
Credit this too: often these very seeds
(From which we are to-day) of old were set
In the same order as they are to-day—
Yet this we can't to consciousness recall
Through the remembering mind. For there hath been
An interposed pause of life, and wide
Have all the motions wandered everywhere
From these our senses. For if woe and ail
Perchance are toward, then the man to whom
The bane can happen must himself be there
At that same time. But death precludeth this,
Forbidding life to him on whom might crowd
Such irk and care; and granted 'tis to know:
Nothing for us there is to dread in death,
No wretchedness for him who is no more,
The same estate as if ne'er born before,
When death immortal hath ta'en the mortal life.

Hence, where thou seest a man to grieve because
When dead he rots with body laid away,
Or perishes in flames or jaws of beasts,
Know well: he rings not true, and that beneath
Still works an unseen sting upon his heart,
However he deny that he believes
His shall be aught of feeling after death.
For he, I fancy, grants not what he says,
Nor what that presupposes, and he fails
To pluck himself with all his roots from life
And cast that self away, quite unawares
Feigning that some remainder's left behind.
For when in life one pictures to oneself
His body dead by beasts and vultures torn,
He pities his state, dividing not himself
Therefrom, removing not the self enough
From the body flung away, imagining
Himself that body, and projecting there
His own sense, as he stands beside it: hence
He grieves that he is mortal born, nor marks
That in true death there is no second self
Alive and able to sorrow for self destroyed,
Or stand lamenting that the self lies there
Mangled or burning. For if it an evil is
Dead to be jerked about by jaw and fang
Of the wild brutes, I see not why 'twere not
Bitter to lie on fires and roast in flames,

Or suffocate in honey, and, reclined
On the smooth oblong of an icy slab,
Grow stiff in cold, or sink with load of earth
Down-crushing from above.

"Thee now no more
The joyful house and best of wives shall welcome,
Nor little sons run up to snatch their kisses
And touch with silent happiness thy heart.
Thou shalt not speed in undertakings more,
Nor be the warder of thine own no more.
Poor wretch," they say, "one hostile hour hath ta'en
Wretchedly from thee all life's many guerdons,"
But add not, "yet no longer unto thee
Remains a remnant of desire for them"
If this they only well perceived with mind
And followed up with maxims, they would free
Their state of man from anguish and from fear.
"O even as here thou art, aslumber in death,
So shalt thou slumber down the rest of time,
Released from every harrying pang. But we,
We have bewept thee with insatiate woe,
Standing beside whilst on the awful pyre
Thou wert made ashes; and no day shall take
For us the eternal sorrow from the breast."
But ask the mourner what's the bitterness
That man should waste in an eternal grief,
If, after all, the thing's but sleep and rest?
For when the soul and frame together are sunk
In slumber, no one then demands his self
Or being. Well, this sleep may be forever,
Without desire of any selfhood more,
For all it matters unto us asleep.
Yet not at all do those primordial germs
Roam round our members, at that time, afar
From their own motions that produce our senses—
Since, when he's startled from his sleep, a man
Collects his senses. Death is, then, to us
Much less—if there can be a less than that
Which is itself a nothing: for there comes
Hard upon death a scattering more great
Of the throng of matter, and no man wakes up
On whom once falls the icy pause of life.

This too, O often from the soul men say,
Along their couches holding of the cups,
With faces shaded by fresh wreaths awry:
"Brief is this fruit of joy to paltry man,
Soon, soon departed, and thereafter, no,
It may not be recalled."—As if, forsooth,
It were their prime of evils in great death
To parch, poor tongues, with thirst and arid drought,

Or chafe for any lack.

Once more, if Nature
Should of a sudden send a voice abroad,
And her own self inveigh against us so:
"Mortal, what hast thou of such grave concern
That thou indulgest in too sickly plaints?
Why this bemoaning and beweeping death?
For if thy life aforetime and behind
To thee was grateful, and not all thy good
Was heaped as in sieve to flow away
And perish unavailingly, why not,
Even like a banqueter, depart the halls,
Laden with life? why not with mind content
Take now, thou fool, thy unafflicted rest?
But if whatever thou enjoyed hath been
Lavished and lost, and life is now offence,
Why seekest more to add—which in its turn
Will perish foully and fall out in vain?
O why not rather make an end of life,
Of labour? For all I may devise or find
To pleasure thee is nothing: all things are
The same forever. Though not yet thy body
Wrinkles with years, nor yet the frame exhausts
Outworn, still things abide the same, even if
Thou goest on to conquer all of time
With length of days, yea, if thou never diest"—
What were our answer, but that Nature here
Urges just suit and in her words lays down
True cause of action? Yet should one complain,
Riper in years and elder, and lament,
Poor devil, his death more sorely than is fit,
Then would she not, with greater right, on him
Cry out, inveighing with a voice more shrill:
"Off with thy tears, and choke thy whines, buffoon!
Thou wrinklest—after thou hast had the sum
Of the guerdons of life; yet, since thou cravest ever
What's not at hand, contemning present good,
That life has slipped away, unperfected
And unavailing unto thee. And now,
Or ere thou guessed it, death beside thy head
Stands—and before thou canst be going home
Sated and laden with the goodly feast.
But now yield all that's alien to thine age,—
Up, with good grace! make room for sons: thou must."
Justly, I fancy, would she reason thus,
Justly inveigh and gird: since ever the old
Outcrowded by the new gives way, and ever
The one thing from the others is repaired.
Nor no man is consigned to the abyss
Of Tartarus, the black. For stuff must be,
That thus the after-generations grow,—

Though these, their life completed, follow thee;
And thus like thee are generations all—
Already fallen, or some time to fall.
So one thing from another rises ever;
And in fee-simple life is given to none,
But unto all mere usufruct.

Look back:
Nothing to us was all fore-passed eld
Of time the eternal, ere we had a birth.
And Nature holds this like a mirror up
Of time-to-be when we are dead and gone.
And what is there so horrible appears?
Now what is there so sad about it all?
Is't not serener far than any sleep?

And, verily, those tortures said to be
In Acheron, the deep, they all are ours
Here in this life. No Tantalus, benumbed
With baseless terror, as the fables tell,
Fears the huge boulder hanging in the air:
But, rather, in life an empty dread of Gods
Urges mortality, and each one fears
Such fall of fortune as may chance to him.
Nor eat the vultures into Tityus
Prostrate in Acheron, nor can they find,
Forsooth, throughout eternal ages, aught
To pry around for in that mighty breast.
However hugely he extend his bulk—

Who hath for outspread limbs not acres nine,
But the whole earth—he shall not able be
To bear eternal pain nor furnish food
From his own frame forever. But for us
A Tityus is he whom vultures rend
Prostrate in love, whom anxious anguish eats,
Whom troubles of any unappeased desires
Asunder rip. We have before our eyes
Here in this life also a Sisyphus
In him who seeketh of the populace
The rods, the axes fell, and evermore
Retires a beaten and a gloomy man.
For to seek after power—an empty name,
Nor given at all—and ever in the search
To endure a world of toil, O this it is
To shove with shoulder up the hill a stone
Which yet comes rolling back from off the top,
And headlong makes for levels of the plain.
Then to be always feeding an ingrate mind,
Filling with good things, satisfying never—
As do the seasons of the year for us,
When they return and bring their progenies
And varied charms, and we are never filled
With the fruits of life—O this, I fancy, 'tis
To pour, like those young virgins in the tale,
Waters into a sieve, unfilled forever.

Tartarus, out-belching from his mouth the surge
Of horrible heat—the which are nowhere, nor

Glossary

Acheron	a river across which Charon was said to ferry the dead to the underworld
Ancus	Ancus Marcius, who lived in the seventh century BCE and was the fourth king of Rome
Carthaginian	the people of Carthage whom Rome fought in the three Punic Wars from 264 to 146 BCE
daedal	intricate, adorned
Democritus	the "laughing philosopher," who lived from about 460 to about 370 BCE and was influential in the development of the atomistic philosophy
divers	diverse, assorted
eld	time, old age
Ether	the upper regions of space; heaven
Heliconian dames	the Muses, a source of inspiration for Homer, who were thought to reside on Mount Helicon in Greece
minished	diminished
Scipio	Publius Cornelius Scipio Africanus, a prominent Roman general who defeated Hannibal in the Second Punic War

Indeed can be: but in this life is fear
Of retributions just and expiations
For evil acts: the dungeon and the leap
From that dread rock of infamy, the stripes,
The executioners, the oaken rack,
The iron plates, bitumen, and the torch.
And even though these are absent, yet the mind,
With a fore-fearing conscience, plies its goads
And burns beneath the lash, nor sees meanwhile
What terminus of ills, what end of pine
Can ever be, and feareth lest the same
But grow more heavy after death. Of truth,
The life of fools is Acheron on earth.

This also to thy very self sometimes
Repeat thou mayst: "Lo, even good Ancus left
The sunshine with his eyes, in divers things
A better man than thou, O worthless hind;
And many other kings and lords of rule
Thereafter have gone under, once who swayed
O'er mighty peoples. And he also, he—
Who whilom paved a highway down the sea,
And gave his legionaries thoroughfare
Along the deep, and taught them how to cross
The pools of brine afoot, and did contemn,
Trampling upon it with his cavalry,
The bellowings of ocean—poured his soul
From dying body, as his light was ta'en.
And Scipio's son, the thunderbolt of war,

Horror of Carthage, gave his bones to earth,
Like to the lowliest villein in the house.
Add finders-out of sciences and arts;
Add comrades of the Heliconian dames,
Among whom Homer, sceptered o'er them all,
Now lies in slumber sunken with the rest.
Then, too, Democritus, when ripened eld
Admonished him his memory waned away,
Of own accord offered his head to death.
Even Epicurus went, his light of life
Run out, the man in genius who o'er-topped
The human race, extinguishing all others,
As sun, in ether arisen, all the stars.
Wilt thou, then, dally, thou complain to go?—
For whom already life's as good as dead,
Whilst yet thou livest and lookest?—who in sleep
Wastest thy life—time's major part, and snorest
Even when awake, and ceasest not to see
The stuff of dreams, and bearest a mind beset
By baseless terror, nor discoverest oft
What's wrong with thee, when, like a sotted wretch,
Thou'rt jostled along by many crowding cares,
And wanderest reeling round, with mind aswim."

If men, in that same way as on the mind
They feel the load that wearies with its weight,
Could also know the causes whence it comes,
And why so great the heap of ill on heart,
O not in this sort would they live their life,

Glossary

Sisyphus	a mythological figure who was condemned eternally to push a boulder up a hill only to see it roll back down as he reached the top
sotted	besotted, drunk
Tantalus	a figure in Greek mythology who was condemned to stand in water beneath the branches of a fruit tree; whenever he reached for a piece of fruit, the branches of the tree would rise out of his reach, and whenever he stooped to drink, the water would recede
Tartarus	the underworld of classical mythology
tilth	the act or occupation of tilling the soil
Tityus	a mythological figure condemned to eternal punishment by being stretched out and having vultures feed on his liver
usufruct	a legal term referring to ownership of property only during the holder's lifetime
Venus	the Roman goddess of love and beauty
villein	peasant

As now so much we see them, knowing not
What 'tis they want, and seeking ever and ever
A change of place, as if to drop the burden.
The man who sickens of his home goes out,
Forth from his splendid halls, and straight—returns,
Feeling i'faith no better off abroad.
He races, driving his Gallic ponies along,
Down to his villa, madly,—as in haste
To hurry help to a house afire.—At once
He yawns, as soon as foot has touched the threshold,
Or drowsily goes off in sleep and seeks
Forgetfulness, or maybe bustles about
And makes for town again. In such a way
Each human flees himself—a self in sooth,
As happens, he by no means can escape;
And willy-nilly he cleaves to it and loathes,
Sick, sick, and guessing not the cause of ail.
Yet should he see but that, O chiefly then,
Leaving all else, he'd study to divine
The nature of things, since here is in debate
Eternal time and not the single hour,
Mortal's estate in whatsoever remains
After great death.

And too, when all is said,
What evil lust of life is this so great

Subdues us to live, so dreadfully distraught
In perils and alarms? one fixed end
Of life abideth for mortality;
Death's not to shun, and we must go to meet.
Besides we're busied with the same devices,
Ever and ever, and we are at them ever,
And there's no new delight that may be forged
By living on. But whilst the thing we long for
Is lacking, that seems good above all else;
Thereafter, when we've touched it, something else
We long for; ever one equal thirst of life
Grips us agape. And doubtful 'tis what fortune
The future times may carry, or what be
That chance may bring, or what the issue next
Awaiting us. Nor by prolonging life
Take we the least away from death's own time,
Nor can we pluck one moment off, whereby
To minish the aeons of our state of death.
Therefore, O man, by living on, fulfil
As many generations as thou may:
Eternal death shall there be waiting still;
And he who died with light of yesterday
Shall be no briefer time in death's No-more
Than he who perished months or years before.

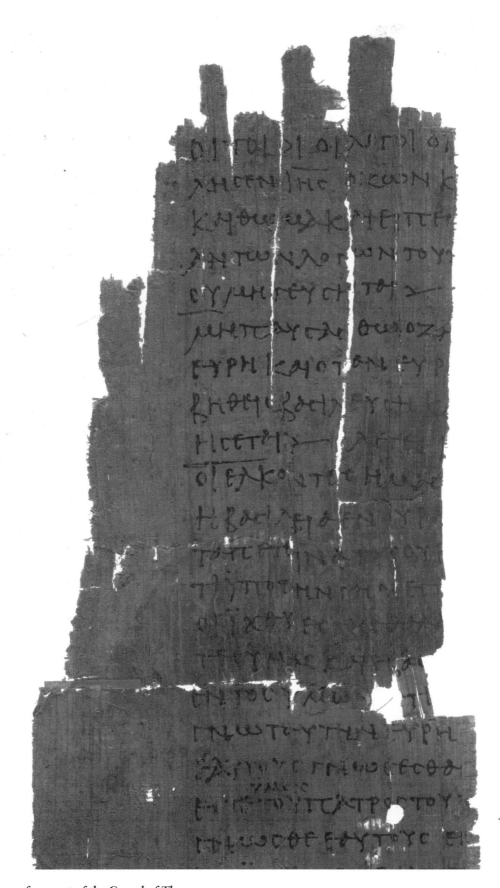

Papyrus fragment of the Gospel of Thomas

(Papyrus 1531, Sayings of Jesus, from the Gospel of Thomas [ink on papyrus], Egyptian School, [3rd Century AD] / British Library, London, UK / The Bridgeman Art Library International)

GOSPEL OF THOMAS

"When you know yourselves, then you will be known, and you will understand that you are children of the living Father."

Overview

The Gospel of Thomas is a collection of 114 logia (utterances) that are alleged to be from the "living" or "life-giving" Jesus. Many of the sayings, or parables, begin with the words, "Jesus said" or "He said," while others are brief conversations between Jesus and his disciples initiated by questions or situations. The document was lost in antiquity until the discovery of a cache of codices (bound books, as opposed to scrolls) in the Egyptian desert near the modern-day town of Nag Hammadi in 1945. The story of the discovery of what has come to be titled the Nag Hammadi Library and its impact upon early Christian studies is both exciting and profound. The collection, written in Coptic, a late Egyptian language, includes thirteen codices in varying conditions, in which forty-six individual writings (tractates) are found. Some of these documents were entirely unknown or known only by title, and they include several gospels, creation mythologies, tracts related to various apostolic figures, commentaries on metaphysical thought, and a few Hermetic writings along with a portion of Plato's *Republic*. The Gospel of Thomas is in Nag Hammadi Codex II and is among the best-known, most celebrated, and most studied tractates of the collection.

Until the end of the nineteenth century, the Gospel of Thomas was known primarily by title from a few ancient sources, particularly the writings of early church fathers, who considered the document theologically suspect (Hippolytus, Origen, and Eusebius). Three papyrus fragments of the gospel were discovered by excavators in the late 1800s at the village of Oxyrhynchus in Egypt. It was not until the discovery of 1945 that the relationship of these fragments to the Gospel of Thomas was confirmed and the complete text became available for study. The full gospel was first published in English in 1959. Since that time analysis has continued unabated, and theories of the document's origin and interpretation have multiplied.

While there is a great deal of scholarly debate regarding the authorship, context, nature, and meaning of Thomas, there are several areas of agreement: The gospel was not written by Thomas, the disciple of Jesus who inspired the title and plays a key role in the text; it was most likely written or edited in Syria, more specifically the northeastern Syrian city of Edessa (now Urfa, Turkey), and it is clearly different from the four canonical Gospels (Matthew, Mark, Luke, and John) in that it lacks a narrative context, its order of sayings seems rather haphazard, and its perspective is more mystical (pertaining to individual enlightenment) and ascetic (involving self-denial).

Context

One of the most disputed issues regarding the Gospel of Thomas is its historical context. While most scholars are willing to identify the document with northeastern Syria because of content and linguistic factors, the timing of this association is deeply debated. Crucial to these matters are the relationship of Thomas to the canonical Gospels, the growth and popularity of a unique type of Christianity in Syria, the thematic content of Thomas, and its relationship with Hermetic and Gnostic traditions.

Over half of the sayings of Thomas have close parallels with the canonical Gospels. Some of them are nearly identical to the New Testament sayings or parables, while others take strange twists or have additional or fewer phrases. The question of the dependence or independence of Thomas in relation to the canonical Gospels is highly debated and difficult to determine. Some scholars argue for numerous types of Christianity stemming from Jesus's first disciples, who understood Jesus and his mission in different ways. Others see diverse types of Christianity developing in later periods as the Christian church sought to determine its relationship with Judaism and encountered the Greek and pagan culture in the Mediterranean world.

A special type of Christianity developed in northeastern Syria and Mesopotamia in the early Christian centuries. This branch of the Christian faith was called Thomasine Christianity, since it claimed to derive from one of Jesus's original disciples, "Judas Thomas." Thomas is alleged to have ministered in the region after Jesus's death and Resurrection and before he departed for the East, where he became associated with India. Unique to Thomasine Christianity was its emphasis upon wisdom, self-knowledge for

Time Line

CA. 30–33	■ Jesus dies by crucifixion in Judea.
CA. 50	■ Numerous scholars date the earliest portions of the Gospel of Thomas to this time.
CA. 55–75	■ The Gospel of Mark is composed, perhaps in Rome.
CA. 60–80	■ The Gospels of Matthew and Luke are composed.
CA. 70–80	■ Some scholars date the completion of Thomas to this early time period.
CA. 85–110	■ The Gospel of John is composed.
CA. 120–140	■ Most scholars date the completion of Thomas to this period.
CA. 172–173	■ Tatian's harmony of the Gospels, the *Diatessaron*, is composed in Syriac; some scholars date Thomas as later than this time, alleging its dependence upon the *Diatessaron*.
CA. 200	■ Scholars date the first Greek fragment of the Gospel of Thomas, discovered at Oxyrhynchus, to this time period.
CA. 200–225	■ Scholars date the *Book of Thomas the Contender* to this time period.
200	■ Hippolytus mentions the Gospel of Thomas in his *Refutation of All Heresies*.
CA. 225	■ Scholars date the *Acts of Thomas* to around this time.
CA. 225–250	■ The second Oxyrhynchus fragment is thought to have been composed.
233	■ Origen mentions the Gospel of Thomas in his *Homilies in Luke*.

salvation, and asceticism or encratism (that is, teachings against marriage, eating meat, drinking wine, and so on).

Several documents related to Thomasine Christianity are significant for this analysis. The *Book of Thomas the Contender,* also discovered at Nag Hammadi and dependent upon the Gospel of Thomas, teaches against sexual intercourse and exhorts the faithful to abstain from lust and other passions. Those who give in to their passions will experience fiery judgment, while those who abstain will inherit life. The *Acts of Thomas* tells the story of Judas Thomas's ministry of preaching and performing miracles in India, where he ultimately becomes a martyr. As Jesus's twin brother and an apostle, he is the recipient of special revelation. The exact relationship between these documents is unclear, but they represent traditions that were prominent in Syrian Christianity in the late second and third centuries.

Whether Thomas was composed in different layers over an extended period of time or was the product of a single author/editor, the complete gospel bears the marks of several influential traditions that were prominent in northeastern Syria from the second century onward. Hermeticism, which had its origins in Egypt and is based upon myths related to Hermes Trismegistus as a revealer of god's wisdom and salvation, became popular in other regions of the Mediterranean world, including Syria, in the second through fourth centuries CE. (Hermes Trismegistus, who combined aspects of a Greek and an Egyptian god, was also considered by some Jewish and Christian writers to have been an ancient pagan prophet.) Several scholars have emphasized thematic parallels between Hermeticism and Thomas, and Hermetic documents were included among the Nag Hammadi codices. Much more debated is Thomas's relationship with Gnosticism, a religion with Platonic, Jewish, and Christian themes that flourished from the second century through the fifth or sixth century. Thomas lacks numerous Gnostic features, such as a creation myth, a fallen Sophia (divine wisdom figure), and the image of an ignorant demiurge (a fallen creator figure). However, it does emphasize Gnostic themes of salvation through knowledge (or gnosis) and a theory of origins to which one is destined to return if salvation is achieved. Further, the discovery of Thomas in a chiefly Gnostic collection may be significant. In the third and fourth centuries, Thomas was a favorite gospel among Manichaeans, a Gnostic group whose founder had family ties with a Jewish-Christian ascetic movement in Syria. Both Hermeticism and Gnosticism were prominent in second-century Syria, but evidence is lacking for their presence in this region in the first century.

There are several features of the Gospel of Thomas that may betray contextual concerns. The first is the idea of "secret" sayings, which may imply not just "hidden" wisdom but also sayings separate from those known in the public or traditional Gospels. References to early disciples of Jesus in the gospel itself may reveal conflicting traditions as early followers of Jesus were seeking to determine, negotiate, and establish the nature of the new faith in the ancient world. In this regard, the identification of other disciples may not have been incidental or historical but rather polemical in purpose.

Since the Gospel of Thomas is mentioned by early church fathers as early as 220, this would pose the latest possible date of composition. The earliest Greek fragment discovered at Oxyrhynchus was dated to the end of the second century; thus, the gospel precedes the date of 200 CE. If its final composition took place in Syria, as most agree, and possibly in the Syriac language, as some propose, then enough time must be allowed for the gospel to be translated into Greek and transported to Egypt. These factors adjust the latest possible date to the last quarter of the second century. Scholars are deeply divided on its earliest possible date of composition, especially if the gospel was written in layers, with some sayings actually spoken by Jesus himself. If the latter is allowed, the earliest possible date would be 30–33 CE, at least for its oral core. Thus, we have a range of possible dates for composition of over a century and a half.

About the Author

Church tradition asserts that the apostle Thomas traveled to Syria, Mesopotamia, and India to spread Jesus's teachings. While the attribution of this gospel to Thomas, the disciple of Jesus, is almost certainly false, the affiliation is not without significance. The prologue is more specific, identifying the recipient of Jesus's secret teachings as "Didymos Judas Thomas." The names Didymos and Thomas both mean "twin," in Greek and Aramaic, respectively, and were also used of one of Jesus's disciples in John 11:16. Some understand the word *twin* to imply that Thomas was Jesus's biological brother, while others suggest imitation. The association of the name "Judas" with Thomas is unparalleled in the New Testament, but the names are linked in the Old Syriac translation of John 14:22; in the early Christian theologian Tatian's harmony of the Gospels, called the *Diatessaron* (ca. 172–173 CE); as well as in several other documents of Syrian provenance. The names for "twin" have special significance in the gospel, as the disciple Thomas is represented to be the one follower most attuned to Jesus in his understanding and imitation of the Master. In fact, Thomas's insight into the indescribable identity of Jesus in Logion 13 earned him Jesus's praise and the comment "I am not your teacher" and entitled him to secret revelations. This situation placed Thomas in a more intimate connection to Jesus than Matthew or Simon Peter, the two disciples who offered more conventional images of Jesus (as "prophet" or "messenger") in the passage. This dissonance may represent competing strains of Christianity in contrast to that represented by Thomas.

Many scholars argue for multiple layers or additions to Thomas over an extended period of time, so many individuals or communities may have contributed to the final content of the document. A final editor, also unknown, compiled the present form of the Gospel of Thomas and very likely added the prologue and title at the end.

Time Line

CA. 250	■ The third Oxyrhynchus fragment is thought to have been composed.
325	■ Eusebius mentions *Thomas* in his *Ecclesiastical History*.
CA. 367	■ Around this year or later, the Nag Hammadi codices are buried in Upper Egypt, near a Pachomian monastery.
1945	■ **December** The Nag Hammadi codices, including Thomas, are discovered in Upper Egypt.
1959	■ The first English translation of Thomas appears.

Explanation and Analysis of the Document

Thomas's character as a sayings source without narrative continuity or obvious logical groupings makes systematic analysis nearly impossible. This factor is consistent with other wisdom writings, such as the biblical book of Proverbs. There is no obvious order to the gospel, and most scholars in the end resort to thematic analysis and topical arrangements. Adding to the complexity of these factors is the deeply debated issue of Thomas's interpretation. Many of the debates evidence a polarization between conservative and more liberal Christian or secular scholars, whose presuppositions and methods yield diverse conclusions. Most important and controversial is the relationship of Thomas to the four canonical Gospels of Matthew, Mark, Luke, and John. Is Thomas dependent upon, foundational to, or independent of the synoptic Gospels (Matthew, Mark, and Luke)? Was the Gospel of John written to refute the ideas represented in Thomas, or does Thomas draw from themes found in John? While these questions are not resolved in the following analysis, they take center stage in the scholarly literature on the subject.

Brackets found in the document text variously indicate an element implied by the original language and supplied by the translators or words that have been restored from a gap in the text or emended from a scribal error. Bracketed ellipses indicate a gap in the manuscript that cannot be satisfactorily restored. Parentheses are used in the usual sense, to indicate parenthetical remarks and narrative asides in the original text.

The apostle Thomas

(The Apostle St. Thomas, c.1619-20 [oil on canvas], Velazquez, Diego
Rodriguez de Silva y [1599-1660] / Musee des Beaux-Arts, Orleans, France
/ The Bridgeman Art Library International)

Introduction

The prologue and first logion provide an introduction for
Thomas as a wisdom book related to salvation. Those who
discover the proper interpretation of Jesus's secret teachings "will not taste death." These "secret" or hidden sayings
were delivered to Didymos Judas Thomas by the "living"
or life-giving Jesus. Since the death and Resurrection of
Jesus are not themes of Thomas, it is unlikely that this is a
reference to the resurrected Jesus. Some early Christians,
called Docetists by modern scholars, taught that Jesus did
not have a real body and thus he could not have died. Some
Gnostic groups embraced this thought as well, concentrating on Jesus's primary role as revealer of truth. Thus, the
epithet here is more likely a reference to Jesus's life-giving
power as a revealer of wisdom and truth. The lack of elevated titles for Jesus—such as "Son of God," "Son of Man," or
"Christ"—in the Gospel of Thomas should be noted, especially in comparison with the canonical Gospels.

♦ Parallels with the Synoptic Gospels

One does not read far in Thomas without discovering that
this gospel has a definite relationship with the four canonical
Gospels of the New Testament (for example, the theme of
seeking and finding in logion 2 can be compared to Matthew
7:7–8). Such themes as the Kingdom of God, discussions on

religious practices, expressions like "anyone here with two
good ears had better listen" (logia 8 and 21; Mark 4:9), and
teaching through parables and sayings sound quite familiar,
yet there is frequently a touch of unfamiliarity in the ultimate teaching in Thomas. How and when these variations
developed is hotly debated. Thomas also includes a number
of characters who were involved in the life of Jesus, including John the Baptist, his family, Thomas, his brother James,
Peter, Matthew, Mary Magdalene, and the disciple Salome.
The most glaring difference is the lack of a storyline or narrative context for Thomas's sayings.

♦ The Kingdom of God

The "Father's imperial rule" or "domain" (where pointed brackets indicate words supplied by the translators) is
parallel to the canonical Gospels' theme of "Kingdom,"
though in Thomas the theme is an individual and present
experience rather than a future or eschatological one (that
is, relating to the end of the world). Those who find the
Kingdom discover it within themselves and through acquiring special knowledge or insight (logia 3, 46, and 113).
At times, Thomas describes the Kingdom in somewhat
ambiguous terms, such as being "inside you and outside
you" (3) and as the place from which you have "come" and
to which you will "return" (49). As in the canonical Gospels, many truths about the Kingdom are taught through
parables. Several parables closely parallel those of the canonical Gospels, such as the parables of the mustard seed
(20), the wheat and the weeds/tares (57), the pearl (76), the
lost sheep (107), and the hidden treasure (109). Thomas
includes several parables of the Kingdom not previously
known (logia 21, of the little children and the field; 97, of
the woman and the jar of meal; and 98, of the man and the
sword). In all, the Kingdom theme is prominent in eighteen
of the 114 logia.

♦ Knowing Self as Salvation

While the canonical Gospels emphasize faith or belief
for salvation (as in John 1:12), Thomas emphasizes knowledge of oneself. When you "know yourselves," you will possess salvation and the Kingdom and will rule over all (logia
3, 50, 67, 111), the gospel tells us. On the other hand, if
you lack this knowledge, you will dwell in "poverty" and "are
the poverty" (logia 3 and 29; compare 28 and 67). These
were important themes in Thomasine Christianity as well
as Gnosticism.

There are other concepts related to salvation in Thomas,
including becoming like children (logia 4, 21, 22, 37, 46, and
106), returning to one's place of origin (logia 18, 49, 50, and
84), achieving rest (logia 50, 51, 60, and 90), bringing forth
what is within oneself (logion 70), and imitation (logion 108).

♦ Asceticism

As mentioned, Thomasine Christianity in Syria emphasized asceticism (self-denial). Expressions such as "single"
(logia 4, 22, and 23), "stand alone" (logia 16 and 75), and
"solitary" (logia 49) are likely indications of a state of personal fullness or completeness and may refer to singleness

"If your leaders say to you, 'Look, the imperial rule is in the sky,' then the birds of the sky will precede you. If they say to you, 'It is in the sea,' then the fish will precede you. Rather, the imperial rule is inside you and outside you. When you know yourselves, then you will be known, and you will understand that you are children of the living Father. But if you do not know yourselves, then you . . . are the poverty."

"His disciples said, 'When will you appear to us, and when will we see you?' Jesus said, 'When you strip without being ashamed, and you take your clothes and put them under your feet like little children and trample them, then [you] will see the son of the living one and you will not be afraid.'"

"Jesus said, 'Be passersby.'"

"Jesus said, 'Congratulations to those who are alone and chosen, for you will find the [Father's] domain. For you have come from it, and you will return there again.'"

"His disciples said to him, 'When will the rest for the dead take place, and when will the new world come?' He said to them, 'What you are looking forward to has come, but you don't know it.'"

"Jesus said, 'If you bring forth what is within you, what you have will save you. If you do not have that within you, what you do not have within you [will] kill you.'"

"Simon Peter said to them, 'Make Mary leave us, for females don't deserve life.' Jesus said, 'Look, I will guide her to make her male, so that she too may become a living spirit resembling you males. For every female who makes herself male will enter the domain of Heaven.'"

or celibacy. This concept may be related to the idea of the union of male and female in one person, also called androgyny, which was believed to be the original state of Adam, primordial man, before the creation of the female out of him (according to Genesis 1–2). Returning to this state is the aspiration of those who would achieve salvation and God's Kingdom (logia 22, 106, and possibly 114). In contrast, "became two" in logion 11 and "divided" in logion 61

may refer to Adam's departure from his androgynous original state (logion 85) and the origin of evil.

The physical body is described as a "poverty" within which the "wealth" of the spirit dwells (logia 29, 87, and 112). This theme has parallels with Platonic and Gnostic thought. Thomas's concept of "disrobing" (logia 21 and 37) may be a reference to putting off the flesh in asceticism or at death when salvation is achieved. The rejection of the body and the world are also prominent in logia 21, 27, 42, 56, 60, 70, 80, 110, and 111. Logion 42, "Be passersby," is the shortest of the 114 sayings and may suggest a transient attitude toward the physical life. The forsaking of family relations (logia 55, 79, 99, and 101) and the comforts of clothing (logia 36 and 78) and food (logion 69) are also ascetic themes.

◆ Disapproved and Approved Rituals

In the Gospel of Thomas, Jesus appears to have a critical attitude toward traditional religious practices (fasting, prayer, charity or giving to the poor, special diets, and so on), especially if they were observed legalistically (logia 6, 14, and 104). Jewish practices of Sabbath-keeping and circumcision are also rejected and given a deeper, more spiritual interpretation (logia 27 and 53). The references to observing the "sabbath day as a sabbath day" and to "true circumcision in spirit" suggest that the Jewish rituals were considered inadequate.

On the other hand, Thomas introduces a new ritual called the "bridal suite" or "bridal chamber" (logia 75 and 104). While this is clearly not a reference to marriage, the bridal suite is portrayed as a place where celibate individuals enter into spiritual union with Christ or their spiritual doubles. The former of these options is the most likely interpretation, as the *Acts of Thomas* makes explicit. The latter interpretation is more consistent with Gnostic thought and is prominent in the Gospel of Philip, which was discovered in the same Nag Hammadi codex as Thomas.

◆ Thomas's Privileged Position

Logia 12 and 13 are among the most important in Thomas, as they provide references to three other prominent disciples of Jesus. James the Just, by tradition a brother of Jesus and the leader of the Jerusalem church, is viewed in a positive light, while Simon Peter and Matthew provide inadequate answers to Jesus's query regarding his identity, calling him a "just angel" and a "wise philosopher," respectively. This is in sharp contrast to the synoptic Gospels' accounts, which do not identify those who offer the answers "John the Baptist," "Elijah," and "one of the prophets" and which present Peter as the one who proclaims the rewarded response, "You are the Messiah, the Son of the living God" (Matthew 16:13–16, Mark 8:27–29, and Luke 9:18–20). Some allege that James is viewed positively in light of his traditional asceticism, while Simon Peter and Matthew may be viewed negatively because of their identification with the canonical traditions of Mark and Matthew, respectively, and their representation of "proto-orthodox" Christianity. (Proto-orthodoxy is the early Christian tradition that would be defined as orthodoxy near the end of the third century). Thomas is obviously elevated above the others as a privileged recipient of hidden revelation and a source of insight and wisdom. Conflict between Thomas and the other disciples may be suggested in logion 13. These passages give insight into the varieties of perspectives in early Christianity.

◆ Anti-Judaism

As Christianity was seeking to determine its own identity in its early history, it often positioned itself over and against Judaism, many times in a critical manner. While this should not be understood as anti-Semitism (that is, as opposition to the Jewish people), it does demonstrate religious conflict. This is evident in Thomas. Beyond the criticism of Jewish rituals, logion 39 charges that the Pharisees and scholars have taken away the keys of knowledge and hidden them, thus denying salvation to others (compare with logia 43 and 102). Similarly, in logion 43, Jesus compares his disciples' lack of understanding with the Judeans'. In logion 52, Jesus appears to diminish the significance of the Jewish prophets and asserts his own primacy. While proto-orthodox Christianity stressed that the Jewish prophets spoke regarding Christ, some groups, particularly the Gnostics, identified the Jewish prophets with the evil creator or demiurge.

◆ Mary's Position in the Community

Logion 114 provides an interesting exchange regarding the position of Mary—understood to be Mary Magdalene—and women in the community of faith. While Peter advocates for Mary's removal, since she is a woman, Jesus defends her place among his disciples. Jesus pledges to guide her in her quest for salvation by helping her become male. While this saying is believed by some to be a later addition to Thomas, the theme of androgyny also appears in logion 22. A similar type of exchange occurs in the Gospel of Mary, a text also found at Nag Hammadi. The positive valuation of maleness and negative valuation of femaleness is found in Plato's writings and was popularized by the first-century Jewish philosopher Philo of Alexandria.

Audience

While the issue of Thomas's audience is deeply connected to the complicated history of the document, several factors can safely be assumed. First, the northeastern Syrian provenance suggests that its final composition was specifically for a community of Christians who would have been encouraged and enlightened by its themes and concerns. Matters of asceticism and knowledge of self as significant for salvation would have been of paramount importance. Further, the fact that Thomas was translated into Greek no later than the end of the second century (if, indeed, it was originally composed in Syriac) and into Coptic no later than the fourth century argues for the appeal of this document to regions beyond Edessa.

One of the thorniest debates in Thomas studies has been its affiliation with Gnosticism, a religion closely related to Judaism and Christianity that began to flourish in the second century CE. Scholars are deeply divided on the nature and definition of Gnosticism and even its real existence as a religious category. If Thomas is indeed Gnostic or semi-Gnostic in character, it may have been compiled for the benefit of a readership akin to that of other apocryphal gospels, including the Gospel of Philip (also found at

Nag Hammadi) and the more recently discovered Gospel of Judas. Renewed interest in Gnostic themes, particularly self-knowledge as salvation, since the late twentieth century has made Thomas a popular source of inspiration to contemporary readers.

Impact

The impact and significance of Thomas in the ancient world is shrouded in the mystery of history's silence; however, such is not the case for the modern period. Ever since its discovery and publication, Thomas has been the source of intense scholarly scrutiny, yielding a vast body of academic and some popular literature. All this has resulted in numerous challenges to traditional understandings of Jesus and Christian origins, sometimes of a sensational nature. This is evident by some scholars giving Thomas the title "The Fifth Gospel" and including it among other apocryphal gospels in works such as *The Complete Gospels, Lost Scriptures,* and even *Lost Christianities.* Some of the questions include these: Is Thomas a more faithful representation of the historical Jesus than the canonical Gospels? Does Thomas represent an earlier, a later, or a parallel Christian community compared with what has traditionally been identified as "orthodox" or "proto-orthodox" Christianity? Were the traditional Gospels composed from literary sources much like Thomas and the sayings of Jesus then given a narrative context by later writers or editors, or is

Thomas a collection of sayings that were remembered or created to serve a community that was forming in an era decades removed from the historical Jesus and in juxtaposition to other forms of Christianity? More dramatically, was Thomas one of many documents suppressed by the "proto-orthodox" Christian church in its attempt to gain supremacy over the early Christian movement, as portrayed, for example, in Dan Brown's popular novel *The Da Vinci Code*?

These questions have generated a plethora of possible answers. At minimum, it is clear that the discovery of Thomas has challenged the old consensus that the New Testament and orthodox Christianity represent the earliest form of the Christian faith and all other forms departed from orthodoxy at a later point in time. Numerous reconstructions of earliest Christianity have been devised by scholars seeking to understand the complexity of its religious origins, including issues of Jesus's nature, teachings, and role as the founder of Christianity. While these questions and potential answers have certainly not overthrown traditional understandings of Jesus and Christianity, they have required a broader picture of early Christian diversity during an age when teachers, texts, and traditions struggled to interpret and preserve the impact of Jesus of Nazareth. One need only peruse the shelves of bookstores or examine religion course offerings at various colleges or universities to see that Christian origins and the historical Jesus are critical issues of modern research. The discovery of the Nag Hammadi documents and most particularly Thomas are central features of this discussion.

Questions for Further Study

1. How does the Gospel of Thomas differ from the four canonical gospels of the New Testament by Matthew, Mark, Luke, and John? Why do you think the work is not regarded as canonical? In general, on what basis are "biblical" books accepted into the canon or rejected? (See, for example, the entry on the Book of Enoch.)

2. What is Thomasine Christianity, and how did it differ from other forms of Christianity? What factors do you think might have influenced the development of varying strands of Christianity in the early decades and centuries of the Common Era?

3. The Gospel of Thomas is described as embodying mystical beliefs. Why do you think mysticism, as embodied in the Gospel of Thomas, Gnosticism, and Judaism (see the entry on the Sefer Yetzirah), was commonplace in that part of the world during that time period?

4. What was the relationship between Judaism and Christianity as the author(s) of the Gospel of Thomas understood Christianity? Explain.

5. Why did the Gospel of Thomas prompt historians of religion to reexamine the development of so-called orthodox Christianity? Why was the gospel's discovery a kind of bombshell?

Further Reading

■ Books

Bock, Darrell L. *The Missing Gospels: Unearthing the Truth behind Alternative Christianities.* Nashville, Tenn.: Nelson Books, 2006.

De Conick, April D. *The Original Gospel of Thomas in Translation: With a Commentary and New English Translation of the Complete Gospel.* New York: T&T Clark, 2006.

Ehrman, Bart D. *Lost Christianities: The Battles for Scripture and the Faiths We Never Knew.* New York: Oxford University Press, 2003.

Ehrman, Bart D. *Lost Scriptures: Books That Did Not Make It into the New Testament.* New York: Oxford University Press, 2003.

Jenkins, Philip. *Hidden Gospels: How the Search for Jesus Lost Its Way.* New York: Oxford University Press, 2001.

Koester, Helmut. "II.2, The Gospel According to Thomas: Introduction." In *The Coptic Gnostic Library: A Complete Edition of the Nag Hammadi Codices,* ed. James M. Robinson, vol. 2. Leiden, Netherlands, and Boston: Brill, 2000.

Meyer, Marvin. *The Gnostic Discoveries: The Impact of the Nag Hammadi Library.* San Francisco: HarperSanFrancisco, 2005.

Miller, Robert J., ed. *The Complete Gospels.* Sonoma, Calif.: Polebridge, 1994.

Pagels, Elaine. *Beyond Belief: The Secret Gospel of Thomas.* New York: Random House, 2003.

Pearson, Birger A. "*Gospel of Thomas,* NHC II,2." In his *Ancient Gnosticism: Traditions and Literature.* Minneapolis: Fortress, 2007.

Perrin, Nicholas. *Thomas, the Other Gospel.* Louisville, Ky.: Westminster John Knox, 2007.

Robinson, James A., ed. *The Nag Hammadi Library in English.* 4th ed. Leiden, Netherlands: Brill 1996.

Smith, Carl B. *No Longer Jews: The Search for Gnostic Origins.* Peabody, Mass.: Hendrickson, 2004.

Uro, Risto. *Thomas: Seeking the Historical Context of the* Gospel of Thomas. New York: T&T Clark, 2003.

Williams, Michael A. *Rethinking "Gnosticism": An Argument for Dismantling a Dubious Category.* Princeton, N.J.: Princeton University Press, 1996.

Yamauchi, Edwin. *Pre-Christian Gnosticism: A Survey of the Proposed Evidences.* Grand Rapids, Mich.: Baker, 1983.

■ Journals

Schenke, Hans-Martin. "On the Compositional History of the Gospel of Thomas." *Occasional Papers of the Institute for Antiquity and Christianity* 40 (1998): 1–28.

Snodgrass, Klyne R. "The Gospel of Thomas: A Secondary Gospel." *Second Century* 7, no. 1 (1989): 19–38.

■ Web Sites

"The Gospel of Thomas." Early Christian Writings Web site.
    http://www.earlychristianwritings.com/thomas.html

"Gospel of Thomas." NT Gateway Web site.
    http://www.ntgateway.com/noncanonical-texts/gospel-of-thomas/

"The Gospel of Thomas Collection." The Gnostic Society Library Web site.
    http://www.gnosis.org/naghamm/nhl_thomas.htm

The Gospel of Thomas Homepage.
    http://home.epix.net/~miser17/Thomas.html

—Carl B. Smith II

GOSPEL OF THOMAS

Prologue: These are the secret sayings that the living Jesus spoke and Didymos Judas Thomas recorded.

1 And he said, "Whoever discovers the interpretation of these sayings will not taste death."

2 Jesus said, "Those who seek should not stop seeking until they find. When they find, they will be disturbed. When they are disturbed, they will marvel, and will rule over all."

3 Jesus said, "If your leaders say to you, 'Look, the imperial rule is in the sky,' then the birds of the sky will precede you. If they say to you, 'It is in the sea,' then the fish will precede you. Rather, the imperial rule is inside you and outside you. When you know yourselves, then you will be known, and you will understand that you are children of the living Father. But if you do not know yourselves, then you live in poverty, and you are the poverty."

4 Jesus said, "The person old in days won't hesitate to ask a little child seven days old about the place of life, and that person will live. For many of the first will be last, and will become a single one."

5 Jesus said, "Know what is in front of your face, and what is hidden from you will be disclosed to you. For there is nothing hidden that will not be revealed."

6 His disciples asked him and said to him, "Do you want us to fast? How should we pray? Should we give to charity? What diet should we observe?" Jesus said, "Don't lie, and don't do what you hate, because all things are disclosed before heaven. After all, there is nothing hidden that will not be revealed, and there is nothing covered up that will remain undisclosed."

7 Jesus said, "Lucky is the lion that the human will eat, so that the lion becomes human. And foul is the human that the lion will eat, and the lion still will become human."

8 And he said, "The human one is like a wise fisherman who cast his net into the sea and drew it up from the sea full of little fish. Among them the wise fisherman discovered a fine large fish. He threw all the little fish back into the sea, and easily chose the large fish. Anyone here with two good ears had better listen!"

9 Jesus said, "Look, the sower went out, took a handful (of seeds), and scattered (them). Some fell on the road, and the birds came and gathered them. Others fell on rock, and they didn't take root in the soil and didn't produce heads of grain. Others fell on thorns, and they choked the seeds and worms ate them. And others fell on good soil, and it produced a good crop: it yielded sixty per measure and one hundred twenty per measure."

10 Jesus said, "I have cast fire upon the world, and look, I'm guarding it until it blazes."

11 Jesus said, "This heaven will pass away, and the one above it will pass away. The dead are not alive, and the living will not die. During the days when you ate what is dead, you made it come alive. When you are in the light, what will you do? On the day when you were one, you became two. But when you become two, what will you do?"

12 The disciples said to Jesus, "We know that you are going to leave us. Who will be our leader?" Jesus said to them, "No matter where you are, you are to go to James the Just, for whose sake heaven and earth came into being."

13 Jesus said to his disciples, "Compare me to something and tell me what I am like." Simon Peter said to him, "You are like a just angel." Matthew said to him, "You are like a wise philosopher." Thomas said to him, "Teacher, my mouth is utterly unable to say what you are like." Jesus said, "I am not your teacher. Because you have drunk, you have become intoxicated from the bubbling spring that I have tended." And he took him, and withdrew, and spoke three sayings to him. When Thomas came back to his friends, they asked him, "What did Jesus say to you?" Thomas said to them, "If I tell you one of the sayings he spoke to me, you

will pick up rocks and stone me, and fire will come from the rocks and devour you."

14 Jesus said to them, "If you fast, you will bring sin upon yourselves, and if you pray, you will be condemned, and if you give to charity, you will harm your spirits. When you go into any region and walk about in the countryside, when people take you in, eat what they serve you and heal the sick among them. After all, what goes into your mouth won't defile you; what comes out of your mouth will."

15 Jesus said, "When you see one who was not born of woman, fall on your faces and worship. That one is your Father."

16 Jesus said, "Perhaps people think that I have come to cast peace upon the world. They do not know that I have come to cast conflicts upon the earth: fire, sword, war. For there will be five in a house: there'll be three against two and two against three, father against son and son against father, and they will stand alone."

17 Jesus said, "I will give you what no eye has seen, what no ear has heard, what no hand has touched, what has not arisen in the human heart."

18 The disciples said to Jesus, "Tell us, how will our end come?" Jesus said, "Have you found the beginning, then, that you are looking for the end? You see, the end will be where the beginning is. Congratulations to the one who stands at the beginning: that one will know the end and will not taste death."

19 Jesus said, "Congratulations to the one who came into being before coming into being. If you become my disciples and pay attention to my sayings, these stones will serve you. For there are five trees in Paradise for you; they do not change, summer or winter, and their leaves do not fall. Whoever knows them will not taste death."

20 The disciples said to Jesus, "Tell us what Heaven's imperial rule is like." He said to them, "It's like a mustard seed. [It's] the smallest of all seeds, but when it falls on prepared soil, it produces a large branch and becomes a shelter for birds of the sky."

21 Mary said to Jesus, "What are your disciples like?" He said, "They are like little children living in a field that is not theirs. When the owners of the field come, they will say, 'Give us back our field.' They take off their clothes in front of them in order to give it back to them, and they return their field to them. For this reason I say, if the owners of a house know that a thief is coming, they will be on guard before the thief arrives, and will not let the thief break into their house (their domain) and steal their possessions. As for you, then, be on guard against the world. Prepare yourselves with great strength, so the robbers can't find a way to get to you, for the trouble you expect will come. Let there be among you a person who understands. When the crop ripened, he came quickly carrying a sickle and harvested it. Anyone here with two good ears had better listen!"

22 Jesus saw some babies nursing. He said to his disciples, "These nursing babies are like those who enter the [Father's] domain." They said to him, "Then shall we enter the [Father's] domain as babies?" Jesus said to them, "When you make the two into one, and when you make the inner like the outer and the outer like the inner, and the upper like the lower, and when you make male and female into a single one, so that the male will not be male nor the female be female, when you make eyes in place of an eye, a hand in place of a hand, a foot in place of a foot, an image in place of an image, then you will enter [the Father's domain]."

23 Jesus said, "I shall choose you, one from a thousand and two from ten thousand, and they will stand as a single one."

24 His disciples said, "Show us the place where you are, for we must seek it." He said to them, "Anyone here with two ears had better listen! There is light within a person of light, and it shines on the whole world. If it does not shine, it is dark."

25 Jesus said, "Love your friends like your own soul, protect them like the pupil of your eye."

26 Jesus said, "You see the sliver in your friend's eye, but you don't see the timber in your own eye. When you take the timber out of your own eye, then you will see well enough to remove the sliver from your friend's eye."

27 "If you do not fast from the world, you will not find the [Father's] domain. If you do not observe

the sabbath day as a sabbath day, you will not see the Father."

28 Jesus said, "I took my stand in the midst of the world, and in flesh I appeared to them. I found them all drunk, and I did not find any of them thirsty. My soul ached for the children of humanity, because they are blind in their hearts and do not see, for they came into the world empty, and they also seek to depart from the world empty. But meanwhile they are drunk. When they shake off their wine, then they will change their ways."

29 Jesus said, "If the flesh came into being because of spirit, that is a marvel, but if spirit came into being because of the body, that is a marvel of marvels. Yet I marvel at how this great wealth has come to dwell in this poverty."

30 Jesus said, "Where there are three deities, they are divine. Where there are two or one, I am with that one."

31 Jesus said, "No prophet is welcome on his home turf; doctors don't cure those who know them."

32 Jesus said, "A city built on a high hill and fortified cannot fall, nor can it be hidden."

33 Jesus said, "What you will hear in your ear, in the other ear proclaim from your rooftops. After all, no one lights a lamp and puts it under a basket, nor does one put it in a hidden place. Rather, one puts it on a lampstand so that all who come and go will see its light."

34 Jesus said, "If a blind person leads a blind person, both of them will fall into a hole."

35 Jesus said, "One can't enter a strong man's house and take it by force without tying his hands. Then one can loot his house."

36 Jesus said, "Do not fret, from morning to evening and from evening to morning, about what you are going to wear."

37 His disciples said, "When will you appear to us, and when will we see you?" Jesus said, "When you strip without being ashamed, and you take your clothes and put them under your feet like little children and trample them, then [you] will see the son of the living one and you will not be afraid."

38 Jesus said, "Often you have desired to hear these sayings that I am speaking to you, and you have no one else from whom to hear them. There will be days when you will seek me and you will not find me."

39 Jesus said, "The Pharisees and the scholars have taken the keys of knowledge and have hidden them. They have not entered, nor have they allowed those who want to enter to do so. As for you, be as sly as snakes and as simple as doves."

40 Jesus said, "A grapevine has been planted apart from the Father. Since it is not strong, it will be pulled up by its root and will perish."

41 Jesus said, "Those who have something in hand will be given more, and those who have nothing will be deprived of even the little they have."

42 Jesus said, "Be passersby."

43 His disciples said to him, "Who are you to say these things to us?" "You don't understand who I am from what I say to you. Rather, you have become like the Judeans, for they love the tree but hate its fruit, or they love the fruit but hate the tree."

44 Jesus said, "Whoever blasphemes against the Father will be forgiven, and whoever blasphemes against the son will be forgiven, but whoever blasphemes against the holy spirit will not be forgiven, either on earth or in heaven."

45 Jesus said, "Grapes are not harvested from thorn trees, nor are figs gathered from thistles, for they yield no fruit. Good persons produce good from what they've stored up; bad persons produce evil from the wickedness they've stored up in their hearts, and say evil things. For from the overflow of the heart they produce evil."

46 Jesus said, "From Adam to John the Baptist, among those born of women, no one is so much greater than John the Baptist that his eyes should not be averted. But I have said that whoever among you becomes a child will recognize the [Father's] imperial rule and will become greater than John."

47 Jesus said, "A person cannot mount two horses or bend two bows. And a slave cannot serve two masters, otherwise that slave will honor the one and offend the other. Nobody drinks aged wine and immediately wants to drink young wine. Young wine is not poured into old wineskins, or they might break, and aged wine is not poured into a new wineskin, or it might spoil. An old patch is not sewn onto a new garment, since it would create a tear."

48 Jesus said, "If two make peace with each other in a single house, they will say to the mountain, 'Move from here!' and it will move."

49 Jesus said, "Congratulations to those who are alone and chosen, for you will find the [Father's] domain. For you have come from it, and you will return there again."

50 Jesus said, "If they say to you, 'Where have you come from?' say to them, 'We have come from the light, from the place where the light came into being by itself, established [itself], and appeared in their image.' If they say to you, 'Is it you?' say, 'We are its children, and we are the chosen of the living Father.' If they ask you, 'What is the evidence of your Father in you?' say to them, 'It is motion and rest.'"

51 His disciples said to him, "When will the rest for the dead take place, and when will the new world come?" He said to them, "What you are looking forward to has come, but you don't know it."

52 His disciples said to him, "Twenty-four prophets have spoken in Israel, and they all spoke of you." He said to them, "You have disregarded the living one who is in your presence, and have spoken of the dead."

53 His disciples said to him, "Is circumcision useful or not?" He said to them, "If it were useful, their father would produce children already circumcised from their mother. Rather, the true circumcision in spirit has become profitable in every respect."

54 Jesus said, "Congratulations to the poor, for to you belongs Heaven's domain."

55 Jesus said, "Whoever does not hate father and mother cannot be my disciple, and whoever does not hate brothers and sisters, and carry the cross as I do, will not be worthy of me."

56 Jesus said, "Whoever has come to know the world has discovered a carcass, and whoever has discovered a carcass, of that person the world is not worthy."

57 Jesus said, "The Father's imperial rule is like a person who has [good] seed. His enemy came during the night and sowed weeds among the good seed. The person did not let the workers pull up the weeds, but said to them, 'No, otherwise you might go to pull up the weeds and pull up the wheat along with them.' For on the day of the harvest the weeds will be conspicuous, and will be pulled up and burned."

58 Jesus said, "Congratulations to the person who has toiled and has found life."

59 Jesus said, "Look to the living one as long as you live, otherwise you might die and then try to see the living one, and you will be unable to see."

60 [He saw] a Samaritan carrying a lamb and going to Judea. He said to his disciples, "[. . .] that person [. . .] around the lamb." They said to him, "So that he may kill it and eat it." He said to them, "He will not eat it while it is alive, but only after he has killed it and it has become a carcass." They said, "Otherwise he can't do it." He said to them, "So also with you, seek for yourselves a place for rest, or you might become a carcass and be eaten."

61 Jesus said, "Two will recline on a couch; one will die, one will live." Salome said, "Who are you, master? You have climbed onto my couch and eaten from my table as if you are from someone." Jesus said to her, "I am the one who comes from what is whole. I was granted from the things of my Father." "I am your disciple." "For this reason I say, if one is [whole], one will be filled with light, but if one is divided, one will be filled with darkness."

62 Jesus said, "I disclose my mysteries to those [who are worthy] of [my] mysteries. Do not let your left hand know what your right hand is doing."

63 Jesus said, "There was a rich man who had a great deal of money. He said, 'I shall invest my money so

that I may sow, reap, plant, and fill my storehouses with produce, that I may lack nothing.' These were the things he was thinking in his heart, but that very night he died. Anyone here with two ears had better listen!"

64 Jesus said, "Someone was receiving guests. When he had prepared the dinner, he sent his slave to invite the guests. The slave went to the first and said, 'My master invites you.' The first replied, 'Some merchants owe me money; they are coming to me tonight. I have to go and give them instructions. Please excuse me from dinner.' The slave went to another and said, 'My master has invited you.' The second said to the slave, 'I have bought a house, and I have been called away for a day. I shall have no time.' The slave went to another and said, 'My master invites you.' The third said to the slave, 'My friend is to be married, and I am to arrange the banquet. I shall not be able to come. Please excuse me from dinner.' The slave went to another and said, 'My master invites you.' The fourth said to the slave, 'I have bought an estate, and I am going to collect the rent. I shall not be able to come. Please excuse me.' The slave returned and said to his master, 'Those whom you invited to dinner have asked to be excused.' The master said to his slave, 'Go out on the streets and bring back whomever you find to have dinner.' Buyers and merchants [will] not enter the places of my Father."

65 He said, "A [. . .] person owned a vineyard and rented it to some farmers, so they could work it and he could collect its crop from them. He sent his slave so the farmers would give him the vineyard's crop. They grabbed him, beat him, and almost killed him, and the slave returned and told his master. His master said, 'Perhaps he didn't know them.' He sent another slave, and the farmers beat that one as well. Then the master sent his son and said, 'Perhaps they'll show my son some respect.' Because the farmers knew that he was the heir to the vineyard, they grabbed him and killed him. Anyone here with two ears had better listen!"

66 Jesus said, "Show me the stone that the builders rejected: that is the keystone."

67 Jesus said, "Those who know all, but are lacking in themselves, are utterly lacking."

68 Jesus said, "Congratulations to you when you are hated and persecuted; and no place will be found, wherever you have been persecuted."

69 Jesus said, "Congratulations to those who have been persecuted in their hearts: they are the ones who have truly come to know the Father. Congratulations to those who go hungry, so the stomach of the one in want may be filled."

70 Jesus said, "If you bring forth what is within you, what you have will save you. If you do not have that within you, what you do not have within you [will] kill you."

71 Jesus said, "I will destroy [this] house, and no one will be able to build it [. . .]."

72 A [person said] to him, "Tell my brothers to divide my father's possessions with me." He said to the person, "Mister, who made me a divider?" He turned to his disciples and said to them, "I'm not a divider, am I?"

73 Jesus said, "The crop is huge but the workers are few, so beg the harvest boss to dispatch workers to the fields."

74 He said, "Lord, there are many around the drinking trough, but there is nothing in the well."

75 Jesus said, "There are many standing at the door, but those who are alone will enter the bridal suite."

76 Jesus said, "The Father's imperial rule is like a merchant who had a supply of merchandise and found a pearl. That merchant was prudent; he sold the merchandise and bought the single pearl for himself. So also with you, seek his treasure that is unfailing, that is enduring, where no moth comes to eat and no worm destroys."

77 Jesus said, "I am the light that is over all things. I am all: from me all came forth, and to me all attained. Split a piece of wood; I am there. Lift up the stone, and you will find me there."

78 Jesus said, "Why have you come out to the countryside? To see a reed shaken by the wind? And to see a person dressed in soft clothes, [like your] rulers and your powerful ones? They are dressed in soft clothes, and they cannot understand truth."

79 A woman in the crowd said to him, "Lucky are the womb that bore you and the breasts that fed you." He said to [her], "Lucky are those who have heard the word of the Father and have truly kept it. For there will be days when you will say, 'Lucky are the womb that has not conceived and the breasts that have not given milk.'"

80 Jesus said, "Whoever has come to know the world has discovered the body, and whoever has discovered the body, of that one the world is not worthy."

81 Jesus said, "The one who has become wealthy should reign, and the one who has power should renounce [it]."

82 Jesus said, "Whoever is near me is near the fire, and whoever is far from me is far from the [Father's] domain."

83 Jesus said, "Images are visible to people, but the light within them is hidden in the image of the Father's light. He will be disclosed, but his image is hidden by his light."

84 Jesus said, "When you see your likeness, you are happy. But when you see your images that came into being before you and that neither die nor become visible, how much you will have to bear!"

85 Jesus said, "Adam came from great power and great wealth, but he was not worthy of you. For had he been worthy, [he would] not [have tasted] death."

86 Jesus said, "[Foxes have] their dens and birds have their nests, but human beings have no place to lie down and rest."

87 Jesus said, "How miserable is the body that depends on a body, and how miserable is the soul that depends on these two."

88 Jesus said, "The messengers and the prophets will come to you and give you what belongs to you. You, in turn, give them what you have, and say to yourselves, 'When will they come and take what belongs to them?'"

89 Jesus said, "Why do you wash the outside of the cup? Don't you understand that the one who made the inside is also the one who made the outside?"

90 Jesus said, "Come to me, for my yoke is comfortable and my lordship is gentle, and you will find rest for yourselves."

91 They said to him, "Tell us who you are so that we may believe in you." He said to them, "You examine the face of heaven and earth, but you have not come to know the one who is in your presence, and you do not know how to examine the present moment."

92 Jesus said, "Seek and you will find. In the past, however, I did not tell you the things about which you asked me then. Now I am willing to tell them, but you are not seeking them."

Glossary

Didymos Judas Thomas	or simply Thomas, the presumed recipient of the wisdom contained in the Gospel of Thomas
James the Just	the leader of the Christian movement in Jerusalem in the decades after the death of Jesus
Judeans	inhabitants of Judea, a portion of the modern state of Israel
Matthew	the author of one of the four canonical gospels of the New Testament
Pharisees	variously a political party, a social movement, and a school of thought among Jews during the Second Temple period before the birth of Jesus
Salome	a follower of Jesus
Samaritan	a member of an ethnic and religious group closely related to Judaism
Simon Peter	one of Jesus's apostles and the first leader—in effect, pope—of the Christian Church

93 "Don't give what is sacred to dogs, for they might throw them upon the manure pile. Don't throw pearls [to] pigs, or they might . . . it [. . .]."

94 Jesus [said], "One who seeks will find, and for [one who knocks] it will be opened."

95 [Jesus said], "If you have money, don't lend it at interest. Rather, give [it] to someone from whom you won't get it back."

96 Jesus [said], "The Father's imperial rule is like [a] woman, who took a little leaven, [hid] it in dough, and made it into large loaves of bread. Anyone here with two ears had better listen!"

97 Jesus said, "The [Father's] imperial rule is like a woman who was carrying a [jar] full of meal. While she was walking along [a] distant road, the handle of the jar broke and the meal spilled behind her [along] the road. She didn't know it; she hadn't noticed a problem. When she reached her house, she put the jar down and discovered that it was empty."

98 Jesus said, "The Father's imperial rule is like a person who wanted to kill someone powerful. While still at home he drew his sword and thrust it into the wall to find out whether his hand would go in. Then he killed the powerful one."

99 The disciples said to him, "Your brothers and your mother are standing outside." He said to them, "Those here who do what my Father wants are my brothers and my mother. They are the ones who will enter my Father's domain."

100 They showed Jesus a gold coin and said to him, "The Roman emperor's people demand taxes from us." He said to them, "Give the emperor what belongs to the emperor, give God what belongs to God, and give me what is mine."

101 "Whoever does not hate [father] and mother as I do cannot be my [disciple], and whoever does [not] love [father and] mother as I do cannot be my [disciple]. For my mother [. . .], but my true [mother] gave me life."

102 Jesus said, "Damn the Pharisees! They are like a dog sleeping in the cattle manger: the dog neither eats nor [lets] the cattle eat."

103 Jesus said, "Congratulations to those who know where the rebels are going to attack. [They] can get going, collect their imperial resources, and be prepared before the rebels arrive."

104 They said to Jesus, "Come, let us pray today, and let us fast." Jesus said, "What sin have I committed, or how have I been undone? Rather, when the groom leaves the bridal suite, then let people fast and pray."

105 Jesus said, "Whoever knows the father and the mother will be called the child of a whore."

106 Jesus said, "When you make the two into one, you will become children of Adam, and when you say, 'Mountain, move from here!' it will move."

107 Jesus said, "The [Father's] imperial rule is like a shepherd who had a hundred sheep. One of them, the largest, went astray. He left the ninety-nine and looked for the one until he found it. After he had toiled, he said to the sheep, 'I love you more than the ninety-nine.'"

108 Jesus said, "Whoever drinks from my mouth will become like me; I myself shall become that person, and the hidden things will be revealed to him."

109 Jesus said, "The [Father's] imperial rule is like a person who had a treasure hidden in his field but did not know it. And [when] he died he left it to his [son]. The son [did] not know [about it either]. He took over the field and sold it. The buyer went plowing, [discovered] the treasure, and began to lend money at interest to whomever he wished."

110 Jesus said, "The one who has found the world, and has become wealthy, should renounce the world."

111 Jesus said, "The heavens and the earth will roll up in your presence, and whoever is living from the living one will not see death." Does not Jesus say, "Those who have found themselves, of them the world is not worthy"?

112 Jesus said, "Damn the flesh that depends on the soul. Damn the soul that depends on the flesh."

113 His disciples said to him, "When will the [Father's] imperial rule come?" "It will not come by watching for it. It will not be said, 'Look, here!' or 'Look, there!' Rather, the Father's imperial rule is spread out upon the earth, and people don't see it."

114 Simon Peter said to them, "Make Mary leave us, for females don't deserve life." Jesus said, "Look, I will guide her to make her male, so that she too may become a living spirit resembling you males. For every female who makes herself male will enter the domain of Heaven."

Michael and his angels fighting a seven-headed dragon, and Saint John seeing a similar seven-headed beast rising out of the sea (Library of Congress)

BIBLE: REVELATION

"They will hunger no more, and thirst no more; the sun will not strike them, nor any scorching heat."

Overview

The book of Revelation, which is more properly called the Apocalypse of Saint John, is the last book in the Christian New Testament, placed there because of its symbolic imagery of the end of time. The book does not carry a date, but most scholars assume that it emerged around 94–96 CE, late in the reign of the emperor Domitian of Rome, at a time when some Christians anticipated persecution. Revelation was addressed to Christian churches around the city of Ephesus, a major urban center in Asia Minor (modern-day western Turkey), where Christianity took root at an early date through the efforts of the apostle Paul.

The book encouraged Christians to endure impending persecution secure in the knowledge that Jesus Christ was in charge of the world and that the unfolding plan of history would see the victory of the Christian faith. However, some interpreters believe that the author intended to address primarily complacent and lax second-generation Christians to remind them that their religious beliefs stood in contrast to the values of the Roman Empire and the popular culture around them. Either way, the book was read during later, more serious persecutions and encouraged many Christians to persevere in their faith. Christians believed that the book was ultimately fulfilled when Christianity became the religion of the Roman Empire in the late fourth century CE, and thus it was placed in the formal New Testament canon, a collection of twenty-seven books officially created in the late fourth and early fifth centuries CE. In later years many people used Revelation to predict the future and imminent arrival of Judgment Day. Invariably they were wrong, and the results often were heartbreak and sometimes death in attempted revolutionary endeavors. Modern biblical scholars and Christian theologians repeatedly stress that the symbols of this book refer to events of the first century CE or in general to any persecution of Christians and are not meant to be used to cast predictions about the future.

Context

Revelation is structured as a letter, or epistle, to seven churches, but in terms of content it is apocalyptic literature, a common literary genre among many people in the ancient world but especially popular among Jews and Christians from 200 BCE to 200 CE. About fifty examples of this type of literature, usually called apocalypses, are still available for us to read today. Most were never placed in a canon of sacred literature. They were written in symbolic language to encourage people to endure persecution or hard times with the promise that God was coming to end the world or radically change history. The typical apocalypse was derived from the experiences of a seer, who, it was believed, was permitted by God to view future events leading up to the end of time either in visions or during a journey to heavenly realms. The visions included details of great persecution before the final arrival of God. Such a vision was written down by the seer and kept until the end of time, when the book would be made public. In actuality, the book was written by an author after most of the predicted events had come true, except for the end of the persecution and the Final Judgment of God. Prediction of events that have already come true is called prediction *vaticinia ex eventu*, or prediction "after the event." This was not really deception, for most listeners understood this symbolic discourse, since it was so common. Even so, the book still gave them hope. Our modern definition of apocalyptic literature describes it as a narrative genre in which God or a celestial being reveals a future temporal reality in bizarre, frenetic, and coded symbolic pictorial images, designed to assure a believers of divine salvation.

The historical context for Revelation is the late first century CE in the eastern half of the Roman Empire. The empire was racked by famine and plague, which served to unhinge the stability of the economic and social order. Severe earthquakes in 60 CE, a major defeat of a Roman army by the Parthian Empire (Persia) in 62 CE, the huge fire in Rome in 64 CE, civil war and the violent deaths of four Roman emperors from 68 to 70 CE, the eruption of Vesuvius in 79 CE, and famine in 92 CE weighed heavily on peoples' minds. Overhanging the provinces of Asia Minor (Turkey) and Syria was the continued threat of invasion

CA. 27 CE	■ Jesus begins his ministry, which lasts for three years.
CA. 40 CE	■ Paul takes up his missionary work, which he continues until 64 CE; during this time he conducts a mission to Ephesus.
CA. 50 CE	■ The writing of the New Testament begins with the Pauline epistles, ending with the Gospel of John ca. 110 CE.
64 CE	■ Nero persecutes the Christians in the Roman Empire, crucifying Peter and perhaps also executing Paul at this same time.
70 CE	■ Jerusalem, the center of the Christian movement, is destroyed during the First Jewish-Roman War.
81 CE	■ The reign of Domitian begins; throughout his reign, which lasts until 96 CE, the Roman Empire faces increasing socioeconomic woes.
CA. 94 –96 CE	■ Revelation is written by "John."

ers). The imposition of this new artificial Roman imperial faith was an attempt to bring together the various peoples in the eastern Mediterranean world under the religious and political unity of Rome. Of course, Christians would not revere these gods, and they faced scorn and possible punishment for treason. With social chaos and the threat of invasion, pressure was increased under the reign of Domitian for people to bow to Roman religious demands, especially emperor worship. Images connected to emperor worship are the most dramatic ones in the book of Revelation.

Domitian became emperor in 81 CE, and throughout his reign the Roman Empire faced increasing social and economic challenges; minorities, like Christians, felt pressures placed upon them to conform. Revelation is thought to have been written between 94 and 96 CE, when Christians most feared impending persecution by Domitian, though we know nothing about its actual creation. The manuscript was probably read aloud in Christian communities around Ephesus in order to strengthen their faith and courage as well as to unveil for them in symbolic language the evil nature of the Roman Empire. The symbols portrayed events that had happened in the previous generation. In subsequent generations the book probably revived in popularity during every fresh persecution. Beyond this we know little of the history of this work for the next two centuries, other than that it was more popular in the eastern Mediterranean world than in the west. Its inclusion in the formal New Testament canon, which was created around 400 CE by decision of several church councils, was highly debated, but its popularity in the eyes of many ensured its ultimate place.

About the Author

According to the first chapter of Revelation, John was exiled on the island of Patmos, where a divine voice commissioned him to write the book of Revelation. The author calls himself John, and early Christians were inclined to equate him with the disciple John, perhaps the last living disciple of Jesus, who may have lived as an old man in Ephesus toward the end of the first century CE. More likely the name is a pseudonym, a symbolic name chosen by the anonymous author, since apocalyptic books usually were written by authors who used names from the distant past, when the works were supposedly written. Perhaps the author of Revelation choose John's name because the disciple was a famous contemporary, or perhaps John was the author's real name, since it was common. The events described by the author appear to refer to many historical events of the forty years previous to the writing of the book (the literary technique of predicting events after their occurrence).

Explanation and Analysis of the Document

Revelation is structured as a letter, or an epistle, written by John to the seven churches of Asia Minor (Ephesus,

by the Parthians. Many Romans believed that the Roman emperor Nero, who had committed suicide in 68 CE, was not really dead but would lead the Parthians in his attempt to conquer Rome. In fact, individuals arose in the eastern part of the empire in 69, 79, and 88 CE claiming to be Nero and causing significant disturbances. Christians could recall Nero's persecution of 64 CE, in which both the apostles Paul and Peter may have died, as well as the horrible war between Romans and Jews from 66 to 70 CE, which saw the destruction of Jerusalem and the Temple. Revelation alludes to all these circumstances but often in general fashion with images like the Four Horsemen, who symbolize Parthian invasion, civil war, famine, and death.

The Roman Empire and regional provincial rulers encouraged the citizenry to worship the emperor as a god associated with the Greek deity Apollo. Moreover, the deity symbolizing the city of Rome, Dea Roma, was propagandized to be the goddess of fertility, thus absorbing all the regional fertility goddesses (Diana of Ephesus, Athena, Cybele, Isis, and oth-

Vesuvius, as seen from Pompeii (Library of Congress)

Smyrna, Pergamum, Thyatira, Sardis, Philadelphia, and Laodicea). The first three chapters of the book are a prologue in which the author makes clever comments that pertain to social, religious, and political issues in those seven cities. The style of the book indicates that it is apocalyptic literature, that is, a work that uses bizarre and highly symbolic imagery in visions to predict the future, which for the audience is actually mostly in the past. Like other apocalyptic writings, Revelation anticipates God's deliverance of faithful believers from persecution. In addition, Revelation is also a highly liturgical work, with many hymnic elements inserted into its visions. The book is twenty-two chapters long; this commentary treats chapters 4–13 and 15–22.

The messages of Revelation are these: Christ is faithful to his people, history will unfold according to the divine plan and see Christ's ultimate victory over evil, those Christians who endure will be blessed, all evil is temporary, and the ultimate victory of God occurred with Jesus's Resurrection, for therein evil was truly defeated—the rest of history until the Second Coming is simply the "mopping-up campaign" of God.

Scholars often have outlined the book of Revelation as seven cycles of symbolic images, though not everyone

agrees on the exact divisions of the text. This is one such outline: Seven Seals (chapters 4–7), Seven Trumpets (chapters 8–11), Seven Visions of the Dragon (chapters 12–13), Seven Visions of the Lamb (chapter 14), Seven Bowls of Wrath (chapters 15–16), Seven Visions of Babylon (chapters 17–19), and Seven Visions of the End (chapters 19–22). Worthy of note is the author's indication that the end of time, or Judgment Day, supposedly comes at the end of the cycles of Seven Seals, Seven Trumpets, Seven Visions of the Lamb, Seven Visions of Babylon, and Seven Visions of the End. (It is probably implied in the other two cycles.) This means that each cycle backs up in time and describes the same period and events leading up to the time of the book's composition. This pattern of repetition of allusions to historical events also occurs in the Old Testament book of Daniel (chapters 2, 4, 7–9, and 11). Thus, different signs can allude to the same events or cultural phenomena.

Scholars are generally loath to make too many connections between symbols in Revelation and historical events of the late first century CE, because the symbols are very generic. For example, the Bowls of Wrath borrow imagery from the Ten Plagues in the book of Exodus, and they simply refer to the various woes that afflict people in many

"Worthy is the Lamb that was slaughtered to receive power and wealth and wisdom and might and honor and glory and blessing."

"They will hunger no more, and thirst no more; the sun will not strike them, nor any scorching heat."

"He will wipe every tear from their eyes. Death will be no more."

"I am the Alpha and the Omega, the first and the last, the beginning and the end."

ages. Symbols in other apocalyptic books, such as Daniel, are more easily connected to specific events of the time when the book was written. The looseness of the symbols in Revelation enabled the book to be used during subsequent Roman persecutions through the second and third centuries CE, because they described recurrent events. It also allowed the book to be referenced randomly in any century to "foretell" the immediate future, as when some people predicted that Judgment Day would come in 1988 (the fortieth anniversary of the modern state of Israel) or 1996 (two thousand years after Jesus's birth). But the loose symbols used by the author also reflect a brilliant literary artistic sense, which sets Revelation apart from so many other apocalyptic works of that age.

Still, we must acknowledge that certain symbols are conceded by most scholars to have specific equivalents to historical events and persons. References to the Son of Man, the Lamb, the baby, the second rider on the white horse, or Michael all point to Jesus. The references to a persecution lasting three and a half years (or 42 months or 1,260 days) is a symbolic allusion to any persecution, since the famous persecution of the Jews that led to Maccabean independence lasted from 167 to 164 BCE—three and a half years. The number 144,000 is created by multiplying 12 (representing the twelve tribes of Israel) times 12 (representing the twelve apostles) times 1,000 (the Hebrew number that stands for eternity) to equal a number that symbolizes the totality of all believers from every age, which, of course, is in the millions. The invading horde, Gog and Magog, the horsemen on the Euphrates, and the frogs all refer to the potential invasion of Parthians out of the country of Persia (modern-day Iran), whose armies were made up primarily of cavalry. This empire in Persia by this time had been the enemies of Rome for two centuries and would continue to be for five more centuries.

Numerous symbols refer to Rome. Babylon is a code name for Rome, not only in Revelation but elsewhere in the New Testament (1 Peter 5:13) as well. We hear of a beast with seven heads and ten horns. The seven heads might refer to the city of Rome, built upon seven famous hills, and the ten horns might be symbolic of those Roman emperors who ruled from the time of Jesus to 96 CE, when the book of Revelation was composed. These emperors are typically considered to be Tiberius (14–37 CE), Caligula (37–41 CE), Claudius (41–54 CE), Nero (54–68 CE), Galba (68–69 CE), Otho (69 CE), Vitellius (69 CE), Vespasian (69–79 CE), Titus (79–81 CE), and Domitian (81–96 CE). (Some scholars, however, omit Galba, Otho, and Vitellius—who ruled during the so-called Year of the Four Emperors—and include other emperors before and after those on this list.) The famous number 666 (also known as the "number of the beast") refers to Nero, for when his name in written in Hebrew and the Hebrew letters are converted to numbers, the total is 666. Even more convincing, however, is the fact that Nero's name can be spelled differently in Hebrew, and the total of those letters is 616. Some versions of the book of Revelation declare that the number of the beast is 616. Only Nero's name can equal both of these numbers. In the book of Revelation, Nero's name is perhaps a symbol for another emperor: Domitian. In later apocalyptic works, like the Pseudo-Sibylline Oracles, book VIII (ca. 150 CE), Nero symbolizes the emperor Hadrian. So in Revelation we have symbols representing other symbols.

For some symbols most commentators show great reluctance to provide equivalent meanings, because our historical evidence is weak. However, it is worth mentioning them. The mark of the beast may refer to stamps or marks placed on business documents or citizenship papers, depending on how people swore allegiance to the emperor when they renewed their papers for the sake of travel permits, building permits, and the right to engage in business. In times of dire economic and political difficulties, people lacking such a stamp were vulnerable to scrutiny, ridicule, and imprisonment for being possible traitors. Perhaps the image of the woman dressed in red and purple is the representation of the Dea Roma, whose veneration the Roman government forced upon citizens in the eastern provinces. Dea Roma was also called the Great Mother, so that the biblical reference to "Babylon the great, mother of whores" may be a veiled reference to Dea Roma, the Great Mother. Thus, much of the imagery in Revelation may be connected to a critique of the cult of emperor worship and the state enforcement of these practices and beliefs, but these observations are very speculative.

♦ Seven Seals

John begins his visionary experience by observing twenty-four elders (probably representing the twelve tribes of Israel and the twelve apostles) seated around a heavenly throne before a sea of glass and four creatures—a lion, an ox, a human face, and a flying eagle (which, in later years, would become symbols for the four evangelists—Mark, Luke, Matthew, and John, respectively). The creatures sing a short hymn, which is characteristic of much of the book of Revelation; many hymnic elements are interspersed throughout the book.

John then views a scroll with seven seals, each opened by the Lamb (Jesus). The first four seals release four horses (white, red, black, and pale) with riders. Scholars postulate that these horses allude, respectively, to a possible Parthian invasion, past civil war in Rome in the late 60s, current famine, and impending death. Of interest is the reference to a quart of wheat and three quarts of barley for a day's pay and the admonishment not to "damage the olive oil and the wine." Scholars note that this passage is a concrete historical allusion to the famous edict of the emperor Domitian, issued in 92 CE in the midst of a famine, when there was an abundance of wine and a shortage of grain. Domitian forbade anyone to plant more vineyards in Italy and ordered that half of existing vineyards be destroyed. The fifth seal describes the appearance of the martyrs, who cry out to God for justice to be meted out to their persecutors, and the sixth seal unveils an earthquake (a common experience for cities around Ephesus, seen as a sign of divine wrath) and cosmic signs, at which time 144,000 saints are sealed by God to protect them from harm. Finally, the seventh seal brings seven angels with seven trumpets to begin the next cycle of visions.

♦ Seven Trumpets

The first trumpet sounds, and hail, fire, and blood fall upon the earth, killing one-third of the population. The second trumpet sounds, and a burning mountain falls into the sea, turning the water to blood—perhaps in reference to the destruction of Pompeii in the eruption of Vesuvius in 79 CE. The third trumpet sounds, and a great star falls into the water and kills many people. This might allude to the bright passing of Halley's comet in 66 CE. The fourth

trumpet causes the sun, moon, and stars to darken. The fifth trumpet opens a bottomless pit out of which come smoke and locusts. The king of the pit is called Abaddon in Hebrew and Apollyon in Greek. Apollyon is another name of the Greek god Apollo, and Roman emperors called themselves Apollo when they wished to be seen as divine. Thus the Roman emperor is king of the pit, and the locusts can be seen as his soldiers. The sixth trumpet releases angels and horses with their riders, who are held back at the Euphrates River. That river was the border between Rome and Parthia; the horsemen are Parthian cavalry. An angel brings seven thunders, followed by two witnesses (possibly referring to Moses and Elijah, who, in turn, represent the apostles Peter and Paul), who are killed but rise from the dead (that is, their message endures). The seventh trumpet brings Judgment Day. In general, these events remind us generically of the Ten Plagues of Egypt brought by Moses according to the Old Testament book of Exodus (river water to blood, locusts, hail, and darkness), and they can describe natural disasters of any age.

♦ Seven Visions of the Dragon

The author begins with a beautiful vision of a celestial woman giving birth to a child (Mary and Jesus). They are confronted by a red dragon with seven heads and ten horns (the seven hills of Rome and the ten emperors). Before the dragon can eat him, the child is snatched away and "taken to God and to his throne," as Jesus ascended into heaven. Then we are told that a "war broke out in heaven," pitting the dragon and his angels against Michael (Jesus) and his angels, with Michael the victor "by blood of the Lamb." This set of events is symbolic of the Resurrection of Jesus. The dragon represents Satan, and his defeat is really the high point of the book; the Resurrection of Jesus is more significant than his Second Coming. Later dragons represent the Roman Empire, and their activity is less important than Satan's, so that God's defeat of them is simply a mopping-up exercise after the great victory. The red dragon (now representing Rome) subsequently persecutes the woman (who symbolizes the Christian Church) for three and a half years (again, the symbolic period of persecution). We then observe a beast rise from the sea with seven heads and ten horns (imperial Rome). One of the heads seems to have received a death blow but has survived (in reference to Nero, who has come back as Domitian). A second beast rises out of the earth (Roman priests) and demands that all people worship the first beast (the emperor) and gives marks to those who do, so that they can buy and sell goods (perhaps referring to business documents or citizenship papers). "No one can buy or sell who does not have the mark, that is, the name of the beast or the number of its name"—that number being 666.

♦ Seven Bowls of Wrath

Seven angels bring seven plagues in bowls. John sees a sea of glass and fire, an allusion to the Red Sea of the Exodus narrative, and then views the "temple of the tent," which alludes to the tent of meeting. This tent was the Hebrew Tabernacle, a portable sanctuary that accompanied Moses and the Israelites on their wanderings in the wilderness. The angels pour forth the contents of their bowls, producing ulcers, a sea of blood, rivers of blood, scorching sun, darkness, a dry Euphrates riverbed to allow kings of the east to travel westward to Harmagedon along with frogs, and finally the fall of Babylon. Ulcers, blood in water, and darkness are simply allusions to the Ten Plagues. Kings in the east refer to the Parthians; frogs are a religious symbol of Ahriman, the god of darkness for the Parthians; and Harmagedon is a valley by Tel Megiddo in central Palestine, north of Jerusalem, where major battles were often fought—a possible battlefield for imminent Roman and Parthian combat. This cycle epitomizes both the general use of Old Testament plague images combined with specific historical allusions.

♦ **Seven Visions of Babylon**

One of the seven angels shows John "the great whore," dressed in red and purple, who rides a scarlet beast with seven heads and ten horns. On her forehead is written "Babylon the Great, mother of whores" (Dea Roma). John is told that the seven heads stand for seven mountains—a clear reference to Rome. The angel further reveals that these mountains are also seven kings. Scholars propose a multitude of theories to equate various emperors with the number seven. Perhaps these are the ten emperors minus Otho, Galba, and Vitellius, or the seven emperors from Nero to Domitian, or even the emperors starting with Caesar Augustus, predecessor to Tiberius, and omitting Domitian, along with Otho, Galba and Vitellius. There is an eighth king, most likely Domitian, who could be counted both as the seventh and the eighth king if we number the seven emperors as Tiberius through Domitian. Alternatively, he

could be counted as a separate king if we number the seven emperors as Caesar Augustus through Titus. Either way he is seen as Nero, who is still alive despite a death blow and has returned from Parthia.

John sees another angel descending from the heavens and announcing the fall of Babylon, which "has become a dwelling place of demons" where merchants "have grown rich from the power of her luxury." The merchants utter a long lament over its destruction. Perhaps Roman merchants wanted a persecution of Jews and Christians to eliminate competition in hard economic times. Ensuing visions speak of rejoicing Christians, rejoicing elders, and how the Lamb (Jesus) will marry the bride (the Church), all with added hymnic material. This cycle of visions illustrates for us how much of Revelation contains hymns.

♦ **Seven Visions of the End**

John sees the heavens open to reveal a rider on a white horse (Jesus), who is called the Word of God. He defeats the beast in battle (the Resurrection of Jesus or Judgment Day). The beast (Rome) is thrown into a lake of fire, and the dragon (Satan) is bound in a pit. Nobody is really sure what these images mean, unless they are meant by the author to be futuristic. A thousand-year reign, or the millennium, then begins. A thousand years can equate with eternity, though most church fathers over the years have thought it referred to the peaceful spread of the Christian church in real time. Some pious Christians have believed that it refers to an actual thousand-year reign brought about by Jesus's return to earth (pre-millennialism) or a thousand-year period of peace and justice instituted by Christians, after which Jesus returns to earth (post-millennialism). Scholars suspect the millennium is symbolic but are uncertain as to its meaning. During this time, martyrs would be with God,

Questions for Further Study

1. How would you respond to a person who says that Revelation is a prediction of the end of the world and that modern events are fulfilling the prophecy of Revelation?

2. What role did the Roman Empire play in the production of the book of Revelation?

3. The book of Revelation is an example of "apocalyptic" literature. What did this word mean in the early years of Christianity, and how does this meaning differ from the way the word is usually used today?

4. Why do you think the numbers 4, 7, and 12 were used so frequently in the book of Revelation? What symbolic significance could these numbers have had?

5. Why do you think the book of Revelation has had such an enduring effect on the works of poets, painters, and artists in general?

and Christians would live on the earth. Eventually, Satan escapes and joins with Gog and Magog to war against God. They ultimately lose, after which a new heaven and earth are created. A long description follows of the New Jerusalem, or heaven.

Scholars do not know if the author of Revelation was referring to something in his own age with this cycle of visions or, more likely, anticipating an event in the near or distant future. Because of the vagueness of the symbols in this cycle, popular religious spokespersons have created many different scenarios to predict human history and the precise coming of Judgment Day. So far, they have always been wrong. But the wild imagery of these symbols endures, particularly in art, literature, and popular religious piety.

Audience

Those who initially heard the book of Revelation read aloud were Christians living in and around Ephesus in the mid- to late 90s, who were concerned because they felt that public opinion was increasingly critical of their faith. They often were called atheists because they denied all gods save one, and their refusal to worship the emperor brought them into a tense relationship with the civil authorities. During hard economic times or the threat of war, minorities are often the target of prejudice, as they are suspected of treasonous behavior. Christians were seen as angering the gods and bringing on the woes that had begun to plague society. As they gathered in Christian worship, they feared that something bad was soon to happen to them. The book sought to allay their fears by declaring that Jesus was in charge and that all things would transpire according to a grand divine plan.

Impact

The impact of the book of Revelation has been great in the past two thousand years, sometimes for good and sometimes for bad. Too many people have used it as a timetable for predicting the future, especially the imminent coming of Jesus, and fomented rebellion among people, particularly poor peasants in the Middle Ages, which generally led to their death. In the modern era, too, many charlatans have convinced people that Jesus was coming because the book's images were being fulfilled in the modern age. As noted, major predictions of this event focused on the possible return of Jesus in September 1988 and again in September 1996.

The book has also been used positively, when it is not taken too literally. When theologians or social reformers seek to inspire change and reform in society by painting the dire consequences of what might happen without change, an appeal to the imagery of these texts often provides cogency and inspiration to their rhetoric. Such rhetoric, for example, inspired Americans who sought to abolish slavery in the nineteenth century and work toward civil rights in our society in the twentieth century. Some contemporary authors maintain that Americans and those in other first world countries need to see ourselves in the imagery of the beast and the third world victims of globalization in the oppressed believers of Revelation. The book should inspire us to disavow our own modern "Roman imperialism."

Ultimately, the book has had a significant impact upon authors, poets, musicians, and especially painters. Images such as the four horsemen, the beasts, and the heavenly city have inspired artistic portrayals—stained-glass windows, woodcuts, lithographs, and paintings. It should not be forgotten that the book itself is a work of art, and the frequent insertion of hymnic material is testimony to this. Biblical scholars define this book as being both apocalyptic literature and liturgical art from the first century CE.

Further Reading

■ Books

Aune, David. *Revelation*. 3 vols. Waco, Tex.: Word Books, 1997–1998.

Bowman, John Wick. "Revelation, Book of." In *The Interpreter's Dictionary of the Bible*, ed. George Buttrick. vol. 4. Nashville, Tenn.: Abingdon Press, 1962.

Caird, G. B. *A Commentary on the Revelation of St. John the Divine*. New York: Harper and Row, 1966.

Collins, Adela. "Revelation, Book of." In *The Anchor Bible Dictionary*, ed. David Noel Freedman. vol. 5. New York: Doubleday, 1992.

Koester, Craig. "Revelation, Book of." In *The New Interpreter's Dictionary of the Bible*, ed. Katharine Doob Sakenfeld. vol. 4. Nashville, Tenn.: Abingdon Press, 2009.

Murphy, Frederick J. *Fallen Is Babylon: The Revelation to John*. Harrisburg, Penn.: Trinity Press International, 1998.

Rowland, Christopher C. "The Book of Revelation." In *The New Interpreter's Bible*, ed. Leander Keck. vol. 12. Nashville, Tenn.: Abingdon Press, 1998.

Thompson, Leonard. *The Book of Revelation: Apocalypse and Empire*. New York: Oxford University Press, 1990.

Wainwright, Arthur William. *Mysterious Apocalypse: Interpreting the Book of Revelation*. Nashville, Tenn.: Abingdon Press, 1993.

—Robert K. Gnuse

BIBLE: REVELATION

◆ Chapter 4

After this I looked, and there in heaven a door stood open! And the first voice, which I had heard speaking to me like a trumpet, said, "Come up here, and I will show you what must take place after this." ²At once I was in the spirit, and there in heaven stood a throne, with one seated on the throne! ³And the one seated there looks like jasper and carnelian, and around the throne is a rainbow that looks like an emerald. ⁴Around the throne are twenty-four thrones, and seated on the thrones are twenty-four elders, dressed in white robes, with golden crowns on their heads. ⁵Coming from the throne are flashes of lightning, and rumblings and peals of thunder, and in front of the throne burn seven flaming torches, which are the seven spirits of God; ⁶and in front of the throne there is something like a sea of glass, like crystal. Around the throne, and on each side of the throne, are four living creatures, full of eyes in front and behind: ⁷the first living creature like a lion, the second living creature like an ox, the third living creature with a face like a human face, and the fourth living creature like a flying eagle.

⁸And the four living creatures, each of them with six wings, are full of eyes all around and inside. Day and night without ceasing they sing, "Holy, holy, holy, the Lord God the Almighty, who was and is and is to come." ⁹And whenever the living creatures give glory and honor and thanks to the one who is seated on the throne, who lives forever and ever, ¹⁰the twenty-four elders fall before the one who is seated on the throne and worship the one who lives forever and ever; they cast their crowns before the throne, singing, ¹¹"You are worthy, our Lord and God, to receive glory and honor and power, for you created all things, and by your will they existed and were created."

◆ Chapter 5

Then I saw in the right hand of the one seated on the throne a scroll written on the inside and on the back, sealed with seven seals; ²and I saw a mighty angel proclaiming with a loud voice, "Who is worthy to open the scroll and break its seals?" ³And no one in heaven or on earth or under the earth was able to open the scroll or to look into it. ⁴And I began to weep bitterly because no one was found worthy to open the

scroll or to look into it. ⁵Then one of the elders said to me, "Do not weep. See, the Lion of the tribe of Judah, the Root of David, has conquered, so that he can open the scroll and its seven seals."

⁶Then I saw between the throne and the four living creatures and among the elders a Lamb standing as if it had been slaughtered, having seven horns and seven eyes, which are the seven spirits of God sent out into all the earth. ⁷He went and took the scroll from the right hand of the one who was seated on the throne. ⁸When he had taken the scroll, the four living creatures and the twenty-four elders fell before the Lamb, each holding a harp and golden bowls full of incense, which are the prayers of the saints. ⁹They sing a new song: "You are worthy to take the scroll and to open its seals, for you were slaughtered and by your blood you ransomed for God saints from every tribe and language and people and nation; ¹⁰you have made them to be a kingdom and priests serving our God, and they will reign on earth." ¹¹Then I looked, and I heard the voice of many angels surrounding the throne and the living creatures and the elders; they numbered myriads of myriads and thousands of thousands, ¹²singing with full voice, "Worthy is the Lamb that was slaughtered to receive power and wealth and wisdom and might and honor and glory and blessing!" ¹³Then I heard every creature in heaven and on earth and under the earth and in the sea, and all that is in them, singing, "To the one seated on the throne and to the Lamb be blessing and honor and glory and might forever and ever!" ¹⁴And the four living creatures said, "Amen!" And the elders fell down and worshiped.

◆ Chapter 6

Then I saw the Lamb open one of the seven seals, and I heard one of the four living creatures call out, as with a voice of thunder, "Come!" ²I looked, and there was a white horse! Its rider had a bow; a crown was given to him, and he came out conquering and to conquer.

³When he opened the second seal, I heard the second living creature call out, "Come!" ⁴And out came another horse, bright red; its rider was permitted to take peace from the earth, so that people would slaughter one another; and he was given a

great sword. [5]When he opened the third seal, I heard the third living creature call out, "Come!" I looked, and there was a black horse! Its rider held a pair of scales in his hand, [6]and I heard what seemed to be a voice in the midst of the four living creatures saying, "A quart of wheat for a day's pay, and three quarts of barley for a day's pay, but do not damage the olive oil and the wine!" [7]When he opened the fourth seal, I heard the voice of the fourth living creature call out, "Come!" [8]I looked and there was a pale green horse! Its rider's name was Death, and Hades followed with him; they were given authority over a fourth of the earth, to kill with sword, famine, and pestilence, and by the wild animals of the earth.

[9]When he opened the fifth seal, I saw under the altar the souls of those who had been slaughtered for the word of God and for the testimony they had given; [10]they cried out with a loud voice, "Sovereign Lord, holy and true, how long will it be before you judge and avenge our blood on the inhabitants of the earth?" [11]They were each given a white robe and told to rest a little longer, until the number would be complete both of their fellow servants and of their brothers and sisters, who were soon to be killed as they themselves had been killed. [12]When he opened the sixth seal, I looked, and there came a great earthquake; the sun became black as sackcloth, the full moon became like blood, [13]and the stars of the sky fell to the earth as the fig tree drops its winter fruit when shaken by a gale. [14]The sky vanished like a scroll rolling itself up, and every mountain and island was removed from its place. [15]Then the kings of the earth and the magnates and the generals and the rich and the powerful, and everyone, slave and free, hid in the caves and among the rocks of the mountains, [16]calling to the mountains and rocks, "Fall on us and hide us from the face of the one seated on the throne and from the wrath of the Lamb; [17]for the great day of their wrath has come, and who is able to stand?"

♦ **Chapter 7**

After this I saw four angels standing at the four corners of the earth, holding back the four winds of the earth so that no wind could blow on earth or sea or against any tree. [2]I saw another angel ascending from the rising of the sun, having the seal of the living God, and he called with a loud voice to the four angels who had been given power to damage earth and sea, [3]saying, "Do not damage the earth or the sea or the trees, until we have marked the servants of our God with a seal on their foreheads." [4]And I heard the number of those who were sealed, one

hundred forty-four thousand, sealed out of every tribe of the people of Israel: [5]From the tribe of Judah twelve thousand sealed, from the tribe of Reuben twelve thousand, from the tribe of Gad twelve thousand, [6]from the tribe of Asher twelve thousand, from the tribe of Naphtali twelve thousand, from the tribe of Manasseh twelve thousand, [7]from the tribe of Simeon twelve thousand, from the tribe of Levi twelve thousand, from the tribe of Issachar twelve thousand, [8]from the tribe of Zebulun twelve thousand, from the tribe of Joseph twelve thousand, from the tribe of Benjamin twelve thousand sealed. [9]After this I looked, and there was a great multitude that no one could count, from every nation, from all tribes and peoples and languages, standing before the throne and before the Lamb, robed in white, with palm branches in their hands. [10]They cried out in a loud voice, saying, "Salvation belongs to our God who is seated on the throne, and to the Lamb!" [11]And all the angels stood around the throne and around the elders and the four living creatures, and they fell on their faces before the throne and worshiped God, [12]singing, "Amen! Blessing and glory and wisdom and thanksgiving and honor and power and might be to our God forever and ever! Amen."

[13]Then one of the elders addressed me, saying, "Who are these, robed in white, and where have they come from?" [14]I said to him, "Sir, you are the one that knows." Then he said to me, "These are they who have come out of the great ordeal; they have washed their robes and made them white in the blood of the Lamb. [15]For this reason they are before the throne of God, and worship him day and night within his temple, and the one who is seated on the throne will shelter them. [16]They will hunger no more, and thirst no more; the sun will not strike them, nor any scorching heat; [17]for the Lamb at the center of the throne will be their shepherd, and he will guide them to springs of the water of life, and God will wipe away every tear from their eyes."

♦ **Chapter 8**

When the Lamb opened the seventh seal, there was silence in heaven for about half an hour. [2]And I saw the seven angels who stand before God, and seven trumpets were given to them. [3]Another angel with a golden censer came and stood at the altar; he was given a great quantity of incense to offer with the prayers of all the saints on the golden altar that is before the throne. [4]And the smoke of the incense, with the prayers of the saints, rose before God from the hand of the angel. [5]Then the angel took the censer and filled it with fire from the altar and threw it on the earth; and there were peals of thunder, rumblings, flashes of lightning, and an earthquake. [6]Now the seven angels who had the seven trumpets made ready to blow them.

[7]The first angel blew his trumpet, and there came hail and fire, mixed with blood, and they were hurled to the earth; and a third of the earth was burned up, and a third of the trees were burned up, and all green grass was burned up. [8]The second angel blew his trumpet, and something like a great mountain, burning with fire, was thrown into the sea. [9]A third of the sea became blood, a third of the living creatures in the sea died, and a third of the ships were destroyed. [10]The third angel blew his trumpet, and a great star fell from heaven, blazing like a torch, and it fell on a third of the rivers and on the springs of water. [11]The name of the star is Wormwood. A third of the waters became wormwood, and many died from the water, because it was made bitter. [12]The fourth angel blew his trumpet, and a third of the sun was struck, and a third of the moon, and a third of the stars, so that a third of their light was darkened; a third of the day was kept from shining, and likewise the night. [13]Then I looked, and I heard an eagle crying with a loud voice as it flew in midheaven, "Woe, woe, woe to the inhabitants of the earth, at the blasts of the other trumpets that the three angels are about to blow!"

♦ **Chapter 9**

And the fifth angel blew his trumpet, and I saw a star that had fallen from heaven to earth, and he was given the key to the shaft of the bottomless pit; [2]he opened the shaft of the bottomless pit, and from the shaft rose smoke like the smoke of a great furnace, and the sun and the air were darkened with the smoke from the shaft. [3]Then from the smoke came locusts on the earth, and they were given authority like the authority of scorpions of the earth. [4]They were told not to damage the grass of the earth or any green growth or any tree, but only those people who do not have the seal of God on their foreheads. [5]They were allowed to torture them for five months, but not to kill them, and their torture was like the torture of a scorpion when it stings someone. [6]And in those days people will seek death but will not find it; they will long to die, but death will flee from them. [7]In appearance the locusts were like horses equipped for battle. On their heads were what looked like crowns of gold; their faces were like human faces, [8]their hair like women's hair, and their teeth like lions' teeth; [9]they had scales like iron breastplates, and the noise

of their wings was like the noise of many chariots with horses rushing into battle. [10]They have tails like scorpions, with stingers, and in their tails is their power to harm people for five months. [11]They have as king over them the angel of the bottomless pit; his name in Hebrew is Abaddon, and in Greek he is called Apollyon. [12]The first woe has passed. There are still two woes to come.

[13]Then the sixth angel blew his trumpet, and I heard a voice from the four horns of the golden altar before God, [14]saying to the sixth angel who had the trumpet, "Release the four angels who are bound at the great river Euphrates." [15]So the four angels were released, who had been held ready for the hour, the day, the month, and the year, to kill a third of humankind. [16]The number of the troops of cavalry was two hundred million; I heard their number. [17]And this was how I saw the horses in my vision: the riders wore breastplates the color of fire and of sapphire and of sulfur; the heads of the horses were like lions' heads, and fire and smoke and sulfur came out of their mouths. [18]By these three plagues a third of humankind was killed, by the fire and smoke and sulfur coming out of their mouths. [19]For the power of the horses is in their mouths and in their tails; their tails are like serpents, having heads; and with them they inflict harm. [20]The rest of humankind, who were not killed by these plagues, did not repent of the works of their hands or give up worshiping demons and idols of gold and silver and bronze and stone and wood, which cannot see or hear or walk. [21]And they did not repent of their murders or their sorceries or their fornication or their thefts.

♦ **Chapter 10**

And I saw another mighty angel coming down from heaven, wrapped in a cloud, with a rainbow over his head; his face was like the sun, and his legs like pillars of fire. [2]He held a little scroll open in his hand. Setting his right foot on the sea and his left foot on the land, [3]he gave a great shout, like a lion roaring. And when he shouted, the seven thunders sounded. [4]And when the seven thunders had sounded, I was about to write, but I heard a voice from heaven saying, "Seal up what the seven thunders have said, and do not write it down." [5]Then the angel whom I saw standing on the sea and the land raised his right hand to heaven [6]and swore by him who lives forever and ever, who created heaven and what is in it, the earth and what is in it, and the sea and what is in it: "There will be no more delay, [7]but in the days when the seventh angel is to blow his trumpet, the mystery of God will be fulfilled, as he announced to his servants the prophets."

[8]Then the voice that I had heard from heaven spoke to me again, saying, "Go, take the scroll that is open in the hand of the angel who is standing on the sea and on the land." [9]So I went to the angel and told him to give me the little scroll; and he said to me, "Take it, and eat; it will be bitter to your stomach, but sweet as honey in your mouth." [10]So I took the little scroll from the hand of the angel and ate it; it was sweet as honey in my mouth, but when I had eaten it, my stomach was made bitter. [11]Then they said to me, "You must prophesy again about many peoples and nations and languages and kings."

♦ Chapter 11

Then I was given a measuring rod like a staff, and I was told, "Come and measure the temple of God and the altar and those who worship there, [2]but do not measure the court outside the temple; leave that out, for it is given over to the nations, and they will trample over the holy city for forty-two months.

[3]And I will grant my two witnesses authority to prophesy for one thousand two hundred sixty days, wearing sackcloth." [4]These are the two olive trees and the two lampstands that stand before the Lord of the earth. [5]And if anyone wants to harm them, fire pours from their mouth and consumes their foes; anyone who wants to harm them must be killed in this manner. [6]They have authority to shut the sky, so that no rain may fall during the days of their prophesying, and they have authority over the waters to turn them into blood, and to strike the earth with every kind of plague, as often as they desire. [7]When they have finished their testimony, the beast that comes up from the bottomless pit will make war on them and conquer them and kill them, [8]and their dead bodies will lie in the street of the great city that is prophetically called Sodom and Egypt, where also their Lord was crucified. [9]For three and a half days members of the peoples and tribes and languages and nations will gaze at their dead bodies and refuse to let them be placed in a tomb; [10]and the inhabitants of the earth will gloat over them and celebrate and exchange presents, because these two prophets had been a torment to the inhabitants of the earth. [11]But after the three and a half days, the breath of life from God entered them, and they stood on their feet, and those who saw them were terrified. [12]Then they heard a loud voice from heaven saying to them, "Come up here!" And they went up to heaven in a cloud while their enemies watched them. [13]At that moment there

was a great earthquake, and a tenth of the city fell; seven thousand people were killed in the earthquake, and the rest were terrified and gave glory to the God of heaven.

[14]The second woe has passed. The third woe is coming very soon. [15]Then the seventh angel blew his trumpet, and there were loud voices in heaven, saying, "The kingdom of the world has become the kingdom of our Lord and of his Messiah, and he will reign forever and ever." [16]Then the twenty-four elders who sit on their thrones before God fell on their faces and worshiped God, [17]singing, "We give you thanks, Lord God Almighty, who are and who were, for you have taken your great power and begun to reign. [18]The nations raged, but your wrath has come, and the time for judging the dead, for rewarding your servants, the prophets and saints and all who fear your name, both small and great, and for destroying those who destroy the earth." [19]Then God's temple in heaven was opened, and the ark of his covenant was seen within his temple; and there were flashes of lightning, rumblings, peals of thunder, an earthquake, and heavy hail.

♦ Chapter 12

A great portent appeared in heaven: a woman clothed with the sun, with the moon under her feet, and on her head a crown of twelve stars. [2]She was pregnant and was crying out in birthpangs, in the agony of giving birth. [3]Then another portent appeared in heaven: a great red dragon, with seven heads and ten horns, and seven diadems on his heads. [4]His tail swept down a third of the stars of heaven and threw them to the earth. Then the dragon stood before the woman who was about to bear a child, so that he might devour her child as soon as it was born. [5]And she gave birth to a son, a male child, who is to rule all the nations with a rod of iron. But her child was snatched away and taken to God and to his throne; [6]and the woman fled into the wilderness, where she has a place prepared by God, so that there she can be nourished for one thousand two hundred sixty days. [7]And war broke out in heaven; Michael and his angels fought against the dragon. The dragon and his angels fought back, [8]but they were defeated, and there was no longer any place for them in heaven. [9]The great dragon was thrown down, that ancient serpent, who is called the Devil and Satan, the deceiver of the whole world—he was thrown down to the earth, and his angels were thrown down with him. [10]Then I heard a loud voice in heaven, proclaiming, "Now have come the salvation and the power and the kingdom of our God and the authority of his Messiah, for the accuser of our comrades has been thrown down, who accuses them day and night before our God. ¹¹But they have conquered him by the blood of the Lamb and by the word of their testimony, for they did not cling to life even in the face of death.

¹²Rejoice then, you heavens and those who dwell in them! But woe to the earth and the sea, for the devil has come down to you with great wrath, because he knows that his time is short!" ¹³So when the dragon saw that he had been thrown down to the earth, he pursued the woman who had given birth to the male child. ¹⁴But the woman was given the two wings of the great eagle, so that she could fly from the serpent into the wilderness, to her place where she is nourished for a time, and times, and half a time. ¹⁵Then from his mouth the serpent poured water like a river after the woman, to sweep her away with the flood. ¹⁶But the earth came to the help of the woman; it opened its mouth and swallowed the river that the dragon had poured from his mouth. ¹⁷Then the dragon was angry with the woman, and went off to make war on the rest of her children, those who keep the commandments of God and hold the testimony of Jesus. ¹⁸Then the dragon took his stand on the sand of the seashore.

♦ **Chapter 13**

And I saw a beast rising out of the sea having ten horns and seven heads; and on its horns were ten diadems, and on its heads were blasphemous names. ²And the beast that I saw was like a leopard, its feet were like a bear's, and its mouth was like a lion's mouth. And the dragon gave it his power and his throne and great authority. ³One of its heads seemed to have received a death-blow, but its mortal wound had been healed. In amazement the whole earth followed the beast. ⁴They worshiped the dragon, for he had given his authority to the beast, and they worshiped the beast, saying, "Who is like the beast, and who can fight against it?" ⁵The beast was given a mouth uttering haughty and blasphemous words, and it was allowed to exercise authority for forty-two months. ⁶It opened its mouth to utter blasphemies against God, blaspheming his name and his dwelling, that is, those who dwell in heaven. ⁷Also it was allowed to make war on the saints and to conquer them. It was given authority over every tribe and people and language and nation, ⁸and all the inhabitants of the earth will worship it, everyone whose name has not been written from the foundation of the world in the book of life of the Lamb that was slaughtered. ⁹Let anyone who has an ear listen: ¹⁰If you are to be

taken captive, into captivity you go; if you kill with the sword, with the sword you must be killed. Here is a call for the endurance and faith of the saints.

¹¹Then I saw another beast that rose out of the earth; it had two horns like a lamb and it spoke like a dragon. ¹²It exercises all the authority of the first beast on its behalf, and it makes the earth and its inhabitants worship the first beast, whose mortal wound had been healed. ¹³It performs great signs, even making fire come down from heaven to earth in the sight of all; ¹⁴and by the signs that it is allowed to perform on behalf of the beast, it deceives the inhabitants of earth, telling them to make an image for the beast that had been wounded by the sword and yet lived; ¹⁵and it was allowed to give breath to the image of the beast so that the image of the beast could even speak and cause those who would not worship the image of the beast to be killed. ¹⁶Also it causes all, both small and great, both rich and poor, both free and slave, to be marked on the right hand or the forehead, ¹⁷so that no one can buy or sell who does not have the mark, that is, the name of the beast or the number of its name. ¹⁸This calls for wisdom: let anyone with understanding calculate the number of the beast, for it is the number of a person. Its number is six hundred sixty-six. . . .

♦ **Chapter 15**

Then I saw another portent in heaven, great and amazing: seven angels with seven plagues, which are the last, for with them the wrath of God is ended. ²And I saw what appeared to be a sea of glass mixed with fire, and those who had conquered the beast and its image and the number of its name, standing beside the sea of glass with harps of God in their hands. ³And they sing the song of Moses, the servant of God, and the song of the Lamb: "Great and amazing are your deeds, Lord God the Almighty! Just and true are your ways, King of the nations! ⁴Lord, who will not fear and glorify your name? For you alone are holy. All nations will come and worship before you, for your judgments have been revealed."

⁵After this I looked, and the temple of the tent of witness in heaven was opened, ⁶and out of the temple came the seven angels with the seven plagues, robed in pure bright linen, with golden sashes across their chests. ⁷Then one of the four living creatures gave the seven angels seven golden bowls full of the wrath of God, who lives forever and ever; ⁸and the temple was filled with smoke from the glory of God and from his power, and no one could enter the temple until the seven plagues of the seven angels were ended.

♦ Chapter 16

Then I heard a loud voice from the temple telling the seven angels, "Go and pour out on the earth the seven bowls of the wrath of God." [2]So the first angel went and poured his bowl on the earth, and a foul and painful sore came on those who had the mark of the beast and who worshiped its image. [3]The second angel poured his bowl into the sea, and it became like the blood of a corpse, and every living thing in the sea died. [4]The third angel poured his bowl into the rivers and the springs of water, and they became blood. [5]And I heard the angel of the waters say, "You are just, O Holy One, who are and were, for you have judged these things; [6]because they shed the blood of saints and prophets, you have given them blood to drink. It is what they deserve!" [7]And I heard the altar respond, "Yes, O Lord God, the Almighty, your judgments are true and just!"

[8]The fourth angel poured his bowl on the sun, and it was allowed to scorch them with fire; [9]they were scorched by the fierce heat, but they cursed the name of God, who had authority over these plagues, and they did not repent and give him glory. [10]The fifth angel poured his bowl on the throne of the beast, and its kingdom was plunged into darkness; people gnawed their tongues in agony, [11]and cursed the God of heaven because of their pains and sores, and they did not repent of their deeds.

[12]The sixth angel poured his bowl on the great river Euphrates, and its water was dried up in order to prepare the way for the kings from the east. [13]And I saw three foul spirits like frogs coming from the mouth of the dragon, from the mouth of the beast, and from the mouth of the false prophet. [14]These are demonic spirits, performing signs, who go abroad to the kings of the whole world, to assemble them for battle on the great day of God the Almighty. [15]("See, I am coming like a thief! Blessed is the one who stays awake and is clothed, not going about naked and exposed to shame.") [16]And they assembled them at the place that in Hebrew is called Harmagedon.

[17]The seventh angel poured his bowl into the air, and a loud voice came out of the temple, from the throne, saying, "It is done!" [18]And there came flashes of lightning, rumblings, peals of thunder, and a violent earthquake, such as had not occurred since people were upon the earth, so violent was that earthquake. [19]The great city was split into three parts, and the cities of the nations fell. God remembered great Babylon and gave her the wine-cup of the fury of his wrath. [20]And every island fled away, and no mountains were to be found; [21]and huge hailstones, each weighing about a hundred pounds, dropped from heaven on people, until they cursed God for the plague of the hail, so fearful was that plague.

♦ Chapter 17

Then one of the seven angels who had the seven bowls came and said to me, "Come, I will show you the judgment of the great whore who is seated on many waters, [2]with whom the kings of the earth have committed fornication, and with the wine of whose fornication the inhabitants of the earth have become drunk." [3]So he carried me away in the spirit into a wilderness, and I saw a woman sitting on a scarlet beast that was full of blasphemous names, and it had seven heads and ten horns. [4]The woman was clothed in purple and scarlet, and adorned with gold and jewels and pearls, holding in her hand a golden cup full of abominations and the impurities of her fornication; [5]and on her forehead was written a name, a mystery: "Babylon the great, mother of whores and of earth's abominations." [6]And I saw that the woman was drunk with the blood of the saints and the blood of the witnesses to Jesus. When I saw her, I was greatly amazed.

[7]But the angel said to me, "Why are you so amazed? I will tell you the mystery of the woman, and of the beast with seven heads and ten horns that carries her. [8]The beast that you saw was, and is not, and is about to ascend from the bottomless pit and go to destruction. And the inhabitants of the earth, whose names have not been written in the book of life from the foundation of the world, will be amazed when they see the beast, because it was and is not and is to come. [9]"This calls for a mind that has wisdom: the seven heads are seven mountains on which the woman is seated; also, they are seven kings, [10]of whom five have fallen, one is living, and the other has not yet come; and when he comes, he must remain only a little while. [11]As for the beast that was and is not, it is an eighth but it belongs to the seven, and it goes to destruction. [12]And the ten horns that you saw are ten kings who have not yet received a kingdom, but they are to receive authority as kings for one hour, together with the beast. [13]These are united in yielding their power and authority to the beast; [14]they will make war on the Lamb, and the Lamb will conquer them, for he is Lord of lords and King of kings, and those with him are called and chosen and faithful." [15]And he said to me, "The waters that you saw, where the whore is seated, are peoples and multitudes and nations and languages. [16]And the ten horns that you saw, they and the beast will hate the whore; they will

make her desolate and naked; they will devour her flesh and burn her up with fire. [17]For God has put it into their hearts to carry out his purpose by agreeing to give their kingdom to the beast, until the words of God will be fulfilled. [18]The woman you saw is the great city that rules over the kings of the earth."

♦ Chapter 18

After this I saw another angel coming down from heaven, having great authority; and the earth was made bright with his splendor. [2]He called out with a mighty voice, "Fallen, fallen is Babylon the great! It has become a dwelling place of demons, a haunt of every foul and hateful bird, a haunt of every foul and hateful beast. [3]For all the nations have drunk of the wine of the wrath of her fornication, and the kings of the earth have committed fornication with her, and the merchants of the earth have grown rich from the power of her luxury." [4]Then I heard another voice from heaven saying, "Come out of her, my people, so that you do not take part in her sins, and so that you do not share in her plagues; [5]for her sins are heaped high as heaven, and God has remembered her iniquities. [6]Render to her as she herself has rendered, and repay her double for her deeds; mix a double draught for her in the cup she mixed. [7]As she glorified herself and lived luxuriously, so give her a like measure of torment and grief. Since in her heart she says, 'I rule as a queen; I am no widow, and I will never see grief,' [8]therefore her plagues will come in a single day—pestilence and mourning and famine—and she will be burned with fire; for mighty is the Lord God who judges her."

[9]And the kings of the earth, who committed fornication and lived in luxury with her, will weep and wail over her when they see the smoke of her burning; [10]they will stand far off, in fear of her torment, and say, "Alas, alas, the great city, Babylon, the mighty city! For in one hour your judgment has come." [11]And the merchants of the earth weep and mourn for her, since no one buys their cargo anymore, [12]cargo of gold, silver, jewels and pearls, fine linen, purple, silk and scarlet, all kinds of scented wood, all articles of ivory, all articles of costly wood, bronze, iron, and marble, [13]cinnamon, spice, incense, myrrh, frankincense, wine, olive oil, choice flour and wheat, cattle and sheep, horses and chariots, slaves—and human lives. [14]"The fruit for which your soul longed has gone from you, and all your dainties and your splendor are lost to you, never to be found again!" [15]The merchants of these wares, who gained wealth from her, will stand far off, in fear of her torment, weep-

ing and mourning aloud, [16]"Alas, alas, the great city, clothed in fine linen, in purple and scarlet, adorned with gold, with jewels, and with pearls! [17]For in one hour all this wealth has been laid waste!" And all shipmasters and seafarers, sailors and all whose trade is on the sea, stood far off [18]and cried out as they saw the smoke of her burning, "What city was like the great city?" [19]And they threw dust on their heads, as they wept and mourned, crying out, "Alas, alas, the great city, where all who had ships at sea grew rich by her wealth! For in one hour she has been laid waste. [20]Rejoice over her, O heaven, you saints and apostles and prophets! For God has given judgment for you against her." [21]Then a mighty angel took up a stone like a great millstone and threw it into the sea, saying, "With such violence Babylon the great city will be thrown down, and will be found no more; [22]and the sound of harpists and minstrels and of flutists and trumpeters will be heard in you no more; and an artisan of any trade will be found in you no more; and the sound of the millstone will be heard in you no more; [23]and the light of a lamp will shine in you no more; and the voice of bridegroom and bride will be heard in you no more; for your merchants were the magnates of the earth, and all nations were deceived by your sorcery. [24]And in you was found the blood of prophets and of saints, and of all who have been slaughtered on earth."

♦ Chapter 19

After this I heard what seemed to be the loud voice of a great multitude in heaven, saying, "Hallelujah! Salvation and glory and power to our God, [2]for his judgments are true and just; he has judged the great whore who corrupted the earth with her fornication, and he has avenged on her the blood of his servants." [3]Once more they said, "Hallelujah! The smoke goes up from her forever and ever." [4]And the twenty-four elders and the four living creatures fell down and worshiped God who is seated on the throne, saying, "Amen. Hallelujah!"

[5]And from the throne came a voice saying, "Praise our God, all you his servants, and all who fear him, small and great." [6]Then I heard what seemed to be the voice of a great multitude, like the sound of many waters and like the sound of mighty thunderpeals, crying out, "Hallelujah! For the Lord our God the Almighty reigns. [7]Let us rejoice and exult and give him the glory, for the marriage of the Lamb has come, and his bride has made herself ready; [8]to her it has been granted to be clothed with fine linen, bright and pure"—for the fine linen is the righteous deeds of the

saints. [9]And the angel said to me, "Write this: Blessed are those who are invited to the marriage supper of the Lamb." And he said to me, "These are true words of God." [10]Then I fell down at his feet to worship him, but he said to me, "You must not do that! I am a fellow servant with you and your comrades who hold the testimony of Jesus. Worship God! For the testimony of Jesus is the spirit of prophecy."

[11]Then I saw heaven opened, and there was a white horse! Its rider is called Faithful and True, and in righteousness he judges and makes war. [12]His eyes are like a flame of fire, and on his head are many diadems; and he has a name inscribed that no one knows but himself. [13]He is clothed in a robe dipped in blood, and his name is called The Word of God. [14]And the armies of heaven, wearing fine linen, white and pure, were following him on white horses. [15]From his mouth comes a sharp sword with which to strike down the nations, and he will rule them with a rod of iron; he will tread the wine press of the fury of the wrath of God the Almighty. [16]On his robe and on his thigh he has a name inscribed, "King of kings and Lord of lords." [17]Then I saw an angel standing in the sun, and with a loud voice he called to all the birds that fly in midheaven, "Come, gather for the great supper of God, [18]to eat the flesh of kings, the flesh of captains, the flesh of the mighty, the flesh of horses and their riders—flesh of all, both free and slave, both small and great." [19]Then I saw the beast and the kings of the earth with their armies gathered to make war against the rider on the horse and against his army. [20]And the beast was captured, and with it the false prophet who had performed in its presence the signs by which he deceived those who had received the mark of the beast and those who worshiped its image. These two were thrown alive into the lake of fire that burns with sulfur. [21]And the rest were killed by the sword of the rider on the horse, the sword that came from his mouth; and all the birds were gorged with their flesh.

◆ Chapter 20

Then I saw an angel coming down from heaven, holding in his hand the key to the bottomless pit and a great chain. [2]He seized the dragon, that ancient serpent, who is the Devil and Satan, and bound him for a thousand years, [3]and threw him into the pit, and locked and sealed it over him, so that he would deceive the nations no more, until the thousand years were ended. After that he must be let out for a little while. [4]Then I saw thrones, and those seated on them were given authority to judge. I also saw the souls of those who had been beheaded for their testimony to Jesus and for the word of God. They had not worshiped the beast or its image and had not received its mark on their foreheads or their hands. They came to life and reigned with Christ a thousand years. [5](The rest of the dead did not come to life until the thousand years were ended.) This is the first resurrection. [6]Blessed and holy are those who share in the first resurrection. Over these the second death has no power, but they will be priests of God and of Christ, and they will reign with him a thousand years. [7]When the thousand years are ended, Satan will be released from his prison [8]and will come out to deceive the nations at the four corners of the earth, Gog and Magog, in order to gather them for battle; they are as numerous as the sands of the sea. [9]They marched up over the breadth of the earth and surrounded the camp of the saints and the beloved city. And fire came down from heaven and consumed them. [10]And the devil who had deceived them was thrown into the lake of fire and sulfur, where the beast and the false prophet were, and they will be tormented day and night forever and ever.

[11]Then I saw a great white throne and the one who sat on it; the earth and the heaven fled from his presence, and no place was found for them. [12]And I saw the dead, great and small, standing before the throne, and books were opened. Also another book was opened, the book of life. And the dead were judged according to their works, as recorded in the books. [13]And the sea gave up the dead that were in it, Death and Hades gave up the dead that were in them, and all were judged according to what they had done. [14]Then Death and Hades were thrown into the lake of fire. This is the second death, the lake of fire; [15]and anyone whose name was not found written in the book of life was thrown into the lake of fire.

◆ Chapter 21

Then I saw a new heaven and a new earth; for the first heaven and the first earth had passed away, and the sea was no more. [2]And I saw the holy city, the new Jerusalem, coming down out of heaven from God, prepared as a bride adorned for her husband. [3]And I heard a loud voice from the throne saying, "See, the home of God is among mortals. He will dwell with them as their God; they will be his peoples, and God himself will be with them; [4]he will wipe every tear from their eyes. Death will be no more; mourning and crying and pain will be no more, for the first things have passed away." [5]And the one who was seated on the throne said, "See, I am making all things new." Also he said, "Write this, for these words are trustworthy and true." [6]Then he said to me, "It is done! I am the Alpha and the Omega, the beginning and the end. To the thirsty I will give water as a gift from the spring of the water of life. [7]Those who conquer will inherit these things, and I will be their God and they will be my children. [8]But as for the cowardly, the faithless, the polluted, the murderers, the fornicators, the sorcerers, the idolaters, and all liars, their place will be in the lake that burns with fire and sulfur, which is the second death."

[9]Then one of the seven angels who had the seven bowls full of the seven last plagues came and said to me, "Come, I will show you the bride, the wife of the Lamb." [10]And in the spirit he carried me away to a great, high mountain and showed me the holy city Jerusalem coming down out of heaven from God. [11]It has the glory of God and a radiance like a very rare jewel, like jasper, clear as crystal. [12]It has a great, high wall with twelve gates, and at the gates twelve angels, and on the gates are inscribed the names of the twelve tribes of the Israelites; [13]on the east three gates, on the north three gates, on the south three gates, and on the west three gates. [14]And the wall of the city has twelve foundations, and on them are the twelve names of the twelve apostles of the Lamb. [15]The angel who talked to me had a measuring rod of gold to measure the city and its gates and walls. [16]The city lies foursquare, its length the same as its width; and he measured the city with his rod, fifteen hundred miles; its length and width and height are equal. [17]He also measured its wall, one hundred forty-four cubits by human measurement, which the angel was using. [18]The wall is built of jasper, while the city is pure gold, clear as glass. [19]The foundations of the wall of the city are adorned with every jewel; the first was jasper, the second sapphire, the third agate, the fourth emerald, [20]the fifth onyx, the sixth carnelian, the seventh chrysolite, the eighth beryl, the ninth topaz, the tenth chrysoprase, the eleventh jacinth, the twelfth amethyst. [21]And the twelve gates are twelve pearls, each of the gates is a single pearl, and the street of the city is pure gold, transparent as glass. [22]I saw no temple in the city, for its temple is the Lord God the Almighty and the Lamb. [23]And the city has no need of sun or moon to shine on it, for the glory of God is its light, and its lamp is the Lamb. [24]The nations will walk by its light, and the kings of the earth will bring their glory into it. [25]Its gates will never be shut by day—and there will be no night there. [26]People will

Glossary

Abaddon	Destruction
Alpha and Omega	the beginning and the end; the first and last letters of the Greek alphabet
another horse, bright red, its rider	war and destruction
Babylon	here, Rome
beast	the anti-Christ; also used to refer to the Roman emperor Nero
black horse	famine
bride	the Christian Church
Euphrates	the river in Iraq that was the eastern border of the Roman Empire
full of eyes	watchful
Gog and Magog	a reference to the nation that will destroy Israel
Hades	the underworld of classical mythology
Harmagedon	generally spelled Armageddon, the hill of Megiddo, the site of several important battles in Israel's history
Judah . . . Reuben . . .	a listing of the twelve tribes of Israel

bring into it the glory and the honor of the nations. ²⁷But nothing unclean will enter it, nor anyone who practices abomination or falsehood, but only those who are written in the Lamb's book of life.

♦ **Chapter 22**

Then the angel showed me the river of the water of life, bright as crystal, flowing from the throne of God and of the Lamb ²through the middle of the street of the city. On either side of the river is the tree of life with its twelve kinds of fruit, producing its fruit each month; and the leaves of the tree are for the healing of the nations. ³Nothing accursed will be found there any more. But the throne of God and of the Lamb will be in it, and his servants will worship him; ⁴they will see his face, and his name will be on their foreheads. ⁵And there will be no more night; they need no light of lamp or sun, for the Lord God will be their light, and they will reign forever and ever.

⁶And he said to me, "These words are trustworthy and true, for the Lord, the God of the spirits of the prophets, has sent his angel to show his servants what must soon take place." ⁷"See, I am coming soon! Blessed is the one who keeps the words of the prophecy of this book." ⁸I, John, am the one who heard and saw these things. And when I heard and saw them, I fell down to worship at the feet of the angel who showed them to me; ⁹but he said to me, "You must not do that! I am a fellow servant with you

and your comrades the prophets, and with those who keep the words of this book. Worship God!" ¹⁰And he said to me, "Do not seal up the words of the prophecy of this book, for the time is near. ¹¹Let the evildoer still do evil, and the filthy still be filthy, and the righteous still do right, and the holy still be holy." ¹²"See, I am coming soon; my reward is with me, to repay according to everyone's work. ¹³I am the Alpha and the Omega, the first and the last, the beginning and the end." ¹⁴Blessed are those who wash their robes, so that they will have the right to the tree of life and may enter the city by the gates. ¹⁵Outside are the dogs and sorcerers and fornicators and murderers and idolaters, and everyone who loves and practices falsehood. ¹⁶"It is I, Jesus, who sent my angel to you with this testimony for the churches. I am the root and the descendant of David, the bright morning star." ¹⁷The Spirit and the bride say, "Come." And let everyone who hears say, "Come." And let everyone who is thirsty come. Let anyone who wishes take the water of life as a gift. ¹⁸I warn everyone who hears the words of the prophecy of this book: if anyone adds to them, God will add to that person the plagues described in this book; ¹⁹if anyone takes away from the words of the book of this prophecy, God will take away that person's share in the tree of life and in the holy city, which are described in this book.

²⁰The one who testifies to these things says, "Surely I am coming soon." Amen. Come, Lord Jesus! ²¹The grace of the Lord Jesus be with all the saints. Amen.

The anti-Gnostic polemicist Epiphanius of Salamis

(Epiphanius, from 'Crabbes Historical Dictionary', published in 1825 [litho], English School, [19th century] / Private Collection / Ken Welsh / The
Bridgeman Art Library International)

PTOLEMY: "LETTER TO FLORA"

"Therefore it is indisputable that here the law of Moses is different from the Law of God."

Overview

Written sometime in the second century CE, the "Letter to Flora," by a Rome-based theologian named Ptolemy, presents a sophisticated critique of the Jewish scriptures from the perspective of one of the major schools of Gnostic thought: Valentinianism. In the letter, addressed to an educated Roman woman named Flora, who was presumably a pupil of his, Ptolemy argues that Jewish law should be divided into different levels of authenticity and evaluated according to this criterion. Whereas some Christian sects in the second century believed that Jewish law came entirely from God, others—radical Gnostics in particular—argued that it came from the Devil. Perhaps responding to questions posed to him by Flora, likely in a previous letter, Ptolemy criticizes both these perspectives and suggests that while some of the law can be shown to come from Moses and the Jewish ancestors, the core of the law was revealed by a just deity subordinate to the perfect God.

This letter is remarkable not only for its clear presentation of a number of key arguments of scriptural interpretation from antiquity but also for its evidence of female participation in ancient theological debates in second-century Rome. Moreover, Ptolemy's interpretation of the Jewish scriptures anticipates modern forms of biblical scholarship, such as source and redaction criticism, in a number of important ways.

Context

In the late second century, the early Christian movement encompassed a wide range of often very different theological opinions and was still in the process of defining its relationship to Judaism, the religion out of which it was born. Two of the most controversial issues at this time were the identity and nature of the Jewish God and the utility of the Jewish scriptures for Christians.

Once the church was opened up to the non-Jewish community, early Christian thinkers, especially in response to the apostle Paul's teaching, began to minimize or even ne-

gate the traditional ritual requirements of the Jewish law. Moreover, some believed that there was a contradiction between the moral messages of Jesus and the sometimes irrational and cruel behavior of the Jewish God. As a result, some Christians wondered if the God of the Jews was in fact the divine father of Jesus. If he was not, then what could be gained from reading and studying the Jewish scriptures devoted to him?

The previous century had been a tumultuous time for both Jewish and Christian communities in the eastern Mediterranean. A violent Jewish revolt near the end of the first century was brutally suppressed by the Roman army, which resulted in the destruction of the Second Jewish Temple, in Jerusalem, in the year 70. The resulting crisis and sense of betrayal led some, probably initially in some quarter of the Jewish community itself, to openly question whether their deity was really the God he claimed to be or some sort of demonic impostor who had led their people to disaster. A myth evolved in which the God of the Jewish scriptures is portrayed as an irrational ruler of the lower material realm, variously known by Aramaic names such as Yaldabaoth ("Child of Chaos") or Saklas ("the Fool"). The true, perfect God could be found existing only beyond the material realm, and knowledge (gnosis) of this divinity is available to only a select few enlightened philosophers, known as "Gnostics" (knowers).

This alternate viewpoint suited some Christian thinkers who wanted to distance themselves from their Jewish roots and develop a distinctly Christian theology using the vocabulary and concepts of Greek philosophy. The fusion of this Jewish critique of the creator god with late Platonic philosophy gave rise to the "Gnostic" tradition within the early church, which saw Jesus as representing the true God beyond the cosmos and as the enemy of the creator. While the precise meaning of the term *Gnosticism* has been fiercely debated by modern scholars, it is nevertheless clear that it represented a significant alternative theological tradition in antiquity and was viewed as a threat by church authorities, especially the "Valentinian" tradition with which Ptolemy was identified.

Valentinus had been an important speculative theologian and Christian philosopher active in Rome during the mid-second century CE. Although he was once

CA. 140	■ The Christian philosopher Valentinus moves to Rome and begins teaching. He is briefly considered as a candidate for bishop of Rome but is not elected.
CA. 150	■ Ptolemy teaches various disciples in Rome. ■ Flora receives Ptolemy's letter.
CA. 160	■ Justin Martyr teaches and writes in Rome.
CA. 250 −300	■ The ideas of the Valentinian School, especially those of Ptolemy and his disciples, are criticized as heretical by anti-Gnostic writers.
374 −377	■ Ptolemy's letter is used as evidence for the refutation of eighty heresies by Epiphanius of Salamis in his *Panarion*.
1945	■ Gnostic manuscripts in Coptic are discovered in Egypt at Nag Hammadi.

considered a candidate for bishop of Rome (an office that later evolved into the Catholic papacy), Valentinus's ideas about the complex nature of the heavenly realm were harshly criticized and rejected by the emerging mainstream church. During the late third century, the ideas of the Valentinian school, especially those of Ptolemy and his disciples, were deemed heretical by anti-Gnostic writers. Valentinus was even caricatured as the "father" of all Christian heresy by anti-Gnostic polemicists such as Irenaeus of Lyons (writing around 180 CE) and Epiphanius of Salamis (in the fourth century), who were typically suspicious of the influence of Greek ideas in Christian theology.

For years the Church had been becoming far more Greek in its outlook and culture and far less Jewish. For instance, Marcion of Sinope, who ran a shipping company on the Black Sea, had argued in the mid-second century that the gods of the Jewish and Christian scriptures were different and that therefore Christians had no real need to study the Jewish Bible, which he viewed simply as a document recording early Jewish history. In fact, Ptolemy himself makes reference to Marcion's argument in his "Letter to Flora." Marcion's ideas gained in popularity and became a threat to the mainstream church as Marcionite communities began to be formed. For the main-

stream Church, however, the Jewish scriptures predicted the coming of Jesus and were thus of enduring value. It is for this reason that the Christian Bible contains both Jewish and Christian writings, since the "New" Christian Testament is thought to complement and supersede the "Old" Jewish one.

The degree to which the Jewish God was seen as entirely good, demonic, or simply inferior varied widely among the many sectarian groups of the early Christian era. Ptolemy, it appears, was attempting in the "Letter to Flora" to stake out a middle ground between the extreme ends of the spectrum of theological opinions by offering a more philosophically nuanced position characteristic of Valentinian teaching.

While the struggle between the emerging mainstream Church and Gnostic Christians eventually resulted in the suppression and destruction of much Gnostic literature, descriptions of their ideas and excerpts from their writings can be found in the words of several church fathers. Ptolemy's "Letter to Flora" is quoted in the *Panarion* (written between 374 and 377), by the fiercely anti-Gnostic author Epiphanius of Salamis, as a typical example of the Gnostic understanding of God and creation. There is no reason to doubt the accuracy of this characterization. Important, too, is that Ptolemy's letter is one of the few Gnostic writings preserved in its original Greek. A large number of Gnostic writings were discovered in the mid-twentieth century at Nag Hammadi in Egypt, but these were Coptic (that is, Egyptian) translations of lost Greek originals. The discovery of these writings revolutionized the study of ancient Gnosticism and shed much light on the diversity that existed between the various Gnostic schools. Two writings in particular, the Gospel of Truth and the Tripartite Tractate, added much to historical knowledge of Valentinian theology. The "Letter to Flora" is likewise important for an overall understanding of Gnosticism, especially in the Greek tradition of the second century of the Common Era.

About the Author

According to the fathers of the church, Ptolemy was one of the main representatives of the Valentinian school of theology. Like Valentinus, Ptolemy likely came from Egypt but pursued his teaching career in the imperial capital of Rome. Even though we know almost nothing about his life, we can infer that Ptolemy was important enough to attract the scorn of rival theologians and influential enough to attract members of the educated Roman elite, such as Flora, to his teaching. It is possible that he was the Christian teacher mentioned by the second-century Christian philosopher Justin Martyr as having been put to death for trying to convert a wealthy Roman woman married to an unsympathetic pagan, although this identification remains unconfirmed. It should also be noted that this Ptolemy is distinct from the famous Greek scientist of the same name who lived at approximately the same time in Alexandria.

Explanation and Analysis of the Document

While some writers attribute a rather complicated Gnostic myth about the tragic fall of divine wisdom to Ptolemy and his followers, the "Letter to Flora" contains none of this sort of elaborate theological speculation. This absence raises the question as to whether Gnostic teachers had two versions of their teaching—a simplified version aimed at beginners and a more detailed version for advanced students. Such an arrangement is not uncommon among religious teachers in various traditions and so would not be unusual in this context. Nevertheless, what we read in the "Letter to Flora" is a coherent argument about scriptural interpretation, not a creation myth.

♦ Paragraphs 1–5

The very first word of the letter introduces its main subject—"the Law"—that part of the Jewish scriptures known as the Torah or Pentateuch (Genesis, Exodus, Leviticus, Numbers, Deuteronomy) and said to have been revealed by God to Moses on Mount Sinai after the Jewish flight from Egypt. The Torah outlines all of the major ethical and ritual requirements of Judaism in often considerable detail. In his letter Ptolemy addresses Flora as "my dear sister," using the family language typical of Christians during this period. It was commonplace for members of the church to address themselves as "brother" and "sister," which sometimes led to charges of incest by hostile Roman observers.

By means of this letter, Ptolemy aims to clarify for Flora the true nature of Jewish law and to explain why the majority of their fellow Christians have failed to understand its origins. Some people, he says, believe that the law was given by "God the Father"—that is, the being to whom Jesus refers in the Gospels. This represents the emerging mainstream, or "proto-orthodox," opinion, which came to be the standard of belief in later centuries. Others suggest that the devil brought forth the law along with the universe itself, an opinion advocated by those Gnostics who rejected the world as a demonic creation. In this way, Ptolemy contrasts two strongly opposed currents of early Christian thought, one that saw the world and its divine ruler as essentially good and the other that condemned them as monstrous and evil. Both, according to Ptolemy, are wrong, because Jewish law is neither completely good, since it contains imperfections, nor completely evil, since it does contain elements of justice. Such contradictions, therefore, refute each of the arguments cited, which Ptolemy then supports through references to Jesus's words from the New Testament. As a Christian, Ptolemy believed that the authority of Jesus supersedes anything contained in the Jewish scriptures. Ptolemy intended to deliver a more "accurate" explanation of Jewish law and of the various sources of that law.

♦ Paragraphs 6–10

According to Ptolemy, if one is to learn the true nature of Jewish law, then one should recognize that not all parts of the law come from the same lawgiver. Some of it certainly comes from God, though other parts come from Moses

Moses and the tablets of the Law

(Moses and the Tablets of the Law, La Hire or La Hyre, Laurent de [1606-56] / Private Collection / Photo © Bonhams, London, UK / The Bridgeman Art Library International)

and still others from the Jewish elders. This multilayered texture, Ptolemy claims, is demonstrated by Jesus's teaching on divorce, in which he states that Moses modified the law of God prohibiting divorce because of the stubbornness of the people (Matthew 19:8). Similarly, Ptolemy cites other examples of Jesus's teaching, in which the Jewish elders are said to have contradicted the law of God. Therefore, for Ptolemy, it is Jesus who has revealed that Jewish law is divided into three parts.

The idea that the Hebrew Bible, especially its early books, is made up of multiple sources is a conclusion reached by modern biblical scholarship, which has attempted to trace the character and origin of these diverse literary sources. In this way, Ptolemy's argument anticipates one of the key findings of modern research on the Bible.

♦ Paragraphs 11–20

The Valentinians seem to have favored three-part, or Trinitarian, structures when explaining their theological ideas, something that would become normative even in the mainstream. For instance, while the law, in general, is divided by Ptolemy into three parts, the portion derived from God is itself divided into three additional parts: the pure law with no imperfections—that is, the divinely revealed core of the Torah (Hebrew for "law"); the imperfect law, containing elements of injustice; and the symbolic law, which is

> *"The Law that was ordained through Moses, my dear sister Flora, has not been understood by many persons, who have accurate knowledge neither of him who ordained it nor of its commandments."*

> *"Therefore it is indisputable that here the law of Moses is different from the Law of God."*

> *"For if the Law was not ordained by the perfect God himself, as we have already taught you, nor by the devil, a statement one cannot possibly make, the legislator must be some one other than these two."*

meant to be interpreted allegorically as referring to higher realities. Again, Jesus is cited as the source of this analysis.

The pure law consists of the "Decalogue," or Ten Commandments, which Jesus claims that he came into the world to complete and reaffirm. The imperfect law is that which contradicts the pure law, such as the vengeance principle of "an eye for an eye," which when taken to its logical extreme can be used to allow revenge killing, an act strictly forbidden by the Ten Commandments' prohibition against murder. The symbolic law is the portion dealing with ritual acts that no longer apply to Christians or, for that matter, Jews. With the destruction of the Jewish Temple in the year 70, many portions of the law regulating its rituals became irrelevant. As a result, such passages were seen to have some other mystical or philosophical meaning. For Ptolemy, this has been shown both by the disciples of Jesus and by Paul, who, in particular, advocated for the nullification of Jewish ritual requirements such as circumcision. It should be noted that Ptolemy's reading of the third "symbolic" part of the law was also promoted by other (more orthodox) early Christian theologians such as Origin of Alexandria. In fact, the "allegorical" method of biblical interpretation was originally developed in Alexandria by Jewish and Christian writers.

♦ **Paragraphs 21–24**

Ptolemy then turns his attention to the question of the identity of the God who revealed the pure portion of the Jewish law. For if it came neither from the perfect God of the Valentinians nor from the devil, then it must have had some other source. For Ptolemy, this being is an intermediary deity, also known as the demiurge or "craftsman," an idea originally expressed by Plato for the creator of the universe. For Ptolemy, this God is neither good nor evil but simply just. Ptolemy's use of this idea underlines the profound influence that later forms of Platonic philosophy had on the Gnostics.

A key part of the Gnostic worldview was the idea that the creator of the universe was a being other than the perfect, transcendent God. While earlier Gnostics, especially in the wake of the destruction of the Temple, had characterized this creator as a malicious ruler who effectively presided over a cosmic prison, Ptolemy seeks to moderate this view by acknowledging both the imperfection of the created world and the justice of Jewish law. Tied to this question is the classic theological quandary known as the "problem of evil." Theologians have long wondered how a God who is the all-powerful and entirely good creator of the world could or would allow wickedness and evil to exist. Either God is not all-powerful or he is not entirely good. The early Gnostics, who sought to preserve the essential goodness and perfection of the true God, responded by saying that he must not be the creator of the world. Later theologians would propose an alternate solution that places the responsibility for evil in the hands of human beings and their freedom to choose between good or evil courses of action.

♦ **Paragraphs 25–27**

Ptolemy's solution raises a number of theological and philosophical problems, although he encourages Flora not to be troubled by them for the time being. Presumably they will be dealt with in future correspondence. Later, he intends to teach her about the origin of the "first principle," the "ungenerated, incorruptible, and good" being that transcends the material cosmos. These arguments, too, will be supported by the teachings of Jesus.

At this point Ptolemy makes a direct appeal to "apostolic tradition," which was a key criterion for judging the value of any Christian teaching. All early Christian teachers had to be able to demonstrate that their ideas were passed down to them from the apostles, who were themselves closest to Jesus, via the later bishops and church leaders. In a debate such as the one reflected in the letter, all sides would claim to have apostolic authority on their side, deriving their ideas from the apostolic legacies of Peter, Paul, Philip, John, Thomas, or even Mary Magdalene. In fact, various schools of early Christian thought developed around each of these apostles and later writings were sometimes attributed to them.

In closing, Ptolemy reassures his pupil that he does not mind engaging in this sort of elementary theological instruction. Presumably, he, like most teachers of his age, relied on upper-class students such as Flora for patronage and support. Once taken to heart, these basic teachings would nourish later insights and bring forth much theological fruit.

Audience

Ptolemy's "Letter to Flora" is important to a number of audiences for very different reasons. We must assume that first and foremost it was intended to be read by Flora herself. Even though we know very little about Ptolemy, we know even less about Flora, which is unfortunately the case for most ancient women. We can, however, infer that she was an educated Roman woman with sufficient wealth and leisure to be interested in religious and philosophical questions and to correspond with a prominent Christian teacher. Still, if we accept that the anecdote recorded by Justin Martyr refers to the Ptolemy who is the author of the letter under discussion, then we would know that she was part of

an unhappy marriage, which Christian teachings encouraged her to abandon.

It is likely, however, that Flora was not the only person for whom Ptolemy's message was intended. Letter writing was a highly developed literary art form in antiquity, with very specific rules and structures. In fact, it was one of the most popular vehicles for philosophical and theological argument of all kinds. For example, the letters of the Roman orator Cicero, of the first century BCE, are still studied by students of Latin today as literary masterpieces. Similarly, the letters of the apostle Paul were highly prized, and even though they were addressed to specific communities, they were also read and studied by other Christian churches. The "Letter to Flora," especially if it was known to Epiphanius in the fourth century, was probably considered to be a classic example of Gnostic writing. As such, it served as an ideal object of refutation, which brings us to the letter's secondary audience.

The letter was also read by those interested in the refutation of Gnosticism. It was used by Epiphanius as a prime example of the point of view that he opposed and of ideas that he hoped his own readers would learn to oppose themselves. In this way, Ptolemy's letter went on to have an audience far broader than its original circulation as Epiphanius's work was copied and read by theologians, monks, and scribes throughout the Middle Ages.

Questions for Further Study

1. In the twenty-first century, Christianity (encompassing numerous religions and sects) and Judaism are clearly regarded as distinct religions. But try to imagine the situation in the first decades and centuries after the founding of Christianity. How would you characterize the relationship between Christianity and Judaism during this period? Be specific.

2. Sometimes the God depicted in the Hebrew Bible, or the Old Testament, has been characterized as an "angry" God, one who was harsh, irrational, and sometimes cruel. What problems did this depiction of God have for early Christians? How were they able to reconcile the Old Testament God with the New Testament message of Christ—or were they?

3. Who were the Gnostics? In what ways did they challenge orthodox religious belief?

4. Read Ptolemy's "Letter to Flora" in connection with the Gospel of Thomas. What do the two documents, taken together, tell you about the state of the early Christian Church—its efforts to formulate a consistent theology and scriptural canon, its relationship with Judaism, the emergence of Eastern and Western branches of the faith, and similar issues?

5. Theologians and philosophers have long been troubled by the "problem of evil"—that is, the question of how a good, just, and loving God could allow evil to exist in the world. How does the "Letter to Flora" address this question? How would Emma Goldman in "The Philosophy of Atheism" address this problem in the twentieth century?

Finally, the "Letter to Flora" is of major interest to modern scholars of Gnosticism. Prior to the discovery of the Egyptian Gnostic manuscripts in 1945, Ptolemy's letter was one of the few surviving documents connected to this ancient movement. At the same time, the fact that it is preserved in its original Greek and is connected to an important Valentinian teacher, rather than an anonymous scribe, means that it continues to be one of the most valued sources in the reconstruction of ancient Gnosticism.

Impact

It is difficult to gauge the impact that Ptolemy's letter would have had in antiquity. It certainly generated sufficient interest to be preserved by both supporters and opponents of its teachings. If we believe Justin Martyr's account, then Ptolemy's interactions with Flora so enraged her husband that he was brought before the Roman authorities and eventually executed. This could have something to do with the notoriety that the letter later received. Still, it was not uncommon for the correspondence of important intellectuals to be preserved for posterity.

The "Letter to Flora" continued to be read as a key piece of evidence in Epiphanius's refutation of the Gnostic heresy. While we cannot know how frequently Epiphanius' work was read through the centuries that it was copied, it would have at least had some readers in the Eastern, Greek-speaking churches, particularly among the monks and scribes who were most commonly exposed to this type of literature. A shortened version of the refutation was used by Saint Augustine in his own antiheretical writings of the fifth century, and Latin versions were published in the sixteenth and seventeenth centuries during the controversies of the Protestant Reformation.

It is likely, however, that more people have read Ptolemy's letter in modern times than in either the ancient or medieval period. It is now considered to be a rare and precious piece of literary evidence documenting an important phase in the development of early Christian theology and not simply a curious specimen of heretical thought.

Ptolemy's reading of the Jewish Bible anticipates some of the modern approaches to biblical scholarship that see the scriptures as being made up of multiple sources with many different authors. While it is difficult to know if Ptolemy's theory of interpretation had any direct impact on these modern developments, we should nevertheless remember that sophisticated critiques of sacred texts are not strictly a modern phenomenon. This more than anything else is perhaps the letter's greatest legacy.

Further Reading

■ Books

King, Karen. *What Is Gnosticism?* Cambridge, Mass.: Harvard University Press, 2003.

Layton, Bentley. *The Gnostic Scriptures.* Garden City, N.Y.: Doubleday, 1987.

Pearson, Birger A. *Ancient Gnosticism: Traditions and Literature.* Minneapolis, Minn.: Fortress Press, 2007.

Rudolph, Kurt. *Gnosis: The Nature and History of Gnosticism.* San Francisco: HarperOne, 1987.

■ Web Sites

"Fragments of Ptolemy." Early Christian Writings Web site. http://www.earlychristianwritings.com/ptolemy.html

The Gnosis Archive Web site. http://www.gnosis.org/welcome.html

—Timothy Pettipiece

PTOLEMY: "LETTER TO FLORA"

The Law was ordained through Moses, my dear sister Flora, has not been understood by many persons, who have accurate knowledge neither of him who ordained it nor of its commandments. I think that this will be perfectly clear to you when you have learned the contradictory opinions about it.

Some say that it is legislation given by God the Father; others, taking the contrary course, maintain stubbornly that it was ordained by the opposite, the Devil who causes destruction, just as they attribute the fashioning of the world to him, saying that he is the Father and maker of this universe. Both are completely in error; they refute each other and neither has reached the truth of the matter.

For it is evident that the Law was not ordained by the perfect God the Father, for it is secondary, being imperfect and in need of completion by another, containing commandments alien to the nature and thought of such a God.

On the other hand, one cannot impute the Law to the injustice of the opposite, God, for it is opposed to injustice. Such persons do not comprehend what was said by the Savior. *For a house or city divided against itself cannot stand*, declared our Savior. Furthermore, the apostle says that creation of the world is due to him, for *Everything was made through him and apart from him nothing was made*. Thus he takes away in advance the baseless wisdom of the false accusers, and shows that the creation is not due to a God who corrupts but to the one who is just and hates evil. Only unintelligent men have this idea, men who do not recognize the providence of the creator and have blinded not only the eye of the soul but also of the body.

From what has been said, it is evident that these persons entirely miss the truth; each of the two groups has experienced this, the first because they do not know the God of justice, the second because they do not know the Father of all, who alone was revealed by him who alone came. It remains for us who have been counted worthy of the knowledge of both these to provide you with an accurate explanation of the nature of the Law and the legislator by whom it was ordained. We shall draw the proofs of what we say from the words of the Savior, which alone can lead us without error to the comprehension of reality.

First, you must learn that the entire Law contained in the Pentateuch of Moses was not ordained by one legislator—I mean, not by God alone, some commandments are Moses', and some were given by other men. The words of the Savior teach us this triple division. The first part must be attributed to God alone, and his legislation; the second to Moses—not in the sense that God legislates through him, but in the sense that Moses gave some legislation under the influence of his own ideas; and the third to the elders of the people, who seem to have ordained some commandments of their own at the beginning. You will now learn how the truth of this theory is proved by the words of the Savior.

In some discussion with those who dispute with the Savior about divorce, which was permitted in the Law, he said *Because of your hard-heartedness Moses permitted a man to divorce his wife; from the beginning it was not so; for God made this marriage, and what the Lord joined together, man must not separate.* In this way he shows there is a Law of God, which prohibits the divorce of a wife from a husband, and another law, that of Moses, which permits the breaking of this yoke because of hard-heartedness. In fact, Moses lays down legislation contrary to that of God; for joining is contrary to not joining.

But if we examine the intention of Moses in giving this legislation, it will be seen that he did not give it arbitrarily or of his own accord, but by the necessity because of the weakness of those for whom the legislation was given. Since they were unable to keep the intention of God, according to which it was not lawful for them to reject their wives, with whom some of them disliked to live, and therefore were in the danger of turning to greater injustice and thence to destruction, Moses wanted to remove the cause of dislike, which was placing them in jeopardy of destruction. Therefore because of the critical circumstances, choosing a lesser evil in place of a greater, he ordained, on his own accord, a second law, that of divorce, so that if they could not observe the first, they might keep this and not turn to unjust and evil actions, through which complete destruction would be the result for them. This was his intention when he gave legislation contrary to that of God. Therefore it is indisputable that here the law of Moses is different from the Law of God, even if we have demonstrated the fact from only one example.

The Savior also makes plain the fact that there are some traditions of the elders interwoven in the Law. For God, he says, *Said, Honour your father and your mother, that it may be well with you, But you,* he says addressing the elders, . . . *have declared as a gift to God, that by which you have nullified the Law of God through the tradition of your elders.* Isaiah also proclaimed this, saying, *This people honours me with their lips, but their hearts are far from me, teaching precepts which are the commandments of men.*

Therefore it is obvious that the whole Law is divided into three parts; we find in it the legislation of Moses, of the elders, and of God himself. This division of the entire Law, as made by us, has brought to light what is true in it.

This part, the Law of God himself, is in turn divided into three parts: the pure legislation not mixed with evil, which properly called *Law*, which the Savior came not to destroy but to complete—for what he completed was not alien to him but needed completion, for it did not possess perfection; next the legislation interwoven with the inferiority and injustice, which the Savior destroyed because it was alien to his nature; and finally, the legislation which is allegorical and symbolic, an image of what is spiritual and transcendent, which the Saviour transferred from the perceptible and phenomenal to the spiritual and invisible.

The Law of God, pure and not mixed with inferiority, is the Decalogue, those ten sayings engraved on two tables, forbidding things not to be done and enjoining things to be done. These contain pure but imperfect legislation and required the completion made by the Savior.

There is also the law interwoven with injustice, laid down for vengeance and the requital of previous injuries, ordaining that an eye should be cut out for an eye, and a tooth for a tooth, and that a murder should be avenged by a murderer. The person who is the second one to be unjust is no less unjust than the first; he simply changes the order of events while performing the same action. Admittedly, this commandment was a just one and still is just, because of the weakness of those for whom the legislation was made so they would not transgress the pure law. But it is alien to the nature and goodness of the Father of all. No doubt it was appropriate to the circumstances, or even necessary; for he who does not want one murder committed, saying, *You shall not kill* and then commanded a murder to be repaid by another murder, has given a second law which enjoins two murders although he had forbidden one. This fact proves that he was unsuspectingly the victim of necessity.

This is why, when his son came, he destroyed this part of the law while admitting that it came from God. He counts this part of the law as in the old religion, not only in other passages but also where he said, *God said, He who curses father or mother shall surely die.*

Finally, there is the allegorical (exemplary) part, ordained in the image of the spiritual and transcendent

Glossary

Because of your hard-heartedness	quotation from the Gospel of Matthew, chapter 19, verse 8
But you have declared as a gift to God	quotation from the Gospel of Mark, chapter 7
Christ our passover has been sacrificed	quotation from 1 Corinthians, chapter 5, verse 7
Decalogue	the Ten Commandments
Everything was made through him	quotation from the Gospel of John, chapter 1, verse 3
For a house or city divided against itself cannot stand	quotation from the Gospel of Matthew, chapter 12, verse 25

matters, I mean the part dealing with offerings and circumcision and the Sabbath and fasting and Passover and unleavened bread and other similar matters.

Since all these things are images and symbols, when the truth was made manifest they were translated to another meaning. In their phenomenal appearance and their literal application they were destroyed, but in their spiritual meaning they were restored; the names remained the same but the content was changed. Thus the Savior commanded us to make offerings not of irrational animals or of the incense of this worldly sort, but of spiritual praise and glorification and thanksgiving and of sharing and well-doing with our neighbors. He wanted us to be circumcised, not in regard to our physical foreskin but in regard to our spiritual heart; to keep the Sabbath, for he wishes us to be idle in regard to evil works; to fast, not in physical fasting but in spiritual, in which there is abstinence from everything evil.

Among us external fasting is also observed, since it can be advantageous to the soul if it is done reasonably, not for imitating others or from habit or because of a special day appointed for this purpose. It is also observed so that those who are not yet able to keep

the true fast may have a reminder of it from the external fast. Similarly, Paul the apostle shows that the Passover and the unleavened bread are images when he says, *Christ our passover has been sacrificed, in order that you may be unleavened bread, not containing leaven (by leaven he here means evil), but may be a new lump.*

Thus the Law of God itself is obviously divided into three parts. The first was completed by the Savior, for the commandment, *You shall not kill, You shall not commit adultery, you shall not swear falsely* are included in the forbidding of anger, desire and swearing. The second part was entirely destroyed, for *An eye for an eye and a tooth for a tooth* interwoven in with injustice, was destroyed by the Savior through its opposite. Opposites cancel out, *For I say to you, do not resist the evil man, but if anyone strikes you, turn the other cheek to him.*

Finally, there is the part translated and changed from the literal to the spiritual, this symbolic legislation which is an image of transcendent things. For the images and symbols which represent other things were good as long as the Truth has not come; but since the Truth has come, we must perform the actions of the Truth, not those of the image.

Glossary

For I say to you, do not resist the evil man	quotation from the Gospel of Matthew, chapter 5, verse 39
God said, He who curses father or mother shall surely die	quotation from the book of Exodus, chapter 21, verse 17, and echoed in the Gospel of Matthew, chapter 15, verse 4
The law is holy, and the commandment is holy and just and good	quotation from the book of Romans, chapter 7, verse 12
the law of commandments in ordinances were destroyed	quotation from the book of Ephesians, chapter 2, verse 15
Moses	the biblical patriarch to whom God revealed his laws in the Ten Commandments on Mount Sinai
Pentateuch	the first five books of the Hebrew Bible (Old Testament): Genesis, Exodus, Leviticus, Numbers, and Deuteronomy
This people honours me with their lips	quoted by Christ in the Gospel of Mark, chapter 7, verses 6–7, from the book of Isaiah, chapter 29, verse 13

The disciples of the Savior and the Apostle Paul showed that this theory is true, speaking of the part dealing with images, as we have already said, in mentioning *The passover for us* and the *Unleavened bread*; for the law interwoven with injustice when he says that *the law of commandments in ordinances were destroyed*; and of that not mixed with anything inferior when he says that *The law is holy, and the commandment is holy and just and good*. I think I have shown you sufficiently, as well as one can in brief compass, the addition of human legislation in the Law and the triple division of the Law of God itself.

It remains for us to say who this God is who ordained the Law; but I think this too has been shown you in what we have already said, if you have listened to it attentively.

For if the Law was not ordained by the perfect God himself, as we have already thought you, nor by the devil, a statement one cannot possibly make, the legislator must be some one other than these two. In fact, he is the demiurge and maker of this universe and everything in it; and because he is essentially different from these two and is between them, he is rightly given the name, *intermediate*.

And if the perfect God is good by nature, in fact he is, for our Savior declared that there is only a single good God, his Father whom he manifested; and if the one who is the opposite nature is evil and wicked, characterized by injustice; then the one situated between the two is neither good nor evil or unjust, but can properly be called just, since he is the arbitrator of the justice which is his.

On the one hand, this god will be inferior to the perfect God and the lower than his justice, since he is generated and not ungenerated—there is only one ungenerated Father, from whom are all things, since all things depend on him in their own ways. On the other hand, he will be greater and more powerful than the adversary, by nature, since he has a substance of either of them. The substance of the adversary is corruption and darkness, for he is material and complex, while the substance of the ungenerated Father of all is incorruption and self-existent light, simple and homogeneous. The substance of the latter produced a double power, while the Savior is an image of the greater one.

And now, do not let this trouble you for the present in your desire to learn how from one first principle of all, simple, and acknowledged by us and believed by us, ungenerated and incorruptible and good, were constituted these natures of corruption and the Middle, which are different substances, although it is characteristic of the good to generate and produce things which are like itself and have the same substance.

For, if God permit, you will later learn about their origin and generation, when you are judged worthy of the apostolic tradition which we too have received by succession. We too are able to prove all our points by the teaching of the Savior.

In making these brief statements to you, my sister Flora, I have not grown weary; and while I have treated the subject with brevity, I have also discussed it sufficiently. These points will be of great benefit to you in the future, if like fair and good ground you have received fertile seeds and go on to show forth their fruit.

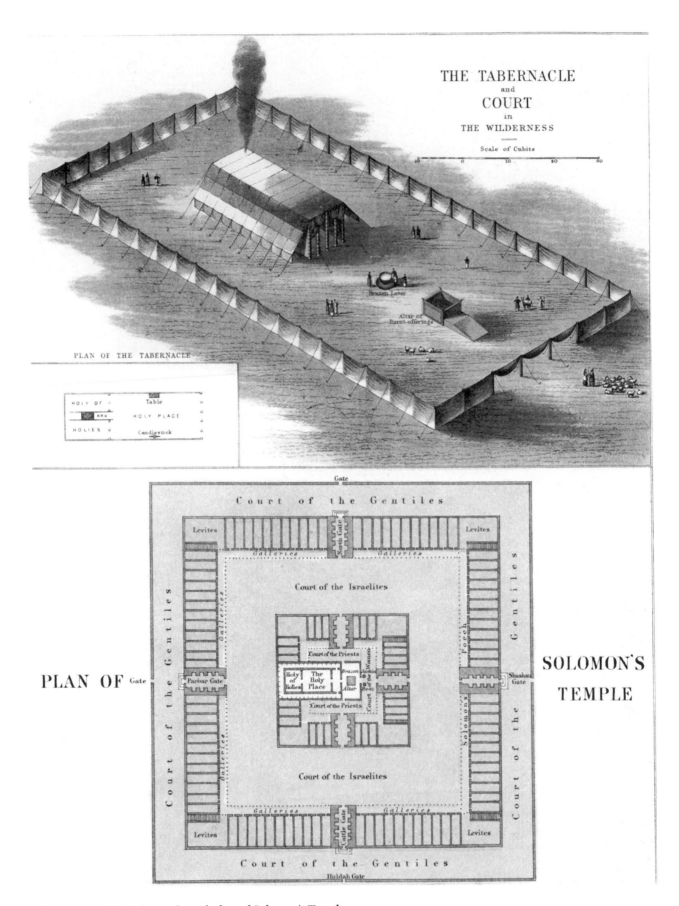

Rendering of the tabernacle and plan of Solomon's Temple

(The Tabernacle and plan of Solomon's temple, English School, [20th century] / Private Collection / © Look and Learn / The Bridgeman Art Library International)

"On three things the world is stayed; on the Torah, and on the Worship, and on the bestowal of Kindnesses."

Overview

Pirke Avot, or "The Sayings of the Fathers," is one of the sixty-three tractates of the Mishnah, the oldest document of classical Jewish (rabbinic) literature, which was composed at the beginning of the third century CE. Apart from its inclusion in the Mishnah, Pirke Avot circulated independently. It is also included in the Talmud, a central text of Judaism composed of rabbinic discussions on Jewish law and ethics. The period from ca. 70 CE until ca. 700 CE is called the Rabbinic Period in Jewish history, and the literature from that period is termed rabbinic literature, with the Mishnah and Talmud being the main works. The sages mentioned therein are the "rabbinic sages," or rabbis.

Unlike other tractates of the Mishnah, Pirke Avot contains almost no religious rules or commandments; rather, it consists of wise sayings. It is therefore usually classified as wisdom or ethical literature. Except for several anonymous proverbs, the wise sayings derive from some sixty-three named sages active from the first to third centuries CE. The tractate was originally written in Hebrew, with short sections in Aramaic. Both languages were spoken in the Land of Israel and are still the common languages in Jewish liturgy. Hebrew is also the original language of the Jewish Bible, called the Old Testament by Christians.

The main topic of Pirke Avot is the Oral Torah. The oldest and main source for Judaism is the Hebrew Bible, particularly the first five books, which are called the Five Books of Moses or the Torah. The Torah is thought to reflect God's will and plan for the people of Israel. It contains the early history of the Israelite people and several collections of law, which were allegedly given by God to Moses and the Israelite people at Mount Sinai. It is also believed that in addition to the Written Torah (the Five Books), Moses received certain other traditions delivered orally. These are called the Oral Torah. The notion of the Oral Torah is notoriously slippery. From a modern critical point of view, the Oral Torah is thought to have been developed by the rabbinic sages to safeguard their authority by demonstrating that their ancestral traditions were in accordance with the Torah.

Pirke Avot consists of six chapters; three of them—chapters 1, 2, and 5—are analyzed here. The first chapter contains very important information on the process of demonstrating rabbinic loyalty to the Torah, an order of transmission that links the rabbinic sages directly to Moses. Moses received the Torah at Mount Sinai and then transmitted it to his successor and so on, until it was finally received by the rabbinic sages through various generations of biblical figures and institutions. The first two chapters of Pirke Avot proceed in a general chronological order, showing the chain of transmission of the Oral Torah through the final editor of the Mishnah, Rabbi Jehuda ha-Nasi. From each of the authorities named in this chain, several wise sayings are mentioned. Most have an ethical content. Many also deal with Torah study, which is a religious act in Judaism.

Context

In 63 BCE, Israel became part of the Roman Empire. At the beginning of the Roman era, most Jews still lived in the Land of Israel (which was part of the larger area known as Palestina in Greek and Roman times). Judaism as we know it today took shape in the first centuries CE, at the same time as Christianity, which originated as a Jewish sect. Of major importance for the development of Judaism was the destruction of the Jewish Temple in Jerusalem in 70 CE by the Romans, following an anti-Roman rebellion of the Jewish population of Israel. In 135 CE a second Jewish rebellion known as the Bar Kochba Revolt occurred; this, too, was put down by the Romans. Thereafter, Jews were banned from Jerusalem and the surrounding areas.

Before the fall of the Temple, the Israelite religion, described in the Hebrew Bible, was centered on the Temple in Jerusalem. In fact, there had been two temples: The first, erected by King Solomon in the tenth century BCE, was destroyed in 586 BCE by the Babylonians, followed by the so-called Babylonian Exile, in which many Israelites were deported to Babylon (present-day Iraq). After their return to Israel from exile, the Jews rebuilt the Temple. Therefore, the latter period is known as the Second Temple Period. Most sages mentioned in chap-

CA. 950 BCE	■ King Solomon, son of King David, builds the First Temple in Jerusalem.
586 BCE	■ The First Temple is destroyed by the Babylonians.
515 BCE	■ The Second Temple is completed by Jews who have returned from the Babylonian Exile.
323 BCE	■ The Greek/Hellenistic Period begins.
63 BCE	■ Rome annexes Judah, and the Roman era begins.
CA. 30 BCE –10 CE	■ Hillel and Shammai, two important Pharisees, are recognized as influential teachers.
70 CE	■ The Second Temple and Jerusalem are destroyed by the Romans.
CA. 80 CE	■ Johannan ben Zakkai founds the rabbinic academy in Javne.
135 CE	■ A revolt against the Romans is led by Simon bar Kochba; the Jews are expelled from Jerusalem and Judea, and Jewish academies move to Galilee (north of Israel).
CA. 200 CE	■ The Mishnah is compiled and edited by Rabbi Jehuda ha-Nasi.

Jews: The priests and their "party," the Sadducees, long at the top of the religious hierarchy, no longer filled that position. In the last decades before the destruction of the Temple, another religious party, the Pharisees, had started to win the popularity of the common people. Whereas the Sadducees were concerned mainly with the sacrifices in the Temple, the Pharisees started to shift the focus of religious attention toward the study of ancestral traditions, which they called Oral Torah. Under their influence, synagogues and study centers were established, nurturing a different kind of religious devotion as an alternative to the Temple service.

After the fall of the Temple, the priests and Sadducees ceased to play any influential role in Judaism, whereas the legacy of the Pharisees became very important. After 70 CE, however, the name *Pharisees* was no longer used, but the rabbinic sages identified themselves as the direct successors of the Pharisees. This is evident in the text of Pirke Avot, where famous Pharisees like Hillel and Shammai are linked in a direct line to the first rabbinic sages. The rabbis managed to give the Jewish religion a new form, with the study of the Torah taking center stage. Beneath this fixation on the study of ancestral traditions was a fear that they would be lost and forgotten in the political and social turmoil surrounding the wars with the Romans. In order to preserve these traditions, the rabbis started to organize and collect them, first in oral form and eventually also in written form. The Mishnah was the direct result of these collection efforts. From an ideological point of view, it is obvious that the rabbis wanted to establish themselves and their predecessors, the Pharisees, as the winners of the religious battle with the Sadducees and priests. The "chain of traditions" in Pirke Avot 1:1 features very few priests: Aaron—Moses' brother and the prototypical biblical priest—is noticeably absent.

About the Author

Like all rabbinic literature, Pirke Avot is a collective, traditional document. It is not possible to designate one person as its author. The document is structured according to a well-conceived plan. Therefore, we can assume that an editor, or several subsequent editors, worked on it to give it its present shape.

Traditionally, a rabbi named Jehuda ha-Nasi (ca. 200 CE) is considered to have been the final collector and organizer of the Mishnah, of which Pirke Avot is one tractate. He is usually called simply "Rabbi." Rabbi is said to have been born in 135 CE. He came from a wealthy family and received an education that included Greek, the common language of the Roman authorities in this part of the Roman Empire. *Nasi* means "patriarch," referring to Rabbi Jehuda's function as the formal leader of the rabbinic community toward the end of the second century CE. Rabbi resided in Beit She'arim and later in Sepphoris—two centers of rabbinic study in Galilee—after all Jewish religious activity was banned from Judah and its capital,

ter 1 of Pirke Avot lived in the Second Temple Period. The sages mentioned in later chapters constitute the early rabbinic generations. Pirke Avot is thus a unique testimony to a crucial period in Jewish history, at the transition between the Second Temple Period and the Rabbinic Period, in which the Jewish religion as we now know it (as distinct from the biblical or Israelite religion) took shape.

All rabbinic literature, starting with the Mishnah and including Pirke Avot, originated from an impulse to preserve Jewish traditions and reorganize the Jewish religion after the disasters of the loss of the Temple and of Jerusalem in the first two centuries CE. In the wake of these disasters came a change in the religious leadership of the

The emperor Antoninus, friend of Jehuda ha-Nasi

(The Emperor Antoninus Pius [colour litho], French School / Private Collection / The Stapleton Collection / The Bridgeman Art Library International)

Jerusalem, by the Romans. He was the first to be formally recognized as *nasi* and served as the spokesperson of the Jews with the Roman authorities. According to rabbinic legend, he developed a close friendship with the Roman emperor Antoninus, who would consult him on worldly and spiritual matters. Rabbi Jehuda was known for his strictly moral way of life. Even though it is unlikely that he composed or even compiled Pirke Avot singlehandedly, its contents seem to reflect the high moral standards that he set for himself and his students.

Explanation and Analysis of the Document

Traditionally, a smaller unit within a chapter of the Mishnah (similar to a verse in the Bible) is called a mishnah. As most of the material contained in Pirke Avot was handed down orally over a long period of time, it cannot be assumed for all sayings (mishnahs) attributed to named sages that they actually originated with these sages. Certain sayings appear to be traditional proverbs, of which variations already appear in the Hebrew Bible or in other sourc-

"On three things the world is stayed; on the Torah, and on the Worship, and on the bestowal of Kindnesses."

"If I am not for myself who is for me? And being for my own self what am I? If not now when?"

"There are four characters in those who sit under the wise: a sponge, a funnel, a strainer, and a bolt-sieve. A sponge, which sucks up all; a funnel, which lets in here and lets out there; a strainer, which lets out the wine and keeps back the dregs; a bolt-sieve, which lets out the pollard and keeps back the flour."

"Ben Bag-bag said, Turn it [the Torah], and again turn it, for the all is therein, and thy all is therein: and swerve not therefrom, for thou canst have no greater excellency than this."

es, such as Greek works. Some sayings are attributed to different sages in different rabbinic sources. Many sayings are transmitted anonymously. All this is typical for traditional rabbinic literature.

◆ Chapter I

This first chapter of Pirke Avot is known as the "chain of traditions," linking Moses, who received the Torah at Mount Sinai, with the generation of sages before Jehuda ha-Nasi. This is done by establishing an uninterrupted chain of tradents—people who transmitted the material to successive contemporary audiences. The tradents are said to have preserved the (Oral) Torah and handed it down from generation to generation, all the way from Moses to Rabbi Jehuda ha-Nasi, who is mentioned in the first mishnah of chapter 2.

Moses, Jehoshua, the elders, and the prophets—mentioned in mishnah 1—are figures from the Hebrew Bible. Moses led the people of Israel out of slavery in Egypt on a journey of forty years through the desert toward their homeland, Israel. On their way in the desert, they received the Torah on Mount Sinai. Jehoshua, or Joshua, was a disciple of Moses who became the leader of the Israelite tribes after Moses' death. The elders are a body of leaders, who, after Joshua, governed the Israelite people upon their entrance in the Land of Israel. The prophets are Jeremiah, Isaiah, Ezekiel, and so on, whose books are contained in the Bible. According to Jewish tradition, "the men of the Great Synagogue" were a legal body in the time of the return from the Babylonian Exile and the rebuilding of the Temple (515

BCE). What is important here is the unbroken chain of tradition: From Moses until the return from the exile, the Torah was preserved and transmitted by trustworthy people. In the following mishnahs and in the following chapters, this process of transmission continued until the collection of Oral Torah that eventually became the Mishnah.

Besides the chain of transmission, the first chapter offers examples of the content of the traditions that were passed down through the ages as well as the substance of the teachings of the sages who lived out the wisdom of the Torah. Mishnah 1 of the first chapter ends with three pieces of advice from the sages: "Be deliberate in judgment; and raise up many disciples; and make a fence to the Torah." This threefold pattern appears repeatedly throughout the chapter. Numerical lists are characteristic for oral traditions: they help in ordering and memorizing the material.

The third wise saying from mishnah 1, "make a fence to the Torah," refers to the rules that are established to safeguard the precise observation of biblical laws. For example, in Deuteronomy 25:3, a maximum of forty floggings is mentioned for certain types of trespassing. The rabbis make this thirty-nine floggings, so that there would be less chance that the number of floggings would inadvertently surpass forty.

The three pillars of the Jewish religion cited in mishnah 2 are Torah (study); Temple Worship, which after the destruction of the Temple was replaced by prayers in the synagogue; and charity. All three must be balanced carefully in Judaism. Somebody who devotes his attention only to Torah study and not to God (through prayer) or to other people (through charity) is not considered a good Jew. Similar sayings are found throughout the tractate, for example, in Pirke Avot 2:2.

Jose ben Jo'ezer and Jose ben Jochanan, mentioned in mishnah 4, are the first of the famous five "pairs." These are the duos of teachers who continued the "chain of tradition" until the great sages Hillel and Shammai. It is characteristic for the rabbis to operate in pairs. They were study partners, often of opposite disposition, who discussed matters of Torah and made legal decisions together. Even in the twenty-first century, it is customary in Jewish learning to study in pairs. Discussion is believed to encourage deeper insight into the subject matter.

The importance of education, study, and learning in general is evident in mishnah 4. "Let thy house be a meeting-house for the wise," the sages say, "and drink their words with thirstiness." A love of learning and a desire for knowledge are viewed as fundamental attributes of a righteous man. Similarly, the advice to make oneself a master (or a teacher) and an associate (or a study partner) in mishnah 6 is typical for rabbinic learning, where, as mentioned earlier, learned sages formed "schools" of disciples and students studied in pairs. Mishnah 7 makes it clear that good or bad social contacts have a profound effect on one's moral life. A good and righteous Jew should associate with like-minded individuals. Note how sayings about Torah study alternate with ethical sayings. Torah study and a good way of life are equally important for the rabbinic sage.

In the midst of these sayings about learning is a cautionary message: The third saying of Jose ben Jo'ezer in mishnah 5 is in line with a general contempt for women in the ancient world (among Greeks, Jews, and Christians). The passage between square brackets (beginning with "His own wife") is probably a later addition, as shown by the disruption of the threefold pattern of sayings. "Gehinnom" is the Jewish equivalent of hell, and women were viewed by the ancients as a source of temptation that might very well derail a man's study of the Torah, which would ultimately lead to his downfall.

Mishnahs 8 and 9 deal with practices in the courtroom. One of the scholarly theories about the origin of Pirke Avot is that it served as moral code for judges and magistrates. Legal commentary gives way to political commentary in mishnah 10, with the latter two sayings of Shema'iah referring to the complicated relationship of the Jews with the Roman authorities. "Hate lordship" means that one should not try to obtain a powerful (political) position. The third saying warns against collaboration with the government. There are individual differences between the rabbinic sages in their attitude toward the authorities. Politically as well as ideologically, the rabbis were not a uniform body. A similar saying is found in Avot 2:3.

In mishnah 11, "the place of evil waters" from which one might "drink" is a form of allegorical speech, the meaning of which has posed a problem in all traditional commentaries. It probably refers to some sort of heresy. Rabbinic Judaism was only one form of Judaism in the first centuries. Several Jewish religious movements existed, which often considered each other heretical.

Hillel and Shammai (in misnahs 12–15) are the most famous pair of sages of the late Second Temple Period. They were Pharisees, the predecessors of the rabbinic sages. Hillel is known for his patient and gentle disposition and his leniency in Jewish law. Shammai is known as the impatient and strict teacher. In later tradition, such as in the Talmud, the rulings of Hillel usually prevail over those of Shammai, probably because of the former's leniency. This prevalence is already made clear by the fact that nine sayings of Hillel are quoted here, as opposed to only three of Shammai. Both founded a school of students that continued their way of interpretation of the Torah. Mishnah 14 contains an enigmatic but very famous saying by Hillel. It suggests that everyone is, in the first place, responsible for his or her own actions and that one should take up that responsibility as soon as that awareness arises. It is interesting that Shammai, who is usually portrayed as a stern figure, recommends a "pleasant expression of countenance" in mishnah 15. Perhaps, as some observers have suggested, his true nature was more amiable than his later reputation, which no doubt was influenced by the school of Hillel.

Rabban Gamliel, thought to be Hillel's grandson, is known in Christian circles as the teacher of the Apostle Paul (Acts 22:3). The injunction not to tithe "by estimation" in mishnah 16 refers to the obligatory donation of one-tenth of one's harvest to the poor. This should be done in a complete and precise fashion because the poor's welfare depends on it. Shime'on ben Gamliel (mishnah 18) seems to be the same as "Shime'on his son" (mishnah 17), *ben* meaning "son of" in Hebrew. Shime'on ben Gamliel was active during the Jewish War (68 CE) and is mentioned by the Jewish-Roman historian Flavius Josephus. Compare the threefold saying in mishnah 18 with the one in mishnah 2. Shime'on ben Gamliel's is more universalist, less specifically Jewish.

◆ Chapter II

The second chapter jumps ahead chronologically by about 130 years, to Rabbi Jehuda ha-Nasi (Rabbi), the final editor of the Mishnah, and his son, also called Rabban Gamliel. Rabbi and his son's sayings focus on the study of Torah, a religious act for which one will be rewarded—if not in this life, then in the world to come—and on an ethical and honest way of life. The saying of Gamliel in mishnah 2 puts Torah study in its proper perspective: It should be balanced with the normal daily business of life.

In mishnah 5, the text jumps back again in time to Hillel the Elder, mentioned in chapter 1. Some scholars think this is another Hillel, the grandson of Rabbi. Whichever is the case, it is clear that the sayings of the earliest sages are juxtaposed with those of some of the latest authorities quoted in the Mishnah and that all are seen as part of the same tradition.

Jochanan ben Zakkai, cited in mishnah 8, was the leading sage at the end of the Second Temple Period and is considered the founder of rabbinic Judaism. According to rabbinic legend, he fled Jerusalem during the revolt against Rome in 68 CE, hidden in a coffin and carried by his students out of the city walls. He is said to have been brought before Vespasian, then a Roman officer, and predicted that he would become emperor. As a reward, he was allowed to open a rabbinic academy in Javne, outside Jerusalem. In this and the following mishnahs, his five most important students are mentioned, each showing a different desirable characteristic for a Torah student: "Plastered cistern" refers to a great capacity for memory and the ability to retain knowledge. "Welling spring" points to intellectual creativity.

Mishnahs 10–14 are sayings by the five students of Jochanan ben Zakkai. Again the contents of the sayings vary between more religious and more worldly oriented insights, in line with the rabbinic idea that Torah affects every aspect of life. The "Shema" and the "Prayer"—that is, the Eighteen Benedictions Prayer—mentioned in mishnah 13 are the two main Jewish prayers, said every morning and evening, whether in the synagogue or at home. Rabbi Shime'on points out here that one should pray with intention and not out of a sense of obligation. This is pertinent for Jewish prayer, which is said at fixed times, with always more or less the same words.

"Epicurus" in mishnah 14 is a rabbinic term for an unbeliever. It is derived from the name of the ancient Greek philosopher Epicurus (341–270 BCE), whose philosophical school of Epicureanism stressed the pursuit of pleasure without the fear of punishment in the afterlife. According to Epicurus, the soul ceases to exist when a person dies, making anxiety over retribution for past deeds unnecessary. Rabbi Tarfon's sayings in mishnahs 15 and 16 are examples of metaphoric speech. The "Master of the house" is God, "work" refers to Torah study, and the "workmen" are the students.

♦ **Chapter V**

This chapter consists mainly of anonymous sayings in numerical groupings. Mishnahs 1–5, featuring the number 10, treats events described in the Hebrew Bible in chronological order. The "ten sayings" by which the world was created refer to the tenfold "and God said" elements in the biblical story of Creation (Genesis 1:3–2:18). The ten temptations of Abraham, the ten plagues, and the ten miracles in the time of the Exodus from Egypt are all biblical facts "counted" by the rabbis in order to make lists of ten. The Sanctuary is the Temple, which at the time of the writing of Pirke Avot had been destroyed. The ten miracles mentioned here are a nostalgic idealization of the sacrifices and events that took place in the Temple.

The things created "between the suns" in mishnah 6 are extraordinary creations that occurred at twilight between the sixth day and the beginning of the Sabbath day, according to the Creation story in Genesis. This creation at twilight is a rabbinic idea, not found in the Bible, but most of the facts described (the manna, the ram, and so on) are biblical. The "tongs made with tongs" reference addresses one of those logical dilemmas that has plagued believers throughout the centuries. It takes a pair of tongs to shape a second pair over a fire. Who made the first pair? It could only have been an act of God, made not during the six days in which he created the natural world, but as a special gift to allow man to cultivate the world.

Mishnahs 7 and 8 feature the number 7, which often has symbolic meaning in the Bible, denoting something that is "whole," such as the days of the week, culminating in the Sabbath, and the cycle of seven years, with the seventh year being referred to as the Sabbath Year. The "seventh year fruits" at the end of mishnah 8 refer to the Sabbath Year (Leviticus 25:1–7), during which the land should lay bare. Only fruits and vegetables that grow spontaneously or crops stored from the harvest of the sixth year can be eaten during this time. Transgressions of this law would lead to divine punishment.

Mishnahs 8 and 9 in chapter 5 deal with divine punishments in the form of natural disasters that will come upon Israel if the people do not obey the biblical laws. The laws dealt with here all have a social function: they are designed to protect the poor and to divide the natural resources over all inhabitants of the land. The "tithing" mentioned in mishnah 8 refers to the 10 percent of each crop that an Israelite farmer had to give by way of Temple tax, used to pay the priests but also to help needy people. After the fall of the Temple, there was still a habit of donating 10 percent of one's income to charity to help people in need. Mishnah 9 also features a thematic transition from the number 7 to the number 4. Again, the laws mentioned here pertain to helping the poor.

The sayings in mishnahs 10–15 are associated with the number 4 as well and contain ethical and pedagogical principles. According to some scholars who see Pirke Avot as a work designed mainly for Torah students, these sayings may be the reason why this chapter was included in the tractate. "The character of Sodom" refers to the sins of Sodom related in Genesis 18–19; the main sins of Sodom in the Jewish tradition are lack of hospitality and taking advantage of strangers. For people to care only about their own good is apparently judged as worse than their being "indifferent" by some sages. 'Am ha-arets, literally meaning "people of the land," denotes illiterate, simple people. Mishnah 14 again focuses on the necessary balance between Torah study and living according to the principles of the Torah.

Mishnah 15 compares four types of students to the way various household tools handle different types of food. The sponge is a metaphor for one who sucks up knowledge and retains it, not unlike the plastered cistern in Avot 2:8. The funnel is one who learns easily but forgets quickly. The strainer is the student who remembers the wrong things and forgets the good. The "bolt-sieve" student does the opposite: He retains the good information and lets go of unnecessary things. Mishnahs 16–19 are structured according to a similar pattern: Two opposite kinds of attitudes are presented, which are then illustrated with reference to two biblical or rabbinic figures.

For instance, of the two types of love mentioned in mishnah 16, the last type does not depend on a transitory thing, such as beauty or money. Possibly the love for Torah is intended here. The examples come from the Bible: Amon, the son of King David (2 Sam. 13), was in love with his half-sister, Tamar, who was very beautiful. After he raped her, it is said that he hated her with the same intensity as he had loved her before. His father, David, to the contrary, had an ever-lasting friendship with King Saul's son Jonathan, despite the fact that Saul was at times his enemy.

"Gainsaying" in mishnah 17 is controversy. The controversies between Hillel and Shammai, discussed in chapter 1, advanced insight in the Torah because they showed different standpoints and interpretations of the precepts therein. Number 16 relates how the Levite Korach led a rebellion against Moses and Aaron, questioning their leadership. God punished Korach and his family by having the earth swallow them up alive. Similarly, mishnah 18 demonstrates by means of the examples of Moses and King Jeroboam how a leader can make his subjects righteous or sinful by the example of his own behavior. Jeroboam was guilty of idolatry, and the people followed his lead.

Mishnah 19 picks up the numerical line, this time focusing on the number 3 in presenting the biblical figures Abraham and Bile'am in opposition. Bile'am is a non-Israelite prophet with a mixed reputation in Jewish tradition. On the one hand, he prophesied Israel's victory in Numbers 22–24, speaking in the name of the God of Israel. On the other, later Jewish tradition made him the prototype of the antiprophet. This might be owing to the fact that, immediately after the presentation of the Bile'am story in Numbers 21–24, the Bible relates how the Israelites started to commit harlotry with foreign women (Numbers 25).

The last mishnahs in this chapter appear as loose ends, featuring the sayings of three rather unknown sages. Jehuda ben Thema's saying in mishnah 20 might have been linked to the previous mishnah because of the occurrence of Gehinnom and the Garden of Eden. A renowned sixteenth-century Jewish commentator, Judah Loew ben Bezalel, a rabbi also known as the Maharal of Prague, explains Jehuda's saying as follows: Be tough-minded like a leopard in deciding to do a good deed; be light like an eagle to take action; be swift as a deer to approach the good deed quickly, dodging and dissuading voices from within and without; and be strong like a lion to complete the task as a lion that consumes its prey. The "building of the city in our days" refers to the reconstruction of Jerusalem with its Temple. A similar prayer is still said in synagogue liturgy today.

Mishnah 21 is not included in all versions of Pirke Avot. As it is, it gives insight in the rabbinic study curriculum still followed in traditional Jewish circles: First the Bible is studied, starting at age five, and then the Mishnah, at age ten. Thirteen is the bar mitzvah age, when a boy (in progressive circles also a girl) is considered old enough to keep the religious commandments.

The famous saying of Ben Bag-bag refers to the Torah: According to rabbinic ideology, the Torah is self-sufficient. The notion that you can "turn it and turn it" points to the never-ending process of Torah interpretation, in which new discoveries will be made each time it is studied. Both Ben Bag-bag and Ben He-he are believed to have been converts to Judaism and disciples of Hillel. In another rabbinic source, these two last sayings are attributed to Hillel, showing again that this is traditional wisdom literature, the voice of a group rather than of individuals.

Audience

Scholars are divided over the original target audience of Pirke Avot. Because of its focus on Oral Torah and the proper balance between study and daily life, knowledge, and good deeds, most traditional and modern commentators think the tractate served as a spiritual guide for Torah students. On the other hand, there is the opinion of the medieval Jewish scholar Maimonides, shared by some modern scholars, who thought of it as an ethical code for judges and magistrates. This makes sense, because Avot is included in the section of the Mishnah that deals with legal issues and because quite a few of the sayings deal with judicial matters.

Throughout Jewish history, diverse communities adopted different practices for reading Pirke Avot: In the Babylonian academies of the fifth and sixth centuries CE, it was read every Sabbath as part of the liturgy. In most present-day American Jewish communities, it is read chapter by chapter during a certain period in the spring or in the summer. To this day it is studied by students all over the Jewish world as an essential part of the religious curriculum.

Of all rabbinic documents, Pirke Avot is the one that is most frequently read by non-Jewish people, who are inspired by its practical wisdom and worldview. In Christian circles, it is increasingly popular to read rabbinic texts in order to better understand the cultural context in which Jesus lived and early Christianity developed. Pirke Avot is one of the choice texts that is often read in adult education or other popular study venues.

Impact

In the Jewish world, the popularity and impact of a work can be measured by the amount of commentary generated, the number of new editions and reprints released, and the number of translations made into other languages. Judged from the number of commentaries on Pirke Avot, it became an influential document as soon as it was composed. The earliest commentary is Avot d'rabbi Natan (late third century CE), which, like Pirke Avot, is included in the Talmud, the main rabbinic work (sixth century CE). After that, many famous Jewish authorities wrote commentaries on it, most notably Moses Maimonides in the twelfth century. To this day, ever-new commentaries on Pirke Avot are being written. (See, for example, *Pirke Avot: A Modern Commentary on Jewish Ethics*, a very readable translation and commentary by Leonard Kravitz and Kerry Olitzky.) Avot has been reprinted more often than any other rabbinic text. It is the only rabbinic text that is included in its entirety in the Jewish prayer books, traditional and contemporary. For this reason, even Jews who are not so scholarly are familiar with the work.

Because of its generally appealing content of brief wise sayings, popular Hebrew songs take as their lyrics lines from Pirke Avot (for example, Avot 1:2). Pirke Avot is translated in many languages for non-Jewish and Jewish audiences. A 1996 Chinese translation is just one example of its cross-cultural impact. A recent interfaith commentary (noted in Ronald W. Pies's book *The Ethics of the Sages*) featuring Christian, Confucian, Hindu, and Muslim parallels is yet another.

Further Reading

■ Books

Danby, Herbert. *The Mishnah*. New York: Oxford University Press, 1991.

Kravitz, Leonard, and Kerry M. Olitzky. *Pirke Avot: A Modern Commentary on Jewish Ethics*. New York: UAHC Press, 1993.

Lerner, M. B. "The Tractate Avot." In *The Literature of the Sages— Part One: Oral Torah, Halakha, Mishna, Tosefta, Talmud, External Tractates*, ed. Shmuel Safrai. Philadelphia: Fortress Press, 1987.

Pies, Ronald W. *The Ethics of the Sages: An Interfaith Commentary of Pirkei Avot*. Lanham, Md.: Rowman and Littlefield, 1999.

Strack, H. L., and Günter Stemberger. *Introduction to the Talmud and Midrash*, trans. and ed. Markus Bockmuehl. Minneapolis: Fortress Press, 1996.

■ Web Sites

"The Book of Principles: The Ethical Classic Pirkei Avot." Jewish Institute for Youth and Family Web site.
   http://mentsh.com/pirkei_avot.html

"Pirkei Avot: Ethics of Our Fathers." My Jewish Learning Web site.
   http://www.myjewishlearning.com/texts/Rabbinics/Talmud/ Mishnah/Seder_Nezikin_Damages_/Pirkei_Avot.shtml

   —Lieve Teugels

Questions for Further Study

1. Compare this document with the Sefer Yetzirah. The date attached to both is 200 CE, yet the two documents and the motivations behind them differ widely. Explain how. Specifically, explain how the two documents represent divergent strands in Jewish thought.

2. A considerable amount of religious literature consists of wisdom passed down from seminal thinkers to followers throughout the ages. Locate another document that consists of such wisdom; an example might be the "Instructions of Ptahhotep." How does each document represent a different set of cultural traditions?

3. What was significant about the so-called Rabbinic Period? What historical circumstances gave rise to the Rabbinic Period?

4. Why would a non-Jew show any particular interest in the Pirke Avot?

5. What is the fundamental difference between the Oral Torah and the Written Torah, other than the obvious difference suggested by the names? How did the distinction between the two play out in Jewish history and in the development of a uniquely Jewish culture and set of traditions?

PIRKE AVOT

Chapter I.

1. Moses received the Torah from Sinai, and he delivered it to Jehoshua, and Jehoshua to the elders, and the elders to the prophets, and the prophets delivered it to the men of the Great Synagogue. They said three things: Be deliberate in judgment; and raise up many disciples; and make a fence to the Torah.

2. Shime'on ha-Tsaddik was of the remnants of the Great Synagogue. He used to say, On three things the world is stayed; on the Torah, and on the Worship, and on the bestowal of Kindnesses.

3. Antigonus of Soko received from Shime'on ha-Tsaddik. He used to say, Be not as slaves that minister to the lord with a view to receive recompense; but be as slaves that minister to the lord without a view to receive recompense; and let the fear of Heaven be upon you.

4. Jose ben Jo'ezer of Tseredah and Jose ben Jochanan of Jerusalem received from them. Jose ben Jo'ezer of Tseredah said, Let thy house be a meeting-house for the wise; and powder thyself in the dust of their feet; and drink their words with thirstiness.

5. Jose ben Jochanan of Jerusalem said, Let thy house be opened wide; and let the needy be thy household; and prolong not converse with woman. [His own wife, they meant, much less his neighbour's wife. Hence the wise have said, Each time that the man prolongs converse with the woman he causes evil to himself, and desists from words of Torah, and in the end he inherits Gehinnom.]

6. Jehoshua ben Perachiah and Nittai the Arbelite received from them. Jehoshua ben Perachiah said, Make unto thyself a master; and possess thyself of an associate; and judge every man in the scale of merit.

7. Nittai the Arbelite said, Withdraw from an evil neighbour; and associate not with the wicked; and grow not thoughtless of retribution.

8. Jehudah ben Tabai and Shime'on ben Shatach received from them. Jehudah ben Tabai said, Make not thyself as them that predispose the judges; and while the litigants stand before thee, let them be in thine eyes as guilty; and when dismissed from before thee let them be in thine eyes as righteous, because they have received the doom upon them.

9. Shime'on ben Shatach said, Make full examination of the witnesses; but be guarded in thy words, perchance from them they may learn to lie.

10. Shema'iah and Abtalion received from them. Shema'iah said, Love work; and hate lordship; and make not thyself known to the government.

11. Abtalion said, Ye wise, be guarded in your words; perchance ye may incur the debt of exile, and be exiled to the place of evil waters; and the disciples that come after you may drink and die, and the Name of Heaven be profaned.

12. Hillel and Shammai received from them. Hillel said, Be of the disciples of Aharon; loving peace, and pursuing peace; loving mankind, and bringing them nigh to the Torah.

13. He used to say, A name made great is a name destroyed; he who increases not decreases; and he who will not learn (or teach) deserves slaughter; and he who serves himself with the tiara perishes.

14. He used to say, If I am not for myself who is for me? And being for my own self what am I? If not now when?

15. Shammai said, Make thy Torah an ordinance; say little and do much; and receive every man with a pleasant expression of countenance.

16. Rabban Gamliel said, Make to thyself a master, and be quit of doubt; and tithe not much by estimation.

17. Shime'on his son said, All my days I have grown up amongst the wise, and have not found aught good for a man but silence; not learning but doing is the groundwork; and whoso multiplies words occasions sin.

18. Rabban Shime'on ben Gamliel said, On three things the world stands; on Judgment, and on Truth, and on Peace.

Chapter II.

1. Rabbi said, Which is the right course that a man should choose for himself? Whatsoever is a pride to him that pursues it, (and) brings him honour from men. And be attentive to a light precept as to a grave, for thou knowest not the assigned reward of precepts; and reckon the loss for a duty against its gain, and the gain by a transgression against its loss. And consider three things, and thou wilt not

fall into the hands of transgression: know what is above thee—a seeing eye, and a hearing ear, and all thy deeds written in a book.

2. Rabban Gamliel, son of R. Jehudah ha-Nasi, said, Excellent is Torah study together with worldly business, for the practice of them both puts iniquity out of remembrance; and all Torah without work must fail at length, and occasion iniquity. And let all who are employed with the congregation act with them in the name of Heaven, for the merit of their fathers sustains them, and their righteousness stands for ever. And ye yourselves shall have reward reckoned unto you as if ye had wrought.

3. Be cautious with (those in) authority, for they let not a man approach them but for their own purposes; and they appear like friends when it is to their advantage, but stand not by a man in the hour of his need.

4. He used to say, Do His will as if it were thy will, that He may do thy will as if it were His will. Annul thy will before His will, that He may annul the will of others before thy will.

5. Hillel said, Separate not thyself from the congregation, and trust not in thyself until the day of thy death; and judge not thy friend until thou comest into his place; and say not of a word which may be heard that in the end it shall be heard; and say not, When I have leisure I will study; perchance thou mayest not have leisure.

6. He used to say, No boor is a sinfearer; nor is the vulgar pious; nor is the shamefast apt to learn, nor the passionate to teach; nor is every one that has much traffic wise. And in a place where there are no men endeavour to be a man.

7. Moreover he saw a skull which floated on the face of the water, and he said to it, Because thou drownedst they drowned thee, and in the end they that drowned thee shall be drowned. He used to say, More flesh, more worms: more treasures, more care: more maidservants, more lewdness: more menservants, more theft: more women, more witchcrafts: more Torah, more life: more wisdom, more scholars: more righteousness, more peace. He who has gotten a good name has gotten it for himself. He who has gotten to himself words of Torah, has gotten to himself the life of the world to come.

8. Rabban Jochanan ben Zakai received from Hillel and from Shammai. He used to say, If thou hast practised Torah much, claim not merit to thyself, for thereunto wast thou created. Five disciples were there to Rabban Jochanan ben Zakai, and these were they: R. Eli'ezer ben Hyrcanos, and R. Jehoshua ben Chananiah, and R. Jose the Priest, and R. Shime'on ben Nathanael, and R. Ele'azar ben Arak. He used to recount their praise: Eli'ezer ben Hyrcanos is a plastered cistern, which loseth not a drop; Jehoshua ben Chananiah—happy is she that bare him; Jose the Priest is pious; Shim'eon ben Nathanael is a sinfearer; Ele'azar ben Arak is a welling spring. He used to say, If all the wise of Israel were in a scale of the balance, and Eli'ezer ben Hyrcanos in the other scale, he would outweigh them all. Abba Shaul said in his name, If all the wise of Israel were in a scale of the balance, and Eli'ezer ben Hyrcanos with them, and Ele'azar ben Arak in the other scale, he would outweigh them all.

9. He said to them, Go and see which is the good way that a man should cleave to. Rabbi Eli'ezer said, A good eye; R. Jehoshua said, A good friend; and R. Jose said, A good neighbour; and R. Shime'on said, He that foresees what is to be; R. Eleazar said, A good heart. He said to them, I approve the words of Ele'azar ben Arak rather than your words, for his words include your words. He said to them, Go and see which is the evil way that a man should shun. R. Eli'ezer said, An evil eye; and R. Jehoshua said, An evil companion; and R. Jose said, An evil neighbour; and R. Shime'on said, He that borroweth and repayeth not—he that borrows from man is the same as if he borrowed from God (blessed is He)—for it is said, *The wicked borroweth, and payeth not again, but the righteous is merciful and giveth* (Ps. 37:21). R. Ele'azar said, An evil heart. He said to them, I approve the words of Ele'azar ben Arak rather than your words, for your words are included in his words.

10. And they said (each) three things. R. Eli'ezer said, Let the honour of thy friend be dear unto thee as thine own; and be not easily provoked; and repent one day before thy death. And warm thyself before the fire of the wise, but beware of their embers, perchance thou mayest be singed, for their bite is the bite of a fox, and their sting the sting of a scorpion, and their hiss the hiss of a fiery-serpent, and all their words are as coals of fire.

11. R. Jehoshua said, An evil eye, and the evil nature, and hatred of the creatures put a man out of the world.

12. R. Jose said, Let the property of thy friend be precious unto thee as thine own; set thyself to learn Torah, for it is not an heirloom unto thee; and let all thy actions be to the name of Heaven.

13. R. Shime'on said, Be careful in reading the She-ma and in Prayer; and when thou prayest, make not thy prayer an ordinance, but an entreaty before God, blessed is He, for it is said, *For God is compassionate and easily-entreated, longsuffering, and plenteous in grace* (Joel 2:13); and be not wicked unto thyself.

14. R. Ele'azar said, Be diligent to learn Torah, wherewith thou mayest make answer to an Epicurus; and know before whom thou toilest; and who is the Master of thy work.

15. R. Tarphon said, The day is short, and the task is great, and the workmen are sluggish, and the reward is much, and the Master of the house is urgent.

16. He said, It is not for thee to finish the work, nor art thou free to desist therefrom; if thou hast learned much Torah, they give thee much reward; and faithful is the Master of thy work, who will pay thee the reward of thy work, and know that the recompence of the reward of the righteous is for the time to come. . . .

Chapter V.

1. By ten Sayings the world was created. And what is learned therefrom? For could it not have been created by one Saying? But it was that vengeance might be taken on the wicked, who destroy the world that was created by ten Sayings; and to give a goodly reward to the righteous, who maintain the world that was created by ten Sayings.

2. Ten generations were there from Adam to No-ach, to shew how great was His longsuffering; for all the generations were provoking Him, till He brought the deluge upon them.

3. Ten generations were there from Noach to Abraham, to shew how great was His longsuffering; for all the generations were provoking Him, till Abraham our father came, and received the reward of them all.

4. With ten temptations was Abraham our father tempted, and he withstood them all; to shew how great was the love of Abraham our father. Ten miracles were wrought for our fathers in Egypt; and ten by the sea. Ten plagues brought the Holy One, blessed is He, upon the Egyptians in Egypt; and ten by the Sea. With ten temptations did our fathers tempt God in the wilderness, for it is said, *And they have tempted me now these ten times, and have not hearkened to my voice* (Numb. 14:22).

5. Ten miracles were wrought in the Sanctuary. No woman miscarried from the scent of the holy meat; and the holy meat never stank; and an unclean-ness befel not the highpriest on the day of the Atonement; and a fly was not seen in the slaughterhouse; and a defect was not found in the sheaf; nor in the two loaves; nor in the shewbread; and rains quenched not the pile; and the wind prevailed not against the pillar of smoke; they stood serried, and bowed down at ease; and serpent and scorpion harmed not in Jerusalem; and a man said not to his fellow, *The place is too strait for me* (Is. 49: 20) to lodge in Jerusalem.

6. Ten things were created between the suns. The mouth of the earth; and the mouth of the well; and the mouth of the ass; and the bow (Gen. 60:13); and the manna; and the rod; and the shamir-worm; and the character; and the writing; and the tables. And some say, the spirits also; and the sepulchre of Moses (Deut. 34:6); and the ram of Abraham our father (Gen. 22:13). And some say, tongs also, made with tongs.

7. Seven things are in a clod, and seven in a wise man. The wise man speaks not before one who is greater than he in wisdom; and does not interrupt the words of his companion; and is not hasty to reply; he asks according to canon, and answers to the point; and speaks on the first thing first, and on the last last; of what he has not heard he says, I have not heard; and he acknowledges the truth. And their opposites are in the clod.

8. Seven kinds of punishments come on account of seven main transgressions. When some men tithe, and some do not tithe, dearth from drought comes: some of them are hungry, and some of them are full. When they have not tithed at all, a dearth from tumult and from drought comes. And when they have not offered the dough-cake, a deadly dearth comes. Pestilence comes into the world for the capital crimes mentioned in the Torah, which are not brought before the tribunal; and for the seventh year fruits. The sword comes upon the world for suppression of judgment; and for perversion of judgment; and for explaining Torah not according to canon.

9. Noisome beasts come into the world for vain swearing; and for profanation of the name of God. Captivity comes upon the world for strange worship; and for incest; and for shedding of blood; and for (not) giving release to the land. At four seasons the pestilence waxes: in the fourth (year); in the seventh; at the ending of the seventh; and at the ending of the Feast in every year. In the fourth (year), on account of the poor's tithe in the third; in the seventh, on account of the poor's

tithe in the sixth; and at the ending of the seventh, on account of the seventh year fruits; and at the ending of the Feast in every year, on account of the largesses of the poor.

10. There are four characters in men: He that saith, Mine is mine, and thine is thine, is an indifferent character; but some say, It is the character of Sodom; (He that saith) Mine is thine, and thine is mine, is 'am ha-arets; Mine and thine are thine, pious; Thine and mine are mine, wicked.

11. There are four characters in dispositions. Easily provoked, and easily pacified, his gain is cancelled by his loss; hard to provoke and hard to pacify, his loss is cancelled by his gain; hard to provoke, and easily pacified, pious; easily provoked, and hard to pacify, wicked.

12. There are four characters in scholars. Quick to hear and quick to forget, his gain is cancelled by his loss; slow to hear and slow to forget, his loss is cancelled by his gain; quick to hear, and slow to forget, is wise; slow to hear, and quick to forget, this is an evil lot.

13. There are four characters in almsgivers. He who is willing to give, but not that others should give, his eye is evil towards the things of others; that others should give, and he should not give, his eye

is evil towards his own; he who would give and let others give, is pious; he who will not give nor let others give, is wicked.

14. There are four characters in college-goers. He that goes and does not practise, the reward of going is in his hand; he that practises and does not go, the reward of practice is in his hand; he that goes and practises is pious; he that goes not and does not practise is wicked.

15. There are ba in those who sit under the wise: a sponge, a funnel, a strainer, and a bolt-sieve. A sponge, which sucks up all; a funnel, which lets in here and lets out there; a strainer, which lets out the wine and keeps back the dregs; a bolt-sieve, which lets out the pollard and keeps back the flour.

16. All love which depends on some thing, when the thing ceases, the love ceases; and such as does not depend on anything, ceases not for ever. What love is that which depends on some thing? The love of Amnon and Tamar. And that which does not depend on anything? This is the love of David and Jonathan.

17. Whatsoever gainsaying is for the name of Heaven will in the end be established; and that which is not for the name of Heaven will not in the end

'am ha-arets	literally "people of the land," or illiterate, simple people
Amon	the son of King David, who was in love with his half-sister, Tamar
Bile'am	a non-Israelite prophet
Epicurus	a rabbinic term for an unbeliever, derived from the name of the ancient Greek philosopher Epicurus, whose philosophical school of Epicureanism stressed the pursuit of pleasure
Gehinnom	the Jewish equivalent of hell
hate lordship	that is, do not try to obtain a powerful position
Hillel and Shammai	the most famous pair of sages of the late Second Temple Period and predecessors of the rabbinic sages
Jochanan ben Zakkai	the leading sage at the end of the Second Temple Period and considered the founder of rabbinic Judaism
Jose ben Jo'ezer and Jose ben Jochanan	the first of the famous five pairs of teachers who continued the chain of tradition until the sages Hillel and Shammai
Joshua	one of the leaders of the Israelites who governed them after they reached Israel
King Jerobeam	the first ruler of the Northern Kingdom of Israel after ten of the twelve tribes of Israel broke away
Korach	a rebel who led a revolt against Moses

be established. What gainsaying is that which is for the name of Heaven? The gainsaying of Shammai and Hillel. And that which is not for the name of Heaven? This is the gainsaying of Korach.

18. Whosoever makes the many righteous, sin prevails not over him; and whosoever makes the many to sin, they grant him not the faculty to repent. Moses was righteous, and made the many righteous, and the righteousness of the many was laid upon him, for it is said, *He executed the justice of the Lord and His judgments, with Israel* (Deut. 33:21). Jerobe'am sinned, and caused the many to sin, (and) the sin of the many was laid upon him, for it is said, *Because of the sins of Jerobe'am who sinned, and made Israel to sin* (I Kings 14:16; 15:30).

19. In whomsoever are three things, he is a disciple of Abraham; and three (other) things, a disciple of Bile'am. A good eye, and a lowly soul, and a humble spirit (belong to) the disciple of Abraham; an evil eye, and a swelling soul, and a haughty spirit, to the disciple of Bile'am. And what difference is between the disciples of Abraham and the disciples of Bile'am? The disciples of Bile'am, go down to Gehinnom, for it is said, *But thou, O God, shalt bring them down into the pit of destruction* (Ps. 55:24), but the disciples of Abraham inherit the Garden of Eden, for it

is said, *That I may cause those that love me to inherit substance; and I will fill their treasures* (Prov. 8:21).

20. R. Jehudah ben Thema said, Be bold as a leopard, and swift as an eagle, and fleet as a hart, and strong as a lion, to do the will of thy Father which is in Heaven. He used to say, The bold of face to Gehinnom; and the shamefaced to the garden of Eden. May it be well-pleasing in thy sight, Lord, our God, and the God of our fathers, that thy city may be built in our days; and give us our portion in thy Torah.

[21. He used to say: At five years old for the Scripture, at ten years for the Mishnah, at thirteen for the fulfilling of the commandments, at fifteen for the Talmud, at eighteen for the bride-chamber, at twenty for pursuing a calling, at thirty for authority, at forty for discernment, at fifty for counsel, at sixty for to be an elder, at seventy for gray hair, at eighty for special strength, at ninety for bowed back, and at a hundred a man is as one that has already died and passed away and ceased from the world.]

22. Ben Bag-bag said, Turn it, and again turn it, for the all is therein, and thy all is therein; and swerve not therefrom, for thou canst have no greater excellency than this.

23. Ben He-he said, According to the toil is the reward.

men of the Great Synagogue	a legal body at the time of the return from the Babylonian Exile and the rebuilding of the Temple
Moses	the biblical patriarch who led the people of Israel out of slavery in Egypt
place of evil waters	probably an allusion to heretical thinking
prophets	Jeremiah, Isaiah, Ezekiel, and others whose books are contained in the Bible
Rabban Gamliel	possibly Hillel's grandson, known in Christianity as the teacher of the Apostle Paul
Rabbi Jehuda ha-Nasi	or "Rabbi," the final editor of the Mishnah
Sanctuary	the Temple, which at the time of the writing of Pirke Avot had been destroyed
seventh year fruits	the Sabbath Year, during which the land should lay bare
Shema and the Prayer	the two main Jewish prayers, said every morning and evening in the synagogue or at home
Shime'on ben Gamliel	a man who was active during the Jewish War of 68 CE
ten sayings	that is, the ten sayings by which the world was created, referring to the tenfold "and God said" elements in the biblical story of Creation
tithing	refers to the 10 percent of each crop that an Israelite farmer had to give by way of Temple tax, used to pay the priests but also to help needy people

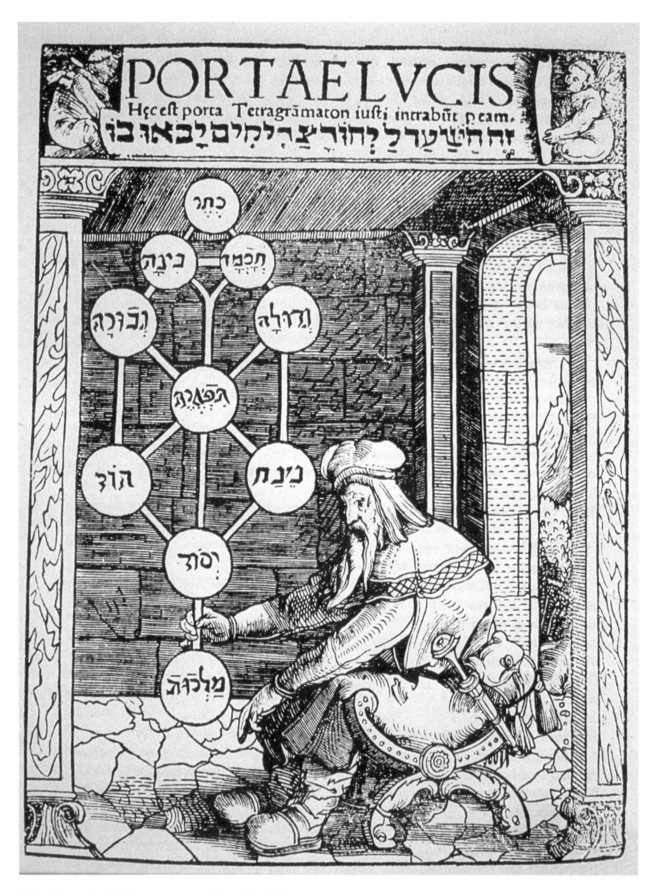

A Jewish mystic holding a representation of the Sefirot

(Jewish cabbalist holding a sephiroth, copy of an illustration from 'Portae Lucis' by Paul Ricius, 1516 / Private Collection / The Bridgeman Art Library International [engraving])

SEFER YETZIRAH

"The proof of this is revealed in the universe, the year and the soul."

Overview

The Sefer Yetzirah, considered the oldest book on kabbalistic philosophy, is translated as the Book of Formation or Book of Creation or Book of Tradition. It was first put into writing possibly around 200 CE, although this is a matter of much dispute. Jewish traditional scholars propose that the patriarchs (Abraham, Isaac, and Jacob) wrote the Sefer Yetzirah, but there is no actual documentary evidence to support that view, and the book always attracts debate about its date of origin and its authorship. Despite the title, the text is not an alternate version of Genesis or even a story about Creation itself. Rather, it presents a mystical, esoteric version of the origin of the universe and humanity, and thus it is a key document in the history of Jewish mysticism. Unlike other kabbalistic writings, the Sefer Yetzirah is written in Hebrew and not Aramaic. It exists in more manuscripts than any other Hebrew work except the Torah itself. There are four "families," or versions, of the Sefer Yetzirah: the Short Version, the Saadia Version, the Gra Version, and the Long Version; the translation reproduced here is based on the Saadia Version. All the variants are quite similar in content, with the differences being in structure, order, and length; the work is usually presented as thirty-three paragraphs within six chapters, although older versions will include a chapter at the end called "The Letters of our Father Abraham."

Context

The Sefer Yetzirah occupies a key place in the history and development of Jewish mysticism. Since about the second century CE, many Jews have tried to find a way of approaching God outside of traditional, orthodox religious thought and practice. These people have sought a more personal and intimate relationship with God, a union that cannot be achieved through rational thought and the intellect. The result of this quest was the development of sects and groups that sought God through direct mystical experience. The best known of these mystical approaches is the kabbalah (or cabala), a word that means "receiving." Kabbalah began

to flourish about the twelfth century CE. Its roots, however, extend back at least a millennium before that.

Jewish mystics accept that the Hebrew Bible, specifically the Tanakh (commonly called the Old Testament), is the divinely revealed word of God and the source of all truth. This truth was revealed by God to the ancient patriarchs and prophets and passed down through the Jewish community in the centuries that followed. Jewish mystics, however, believe that this truth is best accessed through a particular interpretation of the ancient texts. In this respect, two distinct strands of mystical thought developed. One strand said that the way to arrive at mystical truth was through dreams, visions, and intuition. Ancient mystical texts that reflect this strand tend to feature vivid, dramatic visions of God and the divine realm. The other strand emphasized esoteric interpretations of biblical verses and the Talmudic sayings. (The Talmud is a vast collection of rabbinic interpretations and explanations of the Torah, or the first five books of the Tanakh: Genesis, Exodus, Leviticus, Numbers, and Deuteronomy). These esoteric mystics saw themselves as conduits for the transmission of ancient secret wisdom that God had revealed to previous generations and lay concealed in the ancient texts. The Sefer Yetzirah belongs to this second tradition—explaining why the title is sometimes translated as "Book of Traditions."

According to Jewish tradition, God first revealed these mystical truths to the angels before the world was created. The truths were revealed to humankind through three men. The first was Adam, who received the truths from the archangel Raziel (whose name in Hebrew means "Secrets of God" and who is sometimes called the Angel of the Secret Regions) as he and Eve were being expelled from the Garden of Eden. The secrets were lost until the patriarch Abraham received them, perhaps about 1700 BCE. Abraham was initiated into the mystical secrets by Melchizedek, an enigmatic high priest mentioned only twice in the Hebrew Bible (Genesis 14:18–20 and Psalm 110:4). The secrets were lost again after Abraham's descendants were enslaved by Egypt, though one tradition holds that the Sefer Yetzirah was written down by Abraham and hidden in a cave to be rediscovered later. The mystical secrets were revealed again to Moses after he released the Israelites from bondage in Egypt and led them to Mount Sinai. According to mystical

63 BCE	■ The Jews in Palestine fall under Roman rule.
120 CE	■ Rabbi Akiba Ben Joseph may have written down the Sefer Yetzirah, according to some historians.
200	■ Some scholars believe that the Sefer Yetzirah was written about this time.
300	■ The Sefer Yetzirah may have been written down after this date, with sections added as late as 700.
CA. 312	■ The emperor Constantine decrees imperial tolerance of Christianity, clearing the way for its eventual emergence as the state religion of the Roman Empire.
CA. 1200	■ Kabbalah begins to flourish.
1900	■ Aryeh Kaplan publishes *Sefer Yetzirah: The Book of Creation in Theory and Practice*, considered the most thorough verse-by-verse examination in English.

tradition, when he went up to Mount Sinai the first time, he received the Ten Commandments. But he returned to Sinai to receive the secrets that would become the kabbalah. Followers of the kabbalah refer to the Ten Commandments as the "outer teaching" (or "Written Law") and the kabbalistic truths as the "inner teaching" (or "Oral Law").

For centuries Jewish mystics kept their interpretations of the Torah secret—not only from people in general but even from religious and political leaders. Jews in Palestine came under Roman (later Byzantine) rule in 63 BCE, and they remained so until the Muslim conquest of the 630s. The Roman Empire was often brutal in its treatment of Jews, who revolted in 66 CE. The revolt was put down, and in 70 CE the Romans destroyed the Second Temple in Jerusalem. Later revolts included the Kitos War of 115–117 and the Bar Kokhba revolt of 132–136, when much of the Jewish population of central Judea was killed or sold into slavery. Meanwhile, early Christians, regarding Jews as the "murderers" of Jesus Christ, also persecuted Jews. Once Christianity became the state religion in the fourth century, pressure was placed on Jews to convert.

Because Jewish mystics held views that contradicted the teachings of both orthodox Judaism and the new religion of

Christianity, they observed a self-imposed silence. But it can be speculated that the turmoil of the early Common Era, coinciding with the swelling of the Jewish diaspora (or "scattering") through the known world, prompted Jewish mystics to create texts that would preserve the mystical teachings from the kind of disappearance that had occurred during the times of Adam and Abraham. Hence, the Sefer Yetzirah may have been committed to writing at around this time.

About the Author

The exact origins of the Sefer Yetzirah are shrouded in mystery. The author or authors created the text as a giant puzzle or riddle. To decipher the sayings in the manuscript is to unravel the mysteries of life. While the earliest surviving manuscript dates from the tenth century, it is possible that Rabbi Akiba Ben Joseph was the first to set down a written version in the second century BCE. But the content of the Sefer Yetzirah certainly existed in prior oral tradition, and its sayings were attributed to Abraham and Moses, the great Jewish patriarchs of the second millennium BCE. Many scholars allege that Abraham was the first to write it down and should therefore be considered the original author. Jewish tradition also avers that God gave Moses not only the "Written Law," or the Ten Commandments, on Mount Sinai, but also the Sefer Yetzirah, or the "Oral Law."

In any event, the sayings of the Sefer Yetzirah were likely passed down from generation to generation until they were finally committed to writing. Over the years, many rabbinic as well as nonrabbinic scholars added to it, changed some of its parts, or wrote commentaries that were hotly debated. In the tenth century CE, Saadia Gaon, whose version of the text is presented here, argued that ancient historians said that Abraham wrote the Sefer Yetzirah. Other Kabbalistic texts, such as the *Zohar* and *Sefer Raziel*, also maintain this view.

Explanation and Analysis of the Document

The Sefer Yetzirah sets the background for all kabbalistic teachings and philosophy. Its contents have sparked debates and controversy over thousands of years. Since the book is mysterious and filled with riddles, the reader also needs to be knowledgeable about the Tanakh, or Hebrew Bible, and the Midrash, a compilation of commentaries on Hebrew scriptures.

Because of its mystical style, this is a very difficult book to understand. The work shows how the twenty-two letters of the Hebrew alphabet have formed all the words that have ever existed or will exist and explains how God used the energy of the Hebrew alphabet to create the universe. Various powers are attributed to the letters of the Hebrew alphabet. Each letter, number, and sound has its own power, which God uses to create time, the planets, the stars, and the cosmos. Since the letters of the Hebrew alphabet were the building blocks of Creation and the channels of God's creative consciousness, the manipulation of those twenty-two letters and ten numbers offers access to the divine order.

All twenty-two letters are said to derive from one name, *tetragrammaton*, the sacred name of God. *Tetragrammaton* is simply a Greek term for a word of four letters; the actual Hebrew, usually transliterated YHWH (whence "Yahweh" or "Jehovah"), is considered too sacred for human utterance, which is why some modern Jews simply write "G-d." Letters and numbers are the basis for the foundation of creation, quality, and quantity. The qualities of something can be expressed by words formed out of letters. Similarly, quantities can be expressed in numbers and in words.

♦ **Chapter 1**

The first chapter discusses the formation and development of the universe. The thirty-two "mysterious paths of Wisdom" (verse 1) are the thirty-two sounds of the Hebrew alphabet, represented by twenty-two letters. The author divides the twenty-two Hebrew letters into ten double and twelve simple letters, representing the thirty-two sounds; a double letter contains two sounds, while a single contains one. The letters of the alphabet are called foundation letters because they are the basis of the universe. The first paragraphs establish the belief that God created the universe with Hebrew letters.

Wisdom is part of the ten Sefirot (verse 2), which in kabbalah study are essentially the ten attributes or ways in which God reveals himself. They are the divine life and energy force that give meaning to everything. Wisdom is thought to be the state of mind that has not been broken up into many pieces. It is possible to express all numbers by the ten Sefirot. Many kabbalists argue that the thirty-two paths are alluded to in the Torah by the thirty-two occurrences of a specific name for God, "Elohim," in the first chapter of the book of Genesis.

The Sefer Yetzirah centers on three "mother" letters (Alef, Mem, and Shin), seven "double" letters, and twelve "elemental" (or simple) letters. The mother letters correspond to the seasons of the year (summer, winter, and the two intermediate seasons of spring and autumn). The double letters correspond to the days of the week, while the elemental letters correspond to the months of the Hebrew calendar. Each letter of those categories relates to a dimension of reality: space, time, and the soul. Again, in kabbalah, these letters are the foundation blocks of creation.

♦ **Chapter 2**

The three mothers serve as an introduction to the letter-oriented meditative techniques of the Sefer Yetzirah. There is oscillation between different states of consciousness (of which there are understood to be about thirty-two); the three mothers serve to create a balance between those states. Finding that balance enables one to attain a mystical union with the divine. The three mothers also represent the three columns of the Sefirotic tree, or the "tree of life" (verse 5), by which creation came into existence. (This "tree" is sometimes imagined as a triangle or even a circle.) The right-hand column is represented by the letter

The meeting of Abraham and Melchizedek
(Abraham and Melchizedek, from the Altarpiece of the Last Supper, 1464-68 [oil on panel], Bouts, Dirck [c.1415-75] / St. Peter's, Louvain, Belgium / Giraudon / The Bridgeman Art Library International)

Mem, the left-hand column is represented by Shin, and the middle column is represented by Alef. Mem is associated with water and tranquility, Shin with judgment and fire, and Alef with air and also divine mercy. The sounds and pronunciations of the letters when spoken highlight the importance of the letters and reflect a deeper significance in them, pointing one toward an understanding of the particular divine potencies of these letters. The three mothers are air, water, and fire. Fire + water = steam (or moist air), which equates to Shin + Mem = Alef. Strong emphasis is placed on the opposites in the universe. For instance, "the opposite of life is death, the opposite of peace is evil [or 'harm'], the opposite of wisdom is foolishness."

This chapter is replete with philosophical remarks on the twenty-two sounds and letters of the Hebrew alphabet, which are connected with the air by speech. Where the letters are used to form words, these words, in turn, are the signs of ideas and highlight material substances. The seven double and twelve simple Hebrew letters are discussed here as well. The seven doubles are Bet, Gimel, Dalet, Kaf, Peh, Resh, and Tav (verse 3). The twelve simple letters formed the boundaries of the universe, and they are He, Vav, Zayin, Het, Tet, Yod, Lamed, Nun, Samech, Ayin, Tsadeh, Qof (verse 4).

The Creator put the twenty-two Hebrew letters on a wheel and turned the wheel forward and backward. This

"In thirty-two mysterious paths of Wisdom, Yah, Eternal of Hosts [Yod-Vav-Yod], God of Israel, Living Elohim, Almighty God, High and Extolled, Dwelling in Eternity, Holy Be His Name, engraved and created His world in three Sefarim: in writing, number and word. Ten Sefirot out of nothing, twenty-two foundation letters, three mothers, seven doubles and twelve simples."

"Twenty-two foundation letters: three mothers, seven doubles and twelve simples. Three mothers: Alef, Mem, Shin: a great mystery, concealed, marvelous and magnificent whence emerge fire, wind [air, spirit, breath] and water, whence everything was created. Seven doubles: Bet, Gimel, Dalet, Kaf, Peh, Resh, Tav, which are to be pronounced in two tongues: Bet, Vayt, Gimel, Ghimel, Dalet, Dhalet, Kaf, Khaf, Peh, Feh, Resh, Rhesh, Tav, Thav, a pattern of hard and soft, strong and weak."

"The proof of this is revealed in the universe, the year and the soul. The twelve are below, the seven are above them, and the three are above the seven. Of the three, He has formed His sanctuary and all are attached to the One: a sign of the One who has no second, a solitary King in His Universe is One, and His Name is One."

"He created reality from Tohu [Tav-He-Vav] and made His existence out of His nothingness, and He hewed great pillars from the intangible air."

"He made the letter Alef King in Spirit and bound to it a crown and tested this one with this one, and formed of it: air in the universe, abundant moisture in the year, and body in the soul, male and female; with the male: Alef, Mem, Shin, and with the female: Alef, Shin, Mem."

"And when Abraham our father had formed and combined and investigated and reckoned and succeeded, then He-Qof-Bet-He, 'The Holy One Blessed Be He' was revealed unto him, and unto Abraham He called this convocation: 'Before I formed thee in the belly, I knew thee, and before thou left the womb, I sanctified thee, and I placed thee like a prophet amidst the nations.'"

wheel, or sphere, connects each pair of Hebrew letters and forms 231 gates. There are numerous combinations with the Hebrew letters at work here. Uncovering their mysticism through meditation is thought to give one the mysteries of the universe and God.

◆ Chapter 3

The next chapter is preoccupied with the three mothers, known as the Triad. The mothers, Alef, Mem, and Shin, were developed in three directions in the universe. Alef is the balance between Mem and Shin, and it has a value of 1. As the first letter of the kabbalistic alphabet, Alef symbolizes a sacred breath, the wind, and the air; thus, Alef is the sound that carries the air that is necessary to pronounce all of the other Hebrew letters. The unique combinations formed between Alef and the rest of the letters produce the sounds of the Hebrew alphabet.

The seven doubles and the twelve simples are discussed again in verses 3 and 4. The doubles represent the opposites in life—such as strong and weak, life and death, and wealth and poverty. This theme is echoed in many parts of the Sefer Yetzirah. The twelve simples were engraved, hewed, tested, weighed, exchanged, and combined by God.

Out of these letters, the God of Israel, "Dwelling in Eternity," carved out the universe (verse 5) and continues to carry and maintain its "height and depth." His reign shall last forever without interruption. Proof of all this is revealed in the universe itself (verse 6), which includes the years, planets, days of the week, and the soul of man. God is the water and tree of life; he is strength and is sufficient, too. He has formed everything around the Hebrew alphabet.

◆ Chapter 4

The Heptad, or the powers and properties of the seven, is emphasized in the fourth chapter. There is a threefold attribution of the numbers and letters to the universe, the year, and to the human being. Some modern editions identify the letters of the Heptad with the planets, the days of the week, human attributes, and the senses ("apertures [of the head]," which are itemized in verses 5–11). God's universal Creation out of the twenty-two letters of the Hebrew alphabet is continuously reaffirmed. He created the four dimensions of heaven (east, west, north, and south) and a wind for each direction (verse 2). God created reality and existence out of nothing as well. As scholars understand, the east and the south are considered male, while the west and north are female.

There are certain words that one should pronounce at the end of the tongue, others at the place of swallowing, on the palate, between the teeth with the tip of the tongue, on the middle of the tongue, and so on. Everything that God decides to be created in the future will come from these words. The 231 gates of verse 4 refer to the 231 connections between every pair of Hebrew letters. The twenty-two foundation letters can be placed in a circle like a wall with 231 gates, whereby the circle oscillates back and forth. Kabbalists insist that meditating upon this circle and its numerous combinations will reveal the mysteries of God,

humankind, and the universe. Creation came through the manipulation of these letters.

God created his own existence out of nothing, and he created great structures out of the air. Certain specifics of Creation are listed, among them, making dust, mud and clay, snow, water, and the earth itself. The seven doubles also parallel the seven extremities, which are up, down, east, west, north, and south, with the Holy Palace in the middle holding them all up. God created these seven extremities.

◆ Chapter 5

The seven doubles are discussed here, namely, Bet, Gimel, Dalet, Kaf, Peh, Resh, Tav. Their foundation is life, peace, wisdom, wealth, grace, seed, and dominance. Each has two sounds, a structure of hard and soft, and a structure of strong and weak. The seven doubles each contain a pair of opposites: life and death, peace and evil, wealth and poverty, wisdom and folly, "seed" and desolation, grace and ugliness, and dominance and subjugation. The seven doubles make up the planets of the universe, days in the week, and gates in the soul. Seven, therefore, is the beloved number in all the heavens.

Attached to each letter is a crown to display its majesty. The letter is also linked to a planet, a day of the week, and a human body part. Again, this highlights the importance of the Hebrew letters in the creation of the human and the universe.

◆ Chapter 6

Chapter 6 is the culmination of the preceding five chapters. It suggests that humankind and the universe should witness the truth regarding the scheme of the distribution of powers of the numbers among created forms. There are twelve letters/elementals discussed in verses 4–15, each with a different foundation: He (sight), Vav (hearing), Zayin (smell), Het (speech), Tet (taste), Yod (coition), Lamed (action), Nun (motion), Samech (anger), Ayin (laughter), Tsadeh (thought), and Qof (sleep). God combined the twelve simple letters to form the twelve months of the year, the twelve constellations of the zodiac, and twelve organs of the human body.

◆ Chapter 7

The three mothers are listed in this section, as are the signs of the zodiac. The planets, days of the week, and parts of the human body are connected with one another in verse 2. The Creator made everything to have an opposite or symbolically opposing force, including the body parts, days of the week, and planets. He assigns Hebrew letters to everything. For example, Hebrew letters are assigned to "Saturn, Sabbath, the mouth. / Jupiter, Sunday, right eye. / Mars, Monday, left eye" and so forth. All of the planets, days, and body parts are thus set into divinely ordained relationships.

◆ Chapter 8

The twelve elementals also depict the twelve constellations of the zodiac, the twelve months of the year, and twelve body parts, or directors, of the soul: two hands, two feet, two kidneys, the spleen, the gall bladder, the liver, the hemsess, the kivah, and the korkeban. (The translation of the last three of these items is disputed, but some translators render them, respectively, as the third stomach of ruminating animals, the fourth stomach in ruminating animals, and the gizzard in fowl.) This chapter specifies that with the three mothers God formed many things. For instance, with Alef he created air, spirit-wind, the chest, the tongue, and the time between seasons. With Mem he formed water, the earth, cold, the belly, and the balance of guilt. With Shin he formed fire, heaven, heat, the head, and the balance of innocence. Other Hebrew words are listed, and detail is given about what God created out of them.

The end of this chapter, which is the end of the book, says that God and the distribution of powers among created forms were revealed to the Jewish patriarch Abraham. God told him that he knew him before he placed him in the belly and the womb. God was the one who made him his prophet on earth. God was the one who made sure Abraham was his friend and made a covenant with him and his descendants for eternity.

Audience

Rabbi Moses Botarel, a Renaissance Spanish scholar, argued in a 1562 commentary that Abraham wrote the Sefer Yetzirah to condemn the doctrine of the pessimistic sages of the time, who were unsure about the existence of but a single divine power. In addition, Rabbi Judah ha-Levi, a twelfth-century Spanish scholar and physician, maintained that the Sefer Yetzirah teaches everyone the existence of a single divine power because the unity and harmony in the universe could derive from only one Supreme Being. These two rabbis highlight why and for whom the document was written. It was written to convince Jews that order, harmony, and stability in the universe could be the work of only the One God of the Hebrews, the same divine power that led the Israelites out of Egypt and into the Promised Land of Canaan. Equally important, God used the Hebrew alphabet to create the universe and everything around it. The authors of the Sefer Yetzirah wanted to demonstrate just how powerfully complex that God could be by describing the Creation of everything in codes, numbers, and letters.

Questions for Further Study

1. The Sefer Yetzirah is a principal document in the history of Jewish mysticism. Why do you think there has been such a noteworthy strand of mystical thought in Judaism, particularly given that Judaism generally places considerable emphasis on law as reflected in the biblical books of Genesis and Exodus (and the Torah as a whole)?

2. A number of religious traditions place emphasis on esoteric interpretations of ancient texts. Compare the Sefer Yetzirah with one of these texts: the Gardnerian *Book of Shadows*, the Book of Enoch, *Fama Fraternitatis*, **The Meccan Illuminations**, or the Bab: Persian Bayan. What differing emphases do the texts have? How does each reflect the religious and social culture that produced it?

3. Presumably, adherents of the mystical strain of thought contained in the document believed it to be true and therefore might have wanted to promulgate their views to a wider audience to convince readers of their viewpoint. Why, then, do you think that the Sefer Yetzirah is such a puzzling document, one that resists easy interpretation?

4. The words *kabbalism* and *kabbalistic* gave rise to the modern English word *cabal*, used to refer to a secret society that seeks power through intrigue or to a plot or conspiracy. Indeed, the Cabal is even the name of a Marvel Comics secret society of antiheroes and supervillains. Explain the connection between this modern use of the word and the more ancient use—particularly since *Kabbalah* comes from a Hebrew word that literally means "receiving."

5. Respond to the following question: If God could have created the universe by separating the light from the darkness, as stated in the book of Genesis, why could God not just as well have created the universe out of sound rather than light?

The impact of the Sefer Yetzirah has been both profound and widespread. To begin with, it is thought to be one of the earliest texts of the kabbalah. It has been often quoted, and numerous commentaries, articles, essays, and books have been devoted to it. The work has also sparked heated academic discourse. It helped place strong emphasis on letters and sounds in kabbalistic study. Medieval Jewish philosophers such as Saadia Gaon and Judah ha-Levi wrote commentaries on this work, and Jewish mystics were heavily involved in its interpretation. They admitted that God created everything in the universe out of the Hebrew letters, and they implied that an artificial man, Golem, could be created as well. Much of their interpretation of the work had to do with how things were created. Jewish mystics thus guided the Sefer Yetzirah into being considered a work about the creation of all things in the universe.

This work set the tone for kabbalistic philosophy. Today there are many adherents of kabbalah, who study not only the Sefer Yetzirah but also such other kabbalistic classics as the *Bahir*, the *Sefer Raziel HaMalakh*, and the *Zohar*. Jews and non-Jews alike study kabbalah as they seek to maintain a healthy relationship with God and all of God's creation. The Sefer Yetzirah is very much relevant today and forms the basis for mystical interpretations of letters, numbers, and language itself. Scholars argue that it presents an allegorical parallel between the universe and the ideal realm of numbers and letters. It may also have given inspiration to later mystical groups and societies such as the Rosicrucians (a seventeenth-century mystical sect) as well as Freemasonry and adherents of the Tarot (a means of divination via a deck of cards).

Dennis, Geoffrey. *The Encyclopedia of Jewish Myth, Magic, and Mysticism*. St. Paul, Minn.: Llewellyn Worldwide, 2007.

Feldman, Daniel Hale. *Qabalah: The Mystical Heritage of the Children of Abraham*. Santa Cruz, Calif.: Work of the Chariot, 2001.

Fine, Lawrence, ed. *Essential Papers in Kabbalah*. New York: New York University Press, 1995.

Hoffman, Edward, ed. *The Kabbalah Reader: A Sourcebook of Visionary Judaism*. Boston: Shambhala Publications, 2010.

Idel, Moshe. *Kabbalah: New Perspectives*. New Haven, Conn.: Yale University Press, 1988.

Sherwin, Byron L. *In Partnership with God: Contemporary Jewish Law and Ethics*. Syracuse, N.Y.: Syracuse University Press, 1990.

■ Web Sites

Barenblat, Rachel Evelyne. "Jewish Mystics: Using Language, Transcending Language, Becoming Language." Servants of the Light Web Site.
   http://www.servantsofthelight.org/QBL/Books/Yetz_Comm_02.html

Gigi, Daniel. "The Sefer Yetzirah, Book of Creation: The Foundation of Kabbalistic Wisdom." Suite101.com Web site.
   http://kabbalah.suite101.com/article.cfm/the-sefer-yetzirah-book-of-creation

"The Hebrew Letters: The Hebrew Letters of the Day." Gal Einai Institute Inner.org Web site.
   http://www.inner.org/hebleter/letterof.htm

—David Treviño

Sefer Yetzirah

I. Chapter 1

1. In thirty-two mysterious paths of Wisdom, Yah, Eternal of Hosts [Yod-Vav-Yod], God of Israel, Living Elohim, Almighty God, High and Extolled, Dwelling in Eternity, Holy Be His Name, engraved and created His world in three Sefarim: in writing, number and word. Ten Sefirot out of nothing, twenty-two foundation letters, three mothers, seven doubles and twelve simples.

2. Ten Sefirot out of nothing according to the number of the ten digits [fingers and toes], which are five against five and a single covenant to be determined in the center. In word and tongue and mouth, they are ten extending beyond limit: depth of beginning, depth of end, depth of good, depth of evil, depth above and depth below, depth of east and depth of west, depth of north and depth of south, and the sole Master and lofty King faithfully governs them all from his Holy dwelling in Eternity forever.

3. Twenty-two foundation letters: three mothers, seven doubles and twelve simples. Three mothers: Alef, Mem, Shin: their basis is a scale of innocence and a scale of guilt and a tongue ordained to balance between the two. Seven doubles: Bet, Gimel, Dalet, Kaf, Peh, Resh, Tav. Their foundation is life and peace, wisdom and wealth, fruitfulness, grace and government. Twelve simples: He, Vav, Zayin; Chet, Tet, Yod; Lamed, Nun, Samech; Ayin, Tsadeh, Qof. Their foundation is seeing, hearing, smelling, swallowing, copulating, acting, walking, raging, laughing, thinking, and sleeping.

4. By means of these media, Yah, Eternal of Hosts, God of Israel, Living Elohim, Almighty God, High and Extolled, Dwelling in Eternity, Holy Be His Name traced out [carved] three fathers and their posterity, seven conquerors and their hosts, and twelve diagonal boundaries. The proof of this is revealed in the universe, the year, and the soul, which rule ten, three, seven and twelve. Over them rule Tali (the dragon), the wheel, and the heart.

II. Chapter 2

1. Ten Sefirot out of nothing. Ten and not nine, ten and not eleven. Understand in Wisdom and be wise in Understanding. Examine them, investigate them, think clearly and form. Place the word above its Creator and reinstate a Creator upon His foundation; and they are ten extending beyond limit. Observe them: they appear like a flash. Their boundary has no limit for His word is with them: "and they ran and returned." And they pursue His saying like a whirlwind [vortex]; and they prostrate themselves [bend] themselves before His throne.

2. Twenty-two foundation letters: three mothers, seven doubles, and twelve simples. Three mothers: Alef, Mem, Shin: a great mystery, concealed, marvelous and magnificent whence emerge fire, wind [air, spirit, breath] and water, whence everything was created. Seven doubles: Bet, Gimel, Dalet, Kaf, Peh, Resh, Tav, which are to be pronounced in two tongues: Bet, Vayt, Gimel, Ghimel, Dalet, Dhalet, Kaf, Khaf, Peh, Feh, Resh, Rhesh, Tav, Thav, a pattern of hard and soft, strong and weak. The doubles represent the contraries [syzygies]. The opposite of life is death, the opposite of peace is evil [or 'harm'], the opposite of wisdom is foolishness, the opposite of wealth is poverty, the opposite of fruitfulness is barrenness, the opposite of grace is ugliness, the opposite of dominion is slavery.

3. Seven doubles: Bet, Gimel, Dalet, Kaf, Peh, Resh, Tav. Seven and not six, seven and not eight. Six sides in the six directions, and the Holy Palace [Heikhal] ruling in the center. Blessed is the Eternal [Yod-Vav-Yod] in His dwelling. He is the place of the universe and the universe is not His place.

4. Twelve simples: He, Vav, Zayin; Het, Tet, Yod; Lamed, Nun, Samech; Ayin, Tsadeh, Qof. Twelve and not eleven, twelve and not thirteen. Twelve diagonal boundaries divide the directions and separate the different sides: the extremity of the northeast, the extremity of the eastern height, the extremity of the eastern depth, the extremity of the northwest, the extremity of the northern height, the extremity of the northern depth, the extremity of the southwest, the extremity of the western height, the extremity of the western depth, the extremity of the southeast, the extremity of the southern height, the extremity of the southern depth.

5. By these means, Yah, Eternal of Hosts, God of Israel, Living Elohim, Almighty God, High and Extolled, Dwelling in Eternity, Holy Be His Name traced twenty-two letters and fixed them upon a wheel. He turns the wheel forwards and backwards, and as a sign of this, nothing is better than to ascend in delight [Ayin-Nun-Gimel,], and nothing is worse than to descend with the plague [,Nun-Gimel-Ayin].

6. The proof of this is revealed in the universe, the year and the soul. The universe is calculated according to ten: the three are fire, air, and water; the seven are the seven planets; the twelve are the twelve signs of the zodiac. the year is computed by ten: the three are winter, summer and the seasons between; the seven are the seven days of Creation; the twelve are the twelve months; the living soul is calculated according to ten: three are the head, chest and stomach; seven are the seven apertures of the body; the twelve are the twelve leading organs.

III. Chapter 3

1. Ten Sefirot out of nothing. Stop your mouth from speaking, stop your heart from thinking, and if your heart runs (to think) return to a place of which it is said "they ran and returned"; and concerning this thing the covenant was made; and they are ten in extent beyond limit. Their end is infused with their beginning, and their beginning with their end like a flame attached to a glowing ember. Know, think [reflect, meditate] and imagine that the Creator is One and there is nothing apart from Him, and before One what do you count?

2. Twenty-two foundation letters: three mothers, seven doubles, and twelve simples. Three mothers: Alef, Mem, Shin are fire, wind [air] and water. The nature of the heavens is fire, the nature of air is wind [ruach], the nature of earth is water. Fire ascends and water descends and wind balances between the two. Mem is silent, Shin is sibilant, and Alef balances between the two. Alef, Mem, Shin are signed in six rings and enveloped in male and female. Know, meditate and imagine that the fire supports water.

3. Seven doubles: Bet, Gimel, Dalet, Kaf, Peh, Resh, Tav which are to be pronounced in two tongues: Bet, Vet, Gimel, Ghimel, Dalet, Dhalet, Kaf, Khaf, Peh, Feh, Resh, Rhesh, Tav, Thav, a pattern of hard and soft, strong and weak. The doubles represent the contraries. The opposite of life is death, the opposite of peace is evil, the opposite of wisdom is foolishness, the opposite of wealth is poverty, the opposite of fruitfulness is barrenness, the opposite of grace is ugliness, the opposite of dominion is slavery.

4. Twelve simples: He, Vav, Zayin; Het, Tet, Yod; Lamed, Nun, Samech; Ayin, Tsadeh, Qof. He engraved them, hewed them, tested them, weighed them, and exchanged them. How did he combine them? Two stones build two houses. Three stones build six houses. Four stones build twenty-four houses. Five stones build one hundred twenty houses. Six stones build seven hundred twenty houses. Seven stones build five thousand forty houses. Thenceforth, go out and calculate what the mouth is unable to say and what the ear is unable to hear.

5. Through these media, Yah, Eternal of Hosts, God of Israel, Living Elohim, Almighty Master, Lofty and Extolled, Dwelling in Eternity, Holy Be His Name traced [carved] (His universe). Yah [Yod-He] is composed of two letters; YHVH [Yod-He-Vav-He] is composed of four letters; Hosts [Tsvaot]: it is like a signal [sign, ot] in his army [tsava]; God of Israel: Israel is a prince [Sar] before God [El]; Living Elohim: three things are called living, Living Elohim, the water of life and the Tree of Life; El [Alef-Lamed]: strength, Shaddai [Shin-Dalet-Yod]: He is sufficient to this point; Lofty [Ram]: because he dwells in the heights of the universe and is above all elevated being; Extolled [Nisah]: because he carries and maintains the height and depth whilst the bearers are below and their burden is above. He carries and maintains the entire creation; Dwelling in Eternity [Shochen ahd]: because His reign is eternal and uninterrupted; Holy Be His Name [Qadosh Shmo]: because he and His servants are sacred and they declare unto Him every day: Holy, Holy, Holy.

6. The proof of this is revealed in the universe, the year and the soul. The twelve are below, the seven are above them, and the three are above the seven. Of the three, he has formed His sanctuary and all are attached to the One: a sign of the One who has no second, a solitary King in His Universe is One, and His Name is One.

IV. Chapter 4

1. Ten Sefirot out of nothing. One: Spirit-wind of the Living Elohim, Life of the Universe, whose throne strengthens all eternity, Blessed and Be-

neficent Be His Name, constant and eternal: this is the Holy Spirit.

2. Spirit from Spirit engraved and hewed: He cut the four dimensions of Heaven: the east, the west, the north and the south, and there is a wind for each direction.

3. Twenty-two foundation letters: three mothers, seven doubles, and twelve simples. He hewed them in spirit, carved them in voice, fixed them in the mouth in five place: Alef, He, Het, Ayin [ahacha]; Bet, Vav, Mem, Feh [bumaf]; Gimel, Yod, Khaf, Qof [gikhaq]; Dalet, Tet, Lamed, Nun, Tav [datlanat]; Zayin, Samech, Tsadeh, Resh, Shin [zsats'ras]. Alef, He, Het, Ayin are pronounced at the end of the tongue at the place of swallowing; Bet, Vav, Mem, Feh between the teeth with the tip of the tongue; Gimel, Yod, Khaf, Qof on the palate; Dalet, Tet, Lamed, Nun, Tav on the middle of the tongue and pronounced with the voice; Zayin, Samech, Tsadeh, Resh, Shin between the teeth with the tongue at rest.

4. Twenty-two letters: He carved them, hewed them, refined them, weighed them, and combined them, and He made of them the entire creation and everything to be created in the future. How did He test them? Alef with all and all with Alef, Bet with all and all with Bet, Gimel with all and all with Gimel, and they all return again and again, and they emanate through two hundred and thirty-one gates. All the words and all the creatures emanate from One Name.

5. He created reality from Tohu [Tav-He-Vav] and made His existence out of His nothingness, and He hewed great pillars from the intangible air.

6. Three: water of spirit carved and hewed of it Tohu [Tav-He-Vav] and Bohu [Bet-He-Vav], mud and clay. He made them like a garden bed, put them into position like a wall and covered them like a fortification. he poured water upon them and made dust, for He saith to the snow: be earth. (Tohu: this is the green line which encircles the entire world; Bohu: this refers to the rocks split and submerged in the abyss where the water has its source.) As it is said: He spread out the line of Tohu and the rocks of Bohu upon it [the water].

7. Four: fire from water, He engraved and hewed from it a throne of glory and the host dwelling in the heights, as it is written: Who maketh the winds His messengers, the flames of fire His ministers.

8. Five: He chose three simples and fixed them to His great Name, and with them He sealed six extremities. He sealed the height, turning upwards and sealed it with Yod-He-Vav. Six: He sealed the depth and He turned below and sealed it with Yod-Vav-He. Seven: he sealed the east and turned forwards, and sealed it with He-Vav-Yod. Eight: He sealed the west and turned backwards and sealed it with He-Yod-Vav. Nine: He sealed the south and turned to His right and sealed it with Vav-Yod-He. Ten: He sealed the north and turned to His left and sealed it with Vav-He-Yod. These are the ten Sefirot out of nothing, One: Spirit of the Living Elohim; two: wind of the spirit; three: water of the wind; four: fire from the water, height and depth, east and west, north and south.

V. Chapter 5

1. He made the letter Alef King in Spirit and bound to it a crown and tested this one with this one, and formed of it: air in the universe, abundant moisture in the year, and body in the soul, male and female; with the male: Alef, Mem, Shin, and with the female: Alef, Shin, Mem.

2. He made the letter Mem King in Spirit and bound to it a crown and tested this one with this one, and formed of it: earth in the universe, cold in the year, and belly in the soul (male and female).

3. He made the letter Shin King in Spirit and bound to it a crown and tested this one with this one, and formed of it: Heaven in the universe, heat in the year, and head in the soul, male and female. How did He combine them? Alef, Mem, Shin, Alef, Shin, Mem, Mem, Shin, Alef, Mem, Alef, Shin, Shin, Alef, Mem, Shin, Mem, Alef. Heaven is from fire, the atmosphere is from air, the earth is from water. The head of Adam is fire, his heart is of the spirit-wind, and his stomach is from water.

4. Seven doubles: Bet, Gimel, Dalet, Kaf, Peh, Resh, Tav. He carved them, hewed them, tested them, weighed them, and combined them. He made of them: the planets, the days (of the week), and the apertures (of the head).

5. He made the letter Bet King and bound to it a crown and tested this one with this one, and formed of it: Saturn in the universe, the Sabbath in the year, and the mouth in the soul.

6. He made the letter Gimel King and bound to it a crown and tested this one with this one, and formed of it: Jupiter in the universe, Sunday in the year, and the right eye of the soul.

7. He made the letter Dalet King and bound to it a crown and tested this one with this one, and formed of it: Mars in the universe, Monday in the year, and the left eye of the soul.

8. He made the letter Kaf King and bound to it a crown and tested this one with this one, and formed of it: Sun in the universe, Tuesday in the year, and the right nostril of the soul.

9. He made the letter Peh King and bound to it a crown and tested this one with this one, and formed of it: Venus in the universe, Wednesday in the year, and the left nostril of the soul.

10. He made the letter Resh King and bound to it a crown and tested this one with this one, and formed of it: Mercury in the universe, Thursday in the year, and the right ear of the soul.

11. He made the letter Tav King and bound to it a crown and tested this one with this one, and formed of it: Moon in the universe, Friday in the year, and the left ear of the soul.

12. He separated the witnesses and He bestowed a portion to each of them: a portion to the universe, a portion to the year, and a portion to the soul.

VI. Chapter 6

Twelve simples: He, Vav, Zayin; Het, Tet, Yod; Lamed, Nun, Samech; Ayin, Tsadeh, Qof. He carved them, hewed them, tested them, weighed them, and combined them. He formed of them: the signs of the zodiac, the months [of the year], and the leading organs of the body; two are agitated, two are tranquil, two are advising, and two are joyous (these are the two intestines), the two hands, and the two feet.

1. He made them like contenders and set them up like a kind of war; Elohim made them one against the other.

2. Three, to each a portion; seven divided into three above, three [below], and the one rules as a balance between the two. Twelve are arranged in battle: three are friends, three are enemies, three are murderers, and three are resurrectors; and they all are attached one to another. As a sign of this thing, twenty-two inclinations and one body.

3. How did He combine them? He, Vav, Vav, He; Zayin, Het, Het, Zayin; Tet, Yod, Yod, Tet; Lamed, Nun, Nun, Lamed; Samech, Ayin, Ayin, Samech; Tsadeh, Qof, Qof, Tsadeh.

4. He made the letter He King and bound to it a crown and tested this one with this one, and formed of it: Aries in the universe, Nisan in the year, and the liver of the soul.

5. He made the letter Vav King and bound to it a crown and tested this one with this one, and formed of it: Taurus in the universe, Iyyar in the year, and the gall-bladder of the soul.

6. He made the letter Zayin King and bound to it a crown and tested this one with this one, and formed of it: Gemini in the universe, Sivan in the year, and the spleen in the soul.

7. He made the letter Het King and bound to it a crown and tested this one with this one, and formed of it: Cancer in the universe, Tammuz in the year, and the intestine in the soul.

8. He made the letter Tet King and bound to it a crown and tested this one with this one, and formed of it: Leo in the universe, Ab in the year, and the right kidney in the soul.

9. He made the letter Yod King and bound to it a crown and tested this one with this one, and formed of it: Virgo in the universe, Elul in the year, and the left kidney in the soul.

10. He made the letter Lamed King and bound to it a crown and tested this one with this one, and formed of it: Libra in the universe, Tishri in the year, and the intestines in the soul.

11. He made the letter Nun King and bound to it a crown and tested this one with this one, and formed of it: Scorpio in the universe, Marheshvan in the year, and the stomach in the soul.

12. He made the letter Samech King and bound to it a crown and tested this one with this one, and formed of it: Sagittarius in the universe, Kislev in the year, and the right hand of the soul.

13. He made the letter Ayin King and bound to it a crown and tested this one with this one, and formed of it: Capricorn in the universe, Tevet in the year, and the left hand of the soul.

14. He made the letter Tsadeh King and bound to it a crown and tested this one with this one, and formed of it: Aquarius in the universe, Shvat in the year, and the right foot of the soul.

15. He made the letter Qof King and bound to it a crown and tested this one with this one, and formed of it: Pisces in the universe, Adar in the year, and the left foot of the soul.

16. He divided the witnesses and bestowed a portion to each of them: a portion to the universe, a portion to the year, and a portion to the soul.

VII. Chapter 7

1. Air, between seasons ["abundant moisture"], trunk [i.e. torso].

Earth, cold, belly.

Heaven, heat [summer], the head:

These are Alef, Mem and Shin.

2. Saturn, Sabbath, the mouth.
Jupiter, Sunday, right eye.
Mars, Monday, left eye.
The Sun, Tuesday, right nostril.
Venus, Wednesday, left nostril.
Mercury, Thursday, right ear.
Moon, Friday, left ear:
These are Bet, Gimel, Dalet, Kaf, Peh, Resh and Tav.

3. Aries, Nisan, liver.
Taurus, Iyyar, gall-bladder.
Gemini, Sivan, spleen.
Cancer, Tammuz, intestine.
Leo, Ab, right kidney.
Virgo, Elul, left kidney.
Libra, Tishri, intestines.
Scorpio, Marheshvan, stomach.
Sagittarius, Kislev, right hand.
Capricorn, Tevet, left hand.
Aquarius, Shvat, right foot.
Pisces, Adar, left foot:

These are He, Vav, Zayin; Het, Tet, Yod; Lamed, Nun, Samech; Ayin, Tsadeh, Qof.

VIII. Chapter 8

With Alef have been formed: the spirit-wind, air, the between seasons, the chest, the tongue.

With Mem have been formed: water, earth, cold, belly, and the balance of guilt.

With Shin have been formed: fire, Heaven, heat, the head, and the balance of innocence.

With Bet have been formed: Saturn, the Sabbath, life and death.

With Gimel have been formed: Jupiter, Sunday, the right eye, peace and harm.

With Dalet have been formed: Mars, Monday, the left eye, wisdom and foolishness.

With Kaf have been formed: the Sun, Tuesday, the right nostril, wealth and poverty.

With Peh have been formed: Venus, Wednesday, the left nostril, fertility and desolation [barrenness].

With Resh have been formed: Mercury, Thursday, the right ear, grace and ugliness.

With Tav have been formed: the Moon, Friday, the left ear, dominion and slavery.

With He have been formed: Aries, Nisan, the liver, vision and blindness.

With Vav have been formed: Taurus, Iyyar, the spleen, hearing and deafness.

Glossary

Alef, Mem . . .	letters of the Hebrew alphabet
doubles	letters in the Hebrew alphabet that contain two sounds
Elohim	a name for God found in the book of Genesis
foundation letters	the letters of the alphabet, the basis of the universe
mothers	the three letters of the Hebrew alphabet, Alef, Mem, and Shin, from which all the other letters are formed
Nisan	the name of a month in the Hebrew calendar, along with Iyyar, Sivan, Tammuz, Ab, Elul, Tishri, Marheshvan, Kislev, Tevet, Shvat, and Adar
sibilant	a "hissing" sound produced when pronouncing such letters as *s*
simples	letters in the Hebrew alphabet that contain one sound
Ten Sefirot	the ten numbers, or the ten attributes or ways in which God reveals himself
Yah . . .	one of many mystical names for God included in the document
YHVH	that is, Yahweh, a name for God

With Zayin have been formed: Gemini, Sivan, the gall, odor and odorlessness.

With Het have been formed: Cancer, Tammuz, the intestine, the word and silence.

With Tet have been formed: Leo, Ab, the right kidney, eating and hunger.

With Yod have been formed: Virgo, Elul, the left kidney, copulating and castration.

With Lamed have been formed: Libra, Tishri, the intestines, acting and impotence.

With Nun have been formed: Scorpio, Marheshvan, the gullet, walking and limping.

With Samech have been formed: Sagittarius, Kislev, the right hand, rage and loss of faith.

With Ayin have been formed: Capricorn, Tevet, the left hand, laughing and the loss of spleen. With Tsadeh have been formed: Aquarius, Shvat, the right foot, thinking and loss of heart.

With Qof have been formed: Pisces, Adar, the left foot, sleeping and languor.

And they are all fixed to the Dragon [Tali], the wheel, and the heart. Tali in the universe is like a king upon his throne, the wheel in the year is like a king in his empire, and the heart in the body is like a king at war. To recapitulate: some reunited with the others, and those reunited with the former. These are opposed to those and those are opposed to these. These are the contrary of those and those are the contrary of these. If these are not, those are not. And if those are not, these are not; and they are all fixed to Tali [the Dragon], the wheel and the heart.

And when Abraham our father had formed and combined and investigated and reckoned and succeeded, then He-Qof-Bet-He, "The Holy One Blessed Be He" was revealed unto him, and unto Abraham He called this convocation: "Before I formed thee in the belly, I knew thee, and before thou left the womb, I sanctified thee, and I placed thee like a prophet amidst the nations." And He made Abraham a beloved friend, and cut a covenant with him and his seed forever and ever.